William Garden Blaikie

A MANUAL of BIBLE HISTORY

in Connection with the General History of the World

William Garden Blaikie

A MANUAL of BIBLE HISTORY
in Connection with the General History of the World

ISBN/EAN: 9783741123450

Manufactured in Europe, USA, Canada, Australia, Japa

Cover: Foto ©Lupo / pixelio.de

Manufactured and distributed by brebook publishing software (www.brebook.com)

William Garden Blaikie

A MANUAL of BIBLE HISTORY

BIBLE HISTORY

IN CONNECTION WITH

The General History of the World.

By the

REV. WILLIAM G. BLAIKIE, D.D., LL.D.

New Edition, Revised and Enlarged.

London:
T. NELSON AND SONS, PATERNOSTER ROW.
EDINBURGH; AND NEW YORK.
1882.

PREFACE.

The purpose of this work is to enable students of the Bible to grasp the whole course of history which it contains, both in its outline and in its details, and to indicate and apply the great lessons which the history is designed to convey. For this end—

1. It follows the stream of the Bible narrative, arranging and classifying the leading facts, so as to aid the eye and the memory in grasping the whole.

2. It keeps in view, throughout, the great spiritual purpose of Revelation, and shows its gradual development.

3. For illustrating the narrative, it takes advantage of the mass of Biblical illustration of which recent years have been so prolific, in researches, monuments, travels, and expeditions in Bible lands.

4. It notices briefly the chief countries, towns, and other scenes of Bible history as they occur; bringing before the reader the facts that contribute most to the full understanding of what is said of them in the Bible.

5. It glances at the parallel history and progress of the leading nations of the world,—showing what was going on elsewhere while the history of the Bible was being enacted.

6. It traces the progress of religious knowledge, and of the revelation by which it was made known, and the state of social

and spiritual life at different periods, partly in other nations, but especially among the Israelites.

7. It fills up the interval between the Old Testament and the New, so as to throw light on the great changes that had occurred between the time of Malachi and the appearance of our Lord.

It is generally acknowledged that in these days of diligent learning and competitive examinations, Bible knowledge is not so much attended to as it ought to be. The present work is intended to aid in remedying that defect. In an elementary book on the same subject, entitled "Outline of Bible History and Geography," the bare facts will be found in a convenient and compendious form; in this treatise the facts form the groundwork, but it has been attempted to bring flesh and skin over them, and turn the whole into a continuous and lively narrative.

W. G. B.

CONTENTS.

CHAPTER I.
THE CREATION AND THE FALL.

Sect. 1. Introductory,	9
.. 2. The Creation,	10
.. 3. Traditions and Traces of Creation,	13
.. 4. Paradise and the Fall,	16
.. 5. Traditions of Eden and the Fall,	20

CHAPTER II.
THE FLOOD.

Sect. 1. The Antediluvian World,	25
.. 2. Noah and the Flood,	32
.. 3. Traditions and Traces of the Flood,	35
.. 4. Repeopling of the Earth,	37

CHAPTER III.
THE DISPERSION.
FROM THE FLOOD TO THE BIRTH OF ABRAHAM.

Sect. 1. Settlements of Noah's Sons,	40
.. 2. The Tower of Babel and Confusion of Tongues,	44
.. 3. Cities and Empires of the Period,	47
.. 4. The Rise and Spread of Idolatry,	51

CHAPTER IV.
THE HEBREW PATRIARCHS.
FROM THE BIRTH OF ABRAHAM TO THE DEATH OF JOSEPH.

Sect. 1. Career of Abraham,	55
.. 2. Career of Isaac and of Abraham's other Sons,	73
.. 3. Career of Jacob,	75
4. Career of Joseph, and Removal of Jacob to Egypt,	79
.. 5. Social and Religious Life of the Period,	84

CHAPTER V.
EGYPT.
FROM THE DEATH OF JOSEPH TO THE DEPARTURE FROM EGYPT.

Sect. 1. Egypt and the Egyptians,	89
.. 2. The Progress of the Israelites,	100
.. 3. Early Life of Moses,	107
.. 4. The Deliverance,	113
.. 5. Effects of Egypt on the Israelites,	117

CHAPTER VI.
THE WILDERNESS OF SINAI AND THE EAST OF JORDAN.
FROM THE DEPARTURE FROM EGYPT TO THE DEATH OF MOSES.

Sect. 1. The Journey to Sinai,	121
.. 2. The Law-Giving,	128
.. 3. The Forty Years' Wandering,	137
.. 4. The Advance to Canaan,	140
.. 5. Conquest of East Side of Jordan,	144
.. 6. Moab and Midian,	151
.. 7. Death of Moses,	156
.. 8. Social and Religious Condition of the Period,	158

CHAPTER VII.
JOSHUA AND THE CONQUEST OF CANAAN.
FROM THE DEATH OF MOSES TO THE DEATH OF JOSHUA.

Sect. 1. General Description of the Land,	164
.. 2. Joshua's Campaigns,	170
.. 3. The Allotments of the Tribes,	177
.. 4. Joshua's Death,	190

CHAPTER VIII.
THE JUDGES.
FROM THE DEATH OF JOSHUA TO THE ACCESSION OF SAUL.

Sect. 1. The Six Great Invasions,	193
.. 2. Domestic and Religious Life,	208
.. 3. Illustrative Memoirs,	212
.. 4. History of other Nations,	215

CHAPTER IX.
THE UNITED KINGDOM—SAUL, DAVID, SOLOMON.
FROM THE ACCESSION OF SAUL TO THE DEATH OF SOLOMON.

Sect. 1. Reign of Saul,	222
.. 2. Early Life of David,	229

Sect. 3. Reign of David,	243
.. 4. Reign of Solomon,	257
.. 5. Social and Religious Life,	262

CHAPTER X.

KINGDOM OF ISRAEL, OR THE TEN TRIBES.

FROM THE REVOLT UNDER REHOBOAM TO THE CAPTIVITY.

Sect. 1. The Revolt,	267
.. 2. Dynasties of Jeroboam, Baasha, and Zimri — Idolatry taking root,	271
.. 3. Dynasty of Omri, and era of Elijah and Elisha—Idolatry rampant,	275
.. 4. Dynasty of Jehu, and era of Jonah, Amos, and Hosea—Idolatry slightly checked,	290
.. 5. Closing Reigns—Idolatry terminates in destruction,	296

CHAPTER XI.

KINGDOM OF JUDAH.

FROM THE SEPARATION OF THE KINGDOMS TO THE CAPTIVITY.

Sect. 1. Outline of the History,	300
.. 2. First Decline and First Revival,	303
.. 3. Second Decline and Second Revival,	307
.. 4. Third Decline and Third Revival,	313
.. 5. Final Decline,	322
.. 6. Social and Religious Life,	327
.. 7. Contemporary History,	330

CHAPTER XII.

THE CAPTIVITY.

Sect. 1. Captivity of the Ten Tribes,	338
.. 2. Captivity of Judah,	342
.. 3. Further Career of Nebuchadnezzar,	348
.. 4. Later Days of the Babylonian Empire,	351
.. 5. Social and Religious Life,	355

CHAPTER XIII.

THE RESTORATION.

FROM THE EDICT OF CYRUS TO NEHEMIAH.

Sect. 1. The Expedition of Zerubbabel,	359
.. 2. The Persian Empire, from Darius Hystaspes to Artaxerxes Longimanus.	364
.. 3. Story of Esther,	368
.. 4. Labours of Ezra,	371
.. 5. Reforms of Nehemiah,	373
.. 6. Contemporary History,	376

CHAPTER XIV.

INTERVAL BETWEEN THE OLD TESTAMENT AND THE NEW.

FROM THE TIME OF NEHEMIAH TO THE BIRTH OF CHRIST.

Sect. 1. Palestine under the Persians: to B.C. 333,	382
.. 2. Palestine under Alexander: B.C. 333 to 323,	386
.. 3. Palestine under the Ptolemys: B.C. (about) 324 to 204,	388
.. 4. Palestine under the Macedonian Kings of Syria: B.C. 204 to 165,	391
.. 5. Palestine under the Maccabees: B.C. 165 to 63,	397
.. 6. Palestine under the Romans: B.C. 63 to 4,	398
.. 7. The Jews of the Dispersion,	405
.. 8. State of the Gentile World,	408

CHAPTER XV.

GOSPEL HISTORY.

Sect. 1. Birth and Childhood of Jesus Christ,	412
.. 2. Preparation for Public Work,	423
.. 3. Earlier Part of our Lord's Ministry,	428
.. 4. Middle and Later Parts of our Lord's Ministry,	433
.. 5. Closing Scenes of Christ's Life and Ministry,	442

CHAPTER XVI.

APOSTOLIC HISTORY.

Sect. 1. The Church of Jerusalem,	451
.. 2. Early Life of Paul,	456
.. 3. Preparations for Church Extension,	460
.. 4. Paul's First Missionary Tour,	465
.. 5. Paul's Second Missionary Tour,	470
.. 6. Paul's Third Missionary Tour,	477
.. 7. Closing Scenes of Paul's Life,	479
.. 8. Labours of the other Apostles,	486
.. 9. Destruction of Jerusalem, and Contemporary History,	493

GENERAL INDEX, 496

MANUAL OF BIBLE HISTORY.

CHAPTER I.

THE CREATION AND THE FALL.

GENESIS i.-iii.

SECTION I.—INTRODUCTORY.

Object of Bible history—Its connection with general history—Use of ancient geography, history, &c.

Object of Bible History.—In entering on the study of Bible History we ought to bear in mind that its object is not the same as that of other histories. Ordinary histories record the achievements and progress of particular races or nations, telling how they arose, what territories they occupied, in what manner they were governed, what battles they fought, what progress they made in arts and sciences, and, at last, probably, how they fell. The object of Bible history, on the other hand, is to record the progress of true religion. In particular, it seeks to unfold the revelation of himself which God has made to man, and especially his revelation of a way of mercy and blessing for the guilty. How this revelation was received from time to time, and what effects it produced: how in many cases men would not listen to it, and how wicked and miserable they then became; how in other instances God's message was received in love, and what happiness and prosperity followed; how, amid these changes, the way was prepared for the coming in the flesh of the Divine Redeemer, and how at last he came, and lived and died to redeem the lost;--it is with these and such matters as these that Bible history has chiefly to do. The ordinary events that make up common history are, indeed, often touched on, but chiefly as they bear on this great subject—the revelation of God to man, and the relation of man to God. In one word, Bible history is the history of God's kingdom upon the earth.

Connection with General History.—For nearly two thousand years before the birth of Christ, the more special revelations of God's will were made to a single nation—the seed of Abraham. This is the reason why the history of the Hebrew race is given so much more fully in the Bible than that of any other great nation. It is remarkable, however, that Bible history comes into contact with almost every great nation of the ancient world. Among the greatest countries of antiquity were Egypt, Assyria, Babylonia, Phœnicia, Syria, Arabia, Medo-Persia, Greece, and Rome. There is not one of these countries which Bible history does not touch.

Use of Ancient Geography, History, &c.—Some knowledge of the history of these countries, and especially of their condition when the Bible comes into contact with them, is therefore essential to a thorough understanding of the Bible narrative. Some acquaintance with the geography and scenery of the places where the great events of the Bible occurred is very desirable. Little, indeed, absolutely new can be brought to light by this means; but what is already known may become more vivid and more interesting. Such knowledge may be especially helpful to the young, by enabling them to picture the events of Bible history as if they had happened before their eyes. To throw such side lights on the Bible narrative is one of the objects of the following treatise.

SECTION II.—THE CREATION.

The first words of Genesis—Creation and cosmogony—Creation of man—Order of creation—The blessing.

The First Words of Genesis.—When God purposed to create the race of Man, it was necessary that a dwelling-place should be made ready for him. The first sentence of the Bible tells us, with majestic simplicity, that "in the beginning God created the heaven and the earth." From this simple statement we learn—1. That neither the heaven and the earth, nor the matter out of which they are formed, were eternal. 2. That they did not come into existence by chance, or, as the phrase is, "by a fortuitous concourse of atoms." 3. That they were not created by many gods (polytheism), nor by two gods (dualism), but by one God (monotheism or monism). 4. That the creation took place "*in the beginning;*" that is, as soon as God began to manifest himself by working. We are not told when that was, nor have we any information as to how long the heaven and the earth existed before they were fashioned and furnished as they are now.

Creation and Cosmogony.—The force and beauty of the first sentence of the Bible will be appreciated more fully if we think of the many wild speculations of ancient philosophers, and of the many strange fancies of popular mythologies, respecting the creation of the world. Most of the philosophers held that matter was eternal, and their inquiries turned on the point how it came into its present state. This was the science of Cosmogony. Some ascribed the world to the operation of a principle inherent in matter, working out all things as they now are during long periods of time. Others held that all things emanated from a common divine substance, working everywhere in nature. The one set were materialists, the other pantheists. The popular mythologies were usually grotesque, and even laughable. The doctrine that all things were created, or formed at the beginning out of nothing, by one eternal God, is emphatically the doctrine of the Bible. This doctrine gives us a very lofty conception of God's power and glory,—it places him, as the one all-sufficient Creator, on a height infinitely above every other being; and it is well fitted to remind us of our dependence on him, of our responsibility to him, and of our obligation to submit to his authority, and to live for his glory.

The Creation of Man: Order of Creation.—When the earth was about to be prepared for the residence of man, the Spirit of God moved over it, and spread order and beauty on every side. The work of preparing and ordering it occupied six days, or periods of successive darkness and light. 1. On the first day, light was divided from darkness. 2. On the second, a firmament was formed, dividing the waters above from the waters below; that is, dividing the clouds from the water on the earth's surface. 3. On the third, the dry land was separated from the water, and the vegetable kingdom came into being. 4. On the fourth, the great lights, sun, moon, and stars, appeared in the firmament. It is not said that they were "created" then, but "made;" that is, made as they now are, and adjusted to the earth, which was to depend on them for light, and for the measurement of time. 5. Fish and fowl were the products of the fifth day. 6. On the sixth, the higher orders of animals were formed, and last of all Man, made from the dust of the earth, but in the image of God, with the breath of life breathed by God into his nostrils. The formation of woman was very peculiar—from a rib taken from the side of the man. Some naturalists trace a resemblance here to the propagation of plants by the process of budding. It seems better to admit that as the formation of the man was supernatural, so was the formation of the woman. To denote his dependent condition, the man was made of the dust of the earth; the woman, again, was made from part of the man, to denote her dependence on him, and, at the same time, to show the closeness of their relation to each other, and the obligation of the man "to love his wife as his own flesh."

The Blessing.—The blessing of the Creator was given to the first pair; the earth was bestowed on them to be possessed, replenished, and subdued; divine approval was expressed of the whole work of creation; and the seventh day was consecrated to holy rest—"God blessed the seventh day, and sanctified it: because that in it he had rested from all his work which God created and made."

SECTION III.—TRADITIONS AND TRACES OF CREATION.

Geological traces—"The Chaldæan Genesis"—The week and the sabbath—Man formed from the dust.

Geological Traces.—It has been attempted to be shown that "the testimony of the rocks," that is, the evidence which they present of the order of creation, agrees with the order given in Genesis. The order is not quite the same, but there seems to be more than a casual coincidence. "It has been said that the phenomena under the earth's surface correspond with the succession as described in this chapter;—first, a period of comparative gloom, with more vapour and more carbonic acid in the atmosphere; then of greater light, of vegetation, of marine animals, of birds and beasts; and lastly, of man (Kurtz; Hugh Miller). ......Some few points seem clearly to come out. In Genesis, first of all, creation is spoken of as 'in the beginning,' a period of indefinite, possibly of most remote distance in the past; secondly, the progress of the preparation of the earth's surface is described as gradually advancing from the rocks to the vegetable world, and the less perfectly organized [parts of the] animal creation; then gradually mounting up, through birds and mammals, till it culminates in man. This is the course of creation as popularly described in Genesis; and the rocks give their testimony, at least in the general, to the same order and progress. The chief difference, if any, of the two witnesses, would seem to be that the rocks speak of (1) marine plants, (2) marine animals, (3) land plants, (4) land animals, in their successive developments; whereas Moses speaks of (1) plants, (2) marine animals, (3) land animals—a difference not amounting to divergence. As physiology must have been nearly, and geology wholly, unknown to the Semitic nations of antiquity, such a general correspondence of sacred history with modern science is surely more striking and important than any apparent difference in details." *

"**The Chaldæan Genesis.**"—This is the name given by the

* Bishop Harold Browne in Speaker's Commentary.

late Mr. George Smith, a distinguished Oriental antiquary, to a series of terra-cotta tablets found in the ruins of Nineveh, containing records in the cuneiform character of the ancient Chaldæan traditions of the creation, and of other events recorded in Genesis. The tablets that seem to record the creation are mostly in a very imperfect condition. Mr. Smith says: "The story, so far as I can judge from the fragment, agrees generally with the account of the creation in the Book of Genesis, but shows traces of having originally included much more matter." Of the beginning of the first fragment of the story, the following is his translation: "When above were not raised the heavens; and below, on earth, a plant had not grown up; the abyss also had not broken open its boundaries; the chaos (or water), Tiamat (the sea), was the producing mother of the whole of them." The fifth tablet of the series gives an account of the creation of the heavenly bodies. Part of it runs thus: "It was delightful, all that was fixed by the great gods. ['God saw all that he had made, and, behold, it was very good.'] Stars, their appearance [in figures] of animals, he arranged. To fix the year through the observation of their constellations, twelve months (or signs) of stars in three rows he arranged, from the day when the year commences unto the close." Another fragment, not of the same series, describes the order of the creation of animals—"Cattle of the field, beasts of the field, and creeping things of the field;" agreeing with Genesis—"God made the beast of the earth after his kind, and cattle after their kind, and every thing that creepeth on the earth after his kind; and God saw that it was good." Mr. Smith remarks, in reference to what might have been found if the tablets had not been so much injured:—"The fragment of the first tablet of the creation series showed that that was rather introductory, and dealt with the generation of the gods more than with the creation of the universe; and the fact that the fifth tablet contains the creation given in Genesis under the fourth day, while a subsequent tablet, probably the seventh, gives the creation of the animals, which, according to Genesis, took place on the sixth day, leads to the inference that the events of each of the days of Genesis were recorded on a separate tablet." In some of the legends the first men are called Admi, or Adami, "the dark race." *

It is remarkable that one of the Assyrian tablets contains an account of a revolt in heaven, which, though not recorded in Genesis, is alluded to in other parts of Scripture (Jude 6). The following lines are from this tablet: —

> "The god of holy songs, lord of religion and worship,
> Seated a thousand singers and musicians; and established a choral band,
> Who to his hymn were to respond in multitudes....
> With a loud cry of contempt they broke up his holy song,
> Spoiling, confusing, confounding his hymn of praise.
> The god of the bright crown, with a wish to summon his adherents,
> Sounded a trumpet blast which would wake the dead,
> Which to these rebel angels prohibited return.
> He stopped their service, and sent them to the gods who were his enemies.
> In their room he created mankind
> The first who received life dwelt along with him." †

The Week and the Sabbath. "The [Chaldæan] month was divided into two halves of fifteen days each, these being further subdivided into three periods of five days. But a week of seven days was also in use from the earliest ages. The days of the week were named after the sun, moon, and five planets; and our own week-days may be traced back to the active brains of the long-forgotten people of Chaldæa [the Accadians]. The seventh, fourteenth, nineteenth, twenty-first, and twenty-eighth days of the month were termed 'sabbaths,' or 'days of rest,' when the king was forbidden to eat 'cooked fruit' or 'meat,' to change his clothes or wear white robes, to drive his chariot, to sit in judgment, to review his army, or even to take medicine should he feel unwell." ‡

Three lines of the fifth tablet of creation are thus rendered by Mr. Talbot, another eminent Oriental archæologist:—

> "On the seventh day he appointed a holy day,
> And to cease from all business he commanded
> Then arose the sun in the horizon of heaven in [glory]."

"It has been known for some time," Mr. Talbot adds, "that

---

* See Smith's Chaldæan Account of Genesis, pp 61-86
† Transactions of the Biblical Archæological Society, vol. iv , p 349.
‡ Sayce's Babylonian Literature, pp. 54, 55.

the Babylonians observed the Sabbath with considerable strictness."*

Man Formed from the Dust.—The Egyptians had a tradition that they were formed from the clay of the soil. Other nations had a similar tradition.

SECTION IV.—PARADISE AND THE FALL.

Occupation for man—Locality of Eden—Highlands of Armenia—Trees of the garden—
The tempter—The fall and the punishment—The promise.

Occupation for Man.—No sooner was man created than occupation was provided for his whole nature—body, mind, and soul; for even in the state of innocence and holiness, improvement and development were to be gained by exercise. His body was to be exercised in dressing and keeping the garden in which he was placed; his mind, in observing the works of God and in giving names to the animals; and his soul, in fellowship with his helpmeet, Eve, and in loving, praising, and serving his God.

Locality of Eden.—But in what part of the world was man first placed? In the Bible we read: "God planted a garden eastward in Eden......And a river went out of Eden to water the garden; and from thence it was parted, and became into four heads. The name of the first is Pison: that is it which compasseth the whole land of Havilah, where there is gold; and the gold of that land is good: there is bdellium and the onyx stone. And the name of the second river is Gihon: the same is it that compasseth the whole land of Ethiopia. And the name of the third river is Hiddekel: that is it which goeth toward the east of Assyria. And the fourth river is Euphrates."

Notwithstanding this minute account of the situation, it is not easy to determine the locality of Eden. The word itself means in Hebrew "a delight," but it is not now the name of any particular locality. We find it applied in Scripture to two localities—one in Mesopotamia (2 Kings xix. 12), and the other in the neighbourhood of Damascus (Amos i. 5), but not in con-

* Transactions of the Biblical Archaeological Society, vol. v., p. 427.

nection with the primitive Eden. It is the description of the four rivers which has made identification so difficult.

"The three continents of the Old World have been subjected to the most rigorous search; from China to the Canary Islands, from the Mountains of the Moon to the coasts of the Baltic, no locality which in the slightest degree corresponded to the description of the first abode of the human race has been left unexamined. The great rivers of Europe, Asia, and Africa have in turn done service as the Pison and Gihon of Scripture, and there remains nothing but the New World wherein the next adventurous theorist may bewilder himself in the mazes of this most difficult question." *

Highlands of Armenia.—No district corresponding with what is said of the four rivers being known, some have thought the meaning of the passage to be, that the garden of Eden was so well watered that, on leaving it, its waters formed four rivers.† This were, certainly, to use a liberty with the words; the prevalent notion, however, has been that the garden lay in the highlands of Armenia, where the Euphrates and the Tigris, and two other great rivers, now called the Kizil-Ermak and the Araxes, have their rise. In many particulars the account of Eden given in Genesis agrees with what ancient history and modern research tell us respecting this district. The Pison, it is said, traversed the whole land of Havilah, where there were gold, bdellium, and the onyx stone. The Kizil Ermak flows into the Black Sea, not far from the ancient Colchis, which was celebrated for its gold; for, according to the ancient story, it was thither that the Argonauts sailed from Thessaly to fetch the golden fleece. Many other stories are told illustrating the abundance of gold in the district. Onyx and bdellium (which some consider to be *pearl*, and others *beryl*) and other precious stones, are abundant, and of many varieties. "The land of Ethiopia," encompassed by the Gihon, was not necessarily Ethiopia in Africa; literally, it is "the land of Cush," who was a grandson of Ham, and whose descendants

---

* Smith's Dictionary of the Bible, article *Eden*.
† Kurtz, History of the Old Covenant, i. 73.

peopled various districts, some of them, certainly, in this neighbourhood (Gen. x. 8-10).

This district has quite a garden-like character, being full of beautiful valleys and fertile plains, with groves, orchards, vineyards, gardens, and villages. From the great beauty of its valleys, one of the mountains amid which the Euphrates rises is called Jaghi Tagh, or the Mountain of Flowers. The gardens yield abundance of grapes, oranges, peaches, nectarines, figs, apples, pomegranates, and other fruits. In the eastern part is Lake Van, a great sheet of water, whose shores are bright with poplars, tamarisks, myrtles, and oleanders, while numerous verdant islands scattered over its quiet bosom lend to it the enchanting look of fairy-land. The climate is temperate, and the sky almost always bright and clear.* Mount Ararat, on which the ark of Noah rested, is at no great distance. If all kinds of charming products may identify the spot, we may readily believe that it was in this neighbourhood that Adam first looked on the fair earth of which he was to be the lord; and that it was some of these plains and islands that gave birth to the images of Elysian Fields and Fortunate Islands, that continued, age after age, to gild the traditions of the world.

Trees of the Garden.—Among the trees of this memorable garden, two were conspicuous, but more for their symbolical than for their natural character—" the tree of life in the midst of the garden, and the tree of the knowledge of good and evil." The tree of life seems to have been meant as an emblem and a pledge of a higher and more confirmed state of life, to which Adam and Eve were encouraged to look forward as the reward of obedience. The other tree, of whose fruit they were strictly forbidden to eat—the tree of the knowledge of good and evil—was designed to test their obedience—whether they would follow good or evil.

The Tempter.—For evil already existed in the universe. There was already a race of fallen intelligences, of which Satan was the head, possessing that mysterious power of tempting

* Many other interesting particulars of the district will be found in Chesney's Expedition to the Euphrates, vol. 1., p. 274, &c.

others to follow their example which God has been pleased to allow, under certain limitations, to the wicked. Assuming the form of a serpent—the creature least likely to cause suspicion, "being more subtil than any beast of the field"—this fallen spirit appeared to Eve, knowing her to be the weaker of the two, and skilfully contrived, through her, to effect the ruin of mankind.

The Fall and the Punishment.—First, the tempter placed God's restriction in a harsh light: "Yea, hath God said, Ye shall not eat of every tree of the garden?" Then he contradicted God, and promised safety in sinning: "Ye shall not surely die." Next, he insinuated that God was jealous of their happiness, and had on that account kept the truth from them. And, finally, he promised them great advantage in sinning: "God doth know that in the day ye eat thereof, then your eyes shall be opened, and ye shall be as gods, knowing good and evil." At last he induced the woman to eat the forbidden fruit. Adam, following her example, speedily shared her transgression. An act of high disobedience to God's command was thus deliberately committed, involving, too, the spirit of suspicion, unbelief, and unhallowed ambition; the sin being aggravated by the goodness which God had shown them, and by the fact, of which we can hardly suppose them to have been ignorant, that the condition of their posterity, likewise, would be affected by their sin. A great change passed over them, well indicated by the expressive word commonly applied to the event—the Fall. Death, in a special sense, became their heritage. The body became subject to temporal death, to separation from the animating spirit on which all its powers—sight, hearing, moving, and the like—depend. The soul in like manner lost its communion with God, and, in consequence, became corrupt and disorderly; it died spiritually. The greatness of the change that had taken place in Adam was seen from his running to hide himself when he heard the Lord's voice in the garden. Punishments were ordained for the man and the woman, and a curse was pronounced on the serpent, and on the ground for man's sake. Adam and Eve, now unfit for holy society, were driven from the garden; and cherubim and a flaming sword were placed at the east of the garden, to keep the way of the tree of life.

The Promise.—The infliction of the punishment, however, was accompanied by a remarkable promise, usually known as the first promise of a Saviour. In pronouncing sentence on the serpent, or rather on the seducer who had assumed the form of a serpent, God said, " I will put enmity between thee and the woman, and between thy seed and her seed; it shall bruise thy head, and thou shalt bruise his heel." The promise implied that from the seed of the woman there should come one to crush the head of the serpent and repair the ruins of the Fall. Besides giving the hope of a personal Deliverer, who should contend with Satan and overcome him, the prophecy implied also that there would always be two opposing seeds or parties in the world,—the " seed of the serpent," and the seed or spiritual family of the Deliverer. The two parties would be in conflict with each other, but the one would but bruise the heel of his opponent, while his opponent would ultimately bruise his head. Cain and Abel, the first-born of Adam's sons, represented the two seeds or parties. The whole Bible is full of their conflicts; in the days of Christ, " *the* seed of the woman," these conflicts reached their climax. It was by corrupting this great truth that the Persians were led to believe in two opposite spirits or gods, one good and the other evil, contending for the dominion of the world, and nearly equal in power. Nowhere are the conflicts of the seed of the woman and the seed of the serpent portrayed more vividly than in the Apocalypse: they go on to the very end, never coming to a close till Christ returns to reign, and his adversary is cast into the bottomless pit.

SECTION V.—TRADITIONS OF EDEN AND THE FALL.

Primitive state of happiness—Trees of the garden: Chaldæa, Africa—The serpent—Other traditions of the fall—The serpent's curse.

Primitive State of Happiness.—It was quite to be expected that the memory of Eden and the Fall, and of the promise of a

Deliverer that followed, would be long preserved among the traditions of ancient nations. Accordingly we find traces of them more or less distinct in many quarters. There seems, indeed, to be an instinctive conviction in the human mind that at one time there was a purer, better, and happier world than there is now, just as there is also an instinctive longing and hoping for better days to come. The classical legend of the golden age evidently had its origin in the history of Paradise. Hesiod, Virgil, Tibullus, and Ovid have sung of this bright morning of the world; Ovid, in particular, not only commemorating the golden age, but the silver, brass, and iron ages which followed, each bringing increasing wickedness and woe.

The Trees of the Garden.—"In several places in the Genesis legends [of Chaldæa], and especially in the legends of Isdubar, there are allusions to the tree, grove, or forest of the gods; and this divine tree or grove is often represented on the sculptures, both on the Babylonian gem engravings and on the walls of the Assyrian palaces and temples. When the representation is complete, the tree is attended by two figures of cherubim, one on each side of the sacred emblem." *

Even in the wilds of Africa travellers meet with sacred trees. Dr. Livingstone writes, regarding the fig-tree, which is always planted near native villages: "It is a sacred tree all over Africa and India; and the tender roots which drop down toward the ground are used as medicine—a universal remedy. Can it be a tradition of its being like the tree of life, which Archbishop Whately conjectures may have been used in Paradise to make men immortal?" †

What was the tree of which our first parents were forbidden to eat? "Rabbi Mayer says it was a wheat-tree; Rabbi Jehuda, a grape-vine; Rabbi Aba, a Paradise apple; Rabbi Jose, a fig-tree—therefore it was that when driven out of Paradise they used its leaves for a covering. The Persian story, adopted by the Arabs, is, that the forbidden fruit was wheat, and that it grew on a tree whose trunk resembled gold and its branches

---

* Smith's Chaldæan Account of Genesis, p. 88.
† Livingstone's Last Journals in Central Africa, vol. i, p. 141.

silver. Each branch bore five shining ears, and each ear contained five grains as big as the eggs of an ostrich, as fragrant as musk, and as sweet as honey. The people of South America suppose it was the banana, whose fibres form the cross; and they say that thus in it Adam discovered the mystery of redemption. The inhabitants of the island of St. Vincent think it was the tobacco plant." *

Instrumentality of the Serpent in the Temptation.—"It is quite clear that [in the Chaldæan legends] the dragon of Tiamat, or the sea, is connected with the Fall, like the serpent in the Book of Genesis; and, in fact, is the equivalent of the serpent......The form of this creature, as given on the gems, is that of a griffin or dragon, generally with a head like a carnivorous animal, body covered with scales, legs terminating in claws, like an eagle, and wings on the back......One striking and important specimen of early type in the British Museum collection has two figures, sitting one on each side of a tree, holding out their hands to the fruit, while at the back of one is stretched a serpent. We know well that in these early sculptures none of the figures were chance devices, but that all represented events, or supposed events, and figures in their legends; thus it is evident that a form of the story of the Fall similar to that of Genesis was known in early times in Babylonia. The dragon which, in the Chaldæan account of the creation, leads man to sin, is the creature of Tiamat, the living principle of the sea and of chaos; and he is an embodiment of the spirit of chaos or disorder, which was opposed to the deities at the creation of the world." †

The promise of recovery through the destruction of the serpent may perhaps be traced in various legends, both classical and Oriental, where the serpent is introduced. In the garden of the Hesperides, three sisters, assisted by the dragon Ladon, guarded a tree that bore golden apples. It was one of the labours of Hercules to obtain possession of these apples, and some of the classical fables say that he effected this by slaying the dragon. The legend of Hercules strangling, in his cradle,

* Baring-Gould's Legends: Old Testament Characters, vol. i., p. 26.
† Smith's Chaldæan Account of Genesis, pp. 90, 91.

the serpent sent by Juno to destroy him, and that of Apollo killing the celebrated serpent Python, may have come from the same source. In the traditions of the Hindus, the king of evil demons is called the king of serpents; and their hell is formed of those poisonous creatures folded together in horrible contortions.* Krishna, one of the incarnations of the Almighty, attacked the great serpent, and destroyed him; and in some of the Hindu pictures he is represented with his feet on the serpent's head. In all nations there seems to be an instinctive horror of serpents, and a feeling that without pity or remorse they are to be trampled under foot. It may be that this has no connection with the tragedy of the Fall; but it cannot be denied that a creature that is destitute of all sympathy with man, incapable of kindly feeling towards him, full of deadly poison, cold and slimy, stealing along by a silent and stealthy motion, and often not suspected to be present till its deadly fangs are fastened in its victim, furnishes much the most suitable emblem of a tempter among the creatures of the earth. At the end, as at the beginning of the Bible, "that old serpent the devil" is the inveterate enemy of God and man.

Other Traditions of the Fall.—The most remarkable traditions of the Fall are those preserved in Eastern countries. "With some," says Canon Rawlinson, "the Fall is more gradual than with others. The Greeks pass by gentle degrees from the golden age of primeval man to the iron one, which was the actual condition of human kind when the first writers lived. The Hindus similarly bring man through a second and a third age into that fourth one which they recognize as existing in their day. But with some races the Fall is sudden......In the later Persian writings, which are of uncertain date, a narrative appears which is most strikingly in accordance with that of Genesis. The first man and the first woman live originally in purity and innocence. Perpetual happiness is promised to them by Ormuzd if they persevere in their virtue. They dwell in a garden wherein there is a tree on whose fruit they feed, which gives them life and immortality. But Ahriman, the Evil Principle, envying their

* Kitto's Daily Bible Illustrations, vol. i., p. 67.

felicity, causes another tree to spring up in the garden, and sends a wicked spirit, who, assuming the form of a serpent, persuades them to eat of its fruit, and this fruit corrupts them. Evil feelings stir in their hearts; Ahriman becomes the object of their worship, instead of Ormuzd; they fall under the power of demons, and become a prey to sin and misery."* It is generally believed that this account must have been derived by the Persians from the writings of Moses. The Chinese traditions represent man as originally innocent and happy, but as having fallen, through an inordinate thirst of knowledge, or through flattery, or the temptation of the woman.

The Serpent's Curse.—"It is clear that [in the Chaldæan legends] the dragon is included in the curse for the Fall, and that the gods invoke on the head of the human race all the evils which afflict humanity. Wisdom and knowledge shall injure him (line 22); he shall have family quarrels (line 23); he shall submit to tyranny (line 24); he will anger the gods (line 25); he shall not eat the fruit of his labour (line 26); he shall be disappointed in his desires (line 27); he shall pour out useless prayer (lines 28 and 30); he shall have trouble of mind and body (lines 29 and 31); he shall commit future sin" (line 32).†

* Rawlinson's Historical Illustrations of the Old Testament, pp. 11, 12.
† Smith's Chaldæan Account of Genesis, p. 91.

CHAPTER II.

THE FLOOD.

Genesis iv.-ix.

SECTION I.—THE ANTEDILUVIAN WORLD.

The east gate of Eden—Birth of Cain and Abel—Their offerings—Cain's punishment—Cain and Seth—The two races: Cain's and Seth's—Common parentage of mankind—Primitive civilization—Length of life—Traditions of longevity—Wickedness of the world

The East Gate of Eden.—The cherubim and the flaming sword which guarded the tree of life were placed at the east of the garden. From this we may infer that Adam and Eve took up their residence on the eastern border of the district; probably not far from the present boundary between Turkey and Persia. Even after the Fall there seems to have been a spot, probably beside this east gate of Eden, at which the presence of God was manifested by a shining light or otherwise, and which got the name of "The face of the Lord" (see Gen. iv. 14). This was the sanctuary, or place of worship, where our first parents and their family would present their offerings. There is some reason to believe, although it has been much disputed, that the rite of bloody sacrifices was instituted by God immediately after the Fall, as the method by which men were to express to him their sense of sin and their need of pardon. God seems also to have made a distinction at this period between animals clean and unclean; the former alone being allowed for sacrifice. When an offering was pleasing to him, he signified his acceptance of it by some outward token; perhaps by sending fire from "his presence" to consume it. When it was not accepted, no such token was sent.

Birth of Cain and Abel.—It could not have been very long after the expulsion of Adam and Eve from Eden, when Cain and Abel, who seem to have been the eldest of their children, were born. In their occupations, and in some features of character, the brothers did not differ widely from each other. The one was a tiller of the ground, the other was a shepherd. They were both, apparently, regular in their habits, and attentive to the worship of God.

Their Offerings.—But there was a great difference in their offerings, which revealed a corresponding difference in their characters. Cain's offering was of the fruits of the ground, while Abel brought of the animals of his flock. Some have inferred that Cain by his offering would acknowledge God only as the giver of earthly blessings; while Abel, through the shed blood of his lamb, showed his sense of guilt and dependence on God for atoning mercy. However this may be, it would appear from passages in the New Testament (Heb. xi. 4) that Abel's offering was made in faith, in reliance on the promise of God, and (Heb. xii. 24) that he had an apprehension of the truth that "without shedding of blood is no remission" of sin. The token of acceptance was granted to Abel, but not to Cain. In consequence of the preference shown to his brother, the fire of jealousy began to burn in Cain's bosom, and even a remonstrance from the Lord did not extinguish it. That dangerous and deadly passion gained strength, till at last Cain rose up against his brother and slew him. How great must have been the anguish of Adam and Eve, thus doomed to reap so early the bitter fruits of the Fall,—to see in their first-born son a murderer, and in their second the murdered victim of his brother!

Cain's Punishment.—For this frightful offence Cain was called by God to a speedy reckoning. His sin soon found him out. He was driven from the visible presence of the Lord, and from the society of his brethren; the earth was loaded with an additional curse for him; and though his life was spared, it was attended with neither happiness nor peace. Proceeding eastward, he built a city, or fortified settlement, and became the head of a clan. An old Jewish tradition represents him as having at last become insane, in which state he wandered about more like a wild beast than a man. Enoch, the name of his city, became the headquarters of the more godless and worldly branch of the human family.

Cain and Seth.—Another son of Adam, named Seth, who was born when his father was one hundred and thirty years old, seems to have stepped into Abel's place, and become the head and representative of the more godly branch of mankind. It is far from likely that Cain and Seth were the only sons of Adam (Gen. v. 4). An Eastern tradition (of little value, certainly) assigns to Adam and Eve thirty-three sons and twenty-seven daughters. The reason why no other sons are named is, that they were in no way remarkable. Probably those born between Cain and Seth, Abel excepted, resembled Cain in disposition, and joined his clan. It was not till Seth was born that Abel had a like-minded successor,—one who walked "by faith," felt his guilt in God's sight, and by his burnt-offering expressed his reliance on the free mercy of God. For several generations the population of the world attached itself either to Cain or to Seth, like a river that has divided into two great branches; but the godless branch had the start of the other by at least one hundred and thirty years; and it is not surprising that in these circumstances it was the ungodly branch that prevailed.

The Two Races: Cain's and Seth's.—The race of Cain became distinguished for diligence and success in the pursuit of worldly enjoyment and good. The race of Seth, less ardent in worldly pursuits, were, many of them at least, eminent for piety. Cain's descendants applied themselves to arts and manufactures. Jabal introduced tents or movable dwellings, along with the roaming life for which tents are adapted, so favourable to the increase of cattle. Jubal, his brother, brought musical instruments to such perfection as to be accounted the father of the art of music. Tubal-cain, half-brother of Jabal and Jubal, attained similar eminence as a worker in metals. A Jewish tradition ascribes to Naamah, sister of Tubal-cain, the introduction of ornaments in female dress. In the line of Seth, mention is made of no one who attained great eminence in such pursuits as these. It was the great glory of this race that it gave birth to men like Enoch, who walked with God and was translated without dying; and Noah, who, for his eminent faithfulness, was selected to build the ark, and to become the second father of mankind.

Common Parentage of Mankind.—It appears, from the Scripture account, that the human race sprang from a single pair; that they began life in a state of simple civilization, but without much knowledge; and that it was by degrees that they attained to the knowledge both of the useful and of the ornamental arts. On the other hand, it has been affirmed by some that there are such essential differences between the various existing races—the fair-skinned, energetic Anglo-Saxon, the black-skinned, indolent negro, and the saffron or copper-coloured races of Asia, Australia, and America—as to imply that originally they must have been different races. There are, no doubt, difficulties in the case; and yet, if we consider what changes are wrought both on human beings and on the lower animals, in the course of long periods, by difference of climate, food, education, and employment; and if we further take into account that at first these causes of diversity may have been much more active and powerful than they are now, just as the causes that led men to form and use different languages must have been much more active and powerful in early times,—we shall not find the Scripture account of the origin of man at variance with experience. The fact that sin in many similar forms has spread through all mankind; and also the fact that the gospel has won converts in all, even in the lowest races, that it has been accepted on a large scale by many of them, and that, wherever accepted, it has effected a wonderful transformation, and has produced many striking resemblances to the higher races,—are conclusive proofs that in essential qualities mankind are one, and that they originally constituted a single family.*

---

* "In reference to the status of the African among the nations of the earth," writes Dr. Livingstone. "we have seen nothing to justify the notion that they are of a different breed or species from the most civilized. The African is a man with every attribute of human kind. Centuries of barbarism have had the same effects on Africans as Pritchard describes them to have had on certain of the Irish who were driven some generations

Primitive Civilization.—By some it has been held that the human race was formed in a state of barbarism, and that it has slowly worked its way to civilization, which has always a tendency to increase. The remains of weapons and of implements that have been found belonging to the early inhabitants of various countries, point to a flint age, a bronze age, and an iron age, according as men understood how to fashion such materials. It is to be observed that from the original standard of simple but not very enlightened civilization, men were capable either of falling or of rising; and there is every reason to believe that some fell while others rose. Civilization has certainly not been always in a state of advance. In Central America there are abundant remains of a state of high civilization, which must have been utterly lost, and which was followed by the era of the Red Indians, a people of the rudest character, who gained their livelihood by hunting. In China, civilization has remained stationary for many centuries. There is really nothing in the true history of civilization to impair, but much to confirm, the Scripture account that man was made in a state of simple civilization, with the whole world of invention and discovery lying before him; and that while some fell, and fell deeply, others rose in the knowledge both of nature and of the arts.

Length of Life.—A leading and very remarkable feature of this period was the extraordinary length to which human life was protracted. Adam himself lived nine hundred and thirty years. Methuselah, whose age is the longest recorded, died at nine hundred and sixty-nine. Most of the others were nearly as old. This remarkable arrangement was obviously intended to promote the rapid increase of the human race, the rapid advancement of knowledge and art, and the preservation of the primitive revelation respecting the true God and his worship, and the coming of a Saviour. We shall by-and-by see that it was perverted to very different purposes. It is quite in accordance with what we might have expected, that the traditions of ancient nations should take

back to the hills of Ulster and Connaught; and these depressing influences have had such moral and physical effects on some tribes, that ages probably will be required to undo what ages have done."—*The Zambesi and its Tributaries*, p. 596.

notice of a fact so striking as the longevity of the antediluvians, as well as of the corresponding fact that "there were giants in those days." Josephus has a remarkable passage on the subject. "Let no one," he says, "on comparing the lives of the patriarchs with our lives and with the few years that we now live, think that what we have said of them is false; for those ancients being beloved of God, and made recently by God himself, and because their food was then fitter for the prolongation of life, might well live so great a number of years: and besides, God afforded them a longer time of life on account of their virtue, and the good use they made of it in astronomical and geometrical discoveries, which would not have afforded the time of foretelling unless they had lived six hundred years, for the great year is completed in that interval. Now I have for witnesses to what I have said all those that have written Antiquities, among both the Greeks and the barbarians; for even Manetho, who wrote the Egyptian History, and Berosus, who collected the Chaldæan Monuments, and Mochus, and Hestiæus, and besides these, Hieronymus the Egyptian, and those who composed the Phœnician History, agree to what I here say. Hesiod also, and Hecatæus, Hellanicus, and Acusilaus; and besides these, Ephorus and Nicolaus relate that the ancients lived a thousand years." [*]

Traditions of Longevity.—"It is beyond a doubt," says Rawlinson, "that there is a large amount of consentient tradition to the effect that the life of man was originally far more prolonged than it is at present, extending to at least several hundreds of years. The Babylonians, Egyptians, and Chinese exaggerated these hundreds into thousands. The Greeks and Romans, with more moderation, limited human life within a thousand or eight hundred years. The Hindus still further shortened the term. Their books taught that in the first age of the world, man was free from disease, and lived ordinarily four hundred years; in the second age the term of life was reduced from four hundred to three hundred; in the third it became two hundred; and in the fourth and last it was brought down to one hundred. So certain did the fact appear to the Chinese, that an emperor, who

[*] Antiquities of the Jews, l. iii. 9.

wrote a medical work, proposed an inquiry into the reasons why the ancients attained to so much more advanced an age than the moderns." *

On grounds of science it has been denied that such longevity is possible. But all that science can lawfully say is, that with its present organization the human frame could not last so long. The most cautious naturalists, such as Von Haller and Buffon, have declared that it is impossible to say what may have happened under conditions of which we are ignorant. Originally the body of man was not subject to death; and even after it became subject, the process of decay may not at first have been so rapid. The blood was free from taint of hereditary disease, and other causes that tend to shorten life had not begun to operate. It seems wiser to hold with Von Haller and Buffon, than to accept the more confident objections of modern times.†

Wickedness of the World.—In its moral effects, instead of tending to the good of the species, the great length of life seems generally to have been perverted to evil. For nearly a thousand years, death would be almost unknown in the human race, and that restraint on sinful inclinations which arises from the fear of death and judgment could scarcely exist. Good men had to be always reminding the world of a coming retribution. The substance of Enoch's prophecy, recorded in the Epistle of Jude (ver. 14, 15), shows how much the men of those days lived in forgetfulness of the judgment to come. It is remarkable that corruption of religion and morals advanced most rapidly in the line of Cain, where the greatest progress had been made in art and in science; thus showing that knowledge and civilization, apart from religion, have no power to purify the heart, or to preserve society from corruption. In the course of time, Lamech, a descendant of Cain, seems to have been the first to marry more wives than one. The corruption which had become so great in the line of Cain, became all but universal when the two races, that of Cain and that of Seth, began to intermarry (Gen. vi. 5). Here and there, no doubt, in the

---

* Historical Illustrations, p. 15. See also Pliny, Hist. Nat. vii. 48.
† See the Speaker's Commentary, Gen. v.

Sethite district, a bright star might occasionally be seen in the firmament; but, with a few such exceptions, the moral darkness of the Cainites now overspread the entire horizon. The wickedness of man was very great on the earth. Everywhere the heart, like a fountain, poured forth streams of guilty imaginations. Deeds of violence were perpetrated over the world from end to end. Murder appears to have become extremely common; life ceased to be held sacred; the whole earth was filled with violence and blood; and God, deeming all ordinary chastisements or corrections insufficient for the magnitude of the evil, resolved to destroy the world by a flood.

SECTION II.—NOAH AND THE FLOOD.

Building of the ark—The flood—Leaving the ark—The sacrifice—The rainbow—The covenant with Noah.

Building of the Ark.—Amid the universal wickedness that overspread the world, one faithful man was found among the faithless. Noah was the son of Lamech,—a godly man, who had felt deeply the burden of the curse of the ground, and, under inspiration, had foretold, at the birth of his son, that he should be a source of comfort. But more than six hundred years had to run ere that prophecy was fully verified. Noah was about five hundred years of age when God announced to him his purpose to destroy the world by a flood, and commanded him to build an ark for the preservation of his family, and of the inferior animals. It is generally understood that the ark occupied one hundred and twenty years in building; that during that time the world had a respite; and that Noah, who is called a preacher of righteousness, summoned men, but summoned them in vain, to repentance and reformation. The length of the ark was 300 cubits, its breadth 50, and its depth 30. Estimating the cubit (with Kitto) at about 22 inches, these dimensions are 547 feet, 91 feet, and 47 feet respectively. It need not be supposed that the building of such a vessel was an achievement beyond the mechanical resources of that age. In the early ages men seem to have had a great fancy for colossal works. The progress of the mechanical arts may have been great enough to admit of the building of such a vessel. Within this ark, besides Noah, his wife, his three sons and their wives, were gathered all the different species of beasts and fowls and creeping things, seven of each of the clean species, and two of the unclean. When all was ready, the door of the ark was shut by the hand of the Almighty, and the windows of heaven and the fountains of the deep began to discharge the element of destruction, and continued in active operation for forty days and forty nights.

The Flood. The Bible does not give us so much as a single picture of the dreadful scenes that followed. It merely tells us that the tops of the mountains were covered, and that every living creature that moved on the earth died. It leaves us to conceive the dreadful realities which that statement implies. First of all, there rises before the fancy a scene of terrible conflict,— brawny men fighting with the tempest, carrying their families from height to height, but still pursued by the remorseless foe. The next scene is one of defeat and death. Bleached and bloodless corpses float everywhere, like pieces of wreck over a shoreless sea. Last of all, there is a scene of awful stillness and desolation; not one object being seen but the dull expanse of the ocean; nor one sound of life heard,—only the low moan of its surging waters. Within the ark solemn feelings must have prevailed. The eight souls elected to salvation, while the whole world was engulfed, must surely have been filled with holy awe, and must have poured out their hearts in wonder and praise.

Leaving the Ark. For many months the ark floated over a shoreless sea, until at length signs of assuaging began to appear. Seven months after Noah had entered it, the vessel grounded among the mountains of Ararat. Another period nearly as long elapsed before Noah got instructions to leave his temporary prison. Before leaving the ark, he had sent forth a raven, which returned no more; and along with it a dove, which came back to the ark: a week later he had sent forth the dove, and she had returned in the evening, bringing in her mouth an olive-leaf: after another week he again sent forth the dove, and she did not return.

The Sacrifice.—When he left the ark, his first act was to build an altar, and offer on it such a sacrifice as had probably never before been presented to the Lord: "He took of every clean beast, and of every clean fowl, and offered burnt-offerings on the altar." The fragrance of the offering was pleasant to Jehovah; and in order to calm the spirit of Noah and his family, who could not but dread the return of a similar visitation, God said that no such flood should again be sent upon the earth.

The Rainbow.—The rainbow was given to Noah as a pledge of this promise, and of the covenant made with him. Whether (as some think) the "triumphal arch" appeared now for the first time, or whether it was only appropriated as the seal of this covenant, we are not told. The poet Campbell has pictured the scene:—

> "When o'er the green undeluged earth
> Heaven's covenant thou didst shine,
> How came the world's gray fathers forth
> To watch thy sacred sign!
> And when its yellow lustre smiled
> O'er mountains yet untrod,
> Each mother held aloft her child,
> To bless the bow of God."

The Covenant with Noah.—God now blessed Noah and his sons; the earth was again gifted to him as it had been to Adam; his charter of dominion over the lower animals was renewed: their flesh was now, for the first time, allowed him for food, it being carefully provided that the blood, in which the life was seated, was not to be eaten, and that any one who should shed the blood of his fellow-man should forfeit his own life by the guilty deed. Thus the human race started anew, under the blessing of God, as a race of saved men, rescued from destruction by the faith of their father Noah.

SECTION III.—TRADITIONS AND TRACES OF THE FLOOD.

Number and variety of the traditions—Chaldæan traditions—Greek traditions—Chinese and American traditions—Depression of the land near Ararat.

Number and Variety of the Traditions.—No event in Scripture history has been so remarkably preserved in ancient traditions and legends as the flood. It occurs alike in the traditions of the three great branches into which the human race has been divided by scholars—the Semitic, the Aryan, and the Turanian. As might have been expected, the traditions were generally most accurate and minute in the countries that lay nearest to the spot where the ark was deposited.

Chaldæan Traditions.—The Chaldæan traditions are remarkable for their close correspondence to the narrative of Genesis. The tradition preserved by the historian Berosus makes the god Kronos appear to Xisuthrus, announcing to him that there is to be a flood by which mankind will be destroyed, and enjoining him to build a vessel, in which he and his friends, together with all the different animals, should commit themselves fearlessly to the deep. When the flood has begun to abate, birds are sent out from the vessel, which return the first time as they went; the second time their feet are tinged with mud; and the third time they return no more. The vessel is found to be stranded on one of the mountains of Armenia.

A more minute account of the flood has lately been deciphered by Mr. Smith, from the Chaldæan inscriptions found in Assyria. Izdubar (supposed by him to be Nimrod) goes to Hasisadra, the holy man who survived the flood, and gets an account of it from him. Hasisadra relates that the god Hea appeared to him, announced the purpose of the gods to destroy men for their sins, and ordered him to make a ship of certain dimensions (not clearly deciphered), therein to gather his grain, furniture, and goods, his wealth, women-servants, female slaves, young men, the beasts and animals of the field—Hea promising to close the door. Hasisadra remonstrates, says he will be mocked and so forth, but proceeds with the ship, the process of building which is detailed; and it is mentioned that there were poured over it when it was finished three measures of bitumen inside, and the same outside. "Shamas," the sun-god, sent the flood, which raged fiercely, and "destroyed all life from the face of the earth." On the seventh day the deluge ended. Seven days after, Hasisadra sent forth a dove, which came back; then a swallow, which also returned; then a raven, which returned not. On the peak of the mountain where his ship rested he built an altar, and the gods collected "like flies" at the burning of the herbs, etc., which he placed on it. The god Bel wished to destroy him, but was appeased by Ninip; and Hea came to Hasisadra, took him by the hand, led him to the country, and made a covenant with him. This story differs in some details from the Bible narrative, but in substance it is very like it. We see in it clear traces of a prevalent polytheism, to which it has been adapted. Generally all these narratives are marked by a tendency to wordy embellishment: the severe simplicity of the Bible history bears inward evidence of its truth.*

Greek Traditions.—Among Aryan or Indo-European nations, the tradition preserved among the Greeks is worthy of special notice. The accounts of it vary, but according to Lucian the flood was sent as a punishment of the sins of mankind, and the whole race perished with the exception of Deucalion and his family, he being preserved on account of his piety. A chest was provided for his safe custody; and as he was entering it, all kinds of beasts and reptiles came running to him, and were admitted into the chest. The gods instilled such a spirit of peace into them, that they all lived quietly; and when the flood was past they were released from the vessel. The vessel came to land on the top of Parnassus. Ovid has given a somewhat different and more poetical account of the flood.

Chinese and American Traditions. Among Turanian races, the Chinese traditions are interesting, but those preserved by

---

* Smith's Chaldæan Genesis, p. 261, &c. Mr. Smith enumerates twenty-three points of correspondence between the Chaldæan account of the flood and that in Genesis, though the details are sometimes different. The difference of detail shows that the one could not have been taken from the other.

the early Americans are more remarkable. In Mexico, there have been found paintings representing a man and his wife in a boat or raft; a mountain rising beside them; and also birds, such as the dove and the vulture. The Cherokee Indians of North America had a tradition of a flood which destroyed all men, except a single family that were saved in a boat.—These are but samples of the traditions of the flood that have prevailed everywhere: they go to confirm the account of Scripture that the flood was no myth or vision, but a true historical event.[*]

Depression of the Land near Ararat.—In connection with the locality where the ark is said to have rested, it is a remarkable fact that the district lying to the east of Ararat bears traces of having at one time been under water. It is a peculiarly depressed region, lying lower than the districts around, and thus affording peculiar facilities for such a submersion. The level of the Caspian is eighty-three feet below that of the Black Sea; and vast plains, white with salt and charged with sea-shells, show that at no distant period the Caspian was much more extensive than now. From Herodotus and other ancient writers it appears that at one time the Sea of Azof (the *Palus Mœotis* of the ancients) was nearly equal in extent to the Black Sea.

SECTION IV.   REPEOPLING OF THE EARTH.

Ararat—The cradle of the human race—Seeds of life—Man's new career.

Ararat.—Ararat is the name of the mountains where the ark rested, or more probably, perhaps, of the district where the mountains were situated (see Isa. xxxvii. 38, *margin;* and Jer. li. 27); and the plains in their neighbourhood must have been the first settlements of the new fathers of mankind. Ararat has in one respect shared the fate of Eden; its honours have been claimed by many mountains in different countries. But there is no good

---

[*] Rawlinson's Historical Illustrations, p. 20, &c.; Kitto's Bible Readings, vol. i. p. 158, &c.

reason for doubting that the mountain on which the ark rested was one of the mountains in Armenia which still bear the name. Ararat is the name of a district watered by the river Araxes, and lying between the Black and Caspian Seas. In this province there is a mountain with a double peak, to which the name Ararat is commonly given, the smaller of the two peaks being called the Little Ararat. The taller summit rises to the height of 17,750 feet above the level of the sea, or 1,500 feet higher than Mont Blanc. The Persians call it Kuhi Nuch, or Noah's Mountain. The difficulties of the ascent are so great that it has seldom been attempted. According to a monkish tradition, the ascent is impossible: St. Gregory, who attempted it, fell asleep repeatedly from exhaustion, and always found on awaking that he had been carried back unconsciously to the spot whence he set out. But in the year 1829, Professor Parrot, a German, after two failures, at length succeeded in reaching the summit.* He found it to consist of a circular platform, about 220 feet in diameter, composed of eternal ice, unbroken by rock or stone. All travellers speak of the general appearance of Mount Ararat in terms of the highest rapture. "Nothing," says Morier, "can be more beautiful than its shape, more awful than its height. All the surrounding mountains sink into insignificance when compared with it. It is perfect in all its parts: no hard, rugged features; no unnatural prominences; everything is in harmony, and all combine to render it one of the sublimest objects of nature." Sir Robert Ker Porter says: "From the spot on which I stood, it appeared as if the hugest mountains of this world had been piled upon each other to form this one sublime immensity of earth and rock and snow. The icy peaks of its double head rose majestically into the clear and cloudless heavens; the sun blazed bright upon them, and the reflection sent forth a dazzling radiance equal to other suns."† The tradition that the ark rested on the summit of this particular mountain is very improbable, and of little value: it probably arose from the very grandeur of the

* It was ascended by Professor Bryce of Oxford in 1876.
† Kitto's Bible Illustrations, i. 174.

mountain. The expression in the Bible is, that "the ark rested upon the mountains," or mountainous region, "of Ararat."

The Cradle of the Human Race.—The garden of Eden, as we have seen, probably lay near the eastern foot of Ararat; and it would seem that Noah and his sons went forth from the ark to repeople the earth near the very spot where Adam had settled when he went out from Eden. This part of Western Asia is thus distinguished pre-eminently as the birth-place of the human family.

Seeds of Life.—It was not with the seeds of physical life only that this region was charged; intellectual life, and still more, spiritual life, had their sources, not in the same spot, but in the same district. A circle, with its centre at Haran, and a radius of four hundred miles, would embrace Eden and Ararat; Babylon and Nineveh, early seats of learning and science; Mesopotamia, where God revealed himself to Abraham; Phœnicia, where commerce and many of the arts of peace arose; Palestine, the birth-place of prophets, apostles, and evangelists innumerable, and the scene of the birth, labours, and death of our blessed Lord; Tarsus, where Paul was born; and part of Asia Minor, where the labours of the apostles were chiefly carried on. Over this wonderful district, where life was once so abundant, darkness and death have brooded for centuries: the sword of the Turk and the bigotry of the Mohammedan have made it a valley of dry bones, very many and very dry.

Man's New Career.—God had now revealed himself in a very emphatic way: first, as the punisher of the wicked and impenitent; and, second, as the saviour of those who believe. He confirmed these aspects of his character in the covenant he made with Noah, when he gave him anew the earth to be possessed. Noah and his sons started on their new career with a new experience both of sin and of grace. All that had happened was fitted to deepen their fear of God, their sense of his undeserved mercy, and their obligations to serve and worship him in accordance with his holy will.

CHAPTER III.

THE DISPERSION.

FROM THE FLOOD TO THE BIRTH OF ABRAHAM.

GENESIS ix.-xi.

SECTION I.—SETTLEMENTS OF NOAH'S SONS.

Noah's vine—His prophecy—Its fulfilment—Descendants of Japheth—Descendants of Ham—Descendants of Shem.

Noah's Vine.—When Noah left the ark, he probably pitched his tent somewhere on the slopes or in the valleys of Ararat. Directing his attention to the cultivation of plants, he became acquainted with the peculiarities of the vine; he became acquainted, too, to his cost, with the intoxicating property of its juice when fermented, and himself fell once at least under its pernicious influence. But it is only a conjecture that he was the first that discovered the intoxicating quality of wine; it is not likely that the antediluvian world would be ignorant of that. Probably Noah's previous pursuits had been of a different kind; but now the necessity of the case compelled him to be a husbandman, and brought him into personal contact with a process with which formerly he had not had to do.

His Prophecy.—Having made himself drunk from the fruit of his vineyard, the patriarch was found by his son Ham lying in his tent naked and helpless. Instead of respectfully mourning over the sin and humiliation of his father, Ham called his two brothers apparently to enjoy the sport of looking on the shame and helplessness of the old man. But in their better constituted minds the sight raised very different feelings: they hastened to cover and conceal their father's shame. On awaking from his drunkenness, Noah, in the spirit of prophecy, assigned to his three sons the rewards and the punishments of their respective deeds. At that time of the world's depopulation, the few men that were in it seem to have acted more in a representative than in an individual capacity. It was, therefore, the posterity of his three sons rather than themselves that were affected by these rewards and punishments. Canaan, one of the sons of Ham, received the heaviest share of the punishment which his father had provoked. The descendants of Shem were to be blessed; God was to dwell in their tents; and the Canaanites were to become their servants.* "Enlargement" was to be the portion of the descendants of Japheth, indicating that they were to spread over the widest portion of the globe.

Its Fulfilment.—The event corresponded with the prophecy. In general terms, it may be said that most of Africa was peopled by the descendants of Ham; most of Central Asia by those of Shem; and most of Europe by those of Japheth. According to an Armenian tradition, Ham received the region of the blacks, Shem the region of the tawny, and Japheth the region of the ruddy. For a time, some of Ham's descendants, particularly the Egyptians and Phœnicians, and the Cushite founders of Babylonia, were the foremost and most vigorous races of the world; but the period of their ascendency passed away: a great part of the Canaanites were subdued and destroyed by the Israelites; the Cushite Chaldæans were absorbed by Semitic conquerors; and even the Phœnicians, with their mighty daughter, Carthage, ultimately fell before their foes. Though the curse of Ham was formally pronounced on Canaan alone, it has been reflected more or less on the other branches of

---

* The words of Noah's prophecy, "He shall dwell in the tents of Shem," have been understood by some as meaning that Japheth should take possession of Shem's dominions. It is more natural to understand the meaning to be, that God would dwell in Shem's tents, and thereby confer on him the blessing. This he did when he took Abraham into covenant with himself, and through him blessed the world. It is common to say that the British rule in India is an instance of Japheth dwelling in the tents of Shem. But the races of India do not seem to have been Shemites; the resemblance of their languages to those of Europe would rather prove them to be of Japhethic origin.

his family; the black-skinned African became a synonym for weakness and degradation. The blessing of God rested very conspicuously on Shem during the long period of Asiatic ascendency, and especially on the Jews — that branch of the Shemites that overpowered the Canaanites, and in whose tents God had his habitation, in the "tabernacle of Mount Zion." But the Shemites were more a stationary than a progressive race. In vigour, enterprise, and progressive power generally, the race of Japheth has excelled them all. For many an age the Japhethites were little known or heard of; they expended their energy in wild and warlike pursuits on the remote plains of Europe and Northern Asia. But for more than two thousand years they have been the dominant races of the world. Every year the race of Japheth spreads wider and wider over the globe; whole continents are peopled by him, and, either as colonist or as trader, his foot rests upon every soil.

Descendants of Japheth.—*Gomer*, the eldest son of JAPHETH, is thought to have been the ancestor of many of the nations that peopled the continent and the islands of Europe, in some of whose names (for example, Germans, Cimbri, Cambri, Cumbri, Cimmerii, Crimea) the principal consonants in "Gomer," or letters corresponding to them, are still preserved. *Magog* represents the Scythians; *Madai*, the Medes; *Javan*, the Greeks; *Tiras*, the Thracians. *Ashkenaz*, eldest son of Gomer, is believed to have peopled the shores of the Black Sea, which received from him its first designation, Axenus, afterwards changed into Euxine. *Magog*, *Tubal*, and *Meshech* are noticed by Ezekiel (ch. xxxviii. 2, 14, 15) as settled in the north; and perhaps their names may be recognized in the well-known terms, Mogul, Mongolia, Tobolski, Moscow, and Muscovy. From these, or from other descendants of Japheth that peopled "the isles," or remote coasts "of the Gentiles," the great races of Europe, including the Greeks, the Romans, and the more modern nations, must have sprung.

Descendants of Ham.—Of the sons of HAM, the first-born, *Cush*, appears to have peopled more districts than one. One of these was "the land of Cush" (Ethiopia) mentioned in the description of Eden (Gen. ii. 13), a district somewhere near the Caspian Sea; another, and the principal, was the well-known land of Ethiopia beyond Egypt. Cush is also declared to have been the father of Nimrod, a mighty hunter and a mighty conqueror, and the founder of the first great Mesopotamian kingdom. *Misr*, or *Mizraim*, was evidently the ancestor of the Egyptians; in Hebrew, the land of Egypt is invariably called Mizraim, and one of its present designations is the land of Misr. Mauritania and other more remote parts of Africa are thought to have been peopled by *Phut*; while *Canaan*, Ham's youngest son, was father of the Phœnicians, and of the nations that were destroyed or driven out for their sins from the land of Canaan, to make way for the children of Israel. *Heth*, one of the sons of Canaan, is now known to have been the progenitor of a very great people; for the Hittites have been proved to have been one of the greatest nations of the East.

Descendants of Shem.—The sons of SHEM were Elam, Asshur, Arphaxad, Lud, and Aram. *Elam* seems to have settled in Eastern Persia. *Asshur* was represented by the Assyrians. *Arphaxad*, the progenitor of the Shemitic Chaldæans, dwelt in Mesopotamia, north and west of Asshur and Elam, and became, through his grandson *Eber*, the father of the Hebrews. *Lud* is thought to have been the father of the Lydians. *Aram's* settlement embraced the district of Syria near Damascus, and the northern part of Mesopotamia, called Padan-aram. *Uz*, the eldest son of Aram, gave his name to the country where Job went through his unprecedented trials. Though there is great uncertainty as to the exact territories of many of the descendants of Noah's sons, the general position of the settlements of the three great families is tolerably plain. They did not, however, all settle peaceably in their proper territories. Nimrod's kingdom was founded in the very heart of the Shemite district. Another family of Ham's, the Phœnicians, were considerably Semitised, or assimilated to the Shemites, in language and otherwise, when they became prominent in history. It is impossible to draw a distinct line separating all the different families.

SECTION II.—THE TOWER OF BABEL AND CONFUSION OF TONGUES.

The project of the tower—Its probable purpose—Frustrated—Chaldæan traditions—Birs Nimrood: inscription on tablet—The first language.

The Project of the Tower.—The orderly division of the globe among the families of Noah's sons was not effected by quiet and natural means. Mankind had got a very solemn lesson through the flood, that might have taught them their absolute dependence on God on the one hand, and the folly and sin of departing from the pure mode of worship which He required of them on the other. But in a few generations these lessons began to be disregarded, and even to be despised. An intimation appears to have been made of the divine will that men should disperse themselves over the earth; but instead of being humbly obeyed, it awoke the spirit of proud resistance. The Mesopotamian plain, or plain of Shinar, was the head quarters of the human family, and here a conspiracy was set on foot: "Let us build us a city and a tower, whose top may reach unto heaven; and let us make us a name, lest we be scattered abroad upon the face of the whole earth."

Its probable Purpose.—It is not very clear what the specific purpose of the tower really was. Perhaps it was to serve as a rallying-point to keep the people together, and to prevent that eclipse of their greatness and glory which would have resulted from their dispersion over the earth. In any case it was an act of defiance of God, and showed the need of a new chastisement. It is, moreover, probable that idolatry had begun to prevail, and that the tower was to be built in honour of those gods in whom, rather than in the God of Noah, men were disposed to put their trust. The taste for colossal works, which we have already noticed as characteristic of the early periods of the world, was thus shown anew.

Frustrated.—The method which God adopted for frustrating the design of the builders was to confuse their tongues. We have no information as to the way in which this was effected. The narrative implies that hitherto the descendants of Noah had spoken one language, but that now they began to speak several. It is also implied that the change was effected by a direct interposition of the divine will, compelling men to separate from one another, the speakers of each language naturally departing from the rest. It is quite possible that along with this direct interposition of God, certain natural principles operated in the formation and development of the different tongues; for the leading families of languages are distinguished by certain characteristics which seem to be due in a large measure to natural tendencies.

Chaldæan Traditions.—The tower of Babel having been in Chaldæan territory, we naturally inquire whether the Chaldæan histories contain any allusion to it. Mr. George Smith believed that on three Babylonian carvings he found a distorted representation of it; and afterwards on an Assyrian fragment he thought that he had obtained the story of the tower. But the latter fragment was extremely mutilated, and his translation is little better than a guess.*

In one of the early Christian writers it is stated that a belief prevailed in Babylon that "not long after the flood the ancient race of men were so puffed up with their strength and tallness of stature, that they began to despise and contemn the gods, and laboured to erect that very lofty tower which is now called Babylon, intending thereby to scale heaven. But when the building approached the sky, behold, the gods called in the aid of the winds, and by their help overturned the tower and cast it to the ground. The name of the ruin is still called Babel, because

---

* The first column runs thus:—
    Line 1. ....them (?) the father....
    2 and 4. ....of him, his heart was evil,
    3. ....against the Father of all the gods was wicked,
    5 and 7. ....Babylon brought to subjection.
    6 and 8. ....[small] and great, he confounded their speech
    9. Their strong place all the day they founded
    10. to their strong place in the night
    11. entirely he made an end
    12. In his anger also word thus he poured out
    13. [to] scatter abroad he set his face
    14. He gave this (?) command, their counsel was confused.
    15. ..the course he broke
    16. ....fixed the sanctuary
In Transactions of the Biblical Archæological Society, vol. v, p. 304, Mr. Boscawen gives a similar translation.

until this time all men had used the same speech, but now there was sent upon them a confusion of many and diverse tongues."*

Birs Nimrood.—Turning from books to the country itself, we may ask, Are any ruins or remains to be seen that may indicate the locality of the tower? It used to be believed that a vast mound, called Birs Nimrood, about six miles to the west of the modern town of Hillah, on the Euphrates, and near the site of Babylon, was the remains of the tower of Babel. Mr. George Smith held that opinion,† and Professor Sayce‡ supports it, though others think differently. Birs Nimrood is a huge brick mound, oblong in form, measuring about seven hundred yards round, and rising to the height of from one hundred and fifty to two hundred feet. From an inscription deciphered by Sir Henry Rawlinson, it appears that Birs Nimrood was situated, not in Babylon, but at Borsippa, and that its name was "The Stages of the Seven Spheres." It is not unlikely that the tower of Babel was an erection of the same kind. It consisted of seven stages or stories, coloured so as to represent "the seven planets," according to the tints which the Sabaeans considered appropriate to each. The lowest stage was black, the colour for Saturn; the next, orange, for Jupiter; the third, bright red, for Mars (Merodach); the fourth, golden, for the Sun; the fifth, pale yellow, for Venus; the sixth, dark blue, for Mercury; and the seventh, silver, for the Moon. These marks indicated the prevalence of idolatrous worship; and they give probability to the supposition that the tower of Babel was intended to do honour to the Babylonian gods.

Greek Traditions.—In the traditions of the classical nations, we may perhaps trace the story of the tower of Babel in the Greek legend of the giants attempting to pile Mount Ossa upon Pelion, in order to reach Mount Olympus, which was supposed to be the residence of the gods. The gods, it was said, frustrated the attempt, and dispersed the impious conspirators.

The First Language.—That men originally spoke the same language, and that the varieties of human tongues arose from

---
* Eusebius, Preparatio Evangelica. Rawlinson's Historical Illustrations. p. 26.
† Chaldaean Genesis, p. 161. ‡ Babylonian Literature, p. 56.

some remarkable cause, or were greatly promoted thereby, is in some measure supported by philological research. Some authorities affirm that it is possible that all languages sprang from a common source. It is an established position that the various existing languages belong to three great families—Aryan, Semitic, and Turanian; corresponding roughly to the three sons of Noah—Japheth, Shem, and Ham. It is impossible to say what the original language was. It was long supposed to have been Hebrew, because in that language names that were given on account of certain qualities (such as, Eve, Cain, Seth, &c.) bear the meanings on account of which the names are said to have been chosen; but it was so much the custom to translate names by words of corresponding meaning in another language, that this argument goes for little. The old story of Psammitticus, recorded by Herodotus, that he caused two children to be brought up without hearing a word spoken, and that, finding the first word they uttered to be Becos, which in Phrygian means bread, he inferred that Phrygian was the original tongue, is manifestly fantastic and foolish. Hitherto no inscription has been found of sufficient antiquity to throw light on the question.

SECTION III.—CITIES AND EMPIRES OF THE PERIOD.

The two early empires—Nimrod and the Chaldæan empire—The early Accadians Accad and Sumir—The Egyptian empire—Origin of the Egyptians—Unsettled chronology—Monumental records Early civilization.

The Two Early Empires. — After the confusion of tongues, the plain where the tower had been built continued to enjoy pre-eminence in the history of the world. From a period of almost equal antiquity, another plain became celebrated as the home of another great nation. The Chaldæans in the plain on the banks of the Euphrates and the Tigris, and the Egyptians in the plain on the banks of the Nile, were the two nations that attained at the earliest period to a condition of high civilization and influence. It is impossible to say which of these great nations first attained its high civilization. They appear to have started very early in the race, and to have made about equally rapid progress.

Nimrod and the Chaldæan Empire.—The founder of the empire on the Euphrates was Nimrod, a descendant of Ham, whose exploits as a hunter are thought to have helped him to the royal dignity, and who, according to Eastern writers, was the first man who wore a crown. He began to reign at Babel; and among his cities were Erech, Accad, and Calneh, in the land of Shinar. According to our marginal reading, he went out of that district to Assyria, and built Nineveh on the Tigris, and other important cities. Until recently, these short notices in Genesis constituted the whole information men possessed respecting the origin of Chaldæan civilization.

The early Accadians.—Of late years, however, much interesting knowledge has been acquired on this subject from the Chaldæan and Assyrian inscriptions. From these it appears that a people known as the Accadians carried civilization to a high pitch in the Chaldæan plain at a very early period. The language of these Accadians was of the Turanian family, showing that they were not of Semitic origin,[*] and corresponding to the fact stated in Genesis that it was under Nimrod, a Cushite, that the Chaldæan kingdom began.

Accad and Sumir.—When we first come into contact with this ancient Chaldæan people they have two kingdoms, Accad and Sumir; with two capitals, Accad in the northern, and Ur in the southern kingdom. The remains of libraries still surviving show that at a very early period they were in possession of a most extensive literature. The books forming these libraries were on many different subjects, such as history, science, law, and theology, proving that they had given great attention to all these departments, and had made great progress in them. British Oriental scholars are of opinion that it was this Accadian people that laid the foundation of the whole Chaldæan civilization—that Chaldæan literature, astronomy, art, and religion, originated with them. They were a people of original and inventive genius, like the Greeks afterwards, sowing the seeds that came to maturity in later times. The Assyrians, who were of a

---

[*] Smith's History of Babylonia, p. 16. Oriental scholars are not yet quite agreed on this.

different stock, were not original or inventive, and borrowed their civilization from the Chaldæans. It is believed, further, that this Accadian people were subdued at an early period by a Semitic people, who abolished their language, but retained their literature, art, and religion.*

The Egyptian Empire.—The other great centre of early civilization was Egypt. It must have been at a very early period after the dispersion that Mizraim and his company, directing their march southward, settled on the banks of the Nile, and laid the foundations of the great empire of Egypt. "Thus much may be regarded as certain, that the cradle of the Egyptian people must be sought in the interior of the Asiatic quarter of the world. In the earliest ages of humanity, far beyond all historical remembrance, the Egyptians, for reasons unknown to us, left the soil of their primeval home, took their way towards the setting sun, and finally crossed that bridge of nations, the Isthmus of Suez, to find a new fatherland on the favoured banks of the holy Nile." †

Origin of the Egyptians.—The old Egyptians used to boast of a great antiquity, reaching to many centuries before the beginning of our era. A history of Egypt, written some 250 B.C., by Manetho, an Egyptian priest, has unfortunately perished, but some fragments of it have been preserved by the Jewish historian Josephus. The tradition of the country was that at first the gods ruled over Egypt. Then came a dynasty of demi-gods. These traditions are of course mythical, and receive no confirmation from the old monumental inscriptions as these have lately been deciphered. It was about the beginning of this century that a clew was found to the hieroglyphical or sacred writing of the Egyptians,‡ in which the inscriptions were written that cover countless tombs, temples, obelisks, and other monuments, and many rolls of papyrus, recording the

---

* Sayce's Babylonian Literature, p. 6.
† A History of Egypt under the Pharaohs, derived entirely from the monuments. By Henry Brugsch-Bey. Translated from the German. Vol. i , p. 2.
‡ Sometimes the characters employed are images of the objects denoted,—a small circle denoting the sun; or a crescent the moon; or a male and a female figure together, denoting mankind at large: sometimes one object is substituted for another resembling it,— as heaven and a star for night; a leg in a trap for deceit; a man breaking his own head

events of the kingdom. The information that has been obtained by this means respecting the ancient condition and history of Egypt is extensive and most interesting, though not complete.

Unsettled Chronology.—Egyptian archæologists differ in opinion as to the length of the authentic period of Egyptian history. Six writers quoted by Brugsch represent it as having begun at various periods before Christ, ranging from 3150 years to 5702. The period does not exceed by any very great space the time allowed by our ordinary chronology; while the fact that authorities differ to the extent of 2552 years shows how much uncertainty still belongs to the subject. How far the dynasties were contemporaneous, is still an unsettled question.

Monumental Records.—According to Manetho, thirty dynasties of kings ruled Egypt in succession. On the whole, the monuments confirm this statement, and furnish considerable additional information respecting many of the kings. In fact, the knowledge of Egyptian history supplied by these monuments is such that the late Dr. Brugsch, a distinguished German scholar, who spent a great part of his life in Egypt, exploring its monuments and deciphering its inscriptions, proposed to himself the task of writing the history of the country from the monuments alone, from Menes, the first king, to Ismaël Pacha, the late khedive. Part of this intention he fulfilled in the work entitled "Egypt under the Pharaohs." Many of the inscriptions deciphered by him are of great antiquity, and they bear abundant evidence to an advanced state of civilization at a very early period. It is certain that many great monuments of early civilization had been reared before Abraham visited the country; and in particular that the massive forms of some of the largest pyramids were already to be seen in the plain of El-Gizeh. Already the walls of many tombs and tem-

with an axe, for the wicked; or a youth with his finger in his mouth, for a child; and sometimes an enigmatic or emblematic figure is put for the one intended to be represented,—as a hawk for the sun; or a seated figure with a curved beard for a god. The use of these hieroglyphics is immensely ancient. They are found in the Great Pyramid, which is ascribed to the fourth dynasty; and they have the appearance of having been long in use at that time. They are far older than any other known writing. Both the art of writing and the use of the pen are shown to have been common when the pyramids were built. The fact is important, because it proves that Moses may quite easily have found materials for placing on record the history which he was inspired to write.

ples were covered with those inscriptions which the scholars of the present day are translating into our languages.

Early Civilization.—The activity and industry of the Egyptians at this period were wonderful. Their power of erecting large buildings and executing other laborious projects was greatly increased by the large number of captives they took in war, and by the vast masses of spoil, as recorded on the monuments, which they obtained from the captured cities. We shall have occasion in another chapter to describe more particularly the state of Egypt, when the sons of Jacob went to settle within its boundaries. At least twelve of the old dynasties of kings must have reigned in Egypt before that event. During all that time the country was making steady progress in conquest, in wealth, in all kinds of learning and art, and especially in architecture. The monuments quite prepare us for the advanced condition of social progress which Egypt is seen to have attained when Bible history first comes into contact with it.

SECTION IV.—THE RISE AND SPREAD OF IDOLATRY.

Religions of man—Aversion to pure worship—The earliest gods—Origin of polytheism—Debasing influence of idolatry—Agreement of different systems—Overthrow of idolatry.

We have yet to notice the most important of the changes that took place during this period of history— the progress of religious corruption, and the rise and all but universal prevalence of idolatry.

Religions of Man. It is very remarkable that wherever men went, they forsook the pure worship of the true God, as it had been practised by Noah, and instituted religious rites and practices of their own. They did not throw religion to the winds, or live without any sort of worship; but they changed both the object and the forms of worship, as these had been revealed to their fathers by God. The reason why men have never abandoned all worship is, that a religious sentiment is natural to them, and that they cannot rid themselves of the sense of dependence on a higher Power. The sense of guilt needing to be pardoned, of darkness needing light, of disorder needing renewal, and of utter helplessness in the prospect of death and judgment, has always been strong enough in the breasts of men to prevent them from utterly abandoning religious worship.

Aversion to Pure Worship.—But why did they not worship God as he had revealed himself to the fathers of the race, and according to the ordinances which he had appointed? The explanation of this fact seems to lie in the recoil of man's heart from the perfect purity of God's character, and in his unwillingness to deal directly with a Being so much higher and holier than himself. Man shrinks from direct fellowship with the Holy One, as Adam hid from him in Eden; and if he does not know, or does not like the Mediator to whom the first promise pointed, he devises methods and mediators of his own for approaching the Most High. He prefers to pay homage to God through his great works, the sun, the moon, and the stars; or to make images to represent his attributes, and to worship him through these; or to call in the aid of beings inferior to God but superior to himself, and ask them to intercede with God on his behalf. When the mind becomes very dark and degraded, it resorts to magical charms and similar devices as means of obtaining the favour of the powers above.

The Earliest Gods.—In such ways as these idolatry and false worship began. The sun, the moon, and the stars early attracted attention, as manifestations of God, and received religious worship accordingly. In Chaldæa, the earliest gods were Anu, lord of the heavens; Bel, lord of the visible world; and Hea, lord of the sea and the infernal regions. Among the ancient Persians, or fire-worshippers, as they were called, no other worship was allowed but that of the heavenly bodies. In Egypt, homage was also paid to images, and even to inferior animals, such as the ox and the ibis, as representing attributes of God. Departed heroes and saints, eminent for their greatness or their goodness, were constituted, by almost all nations, mediators on behalf of the living.

Origin of Polytheism.—But idolatry has never stopped at

this point. Though in theory idolatrous systems usually recognized One Supreme God, in practice there were always "gods many and lords many." Men began to regard each object of their worship as a separate god. And then arose the notion that the world was divided among the gods, and that each country had gods of its own. The number of gods that were thus recognized is almost incredible. The Greeks had a god for each river, stream, and fountain; and it used to be said that at Athens there were as many gods as there were men.

Debasing Influence of Idolatry.—The most lamentable thing about idolatry was, that when men began to give license to their fancy in fashioning their gods, they often made them like themselves, with their own weaknesses, passions, and lusts. By this means the highest purpose of worship was defeated. Instead of being elevated by fellowship with a Being of purest and noblest character, the worshippers were debased by the contemplation of beings of low passions and propensities, whom it was deemed a duty to imitate. What pollution and degradation were wrought in this way by the worship of the goddess Venus, under the various names by which she was known among different nations, it is impossible to describe, or even to conceive.

Agreement of Different Systems.—In the leading features of idolatry, at all times and in all countries, there has been a wonderful agreement, amid all sorts of outward variation. The old Babylonian idolatry reappeared in many features in the Greek and the Roman worship, and may be traced in even more recent forms. It is not unlikely that idolatry had begun to take shape before the confusion of tongues, and that after that event the various races drifted back into the worship of the same gods, under different names. Very probably it was the old antediluvian idolatry that was then revived.

Overthrow of Idolatry.—Idolatry has ever been regarded by God, not only as dishonouring to himself, but as degrading and ruinous to man. Its rapid growth and diffusion over the world may be said to have sounded anew that knell which brought the flood. But it was not God's purpose again to devote the earth to physical destruction. Idolatry was to be allowed to spread over the world at large, while special means were to be taken to preserve in a single spot the true knowledge and pure worship of the One God. Thereafter, He was to appear in the flesh, who, as God and man in one person, was to show the whole world the way to the Father. After the manifestation of this One Mediator, idolatry would be left without excuse; the times of ignorance would no longer be winked at; a life-and-death conflict would ensue between the doctrine of the One Mediator and that of many mediators; until at last a day should dawn when all idols should be abolished, and GOD IN CHRIST alone be exalted.

CHAPTER IV.

THE HEBREW PATRIARCHS.

FROM THE BIRTH OF ABRAHAM TO THE DEATH OF JOSEPH.

GENESIS xii.-xxv.

SECTION I.—CAREER OF ABRAHAM.

Ur of the Chaldees—Abram's early life—His call—Leaves Ur for Haran—Removes to Canaan—Aspect of the land—Shechem--Beth-el—Egypt—Separation from Lot—Hebron—Beer-sheba—Chedorlaomer: rescue of Lot—Melchizedek—The Mesopotamian kings—The promise renewed—Birth of Ishmael: renewal of the promise Destruction of Sodom—The Dead Sea—Accadian poem—Birth of Isaac—Offering of Isaac—Death of Sarah—The Hittites—Marriage of Isaac—Abraham's death—His character—His Messianic hope.

Ur of the Chaldees.—In consequence of the renewed spread of idolatry, it pleased God to make choice of a family to fulfil the high office of preserving pure and undefiled the true knowledge and worship of himself. Several hundred miles from the foot of Ararat, along the course of the Euphrates, was the residence of the family that was to give to the world its new spiritual father. An old Jewish tradition affirms that the modern Orfah, or Urfah, called also Edessa, was the same with "Ur of the Chaldees," the birth-place of Abram. The Arabs continue to perform pilgrimages to it as the birth-place of their great ancestor, the father of Ishmael, and call it "Ur Chasdim." But as Urfah is situated in upper Mesopotamia, whereas Chaldæa was applied distinctively to the lower part of the district, it is thought by modern authorities that Ur of the Chaldees must have been farther down the river. The name Hûr or 'Ur has been found on cylinders excavated from a ruin now called Mugeyer, on the right bank of the Euphrates, in what was undoubtedly called Chaldæa in ancient times. As has been said, it was one of the most ancient Chaldæan cities, and was once the capital of an Accadian kingdom. Among its ruins is an ancient Chaldæan temple, constructed of brick laid in a bed of bitumen. For many centuries 'Ur was used as a cemetery, and now it is mainly a city of tombs. This seems to have been the birthplace of Abram, and it is distant from Haran several hundred miles. "The city of Ur," says Mr. G. Smith, "was devoted to the worship of the moon-god, called in early times Ur; and the place itself appears to have been named after that divinity 'the city of Ur.' The rise of Ur caused the worship of the moon-god to become famous and to extend over the whole of the country, the Babylonians ever after esteeming this divinity in preference to Shamas, the sun-god; and they always considered the moon to be masculine, while sometimes the sun was represented as the son of the moon, and at other times as a female divinity." *

Abram's Early Life.— In the plain adjacent to this city, in the eighth generation from Noah, the patriarch Terah fed his flocks. Here were born to him his three sons, Abram, Nahor, and Haran; and here he was visited with a great affliction,—the premature death of his son Haran. The birth of Abram is supposed to have taken place about two thousand years before Christ. Up to this period the chronology of Bible history is very uncertain. Though Abram's name is mentioned first, he seems to have been the youngest of Terah's sons. Like his fathers, he engaged in the occupation of a shepherd-farmer, and he seems to have had a large share of prosperity. His flocks and herds increased very rapidly, and from his station in life he was able to procure a sufficient supply of servants to attend to them. Evidently his family was one of high rank in the district. A warm family affection seems to have united its members: for Lot, the child of the deceased Haran, was loved by Abram as a brother; and Sarai, his much-loved wife, was related to him so nearly as to be in a sense his sister. According to a Jewish tradition, Abram's family were persecuted by their Chaldee neighbours in

* Ancient History from the Monuments: Babylonia, p. 65.

Ur for refusing to conform to the idolatry which they had begun to practise; and, owing to the persecution, they were fain to remove to Haran. But it appears, from a statement in Joshua (ch. xxiv. 2, 14), that Terah, who went with Abram to Haran, was not untainted by the prevailing idolatry.

His Call.—As for Abram, his movements were guided by a special divine command. A striking, almost startling, communication had come to him from God. It consisted of a command and a promise. The command was to leave his country and his kindred, and go to a land that should afterwards be shown to him. The promise that accompanied the command gave him the assurance of becoming a great nation, and pointed to the Messiah in its declaration that in him all the families of the earth should be blessed. The command and the promise thus made to Abram indicated a new starting-point for the kingdom of God. In the first place, the gracious regards of God were now to be fixed on a single family, with the view of preserving in it the true worship, and of keeping it free from the idolatry into which all the world was falling. Further, God's dealings with that family were to be remarkably close and intimate : he was to reveal himself to them in an especial way, to take them into covenant with himself, and to make his will known to them much more fully and minutely than it had ever been made known before. And, thirdly, he was to raise up from that family one in whom all the families of the earth should be blessed,—the promised Seed of the woman, who was to bruise the head of the serpent. The call of Abram was the most important event in the history of God's kingdom that had occurred since the Fall.

Leaves Ur for Haran.—Leaving Ur of the Chaldees, in a fine spirit of submission to the divine will and of trust in the divine promise, Abram proceeded first of all to Haran (probably the place which still bears that name),—the Carrhae of the Romans,—situated about twenty miles to the south of Urfah. It continued to be his dwelling-place for only a few years; but his brother's family seem to have made it their permanent abode, for when Rebekah directed her son Jacob where to find her relations, it was to Haran in

Mesopotamia that she sent him. About two thousand years afterwards the place acquired notoriety in Roman history, as the scene of the defeat and death of the Roman general Crassus, in his disastrous encounter with the Parthians. Its plains are still remarkable for their fertility, but are now so thinly peopled that sometimes they are cropped only once in three years.

Removes to Canaan.—Abram continued to dwell at Haran until his father Terah died. But the communication which he had received from God required him to go to a much greater distance from home. He now prepared to obey that command in all its extent. To move such an establishment as his —consisting of thousands of sheep and goats, oxen and asses, hundreds of camels, and scores of servants, with tents, furniture, and implements to correspond—was, in any circumstances, an undertaking of great difficulty and labour. But to transport such a host several hundred miles across the Syrian desert involved a degree of labour and peril that might have appalled an ordinary heart. It spoke volumes for Abram's trust in God, that, when commanded to leave Haran, "he went forth, not knowing whither he went." And it showed how extraordinary an influence he wielded over his large household, that he was able to prevail on them to face with him the perils of the desert, though at the time he was unable to tell them whither he was going. His act of trust in these circumstances was only less sublime than a subsequent act of Moses, when, in obedience to the divine word, he marched his whole people, with their cattle, into the heart of the wild desert of Sinai.

Aspect of the Land.—At last the perils of the wilderness journey are over, and Abram reaches the northern frontier of Palestine. After passing through the green orchards of Damascus, and watering his flocks in the Pharpar or the Abana, he probably crossed the shoulder of Mount Hermon, and from its heights looked down for the first time on the goodly land which God had destined as the inheritance of his seed. The view could not fail to be most interesting. On the right, the towering range of Lebanon formed a bulwark that no enemy could easily force. On the left, the rich pastures of Gilead and the green forests of Bashan seemed as if created for flocks and herds. In front gleamed the blue waters of the Sea of Galilee, whence the Jordan wound luxuriously through plains that seemed at that time like the garden of the Lord. The country formed a succession of hills and valleys, fertile plains and small streams—running on the one side to the Jordan, and on the other to "the great sea," the Mediterranean, now beheld for the first time by Abram. It was a very different scene from that to which he had been accustomed on the rich, level banks of the Euphrates—much more picturesque, undoubtedly, but not so productive nor so easily tilled.

Shechem.—As yet he did not know whether or not this was to be his home and the home of his seed; but with the true pilgrim spirit, and in simple dependence on the word of God, he crossed its frontier. In the same spirit, in obedience to the divine impulse, he continued to journey southward until he reached the centre of the country. At Shechem, in the plain of Moreh, he built his first altar to the Lord. Here, too, he received his first intimation that the land on which he stood was to be the inheritance of his seed. Awaking from the vision, he would look out on a long green vale, remarkably fertile,—he would hear the gurgling streams as they rolled along their wooded banks, and see the giant sentinels, Mounts Ebal and Gerizim, keeping watch at the head of the valley. It would have been pleasant to linger in so sweet a spot,—one of the most delightful in all Palestine.* But the Canaanite dwelt in the land, and was probably unwilling to yield up to Abram so choice a vale. Throughout the whole course of Bible history Shechem occupies a prominent place, down to the time when Jesus met there the woman of Samaria; but as yet it could be

---

* "Nothing that I had yet seen in Palestine appeared to me so charming as that dale. The awful gorge of the Leontes, with its eagles' nests and leopards' dens, is beyond all description grand and bold. The hills of Lebanon at Ronm, over against Sidon, are magnificent and sublime; the valley of the hills of Naphtali is rich in wild oak forest and brushwood; those of Asher present a beautiful combination of wood and mountain stream; Carmel, with its wilderness of timber trees and shrubs, of plants and bushes, still answers to its ancient reputation for magnificence; but the vale of Shechem differs from them all. Here there are no wild thickets; yet there is always verdure, always shade,—not of the oak, the terebinth, the garoub-tree, but of the olive grove, so soft in colour, so picturesque in form, that for its sake we can willingly dispense with all other wood."—*Van de Velde's Syria and Palestine*, i. 386.

taken possession of only by faith,—other scenes were appointed for the pilgrimage of Abram.

Beth-el.—Removing from under the oak, or, as some prefer to translate, terebinth or turpentine tree of Moreh,—Abram pitched his tent on a mountain on the east of Beth-el. Beth-el is some twenty miles south from Shechem, the road to it passing along an elevated ridge that stretches like a backbone along the whole country. Between Beth-el and Ai, the exact spot of Abram's encampment, the traveller finds, as the highest of a succession of eminences, a conspicuous hill; its topmost summit resting on the rocky slopes below, and distinguished from them by the olive grove which clusters over its broad surface above.* This hill would provide at once a fitting base for Abram's altar and a fitting shade for his tent. The district around is "still one of the finest tracts for pasturage in the whole land." † Leaving Beth-el, he continued to move southward, till a famine compelled him to make a journey to Egypt.

Egypt.—The famine was "very grievous." It was probably caused by a failure of the usual rain,—the great cause of famine in those countries; and the loss and misery resulting from it, to both man and beast, must have been very great. Abram was plainly driven to the last extremity, when his only alternative was to remove to a strange and distant country like Egypt. Where was now the God who had made him such ample and glorious promises? Was this burnt-up wilderness the land that God had extolled so highly? The trial was so severe, that Abram's faith seems to have given way for a time. Fearing that, if Sarai were known to be his wife, his life would be in danger, he persuaded her to call herself his sister. He thus showed that, at the time, he did not place full confidence in God as his protector, and that he was not free from that leaven of deceit which is so sad a blot in the character even of the best men among the Jews. In Egypt he finds a court, with a king and princes, and great abundance of wealth. Sarai having been taken to the royal harem, great plagues are sent by God upon

---

* Stanley's Sinai and Palestine, p. 218.
† Robinson's Biblical Researches, vol. i., p. 450.

Pharaoh. Her real relation to Abram is discovered by the king, who, alarmed at what has happened, sends him away laden with presents. In this episode of Abram's history, we see in miniature a chapter of the history of his posterity;—driven by famine, like him, to Egypt; and like him leaving it, under the terror caused by the plagues of Heaven, laden with its spoils. It is a curious fact, that in one of the oldest writings in existence, the Egyptian papyrus containing the "Story of the Two Brothers," in the British Museum, the Pharaoh of the time is represented as fetching, by means of a military force, a beautiful woman to his court, and murdering her husband.* The story is a kind of fable or romance, belonging to the region of the mythical, but it throws light on the present narrative, showing Abram's fear to have been quite justified by Egyptian customs. The name of the king of Egypt during this visit of Abram has not been identified.

Separation from Lot.—The famine that seems to have shaken Abram's faith turned out in the end for his advantage. On returning from Egypt, he settled again at Beth-el, but he found that its pastures were too small for the augmented flocks of Lot and himself. An amicable separation was resolved on, and Abram, with characteristic generosity, allowed Lot to choose whichever district he preferred. From the height between Beth-el and Ai a commanding view of the land was easily obtained.† Surveying this extended panorama, the tract that proved most attractive to Lot was the well-watered plain of the Jordan, near Sodom and Gomorrah; not, as used to be thought, near the Dead Sea (for that is not visible from Beth-el), but

* See Records of the Past, vol. ii., p. 137.
† "To the east there rises in the foreground the jagged range of the hills above Jericho; in the distance, the dark wall of Moab; between them lies the wide valley of the Jordan, its course marked by the tract of forest in which its rushing stream is enveloped; and down to this valley, a long and deep ravine, now, as always, the main line of communication by which it is approached from the central hills of Palestine,—a ravine rich with vine, olive, and fig, winding its way through ancient reservoirs and sepulchres, remains of a civilization now extinct, but in the times of the patriarchs not yet begun. To the south and the west, the view commanded the bleak hills of Judæa, varied by the heights crowned by what were afterwards the cities of Benjamin, and overhanging what in a later day was to be Jerusalem; and in the far distance the southern range on whose slope is Hebron. Northward are the hills which divide Judæa from the rich plains of Samaria." *Stanley.* p. 218. It will be noticed that the shores of the Dead Sea are not included in this description of the view.

...siderably to the north.* In point of morality, it was the most filthy spot on earth; but all its evil savour failed to repel Lot, in whom increase of wealth had brought, as it often brings, increase of worldliness. After the separation, God appeared to Abram; directed him again to survey the panorama on which Lot and he had looked from the height of Beth-el; promised it anew to him and to his seed; and bade him arise and walk through it in all its length and breadth, that he might learn how large and goodly a heritage God had given him, and how countless in number the yet unborn seed should be by whom it was to be possessed.

Hebron.—After this vision, Abram removed to Hebron, and the rest of his life was spent, for the most part, either there or at Beer-sheba in its neighbourhood, close to the southern border of the land. Hebron was one of the oldest cities in the world—"seven years older than Zoan in Egypt" (Num. xiii. 22). It had probably been occupied by Ham's son Mizraim, in his migration southward, till, learning of still richer fields on the banks of the Nile, he had directed his course to Egypt, and laid the foundation of Zoan, its earliest capital. Situated at the head of a valley, on a high table-land, afterwards known as the "hill country" of Judah, it was celebrated then, as it is now, for two things,—the excellence of its pastures, and the luxuriance of its vines.† There still stands a noble oak in the neighbourhood of Hebron, which is said, in the fanciful but baseless traditions of the monks, to be the very oak of Mamre under which Abram had his tent and entertained angels unawares.

Beer-sheba.—Beer-sheba ‡ lies several miles to the south-west

---

* Lieutenant Conder's (of the Palestine Exploration Company) Handbook to the Bible, p. 239.

† "The town lies on the sloping sides of a valley, chiefly on the eastern; but in the southern part extends across also to the western side.... The region around Hebron abounds with vineyards, and the grapes are the finest in Palestine. Each vineyard has a small house or tower of stone, which serves for a keeper's lodge. In this valley everything looked thrifty; and round about were large flocks of sheep and goats, all in good condition."—*Robinson's Researches*, vol. i., p. 214.

‡ Approaching Palestine from the southern desert, "we came upon an open undulating country; the shrubs ceased, or nearly so; green grass was seen along the lesser water-courses, and almost greensward; while the gentle hills, covered in ordinary seasons with grass and rich pastures, were now burned over with drought.... On the northern side of the bed of a torrent, close upon the bank, are two deep wells, still

of Hebron, and marked the southern border of Palestine. Its gentle slopes, covered with green pastures, and its celebrated wells, gave it the attractions which shepherds prized. In this neighbourhood most of the great events of Abram's life were enacted, and here he received most of his visions from God. In the outskirts of Hebron was the famous cave of Machpelah, which he purchased from the Hittites as a burial-place for his family. Under the Turkish mosque which now covers the cave, but which, until a recent visit of the Prince of Wales, had been barred for ages against the entrance of the Christian, the dust of Abraham, Isaac, and Jacob reposes to this hour.

Chedorlaomer: Rescue of Lot.—Abram was dwelling under the oak of Mamre when he heard that a calamity had befallen his nephew Lot. The kings of Sodom and the neighbouring cities had been attacked and defeated by Chedorlaomer and a confederacy of kings from the Mesopotamian plain, and Lot, with all his goods, had been carried away. The battle took place in the vale of Siddim. It is described by Dean Stanley as the first battle of Palestine, but the Egyptian monuments show that there had been earlier fights. Abram's generosity, bravery, and energy were equally shown in the course which he followed after hearing of the disaster to his nephew. He armed the servants of his house, amounting to three hundred and eighteen; procured the assistance of his neighbours; crossed the hills to the Jordan; pursued the eastern kings up the whole course of its valley; surprised and defeated them at what was afterwards called Dan, in the extreme north of the land; then followed them as far as to Damascus, deprived them of their booty, and

---

called Bir es-Seba.—the ancient Beer-sheba. These wells, which are circular, and stoned up with solid masonry, are some distance apart; one 12½ feet in diameter, and 41½ deep, to the surface of the water; the other 5 feet wide, and 42 deep....The water in both is pure and sweet, and in great abundance....Here, then, is the place where the patriarchs, Abraham, Isaac, and Jacob, often dwelt."—*Robinson*, vol. i., pp. 204, 205.

"There was nothing to mark the country in any special way. There were no great features to form a fatherland round which their affections or their patriotism might entwine themselves....It was a fruitful land, no doubt, but a plain and unambitious territory,—very much like the lowly men who occupied it. It was less likely to be coveted than most lands by the stranger: so that here they might sit down in peace, and pass the few days of their pilgrimage in unmolested calm,—walking with God, while they walked with each other in these quiet vales."—*Bonar's Sinai*, pp. 334, 335.

rescued Lot and all his company. Considering the prestige and resources of Chedorlaomer and his allies, this expedition of Abram's was, in a military point of view, one of the most striking ever undertaken. It was hardly inferior to the exploit of Gideon, eight hundred years after, and it must have given Abram indeed the renown of "a mighty prince" in the land.

Melchizedek.—Returning from this expedition, Abram was met by Melchizedek, king of Salem and priest of the most high God. This mysterious person flits like a meteor across the firmament of the history, and vanishes from view as quickly as he appeared. The supposition of some that he was the patriarch Shem must be a mistake: for, apart from chronological reasons, if he really was the patriarch, why should he not have been called by the familiar and venerable name of Shem; and how could Shem be found as a sovereign prince in the very heart of the children of Canaan? Probably Melchizedek was one who had kept up the pure worship of God in days of fearful declension; one whose remarkable attachment to righteousness and peace was denoted by the very name and title which he bore (*Melchi-zedek*, King of righteousness; *Melchi-shalem*, King of peace); and who, for his noble fidelity, was honoured by God with a priesthood so exalted as to be, more than any other, the pattern of Christ's.

The Mesopotamian Kings.—The invasion of the Mesopotamian kings, who came from the country from which God had called Abram, shows how troubled the condition of that country must have been, and how, even in a temporal sense, the command that withdrew Abram from it to Canaan must have turned out for his benefit. These eastern kings seem to have been the chiefs of that Semitic race which had conquered the Accadian inhabitants of Chaldæa, and had established a Semitic in place of a Cushite rule. Some Oriental scholars fancy that Chedorlaomer may have been the same with a Kudur-nakhunta, a king of Elam, mentioned in an inscription by the Assyrian king Assurbanipal (Sardanapalus), as having invaded Chaldæa sixteen hundred and thirty-five years before the date of the monument (about 650 B.C.); but there is too much uncertainty about the meaning of the inscription to justify this inference.* The monuments, however, refer oftener than once to Elamite invasions of Chaldæa. Chedorlaomer was evidently one of those military scourges who are for ever striving to bring all their neighbours under their dominion.

The Promise Renewed.—Soon after these things, another interview took place by vision between God and Abram, which marked an important era in the patriarch's spiritual life. It was declared to him very specifically that he should have a son, born of his own body: he was then taken outside his tent, told to contemplate the stars, asked if he could number them, and assured that his seed should be as numerous as they. "Abram believed God, and it was counted to him for righteousness." He received with unhesitating faith God's declaration, both that his seed should be very numerous, and that blessing should come through it. His ready belief in the divine announcement procured his acceptance—"righteousness was imputed to him" (Rom. iv. 22). A great sacrifice was offered on the occasion, consisting of an heifer, a she goat, a ram, a turtle dove, and a pigeon. An emblematical vision was set before him, representing the sufferings that his seed were to endure for four hundred years at the hands of foreigners, till the iniquity of the Amorites should be full, when, like Abram himself, they should come forth with great substance from Egypt. This was not the first occasion of the exercise of saving faith on the part of Abram; but his faith seems at this time to have shone out with remarkable beauty. He seems to have exhibited very clearly that willingness to receive blessing in God's way, and as God's gift, which is the mark of all true believers. It was substantially the same faith that had been shown by Abel, Noah, and other good men before Abram; but in his case its manifestation was so clear and distinct, that he received as a title, "The Father of the Faithful," or of them that believe.

Birth of Ishmael. Becoming somewhat impatient of the delay in regard to the promised birth of his son, Abram, at the suggestion of Sarai, took Hagar, an Egyptian bond-maid, for his

* Rawlinson's Historical Illustrations, p. 37.

concubine or secondary wife, and became the father of Ishmael. But the birth of Ishmael was only a source of domestic discord, and fourteen years more had to run before the arrival of the child of promise was foretold. After that long interval, the Lord again appeared to Abram; promised that in the following year Sarai should have a son; renewed the covenant, both in its temporal and in its spiritual promises; and instituted circumcision as a pledge or seal of the certainty of its provisions. On this occasion his name was changed to "Abraham,"—that is, Father of a great multitude; and his wife's to "Sarah,"—that is, Princess.

Destruction of Sodom.—In another interview with Abraham, almost immediately afterwards, God announced his purpose to destroy Sodom and Gomorrah, on account of their shocking and unnatural wickedness. The pleading of the patriarch for Sodom was most pathetic, and so effectual, that if but ten righteous men had been found in it the place would have been spared for their sake. Glimpses of the horrible wickedness of the place are given, amply sufficient to justify its doom. Lot with his two daughters was rescued; but the other members of his family were involved in the destruction. Fire and brimstone from heaven burned up the polluted cities. The worldly spirit which Lot, righteous man though he was, had been frail enough to indulge, was terribly chastised, and the curtain drops on him cowering in a dreary cave, and drawn, by the artifices of his daughters, into deeds of the very same class as those for which the guilty cities had perished. Abraham, who was most careful of the purity of his family, did not personally need the lesson taught by this terrible judgment. The inhabitants of the country at large needed it greatly. Probably it had its effect in arresting their wickedness for a season; but by the time that the Israelites came up from Egypt, four hundred years later, the morals of the Canaanites generally were probably as corrupt as those of Sodom and Gomorrah now.

The Dead Sea.—It used to be thought that the "Dead Sea" occupied the plain in which the destroyed cities had stood. Its Arabic name, Bahr Lût (Sea of Lot), tended to foster this belief. It was believed that by volcanic action the level of the plain had been lowered, and that the flow of the Jordan, supposed previously to have passed through the Wady el Arabah to the Red Sea, had been arrested after having formed the lake. The level of the Dead Sea is no less than 1,300 feet below the level of the Mediterranean. The district abounds in bitumen, sulphur, nitre, and other combustible substances; and in one place there is a whole rock of salt, called by the Arabs Usdum, a slight transposition and alteration of the letters of Sodom. Near to Usdum is a singular pillar, which tradition declares to be Lot's wife.* The waters of the sea are so impregnated with salt, that neither fish nor animal of any kind can live in them; but the old belief, that birds were unable to fly across the lake, is now found to be a mistake. Lieutenant Lynch of the United States, who was employed by his Government to survey it, came to the conclusion that some great convulsion of nature had occurred in the locality. The bed of the Jordan, he believed, must have been depressed unnaturally, and the plain along its sides where the cities stood submerged under the waters.† The soundings taken in the Dead Sea showed that its bottom consists of two submerged plains, the one 13 feet and the other 1,300, on an average, below the surface. So strong

---

* "On the eastern side of Usdum we saw a lofty round pillar, standing apparently detached from the rest of the mass, at the head of a deep, narrow, and abrupt chasm.... We found the pillar to be of solid salt, capped with carbonate of lime, cylindrical in front, and pyramidal behind. The upper or rounded part is about 40 feet high, resting on a kind of oval pedestal, from 40 to 60 feet above the level of the sea. It slightly decreases in size upwards, crumbles at the top, and is one entire mass of crystallization."—*Lynch's Narrative*, p. 307.

† Lieutenant Lynch thus describes the scenery of the south part of the Dead Sea, where he believes the submerged cities lie: "It was a scene of unmitigated desolation. On one side, rugged and worn, was the salt mountain of Usdum, with its conspicuous pillar, which reminded us at least of the catastrophe of the plain; on the other were the lofty and barren cliffs of Moab, in one of the caves of which the fugitive Lot found shelter. To the south was an extensive flat, intersected by sluggish drains, with the high hills of Edom semi-girdling the salt plain where the Israelites repeatedly overthrew their enemies; and to the north was the calm and motionless sea, curtained with a purple mist; while, many fathoms deep in the slimy mud beneath it, lay embedded the ruins of the ill-fated cities of Sodom and Gomorrah. The glare of light was blinding to the eye, and the atmosphere difficult of respiration. No bird fanned with its wings the attenuated air, through which the sun poured his scorching rays upon the mysterious element on which we floated, and which alone, of all the works of its Maker, contains no living thing within it."—*Narrative*, pp. 310, 311.

were the corroborations that were obtained by this traveller or the Bible record, that one of his party who was a doubter, and another who was an open unbeliever, became convinced that its narrative was true. A French traveller, De Saulcy, believed that he had discovered the ruins of the cities; but the accuracy of his observations was doubted. He observed many indications of terrible volcanic action—craters of extinct volcanoes, and rocks rent as if by intense heat; also concealed chasms and "slime-pits," into some of which his horses occasionally sank.

These appearances, however, are not really conclusive. The latest and most careful survey of the district shows that the present Dead Sea is not a recent but a very ancient lake; and that in former times, instead of less, there was actually more water than there is now in the valley of the Jordan. The whole region spoken of as the Ciccar or Plain of Jordan appears at one time to have been covered with water. But, as was pointed out long ago by Reland,* there is no reason to suppose that the cities were destroyed by submersion; they are expressly said to have been destroyed, not by water, but by fire. It is said, indeed, that the battle of the kings was fought "in the vale of Siddim, which is the Salt Sea" (Gen. xiv. 3). The Salt Sea covers part of the vale, in the upper or uncovered part of which the battle took place.†

Accadian Poem.—An old Accadian poem describes a rain of fire similar in character and effect to that which destroyed the cities of the plain. Professor Sayce gives the following translation, remarking that the expedition of Chedorlaomer against Sodom makes it not surprising that the destruction of the place should have interested the Accadians:—

"An overthrow from the midst of the deep there came
The fated punishment from the midst of heaven descended,
A storm like a plummet the earth (overwhelmed)
To the four winds the destroying flood like fire did burn.
The inhabitants of cities it had caused to be tormented; their bodies it consumed,
In city and country it spread death, and the flames as they rose overthrew.
Freeman and slave were equal, and the high places it filled.
In heaven and earth like a thunder-storm it had rained; a prey it made

* Palestina, p. 254.   † Conder's Handbook, p. 239.

A place of refuge the gods hastened to, and in a throng collected.
Its mighty (onset) they fled from, and like a garment it concealed (mankind)
They (feared) and death (overtook them)
(Their) feet and hands (it embraced)
Their body it consumed
.... the city, its foundations it defiled
.... in breath his mouth he filled
As for man a loud voice was raised; the mighty lightning-flash descended
During the day it flashed, grievously it fell." *

Birth of Isaac.—After the destruction of Sodom, Abraham was guilty, at Gerar, a city of the Philistines, near Beer-sheba, of the same offence against truth as he had committed in Egypt. Soon afterwards Isaac, the child of promise, was born. Ishmael, having shown a bad spirit towards Isaac, was sent away with his mother. After a narrow escape from death in the wilderness of Beer-sheba, he grew up to manhood, and, having settled in the vast desert tract stretching between Beer-sheba and the extreme south of Arabia, he became the progenitor of the Arabians.

Offering of Isaac.—The next great event in Abraham's life was one of the most memorable. Abraham had already shown that his faith and obedience towards God were strong enough to overcome his love of home and country; now he was called to show that they could overcome even his love of offspring. The child so long waited for, so solemnly promised, and on whose life so many precious hopes depended, had reached, according to Josephus, the age of twenty-five, when Abraham was commanded to offer him up as a burnt-offering on Mount Moriah—usually believed to be the hill of that name in Jerusalem on which the temple of Solomon was afterwards built. The faith of the patriarch stood the test very nobly, sustained by the conviction, as Augustine puts it, that as Isaac's life had been supernaturally given, it would be supernaturally restored; but the Angel of the Lord, by providing a ram for a burnt-offering, saved him from the bereavement. The promises were renewed with increased cordiality and fulness, and Abraham stood out more than ever as "the Friend of God." This transaction has been compared by enemies to the sacrifice of children to Moloch and other heathen gods; but most unjustly, for on the very face of

* Records of the Past, vol. xi., p. 117.

it, it bears the mark of a very different spirit. The spirit of submission was equally beautiful in the father and in the son.*

Death of Sarah.—On the death of Sarah, a place of burial was purchased by Abraham of the Hittites—the cave of Machpelah, near Hebron—the only spot in all the country which he could call his own. Faith was shown in this, as in almost every act of Abraham's life. Nearly four hundred years had yet to elapse before his seed were to obtain possession of the land; and as he deemed it important that the ashes of himself and his family should remain undisturbed during that long period, he took every possible means to obtain sure and indisputable possession of the cave.† To the other patriarchs it was a peculiarly hallowed spot:—

> "The Eden of their earth lay all around
> Machpelah: there God came down in the cool
> Of even to walk with them, and all the ground
> Was therefore holy—therefore beautiful;
> And their free spirits panted for the time
> When they should soar to an unwithering clime.

* For vindication of the whole transaction, see Mozley's Lectures on the Old Testament, chap. ii.

† "The great Haram, or rather the exterior wall which encloses the mosque,... has the appearance of a large and lofty building. The walls are built of very large stones ....and there are no windows in any part of them. At the two northern corners, a long and broad flight of steps, built up and covered along each side of the building externally, leads to a door in each wall opening into the court within. In this court stands the much smaller mosque, which is said to have been once a Christian church. Here, in different parts, the Mohammedans have built tombs for the patriarchs, while their actual place of sepulture is held to be in a cavern below, which even the faithful are not permitted to enter. As Christians are not allowed to enter, and as the height of the outside walls prevents any view of the interior, we know nothing of the cavern which thus represents the cave of Machpelah."- *Robinson*, abridged.

"We were allowed to ascend the wide massy staircase that leads into the interior of the building. The door into the mosque was thrown open, but not a foot was allowed to cross the marble threshold. We were shown the window of the place which contains the tombs of Abraham and Sarah, beneath which is understood to be the cave of Machpelah. It was esteemed a very peculiar favour that we had been admitted thus far, travellers in general being forbidden even to approach the door of the mosque."—*General Assembly's Mission to the Jews*.

When the Prince of Wales visited Palestine in 1862, he was, by dint of great influence, admitted within the mosque, a privilege which had not been enjoyed by any Christian since the time of the Crusades, unless, perhaps, as Mr S. Williams showed at the time, Signor Pierotti, who visited it in company with Sooraya Pasha. Under the mosque is a cave, or double cave, into which even the faithful are not allowed to enter. It is said, indeed, to have no opening, save one of ten inches square; but this is doubted. Within that cave there is no reason to doubt but the remains of the patriarch Jacob, as they were embalmed in Egypt, lie to this hour. (See newspapers of the day.)

> "To them it ceased to be a place of death;
> It was the porch within whose solemn glooms
> They stood till the temple opened; the sweet breath
> Of heaven here soothed their hearts; the lovely blooms
> Of that fair land refreshed their drooping eyes;
> And glimpses came to them from other skies." *

The Hittites.—The contact of Abraham on this occasion with the Hittites, who recognized him as "a mighty prince" among them, leads us to advert to the light that has recently been thrown on the early history of that remarkable people. From the Egyptian monuments we learn that the Khita, as they were called (equivalent to the English word "Hittite"), were at an early period a great people in Western Asia. In Joshua's time their kingdom is defined as extending from the wilderness to Lebanon on the north-west, and to the Euphrates on the north-east (Joshua i. 4). The portion of the people in Palestine proper must have been but a fraction of the whole. Somewhat later, it appears from the monuments that they were able to engage the whole force of Egypt in war; and though they were conquered, the king of Egypt, Rameses II., married the daughter of the Hittite king.† They appear to have been a confederacy of many tribes or kingdoms, with a king at its head.

Marriage of Isaac.—Intensely desirous to preserve among his seed the purity of family life and of religious faith and worship, Abraham could not bear the thought of his son marrying one of the daughters of the Canaanites; he therefore despatched his most confidential servant to his native land, to find there a suitable partner for Isaac. Traversing part of the route along which Abraham had originally come, Eliezer reached the district of Mesopotamia, then called Padan-aram; and in Rebekah, daughter of Bethuel, and grand-daughter of Nahor, Abraham's brother, he found the bride destined for his master's son.

Abraham's Death.—Abraham himself married again, and had six sons born to him by Keturah, his new wife. The future history of these branches of Abraham's family will be referred to afterwards. At last, having reached the age of one

---

* Vision of Prophecy, and other Poems. By J. D. Burns.
† See Brugsch's Egypt, vol. ii., p. 75. Also, Records of the Past, vol. ii., p. 65: Wars of Rameses II. with the Khita. By Professor E. Lushington.

hundred and seventy-five, and seen the children of Isaac and Rebekah in the vigour of early youth, he was gathered to his fathers; and his sons Isaac and Ishmael buried him beside Sarah, in the cave of Machpelah.

His Character.—The character of Abraham is one of the finest and noblest in all history, sacred or profane. Reverence, confidence, love and submission towards the Most High, appear through all his life in colossal proportions. Along with these there were evidently in his character great shrewdness and common sense: he had large knowledge of the world, and much skill in the orderly management of its business; great self-possession, good temper, meekness, and patience; warm domestic affections, and an expansive, genial heart, that looked much to the welfare of others, and was ever ready, for their sakes, to sacrifice his own. He was "not slothful in business," but "fervent in spirit, serving the Lord." His generosity and nobility of disposition gave an elevation to his character which has never been surpassed in any mere man. He had not the stirring and ambitious temper of some great men, that must always be devising enterprises corresponding to their capabilities; but his calm wisdom, his self-possession, and his goodness, were fitted to command the love and confidence of all, and in a time of danger would have made him the mainstay of any community. Of his personal appearance we know nothing; but we can readily fancy it to have been marked by an imposing massiveness and symmetry, corresponding to the remarkable structure of his mind. There could not have been a man more fitted to fulfil the duties and to sustain the honours that devolved on the Father of a Nation and the Patriarch of a Church.

His Messianic Hope.—The most memorable thing in all Abraham's history was the promise given him respecting the Messiah: "In thee and in thy seed shall all the nations of the earth be blessed." This promise was conjoined with that of the land of Canaan, and in his view the two were inseparably connected. The tenacity with which Abraham clung to the land cannot be explained except on the supposition that he believed the double promise. Though Abraham was but a stranger and pilgrim in Canaan, he always felt towards it as his home. He might visit Egypt or Gerar in a famine, but only for a time. When he sent Eliezer to his father's kindred for a wife to Isaac, he bound him by a solemn oath to see to it that she should come to Isaac, and that Isaac should not go to her. When Sarah was to be buried, it was in no sepulchre of her fathers, but in a new tomb in the land of Canaan. Our Lord explained all by saying, "Your father Abraham rejoiced to see my day; and he saw it, and was glad." In connection with such a blessed hope, Abraham could never be prevailed on to forsake the land: whatever it might be in itself, it was the Land of Promise, as his seed was the promised seed; and nothing was ever wanting on his part to keep the land and the seed together. Thus the spirit of *looking forward* was stimulated. Godly men in those times were specially encouraged to this exercise of mind. Whatever new revelation might be given, and whatever new institutions might be set up, they had still to be looking forward. Something better was in the future:—the Hope of Israel had not yet come.

SECTION II.—CAREER OF ISAAC AND OF ABRAHAM'S OTHER SONS.

Isaac: His character—His sons Ishmael: Midian--Edom
Ammon and Moab.

Isaac: His Character. The career of Isaac presents but few points of peculiar interest. The singular gentleness of his disposition was shown in his beautiful submission to the ordeal through which he too had to pass at Mount Moriah. He seems to have had all his father's reverence for God, but little of his energy and force of character. He was of a contemplative, retiring disposition, not adapted for pushing his way through opposition and difficulty, but highly fitted to adorn a quiet and peaceful lot. He showed his father's weakness, by representing Rebekah as his sister to Abimelech, king of Gerar; but, on the other hand, he showed his self-denying love of peace, by readily giving up certain wells about which there was a quarrel between his own and Abimelech's servants. More important than this, he inherited his father's faith, and thus obtained the renewal of the promises which his father had received from God. He seems to have spent most of his life in the quiet neighbourhood of Beer-sheba and Hebron.

His Sons.—His only sons were Esau and Jacob, the twin-children of Rebekah; in neither of whom he could at first have had much satisfaction. Esau early manifested a sad disregard both of the promised blessings of salvation through the coming seed, and of that family order which Abraham had guarded with such care. He carelessly sold his birthright to Jacob, with whatever spiritual privileges it involved. He married two daughters of Hittites, thereby connecting himself with idolatry, and giving his sanction to polygamy and other evils common among the Canaanites. Still, he was his father's favourite; and when the time came for Isaac to mark out, by a solemn form of blessing, the heir of promise, Esau was the son to whom he desired to convey it. By a cunning stratagem, which shows how universal in those times was the tendency to deceit, Jacob, instigated by his mother, obtained the blessing. A deadly feud sprang up between the brothers; and Jacob, to save his life, had to flee to Mesopotamia, and take refuge among his relations at Padan-aram.

Ishmael: Midian.—It may be well here to indicate the settlements of those descendants of Abraham who belonged to other lines than that of Jacob. It has already been mentioned that Ishmael settled in the deserts of Arabia. His descendants adopted that wandering or nomadic life which shepherds and hunters require to follow in a region where but little food is produced either for man or for beast. They appear to have been joined by the sons of Keturah, one of whom was Midian, the ancestor of the Midianites. While most of them followed the wild, roaming life, still familiar to the Arabs of the desert, others engaged in mercantile pursuits; and it is a proof that the Ishmaelites and the Midianites had virtually become one people, that those merchants to whom Joseph was afterwards sold are called, in different verses, by each of these names.

Edom.—The descendants of Esau did not spread over the wide region of Arabia, like the Ishmaelite race, but were chiefly confined to that part of it forming the country of Edom or Seir, which extends over the mountainous tract between the Dead Sea and the Gulf of Akabah. The Israelites came much into contact with them in their subsequent history, and had nowhere more rancorous enemies. They rose to considerable eminence as a nation; and their capital city, Petra, was, as it still is, remarkable for its temples hewn out of the solid rock, and for other extraordinary structures. For many generations Edom was the high-road for the commerce between the north and the south,—between Syria and Babylonia on the one side, and Egypt and India on the other. This makes its present desolation, as foretold in many a prophecy, the more remarkable.

Ammon and Moab.—The Ammonites and the Moabites, the descendants of Lot, also preserved the position of distinct nations. Their territories were situated to the north of those of Edom; and they too, once and again, became conspicuous for their hostile spirit in the subsequent history of Israel.

SECTION III.—CAREER OF JACOB.

Jacob's early history—Vision at Beth-el—At Padan-aram—Recalled to Canaan—Interview with Esau—Wanderings in Canaan.

Jacob's Early History.—Leaving the subordinate branches of the Abrahamic tree, we now confine our attention to Jacob, the divinely chosen child of promise. In natural character, Jacob was in some things more like his grandfather than his father. He had much more of Abraham's strength of will and energy of character than of Isaac's gentleness and love of retirement; but, unlike Abraham, when first introduced to us in Scripture he has obtained no soul-subduing view of the character of God, nor has he learned to make his own will bend to that of the Most High. He wanted, too, the high integrity and the well-balanced mind of Abraham; for while he formed passionate attachments to some, like Rachel and Benjamin, he was barely just to others, like Leah and the majority of his sons. Cunning and selfish, he used his craft to increase his gains. His character was naturally of that kind that needed a powerful and varied discipline to change it; and the course of Providence towards him was evidently ordered with that view. The great sin of his youth, that of deceiving his father, received a signal chastisement. Deceived himself once and again, by his father-in-law, and by his own sons, he had experience of that law of Providence which often makes a man suffer from the very sin in others which he himself has committed.

Vision at Beth-el.—The time of Jacob's chastisements was also a time of mercy. While fleeing from his brother's fury, which he had raised up against himself by his deceit, he had a remarkable vision at Beth-el of a ladder reaching up to heaven; and on that occasion a promise was made to him, similar to that which God had given on the same spot to Abraham. Later in life, when returning homewards, he had a memorable meeting with the Angel of God, and wrestled with him a whole night as if he had been a man: this seems to have been what led him to surrender himself conclusively and wholly to God. In his flight from his father's house he proceeded northward, in the same direction as Eliezer had taken when going to fetch Rebekah; and at last he came to Haran, in Padan-aram, where he found the residence of Laban, his mother's brother.

At Padan-aram.—We need not dwell here on the events of the next twenty years—his engagement as Laban's servant—his attachment to Rachel, Laban's younger daughter—his marriage to both the daughters, Leah and Rachel—the birth of his twelve sons and his daughter, and the circumstances of his leaving Padan-aram and returning to Canaan. These twenty years were spent amid scenes that had been familiar to his grandfather Abraham, the remembrance of whose faith and obedience was fitted to exercise a salutary influence on Jacob.

Recalled to Canaan. At last he was recalled to his native land by a vision and command of God, of the same gracious character as had been vouchsafed so often to his fathers, and to himself at Beth-el. To leave Haran could have been no great trial, for he had little love for his father-in-law; but to return to Canaan, if that should imply meeting with

Esau, was extremely formidable. Weary of Haran, Jacob immediately set about complying with the command; but he showed that the leaven of cunning was still in his nature, by stealing away in secret. He had contrived, in a large measure through his cunning, to accumulate large flocks and herds, which he brought away with him. Pursued by Laban, he was overtaken at Mount Gilead, in the eastern part of Palestine. Through divine interposition matters were amicably arranged between them: they parted in peace, and Jacob had now only his old quarrel with Esau to trouble him.

Interview with Esau.—In dealing with Esau, he showed much greater manliness than in dealing with Laban. Esau was now settled in Mount Seir, in the land of Edom, far to the south (Gen. xxxii. 3). Jacob was on the banks of the Jabbok, close to the Jordan, nearly a hundred miles distant. He might have crossed the Jordan, and quietly settled at Shechem, or at Beth-el, without encountering Esau. But of his own accord he sent messengers all the way to Mount Seir, to tell him of his arrival. What else could have led him to do so but the voice of conscience, testifying that he had wronged his brother, and calling him to make what reparation he could? The messengers, on returning, brought back word that Esau was coming to meet him with four hundred men! The mind of Jacob was greatly agitated, fearing that the meeting might be of a warlike character. After despatching a valuable present to Esau, and arranging his company in suitable order, he betook himself to prayer. He spent the whole night wrestling with the Angel of the covenant, who appeared to him, and from whom he would not part unless he should agree to bless him. In the course of the struggle his thigh was disjointed; but Jacob, disabled in point of natural strength, resorted to the spiritual weapons of prayer and supplication, and by these he prevailed. Perhaps this was meant to teach him very impressively the inefficacy of the carnal weapons of deceit and cunning which he had employed so much in his past life, and the efficacy of prayer and of dependence on God. The blessing he sought was at length most cordially bestowed, and his name was changed to Israel—"The Prince of God." As a manifestation of spiritual earnestness and holy ardour, the scene at Penuel stands unrivalled in Scripture history. When Esau came up, the meeting of the brothers was of the most cordial kind; and after the exchange of compliments and friendly wishes, Esau returned to Mount Seir; and Jacob, after a short halt at Succoth, crossed the Jordan, and settled at Shalem, in the vale of Shechem.

Wanderings in Canaan.—But his residence here was brought abruptly to an end by the perfidious slaughter of the Shechemites by two of his sons, Simeon and Levi, in revenge for the gross and guilty conduct of Shechem, prince of the city, towards Dinah, their sister. The bad odour into which the name of his family was brought by this transaction, compelled Jacob to remove. His course was the same as Abraham had followed more than a century before. First, by divine direction, he came to Beth-el, where God again appeared to him, and renewed his promises. Proceeding southward, past the hills of Jerusalem, he had almost reached the ridge of Beth-lehem, when Rachel, his favourite wife, was taken from him, after having given birth to his youngest son, Benjamin. Griefs of another kind were also preying on his mind as he reached Hebron; for his eldest son had committed an outrage in his family, and the spirit of the young men, generally, was exceedingly wild and reckless. At last he arrived at the residence of his aged father, who was still dwelling, in extreme old age, at Hebron. It must have been with no ordinary feelings that he returned to the familiar scenes of his youth, and gazed on the venerable face he had last beheld in very different circumstances. The discipline of some thirty years, sanctified as it had been, had wrought a vast change upon Jacob; and Isaac, in the latest years of his life, must have found, in the congenial converse of his younger son, abundant cause for the assurance that, foul and false though the method of obtaining it had been, the blessing had come down on the right head after all. It could not have been many years after the return of Jacob when Isaac was gathered to his fathers, at the ripe age of one hundred and eighty; "and his sons Esau and Jacob buried him."

SECTION IV.—CAREER OF JOSEPH, AND REMOVAL OF JACOB TO EGYPT.

Joseph's early life—His life in Egypt—Removal of Jacob and his sons—Death of Jacob—Death of Joseph—A typical history—Patriarchal faith—The lessons of the sojourn in Egypt.

Joseph's Early Life.—The stream of history now follows the life of Joseph, the youngest but one of the sons of Jacob. A remarkable combination of gifts and graces met in his character. He had the calmness, the shrewdness, the large-heartedness, and the faith of Abraham, with the holy reverence and much of the gentleness of Isaac. He had the tender feelings of Jacob, without his ruggedness and impetuosity. His fault was the universal fault of the age,—a tendency to the use of artifice in carrying out his plans,—a want of that perfect honesty which scorns dissimulation, and is now happily recognized as an essential element in the character of a great and good man. Brought early under the fear of God, and thus taught to restrain those feelings which his brothers at the time indulged freely, Joseph soon became the object of their dislike. Their hatred was increased by his informing their father of their doings; and envy was added to hatred, through Jacob's undisguised favouritism. His frankness, perhaps his imprudence, in narrating certain dreams, which pointed to his one day being raised far above them, threw fuel on the flames of their jealousy. Joseph had reached the age of seventeen, when on one occasion he was sent by his father to inquire after the welfare of his brethren. Their flocks had now increased so greatly that they had to go with them for pasture to a distance, and on this occasion they had gone to their old quarters in the vale of Shechem, about fifty miles north from Hebron. Not finding them there, Joseph followed them to Dothan, a fine green plain, nearly twenty miles farther north.* His brethren there conspired against him, and sold him to a trading company of Midianites or Ishmaelites, who were carrying the traffic of Mesopotamia to

---

* Dr. Robinson found here a green hill still bearing the name Dothan, and was told that the great road from Beisan and Jezreel to Egypt still passes through this plain.

Egypt; and by them he was carried to the latter country, and was sold as a slave. Returning home, his brethren pretended that Joseph had been killed by a wild beast. The grief of Jacob, now bereft the second time of the object of his most ardent affection, was of the most passionate and touching kind.

His Life in Egypt.—It is not necessary here to detail, in its successive steps, the beautiful story of Joseph's life in Egypt. Nothing can surpass the beauty and simplicity of the Scripture narrative, telling of his faithful service and noble conduct in the house of Potiphar; his long captivity under the most calumnious of charges, brought against him by Potiphar's wicked wife; his deliverance from prison, and elevation to high honour under Pharaoh, in consequence of his interpretation of the royal dream; his administration of the realm of Egypt during the seven years of plenty which he had foretold, and the seven years of want that followed; his interviews with his brethren when they came from Canaan to purchase corn—his apparent harshness, his making himself known to them, his noble spirit of forgiveness, his unquenched affection for them all. And nothing can be more instructive than the connection which all this is seen to have with Joseph's reverence for God. It was from fellowship with Him that this wisdom and goodness were manifestly derived. Had he not been a godly man, he could neither have stood erect under such temptations, nor have outshone as he did the rest of the world in wisdom and goodness. It might seem at first as if, in the treatment of his brethren, after he had recognized them, his object had been to make them smart under the rod; but on deeper consideration, we see that his object was to ascertain whether they had as little regard then as in former days for the feelings of their father, and as little genuine love for one another. The result showed that a great improvement in these respects had taken place; and the improvement seems to have become still greater under the striking lessons which Joseph's history conveyed. It was made clear to them as noonday that God by his providence rules among men; that he appoints every event that happens in the world; and that he makes all work together for the accomplishment of his purposes.

It was not less clearly shown that the providence of God is of the holiest character;—that wickedness, sooner or later, is sure to be punished; and honest, holy regard to God's will and glory sure to be blessed. When the sons of Jacob came down with their father, at Joseph's invitation, to settle in Egypt, their hearts must have been thrilled with admiration of God's fatherly forbearance and kindness, and with distress for the evil spirit which they had so sadly displayed. The men that came down to settle in Egypt were of a very different temper from the youths that had sold Joseph to the Midianites. Judah, in particular, whose former life had been stained with a great sin, showed in his noble readiness to suffer the penalty that seemed due to Benjamin rather than break the heart of the old man his father, a spirit of self-denying generosity which fitly symbolized that of Christ himself, and justified the eulogium afterwards passed on him by his father,—"Judah, thou art he whom thy brethren shall praise."

Removal of Jacob and his Sons. The sons of Jacob who accompanied him to Egypt were, Reuben, Simeon, Levi, Judah, Issachar, and Zebulun, sons of Leah: Gad and Asher, sons of Zilpah; Dan and Naphtali, sons of Bilhah; Benjamin, full-brother of Joseph, son of Rachel. They and their male descendants, when they arrived in Egypt, with Dinah their sister, amounted to seventy souls. The total number of persons forming their company must, of course, have been considerably larger. The *material* privileges of the birth-right were assigned by Jacob to Joseph, whose family, in the persons of Ephraim and Manasseh, obtained the double portion of the inheritance, due to the first-born; but the *spiritual* privileges of the birth-right, which did not descend by primogeniture, but were allotted according to God's sovereign will, were assigned to Judah. In the subsequent history of the nation, much jealousy sprang up, in consequence of this distinction, between Ephraim and Judah, followed at last by a separation of kingdoms.

Death of Jacob.—Seventeen years after the emigration, a most interesting scene takes place in the bed-chamber of the patriarch Jacob. Feeling his end approaching, he summons all his sons into his presence; and, rapt by the Spirit into future times, foretells the destiny of each. The career of Judah, whose name signifies "praise," is sketched in colours of more than earthly brightness. In the far-distant history of that son's tribe the glorious Messiah is seen, in lion-like strength and majesty, terrible to his enemies, and scattering the richest blessings among his friends.* Exhausted by the effort, the patriarch gathers his feet into the bed, and his spirit passes away. His embalmed remains are carried by his sons to Canaan, and are deposited in the cave of Machpelah.

Death of Joseph.—Fifty years later, Joseph too is removed from the scene of his generous and devoted labours. Like his fathers, he dies full of faith in the promises, strictly enjoining his people to carry up his bones to the Land of Promise, and let them rest in its hallowed soil; thus showing how firmly he clung to the promise of blessing.

A Typical History.—The career of Joseph was remarkable in many respects, but, as it now appears, chiefly as prefiguring the history of the Redeemer. His being hated and cast out by his brethren answered to Christ's rejection by his countrymen; his brethren applying to him in their extremity, and obtaining in him both life and forgiveness, indicated, in general, the kind of reception which all sinners get from Christ, and, in particular, the reception yet to be given when his guilty brethren shall apply to him,—when the Jews shall repent of their great national sin, and apply to the crucified Galilean for pardon and everlasting life. The Redeemer's humiliation and sufferings, and the exaltation and glory which followed, were represented in the corresponding events in the life of Joseph.

Patriarchal Faith.—Whether the good men of the time had any perception of this, it is hardly possible for us to say. The patriarchs were all remarkable for their faith, but it was more an exercise of the heart than of the head. It showed itself in a reverential submission to the word and the will of God, whether he directed them to look to a coming Deliverer for

* The prophecy, "The sceptre shall not depart from Judah, nor a lawgiver from between his feet, until Shiloh come," was regarded by the ancient Jews as a prediction of the Messiah, although in later times other views of it have been advanced.

salvation, or to trust in his providence for present protection and blessing. In the four great patriarchs, faith showed itself under different phases or modes of operation. In Abraham, we admire the firm, unshaken confidence, and the unhesitating obedience of faith, in all its power and fulness. In Isaac, faith is exercised in patient endurance and suffering, in quietness and waiting. In Jacob, it has to wrestle hard with flesh and blood, with the corruptions of the heart within, as well as with the ills of the world without. In Joseph, it is seen both enduring patiently and working laboriously; and it is crowned at last with signal victory. "These all died in faith, not having received the promises, but having seen them afar off, and were persuaded of them, and embraced them, and confessed that they were strangers and pilgrims on the earth."

The Lessons of the Sojourn in Egypt.—In the removal of Jacob's family to Egypt, a great purpose was served in connection with their predestinated history. Had they remained in Palestine, on the same footing as their fathers, they must have been scattered over the country to find food for their cattle, and very probably they would have become mingled with the Canaanite inhabitants. By removing them to Egypt, God made provision at once for their remaining a separate people, and for their pursuing the pastoral life to which they had been trained. He made provision, at the same time, for their profiting by the rough discipline of trial and suffering, and for their learning to look to him for help in trouble. The Hebrew nation, like other great nations, had to encounter a baptism of suffering, and to learn, from hard experience, that it is good for a people, as it is good for a man, to bear the yoke in its youth. The very fact of their removal to Egypt, however, showed that the settled era of their history, and the settled glory of their family, had not yet come. It must be a long time before the great promise to Abraham should be fulfilled. And thus again they were taught the great lesson of their race, to look forward for the Hope of Israel.

SECTION V.—SOCIAL AND RELIGIOUS LIFE OF THE PERIOD.

State of society—State of religion—Idolatry—The three "Pilgrim Fathers"—Time of Job—Its social life—Signs of civilization.

We conclude this chapter with a few remarks on the state of society and of religion during the period we have been surveying.

State of Society.—The state of society was far from barbarous—there are few or no traces of savage life. In the courts of Pharaoh and Abimelech the marriage tie was respected to a certain extent, and a considerable degree of refinement prevailed. In more ordinary life, hospitality and politeness were very generally shown, and the usual forms of speech bore the impress of a courteous spirit. Abraham's interviews with the sons of Heth, and with the strangers who came to the door of his tent, were full of the spirit and language of courtesy. The pastoral life seems to have been the common one, and wealth usually consisted of flocks and herds. Merchants, however, were systematically carrying the products of one district to another; and the precious metals were in use as money. Rebekah's bracelets, ear-ring, jewels set in gold and silver, and fine raiment, Judah's signet-ring, and Joseph's coat of many colours, show that considerable attention was paid to the adornment of the person. In transferring property from owner to owner, regular forms were gone through, as when Abraham bought the cave of Machpelah; and what was thus transferred seems to have been held very sacred, even during the long absence of the rightful possessor. Tents formed the chief dwellings of Abraham, Isaac, and Jacob; but these were adopted in token of their being but strangers and pilgrims in the land. Cities were already the dwelling-places of many; but what are called cities must, in some cases, have been little more than walled villages. The custom of slavery had been introduced, probably as a consequence of war; but in the families of godly men like Abraham, the slaves for the most part were treated with great consideration, and showed a most faithful and attached spirit to their master. The children of even wealthy and important men, like

Jacob, were sent to watch the flocks, and to convey provisions; and every one was provided with active employment. In other communities, we read of kings, princes, chiefs, and dukes; for the spirit of aristocracy early became ascendant in these new communities. In Egypt and Chaldæa learning and the arts were cultivated with great assiduity and success; but among Abraham's seed there is no trace of much progress having as yet been made in these.

State of Religion.—The outward forms of religion among the patriarchs were exceedingly simple. The offering of burnt-sacrifices upon a plain altar was the chief, almost the only, ceremony. There are some indications—especially in the mention of stated periods of seven days—of the observance of the Sabbath as a day of rest and worship. When any of the patriarchs settled in a new place, his first care was to erect an altar to the Lord, and to make an open profession of his worship by calling upon his name. Memorial pillars were sometimes erected, and wine or oil poured out, or other thank-offerings presented, in acknowledgment of particular acts of God's mercy. Male infants, and proselytes from other nations, were circumcised. The practice of offering to God a tenth part of the substance had begun to prevail; for Abraham gave to Melchizedek a tenth of the spoil, and Jacob vowed at Beth-el that he would give back to God a tenth of all that He should give him. Communications from God were made with the patriarchs by visions and dreams. The promise of a Deliverer was unfolded during this period in greater clearness: it was successively announced that the Messiah should come through the line of Abraham, Isaac, Jacob, and Judah; and that the blessings to flow from him should extend to all the nations of the earth. Abraham's special title—"Father of them that believe"—indicates that the spirit of faith had now acquired a broader and more definite form than before. Men, however, were still taught that the great blessing was to come in a future age. Believers were now taught more definitely to renounce their own righteousness, to receive the salvation which God should provide, and to place their entire reliance upon him. Reverence for the character of God, a humble sense of personal unworthiness, a habitual regard to his will as the rule of life, and reliance on his plan of mercy for the guilty, were the great elements of genuine piety. On all occasions of need, prayer was offered up to God, of the most simple, genuine, and spiritual kind. Prominent among the practical fruits of this piety was righteousness—respect for the rights and regard to the feelings of others. Nothing was more sacredly guarded, under the patriarchal economy, than the purity of the family relations. One of Abraham's highest virtues was his admirable faithfulness in training his household to observe the laws of God. One of the great lessons of Providence in the history of Jacob and his family was, that God's displeasure visits the undutiful son and the unkind brother; and that his blessing rests on filial and fraternal love.

Idolatry.—There are some indications that the worship of images was not unknown even in the families of the patriarchs. But, for the most part, the pure knowledge and worship of the one living God was faithfully preserved by them. In other countries, such as Chaldæa and Egypt, idolatry made fearful progress. Still, a recognition of One Supreme God seems to have continued to exist. Among other races, such as the Canaanites, family order and purity were sadly destroyed, and fearful sensual vice prevailed.

The Three "Pilgrim Fathers."—On the whole, the patriarchs furnished a noble pattern of the religious and moral qualities which it was desired that their posterity should exhibit. The three "Pilgrim Fathers" of the Jews—Abraham, Isaac, and Jacob—standing out, as they did, to the eye of posterity the more conspicuously and majestically, by their being alone in their several generations, left to all future ages a very precious example and influence. It showed the sad perversity of the Jewish people, that this, with every other inducement to purity of faith and practice, was so sadly disregarded, and failed often to restrain them even from open profligacy.

Time of Job.—It has generally been believed that the transactions recorded in the Book of Job belong to this period, if not, indeed, to a somewhat earlier time. It is certain that there is no mention in the book of the Hebrew patriarchs, or of the captivity in Egypt, or of the giving of the law, or of any well-known events, like the providential history of Joseph, that would have thrown light on the problem of Job. But while Job belonged to a very early age, it is now the general belief that the Book of Job was not written till about the time of Solomon. If so, the writer evidently studied to make his book a faithful photograph of what belonged only to the patriarchal age, and to some portion of the race outside the chosen family of Abraham and his seed. Job was probably a descendant of Shem; his residence is said to have been "in the east" (Job i. 3),—the term usually applied to the district where the first settlement of men took place (Gen. ii. 8; iii. 24; xi. 2). The Sabæans and Chaldæans were his neighbours; and at the time when he lived, the knowledge of the true God seems to have been preserved without material corruption. The adoration of the heavenly bodies had begun to be practised (Job xxxi. 26, 27), but there seems still to have been a general belief in One Almighty God.

Its Social Life.—The picture of social life in the Book of Job is in many respects extremely beautiful. We dare not regard it as a sample of what was usual over the world, but rather as exhibiting the highest condition of social life that had been attained. There were even then cases of oppression, robbery, and murder; but, for the most part, a fine patriarchal purity and simplicity prevailed. The rich and the poor met together, and to the distressed and helpless the rich man's heart and hand were ever open: "When I went out to the gate through the city, when I prepared my seat in the street, the young men saw me, and hid themselves: and the aged arose and stood up......When the ear heard me, then it blessed me; and when the eye saw me, it gave witness to me: because I delivered the poor that cried, and the fatherless, and him that had none to help him. The blessing of him that was ready to perish came upon me, and I caused the widow's heart to sing for joy." The bonds of family affection retained all their power in the household of Job;—his children feasted by turns in each other's houses; while the affectionate and pious father rose early in the morning to offer sacrifices for them all, lest any of them should have sinned. The simple burnt-offering retained its place as the appointed ordinance of Heaven, and was the sacrifice that Job, as the high priest of his house, presented on behalf of his children.

Signs of Civilization.—In the Book of Job mention is made of kings, princes, nobles, judges, merchants, warriors, travellers, and slaves. The pen of iron had begun to engrave inscriptions upon rocks; the mining shaft was sunk for gold and silver; and palaces that had been built for kings and nobles had fallen into ruin. Astronomy had begun to acquaint men with the heavenly bodies, and many of the stars and constellations had received well-known names. Altogether, the state of civilization was highly advanced. The more closely we study those early times, the more erroneous appears the opinion, that man began his career as a savage, and gradually worked his way up to refinement and civilization.

CHAPTER V.

EGYPT.

FROM THE DEATH OF JOSEPH TO THE DEPARTURE FROM EGYPT.

Exodus i.–xv.

SECTION I.—EGYPT AND THE EGYPTIANS.

Physical aspect of Egypt—Upper and Lower Egypt: Thebes—Memphis—Early relations of Egypt to Eastern tribes: Semitic settlers on the Tanitic branch—The Hyksos invasion—Period of the Hyksos—The title Pharaoh: organization of the kingdom—Parallels to Joseph Egyptian customs referred to in Scripture—Domestic life—Religion—Apis, or sacred bull—Temples and worship: doctrine of retribution.

Physical Aspect of Egypt.—The land of Egypt has well been called "the land of wonders." The nature of the country and the history of its people are equally extraordinary. For the most part, the land of Egypt is but a narrow strip, extending to the breadth of a few miles on each side of the river Nile, but expanding, towards the mouths of that river, into an extensive plain, called, from its resemblance to the Greek letter Δ, a Delta. The length of what used to be called Egypt is about five hundred miles; so that, with Palestine, Greece, Rome, and Britain, it ranks among the very small countries that have had a wonderful influence on the rest of the world. The Egyptian empire, however, covered at times a much larger area. Though encompassed by great deserts on both sides, and though no rain falls in it, it is yet one of the most fertile of countries. This fertility is due to the overflowing of the Nile, which is caused by the rains that fall in the tropical countries where that river has its rise. By means of canals and ditches, extraordinary pains are taken to convey the water of the Nile to every field and corner of the land. The Nile begins to overflow its banks in June, reaches its greatest height in September, and returns to its ordinary level about the end of November. It was regarded by the ancient Egyptians not merely as a sacred river, but (as the Ganges is by the Hindus) as actually a god. Sometimes divine honours were paid to it; and perhaps the Jewish infants that were cast into it, by order of the Pharaoh that knew not Joseph, were intended as offerings to the river god. The water of the Nile was considered the best in the world for drinking. It was so fattening that the priests were not allowed to drink it; and there is a story of a Roman general in Egypt saying, when his soldiers asked for a supply of wine, "What! do you ask for wine when you have the water of the Nile to drink?" It is but recently that the cause of this peculiarity of the Nile water has been discovered. By means of the microscope, Professor Ehrenberg of Berlin found that the mud which the Nile deposits is studded with masses of living animalcules.

Upper and Lower Egypt: Thebes.—Egypt is divided into two chief parts—Upper and Lower. It is with Lower Egypt, or the part nearest the mouths of the Nile, that Scripture history is chiefly connected. The capital of Upper Egypt—"the land of Pathros" of the Bible—was the celebrated Thebes, situated about five hundred miles up the Nile, called in Scripture No, or No-Ammon. (See Jer. xlvi. 25; Nahum iii. 8.) Thebes was a most magnificent city. Homer speaks of its hundred gates. For many centuries the earth poured all her glories into it. The ruins of the Temple of Karnak at Thebes, the colossal statues of the kings, the valley of the tombs, and many other remarkable relics, have no equals in the world.*

---

* "It is impossible to wander among these scenes, and behold these hoary yet magnificent ruins, without emotions of astonishment and deep solemnity. Everything around testifies of vastness and of utter desolation....All is gloomy, awful, grand.... The walls of all the temples are covered with hieroglyphics, representing in general the deeds of the kings who founded or enlarged these structures. Many of these afford happy illustrations of Egyptian history."—*Robinson's Biblical Researches.*

"All that I anticipated of Egyptian magnificence fell short of the reality....I learned to appreciate the spirit of that extraordinary people, and to feel that, poetless as they were, they had a national genius, and had stamped it on the works of their hands,

Memphis.—The capital of Lower Egypt was Memphis, called in the Bible Noph. It seems to have been a chief residence of the Pharaohs in the time of the Israelites. It too was situated on the Nile, a few miles above the modern city Cairo; but nothing now remains to mark its site, save some mounds of rubbish, a colossal statue, and a few fragments of granite. There was lately discovered, however, near Memphis, a wonderful gallery of tombs, cut out of the rock, about two thousand feet long, where, in splendid marble sarcophagi, were deposited the bodies of the sacred bulls that had been kept and worshipped in that city. Near the site of Memphis rise the celebrated pyramids, the tombs of the ancient kings of Egypt,—the oldest structures in the world raised by the hand of man. Some of them are believed to have been built before the time of Abraham.*

Early Relations of Egypt to Eastern Tribes: Semitic Settlers on the Tanitic Branch.—The information recently furnished by the monuments has thrown considerable light on the history

lasting as the 'Iliad.' Willing slaves to the vilest superstition, bondmen to every form and circumstance, adepts in every mechanical art that can add luxury or comfort to human existence; yet triumphing abroad over the very Scythians, captives from every quarter of the globe figuring in those long oblational processions to the sacred shrines in which they delighted after returning to their native Nile,—that grave, austere, gloomy architecture, sublime in outline and heavily elaborate in ornament, what a transcript was it of their character! And where could Clio write their history so appropriately as on the walls of their temples? And never were pages more graphic. The gathering, the march, the melée; the Pharaoh's prowess, standing erect as he always does in his car, no charioteer, the reins attached to his waist, the arrow drawn to his ear, his horses all fire, springing into the air like Pegasuses; and then the agony of the dying transfixed by his dart, the relaxed limbs of the slain,—Homer's truth itself; and lastly, the triumphant return, the welcome home, and the offerings of thanksgiving to Amun-re;—the fire, the discrimination with which these ideas are bodied forth, they must be seen to judge of it."—*Lord Lindsay's Letters.*

* At a distance, the pyramids seem to be composed of small stones, and to have no great elevation. "But as we approached their base and became aware of the full size of the stones, and looked upward along their mountain sides to the summit, their huge masses seemed to swell into immensity, and the idea of their vastness was absolutely overpowering.... Vain pride of human pomp and power! The monuments remain unto this day, the wonder of all time; but their builders, their history, and their very names have been swept away in the dark tide of oblivion!.... The top of the Great Pyramid is now a square platform of 32 feet on each side, at an elevation of 470 feet above the base. The view from it is very extensive: in front, Cairo and numerous villages, with their groves of slender palm-trees; in the rear, the trackless Libyan wastes: on the south, the range of smaller pyramids extending for a great distance along the margin of the desert; and then, in boundless prospect, north and south, the mighty river, winding its way through the long line of verdure which it has won by its waters from the reluctant grasp of the desert upon either side."—*Robinson's Biblical Researches.*

of Egypt *about* the time when Joseph and his kinsmen entered the country, although there is still much obscurity as to the dates, and as to the particular kings who were reigning when the several events took place. Among other things, the relations of Egypt to neighbouring nations have received considerable elucidation. In early times, the Egyptians proper, occupying the Delta, appear to have confined themselves mainly to the space enclosed by the Canopic and Pelusiac branches of the Nile. To the east of this district, and especially to the east of the Tanitic branch, the population was more mixed with foreigners. Coming from Syria, Arabia, and other neighbouring countries, these were commonly of Semitic origin. The principal town, Tanis, or Zoan, a place of great antiquity, "built seven years later than Hebron" (Num. xiii. 23), was essentially a foreign town, as the inscriptions testify. Among the Semitic races who settled in this part of Egypt were " the Shasu from the land of Aduma " * (Edom). Somewhere about the fifteenth or sixteenth century before the Christian era, a body of these Shasu, with their flocks and herds, left their country, driven probably by famine, to seek in the rich fields of the Delta the sustenance which their deserts refused them.

The Hyksos Invasion.—Josephus gives an account of an invasion of shepherds from the east, called Hyksos,† who, apparently with little trouble, dispossessed the old kings, and assumed the government of the country, residing chiefly in the north-east part of it. The new kings were of a much rougher race than the Egyptians. They assumed the Egyptian religion, adopted the Egyptian language, manners, and customs, built temples, and accommodated themselves generally to the existing state of things in Egypt. Their dominion lasted a considerable time, but at last, in the eighteenth dynasty, they were expelled by the old line of kings.

Period of the Hyksos. From the records of the past it may be regarded as established that the dominion of the Hyksos

---

* Circular of the Nineteenth Dynasty, translated by Brugsch, i. 215.
† The name Hyksos in Greek is derived by Brugsch from Hak, "prince," and Shasu, the name of these Arabians from Edom, the two words Hak-Shasu becoming in Greek Hyksos. (Brugsch, i. 232.)

prevailed during some part of the residence of the Israelites in Egypt; but it is matter of dispute whether they were in power when Joseph was carried thither, or their dominion was established later. According to one authority it was some time after the arrival of Joseph and the Israelites that the shepherd kings or Hyksos got possession of the country.* Everything, it is thought, in the account given in Genesis indicates that the kingdom was in a settled state, and highly prosperous; that it was whole and undivided (not likely to have been the case, at first, under the Hyksos); and that its administration was carried on in accordance with the old Egyptian rules and methods. But, according to another authority, the Pharaoh who reigned when Joseph was in power was one of the Hyksos kings.† The considerations in support of the latter view are, we think, the more conclusive. It was natural that the king, if one of the Hyksos, should be friendly to the family of Jacob, for both were of Semitic origin, and both had come from the borders of Syria. It was also natural that a Hyksos king should give them a settlement in the land of Goshen—evidently the north-eastern part of the Delta—for the population of that part was already to a great extent Semitic, and there the Israelites would not be beside the pure Egyptians, in whose eyes every shepherd was naturally an abomination. If the king had shared this feeling against shepherds, he would hardly have welcomed Jacob and his family as he did. If the Hyksos invasion had not occurred before this time, the Egyptians would not have had their strong feeling against shepherds. It appears that the Hyksos were expelled during the residence of the Israelites in Egypt. The king who knew not Joseph was probably a monarch of the old line restored, and was therefore not friendly to any branch of the Semitic people, one section of whom had usurped the government for so long a time. If it be said that at the time of the Exodus the Israelites were dwelling among the Egyptians, the answer is, that after the expulsion of the Hyksos and all their adherents, bodies of pure Egyptians would prob-

---

* Canon Cook: Bearings of Egyptian History on the Pentateuch, in Speaker's Commentary, vol. 1.   † Brugsch.

ably be settled on their lands and in their cities, which were mostly in the north-east of the Delta, where the Israelites had always been. Leaving these points unsettled for the present (light may be cast on them hereafter), we proceed to occupy firmer ground, and to indicate some of the illustrations of the Scripture narrative derived from what the monuments teach of the domestic and foreign arrangements of the kingdom.

The Title Pharaoh: Organization of the Kingdom.—The title Pharaoh, or Perao, in Egyptian means "of the great house." To his subjects the Pharaoh was a god and a lord. At sight of him they were obliged to prostrate themselves, and to touch the ground with their noses. In speaking of him they often used the expression "His holiness." The Pharaoh gives orders to his servants, distributes decorations, such as necklaces and rings, and makes rich presents of lands and servants and maidens. His daughters go out of the royal women's house, and marry the highest and noblest of the land. The royal court is composed of the nobility of the country, and servants of lower rank. The affairs of the court and country are administered by the chiefs or the secretaries, and a numerous class of scribes. Among the officers were several called stewards. One steward had charge of the king's household, another of the wardrobe; another was hair-dresser, took care of the nails of his holiness, and prepared his bath. Other nobles were charged with the administration of the magazines of wheat, dates and fruits in general, of the cellar, of the chamber for oil, of the bakery and the butchery, and the stables. The private domains, the farms, the palaces, and even the lakes and canals of the king, were placed under the care of inspectors. Skilful persons of the order of nobles were placed over the buildings and all kinds of work in stone. The architect was one of the highest nobles of the court. Overseers urged the work-people to toil, by the whip more than by any other means. Judges attended to the administration of justice. The military forces were thoroughly equipped and organized. The hirshesta, or "teachers of the secret," were in possession of various kinds of hidden lore, astronomical and of other kinds. The scribes were divided into many branches, and wrote, with a light reed pen on smooth rolls of papyrus, the events of the kingdom, or recorded in well-kept books the expenditure of their department, or whatever else their masters might require them to preserve. All this vast machinery the records show to have been in a state of excellent organization, moving quietly in all its ramifications under the control of the mighty Pharaoh. It was in virtue of this absolute authority that he was able to place Joseph in so high a position. "Pharaoh said unto Joseph, I am Pharaoh, and without thee shall no man lift up his hand or foot in all the land of Egypt."*

Parallels to Joseph.—The history of Joseph is not altogether without a parallel in these old records. So early as the fourth dynasty, in the reign of Mencheres, we read of a young page who was placed among the royal children, and who, under his successor, King Shepseskaf, married the king's daughter, and is thus described:—"He was esteemed by the king more than any other servant. He became private secretary in everything that the king was pleased to do. He charmed the heart of his master. He was chief steward of the house of provisions, chief of all the works of the mines, prophet (and priest) of the god Sokar, and chief of the temple of this god."†

Some interesting memorials have been found that seem to touch the very time of Joseph. One incident in his life is paralleled by a story recorded on a papyrus, entitled the "Story of the Two Brothers." Anepu, a married man, while in the fields, sends his younger brother on an errand to his house. While engaged in attending to the message, he is solicited by the wife of Anepu, as Joseph was by the wife of Potiphar. He replies: "Thou, O woman, hast been like a mother to me, and thy husband like a father: for he is older than I, for he might have been my begetter. Why this great sin that thou hast spoken to me? Say it not to me another time, then will I not tell it this time, and no word of it shall come out of my heart to any man at all." In the evening, when Anepu returns, he finds his wife in great apparent trouble; and when the cause is

* Egypt under the Pharaohs, vol i., chap. v   † Ibid p 86

asked, she says that the younger brother has made dishonourable proposals to her.

Another recorded incident brings up the years of plenty and of famine. In a tomb at El-Kab, in Upper Egypt, the tomb of one Baba, there is an inscription which Brugsch holds to belong to the seventeenth dynasty. Baba gives an excellent account of himself, of his mildness, his benevolence, and his prosperity. Then he adds: "I collected the harvest, a friend of the harvest god. I was watchful at the time of sowing; and now, when a famine arose, lasting many years, I issued out corn to each city, lasting many years."* The conjecture is, that at the time when Joseph was acting as steward and administrator in the Delta, under a Hyksos king, Baba was employed in like manner in Upper Egypt, under one of the old Egyptian monarchs.

Egyptian Customs referred to in Scripture.—The points in which the Bible narrative coincides with the information derived from other sources respecting ancient Egypt are almost without number. A well-known German writer† notes, among others, the following: the thoroughly Egyptian custom of men carrying baskets on their heads, in the dream of Pharaoh's chief baker (Gen. xl. 16); the shaving of the beard (xli. 14); prophesying with the cup (xliv. 5); the custom of embalming dead bodies and placing them in sarcophagi (l. 2, 3, 26); the basket made of papyrus and covered with asphalt (Ex. ii. 3); the allusion in Numbers xi. 5 to the ordinary and favourite food of Egypt; the Egyptian mode of watering (Deut. xi. 10, 11); the reference to the Egyptian mode of whipping (Deut. xxv. 2, 3); the express mention of the eruptions and diseases of Egypt (Deut. vii. 15, xxviii. 27, 35, 60); and many other things, especially in the account of the plagues, which tally so closely with the national history of that country (Ex. vii.–x. 23).

Domestic Life.—The detailed acquaintance with Egyptian life which we derive from pictures and inscriptions is so full, that with such a work in our hands as Wilkinson's "Ancient

* Egypt under the Pharaohs, i. 260.
† Hengstenberg, Egypt and the Books of Moses.

Egyptians," we can easily realize the appearance of an Egyptian house such as that of Potiphar, or afterwards that of Joseph himself. A large mansion, in the form of a square, encloses a court or garden, planted with palms and other trees; while an elegant corridor, supported on columns, and open to the air on one side, gives access to the different apartments. The mansion is built of brick, covered with stucco, and painted with all the combinations of bright colours- red, green, blue, and yellow. A porch, supported on columns, decked with banners and ribbons, and with statues between, forms the principal entrance. From the flat roof the inmates can look out on the mud huts of the poorer inhabitants, which serve more as store-closets than as dwellings; for their owners may commonly be seen cooking, eating, and even sleeping in the open air. The interior of the great mansion is fitted up with the greatest elegance. The walls of the sitting-rooms are decorated with paintings surrounded by ornamental borders, and with large cornices of flowers and various devices, richly painted. There is no attempt at shading in their paintings, or at perspective drawing;—the colours are all of one shade, and the figures are flat. Everywhere flowers abound. They are formed into wreaths and festoons; they deck the stands that support the vases; they lie in bouquets, ready to be presented to each guest; and they crown the servants who wait on the company. The garden that supplies these flowers is of great extent; it is provided with a water tank for watering it, and it is cultivated with the greatest care. The sitting rooms are carpeted, and the chairs, stools, and couches are of the most elegant finish and shape.* Unlike the great men of the East generally, the lord of the mansion has but one wife; and among the members of the family there is not a little of the intercourse, affection, and endearment which prevail in our Western homes.

* In the tomb of Rameses III "you see arm-chairs like our own, and of the most inviting appearance; ottomans precisely like ours; steps for ascending to bed, at least exactly resembling those used in England for that purpose; and sofas with crescents for the leg and neck to rest upon,—luxurious appendages which Cowper had never heard of when he wrote 'The Task.'" *Lord Lindsay.*

When an entertainment is given, the dinner, which is prepared in a large kitchen by many skilful cooks, is served up at noon. The guests are entertained with music till dinner is ready; water is brought to wash their feet, before they enter the festive chamber; a lotus flower is presented to each guest, who holds it in his hand during the entertainment; sometimes a flower necklace is hung on his neck, and garlands and festoons are strewed around. Each guest has a small round table for himself, the arrangement of the tables being determined by the rank of the guests. They are accustomed to sit at table, not to recline like the Jews and the Romans. The dishes consist of fish; of meat, boiled, roasted, and dressed in various ways; of game, poultry, a profusion of vegetables and fruit, particularly figs and grapes, along with wine of various sorts. After dinner, games, music, dancing, and other amusements are provided for the guests.

The gardens and fields of Egyptian proprietors were carefully cultivated, under superintendence of a steward,—who had charge of the whole establishment. The priests and the soldiers were the privileged classes of Egyptian society; the husbandmen and the artisans were of inferior rank. Besides the native workmen, slaves were employed in manual labour, chiefly in erecting temples, pyramids, and other public works. The priests were often well versed in science and literature: so early as the fourteenth century B.C. large libraries seem to have existed. It is not likely, however, that all this refinement had been reached in Joseph's time; but, undoubtedly, great progress had been made towards it.

Religion.—The religion of Egypt deserves especial notice. Herodotus, a Greek historian, pronounces the people "religious to excess, far beyond any other race of men." The priests held in theory that there was one supreme God; but in practice this doctrine was wholly lost sight of. The Egyptians fell into the habit of deifying the several *attributes* or *qualities* of God, such as his creative power and his wisdom, and of regarding even plants and animals as worthy of divine honours, when they exhibited any of these qualities. In reality, the

Egyptians had a very large number of gods. These gods were of three ranks or orders. Among gods of the first order, were Amun, the great god of Thebes, answering to the Jupiter of the Greeks; Pthah, the father or maker of gods, answering to Vulcan; Khem, the god of nature, answering to Pan;—among the second, were Ra, or Phrah, the Sun; and Thoth, the intellect (Mercury);—and among the third, were Osiris, Isis, and Seth or Typhon. According to the popular belief, Osiris was originally a king of Egypt. He conferred immense benefits on the country, but he was murdered by his brother Typhon, who cut his body in pieces, and threw them into the Nile. Isis was the wife of Osiris. After a long search, she discovered the remains of her husband, and, with the aid of her son, defeated Typhon, and recovered the sovereign power. According to Herodotus, Osiris and Isis were the only gods that were worshipped by all the Egyptians. In each city of Egypt one deity was the chief object of worship: he was the guardian of the town, and had a conspicuous place in the porch of the temple. Each city had also its particular *triad* (as it was called); that is, a cluster of three gods, of whom the third proceeded from the other two.*

Apis, or Sacred Bull. The Egyptian practice of paying divine honour to every manifestation of a divine quality, soon multiplied the number of gods to a prodigious extent. It was on this principle that animals, such as the cat, the crocodile, and the ibis were worshipped. Of sacred animals, the most remarkable was the Apis, or sacred bull of Memphis. This animal, under whose form Osiris was worshipped, was known by certain marks: according to Herodotus, his hair was black, on his forehead was a white triangular spot, on his back an eagle, under his tongue a beetle, and the hair of his tail was double. The Apis was kept in a magnificent temple at Memphis, attended by priests, and worshipped by the people. At his death his body was embalmed, and was carried in divine state by a vast retinue of priests, clothed in the skins of leopards, to a tomb cut out of a rock, where it was laid in a splendid marble coffin.

* See Rawlinson's Herodotus, vol ii, Appendix to chap. iii

Temples and Worship: Doctrine of Retribution.—The temples reared by the Egyptians to their gods were exceedingly magnificent. The remains of some of them are still among the wonders of the world. The priesthood was a large, wealthy, and highly privileged class, with the king himself at its head. Their sacred rites were numerous and varied, and included much that was fitted to dazzle the senses of the multitude. Their religious belief was not without some wholesome elements; among which was the doctrine of future retribution. This was frequently depicted in paintings. "In one instance, a condemned soul is driven away in the shape of a sow; and the word *gluttony* is written over it, to express his crime. The punishments of the bad are frequently depicted; and the rewards of the good, who swim and sport like fishes in the celestial Nile—'the river of the water of life.'" It was the custom, during or after a repast, to introduce a small image of Osiris, in the form of a human mummy, and to show it to each of the guests, as a warning of his mortality and of the transitory nature of human pleasures. The guests were exhorted to love one another, to put a check on their inclinations, and to remember that death, which they should be prepared to meet, must at last close their earthly career.

SECTION II.—THE PROGRESS OF THE ISRAELITES.

Contrast to former life—Land of Goshen—Fortunes of the Israelites—Thotmes III.; his conquests—Neighbouring kingdoms—The Khita or Hittites—Idolatrous tendencies—The new Pharaoh—Oppression of the Israelites.

Contrast to Former Life.—Such were the people among whom the simple shepherds of Palestine went to dwell, when Jacob removed to Egypt. A greater contrast can hardly be conceived than that between the simple, pastoral life of Jacob and his sons, living in tents, following their flocks and herds, and worshipping One God before a stone altar, in the open air, with a simple burnt-offering; and the highly artificial worship and luxurious life of Pharaoh, his nobles, and his people. That

Jacob should have been somewhat unwilling to go to Egypt need not be very surprising, considering, on the one hand, that he inherited all the regard of his fathers for the land of Canaan, as the divinely-chosen theatre on which all the promises were to be fulfilled; and on the other, that his family would be exposed to the risk of so much contamination, by coming into contact with the corrupt but splendid and enticing religion of the Egyptians. At Beer-sheba, however, he obtained the divine sanction to his journey. No doubt he took all possible precautions to prevent his family from being mingled with the Egyptians; and probably it was as the result of these precautions that the land of Goshen was assigned them as their residence.

Land of Goshen.—Goshen is believed to have lain along the Tanitic branch of the Nile, being the part of Egypt nearest to Palestine, and a remarkably fertile district. It is still the most productive part of Egypt, having most flocks and herds, and also most fishermen; and its products at this day, as enumerated by Mr. Lane, a distinguished writer on Egypt, are much the same as those for which the children of Israel lusted in the wilderness. (See Num. xi. 5, xx. 5.) "They consist of millet or maize, milk, new cheese, eggs, small salted fish, cucumbers and melons, and gourds of a great variety of kinds, onions and leeks, beans, chick-pease, lupins," &c. But the testimony of a much more ancient authority than Mr. Lane has lately been brought to light. Describing Pi-Ramessu, the city of Rameses (a later designation of Zoan), an Egyptian letter-writer, on an ancient papyrus roll, thus speaks:—

"Its fields are full of good things, and life passes in constant plenty and abundance. Its canals are rich in fish; its lakes swarm with birds; its meadows are green with vegetables; there is no end of the lentils; melons with a taste like honey grow in the irrigated fields. Its barns are full of wheat and durra, and reach as high as heaven. Onions and sesame are in the enclosures, and the apple-tree (?) blooms. The vine and the almond-tree and the fig-tree grow in its gardens. Sweet is their wine for the inhabitants of Keim. They mix it with honey. The red fish is in the lotus canal, the Borian fish in the ponds; many kinds of Bori fish, besides carp and pike, in the land of Pu-harotha; fat fish and Khiptipennu fish are in the pools of the inundation; the Hanaz fish in the full mouth of the Nile, near the city of the conqueror (Tanis)."*

Zoan or Tanis (afterwards, as we have seen, Pi-Ramessu) was the chief city of the district, and one of the royal residences. The Hyksos kings seem to have lived much here, and after their expulsion their successors might find it convenient to be often at the city which had been the centre of their influence and the abode of so many foreigners. It is plain that before the Exodus, Pharaoh lived much in the neighbourhood of the Israelites, for Moses and Aaron went freely and at once between him and the elders of the people.

Fortunes of the Israelites.—For at least fifty years after the death of Joseph, the Israelites enjoyed peace and plenty in Egypt, witnessing the constant increase of their families and flocks; their fields waving with abundant crops, and their gardens gay with beautiful flowers. It is evident that from the first they had a government of their own—a government of elders. These, as the name implies, were chosen at first on account of their age, but afterwards for their capacity to rule. Other nations, too, had their elders,- the Egyptians (Gen. l. 7), the Midianites (Num. xxii. 4, 7), and the Gibeonites (Josh. ix. 11). The office continued during all the period of the stay in Egypt, and was in full operation while Moses and Aaron were negotiating with Pharaoh (Ex. iii. 16, 18). Occasionally an untoward event took place among the people, like that which happened to some descendants of Ephraim (1 Chron. vii. 21), who were killed in battle with the Philistines, one of the parties having carried off the cattle of the other (compare Ex. xiii. 17). Egypt had by this time achieved great renown for skill in the arts, and probably many of the children of Israel devoted themselves to such pursuits. We read of certain families that wrought fine linen; of others that were potters; and of others who dwelt among plants and

---

* Letter of Panbesa: Records of the Past, vol. vi., p. 11.

hedges, and who dwelt with the king for his work (1 Chron. iv. 21, 23). One of the Hebrews married Bithia, a daughter of the king, and by her had a considerable family (1 Chron. iv. 18), but without thereby acquiring any increase of rank among his own people.

Thotmes III.: His Conquests.—The duration of the sojourn of the Israelites in Egypt is uncertain, but at the least it exceeded two hundred years. From the monumental records we are now enabled to ascertain some important events that happened during that period, both in Egypt and in the surrounding countries. We have already stated that the Hyksos, or shepherd kings, were expelled, and that the royal authority returned to the old line of kings. These kings appear to have spared no pains both to establish their authority at home and to extend their influence abroad. One of these— Thotmes or Thutmes III., who is supposed to have reigned about 1600 B.C.—has been called the Alexander the Great of Egypt. His foreign conquests were on the most extensive scale. In the celebrated Temple of Karnak we find full and important records of his reign. It appears that during a period of twenty years he carried on no fewer than thirteen great campaigns against foreign nations on all sides of Egypt. Among the most important of these were his campaigns to the north-east, including the country called on the monuments Ruthen, and the district of Naharaim or Mesopotamia. Ruthen, or Rutenna, was the general name of the region comprehending Palestine, Phœnicia, and Western Syria. An inscription at Karnak gives a complete list of the towns in Upper Ruthen that had been opposed to him, or rather of the prisoners belonging to them that had been taken in the town of Megiddo. Just as in later times, the plain of Megiddo had been the scene of a great conflict, and the city of that name (which gives the symbolical name Armageddon to the final conflict of the Apocalypse, xvi. 16) had been the scene of one of the earliest military struggles that ever took place in the East. "What gives the highest value to the catalogue," remarks Dr. Brugsch, "is the undisputed fact that more than three hundred years before the entrance of the Jews into the land of Canaan, a great league of peoples of the same race, which the monuments call by the name of the Ruthen, existed in Palestine under little kings, who dwelt in the same towns and fortresses as we find stated on the monuments, and who, for the most part, fell by conquest into the hands of the Jewish immigrants."

The mere lists of booty brought to Egypt after the foreign campaigns of Thotmes III. are elaborate and very imposing documents. Masses of gold and silver and precious stones; vast herds of cattle; stores of wheat, wine, and garments; curiosities of various kinds; and great numbers of men and women reduced to slavery, were added year after year to the stores of Egypt. This royal scourge of the vast territories which he overran and pillaged was an eminently religious man in his way. He built splendid temples in honour of the gods of Egypt, the famous "Hall of Pillars" being one of them; he dedicated to them large portions of booty; he instituted feasts, reared obelisks, erected statues to the memory of his ancestors, vindicating his right to the title of "His Holiness," though in reality he was little better than a wholesale robber and murderer.

These illustrations of the extent of the Egyptian power and dominion enable us to understand better the position of the Israelites. After the conquests of Thotmes III., the power and resources of the Pharaohs were such as would have made any scheme of mere human opposition to them by a people like the Israelites utterly fruitless. Under any circumstances, the escape of the Israelites from Egypt must have demanded supernatural interference. If Egypt was as great and powerful at this time as the monuments indicate, the existence of supernatural help is still more conclusively proved.

Neighbouring Kingdoms.—The monuments throw light also, as we have seen, on the condition and resources of the people by whom the land of Canaan and the adjoining territories were held during the same period. "The whole of the land," says Brugsch, "known under the names of Palestine, Cœle-Syria, and Syria, bore in the inscriptions the appellation of Ruthen-hir, Upper Ruthen (or Luthen). It was divided into a number of small kingdoms, the names of which are commonly connected with one well-fortified capital, and which were inhabited by races with the special designations about which the inquiries of the learned are now eagerly occupied. The great people of the Khita (the Hittites of Scripture) occupies a distinguished place among them; while the kingdoms of Qirkamosh, Kadesh, and Megiddo were looked upon as the most important places for defence and attack, and as places of assembling for the allied kings."

The Khita, or Hittites. Before the rise of the Assyrian empire, the Khita, or Hittites, appear to have been the strongest people in Western Asia. Even before the days of Thotmes III. they had engaged the arms of Egypt. So far away as in the region of the Naharaim (Mesopotamia) the two forces had come into conflict. Rameses II. (supposed to have been the Pharaoh of the persecution) married a princess of the Khita. Though each several tribe might be comparatively insignificant, their practice of fighting in a confederate capacity made them exceedingly formidable. To dispossess any part of this great people of their lands, seemed about as hopeless an enterprise as to rise up against the mighty Pharaoh. Whether regard be had to the character and the resources of the people among whom the Israelites lived in Egypt, or to the character and the resources of the people whom they proposed to dispossess in the west of Syria, their enterprise, without supernatural aid, must be pronounced not only hopeless, but absolutely insane.

Idolatrous Tendencies. It is quite likely that after having been for some time in Egypt, the Israelites showed a tendency to fall into the idolatrous worship of the country. This was so constantly their tendency afterwards, that we cannot doubt that it showed itself now; more particularly if the invasion of the shepherd kings took place during the residence of the Israelites, and if these Semitic invaders showed the example of conforming to the Egyptian religion. It appears to have been God's policy to turn away the hearts of the Israelites from such conformity, by allowing them to be treated in a way fitted to alienate their hearts from everything Egyptian.

The New Pharaoh.—A king was raised up "that knew not Joseph." He was probably one of the old line of kings, restored to their honours after the expulsion of the Hyksos. It is the general belief that he was Rameses II. "The new Pharaoh," says Brugsch, "who knew not Joseph, who adorned the city of Rameses with temple-cities, can be no other than Ramessu II., of whose buildings at Zoan, the monuments and the papyrus rolls speak in complete agreement...... Ramessu is the Pharaoh of the oppression, and the father of that unnamed princess who found the child Moses exposed in the bulrushes on the bank of the river." * The monuments, as yet, have not given us any specific information concerning the affairs connected with the Exodus, "though the hope," says Brugsch, "is not completely excluded that some hidden papyrus may yet give us information as unexpected as it would be welcome."

Oppression of the Israelites.—The king, alarmed, apparently, lest the Hebrews should side with some host of invaders from the east, and so imperil the empire, resolved to cripple and crush them by hard and exhaustive toil. A dark era of oppression, lasting nearly a century, begins with his reign. Brick-making and building, under cruel task masters, are the kinds of work allotted to the Israelites. Pictures on the monuments show abundantly how common such treatment of the subject-races by the Egyptians was. Though nothing has as yet been found which specially identifies the Hebrews with the brick-making, the representations of that labour that survive bear out to the full all that is said in Scripture of its fearful rigour. Many Egyptian buildings are made of bricks dried in the sun, the bricks being often mingled with small pieces of chopped straw. It is a common supposition that the pyramids were built by them: but though the locality might perhaps have answered, as not being very far from Goshen, the time does not suit: for the great pyramids, that of Cheops, for example, of the fourth dynasty, were built before Jacob, even before Abraham visited Egypt.

* Egypt under the Pharaohs, ii. 99.

Finding that the numbers of the people still increased, the king endeavoured, at first secretly, and afterwards openly, to destroy all the male children. He issued an order that they should be thrown into the Nile. It was a terrible blow to the Hebrews, whose passion for offspring, especially male offspring, was proverbial. It does not seem to have continued long in force; and even while it did, it must have been frequently disobeyed. The more the people were oppressed, the more their numbers grew.

SECTION III.—EARLY LIFE OF MOSES.

His birth—His youth and education—His destiny—His trust in God—His trial—His flight—Sinai—Its physical aspect—The burning bush; return to Egypt.

His Birth.—During the subsistence of the order for the destruction of the Hebrew male infants, a man is born that is not only to humble the pride of the Pharaohs and to deliver Israel, but to set up a new economy of religious ordinances, and to introduce a new era in the history of the kingdom of God. Jochebed, wife of Amram, of the family of Levi,[*] a woman full of trust in God, has born a male infant of extraordinary beauty. What is to be done? Is she to conceal him, and thereby endanger the lives of all the family; or to fling him into the river, and think of him no more? Neither the faith nor the feelings of the mother can listen for a moment to the latter proposal. As long as she can she conceals the infant; but, at the end of three months, she finds that she can do so no longer. With many a prayer, she lays the babe in an ark of bulrushes, by the river side; leaves Miriam, his little sister, to watch what shall become of him; and goes home, it may be to meditate on the love and kindness of that heavenly Father who from the jaws of death gave back Ishmael to Hagar, Isaac to Abraham, and Joseph to Jacob. A daughter of Pharaoh coming to bathe in the river, perceives the child. Miriam, advancing at the proper moment, gets leave to call a Hebrew woman—his own mother—to be his

---

[*] It is not necessary to hold (as might at first sight appear) that Moses was literally the grandson of Levi by his mother, and his great-grandson by his father. There may have been several other links in the genealogy which are not enumerated.

nurse. Never, we may believe, did little girl bound home with lighter heart, or on more welcome errand. And nowhere could there have been found a happier household than Amram's, or thanksgivings and prayers more cordial than he would offer that night to God.*

His Youth and Education.—Moses records nothing of his early life while residing at the court of Pharaoh: the purpose for which, under divine inspiration, he wrote the books that bear his name, was not to give his biography to the world, but to show the progress of the kingdom of God. The speech of Stephen (Acts vii. 22) informs us that he was "learned in all the wisdom of the Egyptians, and mighty in words and in deeds." From the papyri published in 1844 by the trustees of the British Museum, belonging apparently to the reign of Rameses II., Egyptologists have illustrated the education which would be given to a youth belonging to the royal household, destined for military or for civil service during the "middle empire;" that is, the middle period of Manetho's thirty dynasties. It appears that a literary education was indispensable even for the lowest appointment in either service. The child, as soon as he was weaned, was sent to school, to which his mother daily carried his food. Reading, spelling, and grammar occupied the earlier years; then composition, both in prose and in verse, the prose style being simple and perspicuous, and the poetical style embracing the parallelisms and antitheses so conspicuous in Hebrew poetry, but more ornate and pretentious than the latter. The art of writing was of no small difficulty, as the intricacies of the sacred or hieroglyphical mode of writing were not easily mastered. Much attention was paid to arithmetic, geometry, and book-keeping. The sacred writings of the Egyptians,

---

* The Assyrian records contain a somewhat similar story of Sargon I., an early Assyrian king, probably of the seventeenth century B.C. "My mother," he is made to say, "was an outcast, my father I knew not, my father's brother ruled the land. In the city Azupirana, on the bank of the river Euphrates, my mother, the outcast, conceived me; in a hiding-place she bore me. She laid me in an ark of rushes; with bitumen its mouth she closed. She gave me to the river, which drowned me not. The river carried me; to Acci the ferryman did it bring me. Acci the ferryman, in the tenderness of his heart, lifted me up. Acci the ferryman as his own child nurtured me. Acci the ferryman as his woodsman made me. And in my woodmanship did the goddess Istar love me."—*Sayce's Babylonian Literature*, p. 10.

dating considerably farther back, had already been the subject of manifold comments and glosses, as is shown in the "Funeral Ritual, or Book of the Dead," translated by Dr. Birch.*

His Destiny.—Little could Pharaoh or his nobles have thought, when they saw the handsome face of the Hebrew child, and remarked his progress in learning, what humiliation awaited Egypt at his hands. Little could the priests have dreamt, when they saw his aptness for learning, and how readily he mastered the treasures of their Hermetic or sacred books, that his fingers were one day to write out a system of laws and government that would be admired and honoured thousands of years after theirs should have perished. Little could they have supposed, as they taught him to read and write the mysterious letters on tomb, temple, and obelisk, intended to immortalize the mighty achievements of Egypt, that ages after those achievements should have been forgotten, the deeds and words of that Hebrew boy would be as fresh and clear in the knowledge of all the nations of the civilized world as if they had been done and spoken but yesterday at their side.

His Trust in God.—For the work that Moses was raised up to do, the great moral quality required was—*trust in God.* It was the spirit for which the patriarchs, whose memory he would be taught to revere, were most remarkable. It was very specially the spirit of his mother. His own natural disposition seems to have been confiding and trustful; and when God sanctified this spirit, and directed it to Himself, it became the ruling principle of his life. To do whatever God might require, to venture on whatever undertaking God might direct, to submit cheerfully to any sacrifice God might appoint, in the full belief that all would be well at last, and that the recompense would infinitely outweigh the sacrifice, became the sacred and binding rule of his life. He was well exercised in the great spiritual lesson of the times, looking forward in reliance on the promises of God,—thinking of a future age, when the great blessing, promised to the seed of Abraham, should be enjoyed.

His Trial.—Ere long, this spirit of faith or trust was subjected

* See Speaker's Commentary Exodus ii 10

to an unexampled ordeal. It was impressed on his mind, in some way not revealed to us, that it was his duty to throw in his lot with his countrymen, and undertake their deliverance from bondage. The mental struggle that followed must have been of no common kind. To renounce all his worldly advantages—to leave the court of Pharaoh, and sink into the position of a mere Hebrew, involved a remarkable exercise of the spirit of trust and submission. But the decisive moment came; the mind of Moses was made up; the world and its attractions were renounced for ever,—it became his only ambition to deliver his countrymen, and to serve his God.

His Flight.—But a new trial awaited him. When he came to his countrymen, he found that they had no disposition to welcome him as sent by God for their deliverance. And having, under a hasty impulse, and perhaps from habits learned in Pharaoh's court, killed an Egyptian who was ill-treating a Hebrew, he was forced to flee for his life, and to direct his steps to the wilderness. He seems for many years afterwards to have been oppressed by the conviction that he had forfeited his influence, and had proved himself unfit for the work of delivering his countrymen.

Sinai.—The district to which he fled was the peninsula of Sinai, a singular and solitary tract, full of barren mountains, lying between the two gulfs into which the Red Sea is divided at its northern extremity. It was the same district in which he afterwards spent forty years as leader and law-giver to the people of Israel. He seems, in his flight, to have gone right across the peninsula, to the farther side of the Gulf of Akabah,* where he fell in with a pastoral tribe of Midianites, and accepted the humble situation of shepherd to Jethro, their priest and

---

* It has recently been considerably disputed whether it was on the eastern or on the western side of the Elanitic Gulf that the settlement of Jethro lay. In favour of the more remote locality it is argued that Moses would not have been safe in the peninsula itself, which was then under the rule and control of the Egyptians, and where they worked their copper mines and carried on a considerable traffic. In favour of the western side of the gulf—the more generally received locality—it is urged that the Towara of the present day, whose settlement is on the west, have been held to be the descendants of the Midianites by Ritter and other geographers, and that the ancient geographers speak of palm groves, springs of water, and a sanctuary with a hereditary priest and priestess having existed there. See Speaker's Commentary, Exodus ii. 13.

chief, whose daughter he ultimately married. A mind so active as that of Moses could not want occupation these forty years. It would be employed partly in devotional thoughts, in communing with that God whose works he now beheld; and partly in digesting the learning and the knowledge of mankind which he had acquired in Egypt, and in considering how these might be turned to account. Unconsciously to himself, Moses would thus be preparing for the arduous task of judging and governing his people, when he should return to them and lead them out of Egypt.

Its Physical Aspect.—The peninsula of Sinai, across which Moses fled, is about one hundred and fifty miles in greatest breadth, and in greatest length two hundred. Its northern part is hilly, rather than mountainous; but towards the southern angle the mountains are crowded together with bewildering profusion; and some of them rise to the height of nine thousand feet. The two great characteristics of the region are,—majesty and desolation. A modern traveller has described its general appearance by comparing it to an ocean of lava, which, while its waves were running mountains high, had suddenly been made to stand still. Another describes the mountains as the "Alps" of Arabia;—but the Alps unclothed; the Alps planted in a desert, and therefore stripped of all the clothing which goes to make up our notions of Swiss and of English mountains,—stripped of the variegated drapery of oak and birch, and pine and fir, and grass and fern,—wild, bare, rugged, desolate: truly a "great and terrible wilderness." This wilderness of mountains is everywhere intersected by ravines, or "wadys," running towards the sea; each of which for a short time in winter forms the channel of a torrent, but during the rest of the year is nearly as dry as the dust of the highway. It is to the absence of water that the desolate character of the district is owing. Notwithstanding, most of these wadys have a thin coating of vegetation, consisting of aromatic and other plants, "the desert's spicy stores;" and in some spots, under the influence of perennial springs, a richer vegetation flourishes, brightening out, here and there, into scenes of considerable luxuriance and beauty. It is the business of shepherds to find out all these green spots, and to lead their flocks to them for refreshment and pasture. The population of the peninsula at the present day does not exceed six thousand; but there are grounds for believing that in former days it was considerably greater. There is evidence that so early as the third Egyptian dynasty, king Senoferu of Egypt worked the copper and turquoise mines in the Wady Magharah, in the peninsula. These continued to be worked till the twelfth dynasty, when operations were transferred to the Sarabit el Khadim. There the mining went on till the twentieth dynasty, or later than the Exodus. There are other evidences of the peninsula having been of more importance in those early times than it is now.*

For forty years Moses had to range over this desert, from valley to valley, in search of food for his flock; living roughly in huts and in sheds; suffering from cold by night, and from heat by day; and liable to be attacked and plundered by hostile tribes. His mode of life demanded a remarkable exercise of patience; and Moses, content with his humble office, did not fail in the spirit of waiting quietly for God's time.

The Burning Bush: Return to Egypt.—The forty years had made no improvement on the outward condition of his people. Indeed, a new king had come to the throne, who treated them worse than his predecessor had done; and all their hopes of relief from the hand of man had now perished. The new king is thought to have been Mineptu II. of the nineteenth dynasty.† In their misery they began to cry in earnest to the Lord, and their deliverance was at hand. Appearing to Moses, in a bush that burned but was not destroyed, God commissioned him to go to Pharaoh and deliver his people from his hand. Moses was most reluctant to undertake the mission; for the spirit of enterprise had died away in him, and his great ruling principle—trust in God—had sunk, from want of exercise, to a very low ebb. But fortified by

---

* See Captain Palmer's Report of Exploration of Sinai.

† Brugsch, ii 128. Birch's Egypt, page 133, with portrait from a statue. Canon Cook, on the other hand, holds that the king was Thotmes II. See Speaker's Commentary, vol. i., p i.

ample promises of divine support, and by the help of his brother Aaron, who was sent to meet him, he at length accepted the appointment, and returned to Egypt to deliver his people.

SECTION IV.—THE DELIVERANCE.

Moses in Egypt: contest with Pharaoh—The ten plagues: their religious significance—Pride of the Pharaohs—Institution of the Passover—Passage of the Red Sea

Moses in Egypt: Contest with Pharaoh. — When Moses reached Egypt, he found his people in a strange state of mind. At times they were disposed to trust him; but when anything went against them, they were ready to despair, and to turn upon him as an enemy and a traitor. The struggle of Moses with Pharaoh was one of extraordinary difficulty. It turned upon a request, that the people should have leave to go three days' journey into the wilderness, to sacrifice to their God. The request was put in this form, to give a religious aspect to the conflict—to show that it was a struggle not merely between Pharaoh and Moses, but between the gods of Egypt, whom Pharaoh represented, and the God of Israel. Both Pharaoh and Moses understood quite well that if this request were once granted, Pharaoh's authority over the people would be entirely at an end. During the contest, Pharaoh seems to have been residing in the royal city of Zoan, which, as we have said, was close to Goshen. The first manifestations of supernatural power went for little, as the Egyptian sorcerers or wise men were able to imitate most of them.*

The Ten Plagues: Their Religious Significance.—The obstinacy of Pharaoh was so great, that the ten plagues of Egypt had to be sent to overcome it. These plagues were—1. The water of the Nile turned into blood. 2. Frogs. 3. Lice (or gnats). 4. Flies (or beetles). 5. Murrain. 6. Boils. 7. Hail.

* The Egyptians who dealt with such things were of various orders. (See the work of M. Chabar: Le Papyrus Magique.) From 2 Tim. iii. 8 we learn that the names of the two principals were Jannes and Jambres. In Egyptian, An (from which Jannes) means a scribe. Jambres may mean scribe of the south. See Speaker's Commentary, Exodus vii. 11.

8. Locusts. 9. Darkness. 10. Death of the first-born. Many of these plagues were well fitted to reprove the idolatry and superstition of the Egyptians, and thus to show them the vanity of the confidence which they reposed in their gods. We have already remarked that the Nile was regarded as a sacred river,—so sacred that, according to one ancient writer, the god Nilus was the rival of Heaven, since he watered the earth without clouds or rain. The *first* plague was very conclusively aimed against this superstition. Other superstitious beliefs were rebuked by the other plagues. Perhaps the most remarkable feature of the religion of the Egyptians was their idolatrous veneration for animals. The number of animals which they deemed sacred was prodigious. Some of them, such as the frog and the beetle (for so "flies" may be better translated), became on this occasion the causes of most intense annoyance to them. On other sacred animals, the murrain and the boils must have fallen with great severity. It is quite possible that the Apis, or sacred bull of Memphis, may have been attacked in the gorgeous temple where he was kept, and that his rotten carcass, which must have defied all the art of the embalmer, may have been carried forth with divine honours to the splendid mausoleum in which it was destined to repose. Amid the universal destruction of the cattle that were supposed to be under the protection of the Egyptian gods, the preservation of every animal of the Hebrews was the more remarkable. But the obstinacy of the king of Egypt was amazing. Under none of the first nine plagues did he yield for more than a short time; and it was not till the death of the first-born in his own and in every other house in Egypt—the first-born both of man and of beast—that he assented to the request of Moses. It had been announced that this plague would be an execution of judgment against all the *gods* of Egypt. At one time it was so difficult to understand this, that a tradition sprang up among the Jewish Rabbins that on that night all the temples of Egypt had been destroyed by lightning. But we now know that as the bull, the goat, the ram, the cat, and even the frog and the beetle, were representatives of deity and objects of reverence to the Egyp-

tians, the destruction of the first-born of beasts could not but be regarded as a direct judgment on their gods.

Pride of the Pharaohs. - How is the extraordinary obstinacy of Pharaoh to be explained? It should be borne in mind that the Egyptian kings were singularly proud. The fact that the pyramids were built by them as their tombs, makes it plain that they had no small idea of their own importance. Another mode in which they were accustomed to give expression to their unbounded pride, was to cause enormous statues of themselves to be set up, very commonly in the neighbourhood of some magnificent temple. Seldom, indeed, were they content with one; whole rows of statues are yet found, all of them representing the same king. Of one of these colossal statues among the ruins of Thebes, thought by some to represent the king in whose reign Moses was born, a recent traveller says: "By some extraordinary catastrophe, the statue has been thrown down. ......But you can still see what he was—the largest statue in the world. Far and wide that enormous statue must have been seen; eyes, mouth, and ears. Far and wide you must have seen his vast hands resting on his elephantine knees...... Nothing that now exists in the known world can give any correct notion of what the effect must have been when he stood erect, resting, in awful majesty, after the conquest of the then known world......In the palace, the same colossal proportions are everywhere observed. Everywhere (in the pictures) the king is conquering, ruling, worshipping, worshipped. The palace is the temple : the king is the priest. He and his horses are ten times the size of the rest of the army. Alike in battle and in worship, he is of the same stature with the gods."* It was to rebuke the towering pretensions of this high-minded race, and to show His own unapproachable greatness in contrast to their littleness, that the ten plagues of Egypt were sent by God. If, after an exile and degradation of more than two centuries, the old royal family of Egypt had reoccupied the throne, we may easily conceive their reluctance to submit to any act of humiliation. And if this act was demanded in the

* Stanley's Sinai and Palestine.

interest of such a people as the Israelites, who, like the Hyksos, were shepherds, the reluctance may easily be conceived to have risen to the height of a determination to resist to the uttermost.

Institution of the Passover.—Immediately before the slaughter of the Egyptian first-born, the ordinance of the Passover was celebrated for the first time by the Israelites. A lamb was slain for each household, and was partaken of by the family in the garb of travellers, while its blood was sprinkled on the door-posts and lintels of their dwellings. This mark indicated to the angel of the Lord the dwellings of the Hebrews, and was the token that they were to be *passed over* when he came forth to destroy the first-born of the Egyptians. Hence the name of the ordinance, which became with the Jews a solemn annual festival. In the course of the night a terrible panic seized the Egyptians, when the eldest son in every house was found dead. Under the excitement, the Israelites were driven out of the land of bondage, laden with jewels and other articles of value, which they had previously borrowed, or rather asked, and which were willingly given by their oppressors. Evidently the Egyptian people felt that the Hebrews had been treated unjustly by them, and that now God was showing his displeasure. As fast as they could, they heaped their treasures upon them, in the hope that God's anger would be pacified, and further judgment averted from Egypt.

Passage of the Red Sea.—Going before them in a miraculous pillar of cloud and fire, God leads them from Rameses to Succoth, thence to Etham on the edge of the wilderness, and thence to Pi-hahiroth, near the shore of the Red Sea. On the third day they are terrified by observing Pharaoh close upon their rear with an army, chiefly of chariots and chariot-warriors, the characteristic arm of Egypt. Their exact situation at the time cannot now be ascertained, but probably they were a few miles south from Suez, shut in by mountains on each side; the Gulf of Suez, some six or eight miles broad, in front; and the Egyptian army behind.* The terror and the anxiety of

---

* No subject has occasioned more debate than the route of the Israelites from Egypt across the Red Sea. Some think that the passage was effected close to Suez, where the

the host of Israel are at their height, when slowly and majestically the pillar of cloud and of fire that had gone before them moves to their rear, and throws a screen between them and their pursuers. A miraculous power imparted during the night to a strong east wind, causes it to lay bare a passage across the gulf, wide enough to allow the whole host to cross. The fiery column sheds its glare before them, and guides them safely to the farther shore. Tempted, amid the darkness of night, to follow them, Pharaoh and all his host are caught and overwhelmed in the returning waters. The body of the proud monarch, for which some lofty pyramid had doubtless been prepared, tossed by the waves, may or may not have been washed ashore. Unspeakably relieved, the people of God, safe on the Sinai shore, pour out their feelings in a song of victory; and to the God of their fathers they ascribe the glory of a deliverance more glorious than they could have ventured to hope for.

SECTION V.—EFFECTS OF EGYPT ON THE ISRAELITES.

Religion of the patriarchs Corrupted by Egypt—Revival of the ancient worship Lessons in the arts of peace—Darkness in other parts of the world.

Thus at last, after a residence of fully two hundred years,* the children of Israel finally left Egypt. In numbers they had increased amazingly. When they first arrived, the number of their males had been about seventy; now there were six hundred thousand able to bear arms.

Religion of the Patriarchs.—But what effects had their resi-

---

gulf is narrow and so shallow that comparatively little miraculous power would have been needed to make a passage; others place the line of passage opposite Ayin Mousa, "the Wells of Moses," five or six miles to the south of Suez; and others place it at a point still more distant. By far the most elaborate attempt to identify the localities is that of Dr. Brugsch, who investigates the meaning of the names specified and the position of the places with great minuteness and care, and makes the sea an arm of the Mediterranean rather than of the Red Sea, in the direction of Port Said. (The Exodus and the Egyptian Monuments.)

* The precise duration of the residence in Egypt is a difficult point. In Exodus xii. 40 it is said to have been four hundred and thirty years. But in Galatians iii. 17 it is said that the law was given four hundred and thirty years after Abraham. This would reduce the sojourn in Egypt to half that period. Stephen adopted the longer period (Acts vii. 6) Our Bible chronology follows the shorter

dence in Egypt produced upon their religious worship and their general character? When they first went down to Egypt, and probably for some time afterwards, their religious worship was very simple and very pure. At the house of each chief of a tribe, probably of each elder (or superintendent of a certain number of families), there would be an altar, with its sacred court around, consecrated to the Lord. Each seventh day the families would assemble around that altar; the burnt-offering would be led out; the elder would kill the animal, pour out its blood before the Lord, then place on the altar the parts to be burned; the congregation, young and old, looking reverently on, till the last wreath of smoke had gone up to heaven. Pious parents would take great pains to instruct their children. The memory of the great events of the past—the fall, the flood, the tower of Babel—would be carefully cherished. The especial dealings of God with the nation—with Abraham, with Isaac, and with Jacob—would be much dwelt on; and his marvellous interposition in the case of Joseph. The promise of God to Abraham would be remembered, and would shine with the light of a bright morning star—" I will be a God to thee, and to thy seed after thee "—" In thee and in thy seed shall all the families of the earth be blessed." There was much to excite their gratitude in the past, there was more to raise their hopes for the future.

Corrupted by Egypt.—All this was extremely simple and pure. No priests, save the heads of families or the elders; no temples, only plain altars; no gorgeous dresses, no images, no imposing processions were here. The religious worship of Egypt was very different. The temples were most magnificent; the priesthood were high in rank and in influence; and the religious ceremonies were most imposing and attractive. The Israelites were soon corrupted. Young persons, not truly pious, would at first be attracted to the Egyptian temples by curiosity; then they would become ashamed of their own simple worship; and by-and-by they would fall completely under the spell of the superstition of the country. When their oppressions began, it is not likely that they were allowed to observe their own Sabbath; so that, as a whole (though with many bright exceptions), they would fall more and more into the prevailing idolatry. That the idolatrous notions of Egypt had been imbibed by the Hebrews, was shown by the singular readiness with which they entered into the scheme for the worship of the golden calf.

Revival of the Ancient Worship.—About the end of their Egyptian bondage, there seems to have been a temporary revival of the spirit of true worship, when, driven to despair, they cried to the Lord. And one great end of the Passover, which was instituted before they left Egypt, was to bring them back to the simple worship of their fathers, and especially to bring out that quiet, *domestic* character, which formed so great a contrast to the splendid temple-worship of Egypt. The more specific design of the Passover was to commemorate the deliverance from the bondage of Egypt. That deliverance was a most impressive type of the great deliverance from the bondage of sin which was afterwards to be achieved, by the shedding of the blood of Him whom the paschal lamb prefigured. The ordinance that constantly looked back on the one deliverance was designed to encourage the faithful to look forward to the other.

Lessons in the Arts of Peace.—In other respects, the Israelites may have learned many instructive lessons from Egypt. Many of the useful arts, including the art of government, of agriculture, of gardening, the useful and ornamental arts, along with science, and other kinds of learning, were prosecuted with great success. Many of the laws of Moses were founded upon arrangements with which the Israelites had become familiar in Egypt. If it had not been for the unbelief of the people, which doomed them to wander in the wilderness till the generation that came out of Egypt died, they would have carried up to Palestine all that was valuable in Egyptian civilization, in union with that pure system of worship which God gave them from Sinai.

Darkness in other Parts of the World. In other parts of the world the state of religion was now becoming darker and darker. We have already, in this chapter, spoken of the religion of Egypt. From the Assyrian inscriptions we learn that in Assyria and in Chaldaea idolatry had by this time been developed to a very deplorable extent. The chief Assyrian god was Asshur—probably the deified patriarch of Gen. x. 11—but they had thirteen principal gods and many minor divinities. The chief god of the Babylonians was called Il, or Ra (often Bel). Besides the chief god, there were twelve principal deities, who were worshipped in suitable temples. The number of inferior deities was enormous. Many of the towns and villages throughout Babylonia and Assyria appear to have had each its own particular deities; and, in an inscription in the reign of Sardanapalus, mention is made of four thousand gods.* Phœnicia, then making rapid progress in commerce and civilization, was particularly addicted to idolatry. The worship of Baal and Ashtoreth was carried on there with extraordinary devotion, and of course was spread abroad with every Phœnician colony. When we think how strongly this awful tide of idolatry was setting in upon the world, we see what a glorious blessing was conferred on it first by the call of Abraham, and then by the ordinances of Moses; and we may realize how difficult and noble was the duty assigned to Abraham and his seed —to be witnesses for the one true God against whole nations of idolaters.

* The other principal deities of the Assyrians and the Babylonians, as stated by Sir Henry Rawlinson, were:—1. Anu; 2. Bilu-Nepru, or Bel Nimrod; 3. Hea, or Hoa; 4. Mulita, or Bilta, the supreme goddess; 5. Iva, god of the sky; 6. San, or Sham, god of the sun; 7. Hurki, or Sin, god of the moon; 8. Nin, or Bar; 9. Bel-Merodach; 10. Nergal; 11. Ishtar, or Astarte; 12. Nebo. See Essay by Sir H. Rawlinson, in G. Rawlinson's Herodotus, vol i., p. 584.

CHAPTER VI.

THE WILDERNESS OF SINAI AND THE EAST OF JORDAN.

FROM THE DEPARTURE OUT OF EGYPT TO THE DEATH OF MOSES.

EXODUS xv.—DEUT. xxxiv.

SECTION I.—THE JOURNEY TO SINAI.

The scene at the Red Sea—Description of the wilderness of Sinai—The wilderness of Sin—Rephidim—Meeting with Jethro—Mount Sinai—The scene of the law-giving.

The Scene at the Red Sea.—It is not difficult to picture the situation of the Israelites on the morning after their miraculous passage of the sea. Here, at the water-edge, are groups of men and women, watching the rolling tide as it casts heavily on the beach the ghastly corpses of Egyptian warriors. Yonder, where the rock juts out into the sea, are clusters of children, who have never before seen the sea, gathering the red sea-weed, and the brilliant shells and corals, or watching the movements of the strange-looking creatures that roam among the pools. Away, dotted over the rocky heights, or in closer masses in the hollows between, are flocks of sheep, of goats, of oxen, and of camels, cropping up the spare herbage of the desert, or making eager journeys in quest of water. Conspicuous above the encampment is the strange column, that appears as a pillar of cloud by day and of fire by night, and becomes from this time the Heaven-sent guide of the host through the wilderness. The whole multitude have that excited look which denotes the recent occurrence of some strange transaction. Everywhere their conversation bears on the great event of the night: intimate friends telling one another what they saw, and how they felt,—tasking their fancy to describe the coloured glow of the waves, "as it were a sea of glass mingled with fire;" or the awful crash of the crystal walls, as they clasped the Egyptians in their merciless embrace. An expression of freedom sits on every face. One countenance, however, may exhibit a mingled expression, as if the spirit of composure and the spirit of anxiety were moulding it by turns. Others may deem their troubles to be past; but that thoughtful, king-like man, with the eagle eye, and the mild expression, and the massive brow, knows that they are but beginning. He knows that desert well. He knows that it contains no sufficient provision for that host, throughout its whole length and breadth. How are they to be fed? How is he to answer them when they ask him for water? He cannot tell. One thing only he knows,—that GOD has brought them there; and that, should He even order them into the very heart of that wilderness, there is no other course to be thought of but to trust and to obey.

Near the spot where the Israelites are usually supposed to have halted on crossing the Red Sea, are the Ayin Mousa, or "Springs of Moses," seven in number, where a clump of palm-trees, tamarisks, and oleanders still greets the traveller.* Marah (that is, "bitter"), where the Israelites found the water bitter (Ex. xv. 23), is thought to be a place now called Huwârah, twenty or thirty miles farther on, where there is a small basin, about five feet in diameter and eighteen inches deep, still containing bitter water.† Elim (Ex. xv. 27),

* "AIN MUSA [Ayin Mousa]. Dr. Robinson counted seven distinct springs, others more recently have made out seventeen....The water leaves a calcareous deposit, like the great fountains of Tyre; and this, having accumulated during long ages, has formed a little mound. A few stunted palm-trees cluster round it, and a few tamarisks bear them company; which they much need in this lonely spot, for the desert spreads all around, bleak and bare as the sea itself."—*Murray's Handbook for Syria and Palestine*, p. 11.

† "AIN HAWARAH [Huwârah], 'the Fountain of Destruction' (sixteen and a half hours [thirty-three miles] from Ain Mûsa), is the next fountain. The water is bitter.... Around are a few stunted palms, and a little thicket of the thorny ghŭrkŭd....Should the thirsty traveller hasten forward now to drink at the fountain, his Arabs will restrain him by the cry, 'Mŭrr! mŭrr!' Bitter! bitter!"—*Ibid.* p. 13.

where they found twelve wells and seventy palm-trees, is probably the Wady Ghŭrundel, five miles from Huwârah, "a gracefully undulated sandy territory, scattered over with thick clumps of the tamarisk-tree and small palms, with fountains in the neighbourhood."*

Description of the Wilderness of Sinai. — The wilderness which the Israelites had now begun to traverse, is not the flat expanse of sand that many suppose it to be. It is a region of rocks and ridges, usually bare, but often grand, and sometimes, in shady nooks and ravines, almost beautiful. "I walked forward for a few miles," says a lady traveller, describing this part of the journey, "past a prodigious black rock, which rose in grand contrast with the brown mountains; the sea, of the deepest blue, opening out at the end of the gorge, and bounded afar by the Egyptian hills, dressed in heavenly hues. We came down upon the sea, and went in and out, between it and the mountains, many times. The rocks were the most diversified I ever saw. I noted them on the spot as being black, green, crimson, lilac, maroon, yellow, golden, and white; and their form was that of a whole host of cones." But the hardships of the desert came apace. Struggling on foot through a steep, narrow, rocky ascent, like a long zigzag staircase, hardly wide enough for a baggage-camel, the traveller could not help thinking—"What a place was this for the Hebrew mothers with their sucking babes! They who had lived on the banks of the never-failing Nile, and drunk their fill of its sweet waters, must have been aghast at the aspect of a scene like this, where the eye, wandering as it will, can see nothing but bright and solemn rocks, and a sky without a cloud!......At every step we found the scriptural imagery rising up before our minds—the imagery of overshadowing

---

* "WADY GHURUNDEL is the next station.....This may be safely identified with Elim. The whole desert is almost absolutely bare and barren, but Wady Ghŭrundel is fringed with trees and shrubs, forming a charming oasis. Here are the stunted palms, with their hairy trunks and dishevelled branches. Here, too, are the feathery tamarisks, with gnarled boughs, their leaves dripping with what the Arabs call manna. And here is the acacia, with its gray foliage and bright blossoms, tangled by its desert-growth into a thicket. Pleasant is the acacia to the sight, wearied by the desert-glare; but it has a higher and holier interest, as the tree of the 'burning bush,' and the 'shittim-wood' of the tabernacle."—*Murray's Handbook for Syria and Palestine*, p. 14.

rocks, sheltering wings, water brooks, and rain filling the pools; —even we, with our comforts, and our well-filled water-skins, relieved our mental oppression with imagery like this. The faith of Moses must have been strong, to bear him up in such a scene; and what must have been the clamour and despair of the slavish multitude, whose hope and courage had been extinguished by that bondage, which yet left their domestic affections in all their strength?"*

The Wilderness of Sin: Rephidim.—After leaving their encampment at Elim, the Israelites proceeded to the wilderness of Sin,—an extensive sandy plain, stretching along the shore of the Red Sea. There the people showed a very offensive spirit, murmuring distrustfully for food. Their murmurings were rebuked; but a daily supply of food, in the form of manna, was sent to meet their hunger. Through the Wady Feirân,† the opening of which still presents so well-clothed and verdant an appearance, that it has been called the "Eden of the desert," and which at one time must have been the seat of a considerable population, it is supposed that they penetrated into the inner and most mountainous part of the peninsula. The next important station was Rephidim (Ex. xvii. 1), whence, at God's command, Moses went with the elders to strike the rock in Horeb, and to procure from it a supply of water. Tradition points out, as the rock which Moses struck, a large block of granite, some twenty feet in height, marked by several horizontal grooves, like mouths,

* "Eastern Life," by Miss Martineau. While referring to this able writer's work, we must take the opportunity of protesting, once for all, against the spirit in which she often writes of the authority of the Bible, and against the disrespect she casts on those who believe it to be the inspired word of God. Since the publication of her Autobiography, the extreme and painful nature of her scepticism has been well known.

† "WADY FEIRAN. The eye is refreshed by the sight of some bushy palms, and verdant gardens, watered from a well at a place called Husseiyeh. About a mile farther, the ruins of an ancient village may be seen, on a mountain to the left..... Half an hour after passing this place, we enter another and much larger palm grove, with whose graceful branches the spreading tamarisk mingles; a little streamlet winds through the thicket in its gravelly bed; hoary, tottering ruins cling to the rugged acclivities around; and the dark openings of rock-hewn hermitages dot the cliffs far overhead. This is Feirân, the Paradise of the Bedawin [Bedouin], and the site of an early ecclesiastical city. Just opposite the ruined city is the mouth of Wady Aleiyât, a wild, picturesque glen, which winds away up southward to the base of Serbâl, whose jagged summits are seen towering over all intervening cliffs."—*Murray's Handbook for Syria and Palestine*, p. 19.

such as might have been formed by the flowing of water. But it is more likely that Moses struck the rock high up the hill, and that the water descended, now by one valley, now by another, while the people were in the wilderness of Sinai, and needed a supernatural supply. It was at Rephidim, too, that they encountered and conquered the Amalekites,—a tribe of Edomites animated by the fiercest jealousy, on account of Jacob's seed having been preferred to Esau's,—who came upon their rear, and annoyed the feeble and helpless of the host. This tribe had probably their usual residence in the Wady Feirân, or in that neighbourhood. Moses, with his hands supported by Aaron and Hur, held his rod outstretched while the battle was going on, in token of dependence on the help of God. While his hands were extended Israel prevailed; when they were let down Amalek prevailed.

Meeting with Jethro.—It was in this neighbourhood that Jethro, the father-in-law of Moses, now came to meet him, bringing with him Zipporah, Moses' wife, and her two sons. The advice which Jethro gave to Moses, when he saw how overburdened he was with his work,— to appoint judges from among the people to decide the ordinary causes, while only those of unusual difficulty should be brought before himself,—led to a thorough organization of the people, and to the appointment of a gradation of rulers,—"rulers of thousands, rulers of hundreds, rulers of fifties, and rulers of tens" (Ex. xviii. 25). In compliance with the invitation of Moses, some at least of the family of Jethro threw in their lot with the Israelites, and accompanied them through the wilderness to Canaan (Num. x. 29-32). They are known in the history as the Kenites, and are occasionally introduced to our notice (Judges i. 16; iv. 11, 17).

Mount Sinai.—The next encampment was in the immediate neighbourhood of Mount Sinai. Here the mountains assume that bold, and lofty, and fearfully bare aspect, which gives to them their peculiar character of majesty and desolation. The chief materials of which the rocks are composed are, granite, porphyry, and sandstone. These rocks are richly tinted with red, and the whole region has a reddish colour. But which of all the hills in the peninsula is the real Sinai, where God manifested his glory and gave forth his holy law? This is a question about which much difference of opinion has long prevailed. Neither the name "Sinai" nor the name "Horeb" is now known among the Arabs. The mountains of the peninsula separate into two or three groups, each of which has a summit higher than the neighbouring mountains;—Mount Serbâl,* in the north-west group, near the Wady Feirân; Mount St. Catherine, in the east; and Um Shomer, in the south-east group, which is the highest of the whole range. Each of these has been put forward as the Sinai of the Bible; but none of them fulfils the conditions required by the history; and for a very long period the mountain to which tradition has chiefly pointed is that called Jebel Mousa, "the Hill of Moses." Jebel Mousa is not a separate mountain, but one of the peaks of a longish ridge, to which the name of Horeb is now commonly given by Christian travellers. Near to Jebel Mousa, on the northern side, stretches an extensive plain, called Wady Er-Râhâh; quite large enough to have contained the whole host of the Israelites, who were encamped close to Mount Sinai when the law was given. There is another large plain on the southern side of the mountain. As the traveller advances on the northern side, the valley opens wider and wider, and is full of shrubs and tufts of herbs; it is flanked on each side by lofty mountains of dark granite—stern, naked, splintered peaks, and ridges of indescribable grandeur; and it is terminated by the bold and awful front of

* "SERBAL, next to Sinai, is the most interesting mountain in the peninsula. It is even more grand and striking in outline than its honoured rival. It rises high above the neighbouring summits,—'all in lilac hues and purple shadows,' as the morning sun sheds upon it his bright beams. It is a vast mass of peaks, which in most points of view may be reduced to five. These are all of granite, and rise so precipitously, so column-like, from the broken ground that forms the roots of the mountain, as at first sight to appear inaccessible..... The view from the summit will amply repay the toil. The highest peak is a huge block of granite. On this, as on the back of some petrified tortoise, you stand and overlook the whole peninsula of Sinai. The Red Sea, with the Egyptian hills opposite,....on the east, the vast cluster of what is commonly called Sinai,....and towering high above all, the less famous but most magnificent of all, the Mont Blanc of these parts, the unknown and unvisited Um Shaumer [Shomer]."—*Murray's Handbook for Syria and Palestine*, pp. 20, 21.

Mount Serbâl is rejected chiefly because the approaches to it are covered with enormous boulders, through which it is hardly possible to find a path.

Horeb, rising in frowning majesty, from twelve hundred to fifteen hundred feet in perpendicular height. On the left of Horeb, in a narrow valley, a convent is situated, called the convent of St. Catherine: the deep verdure of its fruit-trees and cypresses is seen as the traveller approaches,—an oasis of beauty amid scenes of the sternest desolation. This valley is known to the Arabs as Wady Shu'eib, or "the Vale of Jethro," and is said to be the place where Jethro met Moses. (Ex. xviii.) The front of Horeb rises steep like a wall,—truly "the mount that might be touched." (Heb. xii. 18.)

The Scene of the Law-giving.—The ascent of the mountains which form the different peaks of Horeb is very difficult, owing to their excessive ruggedness. On reaching the top of the peak called Jebel Mousa, Dr. Robinson became convinced that it could not have been the summit from which the law was given. No part of it could be seen from the plain Er-Râhâh. There is, however, another brow of Horeb, which overlooks this plain. The highest of the peaks on this part of the mountain is called Râs-es-Sûfsâfeh. The cliff here rises out of a basin to the height of five hundred feet; and the deep hollows, worn by the weather in the granite, have the appearance of architectural ornaments. From this summit the whole plain Er-Râhâh is visible, with the adjacent wadys and mountains. "Here, or on some one of the adjacent cliffs, was the spot where the Lord descended in fire, and proclaimed the law; here lay the plain where the whole congregation might be assembled; here was the mount that could be approached and touched, if not forbidden; and here the mountain brow where alone the lightnings and the thick cloud could be visible, and the thunders and the voice of the trump be heard, when the Lord came down in the sight of all the people upon Mount Sinai."*

It must be added, that some travellers, including Carl Ritter, one of the greatest authorities in Bible geography, still believe Jebel Mousa to have been the real Sinai, and the plain to the south of this peak to have been the place where the children of Israel were encamped. From this plain they could easily have

* Robinson, vol. 1., p. 107

seen the top of the mount. On the other hand, the conductors of the ordnance survey of Sinai,* hold by the view of Robinson. Captain H. S. Palmer thinks that Râs-es-Sûfsâfeh is the peak on which God descended, but that other transactions may have occurred on Jebel Mousa, thus explaining its name and the tradition out of which it arose.

A traveller of eminence, Dr. Beke, in his "Origines Biblicæ," holds that Sinai and Horeb were not in the peninsula at all, but on the eastern side of the Gulf of Akabah, deeming that gulf to have been "the sea" which the Israelites crossed. This view has commended itself to hardly any one; but Captain Palmer thinks it quite possible that the great desert of Arabia, east of Akabah, may have been the scene of the forty years' wandering.

SECTION II.—THE LAW-GIVING.

Modes of communication with the people—The moral law—The ceremonial law—The judicial law—Purpose of the law—Its twofold design—The golden calf—Nadab and Abihu—The Tabernacle—Subsequent history of Sinai.

Modes of Communication with the People.—The communications which God had with the Israelites on Horeb were held partly directly, but chiefly through Moses. All the people heard the divine voice proclaim the law of the ten commandments. The feeling of terror to which this gave rise was so overpowering, that they entreated that they might not hear that voice again. After much solemn preparation, Moses was called up to the top of the mount, and God communicated to him many of the particulars of what we are accustomed to call the Law of Moses. The ten commandments God wrote on two tables of stone, which he delivered into the hands of his servant. He also gave him directions for the construction of a tabernacle, or sacred tent, which was to be the visible shrine, or dwelling place of God; and of a sacred ark or chest, that was to be kept in it, to be called "the ark of the testimony," because

---

* Ordnance Survey of the Peninsula of Sinai, by Captains Wilson and Palmer, under direction of Colonel Sir H. James, R.E., Director-General of the Ordnance Survey, 1869.

it was to contain the law which God had delivered to Moses, and which the people had declared that they would obey. Its name denoted that it would bear testimony against them in case of their disobedience. Instructions were given, also, for the furniture of the tabernacle, and for the garments that were to be worn by the appointed priests of the nation.

The Moral Law.—It has been usual to divide the law of Moses into three parts—the moral, the ceremonial, and the judicial. Clear and bold, on the very front of the whole system, was written the truth, that there is but one God, and that no image or similitude is to be used in his worship. The *moral* law was expressed briefly in the ten commandments: it is the expression of the divine will in reference to duties which arise from the unchangeable distinctions of right and wrong. All through the Bible, to the very close, this moral law is repeated and re-echoed as the fundamental rule for human life.

The Ceremonial Law.—The *ceremonial* law was the part that prescribed the types and symbols by which the great truths of the gospel were now to be prefigured. The most important of these were the sacrifices. Large additions were made to the sacrifices formerly in use: besides the simple burnt-offering, there were now specified the sin-offering, the trespass-offering, the meat-offering, and the thank-offering. An order of priesthood also was now instituted. Instead of each head of a family or elder doing the work of priest, Aaron and his sons were set apart for all the duties of the priesthood, and were invested with robes denoting their office. The members of the tribe of Levi were constituted attendants and assistants to the priests. The necessity of approaching God through a mediator was typified by this appointment: the priests generally, and the high priest in particular, typified Christ, by whom alone sinners have access to the just and holy God. (Heb. iv. 14–16; x. 19–22.)

Minute directions were given as to the manner in which every sacrifice was to be offered and every religious duty performed. It was specially enacted, that when the people should have taken possession of the Land of Promise, all the males should go up three times a year to the centre of the national worship, to observe the festivals of Passover, Pentecost, and Tabernacles. A great feature of the ceremonial law was, that it made use of outward and earthly things as the symbols of things inward and heavenly. The need of an atonement for the sinner's guilt was typified by the shedding of the blood of animals. The same solemn rite indicated that the forfeited life of the sinner could be redeemed only by another life being given up in his room. The need of inward purity was typified by constant washings of the flesh and of the clothes. Heaven was typified by the most holy place in the tabernacle, where the bright light shone indicating God's presence, and into which the high priest could not enter without the blood of sacrifice. Another feature of the ceremonial law was, that the minutest parts of religious duty were most rigidly prescribed by it. Under the New Testament, these ceremonial observances have been superseded, and a freedom unknown to the Jew has been introduced into the service of God. This change is much dwelt on in some of the epistles in the New Testament. Owing to the precise, formal way in which every act of worship was prescribed in the old economy, it was represented as a state of bondage; in contrast to which the more unfettered dispensation of the gospel was an economy of freedom. The one was like Hagar, Abraham's bondmaid; the other like Sarah, who was free. (Gal. iv. 22.)

The Judicial Law. The *judicial* part of the law of Moses was that which regulated the administration of justice, the rights of property, the punishment of criminals, the care of the poor, the education of the young, the numbering and registration of the people, and other matters commonly regulated by civil law in such countries as our own. The land of Canaan was to be divided among all the people, so that each man should have a property and a home of his own. The only exception was to be the tribe of Levi, which, as being consecrated to the Lord, was to be specially provided for. They had no territorial inheritance, but only certain cities for their residence; and in lieu of a share of the land they got a tithe or tenth of the produce of the whole. The usual punishment for theft was, to restore four or five times the value of the article stolen. Persons who had injured others were to have a corresponding injury inflicted on themselves. Murderers were to be put to death. Nothing could exceed the beauty and kindness of the provisions for the treatment of the poor. Slavery was not wholly abolished, but the slave was protected by several enactments made in his favour. Besides many other arrangements, it was provided that each fiftieth year should be a year of jubilee, and that their ancient possessions should return that year to any of the people whom poverty had obliged to dispose of them. Parents were most solemnly charged to instruct their children in the law of God, to explain to them the meaning of the Passover and the other ordinances, and to tell them of all God's wonderful dealings with the nation. The people were encouraged to be kind and courteous in their manners, especially toward strangers, and toward aged and afflicted persons. Holidays and seasons of rejoicing were provided very abundantly, at different periods of the year, especially at the three great annual gatherings, and at the harvest, the vintage, and the sheep-shearing. A happier life than that which God designed for the Israelites there could hardly have been: if only they had been faithful to their covenant, they would have become the envy of every nation.*

Purpose of the Law.—It should be carefully observed that the law of Moses was not designed to be a covenant of eternal life. The people were not led to believe that obedience to the law would secure for them individually the everlasting favour of God. *As a nation*, they enjoyed God's favour before the law was given; and as individuals, the very sacrifices which the law required them to make pointed to the substitution of the Lamb of God in their room, as the means of their deliverance from sin and its punishment. The rewards and the punishments of their law were mainly confined to the present life. It did not in any way interfere with that plan of salvation for sinners through a Redeemer, which God had announced to Adam and

---

* See Michaelis's Commentaries on the Law of Moses; Wines on the Laws of the Ancient Hebrews, &c. It would be quite away from the purpose of this book to enter into the critical question whether all the Hebrew laws were given by Moses. We follow the narrative as it stands.

Eve, and had confirmed by his covenant with Abraham. On the contrary, it pointed to that Saviour. By the greatly increased number and variety of the sacrifices, men were taught more clearly than before that they were guilty beings, that they could not save themselves, and that without shedding of blood there was no remission of sins. But nothing was more common than for men of proud heart to pervert the purpose for which the law was given, and to suppose that, if they obeyed it outwardly, they would personally secure the favour of God. In some of the epistles of the New Testament this error is assailed with great force. It is shown that the law of Moses was meant to be a schoolmaster to bring men to Christ; that their own actions, imperfect and sinful at the very best, could never deserve the favour of God; and that they must be indebted for salvation entirely to the free mercy and love of God in Christ.

Its Twofold Design.—In general terms, it may be said that the design of the law of Moses was twofold;—in the first place, to preserve the Israelites, as a thoroughly peculiar people, distinct from other nations, in their laws, customs, religion, and government; and, in the second place, to supply additional light as to the way of salvation, and to advance the Church's spiritual life. The constitution given to the Hebrew nation was such, that they could not abandon the worship of the true God and become like other nations, without tearing up the very foundations of their prosperity, and plunging themselves at once into an abyss of misery. Though an additional measure of light was imparted as to the way of salvation by means of new sacrifices and other typical ordinances, that great subject was still wrapped in considerable obscurity. It was God's purpose that the grand doctrine of salvation should only dawn by degrees on the eyes of his Church. Spiritual and moral life could as yet, therefore, have but an imperfect development; and we need not wonder that great defects and blemishes appeared in the lives of the best men of the period.

It has sometimes been attempted to be shown that the religious system of Moses was not original, but substantially borrowed from Egypt. But there is hardly anything even of plausibility to recommend this conjecture. Whatever elements of sound natural theology may have been exemplified in the Egyptian religion would of course reappear in the system of Moses; but in most of its important features the system of Moses, instead of resembling that of Egypt, was a contrast to it, and many matters of detail were prescribed apparently with the design of removing as far as possible every trace of Egyptian or other idolatry.

The Golden Calf.—The terror which the Israelites had felt on hearing the voice of God from the top of the mount lasted a very short time, and did not lead to any permanently good result. Moses had been but forty days on the top of the mount, when a great and almost incredible change took place on the spirit of the people. In their hearts, they wished to return to Egypt; and as if to prepare for this, they took steps to institute a form of worship similar to that of the Egyptians. (Acts vii. 39.) Having forced Aaron to join in their project, they induced him to demand of the people the golden ear-rings and ornaments which they had brought in great number from Egypt. Out of these there was constructed a golden calf; and when Moses came down from the mount, he found the people worshipping the image, with all the revelry of a heathen festival, as the god which had brought them up out of the land of Egypt. Without some acquaintance with Egyptian idolatry, from which the notion of the golden calf was plainly borrowed, this particular form of worship could hardly have been resorted to. The worship of the bull was notoriously common in Egypt; especially at Memphis, where, as we have already remarked, the Apis, or black bull, was worshipped with the utmost splendour; and at Heliopolis, where the Mnevis received honours hardly less magnificent. The bull was a representation of Osiris, and was supposed to embody certain divine qualities—such as strength and endurance—that were deemed worthy of homage. The golden calf, on this principle, was probably meant to represent certain divine qualities which had been exhibited in the deliverance of Israel; the figure of the image—a young ox—denoting strength; and the substance of which it was composed gold—signifying richness and glorious splendour. The flagrant contrast between this mode of worship and that enjoined by Moses showed, as we have said, that instead of being founded on the Egyptian system, that of Moses was founded on quite different principles. But the formation and the worship of such an image showed how completely the idolatry of Egypt had taken hold of the people; and the act was, in the circumstances, doubly criminal, inasmuch as God had just given an express prohibition against making gods of silver or of gold. His displeasure with the people was so great, that, had not Moses interceded very fervently for them, they would have been entirely rejected, and deprived of all the blessings of his covenanted people. The self-denial and the patriotic feeling of Moses never shone more remarkably than on this occasion, when God threatened to destroy the nation, and from the seed of Moses to raise up a people more worthy of himself. Moses with all his heart rejected a proposal that would have brought much distinction to his family, and interceded for the people until their ancient position and promises were restored.

Nadab and Abihu.—Another act of defiance of the divine authority took place at Sinai. Nadab and Abihu, two of the sons of Aaron, and of the order of priests, disregarding the divine order, put "strange fire" in their censers when they went to their holy service. "There went out fire from the Lord and consumed them, and they died before the Lord." It is impossible not to be struck with the contrast between the fidelity of the Bible in recording such discreditable acts, and the spirit of national vanity which inspired the inscriptions on the Chaldæan and the Egyptian monuments. If it be objected that on the Egyptian monuments we have no record of the destruction of Pharaoh and his host, and that therefore the whole story is apocryphal, the answer is that disasters had no place in these Egyptian records. They were intended solely to perpetuate the glory of the country. How could the Bible narrative have been constructed in so different a spirit, but for the fact that its object was to record, not the history of a nation, but the progress of the kingdom of God; and that for this end the writers were placed under the guidance of God's Spirit, and recorded not what pleased themselves, but what was according to his will? Josephus makes no mention of the golden calf.

The Tabernacle.—The order for the construction of the sacred Tabernacle had been given before the tragedy of the golden calf, but its execution seems to have taken place afterwards. The great object of the Tabernacle was to represent God dwelling in the midst of his people, and accordingly its place was in the midst of the encampment. It was the scene of the solemn public worship of the nation. The pattern and the mode of execution were communicated by inspiration to Bezaleel, its chief constructer; and the means of erecting it were furnished by the free-will offerings of the people. In the innermost sanctuary, or the Most Holy Place, was the ark of the covenant, containing the tables of the law; above the ark was the mercy-seat, on which, once a year, the high priest sprinkled blood; and on the mercy-seat knelt, face to face, two golden cherubim with outspread wings; denoting that through the appointed propitiation the holy God now held blessed intercourse with his creatures. In the outer sanctuary, or Holy Place, separated by a curtain from the inner, stood various pieces of sacred furniture—the altar of incense, the table of shewbread, the golden candlestick; and here, day by day, the priests came to offer incense with the daily sacrifice. In the court outside of the Tabernacle stood the altar of burnt-offering, on which the daily sacrifices were presented in the sight of the assembled people; and the laver of brass, containing water for the sacred ablutions. The Tabernacle was covered with curtains of rare value and beauty. In the contrast between this simple structure and the highly elaborate stone-temples of Egypt we see the divine mind pointing to simplicity and spirituality as the acceptable qualities of his worship; while the costly and beautiful curtains seem to have been designed to symbolize that holy nature in which God was to be revealed when the Word should become flesh and "tabernacle" among men (John i. 14).

Subsequent History of Sinai.—The people had been encamped at Mount Sinai for about a year, when, the law and all pertaining to it having been given, and the tabernacle and all its appendages having been constructed, the pillar of cloud moved forward, and the host advanced in the direction of the Promised Land. The sacred locality of Sinai and Horeb does not again obtain prominence in the Scripture narrative. Once, and only once, the Bible history returns to Horeb:—when Elijah has fled from Ahab; has advanced a day's journey into the wilderness of Beer-sheba; has seen a vision as he slept under the *retem*, or broom-plant of the desert;[*] has proceeded forty days' journey to Horeb, the mount of God; and has had his memorable meeting there with Jehovah. (1 Kings xix.) It is but a conjecture, that, when the Apostle Paul visited Arabia (Gal. i. 17), he may have gone to Sinai, and have had suggested to him the allegory of the two mountains, which he makes use of in the Epistle to the Galatians (ch. iv.). For the most part, the Jews do not seem to have cared to visit Sinai. Early in the Christian centuries it became a hiding-place for the persecuted Christians of neighbouring countries, among whom was Catherine of Alexandria, whose body (according to the legend), after she had been brought back to Egypt, and had suffered martyrdom there, was carried by angels to the top of the mountain that now bears her name. For centuries Sinai was a favourite resort of monks and anchorets, who, however, suffered much from the Saracens. At Feirân, or Paran, there seems once to have been a town; and the bishop of Feirân, and also the bishop of Sinai, are often mentioned in early Church history. At one time, it is said, six or seven thousand monks and hermits were distributed over the mountains. The Convent of St. Catherine is the only one now remaining, and numbers but from twenty to thirty monks. An archbishop of the Greek Church nominally presides over it; but owing to the exactions of the Bedouins, it is said, he cannot reside there. If he were there, the great gate of the convent would have to be reopened, and for six months every Arab would have liberty to enter, and eat and drink at will. As the convent cannot afford this, the gate has been built up; and the only entrance is by a small door, thirty feet from the ground, to which visitors

[*] Translated "juniper tree" in the English version.

are pulled up by a rope and windlass. It was in this convent that Professor Tischendorf, in 1859, found the celebrated manuscript of the Greek New Testament, now known as the Codex Sinaiticus, one of the oldest in existence, and universally recognized as of first-class authority.

The number of Bedouins, or wandering Arabs, now inhabiting the peninsula of Sinai is reckoned at from four thousand to six thousand. They are professedly Mohammedans, but they have little sense of religion, and they plunder wherever they may.

SECTION III.—THE FORTY YEARS' WANDERING.

Kadesh-barnea: lusting for flesh—The twelve spies—The punishment—Monotony of the forty years—Rebellion of Korah—The budding of Aaron's rod.

Kadesh-barnea: Lusting for Flesh.—When the Israelites left Sinai, and during their subsequent movements, their course was determined by the pillar of cloud and of fire that went before them. "When the ark set forward, Moses said, Arise, Lord, and let thine enemies be scattered; and let them that hate thee flee before thee. And when it rested, he said, Return, O Lord, unto the many thousands of Israel." The wanderers proceeded through the wilderness by a route which we cannot trace now, as the names have almost all perished, till they came to Kadesh-barnea,* on the outskirts of the land of Edom. They had not gone far when the whole multitude "fell a lusting," and expressed a most vehement desire for animal food. The desire was gratified by means of a flight of birds called quails; but the Israelites seem to have fallen on them ravenously, and a plague, which proved fatal to a vast number, came on them as a chastisement. Soon afterwards, Miriam, the sister of Moses, was smitten with leprosy, because, with Aaron, she had spoken disrespectfully of her brother. Moses generously interceded for her with the Lord, and her leprosy was healed.

* The real position of Kadesh-barnea is uncertain, and has given rise to much debate. Robinson places it about twenty-five miles north-west of Petra. Lieutenant Conder, of the Palestine Exploration Society, places it in the same neighbourhood.

The Twelve Spies.—At Kadesh, God allowed the people (comp. Num. xiii. 1 and Deut. i. 22) to send forward twelve men, a man from each tribe, to make a survey of the Land of Promise, and to bring back a report of its appearance, its products, and its inhabitants. These spies, the earliest explorers of Palestine, seem to have proceeded in a due northerly direction, as far as Rehob at the foot of Lebanon, and to have returned as they went, taking Hebron on their way. As a sample of the produce, they brought a bunch of grapes from Eshcol, carried by two of the men on a pole, and also pomegranates and figs. But in regard to the strength of the native inhabitants and the prospect of overcoming them, ten out of the twelve spies brought back so discouraging a report, that a panic spread among the people, and they openly resolved to return to Egypt.

The Punishment.—As a punishment of the gross unbelief and open rebellion shown in this outbreak, they were sentenced to wander for forty long years in the desert; and, with the exception of Joshua and Caleb, the only faithful men among the spies, all above twenty years of age that had come out of Egypt were doomed to die without entering the land. A presumptuous attempt by the people to force their way against an opposing army of Canaanites and Amalekites was defeated, the Israelites being put to flight by these tribes at Hormah, near the southern border of the country.

Monotony of the Forty Years. It must have been wearisome, indeed, to spend forty years in a bare, uninteresting desert, nearly destitute of flowers, trees, animals, and other objects of interest. The delay was another great lesson of patience for the Israelites—another means of exercising the spirit that looked forward to a future time for the blessing. Almost the only break in the monotony took place when the people encamped near the sea (Num. xiv. 25). The part of the sea which they visited at this time was probably the Gulf of Akabah, the eastern arm of the Red Sea. We are told that one of their encampments was at Ezion-geber, at the head of that gulf, afterwards a flourishing sea-port in the time of Solomon, where he, and after him Jehoshaphat, had a navy that traded to Ophir and Tarshish (1 Kings ix. 26; xxii. 48). The sight of the sea, always full of life and interest, must have been a great relief, after the cheerless desolation of the desert. The Gulf of Akabah abounds with shells and coral, interesting objects for a people to behold who had been wandering so long in a waste howling wilderness. They seem to have moved from place to place—an arrangement necessary in order to find food for their cattle. They were enclosed, however, in a kind of prison, and nothing but faith in the divine promise could have afforded any hope of deliverance.*

Rebellion of Korah. Unhappily, when the monotony of the forty years was again disturbed, it was by an event of a very painful nature—namely, the rebellion of Korah, Dathan, and Abiram. The object of this rebellion was to deprive Moses and Aaron of their authority; and, as no fewer than two hundred and fifty "princes of the congregation" are said to have joined in it, it must have been very formidable. The rebellion was put an end to by a miraculous opening of the earth, which swallowed up Dathan and Abiram and their families; by a fire, which consumed the two hundred and fifty princes, with whom probably was Korah; and by a plague, which cut off nearly fifteen thousand of the people.

The Budding of Aaron's Rod. In token of the divine appointment of the house of Aaron, the miracle of the rods took place. Twelve rods were laid in the tabernacle of the congregation, duly labelled, one for each of the tribes; and on the morning it was found that the rod of Aaron was budded, and

---

* Miss Martineau describes a view through a gorge of the mountains of Arabia, with the deep blue of the sky above, and the deeper tint of the sea below, as "like a peep at fairy-land through the mouth of a giant's cave." "Pleasant," says Dr Porter, "is the sight of the waters, after the parched desolation of the rocky wilderness; pleasant, too, is the gentle murmuring of the waves as they break on the pebbly beach, after the death like silence of the glens of Sinai; but pleasanter than all is the fresh breath of the zephyr, which, after playing with the sunlit waves, fans our burning cheeks.... The scenery on the one hand is so wild, so bare, and on the other so ethereal, that one is never tired gazing on it. Now we glance at some new feature of the mountain barrier, and now turn our eyes over the deep blue waters to the beautiful hills of Arabia, whose rich tints are ever changing, as the sun rolls on his course, from the 'russet hue' of early morn to the light azure of noonday and the deep purple of even; and then, besides, the countless shells that strew the beach, exhibiting endless varieties of graceful forms and delicate colours, fill the mind with admiration and wonder"— *Murray's Handbook,* pp. 38, 39.

had brought forth buds, and bloomed blossoms, and yielded almonds. The divine appointment of the family of Aaron for the duties of the priesthood was thus significantly shown, and no further questioning of it appears to have taken place.

SECTION IV.—THE ADVANCE TO CANAAN.

At Kadesh: Miriam's death: striking the rock—Edom, or Idumæa, and Mount Seir—Petra, its wonders and its desolation—Death of Aaron: Mount Hor—Backward march through El Arabah: the fiery serpents—The well at Beer.

At Kadesh: Miriam's Death: Striking the Rock.—At length the destined period of the wandering drew to a close. About thirty-eight years had elapsed, when the people again found themselves at Kadesh, on the borders of Edom, where they had been when the spies brought back their discouraging report. Three events happened there:—Miriam died and was buried: in reply to an outburst of murmuring, Moses again brought water from the rock; but by striking it, instead of speaking to it, he incurred the divine displeasure, in token of which he was told that he should not set foot in the Land of Promise: further, the people were directed to ask permission of the king of Edom to pass peacefully through his borders, on their way to their own land. This permission was angrily refused; and the Israelites, to their great disgust, had to make a long and weary circuit (which we shall by and by describe) in order to reach their own land without passing through Edom.

Edom, or Idumæa, and Mount Seir.—The land of Edom, or Idumæa, is one of no common interest. It stretches along the sides of a rocky ridge—Mount Seir—which extends from the Gulf of Akabah nearly to the Dead Sea. In the centre of the ridge Mount Hor rises in dark and rugged majesty, not far from Petra, or Sela, the renowned and wonderful capital of the kingdom. Esau retired to this district soon after his brother Jacob had fled to Padan-aram; and his descendants held possession of it for many generations, and were always remarkable for the intense bitterness of their hatred to the descendants of Jacob. Though subdued by David, and also by later kings, the Edomites revived from time to time; and when Jerusalem was taken by Nebuchadnezzar, they were a powerful nation. By the Romans, Idumaea was generally treated as a part of Judaea: afterwards, it seems to have been absorbed into the kingdom of Arabia Petraea. For many centuries it was literally an unknown land, noticed by no historian, and visited by no traveller. Only recently has it begun to be visited and known. The interest belonging to it is chiefly derived from the wonderful fulfilment of ancient prophecy which it presents. The predictions of utter desolation pronounced against it were more than usually emphatic, and they have been literally fulfilled. At one time a very populous and fertile kingdom, it is now an expanse of shifting sands and rocky mountains. At one time the busy and crowded highway of commerce between Syria and India, now not a single merchant passes through it.* Though at one time he had his dwelling in "the fatness of the earth," Esau has now become truly "bare" (Gen. xxvii. 39 ; Jer. xlix. 10).

Petra, its Wonders and its Desolation.—The ancient magnificence of the kingdom, and its present degradation and desolation, are both seen in the ruins of Petra. Bozrah appears to have been the ancient capital, but Petra eclipsed its glory. If any city could have defied the ravages of time, that city was Petra. It presents a narrow passage of two miles, lined by precipitous cliffs from four hundred to seven hundred feet high, leading into an oblong space, where the rocks retire to some distance from each other. These rocks were excavated from top to bottom,—tombs, temples, and other buildings, were everywhere chiselled out of the solid stone; but the whole is now a collection of ruins, showing the remains of tombs and temples, of palaces and pillars, strewn on every side, but without a single inhabitant. The unbrotherly act of the

---

* The objection that the prophecy, "none shall pass through it" (Isa. xxxiv. 10), has not been literally fulfilled, inasmuch as travellers have passed through Edom, is evidently frivolous. When the vast streams of traffic that used to pass through Edom have been so withdrawn that not a single caravan is ever seen on the route, the prophecy has surely been abundantly verified.

Edomites in refusing the Israelites a passage through their borders, was the first of the long series of crimes that provoked upon the land and the people of Edom the heavy judgments of God.*

Death of Aaron: Mount Hor.—Ere the Israelites left the neighbourhood of Edom, Aaron was taken from them. When the host had retreated as far as to Mount Hor, he was directed to go to the top of that mountain, in company with Moses and Eleazar his son. Then his priestly robes were put upon Eleazar, and Aaron was gathered to his fathers. A huge, bleak mountain, as desolate as Sinai itself, without grass, or tree, or shrub, seamed and riven by frightful chasms, thus became inseparably associated with the first high priest of Israel. The view obtained from its summit is chiefly remarkable for its utter desolation. Aaron could have seen but little to give him a favourable impression of the Land of Promise. It must have required strong faith to believe that the rocky ridges away to the north and the west indeed belonged to the land flowing with milk and honey. Yet it would cheer his spirit to think that among those heights and valleys had been the haunts and the homes of the patriarchs; and his faith and his fitness for death would be increased by thinking of the promises that

---

* "For nearly an hour we were descending the pass....Now red poppies, and scarlet anemones, and wild oats began to show themselves in corners where there was a deposit of earth; yet the rocks became more and more wild and stupendous, while, wherever they presented a face, there were pediments and pilasters, and ranges of doorways, and little flights of steps scattered over the slopes. A pair of eagles sprang out, and sailed overhead, scared by the noise of the strangers; and little birds flew abroad from their holes, sprinkling their small shadows over the sunny precipices....What a life it must have been, that of the men of old, who led their daily course among these streets and areas of Nature's making, where the echoes, still busy as ever, mingled the voices of men with the scream of the eagle and the gush of the torrent! What a mixture of wild romance with the daily life of a city!....Down we went, and still down, among new wonders, long after I had begun to feel that this far transcended all I had ever imagined. On the right hand now stood a column, standing alone among the ruins of many; while on the left were yet more portals in the precipice, so high up that it was inconceivable how they were ever reached.....At length we came down upon the platform above the bed of the torrent, near which stands the only edifice in Petra (called Pharaoh's Palace)....This platform was richly grown over with a plant of the lily kind—we think, the red amaryllis—which must richly adorn the area when in blossom....The first thing Alee showed us was a scorpion, which he brought from our tent—a hideous, yellow, venomous-looking creature, about two inches long....On reaching the basin where Petra stood, the chief wonder was the number of holes in the rocks, amounting to many thousands. These were either the tombs or the dwellings of the inhabitants. The fulfilment of prophecy in all this is very amazing."—*Miss Martineau.*

had gladdened them. A Mohammedan chapel marks the spot where he is believed to have died, and a subterranean cavity is said to contain his remains. The Pharaohs built lofty pyramids for their ashes, that they might outstrip all others in the magnificence of their tombs; but no Pharaoh had ever pyramid or monument so massive as that which God thus set apart for Aaron.

Backward March through El Arabah : The Fiery Serpents.
It must have been with a desolate heart that Moses descended from Mount Hor, and turned his back on the district where he left the ashes both of his sister and of his brother. The intention was to pass round the southern border of Mount Seir and to advance eastward, so as to reach the east of Palestine without passing through the territories of Edom. Before this was accomplished, the rude voice of war summoned Moses to exertion. Arad, a king in the south of Canaan, having attacked the Israelites, was entirely defeated, and his territories were laid waste as far as to Hormah, where the Israelites had been routed forty years before. The course of the host now lay southward, through what is called Wady el Arabah, a dry valley, that forms on the north a continuation of the hollow of the Dead Sea, and of that of the Gulf of Akabah on the south. All travellers give the same account of the Wady el Arabah, and pity the poor Israelites as they wandered back over "a dreary waste, sand-hills beyond sand-hills, tufted with broom and other bushes, affording excellent pasturage, but still a dreary solitude, a howling wilderness; while the Edomites, from their black mountains, looked down on them in scorn, as they slowly and sadly retraced their steps to Hashmonah." *
It could not have cheered the heart of Moses to hear the generation that had grown up in the wilderness giving way, under the fresh disappointment of this backward march, to that complaining spirit which had been so distressing in their fathers, and from which they had suffered so much. It was, indeed, an exception to the ordinary spirit of the new generation; for they had improved greatly under Moses. A smart

* Lord Lindsay's Letters.

chastisement, in the form of fiery serpents,* brought them rapidly to a confession of their sin; and the means of cure were miraculously provided in the brazen serpent, which afterwards afforded so beautiful an illustration of Christ's salvation (John iii. 14).

The Well at Beer.—Not very long after this incident, the people were again destitute of water. It is evident that the miraculous supply from the rock did not continue with them always. God took a new method to try whether the people would trust him for a supply. The spirit of the people was now admirable, and they showed their confidence in God very beautifully. They were gathered together at Beer, under a promise that God would give them water (Num. xxi. 16-18). Thoroughly believing the promise, they joined in a song, "Spring up, O well!" Suitable means were taken—"the princes digged the well;" but a higher Power is invoked, or rather the well is called to come in obedience to that higher Power. This little incident shows that the long training of the wilderness had not been in vain.

SECTION V.—CONQUEST OF EAST SIDE OF JORDAN.

Kingdom of Sihon Victory of the Israelites at Jahaz—Kingdom of Og: Bashan and its strong cities Og subdued - Argob and its gigantic cities - Proofs of antiquity—Beth-gamul—Fertility of the Hauran; Gilead—Historical importance of the conquests.

Kingdom of Sihon.—Having gone round by the Red Sea (Num. xxi. 14), the host now advanced along the eastern side of Mount Seir. They seem to have been allowed to pass quietly in this way round the eastern borders both of Edom and of Moab,—probably because these were not fortified like the western,—and to have met with no interruption till they reached the brook Arnon, where they were opposed by the Amorites, under Sihon, their king. A peaceful passage was asked through their

---

* "Ayd told me," says Burckhardt, "that serpents are very common in these parts: that the fishermen [on the Red Sea] were much afraid of them, and extinguished their fires in the evening before they went to sleep, because the light was known to attract them."—*Tour in Sinai.*

borders, as had been asked through Edom; but the request was refused (Num. xxi. 23). The Edomites had been spared because they were kinsmen; but there was no such reason for sparing the Amorites. These Amorites were a powerful tribe of Canaanites, which had crossed the Jordan at a former period, and had taken possession of a fertile tract lying between the brooks Jabbok and Arnon, adjacent to the territories of Ammon and Moab. The host of Israel had now arrived in this district. The eyes that had been accustomed for forty years to the bare desolation of the wilderness, must have gazed on the green plains and wooded heights along the banks of the Arnon with feelings of unusual delight.*

Victory of the Israelites at Jahaz.—It is not easy to define the kingdom of Sihon accurately; it seems to have been the "land of Jazer" (Num. xxxii. 1), corresponding to the province now called El Belka. Burckhardt says that the superiority of the pasturage of the Belka over that of all southern Syria causes it to be very keenly contested by rival tribes. The Bedouins have a saying,—"Thou canst not find a country like Belka." Its beef and mutton are preferred to those of all other districts. But, desirable though it was for the cattle of the Israelites, it was in the hands of the Amorites, a powerful and warlike people. Their prowess had been shown at a former time in their contests with the giants, who were the first inhabitants of the district, but whom they had overcome. Indeed, the whole tract of country to the east of the Jordan had at one time been possessed by tribes of gigantic strength and stature; and the present inhabitants enjoyed the renown of having conquered them. (Deut. ii. 20, &c.) In addition to this, the Amorites had driven the Moabites and the Ammonites from

---

* Describing the view about twenty miles from the mouth of the Arnon, at no great distance from the point where the Hebrew host first saw it, Burckhardt says:—"The view which the river here presents is very striking. From the bottom, where it runs through a narrow strip of verdant land, about forty yards across, the steep and barren banks rise to a great height, covered with immense blocks of stone, which have been rolled down from the strata; so that, when viewed from above, the valley looks like a deep chasm formed by some tremendous convulsion of the earth, into which there seems no possibility of descending to the bottom. The distance from the edge of one precipice to that of the opposite one is about two miles in a straight line."—*Travels in Syria.*

parts of the territories formerly occupied by them. A contest with the Amorites was, therefore, a serious prospect. But God encouraged the hearts of his people, and their faith and courage rose to the occasion. A pitched battle was fought at a place called Jahaz. The spirit of faith gave courage to the Israelites: unaccustomed though they were to warfare, they boldly attacked their formidable enemy, and utterly defeated them; Sihon himself was slain; and the victory was so complete, that all the territory that had belonged to Sihon between the Arnon and the Jabbok, with Heshbon its capital, Aroer, and all its other cities, fell into the hands of the Israelites.* (Judges xi. 12-27.)

Kingdom of Og: Bashan and its Strong Cities.—But this victory brought the Israelites into immediate contact with an enemy much more formidable than even Sihon and the Amorites. Og, king of Bashan, ruled over a territory extending a long way to the north and the east of the Amorites, crowded with fortified cities, and filled with a warlike population. The king himself was a man of gigantic stature: his iron bedstead was no less than nine cubits long, and four cubits wide. The number of cities which his dominions contained seems, at first sight, incredible. "I had often observed the statement," says the Rev. Dr. Porter, "that a *portion* of his territory (the region of Argob) contained 'threescore cities, fenced with high walls, gates, and bars, beside unwalled towns, a great many' (Deut. iii. 3-5). I sometimes turned to my atlas, where I found *the whole of Bashan* delineated, and not larger than an ordinary English county. I was surprised......That *sixty walled cities,* besides unwalled towns a great many, should be found at such a remote age, far from the sea, with no rivers and little commerce, appeared quite inexplicable. Inexplicable and mysterious though it appeared, it was strictly true. On the spot,

---
* The most celebrated of the cities thus gained were Heshbon and Aroer. The name of Heshbon is still preserved in the site of a ruined town built upon a hill, about sixteen miles north of the Arnon. In the later period of the history of Israel, it was (with many other towns) seized by the Moabites (or the Ammonites), and is included in the woes and desolations denounced by the prophets against them (Isa. xv. 4; Jer. xlix. 3). Aroer was "by the brink of the river Arnon;" and in this situation, on the edge of the northern precipice, above the valley of Modjeb (Arnon), Burckhardt found the ruins of a town now called Araayr. At Heshbon there is still a large ancient reservoir,—perhaps the "fish-pool of Heshbon," celebrated in the Song of Solomon vii. 4.

with my own eyes, I had now verified it. Lists of *more than a hundred* ruined cities and villages in these mountains alone I had tested, and found correct, though not complete......Here, then, we have a venerable record, more than three thousand years old, containing incidental statements and statistics which few would be inclined to receive on trust, and not a few to cast aside as glaring absurdities, and yet *which close examination shows to be minutely accurate.*"*

Og Subdued.—Undeterred by the fate of his neighbour Sihon, Og, king of this powerful country, came out to meet Moses and the Israelites. The battle was fought at Edrei. The site is matter of dispute, there being two places, ten miles apart, of similar name; but in the opinion of the traveller just quoted, the town Edrei, built on a projecting tongue of rock in the midst of a plain, was a place of almost impregnable strength, and the plain which surrounded it was of unrivalled richness. Such facts need to be known to enable us to form a just conception of the effort of faith and courage that was needed to join battle with so formidable an enemy. But the discipline of forty years had greatly improved the spirit of the Israelites, and the army by which Og was assailed was now a weapon of admirable temper. Og and his army were utterly defeated; the king himself fell in battle; and his kingdom passed into the hands of the Israelites.

Argob and its Gigantic Cities.—The first part of Bashan of which the Israelites got possession was the district of Argob. It is believed to have corresponded with what is now called the Lejah, an oval-shaped district, about twenty-two miles long by fourteen broad. When the Israelites entered it, they must have been greatly astonished at what they saw. Little though they knew of geology, they could not fail to be struck with the strange black basaltic rock of the district, that looked as if it had issued in a liquid state by innumerable pores from the earth, and had flowed out on every side, until the plain was almost covered. The numberless deep fissures and yawning gulfs, the rugged, broken edges, the protuberances and air-bubbles in the rocks,

---

* Five Years in Damascus, vol. ii., pp. 206, 207. See also The Giant Cities of Bashan. By Rev. Dr. Porter.

must have suggested to the least scientific of the people that a dreadful fire had at one time raged below, and have given a terrible significance to Moses' description of the divine wrath in his closing prophecy: "For a fire is kindled in mine anger, and shall burn (*marg.*, hath burned) unto the lowest hell, and shall consume (hath consumed) the earth with her increase, *and set on fire the foundations of the mountains*" (Deut. xxxii. 22). But greater still must have been their astonishment when they entered the cities of Argob. Never before had they seen such houses;—the walls, composed of massive blocks of black basalt, in some instances four feet thick; stone roofs, made of long rafters of the same material; and stone doors consisting of thick slabs, swinging upon pivots fixed into sockets, and fastened by great iron bars. Such structures were as unlike to any that their fathers had seen in Egypt as they were to the tents in which they themselves had lived in the desert. The material, almost as hard as iron, and the enormous masses of it that were heaped together, made the houses truly appear the work as well as the dwellings of giants. Never could a race of shepherds, unaccustomed to war, have gained such victories over a nation of warriors, and subdued such strongholds, had not the hand of the Lord been with them.

Proofs of Antiquity.—"It struck me forcibly," says Dr. Porter, "that many of the houses still standing bear every mark of the most remote antiquity. The few square towers and fragments of buildings, which inscriptions prove to have been erected in the first centuries of the Christian era, are modern in comparison with the massive walls and colossal stone doors of the private dwellings. The simplicity of the plan of these structures, combined with their low roofs, the ponderous blocks of roughly hewn stones of which they are built, and the great thickness of the walls, seem to point to a period far earlier than the Roman age, and possibly even antecedent to the conquest of this land by the Israelites."* Lord Lindsay seems to refer the houses to the Roman period; but Ritter regards "these buildings as eternal witnesses of the conquest of Bashan by Jehovah." Dr. Porter's works contain a minute description of the present state of some

* Five Years in Damascus, vol. ii., p. 195.

of the most celebrated cities of Bashan, including Kunawat, the ancient Kenath (Num. xxxii. 42); Busrah, the ancient Bozrah of Moab (Jer. xlviii. 24); Sŭlkhad, the ancient Salchah (Deut. iii. 10); Kureyieh, the ancient Kerioth (Jer. xlviii. 24); Edhra, the ancient Edrei (Num. xxi. 33), &c.

Beth-gamul.—Another traveller, Mr. Cyril L. Graham, whose travels extended further than Dr. Porter's, gives the following account of a visit to a deserted city now called Um el Jemâl, —believed to be the Beth-gamul of the Bible (Jer. xlviii. 23), originally a city of Bashan (perhaps, from its great size, a capital town), but seized by the Moabites when the ten tribes were carried captive to Assyria:—" This is perhaps among the most perfect of the old cities I saw. It is surrounded by a high wall, forming a rectangle, which seems to enclose more space than the modern Jerusalem. The streets are many of them paved; and I saw here, what I do not think I saw anywhere else, open spaces within the city, such as we call squares. There were some very large public buildings......The houses were some of them very large, consisting usually of three rooms on the ground floor, and two on the first story, the stairs being formed of large stones built into the house walls, and leading up outside. The doors were, as usual, of stone; sometimes folding doors, and some of them highly ornamental. On reaching this city, as indeed was my practice everywhere, I left my Arabs at one particular spot in charge of the dromedaries, and posted a few as sentinels on the towers to watch the approach of any foe; and then, taking my rifle with me, I wandered about quite alone in the old streets of the town—entered one by one the old houses, went up stairs, visited the rooms, and, in short, made a careful examination of the whole place; but so perfect was every street, every house, every room, that I almost fancied I was in a dream, wandering alone in this city of the dead, seeing all perfect, yet not hearing a sound. One of those tales in the 'Arabian Nights' seemed before me, where the population of a whole city was petrified for a century." *

---

* It is fair to add that the views of Dr. Porter and Mr. Graham respecting the origin and antiquity of this town have been called in question by Mr. D. W. Freshfield, in his Travels in the Caucasus.

Fertility of the Haurân: Gilead.—To the east of Argob, or the Lejah, stretches a range of mountains running north and south, now called the Jebel Haurân, on whose sides the Israelites beheld the oak forests for which Bashan was famous. One of the mountains of this range (Shekwet-el-Khudr) rises to the height of five thousand feet, and was probably "the high hill of Bashan" which the Psalmist celebrates (Ps. lxviii. 15). To the west of the Lejah is one of the finest and most fertile plains of the East, the celebrated Haurân, "the granary of Damascus." The kingdom of Bashan comprehended also half of Gilead (the other half having been part of the kingdom of Sihon); and the mountains of Gilead, where the oak likewise flourished, formed its south western barrier. Bashan extended as far north as to Mount Hermon, one of whose off-shoots, the Jebel Heish, was its third mountainous range. Altogether, it was one of the most desirable and delightful provinces in the East. It was much greener and better watered than Palestine itself, but it was necessarily much more exposed to the attacks of enemies. "We were now," says Mr. Buckingham, "in a land of extraordinary richness, abounding with the most beautiful prospects, clothed with thick forests, varied with verdant slopes, and possessing extensive plains of fine red soil.....The landscape varied at every turn, and gave us new beauties from every different point of view; and the park-like scenes that sometimes softened the wildness of the general character as a whole, reminded us of similar spots in less neglected lands." We need not wonder that the dormant love of beautiful scenery, waking up to sudden strength in the susceptible bosoms of the Israelites, and the calmer spirit that could appreciate the value of so fertile fields, made some of them desirous to settle in Bashan. Even the aged Moses felt his enthusiasm stirred by the prospect. The rich glow of poetical feeling that beautifies his farewell song and prophecy is at least in perfect keeping with the interesting scenery amidst which it was composed. It was from Bashan that he borrowed his images, when he pictured Israel "riding on the high places of the earth,"—even "the high hill of Bashan;" "eating the increase of the fields" of the

Haurân, "sucking honey out of the rock, and oil out of the flinty rock,"—the black iron-like basalt of the Lejah,—"butter of kine, and milk of sheep, with fat of lambs, and rams of the breed of Bashan, and goats, with the fat of kidneys of wheat" (Deut. xxxii. 13, 14).

Historical Importance of the Conquests.—The conquest of the kingdoms of Sihon and Og was regarded for many a day as a very remarkable achievement—worthy to rank with the overthrow of Pharaoh and the passage of the Red Sea. Sihon and Og were not petty kings, or chieftains, like many of their neighbours, but "mighty kings," "great kings," "famous kings," kings of prodigious resources and valour. In two of the psalms, the 135th and the 136th, the judgments on Pharaoh and the overthrow of Sihon and Og are dwelt on together, as evincing the greatness of God, and his mercy to Israel. One of these (the 136th) may possibly have been written about this time; the other must have been composed long afterward. But the fact that many hundred years later, when "Zion" and "Jerusalem" had become God's dwelling-place, the conquest of Sihon and of Og was remembered with such peculiar thankfulness, shows what an impression it must have made on the nation, and what a singular display it had afforded of the outstretched arm of God.

SECTION VI.—MOAB AND MIDIAN.

Moab—Subsequent history—Balak—Balaam—His unwilling prophecy—Idolatry of Baal-peor—Midian—Settlement of the east of Jordan—Subsequent history.

Moab.—The land of Moab was the next territory to which the Israelites came. It lay north of Idumæa, extending along the eastern shore of the Dead Sea, and stretching in a northeasterly direction till it met the frontier of Bashan. But the Moabites had been dispossessed by the Amorites of the more level and fertile part of their territory, and were now confined to the mountainous part south of the Arnon and east of the Dead Sea. A dark range of low mountains, east of the Dead Sea, called the Mountains of Abarim, is often referred to by travellers as the "black wall of Moab." The level tract on the east bank of the Jordan, opposite Jericho, bore the name of "the Plains of Moab." The district of Moab was highly fertile and thickly peopled; but it is now, in fulfilment of prophecy, uncultivated and deserted. Canon Tristram's recent account of it is simply a record of ruins.* Infested as it is by wandering and plundering Arabs, its fertile fields lie waste; for no one will sow where he cannot hope to reap.

Subsequent History.--Moab, with his northern kinsman Ammon, survived till after the Babylonian captivity, about which time they disappeared, or were absorbed by the Arabs. The names of most of their chief cities still remain, but their sites are for the most part quite desolate. Prophecy has been very remarkably fulfilled in the utter desolation of these countries, once so rich and flourishing. The idolatry which had its headquarters in Babylon and Nineveh had already become universal among the children of Lot. The apostasy of these nations shows how surely the Israelites would have been sucked into the whirlpool of idolatry, if means so special had not been taken to preserve among them the knowledge and the worship of the true God.

Balak.--The Moabites had allowed the Israelites to pass along their eastern border without troubling them; but now that Sihon and Og were conquered, they became afraid lest they should share the fate of these kings. They either did not know, or did not regard the fact, that God had ordered that the Moabites and the Ammonites should be spared, in consideration of their descent from Lot (Deut. ii. 18, 19). Perhaps they were bent on recovering from the Israelites the territories of which they had been deprived by the Amorites and the Bashanites. Accordingly, Balak their king entered into alliance with such of his cousins and neighbours, the Midianites or Ishmaelites, as he was able to persuade to help him in his attempt to destroy the Israelites. But he sought likewise other allies. He had heard of a prophet or wise man of the east, Balaam by name, a Chaldaean sage of great repute, whose curses and blessings

* See his Land of Moab.

were reported to carry extraordinary effects. It occurred to Balak that such a man might be of great service to him in his war with the Israelites. He saw that they placed great reliance on the favour of their God; and he reasoned that any man who had power to direct the favours and the curses of Heaven might inflict on them irreparable evil.

Balaam.—The belief in a supreme God evidently lingered yet, even amid all the corruptions of idolatry, at least in Balaam's mind. This remarkable man seems to have had the gift, but not the grace, of prophecy—he had supernatural knowledge of future events, but not the self-denied, devoted spirit of the holy prophets, who used that knowledge solely for the glory of God. With the utmost desire to oblige Balak, and to enjoy the rich rewards he offered him, he yet had not courage directly to comply with his request. First of all, a message came from God, forbidding him to go with Balak's messengers; but a second embassy came from Balak to Balaam, offering him a larger remuneration; and on Balaam asking direction from God, he was permitted to go, but was charged to speak only what God should say to him. The permission was given in the way of judgment, for Balaam was in heart most eager to do what was requisite to earn a fee. On his way he received that striking rebuke which came when "the dumb ass, speaking with man's voice, rebuked the madness of the prophet."

His Unwilling Prophecy.—On reaching Balak, and getting only vision after vision revealing how wonderfully Israel was blessed with God's favour, and how awfully any curse pronounced on them would recoil on him who pronounced it, the money-loving prophet was staggered and baffled. He went with Balak to three successive heights,—first to the high places of Baal (or Bamoth-baal), next to the top of Pisgah, and lastly to the top of Peor, hoping that the change of place might bring some intimation of change of purpose on the part of God. But instead of cursing Israel, the Spirit of prophecy within him could not be restrained from pouring out the richest blessing. In singularly beautiful language he pointed to the Messiah, as the Star that should come out of Jacob, the Sceptre that should rise out of Israel, to smite the corners of Moab, and to destroy all the children of Sheth. He thus gave another impulse to the spirit of hope—the Hope of Israel—the spirit that looked forward to a distant future.

Idolatry of Baal-peor.—An open rupture would have taken place between Balaam and the enraged and disappointed monarch of Moab, who, like other godless men, could not brook a prophet showing more respect for the will of God than for the favour of kings; but Balaam was ingenious enough to find a way of gratifying Balak, and so of earning his reward, and at the same time of avoiding direct disobedience to God. Like many other men, though he had not hardihood to go to his purpose right in God's face, he could steal round by a hidden road, and accomplish his end as effectually thereby. He seems to have persuaded Balak to entice the children of Israel, under appearance of friendship, to the idolatrous and impure festivals of the Moabites (Num. xxv. 1; Rev. ii. 14). Baal-peor, the god of the Moabites, was worshipped with services openly impure and licentious. The Israelites, being mostly young, were easily ensnared, and many of them plunged headlong into the abominable revelry. Their own act thus provoked that curse of Heaven which Balaam had no power to draw down. A frightful plague from the Lord immediately destroyed twenty four thousand of the people. Such was the effect of this and of other calamities brought by the Israelites upon themselves, that, when a census of the people was taken soon afterwards, it was found that their number was rather less than it had been when they left Egypt.

Midian.—The last public service of Moses was to despatch an expedition against the Midianites, who appear to have been more guilty than even the Moabites in enticing the Israelites to sin. Selecting a thousand men from each tribe of Israel, he sent them against the Midianites, whom they entirely destroyed. Balaam* did not long enjoy the reward of his cunning villany. He seems to have returned from his place, to which he had gone on the conclusion of his direct business with Balak (Num. xxiv. 25), and being with the Midianites when they were attacked by the Israelites, he was put to the sword (Num. xxxi. 8).

Settlement of the East of Jordan. — The Moabites were now effectually cowed, and there was no one to prevent the Israelites from occupying the lands of Sihon and Og, if God should permit them to do so. As these lands were admirably adapted for pasture, and as the tribes of Reuben and Gad had very extensive flocks, leave was asked by them, and afterwards by the half tribe of Manasseh, to settle in those parts; and it was ultimately arranged that in the meantime their men of war* should leave their families and flocks there, and that they should cross the Jordan to help in the conquest of the country, and, when this should be accomplished, return to settle on the green slopes of Gilead, and on the plains and in the forests of Bashan. The district thus acquired and settled is well known in Scripture history as "the other side of Jordan." The deep valley of that river forms an effectual separation between it and the rest of the country. Up from this valley the ground rises in sloping hills and ridges, intersected by numerous valleys, which are watered by many streams. A glance at the map will show that nearly all the streams which the Jordan receives between the Lake of Galilee and the Dead Sea come from this district.

Subsequent History.—Separated as it was, both by the deep Jordan valley and by the nature of the country itself, from the rest of Palestine, its people did not mingle much in the ordinary events of Jewish history. Its great warriors, such as Jephthah the Gileadite, and its great prophets, such as Elijah the Tishbite, who was among the *inhabitants* of Gilead, whether or not he was a native (1 Kings xvii. 1), burst upon the scene as men who had been scarcely heard of till they were fit for the highest undertakings. It was the hiding-place to which men were accustomed to resort when they fled from danger, or desired a breathing-time from toil and bustle. It was the district to which David fled when Absalom so suddenly seized upon Jerusalem; in one of its forests the battle was fought between the

---

* Or rather a part of the men of war; for only forty thousand, out of more than one hundred thousand, crossed the river (Josh. iv. 13).

two armies; from the boughs of one of its prickly oaks the young rebel hung when Joab slew him. To this district, also, the great Son of David resorted occasionally for retirement and meditation; and in its northern part, called by the Romans Peræa, some of His choicest sayings were spoken, and some of His greatest works were done. In modern times it has been but little visited by travellers. The terror of plundering Bedouins in its wild ravines and forests has commonly restrained travellers from penetrating far into its valleys.

SECTION VII.—DEATH OF MOSES.

The cities of refuge—The last acts of Moses—The scene on the plain of Moab—His last address—The view from Pisgah: death.

The Cities of Refuge.—At various times during the residence in the wilderness, Moses had supplemented his instructions to the Israelites by new ordinances. Among his latest directions was that for the appointment of six cities of refuge, three on the one side, and three on the other side of Jordan, as places of protection for those who had unintentionally killed any one.

The Last Acts of Moses.—After the destruction of the Midianites, the active work of Moses was finished. A little before this event he had been directed solemnly to appoint Joshua as his successor. With his usual readiness he complied with the command, though the feelings of a father would naturally have sought this honour for his own son. A view of the Promised Land from the top of Pisgah had been obtained by him. A public charge to Joshua, and a lengthened and most impressive address to the people, delivered on the plain of Moab, and constituting the Book of Deuteronomy, closed the earthly services of the servant of the Lord.

The Scene on the Plain of Moab.—The scene must have been exceedingly touching. The host of Israel was far too large to be within reach of his voice; but the elders and princes would probably assemble and listen to him from day to day, —each, perhaps, repeating to his own people what he had heard from the lips of their inspired leader. With what veneration must they have gazed on him! That was the head that had been laid by the loving hands of Jochebed in the ark of bulrushes in the far distant days of the persecuting Pharaoh. That was the man who had been called to choose between the attractions of Egypt on the one hand, and the claims of God's people on the other, and who had so nobly chosen to suffer affliction with the people of God. These were the very eyes that, under the shadow of Horeb, had looked on the Angel in the burning bush. That was the hand that had been stretched out over Egypt, and had overwhelmed it with plagues. That was the face that had shone with the reflection of the divine glory on the mount. That was the much-tried man that had been so often unjustly accused, that had borne his many trials so meekly, that had guided the people so faithfully and advised them so wisely, and had refused honours for himself because he loved them so well.

His Last Address.—And now they were listening for the last time to his voice! Never were a people so favourably placed for receiving a lasting impression; and no address could have been more suitable. His great object was to place GOD—the one, living, jealous, yet gracious God of Israel—very vividly before them. He reminded them of all that he had commanded them in his law, and of all that he had done for them in his providence. He pointed to the great Prophet, like himself, that was to arise from among them; thus fostering the spirit that looked forward to the future for the consummation of the promised blessing. He painted in awful colours the frightful doom that disobedience would entail. He described with glowing eloquence the blessings of loyalty to God. He embodied the spirit of the whole in a poem of singular beauty and impressiveness,—intended, probably, to be learned and sung by all. The last echoes of his voice had hardly died away when he was summoned from the scene. When thirty sad days had been spent in mourning for him on the plains of Moab, the people were summoned, under their new leader, to prepare for invading the Promised Land.

The View from Pisgah: Death.—On the east side of the

Dead Sea runs a range of mountains, that rise like a dark wall along the margin of the lake, at some points to the height of three thousand feet. From Pisgah, a point in this ridge which cannot now be discovered, and which, indeed, was purposely concealed, Moses obtained his view of the long-desired Land of Promise. Full in front, as he looked westward, he would see the hills and the upland plains of Judah; distinguishing, perhaps, Hebron, and the cave of Machpelah, where so much venerable dust already lay; and marking "the land of Moriah," and the stronghold of Zion, so rich in coming glories, and so dark with coming crimes. Northward he would see the Jordan, winding like a serpent through its tropical plain, the silver thread widening in the distance into that gleaming expanse along whose shores He was oft to wander in human form who had appeared to him in the bush and on the mount. Still farther, in the utmost border of Naphtali, the snow-clad peaks of Hermon and Lebanon would appear; and filling up the space between, many a fertile plain and sheltered ravine, where happy homesteads might be reared, and much holy worship offered to the Most High. When his eyes were full of the goodly sight, the echo of the divine covenant that had been sworn to Abraham, Isaac, and Jacob, sounded in his ears; and while rejoicing, like them, in promises not yet fulfilled, death closed his eyes, and hands unseen laid his dust in an unknown tomb.

SECTION VIII.—SOCIAL AND RELIGIOUS CONDITION OF THE PERIOD.

State of society in the wilderness—Great change as to religion—Spirit of the people—Religious darkness of the world—Image of Ashtoreth found at Ashteroth-karnaim

State of Society in the Wilderness.—In glancing at the state of society among the Israelites during the period spent in the wilderness, there is little room for remark. It was altogether a very peculiar period, and the people could hardly have acquired settled habits, or have made steady progress in any of the arts of life. It is, indeed, very difficult to fancy the daily occupations of the Israelites during the forty years. In certain parts of the peninsula, especially in a valley near the western shore, called Wady Mokatteb, or "the Written Valley," multitudes of inscriptions are found on the rocks, consisting of figures of animals and words in various characters, of some of which the meaning is quite unknown. Many theories have been framed to account for these inscriptions; and among these is one which ascribes them to the Israelites, during their sojourn in Sinai. But it must be admitted that this opinion is liable to grave objections, and that the subject is yet involved in great obscurity. In the construction of the tabernacle and its furniture, of the robes of the priests, and of other sacred garments, occasion was found, under divine direction, for the exercise of the highest skill that had been attained by Aholiab, Bezaleel, and the other eminent workmen of the time, probably in Egypt. But on the whole, during the forty years, the people must have lost much of what they had learned there. In some points of view this was hardly to be regretted; but if they could have been trusted to turn them to good account, the lessons they had got from the Egyptians, in the arts of building, weaving, pottery, painting, and the like, might have been very valuable. For a long time after they took possession of the Holy Land, they seem to have led a somewhat rude life in reference to such things; it was not till the days of David and Solomon that they attained to a much higher style. It is somewhat singular that there seems to have been no class of men among the Hebrews that devoted themselves to the studies which were prosecuted by the learned among the Egyptians. When, long afterwards, there came to be a learned class, they usually employed their talents in a much less creditable way,—in adding traditions and commentaries to the Law, which commonly served to darken its meaning or to destroy its power.

Great Change as to Religion.—But during the wilderness period a very great change took place in reference to Religion. Formerly the word of God had been handed down orally from parent to child; now it was committed to writing. Formerly the ordinances of public worship had been few and simple; now they were numerous and elaborate. Formerly there was no special class of priests; now the family of Aaron was set apart for the priesthood. Temporal rewards and punishments were now connected with religion more prominently than before. In many ways Christ and his salvation were shadowed forth in types and symbols. How far this was understood by the few, and whether it was at all comprehended by the mass, we do not know; but the New Testament teaches us that the whole scheme of deliverance from Egypt was a type of salvation by Christ. The manna, and the water from the rock, were types of the bread and the water of heaven. The high priest himself, and all the different kinds of bloody sacrifices, were types of Christ. The doctrine of a personal Redeemer, who should come to earth to save, and especially of the union of the nature of man and the nature of God in that Redeemer, was shadowed forth. Probably the most distinct intimations regarding the future Deliverer were those in which Balaam foretold the Star and the Sceptre, and Moses the Prophet like unto him, to whom they were all to give heed. The occasional glimpses obtained of the Divine Angel by whom communications were made to the people, as well as the presence of the Heavenly Light that, in the most holy place, was the mark of Godhead, seemed to point to "the Word becoming flesh and dwelling among men." By all such arrangements and revelations, Israel was now in truth "a people near unto God" (Ps. cxlviii. 14); but it was apparent that the great Hope of Israel was not yet realized.

Spirit of the People.—As to the spirit of the people, that of the generation that came out of Egypt had been haughty, impatient, unbelieving, and rebellious, to a lamentable degree. The spirit of the next generation—the generation that entered the land—was much better. The residence in the wilderness and the institutions delivered to the people there, seem to have effectually cured any tendency to the superstition and idolatry of Egypt. In the early part of the wilderness sojourn the tendency to idolatry was extreme (Ezek. xx. 8). We learn from the speech of Stephen that there "they took up the tabernacle of Moloch, and the star of their god Remphan"

(Acts vii. 43). As a cure for these tendencies, the discipline of the wilderness was not in vain. The idolatries of the neighbouring nations were those that the people were afterwards most prone to imitate. The dreary chastisement of the forty years, the plagues that once and again made such havoc in the host, and the sad fact that the bones of all their fathers were left to whiten in the wilderness, produced a deep impression. Gentler influences, too,—the ever-present hand and help of God, the gift of the land flowing with milk and honey, the remembrance of the faith of the patriarchs, whom Beersheba, Hebron, Shechem, Beth-el, and many other places, would bring vividly before them, the supply of their wants, and the acceptance of their offerings—were doubtless the means of awakening in many a bosom sorrow for sin and loving trust in God. And now that the people were about to cross the Jordan, it is pleasing to think that many a bosom was animated by humble trust in and cheerful obedience to God; that many were treading in the footsteps of the faith of their father Abraham, and were looking, like him, for a city that had foundations, whose builder and maker was God.

Religious Darkness of the World.—Beyond the circle of Israel, the religious state of the world presented an aspect of still increasing darkness. Milton has given us a catalogue of the gods that were now receiving adoration, both in Syria and its neighbourhood, and in other parts of the world, which, though decked out with the usual embellishments of poetry, represents vividly the painful reality.*

* "First Moloch, horrid king, besmeared with blood
Of human sacrifice, and parents' tears;
Though for the noise of drums and timbrels loud,
Their children's cries unheard, that passed through fire
To his grim idol. Him the Ammonite
Worshipped in Rabba and her watery plain,
In Argob, and in Basan, to the stream
Of utmost Arnon....
 Next Chemos, the obscene dread of Moab's sons,
From Aroer to Nebo, and the wild
Of southmost Abarim; in Hesebon
And Horonàim, Seon's realm, beyond
The flowery dale of Sibma clad with vines,
And Eleale, to the asphaltic pool
Peor his other name, when he enticed

Image of Ashtoreth found at Ashteroth-karnaim.—The ancient cities of Bashan have left memorials of their idolatry, as well as of their material-strength, for modern eyes to gaze on. One of the oldest of these cities was Ashteroth-karnaim,—that is, "Ashteroth of the two horns," or crescent. In the days of Abraham it was a stronghold of the Rephaims (Gen. xiv. 5),

> Israel in Sittim, on their march from Nile,
> To do him wanton rites, which cost them woe....
> With these came they, who, from the bordering flood
> Of old Euphrates to the brook that parts
> Egypt from Syrian ground, had general names
> Of Baälim and Ashtaroth : those male,
> These feminine....
>   With these in troop
> Came Astoreth, whom the Phœnicians called
> Astarte, queen of heaven, with crescent horns ;
> To whose bright image nightly by the moon
> Sidonian virgins paid their vows and songs....
>   Thammuz came next behind,
> Whose annual wound in Lebanon allured
> The Syrian damsels to lament his fate
> In amorous ditties, all a summer's day....
>   Next came one
> Who mourned in earnest, when the captive ark
> Maimed his brute image, head and hands lopped off
> In his own temple, on the grunsel edge,
> Where he fell flat, and shamed his worshippers :
> Dagon his name, sea-monster, upward man
> And downward fish....
>   Him followed Rimmon, whose delightful seat
> Was fair Damascus, on the fertile banks
> Of Abbana and Pharphar, lucid streams....
>   After these appeared
> A crew, who, under names of old renown,
> Osiris, Isis, Orus, and their train,
> With monstrous shapes, and sorceries, abused
> Fanatic Egypt and her priests, to seek
> Their wandering gods disguised in brutish forms
> Rather than human....
> The rest were long to tell, though far renowned,
> The Ionian gods, of Javan's issue ;—held
> Gods, yet confessed later than Heaven and Earth,
> Their boasted parents : Titan, Heaven's first-born,
> With his enormous brood, and birthright seized
> By younger Saturn : he-from mightier Jove,
> His own and Rhea's son, like measure found ;
> So Jove usurping reigned : these first in Crete
> And Ida known ; thence on the snowy top
> Of cold Olympus ruled the middle air,
> Their highest heaven ; or on the Delphian cliff,
> Or in Dodona, and through all the bounds
> Of Doric land ; or who, with Saturn old,
> Fled over Adria to the Hesperian fields,
> And o'er the Celtic roamed the utmost isles."

and it subsequently became one of the principal cities of the kingdom of Og (Deut. i. 4; Josh. xii. 4). It was celebrated for the worship of Ashtoreth* or Astarte, the goddess of the moon; from which luminary the crescent or two-horned figure was evidently derived. Among the ruins of this city Dr. Porter found a colossal head, of very striking appearance. Its face was three feet broad, the cheeks were large and out of proportion, the eyes soft and well-formed, the forehead low, and the brow prominent and contracted. On the forehead was a *crescent*, with rays shooting upwards from it, the whole face being encircled with thick tresses. It was doubtless an image of the goddess of the place, before which many a knee had been bent in worship in former times. Who can tell but that it may have been one of those images of "the host of heaven" which apostate Israelites "turned to worship," and which brought upon them at last the Babylonian woe? (Acts vii. 42.)

* The word is Ashtoreth in the singular, and Ashteroth or Ashtaroth in the plural, meaning *images* of the goddess. The Greek form is Astarte. She was the Venus or Aphrodite of Oriental idolatry, called also Dea Syria.

CHAPTER VII.

JOSHUA AND THE CONQUEST OF CANAAN.

FROM THE DEATH OF MOSES TO THE DEATH OF JOSHUA.

Joshua i.-xxiv.

SECTION I.—GENERAL DESCRIPTION OF THE LAND.

Joshua in command- Names of the country—Boundaries and extent—Mountain ranges—The valley between: the Jordan— Fertile spots—A dreary waste—Limestone rocks- -Three natural divisions: Judah or Judæa Ephraim or Samaria -Galilee—The sea-coast—Isolation of the country: its purpose.

Joshua in Command.—The host of Israel is now under the command of Joshua. He assumes the command in the same spirit of high trust in God as he had shown forty years before, when, as one of the twelve spies, he exhorted the people to go up against the land. While he and his army lie encamped in the plains of Moab, preparing to cross the Jordan near Gilgal, it may be useful for us to take a general survey of the land of which they are so soon to take possession.

Names of the Country.—The country is known by various names. On the old Egyptian monuments it is called the land of Ruthen, or Rutenna. In Scripture it is called the land of Canaan before its occupation by the children of Israel; and the land of Israel afterwards. Palestine, the Greek and Latin name, was derived from the Philistines, who inhabited part of the sea-coast, and were earliest known to remote nations. "The Holy Land," though occurring but once in the Bible (Zech. ii. 12), is now the name in most frequent use, on account of the sacred associations with which the country is connected.

Boundaries and Extent.—When God gave to Abraham the promise of the land of Canaan, its boundaries were declared to be from the river of Egypt to the Euphrates (Gen. xv. 18). It was afterwards explained to Joshua that the northern boundary should be beyond Lebanon, at "the entering in of Hamath" (Josh. xiii. 5). In Ezekiel's vision of the Restoration, the eastern boundary is directed to be measured, "from Hauran, and from Damascus, and from Gilead, and from the land of Israel by Jordan, from the border unto the east sea" (Ezek. xlvii. 18). There has been much controversy as to the exact extent of these boundaries, but into this it is not necessary to enter here. It is plain that the territory which God assigned to the seed of Abraham was much larger than that which the Jews actually possessed, until, perhaps, the days of David and Solomon. The district generally understood as Palestine was that which used to be familiarly, though not quite accurately, described as extending from Dan (in the north) to Beer-sheba (in the south); bounded on the west by the Mediterranean, and on the east by the Syrian desert. This district lies between latitude 31° and 33° 30′ north, and between 34° and 37° east longitude. The length of the whole is about one hundred and eighty English miles, and the average breadth about fifty.*

Mountain Ranges.—During the early convulsions of the globe, two lofty ranges of hills were thrown up on the north of Palestine, rising in some places to the height of ten thousand feet, and running parallel to each other—Lebanon and Anti-Lebanon. These two ranges are continued all through the land of Palestine, but at a much lower level, not as mountains, but as table-lands; they run on, indeed, as far as to Sinai and the Red Sea. The range of Anti-Lebanon is continued on the east side of the Jordan, and forms the picturesque highland district of Bashan and Gilead, the mountains of Moab, and Mount Seir, extending all the way to the Gulf of Akabah. The range of

---

* On the east side of the Jordan, the kingdom of Bashan (which fell to Manasseh) extended much further than the old maps used to indicate. More recent maps give that boundary more accurately.

Lebanon is continued on a much lower level throughout the length of Western Palestine, forming a sort of ridge or backbone of table-land along the country, occasionally traversed by flat plains, but more commonly sending out side ridges, like ribs, that run down on the one side to the Mediterranean, and on the other to the Jordan. Many of the chief towns of Palestine, such as Hebron, Jerusalem, Shechem, and Samaria, occupied the highest part of this plateau, while all places on the sea-coast, and in the plain of the Jordan, were situated on a much lower level. Expressions of frequent occurrence in the Bible are thus explained; for example, going *up* to Jerusalem, or going *down* to Gaza, or to Jericho. The descent on the east side was much greater than that on the west, in consequence of the valley of the Jordan and the Dead Sea being depressed many hundred feet below the level of the Mediterranean. The depression, which is slight at its sources, becomes deeper and deeper as the Jordan approaches the Dead Sea, where it is no less than thirteen hundred feet.

The Valley Between: the Jordan.—In the deep valley between the two plateaus lay the three inland lakes of Palestine, Merom and Galilee on the north, and the Dead Sea on the south, the immortal Jordan connecting them. The Jordan rises a few miles to the north of the small lake of Merom, its waters beginning to gush, at one of its sources, from the fountains of Banias, near to the ancient Dan, where Abraham defeated the kings of Mesopotamia. At first the waters of the Jordan flow in several streams, but all meet in the basin of Merom. Issuing from Merom in a single current, the Jordan flows through a valley that begins to be depressed below the level of the Mediterranean, on to the Lake of Galilee. The description of this lake we reserve till we come to the Gospel History, in which it holds so prominent a place. Between the Lake of Galilee and the Dead Sea the direct distance is but sixty miles; but, owing to the perpetual windings of the river, the length of its course is not less than two hundred miles. The "windings" of the Jordan are frequently alluded to in the Bible, but the English translation fails to bring out the force of the allusion. In 1847,

Lieutenant Lynch, with his American expedition, sailed in open boats along the whole course of the Jordan, and found that the river was interrupted by frequent and fearful rapids. He encountered twenty-seven rapids of threatening force, besides a great many of lesser magnitude, and passed a large number of islands. The river itself, whose breadth is from twenty-five to sixty yards, commonly flows in a ravine within a ravine. The stream is enclosed in a narrow, rocky channel, which again is sunk in the Ghor, or valley of the Jordan,—a plain some miles in breadth, bounded by bare mountains on either side. At one time this plain seems to have been more abundantly watered than now. The waters of the Jordan, even in flood, do not spread beyond the inner channel; consequently, while the edge of the river is covered with a rich and rank vegetation, the plain itself is commonly a dry, burned-up wilderness.

Fertile Spots.—It was owing to this peculiarity that, subsequently to the destruction of Sodom and Gomorrah, scarcely any town or village of note existed on the banks of the Jordan, except where the plain happened, as at Jericho, to be fertilized by other waters. Here and there spots of quiet beauty refresh the eye of the traveller;—the pink oleander and the scarlet anemone mingling with the purple bloom of the thistle and the yellow of the marigold; or groves of overhanging willow and creeping plants; or thickets of lofty cane, where the lion and the wild boar have their lair, and the stork her summer haunt; or mountain torrents brawling joyously among the rocks; or tangled masses of shrubs and trees, where the bulbul chatters from his nest, or the swallow darts about in the sunshine. In spots like these, "the river curves and twists, north, south, east, and west, turning, in the short space of half-an-hour, to every quarter of the compass,—seeming as if desirous to prolong its luxuriant meanderings in the calm and silent valley, and reluctant to pour its sweet and sacred waters into the accursed bosom of the bitter sea."

A Dreary Waste.—Farther on, as the river proceeds in its course, all is desolation and sterility. "In the dreary waste there was no sound, for every living thing had retired exhausted from the withering heat and blinding glare....The wind sounded mournfully as it went sweeping over the barren plain, and sighed, even in the broad and gairish day, like the blast of autumn among the marshy sedge, where the cold toad croaks, and the withered leaf is spotted like a leprosy."* Green and beautiful plains once more stretch along the banks of the river, near the springs of Jericho and Gilgal; immediately beyond which the Jordan reaches its grave, and is lost in the dreary expanse of the Dead Sea.

Limestone Rocks.—The rock of which the mountains of Palestine consist is chiefly limestone. There is no kind of rock in which large caverns occur so often; hence the frequent reference to "caves" in Scripture history. In a neglected, uncultivated country, limestone hills have a bare, gray, uninteresting appearance; and at the present day this aspect of desolation is most painfully apparent in many districts of the Holy Land. But there is no soil which can be turned to better account by careful cultivation than that obtained from limestone hills. It is particularly well adapted for the vine and other fruit trees. A hill that would be extremely bare and dreary in a neglected state, becomes clothed and fertile when built up with terraces, row upon row, and planted with vine, olive, pomegranate, and other trees. The Israelites devoted themselves to this species of husbandry, and the produce of their orchards was one great source of their wealth. The plains were well adapted for ordinary grain crops, such as wheat and barley; and there were many extensive tracts unfit for the spade or the plough, usually called "the wilderness," where flocks might be pastured. Compared with Egypt and the desert, Palestine was indeed a land of streams and rivers; but in the dry season these were apt to become empty, and water had to be gathered and kept in store by artificial means. Hence "pools and water-courses" are often mentioned in the Bible, and many remarkable ruins of these still remain. The Jordan was the only stream that could strictly be called a river.

Three Natural Divisions: Judah or Judæa.—Palestine is

* Lynch's Narrative of the United States' Expedition.

literally a land of mountains and valleys. These are so numerous that it would be vain to attempt to recount their names. But there were certain great natural divisions of the surface of the country, that should be carefully marked, because they throw great light on its history. Nature has divided Western Palestine into three great sections—the southern, the central, and the northern. The communications are pretty free between all parts of the district which extends from the southern border to near the thirty-second parallel of latitude, or over a parallelogram with Hebron near the middle of it, and extending twenty-five miles north and the same distance south of that town. It was this district mainly that was afterwards called the kingdom of Judah; and in New Testament times it had the name of Judæa.

Ephraim or Samaria.—A few miles to the north of Jerusalem this district is crossed by several deep valleys and mountain passes, that render the communication with the more northern parts extremely difficult. Accordingly, the district to the north of these passes is to a great degree a separate one; and another parallelogram, with Shechem near its middle, and extending about twenty miles north and twenty miles south, describes in a rough way the district where the tribe of Ephraim—the great rival of Judah—rose to power. This district formed a chief part of the kingdom of the ten tribes, and in New Testament times the region of Samaria.

Galilee.—Still farther to the north lay a district, partly plain and partly mountain, inhabited in Old Testament times by the comparatively unimportant tribes of Issachar, Zebulun, Asher, and Naphtali, and forming in New Testament times the district of Galilee.

The Sea Coast.—The sea-coast line of this country is remarkable for its continuity. There are no natural creeks or bays, adapted to form harbours. Joppa, the best harbour of ancient Palestine, is after all a miserable place for such a purpose. The contrast is very striking between this sea-board and that of Phœnicia, a few miles to the north, where, in consequence of the ridges of Lebanon running down to the sea, the inlets for harbours are numerous. Unlike the Phœnicians, the Hebrews were not a sea-faring people. They seem to have had no love for the sea, for in the Bible it is usually employed as the emblem of danger and unrest.

Isolation of the Country: its Purpose.—It is obvious how well the natural form of the land of Israel was adapted for the purpose for which the people were chosen. That purpose was, that they might preserve the knowledge and the worship of the true God, uncontaminated by the errors and superstitions of the rest of the world. For this end, it was desirable that their land should be shut in—secluded from other nations. The deserts on the south and the east, the sea on the west, and the mountain barrier of Lebanon and Anti-Lebanon on the north, pierced by the deep valley of Cœle-Syria, or Hollow Syria, admirably served this purpose. In this well-protected land it was the purpose of God that the Jews should remain, quietly pursuing the peaceful life of farmers and gardeners, until the fulness of the times should arrive, when their history should take a new departure, and a light should arise upon them destined to spread to all parts of the world.

SECTION 11.—JOSHUA'S CAMPAIGNS.

Capture of Jericho—Its situation—Its history—Roman Jericho—Plan of the campaign—Ai taken—Conquest of the Central district—Scene at Shechem; Mounts Ebal and Gerizim—Stratagem of the Gibeonites—Gibeon—Overthrow of the five kings: conquest of the Southern district—Battle of Merom: conquest of the Northern district.

Capture of Jericho.—At the death of Moses we find Joshua encamped on the east bank of the Jordan, opposite Jericho. Jericho was a most important place. It was situated near the lower end of the Jordan valley, and at the mouth of certain important passes leading westward, which Joshua required to secure before he could lead up his army into the great central division of the land. Unless Jericho had been taken and destroyed, the Israelites could not have advanced a step. It was too important a fortress to be left in the rear. Two spies were sent to examine it. Their presence was detected by the king; but they were hid by Rahab, a remarkable woman, formerly of bad character, who was led to believe that the country was to be given to the Israelites, and from whose faith Joshua drew a great encouragement to go forward. By a miracle the bed of the Jordan was dried up, to afford the Israelites a passage; the descending waters being heaped up at Adam, beside Zaretan, several miles to the north, while the waters below were carried on to the Dead Sea. The ark was carried by the priests in solemn procession to the middle of the river, and remained there till all the people had passed over. Everything was done to remind them of the presence and the power of God. At Gilgal—which means "rolling" or "winding"—circumcision, which had been omitted in the desert, owing to the violation of the covenant, was administered to the males of the congregation, to "roll away their reproach." Here also a solemn observance of the Passover took place. At Jericho the Angel of the Covenant appeared to Joshua, under a military dress and title, as the "Captain of the Lord's host," to give him the assurance of his presence in the series of wars now beginning. While they were besieging Jericho, the ark was carried six successive days round the walls, and on the seventh day seven times, when suddenly the walls fell down. The inhabitants, with the exception of Rahab and her family, were put to the sword, the city was razed to the ground, and a solemn curse was pronounced against any one who should dare to rebuild it.

Its Situation.—Jericho, "the city of palm-trees," was beautifully situated at the foot of a lofty limestone range, close by a number of copious fountains, that still spread beauty and fertility as far as the eye can reach. Trickling through glades of tangled forest-shrub, these streams even yet nourish a luxuriant herbage, and nothing is needed but the hand of cultivation to make the spot one of the richest and most beautiful on earth. From the earliest times Jericho had been famous for its balsam-trees, which nowhere else produced a balm with healing properties so wonderful. In the days of Joshua, a glorious palm-forest—now, like the balsam-trees, utterly gone—stretched along the vale about eight miles in length and three in breadth, Jericho being situated on the west side, and Gilgal (it is believed) on the east of the forest. As the Israelites came up towards Gilgal, those of them that remembered Egypt would be reminded of the great palm-forest of Memphis, close by the pyramids. Emerging from the forest of palms, they would see the lofty battlements of Jericho rising proudly to heaven; and behind, the steep mountain cliffs where the two men who had been sent to spy the city had lain concealed. It was a sight to appal any heart in which faith did not triumph; and it is a proof of the extraordinary courage with which they were now inspired, that they advanced calmly and confidently to an enterprise seemingly so desperate.

Its History.—Jericho would have been a very dangerous place to be held by enemies, and, as a stronghold, it was not needed by the Hebrews, God being their fortress; hence, perhaps, the reason why it was doomed to utter destruction. But, notwithstanding the curse, Jericho was rebuilt once and again (1 Kings xvi. 34). In the days of Elijah and Elisha a school of the prophets flourished at it, and it was a frequent resort of these prophets themselves. At the close of Elijah's career, the two went on from Jericho to the banks of the Jordan, a few miles distant, while the sons of the prophets stood "afar off," on the heights above the city, to witness the departure of the Tishbite. Having crossed to his native side of the river, close to where the Israelites crossed it now, but in the opposite direction, and having arrived near the spot from which Moses departed, Elijah entered the chariot of fire.

Roman Jericho.—When the Romans were masters of Palestine, the palm-groves and balsam-gardens of Jericho were given by Mark Antony to his beautiful but guilty paramour, Cleopatra, queen of Egypt; and afterwards a magnificent mansion was erected for himself at Jericho by Herod the Great.* It was this Roman Jericho through which Christ passed on his last journey to Jerusalem: when he passed along the road beside which grew the sycamore-tree (Luke xix. 4); went up into the wild, dreary mountains; caught from the summit of

---
* Josephus, Antiquities, X. iv. 2.

the pass the first glimpse of the line of way through the long ascent—the scene of his own parable of the Good Samaritan; till he reached the friendly home perched aloft on the mountain side—the village of Bethany.*

Plan of the Campaign.—Having destroyed Jericho, Joshua proceeded to secure the whole country on the west. It requires but little knowledge of military affairs to see how much more favourable the position which he now occupied was for making the attack, than if he had advanced, as Moses had tried to do, through the land of Edom. If that plan had now been followed, the whole confederate forces of the Canaanites, from Dan to Beer-sheba, would have confronted him, and he would have had to fight his way northward across ridge after ridge, every one of which probably would have been defended. The Edomites in his rear might at any time have fallen on him, and he would have been hemmed in between two hostile forces. The long journey round Mount Seir, through the wilderness of the fiery serpents, which had seemed so great a misfortune, turned out to be a great blessing; for now the country east of Jordan, the kingdoms of Og and Sihon, had been subdued, and there was no enemy in Joshua's rear. Moreover, by attacking the country west of the Jordan in the middle, he might cut it in two, and prevent the northern tribes from joining with the southern. Establishing his position in the very heart of the country, he would compel the native tribes to fight a pitched battle; the result of which, if favourable to him, would enable him to occupy much more of the country. Thus it happened, as it happens so often in God's good providence, that present evil issued in future good.

Ai Taken.—From the neighbourhood of Jericho a pass strikes up towards the interior of the country, skirting Ai and Beth-el, which Joshua determined to secure. For this purpose, a select body of troops was sent against the town of Ai. On the first assault, the Israelites were repulsed. This defeat must have occasioned the greatest distress to Joshua, not only as involving the frustration of his plan, but as seeming to imply

Stanley's Sinai and Palestine.

that the divine assistance which had been promised was not to be relied on. The valley of Achor, near which the defeat occurred, was the key to Palestine, and it seemed as if this "door of hope" (Hosea ii. 15) had been shut in the face of the Israelites. But ere long it was discovered that the cause of the defeat lay in an act of disobedience to God, committed by one of the people, named Achan, who had stolen and secreted part of the devoted spoil of Jericho. God's authority was promptly vindicated by the execution of the offender: soon afterwards Ai was taken, its king and its people were destroyed, and the pass from Jericho secured.

Conquest of the Central District.—This victory seems to have given Joshua a firm hold on the central district of Palestine; for immediately afterwards we find him at Mount Ebal, close by Shechem, in the very centre of that district, about twenty miles to the north of Ai. We have already had occasion to speak of this classical spot. It was Abraham's first residence in the land, the scene of one of his earliest promises, and the site of the first altar he built to God. In this fertile plain Jacob, too, had resided: here had been the well which bore his name, and also the piece of ground he had bequeathed to Joseph, where Joseph's bones were now to be laid. The purpose of Joshua in going to Shechem at this time was to fulfil the solemn injunction of Moses, that as soon as they should come into the land, the blessings of the law should be solemnly proclaimed from Mount Gerizim, and the curses from Mount Ebal, in presence of all the congregation.

Scene at Shechem: Mounts Ebal and Gerizim.—The two hills of Shechem, Gerizim on the south, and Ebal on the north, each about six hundred feet in height, are separated by a narrow valley. Six of the tribes stood on the side of the one hill, and six on the side of the other; the priests and the Levites stood in the valley below, and read out the words of the law; the tribes on Gerizim shouted "Amen" to the blessings, and those on Ebal shouted "Amen" to the curses. "It must have been an imposing spectacle: the ark of the covenant in the centre, surrounded by the elders, officers, and judges, with the venerable Joshua at their head; the banners of the tribes marking their different positions, as appointed by God; and the millions of Israel extending in firm phalanx as far as the eye could reach......and when the men, women, and children with one voice shouted 'Amen,' the acclaim must have reverberated among the rocks around with true sublimity, and have swelled in majestic volumes towards heaven."

Stratagem of the Gibeonites.—In consequence of neglecting to ask counsel of God, Joshua was drawn by a cunning stratagem into a treaty with the Gibeonites, a powerful tribe of Hivites in the neighbourhood of Ai. They declared that they had come from a very great distance, and they threw him off his guard by a show of pious humility.

Gibeon.—Gibeon (now El-Jib) stands on the top of a little hill, around which is spread one of the richest plains in Central Palestine, meadow-like in smoothness and verdure, dotted with vineyards and olive-groves, and sending out branches, like the rays of a star-fish, among the rocky acclivities that encircle it. It was at the pool of Gibeon that Abner was defeated and Amasa slain, in the days of David (2 Sam. ii. and xx.); and here, too, it was that Solomon asked and obtained "wisdom" from the Lord (1 Kings iii.).

Overthrow of the Five Kings: Conquest of the Southern District.—Immediately after the Gibeonites had been received, there was formed a great confederacy among all the kings in the southern district of the country, for the purpose of chastising the Gibeonites and opposing Joshua. The head-quarters of the Israelitish army were now at Gilgal. Five kings, whose respective capitals were Jerusalem, Hebron, Jarmuth, Lachish, and Eglon, collected their forces at Gibeon, and must have presented a formidable appearance. But the courage and activity of Joshua were equal to the occasion. Marching his troops by night from Gilgal, he fell unexpectedly on his enemies, who were encamped on the green plain of Gibeon, defeated them with tremendous slaughter, and drove them over the summit of the plateau, down the western passes of Beth-horon, into the valley below. It was on this occasion that the sun and the moon were arrested in their courses, in the valley of Ajalon, that Joshua might have light to complete his conquest.* After the victory, he proceeded to the several capitals of the confederate kings, taking them in succession, and utterly destroying their inhabitants. This campaign gave the Israelites possession of the whole of the southern district of Palestine.

Battle of Merom: Conquest of the Northern District.—The northern or Galilean district now alone remained to be subdued. Here also a powerful confederacy of native tribes was formed, headed by Jabin, king of Hazor. All the princes whose dominions lay near the Sea of Chinneroth (or Lake of Galilee) and the Mountains of Lebanon mustered for this cam-

---

* "On hearing the news, Joshua made a forced march by night up the glens, guided by the pale light of an old moon; and ere the sun rose over the mountains of Moab, the Israelites defiled into the open ground round the hill of Gibeon. Their sudden appearance, immediately followed by their fierce attack, overwhelmed the Amorites. They were driven back in confusion across the plain. Joshua pursued them 'along the way that *goeth up to Beth-horon.*' This was the first stage of the flight—up the gentle slope that leads out of the plain of Gibeon to the rocky heights *east* of Beth horon. Here they [the Amorites] had outstripped their enemies; but when they were in '*the going down* of Beth-horon,'—when they were rushing down the stony declivities from the heights to the village in which we stand, and from the village to the valley away before us,—'the Lord cast down great stones from heaven upon them to Azekah, and they died: they were more which died with hailstones than they which the children of Israel slew with the sword.' The Israelitish chief, leading on his troops, wearied in body with the long night march, but undaunted in spirit, crossed the ridge too, and gained some prominent peak not far above us, from which he saw the vale of Ajalon (now the Merj Ibn 'Omeir) expanding from the ravines away below him, and unfolding itself into the great plain. Below him are the Amorites in wild confusion, clambering down rock and precipice; around him are his 'people of war;' behind him are the heights which just cover Gibeon. But high above those heights stood the sun 'in the midst of heaven;' and in front, over the western vale of Ajalon, was the faint figure of the crescent moon, visible above the hailstorm that was fast driving up from the sea in the valleys below. 'Then spake Joshua to the Lord,....and said in the sight of Israel, Sun, stand thou still upon Gibeon; and thou, Moon, in the valley of Ajalon! And the sun stood still, and the moon stayed, until the people had avenged themselves upon their enemies.' The Amorites were evidently making for their cities, Jarmuth, Lachish, and Eglon, far away on the plain to the south; and though a great part of the day still remained, yet night might come on ere the Israelites could overtake them, and thus favour their escape—hence Joshua's remarkable prayer and command. The Amorites fled down that valley beneath us, and then along the great plain, close to the base of the mountains. Jarmuth was the nearest city, and toward it the five kings ran, turning up the beautiful valley of Elah (now Wady es-Sumt). But Joshua was close upon them ere they could ascend the hill to Jarmuth, and they hid themselves in a cave at Makkedah, in the side of the valley. The Israelites shut up the cave, and continued their pursuit, till they had made an end of pursuing their enemies. From Beth horon to Jarmuth by this route is about twenty-five miles,—a distance that could not have been accomplished by the wearied armies in less than seven or eight hours. The Israelites encamped for the night at Makkedah, and there Joshua hanged the five kings."—*Murray's Handbook for Syria and Palestine*, pp. 223, 224

paign. But it fared no better with them than with their neighbours: a pitched battle was fought near the waters of Merom, in which they were utterly defeated, and the complete conquest of their cities and territories was afterwards accomplished in detail.

SECTION III.—THE ALLOTMENTS OF THE TRIBES.

Joshua and Eleazar divide the land. SOUTHERN TRIBES: *Judah*—Character of the district—*Simeon* and *Dan*—*Benjamin*. CENTRAL TRIBES: *Ephraim* and *Manasseh*—The Plain of Esdraelon—*Issachar*—The battle-field of Palestine. NORTHERN TRIBES: *Zebulun, Asher, Naphtali*—The town of Dan—Phœnicia: Tyre and Sidon—Cœle-Syria—Its scenery—Damascus. EASTERN TRIBES: *Reuben*—*Gad*—The Ammonites—*Manasseh*. Tribe of *Levi*—Ecclesiastical capital: Shiloh—Gatherings of the people—The eastern altar.

Joshua and Eleazar Divide the Land.—The main part of the country being now subdued, it only remained for Joshua, with the help of Eleazar the high priest, and the heads of the tribes, to divide it among the nine and a half tribes that had yet to receive their settlements.

Southern Tribes: Judah.—The first tribe to which a territory was assigned was JUDAH. The tract allotted to this tribe was a large and remarkable district, stretching westward from the Dead Sea, and northward from the southern wilderness, and forming the chief part of what we have called the southern division of the country. Out of this division a part was afterwards taken for Simeon; but Simeon was never an important tribe;—as Jacob prophesied, he was "scattered among his brethren." "The hill country of Judah," or "Judæa," was famous alike in Old Testament and New Testament times. Here, among round hills and broad valleys on every side, "the lion of the tribe of Judah intrenched himself. Well might he be so named in this wild country, more than half a wilderness, the lair of savage beasts, of which the traces gradually disappear as we advance into the interior. Fixed there, and never dislodged, except by the ruin of the whole nation, 'he stooped down, he couched as a lion, and as an old lion; who shall rouse him up?' Throughout the troubled period of the Judges, from Othniel to Samson, Judah dwelt undisturbed within those mountain fastnesses. On these gray hills, and in their spacious caverns, David hid himself when he fled to the mountains like one of their own native partridges, and maintained himself against the whole force of the enemy."*

Character of the District.—The character of this high and rocky district fitted it peculiarly for the cultivation of the vine. Judæa was accordingly celebrated for its vineyards. It was from one of its valleys that the twelve spies bore to Moses the bunch of grapes which had to be carried on their shoulders; and at the present day the grapes of this district are the finest in Palestine. It was to the abundance and richness of its vines, in the literal sense, and perhaps also to the fulness of gospel blessings which this tribe was to send forth, that Jacob's prophecy referred: "Binding his foal unto the vine, and his ass's colt unto the choice vine, he washed his garments in wine, and his clothes in the blood of grapes. His eyes shall be red with wine, and his teeth white with milk." The most distinguished cities in the tribe of Judah were Hebron and Beth-lehem. After the allotment of the tribes, Hebron was given to Caleb, who seems not to have been a member of the tribe by birth, nor of the promised seed, and who therefore got no inheritance at first.† Lachish, Libnah, and other "fenced cities" come into prominent notice in later times. The district was deficient in streams; and though consisting almost entirely of hills, it had no single mountain of great historical name or fame.

Simeon and Dan.—Nestling around the lion of Judah lay Simeon on the south-west, Dan on the north-west, and Benjamin on the north. The districts allotted to Simeon and Dan included the territories of the Philistines;‡ and troubled and

---

* Stanley's Sinai and Palestine.   † See Smith's Dictionary, *art.* Caleb.

‡ The territory of the Philistines extended mainly along the shore of the Mediterranean, in the south-western part of the country. It was remarkable for its luxuriant corn fields, in setting fire to which Samson did them a very serious injury. Dr. Robinson at one spot counted no fewer than thirty herds of cattle treading out grain, and observed grains and fruits of every kind and of the finest quality which the fertile soil produced. The country of the Philistines lay along the direct route between Egypt and Syria; and in the contests between the kings of Egypt and those of Assyria and Babylon, its strong cities were bones of contention, the possession of which was most keenly desired by the rival monarchs. Gaza, the principal city in Samson's time, and the site of the great temple which he overthrew at his death, is now a bald, bare ruin; but a modern Gaza has sprung up in the neighbourhood. This place was besieged by Pharaoh-necho and by Cambyses, and it withstood Alexander the Great five months.

stormy was the life of both these tribes in the immediate neighbourhood of such active foes. The Philistines were scarcely disturbed by Joshua. They cannot be said to have been effectually subdued till the time of David. The names of their great towns, governed by their five lords, were Ekron, Gath, Ashdod, Askelon, and Gaza. Samson, a native of Zorah, of the tribe of Dan, was the man of most mark whom either Dan or Simeon brought to confront their formidable neighbours. Both Dan and Simeon, indeed, dwindled into great insignificance in their allotted settlements; and at an early period a colony of Danites proceeded to the extreme north, and founded the city Dan, familiarly known as the most northerly place in the country.

Benjamin.—The territory assigned to Benjamin lay immediately to the north of Judah. In its general features it resembled Judah, but it was much less in extent. Notwithstanding its narrow limits, it was the scene of many great events. It was "little Benjamin" that furnished the first royal "ruler" to the nation of Israel. Gibeah, Saul's capital, lay within its borders; as did also part of Jerusalem, emphatically "the holy city." Here, too, at first at least (for afterwards it belonged to the kingdom of the ten tribes) was Beth-el, from whose heights Abraham got one of his first views of the Land of Promise, and where Jacob had his wonderful vision. Jericho and Gilgal were also in this tribe; so was Ramah, where the great weeping was heard; and Bethany, where our Lord spent so many peaceful hours. It was in one of the deep passes that intersect Benjamin on the east that Joshua fought his first great battle—the battle of Ai; and at Beth-horon, in the valley of Ajalon, on the western side of the plateau, while the sun and the moon lingered in the heavens to witness his triumph, he completed the rout of the confederate kings. At a later period, we find Sennacherib at

Askelon, the birth-place of Herod the Great, and, according to the legend, of Semiramis, queen of Assyria, is now quite desolate. Ashdod, or Azotus, where the temple of Dagon stood in the time of Samuel, and which withstood a siege by Psammiticus, king of Egypt, for twenty-nine years, is now quite insignificant. Of Gath, where David took refuge with king Achish, there is not now the slightest trace. Mr. Porter thinks that it stood on a hill now called Tel-es-Sâfieh. Ekron, or Akir, is an insignificant place, but without any appearance of antiquity. Thither the ark was sent from Ashdod; and from Ekron it was forwarded to Beth-shemesh. The desolation of the Philistine territory exemplifies very strikingly the fulfilment of prophecy.

Michmash, another celebrated town and pass in this tribe; and after the return from Babylon, Judas Maccabæus, a native of the neighbouring hills, gained his first victory at Beth-horon. Fifteen hundred years after the days of Joshua, the Roman legions were defeated and driven down the pass of Beth-horon, precisely as the confederate kings had been. More than a thousand years later, the Crusaders tried to reach Jerusalem by the same road; and the last halting-ground of Richard Cœur-de-Lion was at a well in the valley of Ajalon. The Mount of Olives was in the tribe of Benjamin, and so were nearly all those places in and around Jerusalem which our Lord's history has crowned with undying fame. Thus though little, in one sense, among the tribes of Israel, Benjamin rivalled them all in greatness and in real interest. It was not the least of its glories that Paul, the great apostle of the Gentiles, was one of the tribe, and could describe himself, with a feeling approaching to exultation, as "an Hebrew of the Hebrews, of the tribe of Benjamin."

Central Tribes: Ephraim and Manasseh.—The portions of Ephraim and Manasseh, which lay to the north of Benjamin, differed considerably in character from those of the southern tribes. The continuous stretch of highland country is here more interrupted; wider plains spread out their fertile bosoms; there are more separate mountains, more running streams, and more continuous tracts of verdure and vegetation. For a long period of the history of Israel, Ephraim was the principal tribe. In the days of Gideon, and again in those of Jephthah, we find the "men of Ephraim" exceedingly jealous when they fancied that they had been treated with neglect, or had been placed in an inferior position. It was a deep mortification to this tribe when Judah obtained the preference, by the appointment of David as king. The revolt of Ephraim, with his allied tribes, in the days of Rehoboam, showed that his wounded jealousy never had been thoroughly healed. Shechem, which had become famous in the days of Abraham and of Jacob, and which Joshua may be said to have made the civil capital of the country, was situated in the tribe

of Ephraim. So was Shiloh, the first ecclesiastical capital, where the ark was solemnly placed, at the end of Joshua's wars. So also was Samaria, which became, under Omri, the capital of the kingdom of the ten tribes. Joshua himself was a man of Ephraim, and must have given no small importance to the tribe. Gideon, one of the most noble of the judges, with his seventy princely brothers, was a native of the adjacent tribe of Manasseh. "The mountain," or mountainous part, "of Ephraim," was frequently the rallying place for the nation, where the appointed deliverers raised the standard of resistance to their oppressors. Deborah, though herself apparently of the northern tribes, dwelt in Mount Ephraim; Tola of Issachar judged Israel in Shamir, in the same mount; Samuel was of Ramathaim zophim, also of Mount Ephraim. In the confines of Ephraim and Manasseh was situated the fine plain of Sharon, celebrated for its excellent pastures and its fragrant plants.*
On the sea-coast lay Joppa, long the chief sea-port of Palestine; and at a later period Cæsarea, which became, under the Romans, the capital of the country.

The Plain of Esdraelon: Issachar.—The hills that form the boundary of Manasseh on the north slope down towards a plain — the most famous in Palestine — called in Scripture Jezreel, sometimes Megiddo, and in modern geography, the Plain of Esdraelon. This fell to the lot of the tribe of Issachar; but though the history of the district is exceedingly memorable, that of the tribe is not closely connected with it. The New Testament district of Galilee commences here. The plain is a wide opening, about twelve miles broad, between the hills of Central Palestine on the south and the loftier heights of Lebanon on the north, running across the country, from the valley of the Jordan on the south-east to the Medi-

---

* "Leaving the gardens of Jaffa behind us, we entered an extensive, fertile, and lovely plain—it was the plain of Sharon. Wherever the ground was cultivated, it brought forth fruit in abundance. We passed two small villages, which were entirely enclosed in olive groves..... The rain had opened nature's flowery treasures; before us was spread a most magnificent carpet, wrought with divers colours of gold, crimson, red, and blue—a carpet made without hands, in comparison with which the most costly Persian in the sultan's harem dwindles into utter insignificance "—*Missionary Labours in Jerusalem.*

terranean on the north-west. For several miles it is bounded by the rocky ridge of Mount Carmel, which juts out into the sea in the form of a bold promontory, and slopes down towards the land till it melts into the plain. As the plain approaches the Jordan valley, it is interrupted by three hills running into it in a north-westerly direction, like three fingers of a hand—Gilboa, Little Hermon, and Tabor. On the north, it is bounded by the mountains of Galilee—the hills that encircle Nazareth being close to its edge. The plain is watered by "that ancient river, the river Kishon," that finds its way to the sea through a narrow opening to the north of Carmel. Another opening, still farther to the north, gives a passage to the Belus, and forms the round bay of Acre or Ptolemais. The plain itself has the aspect of a great corn field, dotted here and there with olives, and interspersed with villages. Jezreel, where Ahab had one of his palaces; Shunem, where Elisha restored the boy to life; En-dor, where Saul consulted the witch; Bethshan, on the walls of which the Philistines fixed the bodies of Saul and his sons; and Megiddo, where Josiah was slain, were among the towns of this district. On the brow of Carmel Elijah had his famous contest with the priests of Baal; and tradition points to Tabor as the scene of our Lord's transfiguration, although recent travellers are disposed to think that that event took place on Hermon, at the head of the Jordan Valley.

The Battle-field of Palestine.—But the chief fame of this plain is derived from its battles. It has, indeed, been the great battle-field of Palestine. It was here that Thotmes III. defeated the Khita, before the Israelites were in possession of the land; here Barak defeated the Canaanites, and Gideon the Amalekites and Midianites; here, in the days of Eli, the Philistines routed the Israelites, and took from them the ark of the Lord; here, in the time of Saul, the Philistines again attacked the Israelites, routing Saul and killing his sons on the mountains of Gilboa; here, long afterwards, king Josiah was slain in a great battle with the Egyptians;—in short, "Esdraelon has been the chosen place of encampment in every great contest carried on in the country, until the disastrous march of Napoleon Bonaparte from Egypt into Syria. Jews, Gentiles, Saracens, Crusaders, Egyptians, Persians, Druses, Turks, Arabs, and French, — warriors out of every nation which is under heaven, have pitched their tents upon the plain of Esdraelon, and have beheld their banners wet with the dews of Tabor and Hermon."* It is probably because the district has been so much signalized by great national struggles that we hear so little of the tribe of Issachar in connection with it. "The strong ass, couching between two burdens," was not likely to make his name famous in a scene of so great exploits.

Northern Tribes: Zebulun, Asher, Naphtali.—North of Issachar, Zebulun, Asher, and Naphtali had their settlements. Living in so remote a part of the country, these tribes did not mingle much in its strifes. It was foretold of Asher that he was to be blessed with children; to "dip his foot in oil," referring to his abundant olive groves; and to be "shod with iron and brass" from mines in Lebanon. Naphtali was to be like a "hind let loose," as our translation has it; or, according to others, a spreading terebinth;—realized in a traveller's description of Kedeshnaphtali as "a natural park of oaks and terebinths." The whole district lies embosomed among the hills that spread out from the foot of Lebanon, and contains many scenes of remarkable beauty. Though seldom noticed in the Old Testament, it is of striking and absorbing interest in the New. Concealed by these round hills of Zebulun, that rise like an enclosure around it, is Nazareth, where the angel rested that announced to Mary the coming birth of Jesus, and where the Word made flesh spent by far the greater part of his earthly life; and away, at the eastern boundary of the same tribe, and the southern "coast" of Naphtali, where the mountains slope down to the lake, is the hallowed region where most of his mighty works were done, and where so many words of life and beauty fell like showers of dew-drops from his lips. Nazareth was a quiet, rural district,—fit scene for the calm meditation and devotion of his youth; the shores of the Lake of Tiberias, with its busy cities and its active population, were the scene of much of his

* Dr. Clarke.

active life. The woe that he pronounced on Chorazin, Bethsaida, Capernaum, and other cities, wherein most of his mighty works were done, has fallen on them with such dreadful severity, that hardly a trace of them now remains to tell the traveller on what spots they stood.

The Town of Dan.—Still farther to the north, near the sources of the Jordan, was the town of Dan, where Jeroboam set up one of his calves; and, in later times, Cæsarea Philippi, where Philip the tetrarch had his palace. It was near this place that Jesus put the memorable question to his disciples, "Whom say men that I am?" and first announced—at the farthest possible point from the destined scene—the terrible sufferings and death that awaited him. It was in this region, too, according to the more modern view, that he was transfigured; perhaps on some part of that magnificent mountain to the north-east, Hermon or Sirion, its top covered with snow,—the purity of which was even rivalled by the whiteness of his raiment. Here, at least, was the northern limit of his wanderings: after a brief rest and refreshment of mind and body amid its glorious scenery, he changed his course, and steadfastly set his face to go up to Jerusalem.

Phœnicia: Tyre and Sidon.—To the north-west of the tribe of Asher stretches the narrow and rocky strip of Phœnicia, or "coasts of Tyre and Sidon." Though the Sidonians were descended from Canaan, they were not expressly specified as doomed to extermination; and the Israelites seem to have thought that they were to be spared, though their territory was included in the promise of the land. They were almost the only neighbours with whom the Israelites lived in habitual friendship. Their country was so secluded that, but for commercial causes, they would have had little or no communication with their neighbours. But the Phœnicians were glad to exchange their manufactures for the farm and garden produce of the Israelites, and a friendly intercourse long subsisted between them. It was to Zarephath, one of the towns of Phœnicia, that Elijah was sent, in the time of a great famine, to bring sustenance to the Syro-phœnician widow and life to her son; and it was somewhere within the borders of this territory that another

Syro-phœnician woman once sought a greater prophet than Elijah, and, after a memorable exhibition of faith, went home rejoicing, her afflicted daughter having been made whole.

Coele-Syria.—A few miles north of Tyre, one of the largest rivers of Syria, the Leontes, enters the Mediterranean. If we ascend its banks, after passing through a deep gorge or ravine that runs across the chain of Lebanon, we enter the celebrated and beautiful province of Cœle-Syria, or Hollow Syria, so called from its lying in the hollow between Lebanon and Anti-Lebanon. Its modern name is El Bukáa, "the valley." This fertile plain seems to have been the refuge of many of the Canaanites who fled northward before the victorious arms of Joshua. Growing here to great numbers, they poured southward in the days of Deborah and Barak, and terrified the Israelites with their frightful chariots of iron. In this plain stood Riblah, a place of sad associations in Jewish history;—where Jehoahaz, king of Judah, was thrown into chains by the king of Egypt; and where afterwards his brother, king Zedekiah, was deprived of his eyes, after witnessing the massacre of his children, by the king of Babylon. South of Riblah stood Baalbec, perhaps a city of Solomon's, and one of the most magnificent ever reared by the hands of man.

Its Scenery.—In the period between the Old Testament and the New, Cœle-Syria continued for a long time a bone of contention between the kings of Egypt and of Syria, passing very frequently from the hands of the one into those of the other. The scenery of the district is remarkably grand. Where the ravine of the Leontes crosses the Lebanon range it is very narrow, the rocks rising perpendicularly, sometimes to the height of one thousand or twelve hundred feet. On the north-west, the valley is bounded by the snowy crest of Lebanon, and on the south-east by the still more snowy crest of Hermon. Green pastures and thriving vineyards fill up the plain. Beyond the sources of the Leontes there is a remarkable opening through the chain of mountains to the sea, believed by many to be "the entering in of Hamath," the northern boundary of the Land of Promise. Not very far from this the slender remains are found of those forests of cedar that at one time seem everywhere to have been "the glory of Lebanon." These cedars, now few in number, stand in a broad cleft of Lebanon, at 6172 feet above the sea.* They are surrounded by a numerous after-growth of younger cedars. Seen from a distance, the whole seems like a green spot, the size of a man's hand—a grove of such tiny dimensions that one might suppose it to be a solitary bush of oak.†

Damascus.—Between the eastern side of Hermon and the northern frontier of Bashan lay several states that are more or less mentioned in the history of the Israelites. Among them was the small kingdom of Geshur, the place to which Absalom fled when banished from Jerusalem, and a daughter of whose king became his wife; the kingdom of Maachah; and the kingdom of Zobah. But by far the most remarkable kingdom in this quarter was that whose capital was Damascus. Even in the time of Joshua, Damascus was a very ancient city; for we read of it in the days of Abraham, the steward of whose house was Eliezer of Damascus. Its situation is very remarkable. It lies in a plain at the eastern foot of Anti-Lebanon, six or eight days' journey from Jerusalem. The plain is watered by the river Chrysorrhoas, anciently called the Barrada, and supposed to be either the Pharpar or the Abana of Naaman (2 Kings v. 12). For many miles the city is girdled by fertile fields and gardens, watered by the Barrada and other streams; and the vegetation is so fresh and green, that, in the East, Damascus is called "a pearl in the midst of emeralds." As the traveller approaches it from Anti-Lebanon, the view is magnificent. A plain, fifty miles in circuit, bordered by blue mountains, lies before him, forming a vast waving grove of walnut, fig, pomegranate, plum, apricot, citron, and other fruit-trees; while in the distance, rising above this vast sea of green, brown, and yellow foliage, are seen the leaden domes, the gilded crescents, and the marble minarets of Damascus. The situation seems as if marked out by Nature as the site of a great and wealthy

---
* Smith's Dictionary of the Bible.
† Van de Velde's Syria and Palestine, vol. ii., pp. 477, 478.

city. In the course of its long history it has passed through many fluctuations of fortune, and has acknowledged many different masters. At the present day, with a population of some one hundred and fifty thousand, it is still one of the most considerable cities of the East.

Eastern Tribes: Reuben.—We have already described, in general terms, the district east of the Jordan, where Reuben, Gad, and the half tribe of Manasseh chose their settlements. Reuben occupied the most southerly district. His lot embraced a considerable part of the kingdom of Sihon, being bounded on the south by the Arnon, and extending on the north to the southern border of Mount Gilead. His southern and eastern flanks were covered by the Moabites, from whom, doubtless, he suffered much annoyance. "Unstable as water, he did not excel." Among the towns in this district were Ashdoth-pisgah, in the neighbourhood of Mount Pisgah; Beth-barah, a celebrated ford of the Jordan; Bezer, one of the six cities of refuge; Heshbon, famous for its fish-pools (Song of Sol. vii. 4); and Jahaz, where Moses defeated Sihon. It was either within or on the confines of Reuben's lot that Moses had his view of Canaan, and that Elijah entered the chariot of fire. In New Testament times it acquired distinction as the scene of the preaching and baptism of John (John i. 28). Probably it was on the ancient lot of Reuben that Jesus himself was baptized, and that the Holy Ghost descended like a dove. The "water," that had at first been only the emblem of Reuben's instability, thus became the symbol of better things; and the fickleness of the first-born of Jacob was redeemed by the glorious steadfastness of the only-begotten Son of God.

Gad.—Gad settled down on the north of Reuben. His lot embraced the remainder of Sihon's kingdom, including the half of Gilead, and ran up in a narrow strip as far as to the Lake of Galilee, between the Jordan and the other half of Gilead, which was given to Manasseh. It included Mahanaim, a place of considerable strength, where the angels met Jacob (Gen. xxxii. 2); where Ishbosheth, son of Saul, had his royal residence; and where David took refuge when he fled from Absalom;—Peniel, where Jacob wrestled with the Angel;—Ramoth-mizpeh, or Ramoth-gilead, where Ahab and Jehoshaphat went to make war with the Syrians; where Ahab was slain, and his son Joram, some years afterwards, was wounded; and where Jehu, by order of Elisha, was anointed king of Israel. Gilead, half of which belonged to this tribe, was a picturesque range of mountains running parallel to the Jordan as far as to the Lake of Galilee.

The Ammonites.—To the east of Gad lay the territories of the Ammonites, with their capital, Rabbah, or Rabbath-ammon, afterwards called Philadelphia. The history of Jephthah shows that the close proximity of the Ammonites must have been as troublesome to Gad as that of the Moabites was to Reuben. The town Philadelphia, which is built on both sides of a stream ("the city of waters," 2 Sam. xii. 27), is remarkable for its fine ruins; but their age is not older than the time of the Greeks and the Romans. Still more celebrated are the ruins found at Jerash (Gerasa), a few miles from the capital of Ammon: the temple of Baal, or the Sun, whose worship was universal over this country, still attracts admiration, and must at one time have been a magnificent building.

Manasseh.—The half tribe of Manasseh obtained for its share the ancient kingdom of Og. This included the northern half of Gilead, the district of Argob, and the whole of Bashan. Among its many cities were Ashteroth-karnaim, and Edrei, the capitals of Og, already mentioned; Jabesh-gilead, whose inhabitants were massacred for refusing to join the war against Benjamin (Judg. xxi. 8), and where Saul routed the Ammonites, and saved the inhabitants from captivity (1 Sam. xi.). Gadara, Bethsaida, and other places near the Sea of Galilee, are believed to have lain within the confines of this tribe; here, too, was "the desert place" to which our Lord used to retire for rest with his disciples, across the Sea of Galilee; and here were some of the mountains on whose tops he would at times spend nights in prayer.

Tribe of Levi.—The only tribe that was not furnished with a territorial home was Levi. This tribe, being devoted to offices connected with the priesthood, and supported by the tithes and offerings of the whole people, had no landed possessions, and was distributed over the whole country. Cities for the residence of the Levites, with surrounding suburbs, were assigned them from the lots of all the tribes. Pre-eminent among these were the six cities of refuge, to which persons might flee who had unintentionally destroyed the lives of others: these were, Hebron in Judah, Shechem in Ephraim, and Kedesh in Naphtali, on the west of Jordan; and Bezer in Reuben, Ramoth in Gilead, and Golan in Manasseh, on the east.

Ecclesiastical Capital: Shiloh.—While the process of allotment was going on, a resting-place was fixed on for the ark of the tabernacle. The place chosen for this purpose was Shiloh, a town in the tribe of Ephraim, situated among the hills to the north of Beth-el. For many generations the ark remained at Shiloh, and thither the Hebrew people went up from year to year, to attend the feasts of the Passover, Pentecost, and Tabernacles. There is nothing striking about the situation of Shiloh. After the ark was removed from it, it sank into insignificance and neglect; and at the present day, Seilun, as it is called, consists of little besides an old tower, with large stones and fragments of columns, indicating an ancient site. Many an interesting scene must have been enacted at that hill-encircled spot. Here it was that Hannah prayed for a son; here she devoted her little Samuel to the Lord; through that narrow valley old Eli, with trembling heart, saw the ark carried out on the fatal day of Aphek; and there the dying, heart-broken mother, widowed in every sense, left the name of I-chabod for the infant that opened his eyes as the glory departed from Israel.

Gatherings of the People.—In Joshua's days, the yearly gatherings at Shiloh must have been deeply interesting. The people, for the most part, were pervaded by the spirit of piety, and were disposed to give God the glory due to him. At each gathering, the mercies they had experienced as a united host would be brought to mind and piously acknowledged; old friendships would be renewed; and more recent tokens of God's goodness would be made known, in connection with the special history of each tribe and family, to cheer the hearts and strengthen the faith of all. The result of all the arrangements is stated in memorable words: "There failed not ought of any good thing which the Lord had spoken to the house of Israel; all came to pass."

The Eastern Altar.—The only occurrence, during Joshua's lifetime, that gave ground for even a suspicion of any open departure from the appointed worship, was the erection of a great altar on the eastern bank of the Jordan, by the tribes which had their residence there. The other tribes dreaded that some rival establishment to that at Shiloh was about to be set up, and made a very spirited remonstrance against such a proceeding. An embassy which they sent over brought back word that no design of this sort was entertained, and that the altar was intended simply as a memorial of the Lord's goodness to the eastern tribes as well as to the rest of the nation. The congregation was satisfied with the explanation, and harmony was restored.

SECTION IV.—JOSHUA'S DEATH.

Joshua's final charge—His character—Judgments on the Canaanites vindicated—Religious spirit of the Jewish people.

Joshua's Final Charge.—About twelve or fourteen years after the final or second division of the country, Joshua, feeling his end approaching, assembled the heads of all the tribes at Shechem and delivered to them his dying charge. It was marked by great earnestness and affection. He entreated them, by all the mercies of the past, and by all the hopes of the future, to cleave to the Lord. The Hebrews were a fickle and an impulsive people, and such an appeal as this had for the moment a resistless power. They vowed again and again never to forsake their God, and never to turn to idols. Joshua was aware of their fickleness, and took all the means in his power to perpetuate the remembrance of their vow. Close to the sanctuary in Shiloh a great stone was set up under an oak, as a perpetual witness of a vow so solemnly sworn. At last, his work being fully done, the Conqueror of Palestine, at the ripe age of one hundred and ten years, was gathered to his fathers, and buried in Mount Ephraim.

His Character.—The character of Joshua is highly instructive. The name Jesus in the New Testament is equivalent to Joshua in the Old (Heb. iv. 8). He was a thorough-going man,—one who "followed the Lord fully." The principle of his life might be stated in these words: "I delight to do thy will, O my God." That combination of courage and gentleness, of the lion and the lamb, which was found in so many Old Testament types of Christ, was well exemplified in his treatment of Achan. Nothing could have been gentler than his way of drawing out a confession: "My son, give, I pray thee, glory to the Lord God of Israel, and make confession unto him; and tell me now what thou hast done; hide it not from me;"—and nothing could have been more firm and fearless than his conduct in executing the offender. It was in the same spirit of implicit obedience to God's authority that he acted in destroying the Canaanites. It was the privilege of Joshua, as a type of Christ, to guide the people to the "rest" of Canaan, though not to the rest of the gospel,—that "rest which remaineth to the people of God."

Judgments on the Canaanites Vindicated.—The judgments which Joshua and his army inflicted on the native races of Canaan were very terrible, but at the same time they were fully deserved. The idolatry of these nations appears to have been very extreme; and, in connection with it, their wickedness was truly awful. It was often wickedness of a very disgusting and degrading character; and, as far as ordinary means were concerned, was incurable. God had borne with it for hundreds of years. The iniquity of the Amorites was now truly full (Gen. xv. 16). Every warning had been set at naught. The utter destruction of these nations was justified as thoroughly as the destruction of the old world, or of Sodom and Gomorrah. The Jews were simply God's instruments in executing the judgment, just as the waters of the flood and the fire and brimstone from heaven had been in the former cases. God might and would have swept away the Canaanites by natural causes, had he not wished to impress the Jews in the most striking manner with the consequences of forsaking the pure worship of the true God. It was constantly represented to them that all the evils which they had inflicted on the Canaanites, and greater evils besides, would be sent upon themselves if they should become idolaters. But, in point of fact, the Canaanites were not wholly destroyed. Many of them seem to have been driven towards the north and the west, and others to have fled to Africa. A remnant, too, remained in the land. The influence which even that small remnant exerted in corrupting the Israelites clearly shows that, had a considerable body of Canaanites remained, the Hebrew religion would have lost all its truth and purity. It was their destruction that secured the preservation of a true faith and a pure worship on the earth. To the doomed nations it was an act of just severity; to the world at large of unspeakable mercy.

Religious Spirit of the Jewish People.—We have already remarked that the religious spirit of the nation in the time of Joshua was highly pleasing. It is touchingly referred to in one of the prophets as the time of Israel's espousals: "Thus saith the Lord, I remember thee, the kindness of thy youth, *the love of thine espousals*, when thou wentest after me in the wilderness, in a land that was not sown" (Jer. ii. 2). A wilderness-training—the discipline of privation and crucifixion to the world—had been greatly blessed. The people were now to have a time of worldly prosperity and comfort; and, as often happens in similar cases, the period of prosperity was to prove more disastrous than the period of suffering had been. Moses' prophecy was soon to be verified: "Jeshurun waxed fat, and kicked: thou art waxen fat, thou art grown thick, thou art covered with fatness: then he forsook God which made him, and lightly esteemed the Rock of his salvation" (Deut. xxxii. 15). For all that Joshua did, he did not give the people rest (Heb. iv. 8). The settlement which they got was not a settlement in the highest sense. A void still remained unfilled. The nation had yet to look forward. The Hope of Israel was yet in the future.

CHAPTER VIII.

THE JUDGES.

FROM THE DEATH OF JOSHUA TO THE ACCESSION OF SAUL.

JUDGES; RUTH; 1 SAMUEL i.-x.

SECTION I.—THE SIX GREAT INVASIONS.

Condition of the Israelites—The principal "Judges"—The six invasions—Insecurity of the eastern tribes—1. Invasion from the north-east: the Mesopotamians; Othniel—2. Invasion from the south-east: the Moabites; Ehud—3. Invasion from the north: the Canaanites; Deborah and Barak—Death of Sisera—4. Invasion from the east: the Midianites—Gideon—Defeat of the Midianites—Celebrity of the exploit—Jealousy of Ephraim—Abimelech—5. Invasion from the east: the Ammonites—Jephthah—War with Ephraim—6. Invasion from the south-west: the Philistines—Samson—Eli and his sons—The ark taken by the Philistines—Samuel and his work—Revival of godliness.

Condition of the Israelites.—For several hundred years after the death of Joshua, the twelve tribes continued as he had left them, except only when any or all of them fell into the idolatrous practices of their neighbours, and, as a punishment from God, were harassed by some powerful enemy. The different tribes did not make so great efforts as they might have made to drive out the remaining Canaanites; and, very soon after the death of Joshua, a messenger from God came up from Gilgal to Bochim to chide them for not having completely destroyed their altars. The chastisements which God sent on the people when they were unfaithful commonly had the effect of humbling them, and of making them cry to him for help. On these occasions their cry was always heard, and officers, named "Judges," were raised up to deliver them from the enemy who was galling them at the time.

The Principal "Judges."—The Book of Judges is so named because it records the exploits of some of those great men. It makes us more or less acquainted with twelve of these judges:— 1. Othniel, of the tribe of Judah; 2. Ehud, a Benjamite; 3. Deborah, a prophetess, who was assisted by Barak; 4. Gideon, of Manasseh; 5. Abimelech, his son; 6. Tola, of Issachar; 7. Jair, of Gilead; 8. Jephthah, also of Gilead; 9. Ibzan, of Beth-lehem; 10. Elon, of Zebulun; 11. Abdon, a Pirathonite; and 12. Samson, of Dan. The office of Samuel was so unlike that of the military judges, that he can hardly be classed among them.

The Six Invasions.—Of several of these judges little or nothing is told us beyond the fact that they judged Israel for a certain number of years. The military judges of greatest eminence were Othniel, Ehud, Deborah (with Barak), Gideon, Jephthah, and Samson. Each of these achieved a great deliverance for his country from a particular enemy;—Othniel, from the Mesopotamians; Ehud, from the Moabites; Deborah and Barak, from the Canaanites; Gideon, from the Midianites and Amalekites; Jephthah, from the Ammonites; and Samson, from the Philistines. It must not be supposed that each of these different enemies brought the whole country under their dominion. Sometimes, indeed, they did; but on other occasions it was only the part of Palestine that lay nearest to their respective territories that suffered from their attacks. The Mesopotamians, the Moabites, the Midianites, and the Ammonites would make their attack on the eastern border, and would, therefore, be most troublesome to the tribes east of the Jordan; the Canaanites would give most annoyance on the north, and the Philistines on the south-west.

Insecurity of the Eastern Tribes. It thus appears that, though the territories on which Reuben, Gad, and the half tribe of Manasseh had set their hearts, were remarkably fertile and beautiful, they were very insecure; and often, no doubt, these tribes must have felt that it would have been wiser for them to have gone with their brethren, and to have had the Jordan and its deep valley between them and their eastern foes. Apostasy from the true faith seems to have broken out oftener among them than among the other tribes, owing to their proximity to so many idolatrous neighbours. For this reason they suffered heavier chastisements, and they were the first to go into captivity.

1. *Invasion from the North-east.*

The Mesopotamians—Othniel.—The first great chastisement of the children of Israel took place not very many years after the death of Joshua. A new generation had now arisen. The people had been marrying into heathen families, forsaking the Lord, worshipping the Canaanite gods, and falling into the horrible immoralities which always attended that worship. A king of Mesopotamia, whose name was Chushan-rishathaim, was sent to chastise them. Josephus speaks of him as a king of Assyria, using the term probably in a general sense. Probably he had conquered all the country lying between the Euphrates and Palestine, making the Israelites, like others, smart under his yoke. It is remarkable that the scourge sent to chastise them for the worship of Baal and Ashtaroth was the king of the country where that worship originated and had its headquarters. For eight years Chushan kept the Israelites in bondage, till Othniel, the nephew of Caleb, was raised up to deliver them. According to Josephus, Othniel first surprised and destroyed the garrisons of the Assyrians in the country; then, mustering forces from all quarters, he fought a pitched battle, in which he obtained a complete victory, and drove the enemy across the Euphrates.

2. *Invasion from the South-east.*

The Moabites—Ehud.—The lesson seems to have had effect for a whole generation; but after forty years the same bad habits were again predominant. The chastisement this time came from the Moabites, whose king, Eglon, in alliance with his neighbours the Ammonites, and some tribes of the Amalekites, attacked the Israelites from the east, crossed the Jordan, and obtained possession of Jericho. Eglon continued to hold his ground for eighteen years, during which time he would, doubtless, inflict great suffering on the eastern tribes, as well as on Benjamin and all who dwelt near Jericho and the valley of the Jordan. The man raised up to deliver Israel from Eglon was Ehud, a Benjamite; he must, therefore, have lived near Jericho, and have known the country well. Having been sent with a present to Eglon, he contrived to get a secret interview with the king, stabbed him, and, having locked the door, escaped unobserved. Climbing the steep precipices or quarries behind Jericho, he hastened to Mount Ephraim, where he gathered an army; he then seized the fords of the Jordan by which the Moabites required to cross to their own country; and, having thus cut off their retreat, he put ten thousand of them to death, not one escaping. After his death there was peace, at least in that part of the land, for the long period of eighty years.

3. *Invasion from the North.*

The Canaanites—Deborah and Barak.—The Philistines were now making themselves troublesome in the south; but the next great national chastisement came from the north, and was inflicted by Jabin, king of Canaan. His followers and forces were the descendants of the original inhabitants that lingered in the possessions of the northern tribes, or occupied the territory beyond them, in the valley between the two ranges of Lebanon. With nine hundred war-chariots, Jabin scoured the plains of Israel, spreading terror and misery. The movement against king Jabin was begun by Deborah, a prophetess of extraordinary faith and courage. She had her dwelling under a palm in Mount Ephraim, between Beth-el and Ramah, where she exercised the functions of judge of Israel, and where her godly example and counsels probably were instrumental in bringing the Israelites to repentance for their sins, and in thus paving the way for their deliverance. At her instigation, Barak, a man of Naphtali, was induced to collect an army of ten thousand men, from the tribes of Zebulun and

Naphtali, and to take the field against Sisera, Jabin's captain. The battle between them took place in the great plain of Esdraelon, on the banks of the Kishon, near the town of Megiddo. The level plain was adapted for the action of the Canaanite war-chariots, of which the Israelites had a great horror, and which they had no proper means of attacking. Barak's little army was drawn up on Mount Tabor, on the east side of the plain. Barak showed uncommon faith and courage, when, of his own accord, he descended with his troops from Mount Tabor, and marched to Megiddo to attack his great enemy. According to Josephus, as the Canaanites were advancing to meet Barak, a tremendous hail-storm dashed from the east upon their faces, terrified their horses, threw them into confusion, and made them an easy prey to their foe. The waters of the brook, swollen by the storm to a prodigious torrent, swept away the Canaanite warriors as they attempted to cross it in order to escape to the north; while the horses, rearing and prancing in their fright, dashed their hoofs against the stones in the bed of the river, and were disabled or destroyed. "The stars in their courses fought against Sisera. The river of Kishon swept them away.......Then were the horse-hoofs broken by the means of the prancings, the prancings of their mighty ones" (Judges v. 20-22).

Death of Sisera.—Escaping on foot, Sisera hastened from the scene of action, and sought refuge in what he deemed the friendly tent of Jael, the wife of Heber, a Kenite,—a descendant of the family of Jethro, who, still retaining the nomadic life, had pitched his tent near Kedesh-naphtali. Sisera was treacherously killed by Jael; and Barak, hastening in pursuit of him, was shown his dead body in the tent. This signal defeat delivered the Israelites from the Canaanites; and, in celebration of the event, a triumphal song, fierce but spirit-stirring, was composed and sung by Deborah. Deborah was evidently a woman of remarkable character—stern and fearless—a woman to rouse a nation. For many a day the influence of her song, holding up distrust and cowardice as it did to scorn and mockery, and exalting faith and courage wherever they appeared, must have been great. Many a pious patriot among the Jews in future times may have been impelled through this song of Deborah to dare and do great things, in dependence on the help of God.

4. *Invasion from the East.*

The Midianites.—Another interval of forty years passed, when the old corruptions again broke out; and another invasion was sent as a punishment. The pastoral hordes of the eastern deserts—Midianites, Amalekites, and other tribes of Arabia—came pouring like locusts into the land of Israel. Their plan seems to have been, to rush with their flocks and herds into the country when the harvest began to be gathered, to seize and consume all its products, to retire on the approach of winter to their own deserts, and to repeat the visitation each returning summer. The Israelites were so terrified, that they had to abandon the plains and the valleys, to retire to their walled towns and intrenchments, and even to hide in caves from their insatiable foes and plunderers. For seven successive seasons this wretched state of things continued; and the enemy had got possession of nearly the whole land before the nation was humbled and made to acknowledge its sin. At last a prophet was sent expressly to remind the people of their wickedness; and his mission had the desired effect.

Gideon.—That prophet was Gideon, a man of Manasseh, who had a meeting with an angel at his house at Ophrah, and was commanded and commissioned to deliver Israel from Midian. It was no easy matter to arouse his faith to the requisite pitch; but once aroused, it stood right nobly. He sounded a note of defiance to the Midianites. In reply, they assembled in the valley of Jezreel, the eastern part of the plain of Esdraelon, in such multitudes as to cover the plain like grasshoppers. His own noble example, the returning spirit of faith and courage in the northern tribes, and the remembrance of Deborah and Barak that lingered on the scene of their exploits, drew to his standard an army of thirty-two thousand men, from the tribes of Manasseh, Asher, Zebulun, and Naphtali. His army was encamped on the slopes of Mount Gilboa; but the number was judged by God too great, and, by two several processes, it was brought down to three hundred. This handful, with their lamps, their trumpets, and their swords, spread themselves by night along one of the heights above the Arab host, that lay wrapped in sleep in the plain below, while their countless camels couched securely around them. Stealing down to their camp, Gideon and a single attendant heard a Midianite tell his neighbour a dream of a barley cake that came rolling into the camp and overturned one of the tents of Midian. The neighbour at once pronounced it a presage of their defeat by Gideon. Greatly encouraged, Gideon and his companion returned to their company, and prepared for action.

Defeat of the Midianites.—On a given signal, the three hundred men broke their pitchers, waved their lamps, and uttered a shout which spread terror among their foes. Roused by the noise, the Arab host was filled with panic, and in their confusion they killed one another. In the morning, the remains of the host were rushing towards the Jordan, to make for their own country, on the other side. Gideon immediately sent word to the Ephraimites to seize the fords of the river, and to cut off their retreat. A second battle took place at the ford of Beth-barah, when Oreb and Zeeb, "the Raven" and "the Wolf," two lesser chiefs of the Midianites, were slain. The two greater chiefs, Zebah and Zalmunna, had already crossed the Jordan with fifteen thousand men; and Gideon and his little band, "faint, yet pursuing," hastened to overtake them. With dauntless faith and courage, the noble Three Hundred penetrated far into the Midianite territory,* attacked and defeated the host, which was little dreaming of such an onset, and caught and slew the fugitive chieftains. Never, before or since, not even in the days of Leonidas and his Spartan band, were greater prodigies done by three hundred men. In the course of their pursuit, they had been haughtily refused

* Nobah, one of the places mentioned past which Gideon went (Judges viii. 11), was at least thirty miles east of the Jordan, near the outskirts of Og's kingdom. It was also called Kenath (Num. xxxii. 42), and now Kunawat. How far Gideon pursued beyond this place, into the Midianite desert, we do not know.

aid by their own countrymen, as they passed through Succoth and Penuel, towns of Gilead,—the people there not dreaming that so small a band could conquer so great an enemy, and fully expecting that, as soon as the Midianites recovered from their panic, they would return and chastise all who had befriended Gideon. Contrary to their confident expectations, Gideon returned victorious; and, fulfilling a threat he had made as he passed in the full confidence of faith, he destroyed the tower of Penuel, and chastised the princes of Succoth with the thorny branches of the acacia groves of their valley.

Celebrity of the Exploit.—The "day of Midian" continued long to be memorable in the history of Israel. In the Psalms (Ps. lxxxiii. 9-11), two or three centuries after, we find the discomfiture of the host of Midian, and especially the destruction of Oreb and Zeeb, Zebah and Zalmunna, referred to as among the most astounding of God's judgments on his enemies. Even after an interval of five hundred years, the prophet Isaiah drew from the "day of Midian" (ch. ix. 4), and the rock of Oreb (ch. x. 26) an emblem of the destruction that was to be brought upon the terrible hosts of Assyria. Gideon is celebrated in the Epistle to the Hebrews as one of those heroes of faith whose reliance on the arm of Jehovah was the secret of their success. The people had such a sense of his noble qualities, that they invited him to become their king. But the piety of Gideon would not listen to the proposal: he knew that God was Israel's king, and he was not the man to usurp His functions. For about forty years he continued to act as judge over his countrymen. But, like other great and good men, he was not invulnerable; and somehow, after his victories, he was induced to apply the gold he had taken from the enemy to embroidering an ephod or priestly robe, which he placed in his house, intending, apparently, to set up some kind of priestly establishment there. It became a snare to him and to his house;—it led them, probably, to irregular and unwarranted worship; and ultimately, perhaps, brought upon them the chastisement of God.

Jealousy of Ephraim.—The triumph both of Barak and of

Gideon had been achieved by the northern tribes, and the great central tribe of Ephraim was chagrined, because it had borne off so small a share of these honours. Its jealousy, indeed, broke out in the very midst of Gideon's victories; and it was only by a clever stroke of flattery that he succeeded at the moment in keeping it down.

Abimelech.—After Gideon's death, Abimelech, who was his son by a concubine of the tribe of Ephraim, resolved to take advantage of his connection with Gideon on the one hand and with the powerful tribe of Ephraim on the other, to set up a claim as king of Israel. Getting rid, by a horrible act of fratricide, of his seventy brothers,—all but one,—who were of the tribe of Manasseh, he got the men of Shechem to proclaim him king, apparently beside the pillar where Joshua had made the people swear that they would serve the Lord. This godless proceeding was attended with no blessing. At the end of three years, a quarrel took place between Abimelech and the Shechemites; and, after a considerable amount of civil broil and fighting, Abimelech was killed by a woman, who threw a piece of a mill-stone on his head as he was setting fire to the tower of Thebez. He seems to have been a thoroughly ungodly and unprincipled man, and to have been in close alliance with the promoters of idolatry; and, no doubt, he did much harm both to his tribe and to the nation at large. His death was declared to be the retribution of Providence for his horrible guilt.

5. *Invasion from the East.*

The Ammonites.—In the course of the next half century some smaller chastisements were inflicted on the Israelites for their old sin; but about the end of that period a terrible scourge was again let loose on the land from the east. The children of Ammon were the chief aggressors on this occasion. Like the Midianites a century before, they not only ravaged the country east of Jordan, but they also spread themselves over the tribes of Judah, Benjamin, and Ephraim. The children of Israel cried in their distress to the Lord; but at first their humiliation and reformation were not sufficient, and God, taunting them with

their idolatry, bade them cry to the gods they had chosen—
"Baalim, and Ashtaroth, and the gods of Syria, and the gods of
Zidon, and the gods of Moab, and the gods of the children of
Ammon, and the gods of the Philistines." Singularly enough,
it was from these very nations, whose gods they were so often
tempted to worship, that their troubles always came. A more
complete confession and reformation followed this taunt, and
God's "soul was grieved for the misery of Israel."

Jephthah.—Jephthah, a Gileadite, the person destined to
deliver them, seems to have had a foreigner for his mother.
He had been driven by his brethren from his father's house,
and with a roving band of followers carried on a desultory
warfare on the borders of the eastern desert. With a profound
regard for God, as the only true God and the God of the
Hebrews, Jephthah seems to have united not a little ignorance
of the way in which he ought to be served. He enjoyed so
great fame as a warrior, that he was earnestly entreated to
take the command of the army of Israel against the Ammonites. Having done so, he entirely defeated the enemy
in a pitched battle near Aroer, not far from the scene of
Sihon's defeat under Moses, and slew vast numbers of them.
But the joy of the victory was turned into bitterness by the
vow which he had made, to offer to the Lord whatsoever
should first meet him on returning home. It turned out to
be his only daughter. Faithful to his vow, Jephthah dealt
accordingly with his daughter. The old interpretation of the
Jews was that he offered her as a burnt sacrifice. At a comparatively recent period the idea arose that she was merely
doomed to perpetual virginity.

War with Ephraim.—Jephthah's character was bold but unenlightened; but the faith he showed, "putting his life in his
hand," and going out in God's name against the Ammonites,
and the thorough trust he reposed in God as the covenant God
of Israel, secured him a place in the muster-roll of the ancient
worthies (Heb. xi. 32). He, too, like Gideon, had to encounter
the jealousy of the haughty and overbearing tribe of Ephraim.
They were offended at not having been called to the war;

crossed the Jordan in great force into Gilead; and, in the fiercest spirit, threatened to burn his house over his head. Unlike Gideon, Jephthah disdained by flattery to smooth their ruffled plumes, and taunted them with having shrunk from the strife when called to take part in it. The result was a fierce civil war between the Gileadites and the Ephraimites. After a decisive battle in Gilead, the victorious Gileadites seized those convenient but terrible places, the fords of the Jordan; and, detecting fugitive Ephraimites by their provincial peculiarity of saying Sibboleth instead of Shibboleth, slew them on the banks of the river—killing, in all, no fewer than forty-two thousand. This prodigious slaughter greatly weakened the tribe of Ephraim, and for a considerable time afterwards they make little figure in the history.

6. *Invasion from the South-west.*

The Philistines.—Another great scourge of apostasy came from the south-west. The Philistines had been troublesome on former occasions, and when they gained any supremacy, they took an admirable way of perpetuating it—they deprived the people of all warlike weapons, and would not even tolerate a forge for sharpening farming tools. In spite of this, however, a great victory had been gained over them long before by Shamgar, who slew six hundred of them with no other weapon than an ox-goad. This defeat kept them at bay for a long time; but now they became more terrible than ever. Their dominion lasted for forty years.

Samson.—At last the prospect of deliverance appeared. A pious couple, living at Zorah, in the tribe of Dan, had obtained a son by express promise from that "Angel of God" who appeared so often to teach the people to connect their sufferings with their sins, and their blessings with the undeserved bounty of Heaven. Samson, the name of this child of promise, was a Nazarite from his birth, set apart expressly for the service of God, and under command that neither wine nor strong drink should ever be drunk by him, and that his hair should never be cut. While fulfilling these conditions he enjoyed supernatural bodily strength. But his will was feeble; and when he happened to be attached to a woman, he could not resist her fascinations. This weakness placed him more or less, from time to time, in the power of the Philistines. Zorah, his place of abode, lay up among the hills of Palestine. From this place it was often his practice to "go down" to the country of the Philistines; sometimes for social relaxation, and sometimes for warlike purposes.* In his youth he married a daughter of the Philistines; and, after her death, another Philistine woman, named Delilah, gained his heart. Both were treacherous to him; but each of them, in different ways, led to his performing prodigious feats of strength and valour against the Philistines. His tearing a young lion to pieces; his killing thirty men of Askelon; his catching three hundred foxes, and setting fire to the corn of the Philistines; his slaying a thousand men at En-hakkore with the jawbone of an ass; his carrying the gates of Gaza up to a hill near Hebron; and last, not least, after he had been treacherously taken and his eyes put out, his destruction both of himself and of the temple and lords of the Philistines, by pulling down the pillars that supported the house, were the greatest feats of bodily strength ever known. Samson may be regarded both as a symbol of the Hebrew nation and as a type of the great Deliverer. Consecrated at first to God;

* "We see around us at Beth-shemesh the native country of Samson, and the scenes of some of the principal events of his life. Standing amid the stones and thistles on the little hill, and turning northward, we have at our feet, running from right to left, Wady Surâr, nearly a mile in width; beyond it rises a steep high ridge—a kind of promontory jutting out from the hills of Judah—crowned with a little white wely: this marks the position of Sûrah, a small, miserable hamlet, situated on the declivity just behind the wely. It contains no traces of antiquity except a cistern and some scarped rocks; yet it is the site of ZORAH, *the birth-place of Samson* (Judges xiii. 2). The intervening wady is most probably the 'valley of Sorek,' the home of the infamous *Delilah* (Judges xvi. 4). About 1½ mile west of Beth-shemesh, but hidden by an intervening ridge, is a village called *Tibneh*, occupying the site of the ancient TIMNATH, where Samson got his Philistine wife (Judges xiv. 1). It was in 'going down' from Zorah to Timnath—somewhere, perhaps, in the rugged sides of the wady—he killed the young lion that 'roared against him;' and it was in the latter place he put forth his celebrated riddle to his Philistine companions—'Out of the eater came forth meat, and out of the strong came forth sweetness' (Judges xiv. 14). It was among these dark hills he afterwards caught three hundred young foxes, and tying them tail to tail, and putting a torch between each two, let them loose over the broad plain to the west among the standing corn of the Philistines. What havoc they must have made! In revenge for this, the Philistines came up to Timnath, and burned Samson's wife and her father with fire."—*Murray's Handbook for Syria and Palestine*, p. 282.

enjoying many privileges while the covenant of consecration was observed; proving unfaithful, losing his strength, and then suffering terrible chastisement; yet restored in the end to a measure of his former strength, his life was a picture of the whole career of Israel. As a type of Christ, he stands by himself, singular and unlike all the rest of the great men of the Old Testament. He was the first that actually and deliberately sacrificed his life for his country, thereby foreshadowing, though in a vague and imperfect way, the great sacrifice of Christ; and perhaps suggesting, long afterwards, by the occasion and the results of his death, the remark of the high priest Caiaphas, that it was "expedient that one man should die for the people."

Eli and his Sons.—Samson was the last of the great military heroes who bore the title of Judge. Contemporary with him, according to our chronology, and exercising the supreme authority of the nation, was Eli, the high priest, personally a good man, but afflicted with an ungodly family, whose disgraceful actings he was too weak and easy-minded to restrain. Flagrant wickedness was always openly punished by God in the Jewish State, for one of God's great ends in connection with the Jewish history was to show his hatred of sin; but such wickedness in his own consecrated priesthood was specially hateful to him, and was strongly and openly denounced. It was foretold that, on account of the gross corruptions which he had tolerated, the priestly office would be removed from Eli and his house for ever.

The Ark taken by the Philistines.—The fulfilment began on occasion of a great battle with the Philistines, fought at Aphek in the plain of Esdraelon. The ark of God had been sent for from Shiloh, and carried by the Israelites into the battle, under the belief that the sacred symbol would be sure to bring victory. But the people found that when they had offended their God, the symbol of his presence could not make up for his actual opposition. The ark was taken; Hophni and Phinehas, Eli's sons, were slain; and the old man, hearing at Shiloh of the fate of the ark, fell from his seat, and was killed. The wife of Phinehas died in giving birth to a child, named by her I-chabod, because, with the ark, the glory had departed from Israel. The Philistines carried the ark to their own country, and placed it at Ashdod, in the temple of their fish-god, Dagon, whose image was found in the morning lying broken on the ground. Plagues were inflicted successively on the men of Ashdod, Gath, and Ekron, to which places the ark was carried in succession, so that it became an object of desire to get quit of it; and at last it was sent off in a cart drawn by unguided cattle, who bore it to Beth-shemesh. The same evil befalling the people there, the men of Kirjath-jearim came and carried it to their city, in the tribe of Judah, where it remained until the time of David. According to our chronology, the death of Samson occurred about the time when the ark was taken in battle. The thought of that great national humiliation may have been the cause of the dying effort of Samson to destroy the Philistines.

Samuel and his Work.—Meanwhile the civil duties of judge passed into the hands of Samuel. The early history of Samuel shows that, great as was the general corruption of the age, there were here and there, in humble life, persons of exemplary piety. His father, who was a member of the tribe of Levi, resided in Mount Ephraim. His childless mother, distressed for want of children, and taunted by Peninnah, Elkanah's other wife, had begged and obtained him as a special gift from God. To his service at Shiloh he had been dedicated before his birth; and the simple, devoted piety of the child showed his fitness for his sacred office. Some time after the death of Eli, he was the means of inducing the people to put away their images of Baal and Ashtoreth, and to return to the worship of the true God. At Mizpeh, in Benjamin,* he held a solemn convocation;

---

* Mizpeh, where the solemn convocation was held, was a remarkable place in Jewish history. It was in its neighbourhood that Samuel set up the stone of help Eben-ezer —saying, "Hitherto hath the Lord helped us" (1 Sam. vii. 6-12). Here, too, the people assembled to choose their first king (1 Sam. x. 17-24). During the Babylonish captivity, the Chaldæan governor, Gedaliah, resided at Mizpeh; and here he was murdered by Ishmael (Jer. xli. 1, 2). Dr. Robinson and Dr. Porter are both of opinion that the modern "**Neby Samwil**" is the ancient Mizpeh. The situation corresponds admirably and at that time a considerable revival of true religion seems to have taken place. Hearing of this assembly, the Philistines went up to Mizpeh against the Israelites to battle; but, at Samuel's earnest intercession, God sent a thunder-storm on their host, which made them an easy prey to the Israelites. Othniel had delivered the people by his spear, Ehud by his dagger, Shamgar by his ox-goad, Gideon by his sword, and Samson by the jaw-bone of an ass; but Samuel's weapon was prayer. This defeat crushed the Philistines, and kept them for a long time at bay. Samuel continued to the end of his life to perform the civil functions of judge. His head-quarters were at Ramah; but he was accustomed to make circuits, especially to Beth-el, Gilgal, and Mizpeh, where he exercised his functions among the people.

Revival of Godliness.—The holy impression made by Samuel on the tribes of Benjamin and Judah remained long uneffaced. Never was a single man of God more instrumental in sowing the soil of a district with the enduring seeds of godliness. It seems to have been mainly through his influence that piety found a home in Judah and Benjamin, when it was banished from the rest of the country. Humanly speaking, David would not have been king if Samuel had not prepared the way. He was to king David what John the Baptist was to Christ. Unquestionably, he is to be ranked among the very greatest and best of the Hebrew worthies. A considerable part of his life was contemporary with the reign of Saul, and falls, therefore, not so much under the period of the Judges as under the period of the Kings.

with the name Mizpeh—"a watch-tower." It is a hill 500 or 600 feet high, about four miles north-west from Jerusalem, which commands a wider view than any other peak in the south of Palestine. From its summit, "Central Palestine is spread out round us, like an embossed map. On the north, at our feet, is Gibeon, encircled by its plain....To the right is the rock Rimmon; and more to the eastward the conical tell, crowned by the village Er-Ram, the Ramah of Benjamin. Further to the right we see the bare top of Tuleil el-Fûl, on which 'Gibeah of Saul' once stood....Over the bleak gray ridge on the south-east are the domes and minarets of Jerusalem, looking as if sunk in a valley... Southward the eye ranges over the summits of the Judæan hills, as far as the environs of Hebron. On the west, at the base of the mountains, is the plain of Philistia, on which we can distinguish Ramleh, Lydda, and even Joppa, washed by the waves of the Mediterranean."—*Murray's Handbook*, p. 226.

SECTION II.—DOMESTIC AND RELIGIOUS LIFE.

Domestic life—The farms; size and products—Seasons of the year—Trees, flowers, and vegetables—Religious festivals—Government—State of religion—A chequered period—The mode of divine teaching.

Domestic Life.—Most of the events that have now been noticed were only among the striking or outstanding occurrences of four or five hundred years. It is very useful to inquire how the people spent their ordinary life during that time—what were their ordinary employments, habits, opinions, and feelings. The materials of the Bible will enable us to give a brief sketch of the daily life of the Hebrews in the days of the Judges.

The Farms; Size and Products.—The Jews were a nation of farmers, and each farmer was the proprietor of his own farm. The size of the farm allotted to each family may at first have averaged from twenty to fifty acres; and as there were very few servants or labourers, except such hewers of wood and drawers of water as the Gibeonites, each family had to cultivate its own estate. The houses were seldom built apart from each other, like the farm-houses of our own country,—that would have been too insecure: they were placed together in villages, towns, and cities; and when the place was very much exposed, and of great importance, it was surrounded by a wall. The lands were adapted chiefly for three kinds of produce—grain, fruit, and pasture. Wheat, millet, and barley were the principal kinds of grain; flax and cotton were also cultivated, and small garden herbs, such as anise, cummin, mint, and rue (Matt. xxiii. 23). The orchards were exceedingly productive. The olive, the sycamore, the fig, the pomegranate, the vine, the almond, and the apple were all common; and a great part of the time of the Hebrews, in days of peace, must have been spent in cultivating these fruit-trees. As beasts of burden, they had the ox, the camel, and the ass; while sheep and goats constituted the staple of their flocks.

Seasons of the Year.—Their grain harvest began about the beginning of our April, and lasted for about two months. Summer followed, in June and July, and was the season for gathering the garden fruits. The next two months were still warmer, so that the sheep-shearing would have to be overtaken before they set in. During all this time little or no rain falls in Palestine. The country becomes parched, the brooks and springs dry up, and almost the only supply of water is obtained from the pools and reservoirs that have been filled in winter. October and November are the seed-time. "The former rain" falls then. It often falls with violence, fills the dry torrent-beds, and illustrates our Saviour's figure of the rain descending, and the floods coming (Matt. vii. 25, 27). December and January are the winter months, when frost and snow are not uncommon; February and March are also cold. "The latter rains" fall at this season. About the end of it, "the winter is past, the rain is over and gone; the flowers appear on the earth; the time of the singing of birds is come, and the voice of the turtle is heard in our land; the fig tree putteth forth her green figs, and the vines with the tender grape give a good smell" (Song of Sol. ii. 11-13).

Trees, Flowers, and Vegetables.—Among the wild trees and the vegetable products of the country were the cedar, strong and lofty, an emblem of stability and beauty (Ps. xcii. 12); the oak, both the smooth and the prickly sort, which grew in great luxuriance in Bashan; the terebinth, or turpentine-tree—also translated *oak*, and occasionally *elm* (Hosea iv. 13), and *teil* (Isa. vi. 13), in our Bibles; the fir, the cypress, the pine, the myrtle, and the mulberry. The oleander and the prickly pear flourished in most situations. The acacia or shittah was found in dry situations, such as the beds of extinct water-courses. The rose and the lily were the common flowers; the red lily, or anemone, was exceedingly abundant and striking (Matt. vi. 28). Altogether, the number of vegetable products was large and varied; and, in such a country, Solomon's memory and acquirements could not have been contemptible, when "he spake of trees, from the cedar that is in Lebanon unto the hyssop that springeth out of the wall" (1 Kings iv. 33).

Religious Festivals.—The ordinary employments of the

Hebrew farmer were thus ample and varied, but were not very toilsome; and often they were pleasantly interrupted. Thrice a year the males went up to Shiloh, to the three great festivals —Passover, Pentecost, and Tabernacles. Each seventh day was a holy Sabbath to the Lord, devoted to rest and worship. At each new moon there was also a holy day. Each seventh year was a year of rest, at least from the ordinary occupations of the field and the garden: it was probably turned to account in repairing houses, clothes, and implements, and particularly in the religious instruction of the people. The education of the children was chiefly in the hands of their parents, assisted by the Levites, who were scattered over the country, and were paid from the tithes. On the whole, the Hebrews, in times of peace, led during this period a quiet, unambitious, country life. Occasionally, as in the song of Deborah, we meet with proofs that music and song and literary culture were not neglected; and the "divers colours of needlework on both sides," for which the mother of Sisera waited so anxiously at her window, show that the Hebrew ladies had acquired no mean skill in the use of the needle. But neither learning, nor the mechanical arts, nor manufactures, nor commerce, nor the fine arts, were very vigorously cultivated, or made much progress during this period. Each man was content to sit under his vine, and under his fig-tree; and the children of a family were usually quite pleased to divide the possessions, and to follow the occupations, of their father.

Government.—The government of the country was carried on chiefly by local officers. It is not easy to ascertain the precise number and nature of the departments of the government, or of the officers by whom they were conducted. Each of the twelve tribes seems to have had a government of its own. Each city had its elders, and each tribe its rulers and princes. In ordinary cases, justice seems to have been administered and local disputes to have been settled by the tribal authorities. There seem also to have been certain central tribunals. In particular, there was "the whole congregation of Israel,"—a sort of House of Commons or States-general, composed of delegates from the whole nation, by whom matters of vital importance to the country were considered. In ordinary times, the high priest seems to have exercised considerable political influence; and in times of pressing danger, the judges were invested with extraordinary powers. The whole of the twelve tribes were welded together, and had great unity of feeling and action imparted to them, through the yearly gatherings at the great religious festivals. When idolatry prevailed in any district of the country, these gatherings would be neglected, and the unity of the nation would consequently be impaired.

State of Religion.—No important addition was made during this period to the religious knowledge of the people. There was no new revelation of the Messiah, except in as far as the several deliverers who were raised up might foreshadow the great Deliverer. The ceremonial law of Moses was probably in full operation during the periods of religious faithfulness. The great lesson regarding sin,—its hatefulness in God's eyes, and the certainty of its punishment,—was continually renewed by the events of providence. Every public event served to show that righteousness exalteth a nation, and that sin is a reproach to any people. Those who really felt the evil of sin would see, in the sacrifices that were constantly offered up, a proof that God cannot accept the sinner unless his sin be atoned for through the shedding of blood. But even pious men had not very clear ideas of the way of acceptance with God. A humble sense of their own unworthiness, the spirit of trust in God's undeserved mercy for pardon, and a steady, prayerful endeavour to do all that was right in God's sight, were the great elements of true piety in those days. There was great occasion for the exercise of high trust in God, both in believing that prosperity would always follow the doing of His will, and in daring great achievements, like those of Barak and Gideon, under the firm conviction that He would crown them with success.

A Chequered Period.—But in a religious point of view this period was a very chequered one; sometimes one state of things prevailed, sometimes another. The people showed a constant inclination to forsake the pure worship of the true God, and to fall into the idolatry of their neighbours. The oppressions which those very neighbours inflicted on them, and the wars which ensued, generally produced an antipathy to their religious and other customs, which lasted for some years; but the old fondness for idolatry returned again and again. It clearly appeared that a pure, spiritual worship, is distasteful to the natural heart. Men do not relish coming into heart-to-heart contact with the unseen God; they are much more partial to a worship conducted through images and symbols. For this reason the Israelites were always falling into idolatry; idolatry led to immorality; and both drew down on them the judgments of their offended God.

The Mode of Divine Teaching.—Speaking generally, the period of the Judges was remarkable for this, that God taught the nation *by events*. Till Samuel, there was no series of inspired prophets conveying the divine lessons either by word of mouth or through written treatises. The lessons of the nation were communicated by means of facts. Disaster following idolatry, and prosperity coming after the surrender of idols, were never far from their experience. They were taught most impressively that the way of transgressors is hard, but that the fear of God is the highway to blessing.

SECTION III.—ILLUSTRATIVE MEMOIRS.

1. Story of Micah—2. Emigration of the Danites—3. Tragedy of Gibeah—
4. Story of Ruth.

At the close of the Book of Judges several interesting narratives occur, giving us glimpses of the state of religion, of morals, and of manners in general, during this period of Jewish history.

1. **Story of Micah.**—This story illustrates the way in which irregularities in worship sprang up. Micah was a young Ephraimite, who had a liking for religious ceremonies, without inward reverence for God, and, as his mode of getting hold of his mother's property shows, without much honesty in secular

matters. His religion was designed rather to bring credit to himself than honour to God. He set up a small establishment in his own house, consisting of a graven and a molten image, teraphim, or small images, and an ephod : at first he consecrated one of his sons as priest, but afterwards he hired a Levite for that office. Soon after being set up, this establishment was violently seized by a colony of Danite emigrants, and was carried to their city in the extreme north of the country. It remained there for a long time, as a sort of rival to the tabernacle establishment at Shiloh. It was at this place that king Jeroboam afterwards set up one of his calves. Among the northern tribes it was doubtless productive of a great amount of evil.

2. **Emigration of the Danites.**—Another narrative gives us a picture of steps that were once taken when the territory of a tribe was found to be too small for them. Part of the tribe of Dan finding themselves in this position, in consequence of their failing to drive out the Philistines, sent spies to search out the country, and to endeavour to find somewhere a suitable settlement. In the extreme north, among the roots of Mount Hermon, they found a spot inhabited by a peaceful tribe of Zidonians or Phœnicians, whose lands they seized, cruelly murdering the people. The proceeding was alike godless and lawless; for it was this colony that carried with them the schismatical establishment of Micah. The town which they built, and which they called Dan, after the founder of their tribe, became famous as the northern boundary of the country.

3. **Tragedy of Gibeah.**—A third narrative gives us a shocking picture of the brutal state of morals which sometimes prevailed, probably under the influence of an idolatrous apostasy; and of the reckless and awful retribution to which, when a great crime had been committed, their excited passions drove the people. The wife of a Levite, travelling from Beth-lehem to Mount Ephraim, had been savagely abused and murdered in Gibeah, a town of Benjamin. The tribe of Benjamin having refused to surrender the guilty persons, a vast concourse of the other tribes fell upon them with such fury that the whole tribe was exterminated, with the exception of some six hundred men.

The furious impulse that had urged them to this deed of vengeance being spent, the tribes were filled with distress at the wretched result. To provide wives for the six hundred Benjamites, four hundred girls were brought from Jabesh-gilead, the other inhabitants of which were massacred; and on these proving insufficient, a trick was resorted to, and the remaining Benjamites, pouncing on the daughters of Shiloh at a festival time, carried them off, much in the same way as the Romans carried off the Sabine women. Thereafter the tribe of Benjamin was allowed slowly to regain its former place. Phinehas, Aaron's grandson, was high priest at the time of this occurrence (Judges xx. 28), so that it must have happened not very long after the people entered the land.

4. **Story of Ruth.**—In delightful contrast to this blood-stained scene are the sweet pictures of the Book of Ruth. Naomi, a Hebrew matron, goes to the land of Moab in a time of famine; there she loses her husband and her two sons, but gains the attachment of the two Moabite young women whom they had married, one of whom, Ruth, a pattern of filial piety, returns with her to her own country. Ruth attracts the notice of Boaz, a man of wealth and property in Beth-lehem, a relation of her husband's family, who ultimately makes her his wife. Nothing can be more beautiful than the simple, happy, and godly life which the Book of Ruth unfolds. True religion is there seen sweetening the intercourse of rich and poor, lightening the burdens of labour and poverty, and cheering the hearts of the afflicted. This beautiful story had Beth-lehem for its scene, and may perhaps be regarded as a sort of type and picture of the effects of that benign religion with which, thirteen hundred years after, the divine babe of Beth-lehem was to bless the world. The story of Ruth illustrates many of the Jewish habits of this period. We have in it a lively picture of a Jewish harvest—that happy season of exhilaration and charitable distribution, when rich and poor met together and acknowledged the Lord, the maker of them all. We have also illustrations of the land system of the Jews,—the mode of transferring property from one person to another; and also of the manner

in which the rights of down-broken families were maintained, and their property was ultimately restored. And we see also—what is exceedingly interesting—how, occasionally at least, members of other nations were brought to know and love the God of the Hebrews. Israel was becoming, in some instances, "a light to lighten the Gentiles." Amid the abounding instances of Hebrews perverted to worship the gods of Moab and other idols, it is delightful to find even one such case as that of Ruth, the young Moabite widow, whose heart had been completely won by the loving and godly spirit of Naomi, and who so simply, yet beautifully, expressed her deepest feelings to her mother-in-law: "Thy people shall be my people, and thy God my God." The high honour of being a progenitor of the Messiah rewarded the faith of this simple-minded young woman. We may hope that not a few of the other neighbours of Israel were filled with the spirit of Ruth, and, seeing the surpassing grace and glory of the God of Israel, were led to give unto the LORD the glory due to his name.

SECTION IV.—HISTORY OF OTHER NATIONS.

1. Egypt—Material glory—Colonization—2. Assyria, Babylonia, Elam, &c.—Frequent conflicts—3. The Phœnicians—Commercial progress—4. Greece—Early inhabitants—The heroic age—The siege of Troy—Greek prodigies and Hebrew miracles—Religion of Greece—Its want of power.

We have now to glance at the other parts of the world, and to gather up the leading events, so far as they are known, that happened after the departure of the Israelites from Egypt. We have still to grope our way amid much darkness, though rays of light from the monuments fall here and there.

1. *Egypt.*

Material Glory.—Egypt itself seems to have recovered, ere long, from the terrible catastrophe of the Red Sea. For several centuries after the Exodus, that kingdom enjoyed an extraordinary measure of prosperity. "Egypt rose up like a flood, and his waters were moved like the rivers; he said, I will go up, I will cover the earth; I will destroy the city and the inhabitants thereof." The priests continued, for the most part, to enjoy their former influence. Everywhere the most magnificent temples, tombs, palaces, obelisks, statues, sphinxes, and other works of art, were executed during this period. The plain of Thebes was adorned with some of its most wonderful buildings. In point of material glory, Egypt sat as a queen, with no one as yet to dispute her wonderful pre-eminence.

Colonization.—In another species of glory Egypt at this time was not wanting. Colonies were leaving her shores from time to time, to carry her civilization to other climes; and illustrious strangers were attracted to her capital in search of the wisdom and the learning for which she was so renowned. Tradition, at least, used to say that about fifteen hundred and fifty years before Christ, Cecrops headed a colony from Sais, that settled in Attica, and founded Athens; and that about half a century later, another Egyptian, Danaus, proceeded in the same direction, and laid the foundation of Argos.

2. *Assyria, Babylonia, Elam, &c.*

Frequent Conflicts.—We have very little exact knowledge of the progress of these kingdoms during this period. The Assyrians were a growing power, and were extending their dominions in many directions. They had several collisions with the Babylonians, over whom they generally had the advantage. The Elamites, a restless people, also invaded Babylonia from time to time. In the early part of the period, Chushan-rishathaim, king of Mesopotamia, ravaged Syria and Palestine: he is called by Josephus an Assyrian, but probably in a general sense, as his kingdom appears to have been separate from Assyria, though afterwards absorbed by it. The kings of Egypt and Assyria, who were afterwards to be so deadly enemies, were beginning to look one another in the face. With the conquests of the Assyrians, the idolatry which they fostered must have spread further and further, and the remains of a purer worship among the Shemitic nations of Asia would mostly be scattered to the winds.

3. *Phœnicia.*

Commercial Progress.—The Phœnicians appear to have advanced steadily in their commercial career. Tyre, founded by a colony from Sidon, which it soon eclipsed in glory, was built during this period. It used to be thought that Sanchoniatho, or Sanchuniathon, a Phœnician historian, was a contemporary of Joshua. Only a few fragments of his History have come down to us, preserved by a Greek writer—Eusebius. They give an account of the genealogy of the Phœnician gods—of Cœlus and of Saturn, and other deities, afterwards adopted by the Greeks—and of the cosmogony or origin of the world; accounts which Sanchoniatho says he collected from the most ancient historical monuments. But many scholars are disposed to deny the authenticity of the History ascribed to him, and to hold that it was really composed by Philon, who issued a so-called translation of it in Greek in the end of the first century.

4. *Greece.*

Early Inhabitants.—Of all the countries that begin during this period to loom in the horizon of history, the most interesting is Greece. The situation of Greece, and its physical features, marked it out from the beginning as a remarkable land. It juts into the sea, so as to command easy access by sea to three great continents, Europe, Asia, and Africa. It is remarkable for the extraordinary extent of its sea-board, being pierced in every direction by gulfs, bays, and creeks, which invited the settlement of adventurers, and encouraged those enterprises of which its early history was full. Nothing is known with certainty of its earliest inhabitants. The Titans may have been a gigantic race, allied perhaps to the Emim, Horim, and Anakim races of early Palestine; but their history is wrapped in fable. It is common to trace the more civilized inhabitants of Greece to foreign colonies, of which the chief were those of Cecrops and Danaus from Egypt, already mentioned; that of Cadmus from Phœnicia; and that of Pelops from Asia Minor. Yet here also doubt and uncertainty prevail.

The Heroic Age.—But there is no doubt that about 1400 B.C., while the judges were ruling Israel, there appeared in Greece a very remarkable people,—the Hellenes, from whom the country was called Hellas. They were a people of extraordinary energy and spirit, devoted to war and conquest, to adventure and discovery; yet with a wonderful capacity for education; fond, too, of the arts and the pleasures of peace, and ready to bear the restraints of religion and of social order. It was not long ere their stirring spirit spread itself through the other races of the country. For about two hundred years Greece was filled with their exploits and adventures. They furnished the great mine from which the Greek poets drew their materials. The fables of this period tell of Bellerophon mounting on the winged horse Pegasus, and killing the monster Chimaera; of Hercules fighting with lions, boars, and hydras, capturing bulls and stags, rending rocks, and releasing tormented heroes from the infernal regions; of Theseus slaying the Minotaur in the labyrinth of Crete, and overcoming the Amazons; of Jason sailing on the Argonautic expedition, with all the heroes of the age, from Thessaly to Colchis on the shores of the Euxine, to fetch the golden fleece, and gaining possession of it through the magic powers of Medea. All this is so enveloped in fabulous exaggeration, that historians are unable to reduce it to authentic narrative. It exemplifies the true conditions under which fabulous mythologies are formed. They originate before the era of history, in the childhood of nations, before the critical or the sceptical, or even the historical spirit has arisen; they are shadowy and vague as to times and places; they have a weird, unearthly character, as if the events belonged neither to earth nor to heaven, but to some intermediate reigion; they are obviously the offspring of the imagination. Instead of furnishing an analogy, they form a contrast to the miracles of Scripture, which originated under conditions in almost every respect the reverse of these.

The Siege of Troy.—About the end of the heroic age the gray dawn begins to creep over Grecian history, and reveals its numerous tribes assembled in Asia Minor before the walls of Troy.

Troy was a flourishing State on the Asiatic side of the Archipelago, founded probably by some body of Grecian conquerors or emigrants. One of the wild adventures of the time—according to the story, the abduction of Helen, a beautiful princess of Greece, by Paris, son of Priam king of Troy—furnished the occasion of a siege far less remarkable in itself than as calling forth, at an after period, the unrivalled powers of Homer, in his great epic poem the "Iliad." If the fall of Troy happened, as is supposed, about 1184 B.C., it would be contemporary with the age of Eli and Samson; and thus, while the house of Priam was approaching its downfall through the lawlessness of Paris, that of Eli was hastening to its end through the profligacy of Hophni and Phinehas; and the aged king of Troy may have breathed his last, amid the blazing ruins of his capital, at the time when Eli was prostrated by the loss of the ark, and when the great judge, whom a woman had betrayed and ruined, was performing his last achievement against the Philistines.

Greek Prodigies and Hebrew Miracles.—Some writers, not acknowledging the divine authority of the Old Testament Scriptures, have alleged that the miracles and prodigies recorded in them—the marvellous feats of Samson, for example—are to be classed with the fables with which the Greek writers used to adorn the heroic age of their history. But the differences between the two are very great. The minute, matter-of-fact style of the Hebrew narrative is a great contrast to the poetical, fabulous air of the legends of Greece. The fables of Greece have no close or vital relation to the history of the country; whereas the Hebrew history becomes unintelligible and even impossible apart from the miracles: the marvels of Greece had no adequate object to call them forth; whereas the Hebrew miracles were wrought in support of the only revelation of pure religion that existed in the world: the Grecian prodigies developed no qualities of the highest order in those who were said to have performed them; whereas the Hebrew miracles uniformly called into vigorous operation faith in the unseen God: the Grecian prodigies always redounded to the glory of Greece and its heroes; whereas those of the

Hebrews redounded to God's glory,—often, indeed, covering the people themselves with shame, in consequence of their unbelief. It is undeniable, too, that the Hebrews observed certain rites—such as the Passover—throughout their whole history, that could not have been instituted had not the marvels which they commemorated actually happened. Moreover, the New Testament fully attests the miracles of the Old, and dwells with peculiar admiration on the exploits "of Gedeon, and of Barak, and of Samson, and of Jephthae; of David also, and Samuel, and of the prophets: who THROUGH FAITH subdued kingdoms, wrought righteousness, obtained promises, stopped the mouths of lions, quenched the violence of fire, escaped the edge of the sword, out of weakness were made strong, waxed valiant in fight, turned to flight the armies of the aliens."

Religion of Greece.—The rise of so vigorous a people as the Greeks betokened a great change for the world. So active an element of life could not be thrown in among the nations without producing a great fermentation. In matters of taste and intellect, in philosophy, in the science of government, in the constitution, the laws, and the liberties of states, the Greeks taught the world many important lessons. But in religion they only adorned and made more dangerous the idolatry of Egypt and Babylon. The lively genius of the people made the mythology much more sprightly and interesting; but it was the same in principle, and often in detail. One important difference there was in the religious system of the Greeks, and afterwards of the Romans, as compared with the Eastern systems—the absence of a great priestly caste or class, exercising a predominant influence on the affairs of the nation.

Its Want of Power.—The rise and progress, and we may say culmination, of Greek culture about this time, seem to show that it was God's design to test its power under the most favourable conditions for elevating and blessing mankind. If this Greek culture had proved a gospel—if it had proved sufficient to purify, elevate, and bless humanity, or to supply a power tending to this result—no other gospel would have been needed. But Greek culture proved to be no gospel. It left the moral sores of humanity unhealed. It made no contribution to the cause of pure religion. It was as necessary as ever that the pure faith and worship of Judæa should be watched and fostered with unremitting care. The hills of Palestine were still the only soil where the true vine lived and grew: had it languished and died there, the tree of life must have disappeared from the world, and the sterility of the desert prevailed unbroken on every side.

CHAPTER IX.

THE UNITED KINGDOM—SAUL, DAVID, SOLOMON.

FROM THE ACCESSION OF SAUL TO THE DEATH OF SOLOMON.

1 Sam. x.-xxxi.; 2 Sam.; 1 Kings i.-xi.; 1 Chron. x.-xxix.; 2 Chron. i.-ix.

SECTION I.—REIGN OF SAUL.

Demand for a king: choice of Saul—His career—Samuel at Ramah—Saul's great campaigns—Against the Ammonites: Jabesh-gilead—Against the Philistines: Michmash—Third campaign—Against the Amalekites: Southern Desert—Anointing of David—Against the Philistines: Goliath—Against David—Against the Philistines: the Witch of Endor—Mount Gilboa—Saul's character.

Demand for a King: Choice of Saul.—The Israelites at length became tired of the government of the Judges, and wished to be like other nations, and to have a king of their own. Perhaps they thought that a king would be able to heal the increasing jealousies of the different tribes, and to induce them to draw comfortably together; or perhaps, under the impulse of that love of show which is so common in the East, they desired to have among them somewhat of the pomp and splendour of a court. Egypt on the one hand and Assyria on the other, to say nothing of the courts at Damascus, Carchemish, and other seats of royalty, probably excited their emulation. The request appeared to Samuel to involve, not only ingratitude to himself, but also disrespect to their heavenly King, and want of confidence in Him: nevertheless, by God's direction, it was not refused. The people were distinctly warned that they should have to bear many sacrifices and inconveniences in connection with this new arrangement: it would be very far from an unmingled comfort. The lot was employed, as on other solemn occasions, to discover the man on whose head God wished them to place their crown. It fell upon SAUL, the son of Kish, a man of Benjamin, whom Samuel had already designated privately for the office at Ramah. After the election, Samuel, as a means of promoting fidelity to the king of Israel, wrote the manner of the kingdom in a book and laid it up before the Lord.

His Career.—Saul was a young man of king-like figure and appearance, brave and energetic, and, at first, modest and master of himself. At the beginning of his reign he was much impressed with the solemn charges addressed to him by Samuel, to rule the kingdom for God, and in accordance with his laws and will. But the principles instilled by Samuel never took root in his heart, so as to become inbred motives of action; and by-and-by, as always happens in such cases, they were disregarded, and his own wishes and passions became the springs of his conduct. Though he had the name and the status of king, Saul in reality was little more than a military chieftain, who made successful wars upon his enemies, but did little or nothing for the internal improvement of the country. He was a member of the tribe of Benjamin, which had sunk to great insignificance in consequence of the dreadful slaughter that followed the enormity at Gibeah; and for this reason, perhaps, he was at first treated with contempt by many. There was some advantage, however, in his belonging to this small tribe. The tribe of Judah was now beginning to be a rival to that of Ephraim; and a king chosen at this time from either of these would have been sure to excite the bitter opposition of the other. Saul selected as his capital and residence the town of Gibeah in Benjamin—the scene of the tragedy of the Levite's concubine, and of the terrible siege which followed. It was situated on a lofty and isolated hill (now called Tuleil-el-Fûl, or "Hill of Beans"), about six miles north of Jerusalem, and commanded an extensive view in all directions, especially to the east. The remains of a large square tower are now almost the only memorial of the spot.

Samuel at Ramah.—After Saul became king, Samuel seems

to have continued to exercise at Ramah some of his former functions as judge; but probably he devoted himself chiefly to settling quarrels, promoting godliness, and training the young. His "schools of the prophets" were evidently very important and much blessed institutions. Young men, chiefly Levites, were trained in these schools to explain the law of God to the people, and to enforce its claims. An intense glow of devotional feeling seems to have prevailed in them, so warm, that whoever came within reach was for a time inspired with its fervour. Though Samuel was not able to recover the whole nation to sincere, inward piety, he was the instrument of doing much good to individuals, and of bringing the mass of the people to at least outward conformity to the law of God.

Saul's Great Campaigns.—The principal military achievements of Saul were seven:—1. Against the Ammonites at Jabesh-gilead; 2. Against the Philistines at Michmash; 3. Various campaigns against Moab, Edom, Zobah, and other places; 4. Against the Amalekites; 5. Against the Philistines, under the championship of Goliath; 6. Against David; and 7. The last campaign against the Philistines, when he fell on Mount Gilboa, near the plain of Esdraelon.

1. *Campaign against the Ammonites.*

Jabesh-gilead.—In his first campaign Saul showed extraordinary vigour and courage. Jabesh-gilead, lying across the Jordan, sixty or seventy miles from Gibeah, was beleaguered by the Ammonites, and its people were cruelly threatened with the loss of their right eyes, if the place were not relieved within a week. Tidings of the crisis were brought to Saul and to the people; but, considering the distance of the place, the power of the enemy, and the shortness of the respite, the case was regarded as desperate by every one but himself. Full of spirit and energy, he sent messengers throughout the country, appointed a muster of the people at Bezek (a place probably high up the Jordan valley), organized a powerful army, and within the stipulated week fell unexpectedly on the Ammonites, and so completely routed and ruined their army, that no two of them were left together. The renown of this wonderful victory tended greatly to strengthen his throne. Samuel took advantage of the occasion to summon the people to Gilgal, where they renewed the kingdom, and where he gave them a most solemn and touching charge to continue loyal to their heavenly King.

2. *Campaign against the Philistines.*

Michmash.—In Saul's next campaign his chivalrous son Jonathan bore the chief renown. Indeed, at the beginning of it, Saul was guilty of an act of high disobedience to the authority of God, in assuming the function of priest, and in offering sacrifices at his own hand instead of waiting for Samuel. This drew from Samuel the announcement that God was to give the kingdom to another. The Philistines had crossed the central ridge of Palestine, and had formed a garrison at the passage or pass of Michmash, in the neighbourhood of Gibeah. Michmash was a highly important place: it commanded one of the great passes from the Jordan valley to the heart of the country. A ravine separated " the utmost part of Gibeah," where Saul and Jonathan were,[*] from Michmash; but at one spot, the opposite ridges of the ravine were almost joined by two bold crags, that stretched towards each other from either side. The crag on the Michmash side seems to have been guarded as an outpost by a few Philistines, whom Jonathan and a single attendant formed the bold design of surprising. Climbing up the face of the cliff, they got upon the top, and fell upon its defenders, who, though they knew of their presence, little dreamed of being assaulted by a couple of Hebrews. About twenty were slain. The dying shrieks of these men, and perhaps the headlong flight of others, along with an earthquake, caused a panic in the principal garrison, at a little distance, who fell to slaying one another. From the height of Gibeah, which, as has been said, commanded an extensive view, this was observed by the Hebrew watchmen. The Hebrews immediately gave pursuit to the terrified Philistines, chased them from Michmash to Beth-aven, and down the western

[*] The name of the place near which Jonathan made his attempt was *Geba*, as in 1 Sam. xiii. 3; incorrectly rendered *Gibeah* in 1 Sam. xiv. 5. Geba was two or three miles north of Gibeah.

passes into the valley of Ajalon, whither Joshua had chased the Canaanites on the memorable day when the sun stood still. At the end of the day, the rash and hasty temper of Saul showed itself very offensively, by his proposing, for an act of disobedience, to put to death his son Jonathan, the hero of the day; but the people, delighted with his exploit, rescued him from his father's ill-timed severity.

3. *Third Campaign.*

Of Saul's wars with Moab, Ammon, Edom, and Zobah, no particulars are recorded. (1 Sam. xiv. 47.)

4. *Campaign against the Amalekites.*

Southern Desert.—But his next campaign, that against the Amalekites, was in one respect a very unhappy one. Pursuing these tribes far into the southern desert, almost to the borders of Egypt, he had an opportunity of so destroying both them and their property as to fulfil the old prophetic doom denounced against them in the time of Moses. But the command of God was openly violated. He spared all the valuable property of the Amalekites, and reserved it to himself and his people. When Samuel met him at Gilgal, he made false apologies for his conduct. Another and more solemn announcement from the Lord that he had forfeited the kingdom met his unworthy excuses.

Anointing of David.—It was now that Samuel was instructed to anoint another as king in room of Saul. He was directed to go to Beth-lehem, with a horn of oil, and with a heifer for a sacrifice, and to anoint a son of Jesse the Beth-lehemite. In compliance with his instructions, he passed over the first seven of Jesse's sons and anointed the eighth, who was a mere lad engaged in keeping sheep. It would seem that soon after this David, becoming known for his skill on the harp, became Saul's minstrel, and soothed his violent temper by means of its gentle strains.

5. *Campaign against the Philistines.*

Goliath.—All his life Saul had war with the Philistines (1 Sam. xiv. 52). On occasion of one of their invasions, they had for their champion Goliath, a man of gigantic stature. Goliath marched to and fro in front of the Israelites, defying their armies, and demanding an antagonist to fight with in single combat. It was now that David came prominently forward. Sent by his father to inquire after the welfare of his three brothers, who were serving in the army, he heard of the challenge of Goliath, and offered to accept it. Refusing Saul's armour, he desired to fight in simple reliance on the God of Israel, who had already enabled him to conquer savage beasts which attacked his sheep, and who would doubtless strengthen him against an uncircumcised Philistine. Advancing in simple faith against the Philistine, he slung a stone against his forehead, and having brought him to the ground, he cut off his head, and spread consternation through the Philistine host. He was greatly honoured by the king, and became a member of his household.

6. *Campaign against David.*

The history of this part of Saul's reign may be better given under the life of David. Saul's one object was to kill David; but, through the mercy of God, David was time after time delivered from his hands.

7. *Last Campaign against the Philistines.*

The Witch of En-dor.—Saul's last encounter with the Philistines brought the Israelites and their foes face to face once more, on the blood-stained plain of Esdraelon. The Philistines, advancing along the sea-shore, had struck into the plain, and were encamped at Shunem. Behind them, to the north, were the slopes of Little Hermon; while in front, separated by a valley three or four miles broad, lay the heights of Gilboa, occupied by the troops of Saul. The night before the battle, the terrified king of Israel stole along, behind Little Hermon, to En-dor, a place lying half-way between that hill and Mount Tabor, and there had his celebrated interview with the witch. Though he had tried to exterminate the whole race of soothsayers and wizards, he had no resource now but to go to a woman with a familiar spirit, and to ask her to call up the spirit of Samuel, who had been some time dead. His account of himself to Samuel is a vivid picture of the effects of forsaking God. "I am sore distressed; for the Philistines make war against me, and God is departed from me, and answereth me no more, neither by prophets, nor by dreams." Samuel could only foretell his coming defeat and death.

Mount Gilboa.—Next morning the battle began. The Israelites were completely routed. Trying to escape across the heights of Gilboa into the Jordan valley, great numbers of them were slain. Saul and three of his sons were among the dead. When the Philistines found their bodies, they fastened them to the wall of Beth-shan, a town in the valley of the Jordan, near to which they had fallen. Hearing of this, the men of Jabesh-gilead, on the other side of the river, acted a noble part. The panic had spread to their side of the Jordan, and the people there were deserting their cities before the victorious Philistines. Mindful of what Saul had done for them at the beginning of his reign, the men of Jabesh fearlessly crossed the Jordan, travelled all night to Beth-shan, recovered the bodies of the king and his sons, carried them to Jabesh, and buried their bones with customary honours.

Saul's Character.—Thus ended the reign of Saul, which is believed to have lasted forty years. His miserable death was a fearful but faithful commentary on his life. He was pre-eminently marked by the great defects of the Hebrew character generally,—impulsiveness and self-will. As long as he was forming his position, or acquiring influence in the community, he kept his heart in subjection, and acted with modesty and propriety. But when his power was firmly established, he placed no check on his impulsive and wayward nature. His desires at last acquired a frightful, tyrannical influence, that nothing could subdue. The laws of God and the rights of man were alike disregarded in the wild excitement of his self-will. Even his self-respect was completely set at nought, when he applied for counsel to a member of a class which he had tried to exterminate as a nuisance. Occasionally he was visited by impulses of a generous kind, but they were not to be relied on. As he systematically resisted the Spirit of God, he was at length left to the fruit of his own ways, and his death exemplified frightfully the misery of such a situation. The generous, noble, self-denying character of his son Jonathan, the friend of David, one of the most beautiful in all Bible history, forms a fine contrast to the selfish impulsiveness of the later years of Saul.

SECTION II.—EARLY LIFE OF DAVID.

His tribe—His family—His birth-place—His era and education—His appearance and character - Epochs of his life—Anointed by Samuel—Minstrel and armour-bearer to Saul—Conflict with Goliath—His schools of discipline—Saul's jealousy of David—Attempts on his life—The friendship of Jonathan—At Nob—At Gath—In the Cave of Adullam: at Mizpeh—In the Wilderness of Judah—In the Wilderness of Ziph—At Maon—At En-gedi: he spares Saul—At Carmel—At Hachilah: spares Saul a second time—Among the Philistines again—Death of Saul and Jonathan Lessons and Psalms of this period—King of Judah—His first act—The civil war: King of Israel—Capture of Jerusalem—Situation of Jerusalem; its hills—Mount Zion—View from the Mount of Olives.

The reign of DAVID was beyond question the brightest era in the history of Israel, and David himself was perhaps the most remarkable of the great and good men of Old Testament times. Like Abraham and Moses, he marks a new era in the history. His life is recorded in Scripture with great fulness, and the interests and lessons connected with it are singularly rich and varied.

His Tribe.—The new king of Israel was a member of the tribe of Judah, in many ways the leading tribe of the twelve. Its traditions were of a remarkable order. Its founder, Judah, had fallen sadly, as David was to fall after him, through unrestrained lust, but had afterwards shown a noble spirit of self-sacrifice in being willing to become the slave of the governor of Egypt in order that his brother Benjamin might be restored to his father (Gen. xliv. 18-34). Caleb, too, the representative of Judah among the spies, had shown a spirit not less noble in resisting the weak counsels of his brethren, and in calling the people to advance against the Canaanites in simple reliance on the promises of God (Num. xiii., xiv.). Othniel, the son of Kenaz, younger brother of Caleb, was the foremost of his day in valour and chivalry, gaining his wife, Achsah, by the taking of Kirjath-sepher (Judges i. 12, 13). Traditions such as these were well fitted to inspire a young heart with noble aims.

His Family.—The family of Jesse, David's father, evidently held a place of importance in his tribe (1 Chron. ii. 10). He was an old man when his son became famous (1 Sam. xvii. 12), but he lived for some time afterwards; for when David was in trouble, he committed his father and his mother to the protection of the king of Moab (1 Sam. xxii. 3). Jesse was the grandson of Boaz and Ruth, and probably inherited their property, or part of it. His name is embalmed in Holy Writ, leading us to believe that he was a holy man—"There shall come forth a rod out of the stem of Jesse, and a Branch shall grow out of his roots." The kindly and fatherly disposition of Boaz, and the holy devotion and warm attachment of Ruth, were very apparent in the character of their great-grandson.

His Birth-place.—Beth-lehem was situated six miles to the south of Jerusalem, and about twice that distance to the north of Hebron. The present town is built on the slope of a long gray ridge, with one deep valley in front and another behind, which unite at no great distance, and run eastward towards the Dead Sea. Of the place where both David and Jesus were born it may well be said, "What a mighty influence for good has gone forth from this little spot upon the human race, both for time and for eternity!"

His Era and Education.—The birth of David is supposed to have occurred B.C. 1080, about one hundred years later than the date commonly assigned to the Trojan War. Samson, one of the latest of the Jewish heroes, had died but forty years before, so that the memory of his exploits would still be fresh in people's minds. The profligacy of morals which had prevailed under Eli had been succeeded by the revival under Samuel. Ramah, Samuel's head-quarters, was but a few miles from Beth-lehem, and the whole neighbourhood seems to have been under the influence of his holy character and teaching. From a very early period, David must have been influenced by the fear and the love of God. When introduced to our notice, he is the shepherd of the family. This quiet occupation was adapted to foster that habit of meditation and that love of nature which became so remarkable in him. In the absence of other companions, he would find a companion in his harp, on which he became an early proficient; and fellowship of a much higher kind in God his Father, from communion with whom he learned so early to derive both strength and joy. One of his earliest exploits was to slay a lion and a bear that came upon his flock, and in this encounter he was guided by that simple trust in God which shone so wonderfully in his after-life.

His Appearance and Character. — His comely appearance, ruddy complexion, and beauty of eyes (1 Sam. xvi. 12, *marg.*), are specified on his first introduction, and many things indicate that there was a charm about him,—a simplicity, an openness, and a warmth of nature,—that won all hearts (1 Sam. xviii. 1, 7, 20; 2 Sam. xix. 14). In his more mature character, he appeared to unite in himself the high qualities of nearly all who had gone before him. The heavenly conversation of Enoch; the triumphant faith of Abraham; the meditative thoughtfulness of Isaac; the wrestling boldness of Jacob; the patient endurance of Joseph, no less than his talent for administering a kingdom; the lofty patriotism of Moses, as well as his brilliant fancy; the warlike skill and energy of Joshua; the daring courage of Gideon; the holy fervour of Samuel, all met in measure in the character of David. A great king, a great warrior, a great poet, a great religious reformer, he held at once four of the great sceptres that rule the hearts of men. He was among the most eminent of the Old Testament types of Christ; and this likeness impressed the popular mind, for after him the Messiah was spoken of as the Son of David, a term denoting not merely natural descent, but also resemblance of character. (Matt. xv. 22, xx. 30, &c.)

Epochs of his Life.—The life of David divides into five parts, represented by the different places where they were spent: (1) his shepherd life at Beth-lehem; (2) his courtier life in Saul's court at Gibeah; (3) his outlaw life in the wilderness of Judah, and among the Philistines; (4) his royal life at Hebron as king of Judah; (5) his royal life at Jerusalem as king of the whole nation.

Epoch I.—His Shepherd Life.

Anointed by Samuel.—The noble fidelity with which David discharged the duty of shepherd is apparent from the incident of the lion and the bear. Possibly it was not long after this that Samuel was sent to anoint him king. As the prophet passed along, and looked on the fields that had belonged to Boaz and Ruth, we may readily fancy him thinking what a blessing was in store for the country if their pious and amiable spirit should reappear in its future king. Yet even Samuel forgot that it is not majesty of form but purity of character that constitutes, in the eyes of God, fitness for a high office; and in his admiration of Eliab, Jesse's first-born, he had to be reminded that "man looketh on the outward appearance, but the Lord looketh on the heart" (1 Sam. xvi. 6, 7). It was certainly not by chance that, when the holy oil was poured on David's head, he wore the shepherd's dress, and probably had in his hand the shepherd's staff. His earlier employment as shepherd had a direct connection with his later employment as king. The ruler after God's own heart was one who would rule like the good shepherd, seeking the good of the flock, and ready to encounter trouble and peril for their sake. In the Seventy-eighth Psalm we read: "He chose David also his servant, and took him from the sheepfolds: from following the ewes great with young he brought him to feed Jacob his people, and Israel his inheritance. So he fed them according to the integrity of his heart; and guided them by the skilfulness of his hands."

Minstrel and Armour-Bearer to Saul.—The fame of David as a harper procured for him the office, first of minstrel, and then of armour-bearer to king Saul (1 Sam. xvi. 21, 23). The office of armour-bearer seems to have been honorary, not involving more than the obligation to give personal attendance on Saul when required.

Conflict with Goliath.—After this came the conflict with Goliath. David seems to have returned home, after serving for a time as Saul's minstrel; and in passing from a boy to a young man, he is believed to have undergone a change of appearance which prevented his being recognized by Saul as his former armour-bearer. This first of David's fights was also the most memorable. In the whole circumstances we notice—1. His filial obedience to his father's wishes, though he was sent to the army merely to serve his elder brothers. 2. His self-control and meekness under the gibes of Eliab. 3. What in his view was the head and front of Goliath's offending—his defying God by defying His army. 4. The unfaltering courage and faith that made him offer to fight with the Philistine, though to the eye of sight this was only to rush into the jaws of death. 5. The modesty and simplicity of faith with which he vindicated his offer. 6. The decision with which he put aside the untried and unsuitable armour pressed on him by the king. 7. His majestic assertion before the Philistine of the claims and prerogatives of the God of Israel. 8. The perfect coolness and absolute success of his method of attack. Doubtless he was well skilled in the use of the sling, not counting that he could use it rightly till he could use it perfectly. To achieve a great result by simple means is usually the mark of great genius: in this case it was the mark of great genius and great faith combined. In reward for this great achievement, David was now entitled to be the king's son-in-law (1 Sam. xvii. 25).

His Schools of Discipline.—But rapid though his promotion had been, it was destined to receive a painful check. He had to pass through an epoch of great trial before he became king. God saw cause to pass him through a series of schools of discipline in order to complete his education for the throne: first the school of shepherd life, training him to faithful service and devout contemplation; then the school of courtier life, familiarizing him with the routine of courts and the habits of royalty; and then the school of Arab life in the desert, bringing him into contact with the actual materials which his life was to be spent in governing.

We have no conclusive proof that any of his psalms were written during this period. Some think that the Twenty-third belongs to the epoch of the shepherd life; but when we find David speaking of his enemies, and looking forward to his death, we are led to believe that it belongs to a later time.

Epoch II.—His Courtier Life at Gibeah.

Saul's Jealousy of David.—The jealousy of Saul sprang up almost immediately after the encounter with Goliath. The songs of the daughters of Israel, ascribing more honour to David than to Saul, poisoned his heart. He delays to fulfil his promise to give him his daughter in marriage. He sends David forth on dangerous enterprises (as David afterwards sent out Uriah). He gives him his daughter Michal to wife, in order that he might have him more thoroughly in his power. But David enjoyed the protection of an invisible shield; and the reason was the same as in the case of Joseph: "he behaved himself wisely in all his ways; and the Lord was with him" (1 Sam. xviii. 14).

Attempts on his Life.—At least five attempts were made by Saul to kill David while connected with his court. 1. He spoke to Jonathan his son, and to all his servants, that they should kill David (1 Sam. xix. 1). 2. In his house he launched a javelin at his head (xix. 10). 3. He sent to David's house (when David had fled) bidding them send him up on his sickbed (xix. 15). 4. He sent messengers to Ramah to seize him, but when there they were filled with the Spirit (xix. 20). 5. He went to Ramah himself, and for the time experienced the same singular change (xix. 23, 24). Once more he stormed against his son Jonathan for his attachment to David, flinging a javelin at him in the fierceness of his rage (xx. 33). It is interesting to study the variety of ways in which David was delivered from all these dangers. The Fifty-ninth Psalm bears to have been written at this time.

The Friendship of Jonathan.—The greatest human solace that David enjoyed during these trials was the friendship of Jonathan. It was not only a friendship of the warmest kind, but it was most disinterested and pure. All that friend could do was done by Jonathan to soften the jealousy of Saul; but in vain. In the firm faith that David was to occupy the throne, Jonathan asked nothing of him except that he would be kind to his kindred when he should come to his kingdom. Before

David finally left Gibeah the two friends had a meeting, at which, in bidding farewell, they could but fall on each other's neck and weep. In classical and other ancient story, the friendships of young men hold a conspicuous place; but nothing purer or nobler of the kind has ever been known than that of David and Jonathan. Besides its tendency to refresh his spirit, it could not but have another effect on David: by showing him how noble a king would have succeeded Saul in ordinary course, it must have stimulated him to seek corresponding virtues (1 Sam. xx.).

Epoch III.—His Outlaw Life.

Obliged to leave Gibeah, David now entered on his outlaw life. Ten points may be noted in his outlaw career (1 Sam. xxi.–xxxi.).

1. **At Nob.**—His first resort was to Nob, a city of the priests, situated probably between Gibeah and Jerusalem, and occupied by the high priest and the tabernacle after the destruction of Shiloh. At Nob, he pretended to the high priest that he had been sent by the king on an expedition, and thus he induced the high priest to help him by giving him the shew-bread and other things; for which act of hospitality the high priest and his brethren were afterwards massacred by Saul. This carnal expedient of David indicates a decline of faith, and prepares us for further declension from the straight path.

2. **At Gath.**—From Nob, he fled westward to Gath, one of the cities of the Philistines, and, indeed, the old residence of Goliath. The servants of king Achish discover who he is, and speak of him to the king, and he is *sore afraid*. This was comparatively a new sensation to David. In a higher state of faith such a feeling would not have been known. It leads him to feign madness, to scrabble on the doors, and to let spittle fall on his beard, till the king drives him away. The Thirty-fourth Psalm bears to have been written at this time.

3. **In the Cave of Adullam: at Mizpeh.**—Leaving Gath, he returns to the tribe of Judah, and takes refuge in the cave of Adullam. Here he is joined by a number of discontented persons, mostly the victims of Saul's oppression, and becomes the captain of a troop. It would seem that faith revived

now, for some psalms full of the spirit of confidence belong to this period. Tradition points out a large cavern in the limestone rock, which has its entrance in the side of steep cliffs, running in by a long, winding, narrow passage, with small chambers or cavities on either side. How many a persecuted saint, of whom the world was not worthy, has praised God, like David, for the shelter of some such dark, miserable hole! From Adullam, he went to Mizpeh of Moab, but the prophet Gad recalled him to his own country. He was allowed, however, to send his parents to the protection of the king of Moab. About this time he heard that Saul had massacred the priests at Nob—an awful manifestation of his fierce, unhallowed rage. Abiathar, who had escaped, came to him; and so did the prophet Gad, who seems to have been next to Samuel in authority as a man of God. The Fifty-second, Fifty-seventh, and the Hundred and forty-second Psalms bear this period as their date.

4. **In the Wilderness of Judah.**—The wilderness of Judah furnishes his next resort. We find him, among other places, at Keilah, which the Philistines were attacking, but from which they were driven by David, who fell on them full of faith, contrary to the remonstrances of his men. Hearing of him in that quarter, Saul advanced to seize him; and learning from God that the ungrateful Keilites would betray him, David had again to flee.

5. **In the Wilderness of Ziph.**—The wilderness of Ziph was his next place of refuge. Here, in a wood, David and Jonathan had an interview; but Saul could not get hold of him.

6. **At Maon.**—Soon after this the Ziphites invite Saul to return, and they undertake to deliver David into his hand. Saul comes, but finds that David and his men have gone to Maon. Saul is disposing his men so as to surround the hill which David occupies, and thus to cut off his retreat. While David is probably wondering from what quarter his deliverance can come, news is brought to Saul that the Philistines have invaded the land, and in hot haste he leaves David and hurries to encounter the greater enemy. The Fifty-fourth Psalm bears to have been written at this time.

7. **At En-gedi: He spares Saul.**—The strongholds at En-gedi furnish his next retreat. En-gedi is a little oasis amid the barren rocks near the Dead Sea, fertilized by a delicious fountain, that made its camphire a fit emblem of the sweetness of the Beloved (Song of Sol. i. 14). Hearing of his being at En-gedi, Saul took three thousand men, determined to secure him. But David disarmed him by a new weapon. Finding him asleep in a cave, David cut off the skirt of his robe, resisting the advice of his followers to avenge himself and put him to death. Going up boldly to Saul, David showed him what had taken place, and appealed to his justice to let him alone. Momentarily touched, Saul promised fairly, and the two parted in peace.

8. **At Carmel.**—The next trouble of David was at Carmel in the south of Judah, where Nabal, a rich farmer, fed his flocks and herds. David and his men had protected them from the Bedouin robbers, who were never far off; but when they asked for an acknowledgment of their service, insolence was the only reply. Exasperated by his rudeness, David was preparing to inflict on Nabal a signal chastisement, when his purpose was arrested by a visit from his wife Abigail, with an ample subsidy. Nabal dying soon afterwards, David married Abigail. It was about this time that the venerable Samuel was gathered to his fathers. A pillar of strength in the land for all that was upright and holy, he could be ill spared by his country in such a time. But his removal might stir up those whom he had instructed and guided to remember their responsibility and follow his steps. The Sixty-third Psalm would seem to have been written now.

9. **At Hachilah: Spares Saul a Second Time.**—Another perfidious attempt to throw him into Saul's hands was made by the Ziphites, in the neighbourhood of the hill Hachilah, which is before Jeshimon. While Saul lay sleeping, David stole down beside him, but sparing his life once more, carried off his spear and cruse of water, and made a new appeal to his justice and generosity. The appeal was replied to with fair words as before, but so as to carry no evidence of sincerity.

10. **Among the Philistines again.**—David's faith failing, he

feels that if he remain longer in Judah, he must fall before Saul; and therefore he goes back to the Philistines, among whom he remains a year and four months. He gives the king to believe that he will be a loyal subject to him. Ziklag, a border city, is assigned to him and his troop; and from it he attacks and plunders the Amalekites and other desert tribes. The Philistines having resolved on a new war with the Hebrews, David is summoned to attend the king. He must have been in great difficulty; but he is sent back, owing to the jealousy of the Philistine nobles. On returning to Ziklag, he finds that in his absence it has been plundered and burned, and that his wives and property have been carried off. The calamity brings David back to the spirit of trust and prayer. He pursues and defeats the enemy, and brings back all that the Amalekites have taken.—In this narrative we may trace in David's mind — (1.) The rising spirit of distrust. (2.) The dissimulation to which it gave rise. (3.) Difficulties. (4.) Chastisement. (5.) The return to the spirit of trust, and happy outlet from abounding troubles. The Fifty-sixth Psalm seems to refer to this time.

Death of Saul and Jonathan.—Saul and three of his sons having been killed by the Philistines, the outlaw life of David comes to an end. He shows his regard for Saul as the Lord's anointed, and for Jonathan as his friend, first by executing a man who had come to tell him that he had killed Saul, and then by composing a beautiful song celebrating Saul and Jonathan as lovely and pleasant in their lives, and in their death as not divided.

Lessons and Psalms of this Period.— The purpose of God in exposing David to so many bitter trials in his youth seems to have been to prevent the evils which sudden elevation to power is apt to breed. It was necessary that he should learn his own weakness, be humbled under a sense of his infirmities, and be trained to entire trust in God even in circumstances of the most trying and threatening kind. The spirit of dependence and prayer had to be exercised and strengthened. It was desirable that he should know more of the people he was going to rule— of the grievances inflicted on them by Saul, and of the way to manage them, and this end was served by his intercourse with the troop that came to him in the wilderness. Both the weakness and the strength of David are brought out in this period : on the one hand, his occasional loss of faith, his tendency to dissimulation, and his impulsiveness (1 Sam. xxv. 34); on the other hand, his noble generosity in sparing Saul, and his habitual spirit of trust and prayer. The psalms composed at this time abundantly exemplify the last feature. We have specified those that bear on their superscription to have been written at this time, but there are many more of similar character.

Epoch IV.—His Royal Life at Hebron.

King of Judah.—At the age of thirty, David is called to the throne by the men of Judah, Hebron being chosen, by divine direction, as the seat of his government. He reigned there for seven years and a half. Hebron was well adapted to be the capital of the southern part of the kingdom. Its upland situation secured it from attack. It abounded in holy associations, recalling many recollections of ancient worth and many victories of early faith. That wide-spreading oak in the suburbs was perhaps the very tree under which Abraham spread his tent, and welcomed the angels. That quiet vale was the scene of Isaac's meditative walk, when he lifted up his eyes to those hills on the north, and saw the camels coming back from Padan-aram. In the side of that ravine was the cave of Machpelah, where the fathers of the nation slept in God. Beside yon brook, where the vine grew in such luxuriance, the spies had cut down the sample branch; and there stood the house of Caleb, the man that followed the Lord so fully. To live in Hebron and not to feel faith quickened to new life, would have indicated a soul dead to every impulse of patriotism and piety.

His First Act.—David's first act, on coming into power, was to send a message of thanks to the men of Jabesh-gilead for having buried Saul and his sons after the fatal battle of Mount Gilboa. Here he showed a generosity entirely opposed to the usual policy of Eastern kings. In general, when a king of a new line obtained the throne, the practice was to show all possible disrespect to the house of his predecessor, and put as many of them as possible to death, lest they should endanger the new dynasty. David's policy was the very opposite of this; and it proceeded from his deep religious convictions, for Saul had been the Lord's anointed.

The Civil War: King of Israel.—Saul's family, however, did not give up the throne without a struggle. Under the auspices of Abner, captain of the host, Ish-bosheth, a son of Saul, had been proclaimed king, and the northern and the eastern tribes accepted him as such. His capital was fixed at a remote but well-protected town, Mahanaim in Gilead—the place where Jacob had met the angels on his way from Padan-aram; but his general, Abner, took military possession of a more central and commanding place, Gibeon in the tribe of Benjamin. Abner was the real ruler. In a battle at Gibeon, Abner was beaten. Pursued by Asahel, brother of Joab, David's nephew and general, Abner turned and killed Asahel. In the course of time, Abner became dissatisfied, and went over to David. The secession of Abner was followed by his treacherous murder at the hands of Joab, to David's intense regret. Then Ish-bosheth was murdered by two treacherous Beerothites. This and other events at length brought the civil war to a conclusion; and a deputation from all the tribes, whose jealousy was at last overcome, came to David to Hebron, and offered him, handsomely and heartily, the crown of the united kingdom.

Capture of Jerusalem.—This matter happily arranged, David's next act was to lay siege to Jerusalem. That place had never been completely in the possession of the Hebrews. The advantages of its situation, and also the intimation of God's will that it should be called by His name (2 Chron. vi. 6), determined David to make a bold effort to secure it. Hebron was too far south to be the capital of the whole kingdom. Jerusalem was admirably adapted for that purpose. It was situated chiefly in Benjamin, a neutral tribe lying between Judah and Ephraim, only part of it being in Judah. It is supposed to have been the place where Melchizedek reigned; and Moriah, one of the hills beside it, to have been the spot where Abraham was commanded to offer up Isaac. The capture of Jerusalem was far from easy, but it was successfully accomplished. Thereafter David fortified the stronghold of Zion, and prepared a place on that hill to which he soon afterwards brought up the ark from Kirjath-jearim. Then he proceeded to extend the town, and laid the foundation of what, for nearly three thousand years, has been emphatically known as "the Holy City."

Situation of Jerusalem: Its Hills.—The situation of Jerusalem is very remarkable. It stands upon the upland ridge that runs along the country from north to south, about 2,200 feet above the level of the Mediterranean, and 3,500 feet above that of the Dead Sea. The town is flanked on three sides by steep, rocky ravines,— the Valley of Jehoshaphat on the east, and the Valley of Hinnom on the west and the south. These ravines are shaped somewhat like a horseshoe, the open part being towards the north-west. The city itself, lying, as it were, within the horse-shoe, spread ultimately over four hills, or heights, called Zion, Moriah, Acra, and Bezetha. The chief of these hills was Zion; it lay, so to speak, in the western bend of the horse-shoe. In David's time the whole town lay on its northern slope. Additions were made at subsequent times. Between the hills ran valleys, the chief of which, lying between Zion and Moriah, was called by the Romans the Tyropœon; but the seventeen great sieges which Jerusalem is said to have undergone have caused many of these valleys to be filled up with rubbish, and internally the city now is very much changed from what it must have been. On all sides, the neighbouring mountains rise somewhat above the city, verifying the figure of the psalm, "As the mountains are round about Jerusalem, so the Lord is round about his people from henceforth even for ever." The most celebrated of these hills is Mount Olivet. It stretches away to the north-east, in the form of a ridge with several summits, rising to the height of 400 feet above the Valley of Jehoshaphat, and 2,500 above the level of the Mediterranean. South of Olivet is the Hill of Offence; so called because believed to be that on which Solomon built shrines to Chemosh and Moloch. Opposite Mount Zion is the Hill of Evil Counsel; which derived its name from the circumstance that here, in the country house of Caiaphas, the priests and elders took counsel to put Jesus to death. Mount Gihon guards the city on the west, and Mount Scopus on the north. The brook Kidron runs, or rather ran, through the Valley of Jehoshaphat, passing the Garden of Gethsemane near the road to the Mount of Olives and to Bethany.

Mount Zion.—Mount Zion is the most conspicuous of the hills on which Jerusalem is built. It rises abruptly to the height of nearly three hundred feet from the Valley of Hinnom, sloping down more gradually "on the sides of the north," where lay the city of the great King. It was a place of great strength, so that the tabernacle, the palace of David, and the other buildings that stood on it, were remarkably secure (Ps. xlviii.). Part of the hill is now under regular cultivation; thus verifying Micah's prophecy, that Zion should be "ploughed as a field." When the temple was built on Moriah, the associations of Mount Zion were transferred to it, and in many instances, apparently, the name itself.

View from the Mount of Olives.—The view of Jerusalem from some of the neighbouring heights is apt to disappoint the traveller; but from the Mount of Olives it is exceedingly striking. When seen from that point, the hill of Zion justifies the admiring exclamation of the Psalmist,—" Beautiful for situation, the joy of the whole earth, is Mount Zion." "Although the size of Jerusalem was not very great, its situation, on the brink of rugged hills, encircled by deep and wild valleys, bounded by eminences whose sides were covered with groves and gardens, added to its numerous towers and the temple, must have given it a singular and gloomy magnificence, scarcely possessed by any other city in the world. ......It is true, the city beloved by God has now disappeared, and with it all the hallowed spots once contained within its walls. Yet the face of nature still endures; the rocks, mountains, lakes, and valleys are still unchanged, save that loneliness and wildness are now where once were luxury and every joy: and though their glory is departed, a high and mournful beauty still rests on many of their settled scenes. Amidst them a stranger will ever delight to wander; for there his imagination will seldom be in fault: the naked mountain, the untrodden plain, and the voiceless shore will kindle into life around him, and his every step be filled with those deeds through which guilt and sorrow passed away, and life and immortality were brought to light."

SECTION III.—REIGN OF DAVID.

The Ark placed on Mount Zion—Desire to build a temple—Foreign wars—Feebleness of Assyria and Egypt—Kindness to the House of Saul—Trespass with Bath-sheba—His rebuke and punishment—Penitential psalms—David's altered aspect—Domestic troubles—Absalom's rebellion—The restoration—Insurrection of Sheba—Influence of Joab—The famine and the sons of Saul—Another war with the Philistines—Numbering of the people—The punishment—Arrangements for erecting a temple—The last words of David- Last days of David—David's personal character—His character as a ruler—His political administration—His ecclesiastical arrangements—His devotional writings—Classification of the Psalms—David's typical character.

Epoch V.—His Royal Life at Jerusalem.

The Ark placed on Mount Zion.—Jerusalem having been captured, David transferred to it the seat of royalty, making it alike the civil and the ecclesiastical capital of the kingdom. He had two encounters with the Philistines in the Valley of Rephaim, near Jerusalem, resulting in two victories over them. It was probably on one of these occasions that David exclaimed, "Oh that one would give me drink of the water of the well of Beth-lehem, which is by the gate!" and that his three mighty men burst through the enemy and brought him the water (2 Sam. xxiii. 15-17). Thereafter, David's first care was to bring up the ark from Kirjath-jearim, some ten miles to the north-west, and to place it on Mount Zion. On the first occasion he was unsuccessful. The ark having been put on a cart instead of being carried by the Levites, and Uzzah having irreverently touched it, the displeasure of the Lord was signified by the death of Uzzah. A few months later, David returned, brought up the ark in due form, and placed it on Mount Zion with great enthusiasm. This enthusiasm was not shared by Michal, his wife, who despised him for his uncontrolled fervour on the occasion.

Desire to Build a Temple.—It was David's desire to build a permanent temple. At first the prophet Nathan encouraged, but afterwards, in God's name, declined the proposal. David was to be a man of war; his son would be a man of peace, and to him this honour would belong. In connection with this announcement, promises of a long line of posterity were given to David, which he received with such exuberant gratitude as to show that he understood them to mean that he was to be the progenitor of the Messiah. Nor could the disappointment about building a temple have been compensated by any inferior privilege. The Thirtieth Psalm is stated to have been written now; but the psalms from the Twenty-fourth to the Thirtieth inclusive probably belong to this period.

Foreign Wars.—In foreign warfare king David was eminently successful. Besides thoroughly subduing the Philistines, the Moabites, the Edomites, and the Amalekites, he turned his arms against the Syrians, and, after a vehement struggle, brought under his dominion the large tract of country stretching between Palestine and the Euphrates. Thus for the first time the Jewish territory filled up the whole outline originally traced in the promise to Abraham (Gen. xv. 18). The wealth flowing from these conquests was enormous. Evidently David was a great warrior, understanding well the art of war, and no stranger to " the stern joy which warriors feel" when their enemies fall in multitudes before them. Tender-hearted to his own countrymen, he seems to have had the ordinary feelings of an Eastern soldier to all besides. The Sixtieth Psalm has its date at this period.

Feebleness of Assyria and Egypt.—It has appeared to some highly improbable that, with Egypt on the south and Assyria on the north, a small kingdom like that of Israel lying between them should have grown into so large and magnificent an empire. It appears, however, from records recently deciphered that both Assyria and Egypt were in a state of feebleness at this very time. " Assyria, which in the twelfth century (B.C.) bore rule over most of northern Syria, passes under a cloud towards the commencement of the eleventh, and continues weak and inglorious till near the close of the tenth. Egypt declines somewhat earlier, but recovers sooner, her depression commencing about B.C. 1200, and terminating with the accession of Sheshonk about B.C. 990."*

Kindness to the House of Saul.—The spirit that had shown such regard for the family of his predecessor, when he came to the throne, continued to animate David. He did not forget his friendship with Jonathan, nor the vow he had taken to show kindness to his seed. Finding that Mephibosheth, a lame son of Jonathan, still survived, he brought him to Jerusalem and attached him to his court.

Trespass with Bath-sheba.—Notwithstanding all the training which he had undergone in the days of Saul, David, partaking as he did the common infirmities of humanity, was thrown off his guard by his wonderful elevation to absolute power, and fell under a terrible temptation. A quarrel had arisen with the Ammonites, on the other side of Jordan, arising from the insulting treatment practised on messengers of David, sent by him to congratulate king Hanun on his accession, David having received some kindness from his father Nahash. War was declared, and Joab and the army went to besiege Rabbah, the capital of Ammon. Meanwhile, David conceived a guilty passion for Bath-sheba, the wife of Uriah, a Hittite, who was absent as a soldier at Rabbah. To screen himself from exposure, David resorts to various mean artifices, and at last sends a letter to Joab, his general, by Uriah himself, ordering Joab to place him in the hottest part of the battle; which having been done, Uriah was slain. The rise and progress of David's temptation is a remarkable exemplification of the ways of sin. David was idle at the time; he had not gone to battle with his troops. He made no covenant with his eyes, but allowed himself to look on a woman and lust after her. He abused his authority, as king, by sending for the woman that he might gratify his guilty passion. To screen himself from exposure, he resorted to mean and wicked stratagems, trying to make Uriah drunk, returning his faithful service with injustice, robbery, and death, and requiring Joab to take part in an unrighteous act. The crime was aggravated by the position of David as king, the singular goodness of

* Rawlinson's Hist. Illust., p. 104.

God to him, his high religious position and profession, his mature period of life, and the example of Uriah, self-restrained as a man, brave and devoted as a soldier. The crime stands out as one of the darkest recorded in the Word of God. It shows what terrible remnants of sin there are in the hearts even of converted men.

His Rebuke and Punishment.—The prophet Nathan was sent to bring David to a sense of his sin, and he did so by means of the parable of the ewe lamb. By making David unconsciously judge in his own case, he not only made him condemn what he had done, but declare that the man who had done it should be put to death. The application is evident when Nathan says: "Thou art the man!" The arrow seems to have gone deep into David's soul. He was brought to the lowest depths of penitence and abasement. His chastisement was of no light order: the child born of Bath-sheba was to die; but more terrible than this, the sword was never to depart from his own house. All his days his heart would be torn by domestic trial and domestic tragedy. As he had sown, so was he to reap.

Penitential Psalms.—To this period of David's life it has been customary to refer some of the most profound of the penitential psalms. The Fifty-first in particular is ascribed to this occasion; and whatever may be made of particular phrases, the internal evidence is conclusive on the subject. The penitent is crying from the depths. His hand is on his mouth, and his cry is, "Unclean, unclean!" He cannot yet venture to appropriate mercy, though he does not despair of it. The picture is that of the prodigal son coming to himself, touched with a sense of his baseness, and sending on his humble confessions and petitions: "Father, I have sinned against Heaven and in thy sight; make me as one of thy hired servants!" Other psalms —for example, the Hundred and thirtieth, the Thirty-second, and the Fortieth—reveal the same depth of self-abasement, with a more definite and rejoicing apprehension of the mercy that redeems Israel from all his transgressions.

David's Altered Aspect.—From this time forward David has a somewhat broken and haggard look. "His piety takes an altered aspect. It is no longer buoyant, glad, exulting, triumphant;

it is repressed, humble, contrite, patient, suffering. Alas for him! The bird which once rose to heights unattained before by mortal wing, filling the air with its joyful songs, now lies with maimed wing upon the ground pouring forth its doleful cries to God."*

Domestic Troubles.—The fountain of domestic grief, from whose bitter waters Nathan foretold that David's chastisements would spring, was not long in sending out its streams. The number of his wives bred jealousies in his family, and his children were not like himself. Amnon, one of his sons, having behaved shamefully to his sister Tamar, was treacherously slain at a feast by his brother Absalom. On this, Absalom fled from the kingdom, taking refuge with his mother's relations at Geshur, in Syria. Absalom was a favourite of his father, and the king's heart pined for his son. Joab, observing this, employed a wise woman of Tekoah to go to David, to lay before him an imaginary case of a widow, one of whose sons had killed the other, and to ask what was to be done. The result was, that Absalom was allowed to return, at first under restraint and without permission to see the king. By a rude argument —setting fire to Joab's corn-field—Absalom prevailed on Joab to get him restored to his former position. This was granted, but it led to unhallowed results. The very tenderness of David's heart was his weakness, as it is with so many; he could not bear to disappoint his children, or inflict pain on them, however much they needed correction.

Absalom's Rebellion.—As soon as the way was open, the treachery of Absalom's perfidious nature began to show itself: he plotted for the kingdom, and, by subtlety and flattery, undermined the loyalty of the people. Then he had himself proclaimed king at Hebron, and a great part of the people hastened to support him. David was obliged to flee from Jerusalem. Zadok and Abiathar, the priests, remained loyal to David. If the counsel of Ahithophel had been followed by Absalom, he would have fallen on David before he had crossed the Jordan, and the king's cause would have been hopeless. But Hushai, a friend of David, pretending to be on Absalom's

* Kitto's Daily Bible Illustrations.

side, induced Absalom to delay till he had gathered a great army. Meanwhile David had reached Gilead; and, choosing as his head-quarters Mahanaim, where Ish-bosheth had reigned, he calmly awaited the course of events. By-and-by, Absalom crossed the Jordan, followed by an enormous host. A battle took place in the wood of Ephraim—probably not far from the scene of the awful conflict under Jephthah between the Gileadites and the Ephraimites. The district abounds with trees, and among these the prickly oak is pre-eminent. The vast army of Absalom was thoroughly defeated by the troops of David, who were led by Joab; and Absalom was killed. But so tender was the heart of the king, that his grief for the death of his son was actually greater than his joy at the victory of his army.

The Restoration.—After a time, David became composed, and sat in the gate, in no hurry to return to Jerusalem, or to take possession of the throne without an invitation from those who had driven him away. The ten tribes were cordial in their desire for his return. Judah, his own tribe, and the chief supporter of the rebellion, alone seemed cold. To rouse them to their duty, Zadok and Abiathar, the priests, were sent to speak to the elders of the tribe; and Amasa, the leader of the rebel forces, was appointed general of the army in room of Joab. When it was thus seen that the rebellion was not to be further punished, the men of Judah came willingly forward; a new sense of the goodness and generosity of the king took possession of them: "He bowed the heart of the men of Judah, even as the heart of one man; so that they sent this word unto the king, Return thou, and all thy servants." On his way back, the king showed his generosity by pardoning Shimei, an unmannerly Benjamite, who had cursed him as he fled; he restored to Mephibosheth half his possessions, the whole of which had been given to Ziba, on the supposition that Mephibosheth was among the rebels; and invited old Barzillai the Gileadite, from whom, in the climax of his troubles, he had received great assistance, to come and dwell with him at Jerusalem. Barzillai was too old to relish the change, but he accepted the honour for his son Chimham. The faithfulness of God was shown in his restoring David to his capital and his throne under far more agreeable conditions than he could have dreamt of when he was driven ignominiously from both; although a fresh thorn must have lacerated his heart, and a fresh weight oppressed his spirit, as he thought of the untimely end of Absalom. The only psalm formally assigned to this period is the Third; but many more are of similar tone, and seem at least to refer to his troubles at this time.

Insurrection of Sheba.—The remaining years of the life of David were disturbed by another insurrection. Sheba, son of Bichri, a Benjamite, raised the standard of revolt. His complaint was that the ten tribes had not been sufficiently acknowledged in bringing back the king. On this miserable complaint the ten tribes flocked to his standard. The old state of things was reversed. Judah, the rebellious tribe, was now loyal to David; and the ten tribes, that had mostly been loyal, were now rebellious. Amasa was ordered to muster the army, but was too late; and Abishai was sent forth with the household troops. Joab, who had never forgiven the promotion of Amasa, met him on the way, and basely assassinated him. Joab then took command of the troops, and in his bold and vigorous way soon brought the insurrection to an end. Sheba was besieged in Abel of Beth-maachah, and his head was thrown to Joab over the wall by a woman. David was obliged to wink at Joab's atrocities, but his crimes were never effaced from his memory. They cried out for retribution. In his dying charge to Solomon, he insisted that his hoary head should not go down to the grave in peace.

Influence of Joab.—In David's relation to Joab we have a specimen of the trials of kings. No man was better fitted by talents and virtues to be a king than David; but even David was not always his own master. Joab was often really above him; frustrated, doubtless, many noble plans, and interrupted many benevolent schemes; did great service, indeed, by his rough patriotism and his ready valour, but injured the good name of David and the moral reputation of his government by actions which David, so far from approving, detested in his inmost soul.

The Famine and the Sons of Saul.—The kingdom was by-and-by distressed by a new form of calamity. For three successive years famine prevailed. On inquiry being made of God as to the cause, the answer was given—"It is for Saul, and for his bloody house, because he slew the Gibeonites." The matter is obscure. It would appear, however, that among other wicked acts, Saul had broken faith with the Gibeonites, and had massacred them, having for his object to get possession of their vineyards and to give them to his favourites.* "His bloody house," or some part of it, had abetted the massacre. No acknowledgment of the crime had ever been made, and no restitution to the Gibeonites had taken place. When the cause of the famine was discovered, and the wrong that had been done to the Gibeonites was laid bare, it was committed to the remnant of the Gibeonites to fix on the remedy. Their answer was probably an unexpected one. Instead of claiming fresh lands, they claimed seven lives. The request was a strange and awful one, but it was granted. The men whose lives they claimed may have been involved in the spoliation and murder. They were hanged at Gibeah. The event had a tender touch thrown over it by the motherly affection of Rizpah, whose two sons were among the slain. She watched the dead bodies all the season, protecting them from the vultures and beasts of prey. This made a deep impression on David. He collected the bones of Saul and his sons, which had been buried under a tree, gathered also the bones of the men that had been hanged, and buried them all, reverently consigning those of Saul and Jonathan to the family sepulchre. After this we read that God was entreated for the land.

Another War with the Philistines.—These restless enemies of the Israelites were determined to give them no peace so long as they had a champion that could defy them. And David personally was not free from mortal danger. His last warlike achievement was like his first. It was a personal conflict with a son of the giant. But it was like to have ended differently. He was rescued by the prompt assistance of Abishai; and his servants prevailed on him to face no more the hazards of the

* See David, King of Israel. By W. G. Blaikie, D.D. Page 306.

battle-field. The Song of Thanksgiving contained in the Eighteenth Psalm was now composed as an appropriate conclusion to the history of his active life.

Numbering of the People.—Another great chastisement was drawn on David and his people by his determining to number the people. It is not very apparent wherein the sin of this lay; but as even Joab remonstrated with the king on his project, it is evident that in some way the proceeding was most objectionable. In First Chronicles, it is said that "Satan stood up against Israel, and provoked David to number Israel." The numbering of the people was evidently done for a military purpose; the object of it was to see how many of the people were fit to bear arms, and thus to make a great display of military power, in the very spirit of the kings of Egypt and Assyria. It seems to have been this that made the offence of so serious a character. We know how much these nations trusted to their great military equipments, and with how much insolence and inhumanity they filled their minds; and if David was now treading in their footsteps, he was sinfully insulting Israel's God, and forgetting the true source of safety and of glory—"Some trust in chariots, and some in horses; but we will remember the name of the Lord our God."

The Punishment.—The project was carried out—the people were numbered: in Israel, 800,000, and in Judah, 500,000 valiant men were found that drew the bow. But when the process was completed, the king's heart smote him, and he felt how greatly he had sinned. The prophet Gad was sent to him with an offer of three chastisements—seven years of famine, three months of defeat before his enemies, or three days of pestilence. He answered that he preferred to fall into the hand of the Lord, and not into the hand of man. So the Lord sent a pestilence, which was very destructive. It wrung David's heart and awakened its most unselfish feelings. "Lo, I have sinned," he said, "and I have done wickedly: but these sheep, what have they done? let thine hand, I pray thee, be against me and against my father's house." Unlike the men of the world, who are always ready to lay the blame on others and to let them bear the penalty,

David was willing to take on himself even more than his own share. The destroying angel was approaching Jerusalem, when David was directed to meet him on Mount Moriah, at the threshing-floor of Araunah the Jebusite. There a sacrifice was offered, and the anger of God was appeased. This spot afterwards became the site of the Temple; and the rock which Araunah is said to have used as a threshing-floor remains, it is believed, to this day within the sacred enclosure where the Temple stood.

Arrangements for Erecting a Temple.—Towards the close of his life, David, on a very solemn occasion, handed over to Solomon the immense stores which he had set aside for building a temple, and also the pattern which had been given him by divine revelation. By this act he made it plain that as Solomon had been divinely pointed out for this work, so David desired that the succession to the kingdom should go to him.

The Last Words of David.—This is the title given to a remarkable prophecy of David, evidently referring to the coming of the Messiah. The words may not have been the last absolutely spoken, but they expressed the view which filled his mind in the last stage of his life. The prophecy consists of a description of a ruler, and it describes first the foundation, and then the effects of his government. The effects are either saving or destructive. The saving effects are described under a beautiful emblem that often reappears in Scripture, and gives the brightest possible idea of the influence of Christ both on individuals and on communities: "He shall be as the light of the morning, when the sun riseth, even a morning without clouds; as the tender grass springing out of the earth by clear shining after rain." But with this is associated very closely the idea of righteousness. The divine government reposes on righteousness while it exercises mercy; on no other foundation can the government of the universe be carried on (2 Sam. xxiii. 1–7).

Last Days of David.—David was now threescore years and ten, and was visibly approaching his end. The question of his successor began to excite men's minds while the king was yet alive. The usual schemes and manœuvres of Eastern countries began to be set on foot. Adonijah, one of his sons, seemed likely to secure the throne; but, through the intercession of Bath-sheba and the energy of David, backed by Nathan and others, his attempt was defeated, and Solomon, Bath-sheba's son, was made king. And David, after giving him a dying charge against Joab and Shimei, and after counselling him to be strong and of a good courage, was at length gathered to his fathers. After having reigned forty years, he was buried on Mount Zion—the place to which he had been the means of imparting such extraordinary consecration. Thus ended the most memorable period of Hebrew history from the days of Moses till the coming of David's Son and David's Lord.

David's Personal Character.—In reviewing this memorable reign, we are first led to think of the personal character of the king. He comes on the field at first quite naturally, a ruddy shepherd boy, with a warm heart, a ready hand, a simple trust, a fearless courage, and a deep regard for his country and his God. Unlike Moses, he has little book-learning; but he has a great love for the law of the Lord, and rare gifts of music and song. His bravery as a warrior soon makes him famous; and his warm, simple, loving nature endears him to all. Men feel instinctively that the desire of his heart and the aim of his life is to make his people prosperous and happy. His religious feeling is deep, intense, all-pervading; but instead of a repulsive gravity, it genders a bright joyousness, bathing his life in sunshine, filling his heart with peace and joy. Even when clouds darken his sky, and when everything around him seems stormy, he comes out from his closet bright and hopeful, as if he had found a charm against all anxiety and fear. Not that he was uniformly consistent and exemplary. He was not without his share of ordinary infirmity, and in his readiness to multiply wives he fell into one of the great vices of the age. Out of that vice sprang the unguarded state of his heart which led to the awful tissue of sins in the affair of Bath-sheba and Uriah. In the management of his family he was led into an easy-going indulgence, which left unpunished terrible sins. Yet in the deepest abyss of guilt, David shows a heart so broken, a self-reproach so keen, a cry for forgiveness and renewal so piercing, as to leave no doubt of the genuineness of his religion.

His Character as a Ruler.—As a king he was a great contrast to Saul, and still more so, perhaps, to the ordinary run of Eastern kings. He was entirely free from mere selfish aims. He did not fall into the exacting ways of other kings, spoiling his subjects of their possessions, grinding them by taxes, demoralizing them by accepting bribes, seizing them against their will for soldiers, or making them feel that they were mere instruments of enjoyment to him. He sought to make his rule one of mercy and righteousness combined, under which the people might find life and property secure, and might feel that there was some enjoyment in living. The king was for the people, not the people for the king.

His Political Administration.—Under David, the Hebrew nation made a great advance; and from a feeble state, which any neighbouring tribe could humble, it became a first-rate power, honoured by all the East. David excelled greatly in that faculty of orderly arrangement which had belonged to Abraham, Moses, and other chiefs of the nation. Without overturning the ancient tribal government, he extended and improved it, especially by distributing a large portion of the Levites through the country, of whom no fewer than six thousand were made officers and judges (1 Chron. xxiii. 4). For developing the material resources of the country, he had store-houses in the fields, in the cities, in the villages, and in the castles; there were vineyards and wine cellars, and cellars of oil, superintended each by appointed officers; in different valleys herds and flocks grazed under the care of royal herdsmen and shepherds; an officer, skilled in agriculture, presided over the tillage of the fields; the sycamore and olive trees were under the eye of skilful foresters: nothing was wasted, nothing done lazily; all was regularity, order, and care (1 Chron. xxvii. 25–31). By friendly intercourse with Hiram, king of Tyre, a knowledge of the useful and the ornamental arts was promoted among his people (1 Chron. xxii. 2–4). In regard to military organization, the men who bore arms were divided into twelve courses of 24,000 each, which attended on the king at Jerusalem, each for a month at a time (1 Chron. xxvii.). There was also a body of regular troops, sometimes called the Cherethites and Pelethites. There appears to have been also a Legion of Honour—David's "mighty men" (2 Sam. xxiii.). It was three of these that burst through the host of the Philistines to bring water to David from the well of Beth-lehem.

His Ecclesiastical Arrangements.—The first great change in this department was to make Jerusalem the ecclesiastical centre of the country, and to place the ark on Mount Zion. Great attention was bestowed on arranging the priests and Levites, with a view to the effective discharge of their duties. The Priests were divided into twenty-four courses, each to serve in its turn. By far the largest part of the Levites, 24,000, were allocated to the service of the house of God. Another section, 4,000 in number, were porters; 6,000 were officers and judges; and 4,000 were singers (1 Chron. xxiii. 4, 5). These last appear to have been most regularly and skilfully trained; and though they usually served only by turns, yet when, on such great occasions as bringing up the ark, or the dedication of the Temple, or even the great annual festivals, a general muster took place, the combined performances must have been sublime. The use of musical instruments, if not introduced by David into the service of the sanctuary, was carried out in great fulness of detail (1 Chron. xxv.).

His Devotional Writings.—Though not the first, David was undoubtedly the most distinguished writer of the sacred songs of the Hebrews, so that the whole collection has been named after him. Nearly half the collection is ascribed to him in the superscriptions; but as some of these are of doubtful authenticity, the real number of David's psalms is probably not quite so large. Some critics have attempted to cut them down to seven, or even to fewer; but their views have not commanded general assent. David doubtless may be said to have stamped the collection with its unexampled character. For though other religions have their sacred songs (such as the Rig-Veda of the Hindus), none are like the Psalms. If the special glory of the Hebrew collection be inquired for, it may be found in such particulars as these:—1. God, in the Psalms, is the personal friend of his worshipper, offered and accepted and enjoyed as such. They are at one, and there is a happy, confiding, blessed fellowship between them. 2. The worshipper is a real human being, a sinner, a great sinner, consciously unworthy; yet to this poor frail being God has drawn nigh in infinite grace, and given pardon and blessing. 3. The experience of this accepted sinner in trying to serve God—his longings for close communion, his successes, his failures, his hopes and fears—is delineated with a fidelity that comes home to all like-minded hearts. 4. Generally it is a happy experience—from gloom to gladness, from sorrow to joy, from the weeping that endures for a night to the joy that comes in the morning. And the prospect in the end is unspeakably bright. 5. Glimpses of a Saviour are ever and anon presented—a God of salvation—a King who is to reign in righteousness, a Priest after the order of Melchizedek—a worm and no man in his humiliation, but in his exaltation higher than the kings of the earth. 6. Throughout the whole collection the voice of nature is often heard, uttering something of God and for God. But it is not from nature that we know God. We know and love him first as the God of redemption, and then as the God of nature. Hence the Hundred and third Psalm, a beautiful song of redemption, is followed by the Hundred and fourth, a beautiful song of nature.

Classification of the Psalms.—It has been attempted to find for each of David's psalms an event in his life to which it refers; but the attempt has not been very successful. Perhaps they would not have been so generally useful if in every instance the occasion had been definitely indicated. It is better, perhaps, to group them according to their character Taking the psalms formally ascribed to David, we have:—

1. Songs of Nature—8, 19, 29, 65.
2. Songs of Distress and Trust—3, 4, 6, 7, 12, 13, 14, 22, 25, 31, 35, 41, 52, 53, 54, 55, 56, 57, 58, 59, 60, 61, 64, 69, 70, 76, 109, 123, 140, 141, 142, 143.
3. Songs of Contrition—32, 38, 39, 51.
4. Songs of Trust, Thanksgiving, and Triumph—5, 9, 11, 16, 17, 18, 20, 21, 23, 27, 28, 33, 34, 36, 37, 40, 62, 63, 68, 101, 103, 109, 110, 138, 139, 144, 145.
5. Songs of the Sanctuary—15, 24, 26, 30, 122, 133.

David's Typical Character.—Of all the Old Testament types of Christ, David is perhaps the most eminent. His oneness with his people; his uniting, in his kingly office, the gentleness of a shepherd with the might of a warrior—the lion and the lamb; his covenant relation to God, as king of Israel; the incidents of his life,—first, the man of sorrows, then crowned with glory and honour; the intense glow of his loving heart; and last, not least, his singular trust, love, and reverence for God, make him a more *complete* type of Christ than any other Old Testament worthy. This typical relation, appearing everywhere in his psalms, invests him with peculiar interest, and makes the study of his life and experience one of the most profitable in which the Christian can engage.

SECTION IV.—REIGN OF SOLOMON.

Building of the Temple—Its form and arrangements—Intercourse with other countries: Phœnicia, Egypt—Sheba—Solomon's backsliding—His buildings: Tadmor, or Palmyra—Baalath, or Baalbec—Solomon's character—A type of Christ.

Building of the Temple.—In magnificence, wealth, and wisdom, no king was ever known in the East equal to SOLOMON. His first youthful energies were employed in the building of the Temple which David had designed. The site had already been fixed for this great edifice,—Moriah, one of the heights of Jerusalem, separated from Mount Zion by the valley of the Tyropœon, over which a fine bridge was formed, connecting the two hills. The magnificence of the Temple was very great, and the gold and other precious substances expended in embellishing it almost transcend belief. According to the most moderate computation, the value of the precious materials was £120,000,000 sterling.

Its Form and Arrangements.—The building itself was oblong in form, sixty cubits in length from east to west, and twenty cubits in breadth: twenty cubits formed the Holy of Holies, and forty formed the Sanctuary or Holy Place. In the Holy of Holies was placed the ark, along with the mercy-seat overshadowed by cherubim; and *there* shone the mysterious light, the Shekinah, the symbol of the presence of God. No one could enter this inmost Sanctuary save the high priest, and he only once a year, on the great day of atonement, carrying with him the blood of his offering. The Holy of Holies was separated from the Sanctuary or Holy Place partly by a partition and partly by a rich veil or curtain. In the Sanctuary, and in the Most Holy Place, everything, including the floor and the walls, was covered with pure gold. Besides the Temple itself, there were several adjacent buildings, porches, chapels, and courts. Outside of the Temple was the Court of the Priests, where the daily sacrifices were offered up; beyond that, the Court of the Jews; and outside of that, again, the Court of the Gentiles. No such building had ever before been seen within the boundaries of Palestine; for till now the Jews had devoted little or no attention to architecture. The pattern of the building had been supplied by divine inspiration, and probably it had but little resemblance to the temples of Assyria or of Egypt. The dedication must have been a most imposing scene; and as Solomon personally conducted some of the religious services, and that with the utmost earnestness and humility, the occasion must have been as instructive and profitable as it was grand and imposing.

Intercourse with other Countries: Phœnicia, Egypt. — In building the Temple, Solomon had been greatly indebted to Hiram, king of Tyre, one of the potentates of Phœnicia, who supplied him not only with cedar-wood but also with skilled labourers, without whose aid the Temple could not have been built. Friendly intercourse began, too, to be held under Solomon with several other countries, some of them remote from Palestine. Among the chief of these was Egypt. Nearly five hundred years had now elapsed since the Exodus, and during that long period there had been no intercourse between the two countries. Many memorable events had happened in Egypt during the interval. There had been more times of grand conquests, when Egyptian arms subdued Asia, and victorious Pharaohs blazoned their exploits in the temples of Karnak and

Luxor; the arts had risen, some two hundred years after the Exodus,* to the highest degree of excellence of which they were then capable, but had now begun somewhat to decline. Not only did Solomon marry a daughter of Pharaoh, but "he had horses brought out of Egypt, and linen yarn; the king's merchants received the linen yarn at a price. And a chariot came up and went out of Egypt for six hundred shekels of silver, and an horse for one hundred and fifty" (1 Kings x. 28, 29). The latter sum is rather under £20, the former is about £70. But this introduction of chariots and horses was not in accordance with the divine command (Deut. xvii. 16). Other remote places with which Solomon held intercourse were Ophir and Tarshish. From these were brought gold and silver, ivory, apes, peacocks, and algum-wood. Three years are said to have been occupied in the voyage. From the nature of the articles named, and the length of time occupied, it is inferred that these voyages must either have been to India or to some place having access to India. It is known that even at that early period intercourse existed with places more remote than India; for in Egyptian tombs of earlier date there have been found articles which are undoubtedly of Chinese manufacture.

Sheba.—Solomon maintained intercourse also, of a very interesting kind, with the kingdom of Sheba, whose queen came all the way to Jerusalem to verify the wonderful reports of his wisdom. "She came with a very great train, with camels that bare spices, and very much gold, and precious stones." It is believed that this lady was queen of the Sabæan kingdom of Yemen, or "the south," the most southern part of Arabia, within the limits of which the British port Aden now lies. As the British steamers that ply between Egypt and India usually touch at that port, so probably did the ships of Solomon, nearly three thousand years ago, on their way to Ophir, leaving such accounts of their royal master as induced the queen to undertake in person the journey to Jerusalem.

Solomon's Backsliding.—Besides the queen of Sheba, "all the earth sought to Solomon, to hear his wisdom which God put into

* See Rawlinson's Herodotus, vol. ii., p. 367.

his heart." What a lively place Jerusalem must have been in Solomon's days, ever and anon receiving some splendid embassage from a distance, come to express its admiration and homage! What a glorious opportunity for a pious king to spread the knowledge and proclaim the glory of the one living God! But Solomon, most unhappily, following the pernicious example of other Eastern kings, increased the number of his wives, and married the daughters of many of those foreign potentates. The thing, like Gideon's ephod, became a snare to him and to his house. To please his wives, he built shrines or high places for their gods, on the Hill of Offence, to the south-east of Jerusalem. His conduct was so offensive to God, that he sent Ahijah, a prophet of Shiloh, to intimate to his rival, Jeroboam, that the greater part of the kingdom would be rent away from Solomon's family. Solomon had other enemies, among whom were Hadad, an Edomite, and Rezon of Zobah: the former of whom became brother-in-law to the king of Egypt, and would fain have got the aid of Pharaoh against Solomon. After Ahijah announced to Jeroboam the coming disruption of the kingdom, Solomon tried to kill Jeroboam, who fled to Egypt and remained there till Solomon's death.

His Buildings: Tadmor, or Palmyra.—Besides the temple at Jerusalem, many other great buildings and undertakings owed their origin to Solomon. Among the most celebrated of the cities which he built was "Tadmor in the wilderness,"—known, since the time of the Romans, by the name of Palmyra, and now the site of ruins so extensive and magnificent as to fill every traveller with astonishment. Palmyra was situated in a palm-studded oasis of the great eastern or Syrian desert, rendered fertile by the abundance of water, and it lay about one hundred and forty miles north-east from Damascus. It seems to have been built as an emporium of commerce,—where the great merchants from Syria and the Euphrates on the north might exchange their wares with those from Egypt on the south. In the time of the Romans, the produce of India was carried through Palmyra to Rome. In the third century after Christ, the title of King was given by the Roman emperor Gal lienus to a citizen of Palmyra who had been of great service in a war with the Parthians; and after his death his widow, Zenobia, assumed the crown, and, styling herself Queen of the East, asserted her sovereignty over Mesopotamia and Syria. After a vigorous resistance, she was at last defeated, and her prime minister, Longinus, author of a celebrated treatise on the Sublime, was put to death. The ruins of Palmyra extend to nearly a mile and a half in length; but the only inhabitants now are a tribe of Bedouin Arabs.

Baalath, or Baalbec.—Another city, built or improved by Solomon, and still celebrated for its ruins, was Baalath or Baalbec, near Lebanon. Its Temple of the Sun, like that of Palmyra, afterwards built, was among the finest edifices in Syria. Besides Tadmor and Baalbec, he built many other great cities, both within the ancient territory of Palestine and in the more extended empire which he now ruled. The whole district of Lebanon on the north, the whole country reaching to the Euphrates on the east, and on the south to the borders of Egypt, formed part of his magnificent dominion. The most remarkable thing about this greatness was, that it entirely failed to satisfy his heart; and, after declaring all to be "vanity of vanities," he left this as the great practical lesson to be drawn from his experience,—"Let us hear the conclusion of the whole matter: Fear God, and keep his commandments; for this is the whole duty of man" (Eccles. xii. 13).

Solomon's Character.—The character of Solomon is a riddle. His heart seems to have been touched, at a very early period, with true reverence for God: for his choice of wisdom, in answer to God's offer to grant him whatever he should ask, showed an earnest, conscientious, godly spirit; and his prayers at the dedication of the temple were singularly humble and fervent. That such a man should have built temples to the obscene gods of the heathen, within sight of God's holy hill, is strange and disappointing. Allowance, however, should be made for the greatness of his temptations. The world, with its wealth, pleasures, honours, schemes, and boundless flatteries, drew him away from God, with a strong, steady attraction, greater than any other man had ever been exposed to. His backslidings were consequently far more terrible than those of most good men.

A Type of Christ.—Solomon, like David, may be said to have foreshadowed Christ, but under a different aspect. He foreshadowed the peace and the glory of Messiah, as David had done the more warlike aspect of his character. The name Solomon denoted "peace," and the whole circumstances of Solomon's reign might have been thought to indicate that at last the promised blessing had come. If worldly prosperity and tranquillity could ever have realized what was promised to Abraham, it must have been in Solomon's time. But "vanity of vanities" was the motto for this reign as it had been so often the motto before. The Hope of Israel had not yet come. Godly men had still to project their hopes on a distant horizon.

SECTION V.—SOCIAL AND RELIGIOUS LIFE.

Great increase of wealth—Evil consequences—Allusions in the Proverbs—New vices and snares—Soothsaying—Literature and science—State of religion—Character of the people.

Great Increase of Wealth.—It is evident at a glance that, during the period that has now been under review, the state of social life among the Hebrew people underwent a very great change. An immense flow of wealth into the country took place. Through intercourse with other countries, many new habits and fashions were undoubtedly introduced. The people must have lost not a little of their early simplicity of character and life. A splendid court had been set up, and a splendid capital built. Commercial relations had been established with remote parts of the world. A great stride had been taken in the direction of luxury and refinement. There were now in the country a standing army, a large staff of civil officers, and a vast number of menial servants. Besides the ass, the horse and the mule were introduced as beasts of burden; chariots and splendid equipages were set up; and many persons assumed the style and bearing of princes. Private dwellings must have undergone a corresponding change, and all the luxuries of Egypt and Nineveh would become familiar to the Hebrews.

Evil Consequences.—But was all this for good? It appears as if the nation, or its leaders, had now struck out a new path for themselves, in which God rather followed than preceded them, giving them, indeed, at first, a large measure of prosperity, but leaving them more to their own ways and to the fruits of these ways than before. This, at least, was plainly the case under Solomon. The vast wealth circulated in his time over the country did not bring any proportional addition, either to the material comfort, or to the moral beauty, or to the spiritual riches of the nation. There can be no doubt that "haste to be rich" brought all the evils and sins which always flow from it in an age of progress towards worldly show and magnificence.

Allusions in the Proverbs.—The Book of Proverbs throws much light on the age. It appears that in the main the nation had grown and flourished under sound maxims of morality. Sensuality and self-indulgence were contrary to the approved maxims for the young. It was felt that righteousness exalted a nation. Industry, integrity, and devotion to duty were enshrined as moral virtues of great price.

New Vices and Snares.—Yet it is apparent that, in a moral sense, the nation was in a transition state. The sound old moral maxims of the fathers were in some danger of being forgotten, and needed to be revived and riveted anew on the national conscience. It appears, too, that many new vices had been introduced. Many of the counsels of the Book of Proverbs would have been quite inapplicable to a simple, patriarchal, agricultural people; but they were eminently adapted to a people surrounded by the snares of wealth and the temptations of commerce, and very liable to forget or despise the good old ways and counsels of their fathers. The Proverbs will be read with greater interest, if it be borne in mind that this change had just taken place among the Hebrews; and that, as Solomon had been instrumental in giving the nation its wealth, so, perhaps, he was led by the Spirit to write this book, to guard against the fatal abuse of his own gift, and to preserve something of primitive simplicity and primitive morality.

Soothsaying.— The practice of soothsaying, or fortune-telling, was evidently very common among the Hebrews at the beginning of this period. The prevalence of such a practice indicates a low standard of intellectual attainment. It seems to have had its head-quarters among the Philistines (Isa. ii. 6); and very probably, when Saul drove all who practised it from the land, he did so more from enmity to the Philistines than from dislike to the practice itself. It continued, as Saul himself knew, to lurk in the country, even after all the royal efforts to exterminate it (1 Sam. xxviii. 7). Probably it never altogether died out. In New Testament times it was evidently a flourishing trade (Acts viii. 9, xiii. 6). All over the East it was practised to a large extent, and the Jewish sorcerers had the reputation of being the most skilful of any. It was the counterfeit of that wonderful privilege of knowing God's mind and will which the Hebrews enjoyed through the Urim and Thummim of the high priest, as well as through their prophecies. Those who would not seek, or could not obtain the genuine coin, resorted to the counterfeit.

Literature and Science.—In literary and scientific culture the nation must have made a great advance during this period. In a merely literary point of view, the Psalms of David and the writings of Solomon possess extraordinary merits; and we cannot doubt that two literary kings, whose reigns embraced eighty years, or nearly three generations, would exercise a very great influence, and have their example very largely followed among their people. David's talents as a musician, and the extraordinary pains he took to improve the musical services of the sanctuary, must have greatly stimulated the cultivation of that delightful art. What David did for music, Solomon did for natural history. It need not surprise us that all the uninspired literary compositions of that period have perished. If Homer flourished (according to the account of Herodotus, for others give different dates) eight hundred and eighty-four years before Christ, Solomon must have been a century in his tomb before the "Iliad" was written. And if it be considered what difficulty there was in preserving the "Iliad," and how uncertain it is whether we have it as Homer wrote it, it cannot be surprising that all the Hebrew writings of this period have been lost, except such as were contained in the inspired canon of Scripture.

State of Religion.—There were, also, great religious changes during this period of the history. Evidently, under Samuel, a great revival of true religion took place; and the schools of the prophets which he established seem to have been attended with a marked blessing from Heaven. Under David the change was confirmed. In the first place, the coming Messiah was more clearly revealed. It was expressly announced to David, as has been already remarked, that the great Deliverer was to be a member of his family. David, too, as a type of Christ, conveyed a fuller and clearer idea of the person and character of Christ than any typical person that had gone before him. Further, the Psalms of David must have served very wonderfully to give precision, force, and richness to devotional feelings among godly people. Then, too, the distribution of the Levites and the remodelling of the temple service must have secured at least much more attention to the ordinary services of religion. The lyrical compositions of the two royal authors corresponded to the typical character of each. As David's reign was a warlike reign, and Solomon's a reign of peace, so David was the psalmist of storms and struggles, Solomon of tranquillity and rest. The Psalms of David bore marks of the camp, of the tumult of arms, and of the busy bustle of life; while the Song of Solomon, with its images of peace and rest, proclaimed that "the winter was past, the rain was over and gone, the flowers appeared on the earth, the time of the singing of birds was come, and the voice of the turtle was heard in the land."

Character of the People.—It is interesting to inquire how far a religious spirit pervaded the people at large. The question cannot receive a very satisfactory answer. It is plain that even in David's time the mass of the people were not truly godly. The success of Absalom's movement is a proof of this.

Had there been a large number of really godly persons in the tribe of Judah, they would not only not have joined the insurrection, but their influence would have had a great effect in hindering its success. The real state of matters seems to have been, that both in good times and in bad there were some persons, more or less numerous, of earnest piety and spiritual feeling, who worshipped God in spirit, not only because it was their duty, but also because it was their delight; while the mass of the people either worshipped idols, or worshipped God in accordance with the will, the example, or the command of their rulers. But the constant tendency was to idolatry; and the intercourse with foreign nations which Solomon maintained, as well as his own example, greatly increased the tendency. Under Solomon, indeed, idolatry struck its roots so deep, that all the zeal of the reforming kings that followed him failed to eradicate it. It was not till the seventy years' captivity of Babylon that the soil of Palestine was thoroughly purged of the roots of that noxious weed.

CHAPTER X.

KINGDOM OF ISRAEL, OR THE TEN TRIBES.

FROM THE REVOLT UNDER REHOBOAM TO THE CAPTIVITY.

1 AND 2 KINGS—2 CHRONICLES.

SECTION I.—THE REVOLT.

Influence and ambition of Ephraim—Rehoboam's foolish conduct—Jeroboam—Shishak, king of Egypt—The schism completed—Kingdom of Israel—Periods of the history—No godly king—Tabular view of the history of the kingdom of Israel.

Influence and Ambition of Ephraim.—The high pretensions of Ephraim to be the sovereign tribe, which were put forward so prominently in the days of Gideon and in those of Jephthah, had never been altogether abandoned; and whenever a pretext occurred for disputing or renouncing the authority of the sceptre of Judah, it was sure to be seized. During the later part of the reign of Solomon, much dissatisfaction prevailed on account of the public burdens laid by him on the people, to maintain the splendours of his court; and the spirit of discontent had its head-quarters in the tribe of Ephraim. His son REHOBOAM seems to have had no difficulty in getting his claims to the crown admitted by the city of Jerusalem and the tribe of Judah; but at Shechem, and throughout the tribe of Ephraim generally, and the tribes influenced by Ephraim, the state of things was different.

Rehoboam's Foolish Conduct.—It is a proof of the great importance which Ephraim still retained, that Shechem, its capital, was the city selected for the coronation of Rehoboam. A great gathering of the heads of tribes and of houses was held there on occasion of this event. It was deemed by them a fitting opportunity for endeavouring to get a relaxation of the burdens that Solomon had imposed. The result of their respectful application to Rehoboam for this purpose was a scornful refusal, and a threat of more oppressive burdens than before. Insult added to injury aroused the spirit of the people; allegiance to Rehoboam was indignantly refused; the claims of the house of David were repudiated; Adoram, Rehoboam's chief tax-gatherer, was stoned to death in a tumult; and Rehoboam, trembling for his own safety, rushed to his chariot and galloped to Jerusalem.

Jeroboam. The master-spirit in this revolution was JEROBOAM, the son of Nebat, an officer of Solomon's. Jeroboam had early shown a singular talent for administering affairs, insomuch that Solomon appointed him a sort of viceroy or lieutenant "over all the charge of the house of Joseph" (1 Kings xi. 28), —that is, over Ephraim and the tribes allied to it. While on his way to this high office, Ahijah, the prophet of Shiloh, met him, and intimated that, on account of the encouragement which Solomon had given to idolatry, ten of the tribes were to be removed from the allegiance of his son, and committed to the charge of Jeroboam. Hearing with alarm of this announcement, Solomon tried to kill Jeroboam; but he contrived to escape to Egypt, where he was protected by king Shishak.

Shishak, King of Egypt.—Of this Shishak we have lately obtained very curious information. It was previously known that he headed a new dynasty, and this circumstance was held sufficient to account for his hostility to the house of Solomon. According to Dr. Brugsch, inscriptions recently deciphered inform us that Shishak, or Sheshonk, was a son of Nimrod, king of Assyria, who, having gone to Egypt and conquered the country, turned it into an Assyrian dependency. On the death of Nimrod, his son Sheshonk reigned at Bubastis.[*] It was his policy to break up the powerful empire of Solomon,

[*] Egypt under the Pharaohs, ii. 207.

and hence the encouragement he gave to the schismatic kingdom.

The Schism Completed.—On the death of Solomon, Jeroboam returned to his own country, and repaired to Shechem with the other leading men of the nation. It was he that headed the deputation to Rehoboam, and proposed the terms which Rehoboam refused. It was he, too, that headed the revolt, and encouraged the ten tribes to refuse allegiance to the family of David. His great energy of character, the reputation for skilful government which he had acquired under Solomon, and the message which had been sent him from the Lord by Ahijah, secured for him a unanimous offer of the throne of the new kingdom. The tribe of Judah adhered to Rehoboam, with the chief part of Benjamin, and probably a few members of Dan, Simeon, and other tribes. By-and-by, the Levites also joined their brethren of Judah; but with these exceptions, the tribes resorted to the standard of Jeroboam. When the revolt took place, Rehoboam took steps to gather an army, with a view to recover the revolted tribes; but Shemaiah, another prophet of the Lord, was sent to forbid him. The breach was never healed: the kingdom of Judah and the kingdom of Ephraim, or Israel, as it came to be called, pursued their separate courses, sometimes at peace, but far more commonly at war with each other.

Kingdom of Israel.—We shall first follow the course of the kingdom of the ten tribes. It lasted upwards of two hundred and fifty years, and at the end of that period it was destroyed by the Assyrians. During that time it had nineteen kings, belonging to nine different families, of whose history the following table (page 270) gives a summary view.* It was conspicuous for its idolatry; hence it failed to fulfil the divine purpose in connection with the seed of Abraham; and after sufficient time for trial, and many ineffectual calls to reformation, it was finally broken up.

Periods of the History.—There were four leading periods in

---

* Interregnums occasionally occurred, and periods of anarchy; hence a slight discrepancy in the dates.

Leading Feature of Periods.	Dynasties	Kings.	Length of Reigns.	Prophets.	Kings of Judah
I. Idolatry taking root,—about 50 years,	1.	1 JEROBOAM I.	22 years.	Abijah.	Rehoboam, Abijah, Asa.
		2 Nadab.	2 ..		Asa.
	2.	3 Baasha.	24 ..		Asa.
		4 Elah.	2 ..		Asa.
	3.	5 Zimri.	7 days.		Asa.
		6 Omri.	12 years.		Asa.
II. Idolatry rampant,—about 48 years,	4.	7 AHAB.	22 ..	Elijah—Micaiah	Asa and Jehoshaphat.
		8 Ahaziah.	2 ..	Elisha.	Jehoshaphat.
		9 Jehoram.	12 ..		Jehoshaphat, Jehoram, Ahaziah.
III. Idolatry slightly checked,— about 102 years,	5.	10 JEHU.	28 ..		Joash.
		11 Jehoahaz.	17 ..		Joash.
		12 Joash.	16 ..	Jonah.	Joash and Amaziah.
		13 Jeroboam II.	41 ..	Hosea and Amos.	Amaziah.
		14 Zachariah.	6 months.		Uzziah.
IV. Idolatry terminating in ruin, including Interregnums, —from 40 to 70 years, ...	6.	15 Shallum.	1 ..		Uzziah.
	7.	16 Menahem.	10 years.		Uzziah.
	8.	17 Pekahiah.	2 ..		Uzziah.
		18 PEKAH	20 ..	Oded.	Uzziah, Jotham, and Ahaz.
	9.	19 Hoshea.	9 ..		Ahaz and Hezekiah.

the history of this kingdom: in the first, the most prominent king was Jeroboam; in the second, Ahab; in the third, Jehu; and in the fourth, Pekah. During the first period, idolatry took root; during the second, it was in full blow; during the third, it was somewhat checked through the influence of the prophets; and during the fourth, it produced its natural fruit, in the utter destruction of the kingdom.

No Godly King.—It is very singular that not one of the kings of Israel was a godly man. The separation of the ten tribes from the sceptre of Judah, though permitted, and in one sense ordained by God, was never blessed; and few histories of royal families are more tragical than that of the house of Israel. An idolatrous and abominable worship was the established religion of the kingdom; and had there been nothing else to draw down God's anger, the calves of Dan and Beth-el would have sufficed. Perhaps the very predominance of idolatry in the kingdom of Israel served to check it in the rival kingdom of Judah: had it not been for their mutual alienation, the whole country might have been hopelessly overrun by this abominable thing.

SECTION II.—DYNASTIES OF JEROBOAM, BAASHA, AND ZIMRI— IDOLATRY TAKING ROOT.

Jeroboam's fortified towns—The calves at Dan and Beth-el—Reign of Nadab—Policy of massacre—Reign of Baasha—War with Syria—Reigns of Elah and Zimri.

Jeroboam's Fortified Towns.—JEROBOAM began his career by showing that he set no value on the favour of God, as the source of protection and blessing to his people. As a place of strength in the centre of his kingdom, he built or fortified Shechem; and wishing to have a fortified town across the Jordan, he selected for that purpose Penuel on the Jabbok, where Jacob had wrestled with the Angel, and Gideon had destroyed the tower. The former history of these places might have taught him that walls and towers are but poor defences compared with the presence and favour of God; but he paid no attention to lessons of that kind. For his family residence he selected Tirzah (1 Kings xiv. 17). The beauty of Tirzah is celebrated in the Song of Solomon (vi. 4) side by side with that of Jerusalem. If its supposed site, a few miles north-east of Shechem, be the true one, it stood on the top of a hill, surrounded by immense groves of olive-trees planted on all the hills around, and commanding an extensive view. It remained the seat of royalty till the days of Omri, who changed the residence of the court to the still more beautiful and not distant hill of Samaria.*

The Calves at Dan and Beth-el.—But the great offence of Jeroboam, and that which covered with eternal infamy a name that might have been honourable in history, was his setting up two golden calves, one at Beth-el and one at Dan. It is difficult to say whether the cleverness or the impiety of this step was the greater. His object was to prevent the people from going up to Jerusalem to attend the great religious festivals, fearing that if they should do so, they would withdraw their allegiance from him, and transfer it to the king of Judah. The places where the idols were set up were at the northern and southern extremities of his kingdom, so that the whole country lay, as it were, between the two great strongholds of idolatry. Instead of three times a year, he required the attendance of the people but once. The time fixed for this gathering was a month after the Passover, so that it would have been extremely inconvenient for the same persons to attend both at Beth-el and at Jerusalem. Images were made use of, to suit the popular taste for these forbidden but favourite symbols; and the form of the golden calf was probably suggested by what he had seen in Egypt. The whole proceeding indicated a very daring spirit of godlessness. It was solemnly denounced in God's name by a prophet sent from Judah, who declared that a prince of the rival house of David,

---

* "This place [Tirzah] seems to have been to Shechem what Windsor is to London .... It commands a fine view down the eastern declivities of the mountains of Ephraim into the Jordan valley. The village is large and prosperous, with corn-fields in the glens, and immense olive-groves on the surrounding hills. There are no remains of antiquity, except a few rock-tombs and some cisterns. Tirzah was a place of high antiquity, having been the seat of a Canaanitish king before the conquest of the country by the Israelites." *Murray's Handbook*, p. 343.

Josiah by name, should one day execute vengeance on the priests of Beth-el. A slight act of disobedience to God's command, on the part of this prophet, was summarily punished by his death, thus showing to Jeroboam and his people how jealous God was of his authority. But neither this warning, nor another warning delivered to his wife, by Ahijah of Shiloh, when she came in disguise to consult him about her sick child, had any good effect: he made priests of the lowest of the people, and acquired for himself in history the unenviable designation, "Jeroboam, the son of Nebat, who made Israel to sin."

Reign of Nadab.—After a reign of twenty-two years, Jeroboam left the crown to NADAB his son. He followed the bad example of his father; and only two years after coming to the throne, while besieging a town of the Philistines, he was murdered by Baasha, a man of Issachar, having done nothing to signalize his reign.

Policy of Massacre.—In this kingdom, the policy so common in the East, of plots against the reigning king, with the murder and massacre of his relatives, becomes very common. That in the neighbouring kingdom of Judah such plots were rare and exceptional, and that the same dynasty continued for so many generations, is a notable proof of the protection of God, and of his faithfulness to his promise to David.

Reign of Baasha.—BAASHA, the murderer of Nadab, took possession of the kingdom, and for safety's sake destroyed all the house of Jeroboam. He began to build, or rather to fortify, Ramah, to prevent any communication from being held with the kingdom of Judah. Ramah had been the place of Samuel's residence. It was situated near one of the great passes that connect the southern with the middle portion of the country, so that it would have been well adapted, when fortified, to secure the end which he had in view. Like his predecessors, Baasha lived in a state of warfare with the sister kingdom. His rival, Asa, king of Judah, was so much annoyed by him, that he sent a large bribe to Ben-hadad, the king of Syria, to induce him to come to his assistance against Baasha. It will be remembered that Damascus and the country around had been subdued by king David; but under Solomon, one Rezon, a servant of Hadadezer, king of the neighbouring state of Zobah, possessed himself of Damascus, and was an adversary to Solomon all his days. Perhaps it was the loss of his Damascus tribute (which must have been very valuable) that made Solomon, and after him Rehoboam, lay so heavy burdens on his own people. Ben-hadad, whom some suppose, though on rather uncertain grounds, to have been the great-grandson of this Rezon, now occupied the throne. He accepted the bribe offered him by king Asa; and for many years the Syrians of Damascus exercised a powerful influence on the kingdom of Israel, and also on that of Judah.

War with Syria.—The northern frontier of Palestine, which lay nearest to Damascus, soon bore testimony to the power of Ben-hadad. In quick succession he laid waste the towns of Ijon, Dan, and Abel-beth-maachah, with the district around the Lake of Galilee and the tribe of Naphtali. The king of Israel had to abandon his projects at Ramah, and hasten to defend his kingdom on the north. The Syrians seem to have retired without attempting a battle. That Baasha might have no excuse for his wickedness, and might clearly understand the reason of his troubles, a prophet named Jehu was sent to remonstrate with him.

Reigns of Elah and Zimri.—Both Baasha and his son ELAH, who reigned two years, followed in the footsteps of Jeroboam. Elah suffered the same fate at the hands of Zimri, one of his captains, as Nadab had suffered at the hands of Baasha. He was murdered in his palace, with all his house; and with him the second royal dynasty of Israel came to an end. ZIMRI can hardly be said to have formed a dynasty, for his reign lasted but a week. Being besieged by Omri, another claimant of the crown, in the palace of Tirzah, and reduced to desperation, he set fire to the palace and perished in the flames.

SECTION III.—DYNASTY OF OMRI, AND ERA OF ELIJAH AND
ELISHA—IDOLATRY RAMPANT.

Omri builds Samaria—Assyrian inscriptions—Reign of Ahab; Jezebel; Persecution—Appearance of Elijah—Contest on Mount Carmel—Its result—Elijah at Horeb—War with Syria—Defeat of Ben-hadad—Death of Ahab—Naboth's vineyard—The curse on Jericho—Reign of Ahaziah—The Moabite stone—Reign of Jehoram; Elijah and Elisha at Beth-el—At Jericho: at the Jordan—Translation of Elijah—The Mount of Transfiguration—Elijah's work—Miracles of Elisha—Naaman the Syrian—At Gilgal—Naaman's conversion—Gehazi—Effect of Elisha's miracles—More wars with Syria—Elisha at Damascus—Destruction of the house of Ahab—Jehu.

Omri Builds Samaria.—For four years the crown of Israel was contested by two claimants, OMRI and Tibni; but at last Omri secured the prize. When he came to the throne, instead of rebuilding the ruined palace of Tirzah, he bought the neighbouring hill of Samaria, and built the celebrated city of that name,* which was given to it in commemoration of Shemer, the former owner of the hill. The fine swelling hill of Samaria, almost worthy to be called a mountain, stands alone in the midst of a broad, noble basin, surrounded by higher mountains on every side. The ancient town seems to have been partly built on the flattened top of the mountain, thus giving rise to the terms of Isaiah's description, "The crown of pride"—"The glorious beauty which is on the head of the fat valley" (Isa. xxviii. 1–4). The town on the hill of Shemer became the

* "The situation of this royal city, if less beautiful, is more commanding than that of its sister, Shechem. Nearly in the centre of a basin, about five miles in diameter, rises a flattish, oval-shaped hill, to the height of some 300 feet. On the summit is a long and nearly level plateau, which breaks down at the sides 100 feet or more to an irregular terrace or belt of level land; below this the roots of the hill spread off more gradually into the surrounding valleys. The whole is now cultivated in terraces, in the formation of which the stones of the ancient city have been freely used. Groves of luxuriant olives almost cover the southern side, and fill the valley below, while single trees and little groups dot the rest. A wide circuit of picturesque mountains encompasses the basin, having only a narrow opening on the west, through which a winter torrent finds its way to the plain of Sharon. Little villages, with their green cornfields and gray olive-groves, stud the dark mountain sides or crown their summits, making the whole landscape one of the richest and most beautiful in Palestine. The modern village of Sebustieh may contain about sixty houses, with a population of four hundred. It stands u‗ n the broad terrace midway up the eastern side of the hill.... The view from the top is a noble one, embracing the glens and vales round the hill, the circuit of mountains, a section of the plain of Sharon, and the wide expanse of the Mediterranean. No better site for a capital could have been selected in the length and breadth of Palestine,—a strong position, rich environs, central situation, and an elevation sufficient to catch untainted the cool healthy breezes of the sea."—*Murray's Handbook*, pp. 344, 345.

scene of many remarkable events in the future history of the country.

Assyrian Inscriptions.—The reign of Omri was one of no ordinary external prosperity. "In the Assyrian inscriptions of the time, his is the Israelitish name with which they are most familiar. Samaria is known to the Assyrians for some centuries merely as Beth-Omri, the house or city of Omri; and even when they come into contact with Israelite monarchs of the house which succeeded Omri's upon the throne, they still regard them as descendants of the great chief, whom they view perhaps as the founder of the kingdom. Thus the Assyrian records agree generally with the Hebrew in the importance which they assign to this monarch, and specially confirm the fact that he was the founder of the later Israelite metropolis, Samaria." *

Reign of Ahab: Jezebel: Persecution.—Omri was succeeded by his son AHAB, one of the most conspicuous names in the history. Under Ahab the country received a terrible impulse towards idolatry, and consequently towards ruin. The great moving power in this direction was Jezebel, Ahab's wife, a daughter of the neighbouring king of Phœnicia, and a furious and fanatical promoter of the worship of Baal, the Phœnician god. An altar and a temple to this idol were among the earliest structures reared in the new capital, Samaria. The whole power and energies of Jezebel were brought to bear against the worship and worshippers of the true God. She was the Bloody Mary of her day; and had it not been for the wonderful prophet whom God raised up, to display the banner of the truth in those evil days, the cause of pure religion would have utterly perished in the kingdom of Israel.

Appearance of Elijah. From the woody mountains and defiles of Gilead † there suddenly emerged, and presented himself

---

* Rawlinson's Historical Illustrations, p. 112.

† Elijah is thought by some to have been a native of Tishbe in Galilee, but for some reason to have gone in his youth to reside across the Jordan in Gilead. Perhaps, like John the Baptist in the wilderness of Judæa, he was to be trained in that comparatively solitary district for his grand and difficult mission. If king Ahab and his courtiers knew the character of Elijah before his withdrawal to Gilead, his reappearance would probably produce a sensation like that at the Scottish court when it was known that John Knox had landed in Scotland. Others, however, think that Tishbe was in Gilead.

before king Ahab, an extraordinary man, with an extraordinary message. Great must have been the amazement of the king when the strange messenger, surveying the fat valley below, now awaiting, probably, the usual rains, uttered the ominous words, "As the Lord God of Israel liveth, before whom I stand, there shall not be dew nor rain these years, but according to my word." No sooner are the words spoken than the prophet disappears. ELIJAH the Tishbite has entered upon a conflict which is to last all his life, and to be the great characteristic of the reign of Ahab. Having sounded this note of defiance to Ahab, he must now find a hiding-place from his fury. This he got first at the brook Cherith,* probably near Jericho, where the ravens fed him; and afterwards about a hundred miles away, at Zarephath, a town in Phœnicia, where he was miraculously sustained with a poor widow's oil and meal. His gratitude to the woman was shown by a signal miracle—raising her son from the dead. This place of banishment, in the neighbourhood of Zidon, the head-quarters of the worship of Baal, was probably appointed for him that he might see with his own eyes the working of that detestable system which Ahab and Jezebel were now labouring to establish in Israel, on the ruins of the pure worship of Jehovah. By this means his indignation and horror would be the more aroused against idolatry, and his mind braced for his arduous task; just as Luther, after his visit

---

* The "brook Cherith" is believed to be the stream that flows through the *Wady el-Kelt*. This glen (probably the valley of Achor, where Achan was stoned) is "one of the most sublime ravines in Palestine. It is not less than from 400 to 500 feet deep, just wide enough below to give a passage to a little streamlet like a silver thread, and afford space for its narrow fringes of oleander. The sides are almost sheer precipices of naked rock, occasionally pierced by grottoes, apparently inaccessible to anything except the eagles that now hover round them; and yet history tells us that all these uncomfortable dens were once occupied by hermits....From the depths of the wild ravine issues a thread of verdure, gradually spreading out as it advances, until it mingles, at the distance of a mile or more from the base of the mountains, with the thickets that encompass the village of Riha (Jericho)....Away considerably to the north the vegetation and foliage stretch along the plain to the base of the mountains. They are nourished by two living fountains:—'one now, as always, called Dûk' (1 Mac. xvi. 14, 16); the other and larger, as well as more celebrated, now called the Spring 'of the Sultan,' once 'of Elisha;' which pour out, at the foot of the great limestone range, rills that trickle through glades of tangled forest shrub, which, but for their rank luxuriance and Oriental vegetation, almost recall the scenery of an English park. It is these streams, with their accompanying richness, that procured for Jericho, during the various stages of its existence, its long prosperity and grandeur."—*Murray's Handbook*, p. 191.

to Rome, was quickened to greater zeal against the corruptions of Popery.

Contest on Mount Carmel.—Three years after the beginning of the drought, the Lord commanded Elijah again to appear before Ahab. The result of the meeting was the celebrated trial on Mount Carmel between the priests of Baal and himself, to test whether Jehovah or Baal was the true God. The spot where the contest is believed to have occurred is the extreme eastern point of the range of Carmel, commanding a view both of the sea behind and of the great plain in front. Here had stood an altar of the Lord, which Jezebel had thrown down. "Close beneath must have been ranged, on one side the king and people, with the eight hundred and fifty prophets of Baal and Astarte; and on the other side, the solitary and commanding figure of the prophet of the Lord. Full before them opened the whole plain of Esdraelon, with Tabor and its kindred ranges in the distance; on the rising ground, at the opening of its valley, the city of Jezreel, with Ahab's palace and Jezebel's temple distinctly visible; in the nearer foreground, immediately under the base of the mountain, was clearly seen the winding stream of the Kishon, working its way through the narrow pass of the hills into the Bay of Acre. Such a scene, with such recollections of the past, with such sights of the present, was indeed a fitting theatre for a conflict more momentous than any which their ancestors had fought in the plain below." *

Its Result.—The result of the conflict was decisive. By fire from heaven the claims of the true God were vindicated. The defeated prophets of Baal were then brought down the mountain to the bed of the Kishon, and were there put to death. From the slaughter the king went up again to Carmel, to join in the sacrificial feast. Elijah too went up, apparently on another peak, to pray. Seven times he sent his servant to look out over the Mediterranean for signs of rain. At last the welcome sight appeared. A message was sent to the king, bidding him prepare his chariot and return quickly to his palace, lest the rain should swell the torrent of the Kishon, as in the days when it

* Stanley, p. 354.

swept away the host of Sisera, and should intercept his return to Jezreel. The hand of the Lord was upon Elijah; and girding his mantle around his loins, "amidst the gushing storm with which the night closed in, he ran before the chariot to the entrance of Jezreel, distant, though still visible, from the scene of his triumph."

Elijah at Horeb.—The tidings of Elijah's victory only inflamed the jealous rage of Jezebel. The prophet, who perhaps expected that the worship of the true God would now be restored in its purity over the land, was forced to flee for his life. It would have been unsafe to return to Zarephath, so he was compelled to fly southward. Nowhere along the whole extent of the country, not even in the kingdom of Judah, could he find a place which he deemed secure from Jezebel's fury. Jehoshaphat, king of Judah, had made a league with Ahab, and might have had to give up his fugitive subject. At last, worn and weary, having reached the wilderness of Beer-sheba, and feeling like an outcast or outlaw whom no man cared for, he lay down under a "broom" or retem-tree to die. A miraculous supply of food and of strength carried him on through the wilderness till he reached the lonely wilds of Horeb. The scenery carried him back six hundred years. It was amid these valleys that the eye of Moses had caught sight of the burning bush; and thence he had been sent back to Egypt, to unfurl the banner of the truth, when all seemed dark and desperate, and to deliver his people. It was these cliffs that had been crimsoned by the glow of the fiery pillar; it was around that tall jagged peak that the lightnings and thunders had played when God came down in awful majesty. It was here that Moses had interceded for an apostate people, and had obtained their pardon, after the gross idolatry of the golden calf. The scenery was well fitted to revive the prophet's faith and courage. In addition to this, God made a special communication to him of an encouraging kind, and sent him to Damascus, to anoint Hazael to be king of Syria; then he was to anoint Jehu to be king of Israel; and Elisha, of Abel-meholah (near the Lake of Galilee), to be prophet in his room. The journey to Damascus was cheerfully undertaken; the faith and courage of the prophet were wonderfully revived; and the company of Elisha, a man singularly like-minded, was given him to cheer the remainder of his pilgrimage.

War with Syria.—Meanwhile, the attention of Ahab was turned away from matters of religion to the defence of his kingdom. Ben-hadad, king of Syria, again appeared in the land. Since he had invaded Israel his power had greatly increased. No fewer than thirty-two kings, whom he had probably subdued, and attached to his court, now followed his standard; and, passing the places in the north which he had formerly laid waste, he made a bold demonstration against Samaria itself, and sent an insolent message to Ahab, demanding his entire submission. Ahab repelled his demand with spirit, and was soon after informed by a prophet of the Lord that Ben-hadad would be defeated by the young men of the princes of the provinces. It turned out as the prophet had said. But next year Ben-hadad resolved to repeat his attempt. His servants flattered him by suggesting that he would succeed better on the plains, where his cavalry and his chariots might act, than on the mountains; saying that the gods of Israel were only gods of the hills, and not of the valleys.

Defeat of Ben-hadad.—Returning with as great an army as that which had been destroyed the previous year, he avoided the hilly district of Samaria, and pitched at Aphek, in the plain of Esdraelon. A prophet of the Lord was sent to tell Ahab, that on account of the impious saying of Ben-hadad about the God of Israel, he would be totally defeated. A great slaughter of Syrians took place in the field, followed by the destruction of many more by the fall of some buildings in Aphek. Ben-hadad was compelled to humble himself before Ahab, who, with mistaken clemency, spared his life, and made a league with him.

Death of Ahab.—But the war was soon renewed. The scene of the next campaign was at Ramoth, in Gilead, on the eastern side of the Jordan. Ahab had persuaded his neighbour Jehoshaphat, king of Judah, to go with him to the war. The preliminary deliberation of these kings acquired a deep interest from the faithfulness of Micaiah, an honest but ill-treated prophet of the Lord, who warned Ahab against the expedition. The warning of the faithful prophet turned out to be well founded. Ahab was slain in the battle; his army was disbanded; and Ben-hadad was left to do as he pleased on the Gilead side of the Jordan.

Naboth's Vineyard.—Some time before this fatal expedition, Ahab had committed a heinous crime, for which Elijah had to denounce God's judgment against him. He had built a palace at Jezreel,* at the foot of Mount Gilboa, in the great plain of Esdraelon, either because he admired the situation, or perhaps because his wife Jezebel wished to live nearer to her native Phœnicia. The adjacent possession of one Naboth would have been a very convenient addition to the royal demesne, and Ahab had been very eager to secure it for that purpose. But Naboth had stoutly refused to part with the inheritance of his fathers. At the instigation of Jezebel, a false charge of blasphemy had been got up against him, on which he was put to death. As Ahab went to take possession of the coveted vineyard, Elijah had met him and had prophesied that in the place where dogs had licked Naboth's blood they should lick the blood of Ahab. The prophecy was literally fulfilled. The chariot that conveyed the wounded king from Ramoth-gilead,

---

* Jezreel has shared the degradation of its founder. Its present name is Zer'in. It is situated on the crest of a low spur, which projects some distance into the plain from Gilboa. "The modern village is composed of about twenty wretched houses, apparently fast falling to ruin. The only sightly building is a square tower of some antiquity, now used as a medâfeh or inn, where travellers are treated to bare walls, fleas *ad libitum*, and a supper at the public expense.... Yet this is the royal Jezreel where Ahab built his palace.... As we stand on the crown of the ridge, perhaps on the very site of the palace, we open our Bible at 1 Kings xxi., and read the story of poor Naboth and his vineyard. The vineyard was here below us in the plain (ver. 16).... Then turn to 2 Kings ix. 11-37, and the scene is changed; and every incident of that fearful change is illustrated by the natural features of the scene before us. We see how up the valley from the Jordan Jehu's troops might be seen advancing,—how in Naboth's 'field' the two sovereigns met the relentless soldier,—how, whilst Joram died on the spot, Ahaziah drove across the westward plain towards the mountain pass, by the beautiful village of En-gannim ('the garden-house'), but was overtaken in the ascent, and died of his wounds at Megiddo,—how, in the open place which, as usual in Eastern towns, lay before the gates of Jezreel, the body of the queen was trampled under the hoofs of Jehu's horses,—how the dogs gathered round it, as even to this day, in the wretched village now seated on the ruins of the once splendid city of Jezreel, they prowl on the mounds without the walls for the offal and carrion thrown out to them to consume."—*Murray's Handbook*, p. 354.

clotted with his blood, was washed at the pool or water reservoir of Samaria; and the dogs, that prowl in great numbers about Eastern cities, licked up the blood.

The Curse on Jericho.—It is remarkable that in the reign of Ahab another terrible curse was verified. Hiel, a man of Beth-el, who had probably been utterly corrupted by the idolatrous worship of that place, and so had been led to set the word of God at nought, attracted apparently by the beautiful fields and fountains of Jericho, went down to the inviting spot, and proceeded to build up its walls. The death of his firstborn at the laying of the foundation, and of his youngest child at the setting up of the gates, literally verified the curse of Joshua (ch. vi. 26).

Reign of Ahaziah.—AHAZIAH, the son and successor of Ahab, was a man of less force of character, but of the same disposition. His idolatrous and superstitious turn was shown by his sending to Baal-zebub, the god of Ekron, to inquire whether he should recover from the effects of a fall he had received in Samaria. Elijah was ordered by God to go and testify against this open and insulting preference of Baal-zebub to the God of Israel. Hearing of this, the king attempted with a high hand to seize Elijah; but twice in succession fire from heaven consumed the company of fifty soldiers that were sent to arrest him, and the prophet remained secure in the protection of his God. At last, at God's command, he went fearlessly and readily to the king, and told him that, after his insult to the true God, he should not recover. The name of this god of Ekron, Baal-zebub, means literally "lord of flies." Ekron was one of the cities of the Philistines; but that people seem to have borrowed their religion largely from the Phœnicians. It is uncertain whether the name Baal-zebub was a contemptuous nickname invented by the Hebrews, or a name given to the god by his worshippers on account of his supposed usefulness in ridding them of the great nuisance of flies. On some Phœnician coins the figure of an insect has been noticed, which is supposed to have had some reference to this idol.

The Moabite Stone.—It is emphatically recorded that "Moab rebelled against Israel after the death of Ahab." This event has had light thrown on it by the recent discovery of a monument, in the land of Moab, known as "the Moabite stone," erected to commemorate the occurrence. Mesha, king of Moab, a great sheep-master (2 Kings iii. 4, 5), threw off the yoke of Israel, and inscribed on a pillar the series of events connected with that result. The stone bearing the inscription has recently been discovered and deciphered. "It appears from this document that a grievous oppression of the Moabites was begun by Omri, and continued by his son Ahab, who together oppressed the nation for a space which Mesha reckons roughly as forty years. After this, probably in the first year of Ahaziah, the Moabites rebelled. Mesha attacked and took the various towns that were occupied by Israelite garrisons throughout the country, and, after a sharp struggle, made himself master of the whole territory. He then rebuilt such of the Moabite cities as had fallen into decay during the oppression, strengthening their fortifications, and otherwise restoring and beautifying them." *

Reign of Jehoram: Elijah and Elisha at Beth-el.—Ahaziah was succeeded by his brother JEHORAM, who reigned twelve years. The beginning of his reign was signalized by one of the grandest events either of Jewish or of any other history. The work of Elijah was now done. The faithful Tishbite was to receive an honour which had been bestowed but once before, in all the history of the world—he was to be translated to heaven without dying. For some time past he seems to have resided with Elisha near Gilgal, superintending and stimulating the schools of the prophets, now almost the only fountains of true piety in the land. A divine impulse leads them away from Gilgal, probably to some height in the neighbourhood. From thence they are called by the same mysterious power to go down to Beth-el.† There are sons of the prophets even in

---

* Rawlinson's Historical Illustrations, p. 117.

† From the Palestine Exploration Map, just published (1880), it appears that Beth-el is 2890 feet above the sea-level. Very few places in the neighbourhood are higher than Beth-el, so as to justify the expression, "go down to Beth-el." In the map we can find but three or four.

Beth-el. Their minds are oppressed with a dark presentiment of an approaching bereavement; and as they see Elisha, they come to him with solemn and anxious faces, to ask whether he knows that God is to take his master from his head that day. Yes, he knows it; but it is not a thing to be spoken of,—his emotions on the subject are too deep for utterance.

At Jericho: at the Jordan. — Resuming their march, the two prophets go on to Jericho, where the same scene is repeated. The places which they traversed were to be the chief scenes of Elisha's ministry, and the purpose of the journey seems to have been to transfer to him the spiritual charge of the district; but only in so far as he was quite willing to undertake it. Once and again Elisha got leave to remain behind, if he pleased; but each time, with remarkable solemnity, he refused to do so. Another stage brings the two prophets to the Jordan. Afar off, on the cliffs above Jericho, a band of the sons of the prophets have taken their stand, to watch the wonderful manifestation of divine power that is to take place. At the touch of the prophet's mantle the waters of the river separate, and Elijah and Elisha pass over on dry land. The man of God invites his younger brother to make his parting request. It is worthy of the occasion: as the first-born of Elijah's spiritual family, he asks a double portion of his spirit; and the request is not denied.

Translation of Elijah.—Onward and onward they still go, till they have reached the mountains of Nebo,—perhaps the very Pisgah from which Moses disappeared: "And it came to pass as they still went on, and talked, that, behold, there appeared a chariot of fire, and horses of fire, and parted them both asunder; and Elijah went up by a whirlwind into heaven. And Elisha saw it, and he cried, My father, my father! the chariot of Israel and the horsemen thereof!" And so the prophet of Israel was borne away to the presence of the Master whom he had served so faithfully.

The Mount of Transfiguration.—Once again, after the lapse of nearly a thousand years, he appeared on one of the mountains of Israel, in company with Moses, and held communion with his suffering Lord. The scene of this meeting was far from the scene of the translation,—probably, as has already been remarked, on the heights of Hermon. It would be difficult to say whether his translation or his mission to the Mount of Transfiguration was the higher tribute to this noble and faithful warrior of the Lord.

Elijah's Work.—Amid all his discouragements, Elijah did a great work. He counteracted to a very considerable degree the fanatical schemes of Ahab and Jezebel; and he arrested, though he could not avert, the destruction of the kingdom of the ten tribes. Raised up to oppose a mighty tide of corruption, he was necessarily a man of stern and rigid mould,—a man to be admired and honoured rather than loved. He represented the law in its stern severity, rather than the gospel in its winning and tender love. His labours seem to have done much good at Beth-el, Gilgal, Jericho, and other places that were remote from Ahab's residence. As the kings of Israel moved northward, first to Tirzah, then to Samaria, and occasionally, at least, to Jezreel, the southern borders of the kingdom seem to have become more assimilated to Judah, where much true piety was still found. The setting up by Ahab of a temple and an altar to Baal in Samaria seems to have greatly lessened the importance of Dan and Beth-el as seats of idolatrous worship. It was probably from this cause that Beth-el, once the headquarters of idolatry, was now a stronghold of the sons of the prophets. After the memorable contest at Mount Carmel, and especially after the death of Ahab, the open persecution of the Lord's servants ceased, and the holy work of the schools of the prophets was carried on without molestation.

Miracles of Elisha.—After the removal of Elijah, ELISHA is the prominent figure in the history of Israel. The same aspect of stern severity sits upon his character. We find him, after healing the bitter waters of Jericho, going up to Beth-el, thence to Mount Carmel, and thence to Samaria. While he was residing at Samaria the trumpet of war again sounded; and when the kings of Israel, Judah, and Edom went out to fight with the king of Moab, Elisha accompanied the host. Proceeding round the southern angle of the Dead Sea, the armies seem to have advanced into Moab through the territories of Edom, who was then on the side of the allies. Being greatly at a loss for water, advice was sought from Elisha, who was following the camp; and, through his intercession, made solely for the sake of Jehoshaphat, a supply was miraculously secured. The enemy was totally defeated. Next we find Elisha travelling over the country, wherever work was provided for him, doing much to revive and foster the spirit of godliness. In one of these tours, probably near Jericho or Gilgal, he caused a poor woman's store of oil to be multiplied to such an extent, that with the proceeds she cleared her debts and protected her sons from expected slavery. Then we find him at Shunem, in the plain of Jezreel, close to the residence of the king, where a woman of high rank openly countenanced him, and built a chamber for his use, whenever, in his missionary journeys, he should pass that way. At this period he was high in influence, both with the king and with the captain of the guard. Next he is at Mount Carmel, whither the Shunammite woman rides to him when her son is seized with mortal illness: he goes with her to Shunem, and restores the boy to life. Then we find him at Gilgal, miraculously preserving the sons of the prophets from the effects of a poisonous herb, and multiplying a present of bread and fruit that had been given him, so that it served a hundred men.

Naaman the Syrian.—The next incident in his life was a very memorable one. Naaman, captain-general of the great king of Syria, had been seized with leprosy,—one of the most repulsive of Eastern diseases. Among the slaves of his household was a little girl, who had been carried off from her Israelite home in one of the forays of the Syrians, and sold to Naaman. This little child, touched with pity for her master, expressed an earnest wish to her mistress that her lord were with the prophet in Samaria, for he would recover him from his leprosy. Elisha had probably been living in Samaria when the child was stolen from her home, but when Naaman reached Samaria in search of him, his abode was at Gilgal or at Jericho, near the Jordan. When king Jehoram heard his errand, it threw him into consternation; for he seems, like many kings, to have utterly undervalued the servant of the Lord, the truest noble in his kingdom, and to have known little of him, so that when he heard Naaman's message, he fancied that the terrible king of Syria was only seeking an occasion for war.

At Gilgal.—Elisha, hearing at Gilgal what was going on, bade them send the Syrian captain to him. Over the hill of Ephraim, and down the steep and dreary pass that led to Gilgal, the Syrian cavalcade journeyed, and at last it arrived at Elisha's gate. But when the news of the arrival was carried to the prophet, he did not even condescend to appear, but sent a message to Naaman to go and wash seven times in the Jordan. He preferred to hide the genuine kindness of his heart under a stern, almost insulting message. The mighty stranger fumed and fretted at such unceremonious treatment, but yielded at last to the calm arguments of his attendants, and washed in the adjacent river. The spot must have been near the place where the Israelites, under Joshua, crossed the Jordan about six hundred years before. The cure was instantaneous and complete.

Naaman's Conversion.—In a short time Naaman returned to the prophet's dwelling, and overwhelmed him with thanks and the offer of gifts, which Elisha, with noble disinterestedness, declined. And Naaman was not only cured of his leprosy, but was convinced that the God of Israel was the true God. On leaving, he made two singular requests of Elisha. One was, that he might carry with him two mules' burden of earth; thinking that the earth from such a spot would be sacred, and would benefit him in worshipping the God of Israel,— just as the Mohammedan now counts the soil of Mecca sacred, and thinks it a great advantage to have it beneath his head when he prostrates himself. The other request was, that when he should go into the temple of Rimmon, as his master would compel him to do, and should bow before the idol, the act might be pardoned, as it would not imply any real respect. We have no information about Rimmon or his worship; the name does not occur elsewhere in the Bible, or in any ancient writer.

Gehazi.—The departure of Naaman was connected with a memorable incident in the history of Gehazi, Elisha's servant. Naaman would probably proceed northward, up the Jordan valley towards Damascus. When he had gone but a little way, Gehazi hastened after him, saying that two of the sons of the prophets had just come down from Mount Ephraim, and that his master had sent him to beg a silver talent and two changes of raiment. Indignant both at the lie and at the perfidy of Gehazi, as well as at his recklessly counteracting the effects of his own disinterestedness, Elisha doomed him to inherit the leprosy of Naaman: "And he went out from his presence a leper as white as snow."

Effect of Elisha's Miracles.—The next miracle of Elisha was on a humbler platform: an axe, borrowed by one of the sons of the prophets, having fallen into the Jordan, "he cut down a stick, cast it in thither, and the iron did swim."—The effect of these miracles could not fail to be very great; and the cause of true religion must have been placed in a far more favourable position than it had held in the reign of Ahab. But there was one heart unsoftened and unchanged, alike by these and by subsequent wonders done by Elisha. That was the heart of the king. Elisha had removed once more either to Samaria or to the immediate neighbourhood (Dothan); and his presence there, and his fearless and faithful spirit, seem to have so stirred up the king's heart against him, that all his eminent services to his country were of no avail in his favour.

More Wars with Syria.—Another war had broken out with the Syrians. In the first campaign, Elisha saved his country by one of those pieces of cunning which even good men did not shrink from in those times,—in answer to his prayer, the Syrians were smitten with blindness, and were led blindfold into Samaria, when they thought they were going to Elisha's abode in Dothan. In the next campaign, Ben-hadad came with all his forces and besieged Samaria. The famine was awful. Women were devouring their own children. The infatuated king Jehoram laid all the blame on Elisha, and vowed that his head should be struck from his shoulders before night. Unmoved by the impious threat, Elisha calmly foretold that next day the people of Samaria should be revelling in plenty. The prediction was literally verified. The Syrian host was seized in the night with a panic, and fled in disorder to the fords of the Jordan. The people of Samaria, entering their deserted camp, found provisions in abundance, and ate and drank to their heart's content.

Elisha at Damascus.—Some time after this, Elisha visited Damascus. His fame had travelled thither before him. Naaman, the great warrior, had carried it with him from Gilgal; Ben-hadad's officers had brought it from Dothan, and Ben-hadad himself from Samaria. He was received at Damascus with extraordinary honours. A present borne by forty camels was sent him from the king. Ben-hadad was sick, and wished to know whether he should recover. The disease, the prophet said, was not a fatal one; still Ben-hadad was near his end: his successor would be Hazael,—the officer that now spoke to Elisha; and Hazael would be guilty of such horrible cruelties to the people of Israel, that the prophet's flesh crept as he thought of them. The next day Hazael suffocated his master in bed, and usurped the Syrian crown.

Destruction of the House of Ahab.—Another great revolution was at hand. Four kings of the house of Omri and Ahab had now sat on the throne of Israel; but the death-knell of the wicked dynasty had rung. There had been a new war between Syria and Israel; and Ramoth-gilead, as before, was the scene of the contest. King Jehoram had been wounded in battle, and had retired to Jezreel, where his cousin, king Ahaziah of Judah, had come to see him. Jehu, a captain of Jehoram's, was conducting the campaign at Ramoth-gilead. One of the sons of the prophets was sent to Ramoth to anoint this Jehu king of Israel, and to commission him to root out the wicked house of Ahab. Never did a man execute a bloody commission with more hearty zeal. The army having proclaimed him king, Jehu mounted his chariot, crossed the Jordan, and galloped towards Jezreel. As he dashed furiously along, the watchman from the tower of Jezreel caught sight of him and reported his appearance to the king. Both Jehoram and Ahaziah rode out in their chariots to meet him. But they were both of the house of Ahab, and Jehu's sword thirsted for their blood. Jehoram was struck down by an arrow from Jehu's hand, and fell in what had been the inheritance of Naboth. Ahaziah was pursued to Megiddo, where he died mortally wounded. Jezebel was flung down from a window in Jezreel, and was devoured by dogs. Seventy sons of Ahab were put to death in Samaria. The brethren of Ahaziah were put to death in the same place. The priests and the worshippers of Baal were enticed into his temple at Samaria; the doors were then blockaded, and the inmates were killed to a man. And thus in a moment the mighty house of Ahab was brought to desolation, and the fabric of Phœnician idolatry, reared with such care and at such cost, was utterly overthrown.

Jehu.—JEHU now ascended the throne. Notwithstanding his zeal in executing judgment on the house of Ahab, he was for the most part regardless of the will of God. Although the worship of Baal was abolished, the worship of the calves at Beth-el and Dan, as originated by Jeroboam, not only continued, but seems to have revived, after the destruction of Baal's temple at Samaria. In consequence of this unfaithfulness, the territories of the kingdom of Israel began to be lessened in the reign of Jehu; and the whole tract east of Jordan, including Bashan and Gilead, fell for a time into the hands of the Syrians. We learn from the Assyrian monuments that Jehu, who is called in them the son of Omri, was obliged to pay tribute to Shalmaneser, the Assyrian king.

SECTION IV.—DYNASTY OF JEHU, AND ERA OF JONAH, AMOS, AND HOSEA —IDOLATRY SLIGHTLY CHECKED.

Jehu's reign: Jehoahaz: Joash: Death of Elisha –Jeroboam II.--The prophets of judgment—Promises of restoration—Jonah's mission to Nineveh State of Nineveh—Jonah's reluctance—Effect of his preaching Lesson of the gourd— Prophecy of Amos—Hosea, the Jeremiah of Israel Approaching downfall of the kingdom.

Jehu's Reign: Jehoahaz: Joash: Death of Elisha. — The reigns of JEHU, and those of JEHOAHAZ and JOASH or JEHOASH, his son and his grandson, lasted in all about sixty years, but they were not signalized by many remarkable events. Elisha, who seems to have been living in retirement for some time, died, at a very advanced age, in the reign of Joash. His influence must have been exceedingly beneficial over many individuals and in many places; but the nation at large was too confirmed in idolatry to be easily reformed. Still, idolatry appears to have received a check, so that the destruction of the kingdom was arrested for a time.

Jeroboam II. — Joash, too, evidently met with considerable success in battle with the Syrians; as did also his son, JEROBOAM II. Indeed, under these two kings the kingdom of Israel recovered not a little of its former splendour. The reign of Jeroboam lasted forty-one years, and was chiefly memorable for the appearance of some of those prophets who have left permanent writings behind them. Jonah, Amos, and Hosea belonged to this period, and were connected chiefly with the kingdom of Israel.

The Prophets of Judgment. — The prophets who now appeared on the stage were not superior, either in gifts or in grace, to those who had flourished before them, but they had a different function to perform. It was now apparent that in the kingdom of the ten tribes, at least, the disease of idolatry could not be healed by any remedy acting inwardly. It was also apparent that ordinary judgments or chastisements would not produce the desired effect. It was necessary to have a great catastrophe, an overwhelming judgment, that would all but consume the nation, yet would admit, at a distant period, of a resurrection to new life.

Promises of Restoration. — It was of this sweeping judgment that the prophets who were now raised up had to speak, in God's name. It was necessary that they should commit their messages to writing, because the period of time over which this new judgment was to extend would embrace many generations; and both the warnings and the consolations connected with it concerned multitudes who were not living at the time of their utterance. The message of the prophets now becomes preëminently "a burden,"—heavy, painful, distressing. Yet amid these woful utterances many consolations are introduced, for the refreshment of the faithful. Allusions to a happy restoration are found in them all. In some of the prophets who wrote to the ten tribes, these allusions were not very distinct; but in those who were raised up soon afterwards, in the neighbouring kingdom of Judah, they were much more explicit. In these latter, great prominence is given to the coming of the Messiah, in connection with the restoration of the kingdom of God; and in Isaiah, especially, his many sufferings and expiatory death are dwelt on as the foundation of that new and better kingdom which was to be the glory of the latter days.

Jonah's Mission to Nineveh.—Jonah, a native of Gath-hepher, in the tribe of Zebulun, appears to have first come on the field in the reign of Joash (2 Kings xiv. 25). Probably he had been a pupil of Elisha's, and had succeeded him as the public and prominent witness for God in the kingdom. The first prophecy which we are told that he uttered was, that the dominions of Israel, that were now greatly diminished, should again be enlarged,—the result, doubtless, of a partial repentance and forsaking of idolatry. This prophecy was fulfilled in the reign of Jeroboam II., who recovered Hamath, Damascus, and other places that had been lost. But, as usual, the good effects lasted but a very short time; open idolatry broke out anew. To convey a striking and unusual rebuke of this state of things, Jonah was commanded to undertake a mission of a very remarkable kind. He was ordered to go to a great heathen city, and to testify against it, threatening it with destruction on account of its wickedness. God's intention seems to have been "to provoke Israel to jealousy,"—that is, to rebuke their apathy, and to stir them up to penitence, by showing them a great heathen nation, from the king to the beggar, lying penitent and prostrate in the dust, under a single warning from a single prophet. Such a sight as this would have been a great rebuke to a kingdom like Israel, that had been favoured with so many eminent prophets, and had received such earnest warnings. Should the tribes of Israel neglect such a lesson, their final destruction could not be long delayed.

State of Nineveh.—The city to which Jonah was commanded to go was NINEVEH, the capital of Assyria. We cannot say with absolute certainty who was king of Assyria at the time. According to Mr. Smith it was Vul-nizari III.* This king was a great warrior, and, among other places, he directed several campaigns against Syria, pushing his armies on one occasion up to the borders of Manasseh.† Nineveh had not yet acquired all the splendour it achieved under its later kings; but even now it must have been a city of great magnitude and splendour. Jonah speaks of it as requiring a three days' journey to walk round it; and Sir A. H. Layard, the celebrated excavator of its temples and palaces, says that the whole space containing ruins is sixty miles round. This vast space must have been half town, half country. The inner part of the city was surrounded by a lofty wall, the ruins of which still exist, being eight miles round. Already there were palaces and public buildings in Nineveh of which the rare structure and the remarkable magnificence must have made a great impression on Jonah. Slabs with pictures and inscriptions recording the conquests of the kings had probably begun to be erected in public places. On these slabs might be seen ample evidence of the savage and cruel spirit in which enemies were treated. Here might be seen a picture exhibiting a row of captives, each impaled on an iron spike; another, representing a group undergoing the process of being flayed alive; while in a third, a row, with halters round their necks, or hooks in their tongues, were dragged about to feast the eyes of their conquerors, preparatory to their being put to a more terrible death. The wickedness of the place was in proportion to its wealth and magnificence. In some respects it was hardly less guilty than Sodom or Gomorrah.

Jonah's Reluctance.—At first Jonah shrank from his commission to proclaim, to this the greatest city of Asia, perhaps of the world, "Yet forty days, and Nineveh shall be destroyed." His book relates how he tried to flee from the face of the Lord;

* Smith's History of Assyria, p. 67.   † Ibid. p. 69.

how his purpose was defeated; how he was miraculously engulfed in a great fish, and preserved in its belly till he had confessed his sin; and how, gaining at last the requisite faith and courage, he went to Nineveh, and faithfully delivered his message. Scepticism has found the fish of Jonah a great stumbling-block; but if we admit the supernatural to be in Scripture at all, the particular form is only a matter of detail. Jonah was sent out on a very unusual mission, and the whole circumstances of the case justified an extraordinary miracle.

Effect of His Preaching.—Contrary to all anticipation, a great effect was produced by the preaching of Jonah. Nineveh repented, and the Lord resolved to spare it. Jonah was deeply distressed at this forbearance. His mind seems to have been quite filled with the case of his own people Israel; and he seems to have thought that this forbearance would encourage them to continue in sin. If he had gone back to Samaria with the dreadful intelligence that Nineveh, in all its magnificence, had perished, there would have been more likelihood of his own people getting a fright, and repenting of their sins. His fault lay in his want of concern or of consideration for Nineveh.

Lesson of the Gourd.—He was rebuked by a sort of acted parable, connected with a gourd. The gourd is believed to have been a castor-oil plant, common near the Tigris, that grows quickly and flourishes in the driest soil, even among stones and rubbish. A plant of this kind had been very useful to Jonah, it had shielded him from the sun; and when it withered he missed it much, and was greatly distressed. So God taught him that Nineveh—though not, like Israel, a choice vine, but, like this gourd, an outlandish plant—might be very useful in His eyes; there might yet be important work for Nineveh to do for God, so that its destruction ought to have been regarded as ground for deep concern, and its being spared matter rather of satisfaction than of grief. Thus reproved by God, the prophet probably returned to his country; for there is no reason to suppose that the mound at Nineveh, called "The tomb of Jonah," was really his burial-place. Not many years afterwards, one of the purposes for which God had spared Nineveh became apparent. Nineveh was the appointed scourge of the wickedness and impenitence of the ten tribes; and the walls which Jonah would have rejoiced to see prostrate, were yet destined to enclose his captive countrymen.

Prophecy of Amos.—Amos was another of the prophets that flourished in the reign of Jeroboam II. He was originally a herdman of Tekoa, in the kingdom of Judah; but, when called to be a prophet, he appears to have taken up his residence at Beth-el; and there, with great boldness and vehemence, he prophesied of the destruction that was coming on Israel and other kingdoms (Amos vii. 13). He rebuked the corruption of manners and gross luxuriousness prevalent in Israel,—charged the great men with partiality as judges, and with violence towards the poor; he represented, in a series of symbolical visions, the successive punishments that were to be inflicted on the people, and foretold the captivity of the ten tribes in a foreign country. Yet the Lord, he said, would not utterly destroy the house of Israel, but, after sifting and cleansing it among the nations, would raise it again to more than its former glory, when the fallen tabernacle of David should be reared once more.

Hosea, the Jeremiah of Israel.—A third prophet, who also uttered the word of the Lord at this time in the kingdom of the ten tribes, was Hosea. He began to prophesy in the end of the reign of Jeroboam II., and continued to lift up his voice for sixty years, till the days of Hoshea, the last of the kings of Israel. He was to Israel what Jeremiah was to Judah,—its weeping prophet. The extreme tenderness and plaintiveness of some parts of his writings remind us of the Saviour weeping over Jerusalem. His prophecies were addressed almost exclusively to the ten tribes. They give a vivid but sad picture of the degeneracy of the kingdom. "The kings and the princes were murderers and profligates (vii. 3–7); the idolatrous priests had spread their shameful festivals and their deceitful oracles all over the land (iv. 12–14, x. xii. xiii. 2); the great parties in the state resorted for help sometimes to Assyria, at other times to Egypt (2 Kings xv. 19,

xvii. 4); while the whole nation entirely relied on human help (v. 13, vii. 8-11, viii. 9, 10, x. 13, etc.); worldly and sinful objects were pursued with the same eagerness by Ephraim as by Canaan (xii. 7, 8); a listless security blinded all minds (v. 4, xii. 8); giving place in the moment of danger to a repentance merely of the lips (vii. 16); and, what was the root of all other evils, God and his word were forgotten" (iv. 1-6, viii. 12.) *

Approaching Downfall of the Kingdom.—From such representations as those of Hosea, it is plain that before the overthrow of the kingdom, idolatry had entirely recovered from the check which the labours of Elijah, Elisha, and their colleagues, had been the means of producing. Ephraim's goodness had been but as a morning cloud and the early dew. Judgment was now ready to be poured out. Yet better days would also come, when God should be as the dew to Israel, and heal his backsliding. The prophet delights to linger on these happier scenes, and manifests the greatest distress in contemplating what he dared not conceal,—the coming overthrow of the kingdom. Nothing can be more plaintive or affecting than the passage where God is represented as not knowing how he shall be able to execute on Ephraim the fierceness of his wrath (xi. 8). To understand the state of things in which these judgments were announced, it is necessary to study the closing reigns of the kingdom of Israel.

SECTION V.—CLOSING REIGNS—IDOLATRY TERMINATES IN
DESTRUCTION.

The kings, murderers and profligates—An oasis in the desert—Four Assyrian invasions—Total destruction of the kingdom--The ten tribes led captive to Assyria—"The outcasts of Israel."

The Kings, Murderers and Profligates.—The history of the kings that followed Jeroboam II. is only a history of murderers and profligates. ZACHARIAH, son of Jeroboam, was openly murdered after a reign of six months. His murderer, SHAL-

* Angus, Bible Handbook, p. 483.

LUM, sat but one month on the throne, and was despatched by one MENAHEM, who came on him from Tirzah; and after committing revolting cruelties on those who opposed him, he reigned ten years in Samaria. The reign of his son PEKA-HIAH lasted but two years, and was ended by the dagger of Pekah, one of his captains. PEKAH held his place for the unusually long period of twenty years, but was at last murdered by Hoshea. Ten years of tumult and anarchy seem to have elapsed before HOSHEA succeeded in establishing himself on the throne (compare 2 Kings xvi. and xvii. 1.) After a reign of nine years, Samaria was taken by Shalmaneser, king of Assyria, Hoshea and his people were carried captive to the dominions of Shalmaneser, and the kingdom of the ten tribes came to an end.

An Oasis in the Desert. — Without exception, these later kings were unprincipled and profligate; and the abominable practices, so strongly denounced and so plaintively mourned over by the prophets, increased from reign to reign. Still even this dark wilderness of guilt did not want its oasis. A touching incident is recorded in the reign of Pekah. In a furious war with Judah, one hundred and twenty thousand of the men of that kingdom had been slain, and two hundred thousand women and children, with much spoil, were brought to Samaria. At the gate of that city, Oded, a prophet of the Lord, met the victorious army, and warned them not to offend God by wanton cruelty to these poor captives, since their sufferings had been caused by unfaithfulness to their God, and there was a fearful risk that the same cause might bring similar judgments upon themselves. "Are there not with you, even with you, sins against the Lord your God?" The bold appeal was successful. The conquerors treated the captives with singular kindness;—clothed, shod, and anointed them; gave them meat and drink; placed the feeble upon asses, and brought them to Jericho, where they were restored to their brethren. "This beautiful incident comes over our sense as might some strain of soft and happy music amidst the bray of trumpets and the alarms of war. It also proves that, even in the worst of times, a righteous few were found, even in Israel, who honoured the God of their fathers, and stood in dread of his judgments."

Four Assyrian Invasions.—In the course of this period, the kingdom of Israel was invaded or threatened by four several kings of Assyria: (1) by SHALMANESER II., to whom Jehu paid tribute; he is not mentioned in Scripture, but he is referred to on the monuments: (2) by PUL, in the reign of Menahem (2 Kings xv. 19), whose name does not occur in the Assyrian catalogues, but who is supposed to have reigned at Babylon;* (3) by TIGLATH-PILESER II., in the reign of Pekah (2 Kings xv. 29); and (4) by SHALMANESER IV.† The power of the Assyrian monarchy had now reached colossal dimensions; the old jealousy of Egypt prevailed; and in order to reach Egypt, it was desirable to secure the kingdoms that lay between it and Assyria. When Pul made his invasion, Menahem deemed it most prudent to buy him off with a bribe of a thousand talents of silver. The third invasion, by Tiglath-pileser, "lord of the Tigris," was brought about by Ahaz, king of Judah, asking his protection against Pekah, king of Israel, and Rezin, king of Syria, who had conspired against him. Under this invasion all the frontier towns on the north-east were taken,—nearly the same as the king of Syria had taken in the reign of Baasha —Ijon, and Abel-beth-maachah, and Janoah, and Kedesh, and Hazor; along with Gilead, Galilee, and Naphtali; and the inhabitants were carried captive into Assyria. At the same time, Tiglath-pileser defeated and slew Rezin, the king of Syria; took Damascus, and carried off the inhabitants into Assyria; thus putting an end to the Syrian kingdom of Damascus.

Total Destruction of the Kingdom.—In the reign of Hoshea, the remnant of the kingdom of Israel was again threatened, by Shalmaneser, the new Assyrian king. Resistance was vain, and Hoshea agreed to pay him a tribute. After a time the tribute was withheld, and Hoshea was found to be negotiating with So or Sabaco, king of Egypt, who, to repress the old

* See Smith's Dictionary, art. *Pul.*
† The numbers annexed to the names of the kings are from the reconstructed Assyrian History.

enemy of his country, had promised aid to the kings of Israel and Judah. But So did not fulfil his promise; Shalmaneser invaded and ravaged the land of Israel, threw Hoshea into prison, and laid siege to Samaria.

The Ten Tribes led Captive to Assyria. — After three years, "the crown of pride at the head of the fat valley" was thrown to the ground. The Israelites were carried into Assyria, and were placed chiefly in the province of Media. Strangers were brought from various parts of the Assyrian dominions to occupy the deserted kingdom of Samaria. At first they worshipped their idols; but as lions and other wild beasts gave them great annoyance in the depopulated region, they ascribed the evil to the anger of the local deities, recalled an Israelitish priest from exile, got from him instruction in the worship of "the God of the land," and afterwards joined the worship of Jehovah with that of their idols. The Samaritans, of whom we read in the books of Ezra and Nehemiah, and in the New Testament, were the descendants of this mongrel race. A small remnant of that people survive to this day, and have their abode at Nablous, the ancient Shechem.

"The Outcasts of Israel." — But the kingdom of the ten tribes was never restored; nor did "the outcasts of Israel" ever attempt to return in a body to their land. A few of them may have returned along with the Jewish exiles, to whom Cyrus gave permission to go to the land of their fathers. But the mass of the people remained outcasts. Various theories have been framed as to where the descendants of these Israelites are now. There is good reason to believe that some of them are in India, and some in Armenia, and other localities near the scenes of their first captivity. In New Testament times the whole people of Israel were addressed as "the twelve tribes scattered abroad" (James i. 1)

CHAPTER XI.

KINGDOM OF JUDAH.

FROM THE SEPARATION OF THE KINGDOM TO THE CAPTIVITY.

1 AND 2 KINGS; 2 CHRONICLES; ISAIAH; JEREMIAH.

SECTION I.—OUTLINE OF THE HISTORY.

The nineteen kings of Judah—Periods of the history—Table of kings, &c.—Religious declines and revivals—Subsequent history.

The Nineteen Kings of Judah.— The kingdom of Judah lasted about four hundred years after its separation from that of the ten tribes. During that period it was presided over by nineteen kings, all of the same dynasty, and lineal descendants of king David. Although the number of its kings was the same as that of the kings of Israel, its duration was about a century and a half longer than that of the latter kingdom. The frequent assassinations that shortened the lives of many of the successors of Jeroboam explain the fact that while the nineteen kings of Israel reigned only about two hundred and fifty years, the nineteen kings of Judah reigned about four hundred.

Periods of the History.—In a religious point of view, the history of the kingdom of Judah may be divided into four periods, as shown in the table on next page. The various revivals and declines of religion furnish the divisions. It is remarkable how closely the religious character of the several periods corresponded to that of the monarchs who sat on the throne. The official influence of the kings was very great;

OUTLINE OF THE HISTORY. 301

PERIODS	KINGS	LENGTH OF REIGNS.	PROPHETS.	KINGS OF ISRAEL
I. First Religious Decline and First Religious Revival,—about 86 years.........	1 Rehoboam,	17 years.	Shemaiah, Iddo	Jeroboam.
	2 Abijam (or Abijah).	3		Jeroboam.
	3 Asa.	41	Azariah, Hanani.	Nadab, Baasha, Elah, Zimri, Omri.
	4 JEHOSHAPHAT.	25	Jehu, Jahaziel.	Ahab, Ahaziah, Jehoram.
	5 Jehoram.	8		Jehoram.
	6 Ahaziah. (Athaliah.)	1		Jehoram.
		6		Jehu.
II. Second Decline and Second Revival,—about 207 years	7 Joash.	40	Zechariah (son of Jehoiada).	Jehu, Jehoahaz.
	8 Amaziah.	29		Joash, Jeroboam II.
	9 Uzziah (or Azariah)	52	Joel, Zechariah II.	Zechariah, Shallum, Menahem, Pekahiah, Pekah.
	10 Jotham.	16	Isaiah, Micah.	Pekah.
	11 Ahaz.	16		Pekah, Hoshea.
	12 HEZEKIAH.	29	Nahum.	Hoshea.
III. Third Decline and Third Revival,—about 88 years.	13 Manasseh.	55		
	14 Amon.	2	Zephaniah, Jeremiah.	
	15 JOSIAH.	31		
IV. Final Decline,—about 23 years............	16 Jehoahaz.	¼		
	17 Jehoiakim.	11	Habakkuk.	
	18 Jehoiachin.	¼	Obadiah	
	19 Zedekiah.	11		

and when it was maintained with great strength of will and force of character, the effect was overwhelming. Too often this influence was used for evil; but sometimes it was used for good.

Religious Declines and Revivals. — Under Rehoboam and Abijam, religion underwent a decline, from which it began to recover in the reign of Asa; while under Jehoshaphat the revival was decided and complete. A second decline commenced with the reign of Jehoram, the son-in-law of Ahab and Jezebel, and went on through a long succession of reigns — the spiritual thermometer falling lowest in that of Ahaz. The darkest hour of night, however, was succeeded by the dawn; under Hezekiah, the son and successor of Ahaz, the firmament brightened again. With Manasseh there began a new decline, more terrible than any that had preceded it; followed, in the days of his grandson, Josiah, by a new and most interesting revival. But the corruption had become so deeply seated that little genuine reformation took place. The sons and successors of Josiah were not like-minded with himself; the old corruptions broke out afresh; and, with the awful catastrophe of the Babylonian Captivity, the glory departed from the kingdom of Judah.

Subsequent History.—If the subsequent history were to be viewed in the same manner, it might be said that the decline last mentioned was followed by a revival, when Zerubbabel and his company returned to Jerusalem and rebuilt the temple. The rise of the Pharisees, and of the system of tradition which they encouraged, was the leading symptom of a new decline, whose darkest landmarks were the rejection and crucifixion of the Messiah, followed by the destruction of Jerusalem and the dispersion of the Jews. Though this decline has lasted above two thousand years, it is destined, according to the sure word of prophecy, to be followed by the most glorious revival of any, when Judah and Israel shall be united in one, and the receiving of them again shall be "as life from the dead" (Rom. xi. 15).

SECTION II.—FIRST DECLINE AND FIRST REVIVAL.

Rehoboam—Invasion of Shishak—Abijam; war with Israel—Asa; invasion of Cushites—Jehoshaphat; revival—Alliance with Ahab—Rebuked by Jehu—Wars with the Moabites, &c.

Rehoboam.—The first impulse of REHOBOAM, on returning to Jerusalem after his rejection at Shechem, was to muster an army, and to try to force the recusant tribes back to their allegiance. One hundred and eighty thousand men were collected for that purpose; but, through the prophet Shemaiah, the intended campaign was stopped by divine command. Though unable to carry out this project, Rehoboam continued to show a disposition to trust for security to material defences rather than to the favour and blessing of God. He set about fortifying all the principal places in his kingdom, erecting fortresses and placing garrisons in at least fifteen cities throughout the two tribes.

Invasion of Shishak.—Ere long the priests and the Levites scattered over the other tribes flocked to his standard; for Jeroboam probably found that they were not sufficiently ready to comply with his wishes, and drove them from their offices to make way for the lowest of the people. Until he was firmly settled in the kingdom, Rehoboam paid outward regard to the established worship of Jehovah; but, three years after coming to the throne, he appeared in his true colours, and forsook the law of the Lord. His numerous wives probably exerted the same corrupting influence on him that had proved so hurtful to Solomon. Shishak, or Sheshonk, king of Egypt (see page 268), with an enormous army, came up against him, took the cities which he had fortified with so much care, entered Jerusalem, and spoiled the temple and the king's palace of their golden treasures, but was restrained from destroying the city. Sheshonk was a great conqueror, whose exploits are emblazoned at length on the walls of Egyptian temples. It is an interesting fact, discovered by Champollion, that in the long list of towns captured by Sheshonk, found in the great Temple of Karnak, occurs that of *Yuda melchi* — the kingdom of Judah.* This calamity was attended with blessed effects to Rehoboam;—he and his people confessed their sin; and though there was continual war between Jeroboam and Rehoboam, the kingdom of Judah was strengthened, and "things went well."

Abijam : War with Israel.—Rehoboam was succeeded by ABIJAM (or ABIJAH), who reigned three years. He is stigmatized as one "who walked in all the sins of his father, and whose heart was not perfect with the Lord his God." But during his short reign he on one occasion acted a part worthy of the heroes of other days : under one of those great floods of religious enthusiasm which so often gave a momentary impulse to the nation, he encouraged his soldiers, at Zemaraim, a mountain of Ephraim, to fight boldly against the huge army of Israel;—in consequence, Jeroboam was signally defeated, a very great number of his people were slain, and some of the border cities of his kingdom were recovered to Judah. But the state of religion continued depressed, and altars to strange gods, images, and groves abounded in the land.

Asa : Invasion of Cushites.—After Abijam came ASA. His reign lasted forty-one years, nearly corresponding, in point of length, to those of Saul, David, and Solomon. The neighbouring kingdom had been so shattered by the bloody battle of Zemaraim, that Asa enjoyed peace during the first part of his reign. He improved the opportunity by destroying the monuments of idolatry, and repairing the fortified places that had been laid waste by the king of Egypt in the days of his grandfather. In the course of a few years a new danger threatened him from the south. A Cushite or Ethiopian prince, named Zerah, came up against his kingdom, with a million of soldiers and three hundred chariots. At Mareshah, in the valley of Zephathah, the troops of Asa encountered the mighty host; and, strong in faith, completely defeated them, and pursued them to Gerar. The exact localities have not been identified with certainty, but the battle and the pursuit took place

---

* "On the south external wall, behind the picture of the victories of king Ramessu II., the spectator beholds the colossal image of the Egyptian sovereign dealing the heavy blows of his victorious club on the captive Jews." *Brugsch*, ii. 208.

in the neighbourhood of places where Abraham and Isaac had dwelt nearly a thousand years before. It is easy to conceive king Asa recalling on the spot the visions and promises that had been given to them, and having his own faith confirmed by the remembrance of theirs.* The effect of the campaign seems to have been most blessed; and after returning home, Asa, stimulated by the prophet Oded, convened the people, including a great number from the tribes of Simeon, Ephraim, and Manasseh: a solemn league and covenant was sworn—"they entered into a covenant to seek the Lord God of their fathers with all their heart and with all their soul." But in the later part of his reign Asa's faith became comparatively feeble. When Baasha, king of Israel, was fortifying Ramah, in order to block up the kingdom of Judah on the north, Asa, thinking only of meeting force by force, applied for help to Ben-hadad, king of Syria; and, through a gift of money, prevailed on him to attack Baasha's northern frontier. A faithful prophet, Hanani, for pointing out to Asa his lack of faith, was cast into prison. And when the king was attacked by a disease in the feet, "he sought not to the Lord, but to the physicians." It is probable that this backsliding on the part of the king was accompanied by a relapse into idolatry on the part of the people.

Jehoshaphat: Revival.—JEHOSHAPHAT, Asa's son, began his reign, which lasted twenty-five years, three years after Ahab had ascended the throne of Samaria. The ruinous influence of the most wicked of the kings of Israel was, in some sense, balanced by the influence for good of one of the best of the kings of Judah. Under Jehoshaphat, the kingdom regained much of the prosperity which it had enjoyed in the days of

---

* "The plain [between Gaza and Beit Jibrin] is no less fertile than the very best of the Mississippi valley....Isaac reaped an hundred-fold here....About seven hours south of Beit Jibrin is the great valley, Wady Sheriah; and in it, or in one of its fertile branches, there is little doubt that the lost site of Gerar will be found. Arabs who frequent Gaza from that neighbourhood speak of a ruined city somewhere there, which careful examination may yet decide to be the ancient Gerar. The Rev. J. Rowlands says, 'Within Wady Gaza, a deep and broad channel coming down from the south-east and running a little higher up than this spot, is Wady es Sheriah, from the east-north-east. Near Joorf el Gerar are the remains of an ancient city, called Khirbet el Gerar—the Ruins of Gerar.'"—*The Land and the Book, by W. M. Thomson, D.D.*, vol. ii., p. 349.

king David, to whom Jehoshaphat seems to have borne a considerable resemblance (2 Chron. xvii. 3). One of the first undertakings of his reign was a great home-missionary enterprise, in which the princes took part with the Levites in teaching the people. At an after period the king himself seems to have made a missionary tour over the whole kingdom, for the purpose of stirring up the religious spirit of his subjects. When the tokens of divine blessing on Jehoshaphat became apparent, the neighbouring states were filled with dread, and sent him presents. A great military force was at the same time maintained by him, and the judges and officers resumed over the kingdom the duties that had been assigned them by king David.

Alliance with Ahab.—Jehoshaphat seems to have felt deeply the evils of the schism between the kingdoms of Judah and Israel: to heal the breach was beyond his power, but, with the design probably of obviating the worst of those evils, he was induced to form an alliance with king Ahab, and join him in his last campaign against the Syrians at Ramoth-gilead. Evidently the king of Judah had scruples as to the propriety of this step; but when the proposal was made to him, he had not courage to resist.

Rebuked by Jehu.—Ramoth-gilead, now Es-Salt, was a powerful stronghold in the district of Gilead, standing on a hill in the midst of oak-covered mountains, and commanding an important region between Syria and the Jordan. The Syrians had still possession of this stronghold. The attempt of the confederate kings to wrench it from them was unsuccessful; Ahab was killed in the battle, and Jehoshaphat made a narrow escape. Returning home, the king of Judah was met by the prophet Jehu, who rebuked him for helping the ungodly,—making him feel, perhaps, that instead of assisting king Ahab, he ought to have been sheltering the prophet Elijah from his fury.

Wars with the Moabites, &c.—Subsequently, Jehoshaphat showed a better spirit, when engaged in war with the combined forces of Ammon, Moab, and Edom. A vast multitude of these nations had advanced along the western shore of the Dead Sea, as far as to En-gedi, where David had hid from Saul, and Solomon had cultivated the vine; but Jehoshaphat came out against them full of faith, his troops singing psalms as they advanced. It was not necessary to strike a blow; the allies quarrelled among themselves, and before the forces of Jehoshaphat came up to them, the ground was covered with the slain. Much about the same time Jehoshaphat accompanied Jehoram king of Israel, and the king of Edom, against the Moabites, on the occasion (already referred to) when Elisha went with the host (see page 285). Jehoshaphat seems to have been a man of too easy a temper: he had not courage to resist the projects of the more wilful house of Ahab, and was led to give it a measure of open countenance which must have greatly neutralized the good effects of his personal piety. The evil consequences of the alliance with the house of Ahab began to be more openly shown when his son came to the throne. With him a dark era commences, and many generations elapsed before such hands as Jehoshaphat's again held the sceptre of Judah.

SECTION III.—SECOND DECLINE AND SECOND REVIVAL.

Jehoram: his chastisements—Ahaziah—Athaliah: her crimes—Joash: war with Syria—Amaziah—Uzziah Jotham: Pekah and Rezin threaten him—Ahaz: open apostasy—Alliance with Assyria—Hezekiah: revival—War with Sennacherib—Sennacherib's advance—His catastrophe—The "blast"—Effect of the incident—Records on the monuments—Hezekiah's life prolonged—Joel—Isaiah—The two parts of his prophecy—His reference to distant events—His influence—Micah—Nahum—A coming storm.

Jehoram: His Chastisements.—JEHORAM succeeded his father Jehoshaphat at the age of thirty-two, and reigned eight years. The pernicious influence of his wife Athaliah, called the daughter of Omri (2 Chron. xxii. 2), and also of Ahab (2 Chron. xxi. 6), began immediately to be felt. On the impulse of that spirit of cruelty and jealousy which idolatry fosters, he murdered all his brothers when he came to the throne. He encouraged idolatry in his kingdom, and persecuted his people into its abominable practices. Such high-handed treason against the supreme King of Israel could not be long without punishment. By a revolt of the Edomites, and of Libnah, an important fortress in the south ; by harassing invasions of the Philistines, the Arabians, and the Ethiopians, who, advancing probably by Libnah, burst into his kingdom, and carried off his whole family except his youngest son; and by a terrible disease of the bowels, which occasioned his death, Jehoram was made to know that "the way of transgressors is hard."

Ahaziah.—His son AHAZIAH (or JEHOAHAZ) merely tasted the sweets and the bitters of royal life. The evil counsel of his mother Athaliah kept him from profiting by the experience of his father : he followed his wicked example, and was an active promoter of idolatry. He allied himself with Jehoram, king of Israel, his mother's brother, in a fresh attempt to wrest Ramothgilead from the Syrians. In that attempt the king of Israel was wounded ; and, on the occasion of Ahaziah going down to see him at Jezreel, both kings were suddenly attacked and slain by Jehu, Ahaziah having reigned but a single year.

Athaliah : Her Crimes.—The news of Jehu's wholesale massacre of the house of Ahab, including Ahaziah and forty-two of his near relatives, must have spread consternation among the people of Jerusalem. But there was one heart undaunted and unhumbled by these terrible judgments. ATHALIAH, the daughter (it is believed) of queen Jezebel, whose blood the dogs of Jezreel had just licked ; the sister of king Jehoram of Israel, who had just fallen under the bow of Jehu ; the widow of king Jehoram of Judah, whose bowels had dropped out, when stricken by the hand of the Lord ; the mother of king Ahaziah, and of other young men, who had also just fallen under the avenging sword of Jehu,—was neither awed nor humbled by all these frightful judgments. It would be speaking too favourably of this woman to compare her to Lady Macbeth of Scotland. With the news of these awful tragedies sounding in her ears, she arose and destroyed her own grandchildren, and all the seed-royal of Judah,—a single infant, a son of Ahaziah, named Joash, alone escaping the slaughter, unknown to her.

The kingdom groaned for six years under her tyranny, and we may well believe how ill it fared with the faithful servants of the Lord; but at the close of that period a revolution was effected. Under the auspices of Jehoiada, the high priest, the youthful Joash was proclaimed king; and the infamous woman, whose stout heart had brought so much misery on the kingdom, received the just reward of her wickedness. A temple which had been built in Jerusalem to Baal, was at the same time demolished, and the high priest of idolatry was put to death amid the ruins of his altars and images.

Joash: War with Syria.—At the early age of seven JOASH began a reign of forty years. He evidently inherited the easy disposition of his great grandfather Jehoshaphat, rather than the iron will of his grandmother Athaliah. While Jehoiada lived, Joash was induced to pay outward regard to the laws of the Lord; but on the death of that pontiff, he lapsed into the ways of the house of Ahab. So far did he go astray, that Zechariah, the son of Jehoiada, was killed by his orders, for having faithfully reproved his transgressions. During his reign, Hazael king of Syria made an attack on Gath, the ancient city of Goliath the Philistine, and would have besieged Jerusalem, had he not been bought off by a bribe, furnished from the treasures of the house of the Lord. Subsequently, a small body of Syrians defeated an immense host of his people, who were abandoned by God for having been faithless to his covenant. Joash, it is said, was left by the Syrians "in great diseases;" and the wretched man found that he fared no better at the hands of friends than of foes, for his own servants conspired against him, and slew him on his bed.

Amaziah.—AMAZIAH, his son, who reigned twenty-nine years, was of much the same character as his father. His reign was signalized by a war with Edom, in which he triumphed; and a war with Israel, in which he was signally defeated. Though he began by serving the Lord, he was soon drawn into the whirlpool of idolatry, and, with singular infatuation, he brought from Edom the gods of its conquered people, and worshipped them as his own. Like his father, he died a violent death, being assassinated by his servants at Lachish. What a contrast must the state of the kingdom have presented now, both in things civil and in things sacred, to the happy days of Jehoshaphat!

Uzziah.—The reign of his successor UZZIAH (or AZARIAH) was the longest that had yet been known in Judah; it extended to fifty-two years. Uzziah was a king of remarkable activity and talent. His capacity for administration resembled that of king David. As an agriculturist he was eminently successful; and to these talents he added an astonishing turn for engineering, which he showed in the construction not only of forts, but also of armour and of engines for projecting stones and other missiles. Like his predecessors, he paid regard to the laws of God in the early part of his reign, and the kingdom was blessed with a large measure of prosperity. But prosperity stirred his pride and made him forget whose servant he was. He impiously determined to assume the functions of the priests, and to burn incense in the sanctuary on the golden altar; but the disease of leprosy, falling instantly upon him, made him abandon the attempt. The historian of his reign was the prophet Isaiah. Probably it was from his biography that the brief account of him in Chronicles was compiled. From the history of Assyria it appears that Tiglath-pileser, king of that country, struck a blow at Azariah, who had befriended the people of Hamath, while they were in rebellion against the authority of the great king.*

Jotham: Pekah and Rezin threaten him.—JOTHAM, who succeeded Uzziah, and who reigned sixteen years, inherited his talent for material improvements. Besides building cities, castles, and towers in various places, he covered with houses the ridge of Ophel, in Jerusalem, which slopes down from Mount Moriah to the valleys of Kidron and Hinnom. The account given us of Jotham's personal religion is not qualified by the charge of degeneracy in his later days; but his religious convictions were too feeble to make him a reformer

* Smith's History of Assyria, pp. 78, 79.

of the prevailing corruptions. From the testimony of the historian we learn that the people still did corruptly; and the allusions in Isaiah to the prevailing state of morals and religion evidently betoken a lamentable state of things. In the reign of this king the Ammonites were subdued; but, on the other hand, Pekah, king of Israel, and Rezin, king of Syria, began to form a threatening conspiracy against him.

Ahaz: Open Apostasy.—The fruits of this confederacy, however, were not ripened until the reign of AHAZ, the son and successor of Jotham. During the sixteen years of his reign the moral darkness became thicker than it had ever been. Open apostasy was now the order of the day. Images of Baal, altars and high places consecrated to idolatry, did not suffice king Ahaz: he crowned his abominable practices by burning his children in the Valley of Hinnom. The visitation of divine wrath upon guilt so flagrant was swift and terrible. The kingdom of the ten tribes was almost at its last gasp; yet, weakened though it was, it inflicted that terrible defeat upon king Ahaz to which allusion has already been made (p. 297). The Syrians, too, pressed him hard; and, though unable to take Jerusalem, they drove him out of Elath, on the Gulf of Akabah, thus depriving him of the profits of the Indian traffic. At the same time the Edomites and the Philistines annoyed him.

Alliance with Assyria.—Against the remonstrances of Isaiah, he applied for help to the king of Assyria; and in answer to his request, Tiglath-pileser attacked and destroyed Damascus. King Ahaz went to that ancient capital to meet him; but when the king of Assyria came to him "he distressed him, and helped him not." The influence of this king seems to have been most pernicious. Calamity only served to blind his eyes and to harden his heart. The thickening afflictions of the sister kingdom had no effect on him; and had his reign not been cut short by his early death at the age of thirty-six, a similar catastrophe could hardly have been averted from Judah.

Hezekiah: Revival.—But God had better days yet in store

for the tribe which he loved. HEZEKIAH, the son of Ahaz, and grandson by the mother's side of Zechariah (perhaps the prophet who flourished in the reign of Uzziah, 2 Chron. xxvi. 5), gave quite an altered complexion, during the twenty-nine years of his reign, to the religious condition of the kingdom. He was a man of devoted personal piety, and of powerful influence upon others. While the sister kingdom was in its death-throes, he set himself, with heart and soul, to revive the whole economy of Moses, which had fallen into complete neglect. His posts, traversing the whole length of the kingdom of Israel to invite the faithful to the passover at Jerusalem, may be said to have sounded throughout that kingdom the ominous warning, "Come out of her, my people, that ye be not partakers of her sins, and that ye receive not of her plagues."

War with Sennacherib.—The great external event of Hezekiah's reign was his contest with one of the greatest warriors of ancient times—SENNACHERIB, king of Assyria. Samaria had been destroyed by the Assyrians, under Shalmaneser, a few years before, and its captive people had been scattered among the cities of Assyria and Media. Since then, Sargon, one of the most active kings of Assyria, had directed many blows against various parts of Syria.* Several obstacles that had stood between the king of Assyria and the rival kingdom of Egypt were thus removed, but in the kingdom of Judah another remained. It was the policy of the great empires, such as Egypt, to excite the tributary kings of Assyria to insurrection, in order that their powerful rival might have his attention diverted from them. Perhaps it was under such instigation that Hezekiah was led to revolt from the king of Assyria, and to refuse the tribute which his father had promised to pay. In the fourteenth year of Hezekiah, Sennacherib, having succeeded to the Assyrian throne, prepared to invade Judah and to force from Hezekiah the tribute he had refused.

Sennacherib's Advance.—The dreaded hour had now come

---

* Smith's Assyria, p. 93.

when the banners of the terrible king of Assyria were to be seen from Jerusalem moving over the heights of Benjamin. "In the description of Sennacherib's advance upon Jerusalem contained in the tenth chapter of Isaiah, every step of his approach is so graphically portrayed that we can follow him with our eyes. The army is supposed to leave the great northern road near Beth-el, and to turn off eastward to Ai. Advancing to Michmash, the baggage is left there; and the troops, thus disencumbered, cross the ravine, and pass the night at Geba. Ramah, situated only half an hour westward, though hid by an intervening ridge, 'is afraid.' Gibeah of Saul, placed on the top of a conspicuous hill, is *fled*, for the dreaded foe is in sight. In the morning the army continues its march southward. The sites of Gallim and Laish are now unknown; but Anathoth is in the direct line of march—'O poor Anathoth!' The evening finds them at Nob, within sight of the holy city; and from thence the foe shakes his hand against the daughter of Zion." *

His Catastrophe.—Sennacherib, however, deemed it best to attack in the first instance the fenced cities of Judah. These having been taken, Hezekiah was so disheartened that he agreed to pay tribute to the invader. Meanwhile, Sennacherib appears to have gone to Egypt, leaving one of his generals to besiege Ashdod or Azotus, a stronghold of the Philistines, of which mention has been made already. Returning to Palestine, Sennacherib broke his agreement, and again attacked the fenced cities of Judah. He was encamped before Lachish when he sent his general, Rabshakeh, with a threatening and blasphemous message to Jerusalem, summoning Hezekiah to surrender. The faith and courage of Hezekiah, sustained by prayer, stood nobly the most appalling test to which they were ever subjected. The prophet Isaiah foretold that Sennacherib's host should be miraculously destroyed, and that he should return smitten and helpless to Nineveh. The prophecy was fulfilled. "A blast" from the Lord in one night killed one hundred and eighty-five thousand of the Assyrian warriors,

* Murray's Handbook, p. 215.

and Sennacherib slunk home, to vent his rage on the captive Israelites.*

The "Blast."—Some time after this catastrophe, Sennacherib was murdered by two of his own sons. The "blast" is thought by some to have been the poisonous wind, the sirocco, which is sometimes extensively fatal in its effects. Herodotus mentions a story, which may somehow have been a perversion of this singular miracle—that when the king of Assyria was besieging Pelusium in Egypt, a multitude of rats came into his camp, and in one night ate all the shield-straps, quivers, and bow-strings, so that rising next morning the soldiers found their arms useless, and were obliged to retreat.

Effect of the Incident.—The destruction of Sennacherib's host was one of the grandest and most stirring events in Hebrew history. It was worthy to stand side by side with the memorable overthrow of Pharaoh, eight hundred years before. It was admirably fitted to give support to faith and courage in future trials that might arise, if only reliance should be placed on the arm of God. Unhappily, it seems to have been so perverted as to minister only to pride and self-confidence, and to make the people in Jeremiah's time absolutely certain that Jerusalem would not fall into the hands of the Chaldæans; though in the latter case God's word was as explicit in declaring that Jerusalem should fall, as in the former that it should be delivered.

Records on the Monuments.—The Nineveh monuments recently deciphered show Sennacherib to have been a very great warrior, with enormous resources. Many of the events

* " The angel of death spread his wings on the blast,
  And breathed on the face of the foe as he passed ;
  And the eyes of the sleepers waxed deadly and chill,
  And their hearts but once heaved, and for ever were still.

  " And there lay the steed with his nostril all wide,
  But through it there rolled not the breath of his pride ;
  And the foam of his gasping lay white on the turf,
  And cold as the spray of the rock-beating surf.

  " And there lay the rider distorted and pale,
  With the dew on his brow and the rust on his mail ;
  And the tents were all silent, the banners alone,
  The lances unlifted, the trumpet unblown."

of his reign recorded in the Bible are also mentioned in the inscriptions, in particular the destruction of the cities near Jerusalem, and Hezekiah's payment of tribute. Of the catastrophe of the "blast," as might have been anticipated, there is no mention. But it is plain that in some extraordinary way Hezekiah must have been delivered from Sennacherib, for the resources of the one were utterly insufficient to meet those of the other.

Hezekiah's Life Prolonged.—In the course of the year of Sennacherib's invasion, Hezekiah was seized with a remarkable illness which nearly proved fatal, and from which he most earnestly besought recovery. If the hosts of Assyria were preparing to invade him, we may see one reason why he was so very earnest in his prayer. Fifteen years were added to his life, and he was promised protection from his enemies.* Some time after this illness, Merodach-baladan, king of Babylon, which was at that time an independent kingdom, sent messengers to congratulate Hezekiah. Jealous of the growing power of the Assyrians, Baladan seems to have been anxious to cultivate friendship with Hezekiah and to urge him to resistance. Hezekiah allowed a carnal spirit to prevail above higher considerations, by boastfully showing the amount of his riches to the messengers of Baladan. For this the Lord rebuked him by the prophet Isaiah, and informed him that the successor of Baladan should one day prove the bitter enemy of Judah, and that the groans of the captive people should be heard within the walls of his capital.

This period of the history of Judah was signalized by the appearance of some eminent prophets, who left written prophecies behind them.

Joel.—JOEL, son of Pethuel, is thought to have flourished about the time of Uzziah, before the nation had sunk into that state of utter corruption which it reached in the reign of Ahaz. When Joel mentions the enemies of his country, he names the

---

* The period added to his life was fifteen years; if, therefore, his whole reign lasted twenty-nine, this illness must have occurred in the fourteenth year. It is likely that it happened before the actual arrival of Sennacherib. There is some difficulty in adjusting dates. See Trans. Soc. Bib. Arch., vol. ii., p. 322.

Phœnicians, the Philistines, the Idumæans, and the Egyptians; but not the Assyrians or the Babylonians. This prophet gives a most powerful description of an approaching famine, and calls to repentance, fasting, and prayer; promises the removal of impending evils, announces rich evangelical blessings, and foretells the outpouring of the Holy Ghost. There cannot be a doubt, if he flourished at the time usually believed, that his living voice and written testimony must have been instrumental in at least preparing the way for the revival of religion under Hezekiah.

Isaiah.—A more conspicuous share, however, in this great work must have been borne by ISAIAH. Very little is known of the personal history of this great prophet. He began to prophesy in the reign of Uzziah, and came forward prominently during the reigns of Ahaz and Hezekiah. Tradition represents him as a member of the royal family, and even as father-in-law of king Manasseh, by whom it is said that he was sawn asunder.

The Two Parts of his Prophecy.—The prophecy of Isaiah consists of two parts; the first embracing the first thirty-nine chapters, the second the last twenty-seven. The first part consists of a variety of writings, issued at various times, reproving the sins of the Jewish nation; foretelling the destruction of the neighbouring nations—Assyria, Babylon, Moab, Egypt, Philistia, Syria, Edom, and Tyre; giving an account of Sennacherib's invasion and of the destruction of his army, and of the illness and recovery of Hezekiah; with many allusions throughout to the coming of the Messiah, to the conversion of the Jews under the gospel, and to the destruction of the enemies of the Church.

His Reference to Distant Events.—The predictions of the second part relate chiefly to more distant events. "The subjects particularly foretold are, the deliverance of the Jews by Cyrus, about two hundred years before his birth, and the overthrow of their oppressors; the return to Judæa, and the establishment of their ancient polity; the coming, character, appointment, sufferings, and glory of the Messiah; the downfall of idolatry, and the call of the Gentile world; the wickedness of the Jews consummated in their rejection of Messiah, and the consequent rejection of them by God; their future conversion and recovery, and the final triumphant perfection of the Church."

His Influence.—Isaiah appears to have occupied a leading place under Hezekiah in the councils of the nation. It is far from unlikely that Hezekiah himself owed to the instrumentality of this fervent prophet the strong religious convictions by which he was characterized; and it is all but certain that Isaiah was his counsellor and helper in the great reformation which he effected. Amid the desolation of the kingdom of Israel, and the terrible judgments foretold on Judah, the bright visions of future glory presented in the writings of this prophet must have cheered and steadied many a sinking heart. Many an earnest spirit must have been arrested by the striking views presented by him of the humiliation and sufferings, as well as of the glory of the Messiah; but not a few must have felt, like the Ethiopian eunuch in the days of the apostles, that such a passage as his fifty-third chapter was not to be understood without some one to guide them.

Micah.—MICAH prophesied during nearly the same period as Isaiah. He appears to have been a member of the tribe of Judah; his designation, "the Morasthite," denoting probably the town of Mareshah, near which Asa defeated the Ethiopian host. In describing the approaching ruin of both kingdoms, he specifies several of the towns and villages in his own neighbourhood (ch. i.). "He foretells, in clear terms, the invasions of Shalmaneser and Sennacherib; the dispersion of Israel; the cessation of prophecy; the utter destruction of Jerusalem; the deliverance of Israel; the destruction of Assyria, and of the enemies Assyria represents; the birth-place of Christ, and his divine nature; the promulgation of the gospel from Mount Zion and its results; and the exaltation of his kingdom over all nations."*

Nahum.—NAHUM, too, belonged to the same period. Of Elkosh, his native place, nothing is known; but Jerome asserts it to have been in Galilee. "He probably prophesied in Judah,

* Angus's Bible Handbook.

after the ten tribes had been carried captive. He was raised up to reveal the power and tenderness of Jehovah, to foretell the subversion of the Assyrian empire, the death of Sennacherib, and the deliverance of Hezekiah. The destruction of Nineveh is then predicted in the most glowing colours, and with singular minuteness." For the right understanding of this prophecy, it should be read in connection with the book of Jonah, of which it is a continuation. "The two prophecies form connected parts of the same moral history; the remission of God's judgments being illustrated in Jonah, and the execution of them in Nahum."* In the year B.C. 625 these predictions of the destruction of Nineveh were fulfilled.

A Coming Storm.—The deaths of the great instruments of the revival in the kingdom of Judah—Isaiah, Micah, Nahum, and king Hezekiah—do not seem to have been separated by long intervals. When these righteous men perished, no man, perhaps, laid to heart that they were taken from evil to come (Isa. lvii. 1); but scarcely had they been gathered to their fathers when the elements of a frightful storm began to darken the horizon.

SECTION IV.—THIRD DECLINE AND THIRD REVIVAL.

Manasseh: his idolatry—Carried to Babylon—Repentance and restoration—Shebna and Eliakim—Amon: Josiah: the prophet Zephaniah—Jeremiah—Battle of Megiddo—Death of Josiah: grief of Jeremiah—Destruction of Nineveh.

Manasseh: His Idolatry.—MANASSEH, the son of Hezekiah, ascended the throne at the early age of twelve. His reign terminated fifty-five years afterwards, though he can hardly be said to have reigned all that time. He must have been born about the very time when the Lord gave his father the memorable deliverance from Sennacherib; but the only effect of such things upon him seems to have been to rouse him to greater opposition to the ways of the Lord. Probably he fell into the hands of bad advisers, persons who had been secret enemies to Hezekiah and his cause. His insane fanati-

* Angus's Bible Handbook.

cism in the cause of idolatry was not surpassed even by that of the king in modern times who most resembled him—Philip II. of Spain. All the work of his father was undone. Not only were groves and images reared to Baal, but the very temple was polluted by them. His children were burned in honour of the idol; the more pliable part of his people were compelled to join him in his idolatry; and a furious persecution opened against such as continued to revere the God of Hezekiah and Isaiah. Their innocent blood flowed like water through the streets of Jerusalem. In vain did the prophets of the Lord remonstrate with him, and threaten Jerusalem with the fate that had overtaken Samaria during the reign of his father. Remonstrance was thrown away upon Manasseh.

Carried to Babylon.—But the career which defied all attempts to stop it from within, was brought to a close by judgments from without. Esarhaddon was now king of Assyria, and by a victory over the king of Babylon he had added that great city to his empire. He had lately visited the district of Samaria, had carried off any straggling remnants of the ten tribes, and had brought from the east new colonists to supply their place. Advancing to Jerusalem, probably through a desire to wipe out the disgrace that had befallen his father Sennacherib, he took the sacred city, and carried Manasseh a prisoner to Babylon.

Repentance and Restoration.—By the extraordinary mercy of God, Manasseh was converted from his evil ways, and became a miracle of divine grace and power. Ere long, he was set at liberty, and he seems to have had the district of Samaria added to his proper dominions. Probably Esarhaddon placed him under solemn obligations to aid the Assyrians against the Egyptians; for Psammiticus, king of Egypt, pushing his conquests into Asia, was now engaged in the memorable siege of Ashdod, which lasted nine-and-twenty years.

Shebna and Eliakim.—When Manasseh returned to Jerusalem, he exerted himself to undo the mischief he had wrought, and to set up the worship of the true God. It seems to have been at his restoration that a prediction of Isaiah regarding

Shebna and Eliakim was fully verified. Shebna had probably been Manasseh's counsellor to evil. In fulfilment of the prophecy, he was carried to Babylon, and there he died. On Manasseh's restoration, the godly Eliakim was called to office. With "the key of the house of David on his shoulder," he laboured to restore the ancient order of the kingdom. "They hung upon him all the glory of his father's house" (Isa. xxii. 15-25). But Manasseh found how much easier it was to debauch than to reform a kingdom. His efforts to reform it do not seem to have been very successful; and as his end approached, it must have saddened him to think that the godless Amon was to wield the sceptre after him. We may believe, at the same time, that a ray of hope would brighten the future, as he gazed on the gentle face of his grandson Josiah, and observed how already the tender heart of that little child had learned to tremble at the word of the Lord.

Amon: Josiah: the Prophet Zephaniah.—For two years AMON imitated the first and worst practices of his father Manasseh; but his career was cut short by assassination. The child JOSIAH, then but eight years old, ascended the throne. At the age of sixteen he began to devote himself actively to God, and became one of the most energetic and at the same time most lovable of pious kings. The prophet ZEPHANIAH seems to have flourished in the early part of his reign. Perhaps Josiah may have been himself aroused by the stirring proclamation of this servant of the Lord—"Seek ye the Lord, all ye meek of the earth, which have wrought his judgment; seek righteousness, seek meekness: it may be ye shall be hid in the day of the Lord's anger." There can be little doubt that Zephaniah was an active adviser of Josiah in the great scheme of reform which he immediately began. At the age of twenty, Josiah commenced the active work of reformation. Armed with hatchet and mattock, he personally commenced the demolition of the altars and images of idolatry. Six years seem to have been more or less occupied in carrying out the work, not only in Judah, but in the districts of Ephraim and Samaria, that had now, apparently, been added to Judah.

Jeremiah.—A year after that work began, Josiah must have been greatly cheered to learn that in the neighbouring town of Anathoth a new prophet had begun to utter the word of the Lord; and in the youthful and timid, but devoted and gracious JEREMIAH, he must have welcomed a most congenial and delightful friend and helper. The discovery of the long-forgotten Book of the Law, the celebration of the Passover at Jerusalem, and a second tour through his kingdom, for restoring still further the pure worship of God, were the chief things of importance in the next part of his reign.

Battle of Megiddo.—But the auspicious life and reign of Josiah were destined to a disastrous ending. On the banks of the Euphrates, and in the adjacent countries, there was no small stir and conflict, and Pharaoh-necho, king of Egypt, in the old spirit of rivalry and aggression, having undertaken an expedition to those parts, had to pass through Palestine on the way. Hearing of this, and perhaps deeming himself bound by the obligation his grandfather Manasseh had entered into to oppose the Egyptians, Josiah mustered an army, and at Megiddo, in the great battle-field of Esdraelon, awaited their approach. In vain Pharaoh-necho reminded him that with the king of Judah he had no quarrel, and that all that he wished was a passage through his borders. The hostile armies joined battle near Megiddo, beneath the brow of Carmel, where, two hundred years before, Elijah had conquered the priests of Baal; and on the banks of the Kishon, which, seven hundred years before, had witnessed Barak's discomfiture of the Canaanites.

Death of Josiah : Grief of Jeremiah.—Soon afterwards, one of the chariots of the king of Judah might have been seen pushing rapidly towards Jerusalem. As it passed from place to place, we may conceive the eagerness of the inhabitants to hear tidings of the battle, and their horror at learning that the chariot conveyed their beloved king mortally wounded. At Anathoth we may fancy the young priest, Jeremiah, sitting like Eli of old by the way-side, trembling for the ark of God. What must have been his emotion, when he saw the death-stricken face of his beloved friend and king, the sole prop and pillar of God's cause in the land! We read that "Jeremiah lamented for Josiah." Even David's lament for Jonathan could not have equalled the depth of tender feeling, the intensity of longing, that must have breathed in Jeremiah's elegy. In a deeper sense than on the day when the ark was taken, the glory had now departed from Israel; and the dark judgments of an offended God might speedily be looked for in the land.

Destruction of Nineveh.—Necho advanced to the Euphrates, took the stronghold of Carchemish, and established his authority over the country west of the Euphrates. But even more important changes were now going on. The great Assyrian empire was approaching its fall. The Medes and also the Babylonians had revolted from the king of Assyria, and, not content with establishing their independence, had laid siege to Nineveh itself. After several repulses, they at last succeeded. Seeing his cause to be desperate, the king of Assyria shut himself and all his wives up in his palace, set it on fire, and perished in the flames. Nineveh was destroyed; the predictions of the Hebrew prophets were verified, and the "bloody city," as Nineveh is truly named by the prophet Nahum, was reduced to ruins.

SECTION V.—FINAL DECLINE.

Jehoahaz: Jehoiakim—First invasion of Nebuchadnezzar: Daniel, &c., carried to Babylon—Career of Jeremiah: Jehoiachin—Zedekiah—Destruction of Jerusalem—Sufferings of the inhabitants—Cruelties of the Chaldæans—Remnant under Gedaliah—Habakkuk—Obadiah.

Jehoahaz: Jehoiakim.—The sons of Josiah were not like-minded with himself. At his death the people generally seem to have relapsed into idolatry, as a bow returns to its natural shape when the pressure is removed. His immediate successor was JEHOAHAZ, who, however, reigned but three months. Pharaoh-necho, on his return from Carchemish on the Euphrates, threw him into chains at Riblah, in the valley of Lebanon, carried him to Egypt, imposed a heavy tribute on the country, and appointed his brother ELIAKIM, or JEHOIAKIM, king in his room. Jehoiakim reigned eleven years. He was a wicked, godless, reckless king.

First Invasion of Nebuchadnezzar: Daniel, &c., carried to Babylon.—About this time there comes on the stage of history a most important personage—NEBUCHADNEZZAR, son of Nabopolassar, king of Babylon, now acting as his father's coadjutor and lieutenant. Having driven the Egyptians from the fortress of Carchemish, Nebuchadnezzar advanced to recover Syria and Palestine. Jehoiakim, after submitting for a time, rebelled against him; and Nebuchadnezzar appeared before Jerusalem, and took it. He was induced, for some reason, to spare Jehoiakim; but he carried off several of the princes of Judah, among whom were Daniel, Shadrach, Meshach, and Abed-nego. Very probably, when members of the royal family were demanded by Nebuchadnezzar, Jehoiakim made offer of Daniel and his friends for their very piety, thinking it might be well to be rid of cousins whose godly life and character must have constantly reminded him of his father's virtues and his own sins. We may readily fancy the mournful interest with which Jeremiah would view the departure of these godly youths, and how he would feel that the last hope of Israel was now gone from Jerusalem.

Career of Jeremiah: Jehoiachin.—It was probably in the reign of Jehoiakim that Jeremiah, driven by persecution from his native Anathoth, went to reside at Jerusalem (ch. xi. 21; xii. 6). The death of Josiah had made a vast difference on the moral atmosphere there; the genial sunshine of royal countenance was changed at once to the biting frost of persecution. And now began, within the walls of Jerusalem, one of the noblest and most glorious moral contests which the page even of sacred history records. Almost single-handed, for the long period of above twenty years, the gentle and timid Jeremiah, strong in a higher strength, stood forth for the Lord in opposition to the united power and fury of the kings, princes, and priests of Jerusalem. In his communings with his God we have glimpses of the dreadful expense of personal suffering at which this conflict was maintained by him; but in public, whether in prison or at large, in the palace or in the temple, we never see him flinch from uttering the stern message committed to him. JEHOIACHIN, or JECONIAH, for three brief months the successor of Jehoiakim, found that, whoever might be disposed to pay flattery to the new king, Jeremiah continued faithful and fearless as ever.

Zedekiah.—ZEDEKIAH, the last king of Judah, an uncle of Jehoiachin, and another son of Josiah, was placed on the throne by Nebuchadnezzar. Through all the eleven years of his reign he never heard the lips of Jeremiah prophesy smooth things. The corruptions of the community were now quite frightful. The threatened judgment advanced apace.

Destruction of Jerusalem.—During the reign of each of the two last named kings, Nebuchadnezzar attacked Jerusalem. Jehoiachin was carried to Babylon, with ten thousand of the principal inhabitants. Zedekiah exasperated his master by a revolt. After laying siege to Jerusalem, Nebuchadnezzar raised the siege for a time, on a rumour of help coming from Egypt. Jeremiah foretold that he should return and burn the city with fire. It turned out as he had said. In Zedekiah's eleventh year, the city was taken. Zedekiah attempting to flee, in the same direction as David had fled from Absalom, was caught in the valley of the Jordan, and carried to Riblah, in Cœle-Syria, where his brother Jehoahaz had been thrown into chains by the king of Egypt. There he was doomed to witness the execution of his sons: his own eyes were then put out, and he was carried to Babylon. The temple was rifled and was burned to the ground; the walls of the city were overthrown; the palaces and public buildings were reduced to ruins; the inhabitants were carried into captivity; and save in the hearts of the people, JERUSALEM was no more.

Sufferings of the Inhabitants.—The cruelties suffered by the inhabitants, especially during this last siege, were frightful. The "Lamentations" of Jeremiah present us with vivid pictures of these. Enraged by their rebellion and vigorous opposition, Nebuchadnezzar, when he took the city, "had no compassion on young man or maiden, old man or him that stooped for age." How terrible the import of these words is may be gathered from monuments and inscriptions presenting very hideous spectacles of maiming and impaling prisoners, and of skinning them alive. Famine had done its work before the conqueror entered; and children swooning in the streets for hunger, princes raking dung-hills for a morsel, and other ghastly sights, showed the extremities to which the people were driven.

Cruelties of the Chaldæans.—When the Chaldæans rushed through the breach, the usual brutalities were perpetrated by the licentious soldiers. The famished fugitives were pursued with relentless fury. The Chaldæans were hounded on by the Edomites and other neighbours of the Jews, who knew the country well, and like blood-hounds tracked to holes and caves such as had escaped from the city. Dead bodies lay piled in heaps upon the streets. Multitudes of these were mere boys and girls. Princes were hanged by the hand, enduring the slow horrors of crucifixion. Some seem to have been consigned to subterranean dungeons, perhaps on the shores of the Dead Sea, where "waters flowed over their head." Never had so terrible a proof been given of God's hatred of sin. "For the sins of her prophets, and the iniquities of her priests, that shed the blood of the just in the midst of her," the daughter of Zion lay covered under a very cloud of wrath.

Remnant under Gedaliah.—Yet she who had been God's hammer for chastising his people was not to escape. Jeremiah, who had so faithfully warned his countrymen of the calamities that were coming on them from Babylon, denounced no less fearlessly the coming desolation of that cruel and haughty empire. Nebuchadnezzar had given orders that Jeremiah should be treated with kindness; and on the capture of the city, he had his choice between going to Babylon and remaining in Judæa. He preferred the latter. Gedaliah was appointed governor of a remnant of the poor who were left in the land,—probably not being deemed worth the expense of removal to Babylon. Jerusalem not being now habitable, Gedaliah fixed his residence at Mizpeh, in its neighbourhood,—probably the Neby Samwil of the present day. (See p. 206, *note*.) Gedaliah was treacherously murdered by Ishmael, who had been a fugitive in the country of Ammon; and after his death, contrary to the remonstrances of Jeremiah, the remnant, fearing the anger of Nebuchadnezzar, removed to Egypt. Some time afterwards, when Egypt was invaded by Nebuchadnezzar, most of them perished miserably. We have no certain knowledge of the fate of Jeremiah: according to tradition, his countrymen, offended by his faithfulness, put him to death at Tahpanhes, in Egypt.

Habakkuk.—Another prophet who lived during the last years of Jerusalem, was HABAKKUK. Nothing is known of his history. It was his mournful duty to foretell the destruction and desolation of Jerusalem; but his book concludes with a sublime song, pleading for revival and breathing perfect confidence in God. It must have been a most cheering song to pious Jews, amid the heartbreaking calamities of that dark day.

Obadiah.—The Edomites had shown a peculiarly bitter spirit amid the crowning calamities of Judah. Their heartless cries resounded in the ears of the weeping captives, as their harps hung tuneless by the rivers of Babylon, and prompted the cry, "Remember, O Lord, the children of Edom in the day of Jerusalem; who said, Rase it, rase it, even to the foundation thereof." Perhaps it was now that the prophet OBADIAH was raised up to bring down the pride of Esau. He foretells how, in spite of their taunts and defiance, the dwellers in the clefts of the rock, that set their nests among the stars, should be brought to the ground. (See p. 141.) And lest it should be supposed that they were only to share the same judgment that had befallen Judah, the prophet was commissioned to add, that while Edom should be desolate, "upon mount Zion there should be deliverance, and there should be holiness; and saviours should come up on mount Zion, to judge the mount of Esau; and the kingdom should be the Lord's." The ancient promise of a Saviour had not yet been fulfilled; but as God's promise could not fail, a better time was to come, and the blessing was yet to descend. Such was the uniform testimony of the Old Testament prophets; and such was one great lesson of Old Testament history.

SECTION VI.—SOCIAL AND RELIGIOUS LIFE.

Wealth and property: luxurious living—Dress: ornaments: equipages—Intellectual culture—Abounding immorality—Effect of the revivals: the Church still taught to look forward.

The writings of the prophets abound in allusions to the state of society and religion during the monarchy; but our limits admit of only a brief notice of some of the leading particulars. We have not deemed it necessary to make a formal separation of the two kingdoms in the following sketch:—

Wealth and Property: Luxurious Living.—In regard to wealth and property, the moderation and equality of earlier days were now widely departed from. Isaiah denounces those who "join house to house, and lay field to field, that they may be placed alone in the midst of the earth." Notwithstanding, some men, like Naboth, stood up bravely for their paternal rights; and even in Jeremiah's time, the old practice of redeeming possessions survived (xxxii. 7). Many of the people lived in elegant houses "of hewn stone" (Amos v. 11), which they adorned with the greatest care. There were winter-houses, summer-houses, and houses of ivory (Amos iii. 15, and compare Ps. xlv. 8). Jeremiah describes the houses as "ceiled with cedar and painted with vermilion" (xxii. 14); and Amos speaks of the "beds of ivory" and luxurious "couches" on which the inmates "stretched themselves" (vi. 4). Sumptuous and protracted feasts were given in these houses. Lambs out of the flock and calves from the stall, used in early times only for rare entertainments, had now become ordinary fare (vi. 4). At feasts, the person was anointed with "chief ointments;" wine was drunk from bowls; sometimes the drinking was continued from early morning to the sound of the harp, the viol, the tabret, and the pipe (Isa. v. 11, 12).

Dress: Ornaments: Equipages.—The dress, especially of the ladies, was often most luxurious and highly ornamented. Isaiah has given us an elaborate picture of the ornaments of the fine ladies of Jerusalem. He foretells a day when "the Lord will take away the bravery of the ankle-bands, and the caps of network, and the crescents; the pendants, and the bracelets, and the veils; the turbans, and the ankle-chains, and the girdles, and the smelling-bottles, and the amulets; the signet-rings and the nose jewels; the holiday dresses and the mantles, and the robes, and the purses; the mirrors, and the tunics, and the head-dresses, and the large veils." (Isa. iii. 18–23; *Alexander's translation*.) A plain, unaffected gait, would have been far too simple for ladies carrying such a load of artificial ornament: the neck stretched out, the eyes rolling wantonly, and a mincing or tripping step completed the picture, and showed to what a depth of folly woman may sink through love of finery. Splendid equipages were also an object of ambition. Chariots were to be seen drawn by horses, camels, or asses, with elegant caparisons (Isa. xxi. 7); the patriarchal mode of riding on an ass being confined to the poor.

Intellectual Culture.—There are some traces, but not many, of high intellectual culture. Isaiah speaks of "the counsellor, and the cunning artificer, and the eloquent orator," as if these were representatives of classes. We have seen that one of the kings of Judah (Uzziah) was remarkable for mechanical and engineering skill. Amos refers to "the seven stars and Orion," as if the elements of astronomy had been generally familiar to the people. On the other hand, there are frequent references to soothsayers and sorcerers, indicating a low intellectual condition. The prevalence of idolatry could not fail to debase the intellect as well as to corrupt the morals and to disorder society.

Abounding Immorality.—Very deplorable, for the most part, are the allusions of the prophets to the abounding immorality. There is scarcely a vice that is not repeatedly denounced and wept over. The oppression of the poor was one of the most flagrant. Amos declares that the righteous were sold for silver, and the poor for a pair of shoes (viii. 6). From Hosea it appears that wives were bought and sold. The princes and rulers were specially blamed for their covetousness, their venality, their oppressions, their murders (Isa. i. 23, x. 1; Hosea ix. 15). Impurity and sensuality flourished under the shade of idolatry.

In large towns, there was a class that pandered to the vices of the licentious (Amos vii. 17). Robbery, lies, deceitful balances, were found everywhere. Even genuine grief, under affliction and bereavement, had become rare and difficult; and persons "skilful of lamentation" had to be hired to weep for the dead! (Amos v. 16.)

Effect of the Revivals: the Church still Taught to Look Forward.—The revivals under the pious kings of Judah, as far as the masses were concerned, were rather galvanic impulses than kindlings of spiritual life. Yet it cannot be doubted that during those movements many hearts were truly turned to God. The new proofs that were daily occurring of God's abhorrence of sin, would lead many to cry more earnestly for deliverance from its punishment and its power. In the disorganized and divided state into which the kingdom fell, rendering it difficult and even impossible for the annual festivals to be observed, the writings of the prophets, as well as the earlier portions of the written word, would contribute greatly to the nourishment of true piety. The 119th psalm, with all its praises of the word and the statutes of the Lord, if written during this period, is a memorable proof of the ardour with which the godly were drinking from these wells of salvation. Increased study of the word would lead to enlarged knowledge of the Messiah, though even the prophets themselves had to "search what, or what manner of time the Spirit of Christ which was in them did signify, when it testified beforehand the sufferings of Christ and the glory that should follow." One great result of the training of this period was, to carry forward the minds of the faithful beyond the present to the future. In the immediate foreground of prophecy all was dark and gloomy, and hope could find no rest but in the distance. The shades of a dark night were gathering; its long weary hours had to pass before the day should break and the shadows flee away.

SECTION VII.—CONTEMPORARY HISTORY.

1. EGYPT: The Ethiopian dynasty—Submission to Babylon. 2. ASSYRIA: Early obscurity—Contents of the records—Sennacherib—Esarhaddon—Sardanapalus. 3. BABYLON: Destruction of Nineveh. 4. MEDIA: Overthrow of Babylon. 5. PHOENICIA: Commercial greatness—Ezekiel's prophecy. 6. CARTHAGE: Extensive colonization. 7. GREECE: A collection of republics—Sparta and Athens—Grecian literature—New phase of religion. 8. ROME: Contrast with Greece—Historical function.

1. *Egypt.*

The Ethiopian Dynasty.—Reference has already been made to the invasion of Judæa and the capture of Jerusalem, in the reign of Rehoboam, by Shishak or Sheshonk I., king of Egypt. (See p. 268.) Rather more than seven hundred years before the Christian era, towards the end of the kingdom of the ten tribes, Sabaco, a conqueror from Ethiopia, subdued Egypt and usurped the throne. He is called So in Scripture, and was the king on whom Hoshea vainly relied for aid against the Assyrians. (See p. 298.) Tirhakah, another king of the Ethiopian dynasty, was the prince whose rumoured advance against Sennacherib led that king to urge the submission of Hezekiah (Isa. xxxvii. 9).

Submission to Babylon.—A period of disorder occurs about this era in Egyptian history; by-and-by the throne is filled by Psammiticus, who has been already mentioned in connection with the memorable siege of Ashdod or Azotus, that lasted nine-and-twenty years. Psammiticus was followed by Necho, in battle with whom king Josiah was killed. He attempted the union of the Red Sea and the Mediterranean by a canal,—an undertaking that cost the lives of one hundred and twenty thousand men. A naval squadron sent out by him is said to have circumnavigated Africa, and returned to Egypt by the Pillars of Hercules, now the Strait of Gibraltar. His successor was Apries, the Pharaoh-hophra of the Bible (Jer. xliv. 30), who was killed when trying to quell the rebellion of the usurper Amasis. During this period Egypt was coming into closer connection with Greece; her national peculiarities were declining, and the influence of the priesthood was decidedly on the wane. Great efforts were made by her to conquer Asia, but the military genius of Nebuchadnezzar repelled the invaders, and at last Egypt had to pay homage to Babylon.

2. *Assyria.**

Early Obscurity.—Much of the early history of Assyria is shrouded in obscurity. Between the time, in very remote antiquity, when it absorbed Babylon and became the ruling power in that part of the world, and the time when it was itself destroyed and absorbed by Babylon, several revolutions occurred, and several dynasties of kings occupied the throne. Nineveh was not at all times the capital, or at least the seat of monarchy; but it seems to have been always the largest and noblest city of the empire,—in its palmy days no other could be compared to it either in size or in magnificence.

Contents of the Records.—In the records of Nineveh that have been deciphered we find chiefly two things—lists of campaigns and conquests on the one hand, and accounts of the great public buildings erected by the several kings on the other. The great palaces, whose ruins have lately been laid bare, were built by various kings. Sardanapalus I., about the year B.C. 930, built the north-west palace at Nimroud, which, next to that of Sennacherib at Koyunjik, is the largest and most magnificent of all the Assyrian palaces. A close analogy (says Professor Rawlinson) has been pointed out between this style of building and the great edifices of the Jews as described in Scripture and by Josephus, though the dimensions of the palace of Solomon fell far short of those of the Assyrian monarchs.†

Sennacherib.—Sennacherib, who at vast cost repaired and beautified Nineveh, erecting the great Koyunjik palace, with its magnificent halls and galleries, reigned about B.C. 705 to 681. His warlike achievements were such as to enable us to understand his boastful language to king Hezekiah. In Chaldæa, he

---

* Reference has been made repeatedly to Assyrian history in the course of this chapter. Much more is known of it now than a few years ago. A convenient summary will be found in Mr. Smith's little volume, already referred to, on Assyria, in the series of Ancient History from the Monuments.

† The palace of Solomon was 150 feet long and 75 broad,--a space only 1-10th that of the palace of Sardanapalus, and not 1-30th of that of Sennacherib.

destroyed 79 cities and 820 villages. From the Nabatæans and Hagarenes he carried off more than 200,000 prisoners. Viewed in the light of his vast military prestige and resources, the resistance of Hezekiah to Sennacherib becomes sublime.

Esarhaddon. — Esarhaddon, who carried Manasseh captive to Babylon, was also a great conqueror as well as a great improver of the empire. Thirty temples, "shining with silver and gold, as splendid as the sun," were built by him, and at least three new palaces.

Sardanapalus. — Assur-bani-pal, called by the Greeks Sardanapalus, succeeded Esarhaddon. Invading Egypt, he defeated Tirhakah, and took possession of the country. In the famous and beautiful city of Thebes he committed great ravages. Ultimately he was driven from Egypt. In another campaign, undertaken against the Elamites, he was successful; but the cruelties practised by him on his victims were appalling. In a procession, Gunanu, king of Gambuli, and his brother Samgunu, marched with the severed heads of the king of Elam and his son hung around their necks. Thereafter Gunanu and other chief prisoners were fastened to the ground with four stakes, their tongues were torn out, and their skins flayed off. Others had their limbs torn off; and all were put to death with great cruelty. Such was the savage and awful spirit of the time, from which, in the day of their calamity, the kingdoms of Judah and Israel were both doomed to suffer. The classical writers represent Sardanapalus as the king who burned himself in his palace; but there is reason to think that it was a later king who was reduced to this strait.

3. *Babylon.*

Destruction of Nineveh. — The early history of Babylon, like that of Assyria, is very obscure. It seems for a long time to have been a dependent kingdom under Assyria. Occasionally its kings asserted independence. In the time of Hezekiah, Merodach-baladan was an independent king; but the kingdom was soon afterwards conquered by the Assyrians. The last Assyrian king appointed Nabopolassar governor of Babylon.

Nabopolassar proved treacherous, and became founder of the new Babylonian empire. In union with Cyaxares, the Median monarch, he attacked Nineveh, and destroyed it. Nabopolassar was succeeded by his son Nebuchadnezzar, the destroyer of Jerusalem.

4. *Media.*

Overthrow of Babylon.—The Medes are thought to have been a people of Eastern origin, who emigrated from near the Indus to the country to which they gave their name. For a long time their kingdom seems to have borne some sort of dependent relation to the great dominating power of Assyria. At length, under their king Cyaxares, having achieved their independence, they joined with the Babylonians in destroying Nineveh. Under Cyrus, the Medes and the Persians united, and founded the great empire that succeeded the Babylonian.

5. *Phœnicia.*

Commercial Greatness.—Phœnicia, though not altogether a stranger to arms and war, continued for the most part to prosecute her maritime and commercial pursuits. It was during this period that Tyre reached its zenith. As the prophet Elijah passed through it on his way to Zarephath, he could not have been less astonished at what he beheld than Jonah in Nineveh. Never had he seen such markets, such warehouses, such ships. If his visit was paid during one of the great fairs, the contrast with the quiet cities of Israel must have been overwhelming. Proud is the flag of embroidered Egyptian linen, known in every sea-port of the world, that floats over the vessels, with the blue and purple awnings, in yonder harbour. The market-place of the town would only have had to be covered with a roof of Phœnician glass to become "a crystal palace"—an exposition of the industry of all nations (Ezek. xxvii.). Every country that possesses a valuable commodity of any sort is represented there. From the distant West, Tarshish sends silver, iron, tin, and lead,—the tin, possibly, from the mines of Cornwall. Armenia sends horses, probably of the famous Nisæan breed.

Arabia sends horns and ivory, cassia and calamus, lambs and goats. Syria exhibits precious stones, fine linen, and broidered work. From the land of Israel have come wheat and honey, oil and the balm of Gilead. Damascus sends wine, the famous chalybon of the Greeks, and unwrought wool. From the ancient dominions of the queen of Sheba have come spices, precious stones, and gold. From Assyria have been forwarded cedar boxes, bound with cords, containing rich apparel, the blue cloth of the Assyrian uniforms, and broidered work. True to the idea of an Eastern market, a space is allocated for the exposure of slaves, and Javan, Tubal, and Meshech send up the miserable creatures whose descendants from Georgia and Circassia, in the same locality, are still bought and sold in the markets of the East.

Ezekiel's Prophecy.—What would the "merchant princes" of Tyre have thought, in the midst of all this greatness, had some one read to them a verse which a Hebrew prophet, on the banks of the Chebar, was inditing at the very time when their pride had received a new accession by the fall of Jerusalem?—" Thy riches, and thy fairs, thy merchandise, thy mariners, and thy pilots, thy calkers, and the occupiers of thy merchandise, and all thy men of war, that are in thee, shall fall into the midst of the seas in the day of thy ruin"! (Ezek. xxvii. 27.)

6. *Carthage.*

Extensive Colonization. — The great empire of Carthage, which was long the dominating power in North-Western Africa and Western Europe, sprung from a colony of Tyre. It was founded about 880 B.C.,—about the time when Jezebel, a native of the same district, was forcing on the Israelites the worship of Baal. The territories of Carthage were gradually extended, and through her vigorous system of colonization, most of the islands and sea-coasts in the west of Europe fell into her hands. It is probable that the rapid extension of the Carthaginians tended to spread the impure, idolatrous worship which they had brought from Tyre. Whatever commercial advantages they may have contributed to circulate among the barbarous nations with whom they came into contact, religious light was certainly none of their gifts. The religious darkness of Western Europe at that time must have been fearfully deep.

7. *Greece.*

A Collection of Republics. — For a long period after the Trojan War, Greece remained in a very unsettled state. When the fermentation subsided, monarchy had been abolished, and republican constitutions had been introduced in nearly all its States. The country was parcelled out among a number of small States, that were not united by any common political bond, though a sort of unity was produced through their national games and other institutions.

Sparta and Athens.—In the course of time, two of the Greek States — Sparta and Athens — raised themselves high above their neighbours. Sparta, situated in the peninsula of Peloponnesus, was remarkable for the hardy manner in which its people were brought up, and for the efforts made to secure and support a vigorous and uncorrupted race of men. Its great lawgiver, Lycurgus, who flourished about 880 B.C., was a contemporary of Elijah and Jehoshaphat. Athens, the capital of Attica, one of the States north of the Peloponnesus, was as remarkable for its devotion to all kinds of intellectual and social culture and refinement as Sparta was for its contempt of such things. About the end of the period now before us, Solon, the greatest lawgiver of Athens, was propounding his laws to the Athenians. He was a contemporary of Daniel, Jeremiah, and Ezekiel. It is remarkable that both he and Lycurgus had visited Egypt in search of knowledge and wisdom. The internal contests that raged among many of the Greek States were incessant. In many respects their history is most painful; there was often a vast expenditure of life, energy, and enthusiasm for objects that were unworthy of the sacrifice.

Grecian Literature.—In the period which we have now been surveying we place the dawn of Grecian literature. If, according to Herodotus, Homer lived about 900 B.C., he must have been composing the "Iliad" when Elijah and Elisha were maintaining God's cause in Israel, and when Jehoshaphat was fighting the same battle in Judah. Hesiod, Tyrtæus, Alcæus, and Sappho sung their verses in the seventh century before Christ; and Æsop may have published his fables at Athens while Jeremiah was announcing his prophecies at Jerusalem.

New Phase of Religion.—Besides giving an immense impulse to literature, philosophy, and art, the Greeks were destined to introduce a new phase of religion. Borrowing largely from the East, they gave a new aspect to the religion which they accepted, by the much more vivid and sprightly spirit which they breathed into the old mythology; but in the Greek religion we do not find anything that is in reality better adapted to meet the wants of man. It was in the poetry of religion that the Greeks excelled. Everything was made bright, lively, and beautiful; but there was really no effectual provision for removing the guilt of man, for bringing him into loving fellowship with God, and for elevating him to a life worthy of his high capacities. When men like Socrates and Plato began to grapple with these questions, they found little help in the popular religion, and they were able to contribute but little from their own resources. In Greece we do not find much moral earnestness, or much sense of sin. The very gods were represented as amusing themselves with the infirmities of humanity, so that instead of serving to raise men up, they rather helped to sink men deeper in the gulf of sin.

8. *Rome.*

Contrast with Greece.—In the south of Europe a new nation now begins to raise its head. The Romans were in many points a contrast to the Greeks. Instead of the endless diversity of the latter in manners, society, arts, and government, the Romans presented a rigid unity; and the lively, elastic, chivalrous spirit of the one was a great contrast to the sombre, prosaic uniformity of the other. The Romans were remarkable for their sturdy, plodding, indomitable purpose; they were painstaking and sagacious, constantly on the alert to discover anything in their favour, successful and victorious to an extraordinary degree. In the more advanced periods of their history, conquest was the avowed object of their existence—they lived for it alone. Their rod was a rod of iron, and the world was made to feel its severity.

Historical Function.—Rome is said to have been founded B.C. 752,—about the time when the king of Assyria was beginning to invade the kingdom of Israel. The history of the Romans under their kings is admitted to be full of legend and fable; and till a later period we have scarcely an authentic fact regarding the people that were destined, in the wonderful purpose of God, to be the connecting link between the great continents of Asia, Europe, and Africa, and thus, all unconsciously to themselves, to prepare the way for the universal empire of Messiah.

CHAPTER XII.

THE CAPTIVITY.

JEREMIAH, EZEKIEL, DANIEL.

SECTION I.—CAPTIVITY OF THE TEN TRIBES.

The seed of Jacob scattered—The several Assyrian captivities—Testimony of the Assyrian monuments—Trials of the Israelites—Story of Tobit—The Israelites in Media—Ultimate fate of the ten tribes.

The Seed of Jacob Scattered.—The seed of Jacob, whose history we have heretofore followed in the land of Canaan, was now dispersed in four or five different countries. Assyria, Media, Chaldæa, Egypt, and Palestine, contained each a section of the chosen people. The prophecy of Moses, uttered eight or nine hundred years before, had received its first but not its only fulfilment; on account of their sins and provocations, the chosen people, whom God loved so well, were scattered among the heathen.

The Several Assyrian Captivities.—The successive invasions of the kingdom of the ten tribes by the kings of Assyria, with the results of each, may be seen at a glance in the following table:—

YEAR B.C.	ASSYRIAN KINGS.	KINGS OF ISRAEL.	PEOPLE CARRIED OFF	KINGS OF JUDAH	YEAR BEFORE DESTRUCTION OF JERUSALEM.
771.	Pul	Menahem.	Reuben, Gad, &c.	Uzziah.	183.
740.	Tiglath-pileser.	Pekah.	Gilead, Galilee, &c.	Ahaz.	152.
721.	Shalmaneser.	Hoshea.	All Israel.	Hezekiah.	133.

Testimony of the Assyrian Monuments.—It is an interesting fact, that the inscriptions on the monuments that have lately been discovered in the ruins of Nineveh agree generally with the Scripture account of the captivity, though they do not notice the captivity of Israel. Many of the monuments are records of the conquests of the kings of Assyria. In some of these, two things may be particularly noticed. One is, that the king in his wars always invokes the help of Assarac, the supreme god of heaven, and ascribes his conquests to him. This shows that the wars of the Assyrians were regarded as contests with the gods of the different countries not less than with their peoples; and that, if the Israelites had been faithful to their God, they would never have been allowed to be vanquished. The other remarkable circumstance is, that the king is generally said to have "carried off the inhabitants, with their most valuable effects, into captivity in Assyria, replacing the people with colonists drawn from the nations immediately subject to him, and appointing his own officers and prefects to the charge of the colonists and the administration of the new territory."* The king's object in this, probably, was to weaken and divide the power of the conquered nations, so as to prevent them from combining in any rebellion or insurrection against him. It was in this way as we learn from the Scripture narrative, that he dealt with the kingdom of Israel: colonists were brought to the land of Israel from Babylon, Cuthah, Ava, Hamath, and Sepharvaim, while the Israelites were carried to Assyria and Media.

Trials of the Israelites.—There can be no doubt that dreadful cruelties and hardships were suffered by the Israelites during their wars with the Assyrians; for, with all their outward refinement and civilization, the Assyrians in their wars committed frightful atrocities. It was quite common in those wars for women and children to be torn asunder or dashed to pieces. It must have been with terribly dejected hearts that the captive Israelites marched towards Assyria from the land of their fathers; gazed for the last time on the snowy peaks of Lebanon

* Rawlinson.

and Hermon; remembered, as they passed through the green orchards of Damascus, how Abraham, twelve hundred years before, had there defeated the Assyrian kings that were carrying off Lot, and sighed to think that there was no one to rescue them; saw in the columned temples and palaces of Palmyra the remains of that magnificence which their country had possessed in the days of Solomon; and at last, after a weary march of many weeks through the Syrian desert, entered the mighty gates of Nineveh, and, in its strange palaces and temples, witnessed the marvellous memorials of the glory of their conquerors.

Story of Tobit.—Some of these captive Israelites appear to have remained in Nineveh; and, as afterwards among their brethren in Babylon, individuals rose to considerable distinction. The apocryphal book of Tobit professes to give the history of one of these. Though forming no part of the canonical Scriptures, and though marked in some places by great faults, it is not unlikely that this book contains the substance, at least, of a genuine narrative. Tobit, one of the captive Israelites, a man of wealth, pious and charitable, rose to be purveyor to Shalmaneser; and his nephew, Achiacharus, became his cup-bearer. He represents his brother-captives as sometimes suffering much hardship at the hands of the Assyrian king. Particularly, when Sennacherib returned from his attempted conquest of Hezekiah at Jerusalem, after the signal judgment inflicted on him, he vented his rage upon the captive Israelites, and cast the dead bodies of those whom he destroyed beyond the walls of Nineveh, to remain there unburied. Tobit made a point of burying at night the bodies of all whom he found thus exposed. The removal of the bodies caused suspicion to fall on him, and, to save his life, he had to flee from Nineveh. Soon afterwards, Sennacherib, whose tyranny had become intolerable, was killed by two of his sons, while worshipping in the temple of his god, Nisroch — probably the Assarac of the inscriptions.

The Israelites in Media.—But though a few of the captive Israelites remained in Nineveh, the greater part were placed in the province of Media. Media lay to the east of Assyria. Its aspect was wild and mountainous, thus forming a great contrast to the flat plains of Assyria and Mesopotamia. Its northern boundary was formed by the great chain of mountains that spread out on either side from Ararat, and that sometimes rise to heights that are almost lost to view in the skies. The Israelites were thus brought back to the neighbourhood of the first settlements of the human race. Some of them would drink from rivers cooled by the snows of Ararat; and though the general aspect of the country was somewhat barren, yet here and there Eden itself might be recalled by some lovely valley, encircled by wooded mountains, with silvery rills streaming down to the lake below, from whose still bosom were reflected the hues of roses, hyacinths, and all sorts of flowers. The remote position and the highland character of Media, separated by a high chain of mountains from the countries to the west, may partly explain the circumstance of our hearing so little ever after of the captive ten tribes.* God designed that, as a nation, they should pass out of sight, and consequently caused them to be carried off to this remote province.

Ultimate Fate of the Ten Tribes.—But it is likely that they would obtain here a tolerable measure of tranquillity and comfort. A few years after they were placed in it, Media attained the position of an independent kingdom. It was in the reign of Sennacherib that Media revolted from Assyria, and chose as its king Deioces (called Arphaxad in the apocryphal book of Judith), who made Ecbatana his capital. The social condition of the Israelites in Media must have been greatly improved, when they passed from under the yoke of the cruel and persecuting king of Assyria, and became a constituent part of an independent kingdom. Probably they obtained lands and

* They are said to have been placed in Halah and Habor by the river of Gozan, and Hara, and other cities of the Medes (2 Kings xvii. 6, xviii 11; 1 Chron. v. 26). Halah is believed by Sir H. Rawlinson to be the Calah of Asshur (Gen. x. 11), afterwards known by the names of Cálah or Halah, and now called Holwan, situated on the high-road between Bagdad and Kirmanshah, about longitude 46° east, and latitude 34° 30' north. Habor, by the river of Gozan, is regarded by Major Rennel as the same with Abhar, situated on a branch of the river Kizil-Ozal, and believed to be a very ancient place. Hara is thought by Rawlinson to have been Ecbatana (in Atropatenia), once called Airyana. The only other cities of the Medes mentioned in the accounts of the captivity are Rhages (in Tobit),—thought to be the same as Rei, a ruined city four miles south of Teheran; and Ecbatana (Apocrypha) or Achmetha (Ezra vi. 2),—probably the Median Ecbatana, now called Hamadan.—*Kitto's History; M'Leod's Atlas.*

houses and many other material comforts in Media. But there is little reason to think that they improved much in religious character. Before their captivity, they had sunk as a kingdom to a much more hopeless state than that of Judah, and the better disposed members of the nation had joined that kingdom. In their captivity there were, doubtless, faithful individuals, who continued to worship the God of their fathers, and who perhaps found their way back to the land of Israel; but the mass of the nation probably conformed to the corrupt worship around them, and, as a body, never returned to their own land. In the course of a few generations, under Darius the Mede, the empire of Medo-Persia swallowed up both Babylon and Assyria, and the Median, Assyrian, and Chaldæan Jews became subjects of the same king. What ultimately became of these ten tribes is one of the unsolved problems of history. Some think they are to be found in the Nestorian Christians of Turkey in Asia; others, in the Afghans of India; and others think they have gone to places more remote.

SECTION II.—CAPTIVITY OF JUDAH.

Successive detachments of captives—Empire of Nebuchadnezzar: Babylon—Learning of the Chaldæans: the Magi—Daniel: Nebuchadnezzar's dream—Noble conduct of Daniel's companions: influence on their countrymen—Second detachment of Jews in Chaldæa—Distress of the captives—Prophecies of Ezekiel.

Successive Detachments of Captives.—In the kingdom of Judah, as in that of the ten tribes, the captives had been carried off in three detachments. The following table exhibits the whole process:—

YEAR B C	KINGS OF JUDAH.	THE CONQUEROR.	PEOPLE CARRIED OFF.
607	Jehoiakim.	Nebuchadnezzar, acting for his father.	Daniel and other princes.
599	Jehoiachin.	Nebuchadnezzar.	10,000 chief people.
588	Zedekiah.	Nebuchadnezzar.	Nearly all the people.

A small remnant was still left in the land, under Gedaliah, most of whom were massacred by Ishmael; of the remnant, the greater part went to Egypt with Johanan, while a very small fragment continued to hover about their ancient seats.

Empire of Nebuchadnezzar: Babylon.—We have already seen how the Chaldæan empire separated from that of Assyria, and rose on its ruins. Under the vigorous rule of Nebuchadnezzar, the new empire rapidly increased; and Babylon, its capital, assumed an aspect of the greatest magnificence. Besides the countries in the Mesopotamian plain, and the highland regions beyond, Arabia, Syria, and Palestine were now parts of the empire, and other important provinces were added to it soon afterwards. Babylon is commonly believed to have occupied the site of the ancient Babel. It was situated in a flat, fertile plain, on the banks of the Euphrates. Some ancient writers give a very singular account of the city. Its walls were drawn about it in the form of a square, each side of which was fifteen miles long. Twenty-five streets ran in one direction, and twenty-five across them at right angles, terminating in a hundred gates, and dividing the city into upwards of six hundred squares. The middle of each square was laid out in gardens. Nebuchadnezzar bestowed immense pains on the embellishment of Babylon, and among other great works, including splendid palaces and temples, he constructed its famous hanging gardens, which consisted of several large terraces, piled one above the other, till the height equalled that of the walls of the city. They are said to have been constructed to please Amyitis, his Median queen, who missed, in the flat plains of Babylonia, the bold scenery of her highland home. We cannot but suspect this account of the size and structure of Babylon to be exaggerated; but beyond all doubt the city was a very wonderful one.* Nebuchadnezzar seems to have been one of the most powerful, perhaps the most powerful, of all the kings that ever reigned in the East.

Learning of the Chaldæans: the Magi.—Hither, then, in the third year of Jehoiakim, eighteen or nineteen years before

---

* The name of Nebuchadnezzar has been distinctly deciphered on the bricks that are yet found among the ruins of Babylon.

the destruction of Jerusalem, were brought Daniel and his companions, to be instructed in the learning and the tongue of the Chaldæans. It is from this period that the commencement of the seventy years' captivity is usually reckoned. The Chaldæans had prosecuted learning from a very early period. In the time of Alexander the Great they boasted that their ancestors had made astronomical observations for four hundred and seventy thousand years! This period was afterwards cut down to nineteen hundred and three years. Their Magi, or learned men, were a numerous and important class. The movements of the heavenly bodies, the qualities of metals and minerals, prognostications of the future, explanations of dreams, and similar subjects, constituted their studies; and as they claimed great skill in the art of foretelling the future, they acquired a position of extraordinary influence. They were the priests of the Chaldæan nation, and they taught the worship of the sun, the moon, and the planets. In their creed, they acknowledged one Supreme Being, the maker and governor of the world; but practically, as in the case of the Egyptians, this sublime truth was lost under the popular notion of many gods. Bel, or Belus, the supreme god of Babylon, was worshipped with extraordinary honours; and a magnificent temple was built for him by Nebuchadnezzar. The Chaldæan language was a branch of what is called the Aramean family. There were two main branches of the Aramean: the western, including Syriac and Hebrew; and the eastern, including the Assyrian and the Babylonian. Though similar in structure, they were so far different, that without special study those familiar with the one could not understand the other.

Daniel: Nebuchadnezzar's Dream.—Flung in among the cunning priests of Babylon, Daniel and his companions were exposed to the greatest danger. They were mercifully enabled, from the very first, to make a decided and prudent stand against Babylonian luxury; and afterwards a still more noble stand against Babylonian idolatry. Their spirit was a great contrast to that yielding, accommodating temper in religious matters, which had always been a prominent weakness of the mass of the Jews. Their names formed worthy additions to the illustrious roll of faithful Hebrews, headed by Abraham, who renounced all that was dear to flesh and blood, and braved all terrors, rather than prove unfaithful to their God, and who form the brightest and noblest galaxy that ever threw lustre on any nation. Their position was greatly strengthened by the success of Daniel in recalling and explaining to Nebuchadnezzar a dream which had baffled all the wise men of Babylon. The dream showed a great image, of various materials, gold, silver, brass, iron, and clay, smitten and broken in pieces by a stone cut out without hands, which became a great mountain and filled the earth. The head of the image represented the kingdom of Nebuchadnezzar; and the stone the kingdom which the God of heaven was to set up, never to be moved. This happened in the second year of Nebuchadnezzar's reign as sole monarch, his father having lately died;* and probably about the seventh year of Jehoiakim, or four years after the arrival of Daniel in Babylon.

Noble Conduct of Daniel's Companions: Influence on their Countrymen.—It may have been soon after this that Nebuchadnezzar set up a golden image on the plain of Dura, which all were commanded to worship, on pain, if they should refuse, of being cast into a burning fiery furnace. Daniel must have been absent on this occasion, for he certainly would not have yielded; and the main body of the Jews could not yet have been in Chaldæa, for it is incredible that his three companions, Shadrach, Meshach, and Abed-nego, should in that case have stood alone in their refusal to bow down before the image. A signal miracle delivered them from the burning fiery furnace, after they had been thrown into it, their deliverer appearing in person as the Son of God. The miracle and the deliverance made a deep impression on Nebuchadnezzar for the time, and in his decree he claimed from all men the highest honour for the God of Israel. But all this must have been forgotten by him when, about twelve years later, he destroyed the temple of that same God

---

* For removal of chronological difficulties as to Nebuchadnezzar's reign, see Rawlinson, Historical Illustrations, p. 158.

at Jerusalem. Yet the noble stand of the three Jewish princes could not but make a deep impression at Babylon, and must have secured respect for their religion, the benefit of which would be extended to the nation when they joined them in their captivity. The Jews were generally disposed to pay great regard to their royal family; and when they found ground so decided taken up against idolatry by the captive princes, they would be strongly disposed to support them. And thus, at the very beginning of the captivity, the decided conduct of three young men, who were full of the spirit of faith and prayer, served materially to accomplish the grand purpose of the captivity,—to wean the whole nation from idolatry. The miracle had a great religious and national purpose, and that purpose was fulfilled.

Second Detachment of Jews in Chaldæa.—About eight years after the arrival of Daniel and his companions, the second detachment of Jews was brought to Chaldæa. In this company came the prophet Ezekiel, who naturally reckons the captivity from the year when he was made a prisoner, which he calls the year of Jehoiachin's captivity (i. 2). He and many of his countrymen were settled on the banks of the river Chebar (now the Khabur), a tributary of the Euphrates, that flows into it about three hundred miles above Babylon. Here they were close to the celebrated fortress of Carchemish (now Kerkisiyeh or Kerkisijieh), for which the Egyptians, Assyrians, and Hittites had had so many contests. Soon after reaching the scene of their bondage, and before Ezekiel received his commission, false prophets arose among the captives, who promised them a speedy return from captivity. On hearing this, Jeremiah, who was still at Jerusalem, wrote to inform the captives that such hopes were utterly vain, and that the captivity would last seventy years (Jer. xxix. 10). This period is to be reckoned from the beginning of the captivity, when Daniel and his companions were carried away (Dan. ix. 2).

Distress of the Captives.—Many a bitter insult had to be borne by these captive Jews. The flat marshy surface of the country is favourable to the growth of the willow. So abundant is that tree, that wicker boats constructed of it may be seen at all times passing along the rivers.* The beautiful words of the 137th psalm give a vivid picture of the heart-broken captives : " By the rivers of Babylon, there we sat down, yea, we wept, when we remembered Zion. We hanged our harps upon the willows in the midst thereof. For there they that carried us away captive required of us a song; and they that wasted us required of us mirth, saying, Sing us one of the songs of Zion. How shall we sing the Lord's song in a strange land? If I forget thee, O Jerusalem, let my right hand forget her cunning. If I do not remember thee, let my tongue cleave to the roof of my mouth ; if I prefer not Jerusalem above my chief joy."

Prophecies of Ezekiel.—It was not long after Jeremiah's mournful message had reached the captives at Chebar, intimating a captivity of seventy years, that a great prophet was raised up among themselves, whose visions amply confirmed the words of his brother at Jerusalem. In the fifth year of the reign of Zedekiah, and therefore the fifth after the second deportation from Jerusalem, prophetic visions began to be sent to EZEKIEL, on the banks of the Chebar. These visions spread over a considerable period. Among the earliest were those of the complete destruction of Jerusalem, and the desolation of Judæa. The treacherous conduct of the Egyptians, in deserting the Jews in the extremity of their distress, furnished occasion for a blast against Pharaoh-hophra, whose destruction, with the desolation of Egypt, is also foreseen and foretold. Tyre, also, which latterly had been a bitter enemy of the Jews, was doomed to speedy destruction. But Ezekiel's later visions were full of mercy and peace. They not only foretold the restoration of the captive people, but also the far higher and richer mercies of the gospel ; and his sun, like that of Isaiah, went down pouring both on Jews and on Gentiles the golden lustre of Messiah's reign. Mercy was thus graciously mingled with judgment; and while the people were faithfully reproved for their sins, the penitent and believing were encouraged to hope in the not very distant advent of better times.

* Chesney's Narrative.

SECTION III.—FURTHER CAREER OF NEBUCHADNEZZAR.

Conquest of Syria, Tyre, Ammon, &c.—Conquest of Egypt—Dream and humiliation of Nebuchadnezzar—His death—Purpose for which he was raised up—Evil-merodach and Jehoiachin.

Conquest of Syria, Tyre, Ammon, etc.—Soon after the destruction of Jerusalem, Nebuchadnezzar went forth to subdue some of the neighbouring nations, and to measure strength with Egypt, still the great rival empire of the South. Tyre, the great mart of the commerce of the world, withstood him and his generals for thirteen years. At last he succeeded in taking it;* but the inhabitants had removed all their effects to an island half a mile from the shore, where New Tyre was built—the city which afterwards nearly baffled the skill of Alexander the Great. The Tyrians had gloried over the captivity of their neighbours, the Israelites; and the destruction of their city by Nebuchadnezzar was a divine retribution for their sin. The few Jews still remaining in the land of Israel were now collected and sent to Babylon. The Ammonites were completely subdued; Rabbah their capital was destroyed, and themselves and their king were carried captive to Babylon. A similar fate seems to have befallen most of the other neighbouring nations—the Philistines, the Moabites, and the Edomites. Most of these nations now disappear as such from the field of history. The policy of Nebuchadnezzar, not only in annexing kingdoms, but actually in changing their inhabitants, effected an entire change in the social condition of that part of the world, and laid the foundation of the vastly altered state of society that we meet with in the New Testament.

Conquest of Egypt.—Palestine and Syria having been completely subdued, Nebuchadnezzar's arms were next directed to Egypt. Meeting with no serious opposition, he ravaged the country from end to end. The remnant of Jews that had fled thither under Johanan, met with the miserable fate which Jeremiah had foretold: many of them were put to death, and the

---

* Considerable obscurity rests on this part of the history.

rest were sent to Babylon. The king of Egypt himself, who had made it his boast that even God could not strip him of his greatness, was strangled in his capital. The predictions of Ezekiel were thus fully verified. Nebuchadnezzar returned, laden with spoils and with glory; and having now rest from all his enemies, he applied himself to the embellishment of Babylon.

Dream and Humiliation of Nebuchadnezzar.—But a strange dream of a great tree that was hewn down to the ground was explained to him by Daniel to foreshadow a great humiliation that was about to befall him. The prophet strongly counselled a course of righteousness and clemency,—which implies that Nebuchadnezzar was both unjust and merciless; but the advice was disregarded. He went on embellishing and glorifying Babylon. The vast plunder he had gathered, and the multitudes of captives whose labour he could command, enabled him to perform works of prodigious magnitude. Surveying one day the marvellous results of his genius, enterprise, and power, perhaps from the highest terrace of the hanging gardens, or from some eminence connected with his palace, he heard a voice from heaven, which doomed him, as the punishment of his pride, to seven years' insanity. The sentence was literally carried into effect. No notice of this strange event has yet been found in any Babylonian records;[*] and probably there was a purposed omission of a fact so humiliating to one of the greatest kings that had ever reigned in the East.

His Death.—After recovering from his illness, Nebuchadnezzar seems to have reigned a year. He died after a reign of forty-three years, or forty-five from his first going into Syria. His acknowledgment of the Most High, after his recovery, is cordial, and seems to indicate a chastened heart. The events of his reign must have had a great effect in exalting the true God in the estimation of Eastern nations, and perhaps in drawing attention to and in procuring respect for the sacred books of the Jews. And as the predictions of the Messiah in Daniel's writings were now clear and full, the attention of earnest spirits must have been largely drawn to the coming Deliverer. The

[*] There are, however, hints of it. See Rawlinson's Historical Illustrations, p. 168.

foundation would now be laid of that expectation of a great King of the Jews, unlike all other kings, which long after led the wise men of the East to interpret as they did the mysterious star that appeared at Christ's birth, and drew them to Jerusalem in search of him. Thus, in the wisdom of that God who ruleth over all, the destruction of the nation, the city, and the house of God—of all, in a word, that had been visibly connected with his name—proved the means of really advancing his cause.

Purpose for which he was Raised Up.—The conquests of Nebuchadnezzar, uniting many kingdoms into one, formed an important link in the long chain of events designed by God to prepare the way for the kingdom of Christ. If Christianity had been introduced at an earlier period than it was, it would have found the world divided into a large number of independent kingdoms, commonly at war with one another. There was no mutual affinity among them, no bond of connection, but every element of repulsion. The success of Christianity in any of these kingdoms, so far from promoting its success in the rest, would rather have secured its rejection. No apostle could have travelled from kingdom to kingdom but at the risk of his life. It pleased God, therefore, to raise up a succession of great conquerors, whose work was to bring the kingdoms of the world into one. First, NEBUCHADNEZZAR arose, and brought into one empire Chaldæa, Assyria, Arabia, Palestine, Egypt, and other countries. Next, CYRUS the Persian was raised up, under whom nearly the whole of Asia was brought under one sceptre. Then followed ALEXANDER of Macedon, whose territories embraced the east of Europe besides. And lastly, the ROMANS, who, though not extending quite so far on the side of Asia, added the north-west of Africa, and the south and south-west of Europe. And thus, when Christianity was introduced, it had only to be planted in a single centre; and from that centre it was able to spread out, east and west, north and south, over the length and breadth of the Roman empire. The apostle Paul could travel from Arabia on the east to Spain on the west without ever losing the benefit of his Roman citizenship and the protection of the laws of Rome, and without exposing his life to any dangers but those which arose from the lawlessness and turbulence of evil-disposed men.

Evil-merodach and Jehoiachin.—Jerome mentions a tradition, that while Nebuchadnezzar was laid aside, his son Evil-merodach administered the kingdom, but did it so ill that when his father recovered he threw him into prison. In this prison, it is said, he met with Jehoiachin, ex-king of Judah, now in the thirty-seventh year of his imprisonment, for whom he conceived a great affection. Be that as it may, it is certain that when Evil-merodach came to the throne, he removed Jehoiachin from prison and gave him a high place in the kingdom of Babylon. But his reign lasted only two years, and was marked alike by wickedness and by folly. He was succeeded by Neriglissar, his brother-in-law; and about the same time Jehoiachin left to his son Salathiel the nominal succession to the throne of David.

SECTION IV.—LATER DAYS OF THE BABYLONIAN EMPIRE.

Cyrus, the Persian—Nabonadius and Belshazzar—Daniel's vision of the four beasts—Crœsus, king of Lydia—Conquests of Cyrus: capture of Babylon—Daniel's promotion: the den of lions—A promise of deliverance—Cyrus succeeds Darius: release of the Jews.

Cyrus, the Persian.—About this time there comes on the field of history a prince of singular character and great ability—CYRUS, founder of the Medo-Persian empire, who had been designated by Isaiah long before as the appointed deliverer of the Jews. Xenophon, a Greek general and historian, has written an account of the education of Cyrus, in which he is exhibited as the model of a wise, able, and excellent prince; but his early history is involved in considerable obscurity, for Xenophon's work is rather a romance than a history. He was the son of Cambyses, a Persian noble, and of Mandane, daughter of Astyages, king of the Medes. A great warrior, Cyrus pursued a career of conquest, and in process of time turned his arms against the Babylonians.

Nabonadius and Belshazzar.—The accounts of the historians while substantially agreeing with that of the Bible respecting the capture of Babylon by Cyrus, show some apparent discrepancies. The king of Babylon is said to have been Nabonadius, but he had retired to the neighbouring city Borsippa, which he surrendered to Cyrus, his life being spared. A comfortable residence was given him in Carmania, where he died. The ordinary historians, while recording the sudden capture of Babylon by Cyrus, do not name Belshazzar. Recently, however, certain inscriptions deciphered by Sir Henry Rawlinson, have cleared up the mystery. It appears from these that the eldest son of Nabonadius was named Bel-sharezar, contracted Belshazzar, and admitted by his father to a share in the government.

Daniel's Vision of the Four Beasts.—In the first year of the reign of Belshazzar, Daniel saw a vision of four beasts, representing the four great empires—the Babylonian, the Medo-Persian, the Grecian, and the Roman; and of the rise, persecution, and final triumph of the kingdom of Christ. Two years afterwards, while employed at Shushan, in the neighbouring province of Elam, he had another vision, in which the succession of these empires was more fully set forth, the Medo-Persian, as well as the Grecian, which was to succeed it, being mentioned by name. These visions indicated the approaching downfall of the Babylonian empire,—an event which the arms of Cyrus were fast accomplishing.

Crœsus, King of Lydia.—It was the policy of the Babylonian monarch to enlist all the allies he could prevail on, to take arms against the Medes and Persians. The most eminent of his allies was Crœsus, king of Lydia, a country in the west of Asia. Lydia, with its capital, Sardis, was a very ancient kingdom; and its people appear to have been civilized, industrious, and wealthy,—practising commerce, agriculture, and manufactures, and acquainted with various arts; but, like other nations of Asia, lax in their morals. Crœsus had the reputation of being the wealthiest of men. But he was quite unable to withstand the arms of Cyrus, who suddenly appeared before Sardis, took it, and condemned Crœsus to be burned to death.

It is said that, as the king stood before the funeral pyre, he cried out, with a deep sigh, "O Solon, Solon, Solon!" The curiosity of Cyrus was roused by the circumstance, and he learned that, when Solon, the Athenian sage, was at Sardis, Crœsus had showed him all his wealth and magnificence, and, expecting a compliment, had asked him who was the happiest man he had ever seen? Solon had named two comparatively obscure Greeks, and had then remarked that he could pronounce no man happy as long as he lived, because no one could foresee what might happen to him before he died. The striking application of this remark to his own altered circumstances made such an impression on Crœsus, that he could not refrain from calling out the name of Solon. When the matter was reported to Cyrus, he spared the life of Crœsus, and made him his friend.

Conquests of Cyrus: Capture of Babylon.—The conquests of Cyrus had now brought under the dominion of the Medo-Persians the largest empire over which one man had ever ruled. It extended from the Indus to the Nile, and embraced nearly all the intervening territory. But for a long time Babylon maintained its independence. Surrounded by walls of enormous height and strength, and having provisions for twenty years, even Cyrus would have had to leave it in despair, but for a stratagem. Nabonadius was absent from the capital, which was left in charge of Belshazzar. A great festival was going on within the city, during which Belshazzar was guilty of an act of excessive profanity,—using the sacred vessels of Jerusalem for convivial purposes, and extolling meanwhile the gods of gold, silver, brass, iron, wood, and stone, which he and his people worshipped. A mysterious hand was seen on the palace wall, tracing letters which none of the Babylonian wise men could read. The queen mother, Nitocris, remembering the wisdom of Daniel, caused him to be sent for. He was promised the position of *third* ruler of the empire— implying that there were already two rulers, Nabonadius and Belshazzar, that could not be superseded. Daniel at once deciphered the letters, and boldly announced, as their import, that the kingdom was taken from Belshazzar and given to the Medes and Persians. Meanwhile Cyrus, by drawing off the waters of the Euphrates, which ran through Babylon, obtained an entrance for his soldiers, who, advancing to the palace, killed Belshazzar, and was soon in undisputed possession of the city.

Daniel's Promotion: the Den of Lions.—Though Babylon was taken by Cyrus, its nominal master was Cyaxares, king of the Medes, the uncle, and afterwards the father-in-law of Cyrus. He is called in Scripture Darius the Mede. He and Cyrus divided their vast empire into one hundred and twenty provinces; over which they placed three presidents, of whom Daniel was the first. While Cyrus was absent on a warlike expedition, Daniel's enemies accused him to Darius, and got him cast into a den of lions. His miraculous escape from the lions must have raised him to a position of higher influence than ever.

A Promise of Deliverance.—In the first year of the reign of Darius, Daniel, believing that the end of the captivity was at hand, was engaged in a special service of confession and prayer on behalf of his people, when an angel assured him that the time of their deliverance was come, and foretold, in very precise terms, the period when Messiah should appear.

Cyrus Succeeds Darius: Release of the Jews.—In the course of two years Darius died, and Cyrus succeeded to the magnificent Medo-Persian empire. It is hardly a stretch of fancy to imagine an interview between him and the venerable Hebrew prophet, who had risen so high in the councils of the Babylonian kings. We may easily suppose Daniel, after being presented to Cyrus, opening the book of the prophet Isaiah, and reading to the king the first few verses of the forty-fifth chapter. Great must have been the astonishment of Cyrus to find himself mentioned by name in that old Hebrew document- described as breaking in pieces "the brazen gates" of Babylon; as receiving from God "the hidden riches" of Croesus and other wealthy kings; and as God's appointed instrument for setting his people free. Great, too, must have been the impression made on him by the magnificent description of the majestic power of the great God, whom Cyrus and the Persians believed to be little more than coördinate with the principle of Evil,—"I form the light and create darkness; I make peace and create evil; I the LORD do *all these things.*" Yielding to the impression of such truths, Cyrus, among his very first acts, issued a decree permitting the Jews to return and build the temple of the Lord at Jerusalem. This permission was given with the utmost cordiality. No Jew or Israelite disposed to take part in the work could now be detained against his will in Babylon or the neighbourhood; and though, in point of fact, many did not return then, and some never returned at all, yet, as a state of compulsory bondage, the Babylonian Captivity was at an end.

SECTION V.—SOCIAL AND RELIGIOUS LIFE.

Employments of the captives—The new generation—Preservation of genealogies—Change in language—Great change in religion—Additions to the canon.

Employments of the Captives.—The employments of the Jewish captives, both in Assyria and in Chaldæa, must have been very varied. The general superiority of the Hebrew character, both intellectually and morally, to that of other Eastern nations, would commonly secure the advancement and prosperity of the captives. Some rose to the very highest situations, such as Daniel, who became prime minister; Shadrach, Meshach, and Abed-nego, who also got high promotion; and afterwards Nehemiah, who became cup-bearer to the king of Persia. Many would be employed as craftsmen or artisans. We find the goldsmiths and the apothecaries, for example, taking a considerable share in repairing the walls of Jerusalem under Nehemiah (Neh. iii. 8). Many who had been accustomed to agriculture and gardening doubtless followed the advice of Jeremiah in the land of their captivity—"Build ye houses, and dwell in them; and plant gardens, and eat the fruit of them" (Jer. xxix. 5, 28).

The New Generation.—As a rule, the captives were not now exposed to grinding tyranny; for it was the interest and policy of Nebuchadnezzar to make them comfortable. The laceration of their feelings was doubtless their chief misery; but the generation born in Babylon would be less sensible of that pain than their fathers. Probably many who were settled in the country districts on comfortable farms and in productive gardens became so fond of them as not to desire to return home. The companies that returned were probably gathered mainly from the more enterprising and more movable population of the towns. The total number of horses, camels, mules, and asses brought back to Jerusalem was exceedingly small— not exceeding eight thousand. It is a proof that the spirits of the people must have revived somewhat, after the time when they hung their harps upon the willows, that the cultivation of their musical gifts was not neglected. In the first company that returned there were two hundred singing men and women.

Preservation of Genealogies.—However they may have been scattered at first, or tossed hither and thither in Babylon and Chaldæa, they contrived very wonderfully, for the most part, to preserve their genealogies. A few were unable to trace their pedigree when the restoration took place, but the greater part had preserved it as carefully as if they had been at home. In the arrangements adopted at the rebuilding of Jerusalem, strict regard was had to each person's family. Perhaps the prophecies of Ezekiel, who foretold the restoration of each tribe individually, stimulated them specially to the careful preservation of their genealogies.

Change in Language.—The spoken language of the people underwent a change. To a considerable degree they adopted the Chaldee dialect. When Ezra read the law in Hebrew, at the restoration, he had to give the sense in the spoken dialect, in order to make the people understand the meaning.

Great Change in Religion.—But the greatest change of all took place in religion. The old love of idolatry was now rooted out. Never again, in any part of their history, did the Jews show any tendency to worship idols. The change seems to have been brought about more by the action of natural feelings than by any spiritual revival. The idolatry of the Chaldæans would be viewed by them with disgust, because it was the religion of their spoilers. A people banished and denationalized have always a strong inclination to cherish and cling to their national institutions and distinguishing glories. Those of the Jews were peculiarly their religious ordinances. That sense of superiority which refused to humble itself even under a Babylonian captivity would intrench itself amid the venerable institutions of Moses. Hence, perhaps, the reason why the love of idolatry that had characterized them in their earlier period was succeeded in their later by national pride, by expectations of carnal glory under the Messiah, by reliance on their own works and righteousness, and by a tendency to overrate trivial observances and to undervalue the weightier matters of the law.

Additions to the Canon.—Nevertheless, the path of the true Israel—the election according to grace—waxed brighter and brighter unto the perfect day. Many psalms were added to the canon during this period, along with the prophecies of Ezekiel and Daniel. The promises became clearer and brighter. The doctrine of the Messiah was presented with greater distinctness in the writings of Daniel; his spiritual work became better understood—"to finish transgression, make an end of sin, make reconciliation for iniquity, and bring in everlasting righteousness." The doctrine of the resurrection of the body began now to assume a more definite form (Ezek. xxxvii. 12; Dan. xii. 2). Ezekiel presented the doctrine of the new heart and the life-giving power of the Holy Spirit more vividly than any former writer had done. Sacrifices continued to be offered. Daniel speaks of "the evening oblation;" and doubtless there was some place in Babylon where as much of the temple service as possible continued to be celebrated. But in general there must have been a great lack of religious ordinances; and the pious would be more and more thrown on private and family exercises of devotion. Thrice a day was Daniel accustomed to offer prayer in his house; and on certain occasions he observed long seasons of special devotion. The way was gradually being prepared for a more spiritual religion, although more than five hundred years had to run before Christ should proclaim that the time had come when neither in Mount Gerizim nor yet at Jerusalem were men to worship the Father, but when true worshippers were everywhere to worship him in spirit and in truth.

CHAPTER XIII.

THE RESTORATION.

FROM THE EDICT OF CYRUS TO NEHEMIAH.

DANIEL, EZRA, NEHEMIAH, ESTHER, HAGGAI, ZECHARIAH, MALACHI.

SECTION I.—THE EXPEDITION OF ZERUBBABEL.

The several expeditions to Jerusalem—The company of Zerubbabel—Opposition to the work of restoration—Reigns of Cambyses and Smerdis—Reign of Darius Hystaspes—Completion of the temple—Haggai and Zechariah—Intercourse with Jews at Babylon—Revolt, capture, and destruction of Babylon.

The Several Expeditions to Jerusalem.—In the history of the restoration of the Jews to their own country, the names of three Jewish leaders and of three Persian kings are prominent:—

1. The first Jewish leader was ZERUBBABEL, who left Babylon when CYRUS came to the throne, B.C. 535. After an interval of about twenty years, he was enabled to complete the rebuilding of the temple, in the reign of DARIUS HYSTASPES.

2. The second Jewish leader was EZRA, who went up from Babylon about eighty years after Zerubbabel, B.C. 458, in the seventh year of ARTAXERXES LONGIMANUS. He laboured chiefly to restore the institutions of Moses.

3. The third Jewish leader was NEHEMIAH, who went up from Susa, or Shushan, in the twentieth year of the same Artaxerxes,* B.C. 445. He rebuilt the wall and set up the gates of

---

* A recent writer in the "Transactions of the Society of Biblical Archæology" (vol ii., p. 110) tries to show that Ezra and Nehemiah went up together to Jerusalem, the years of Artaxerxes' reign being computed from different beginnings. But this is altogether an assumption.

Jerusalem, and promoted many reforms. After returning for a time to Susa, he paid a second visit to Jerusalem; soon after which the prophet Malachi closed the canon of the Old Testament. The story of Esther comes in a few years before the time of Ezra.

The Company of Zerubbabel.—As soon as the edict of Cyrus was issued, preparations began to be made for the return of a part of the Jews. As Daniel deemed it right to remain at his post in Persia, this expedition was intrusted to ZERUBBABEL and JESHUA; the one, the son of Shealtiel or Salathiel, and therefore representative of the royal family of Judah; the other, the hereditary high priest. The total number of the party was about fifty thousand. Most of them were of the tribes of Judah, Benjamin, and Levi, but there were a few belonging to the ten tribes also. From this time, owing to the predominance of the tribe of Judah, the people are known as "the Jews." The only other considerable emigration was that which came with Ezra, about eighty years afterwards, amounting to about six thousand persons. The great mass of the exiles, therefore, remained in Chaldæa, Persia, and Media. By remaining in the East, they helped to diffuse the knowledge of the true God over Eastern countries, and thus to prepare the way for the gospel. It was now that "the missionary era" of the Jews began. From this time they became "a light to lighten the Gentiles,"—a witness for God to the ends of the earth.

Opposition to the Work of Restoration.—The select company that followed Zerubbabel must have consisted of the most earnest, godly, and enterprising members of the captive nation. It took them four long months to traverse the seven hundred miles between Babylon and Jerusalem. One year after they had reached their country, they began to rebuild the temple. The Samaritans (the descendants of the Assyrian colony planted by Shalmaneser in the district of Samaria) asked, but were refused, permission to join them in this work; and, in consequence of the refusal, they began to give annoyance and to make opposition. Probably it was when he heard of this opposition, that

Daniel, in the third year of Cyrus, held the solemn fast of which he gives an account in his tenth chapter, and had the very remarkable visions of the events that were coming, contained in the eleventh and twelfth.

Reigns of Cambyses and Smerdis.—The opposition of the Samaritans continued during the whole reign of Cyrus, and during the reigns of his successors, Cambyses (called Ahasuerus), and Smerdis (called Artaxerxes). Cambyses was a man of violent temper, and was by no means disposed to pay regard to religious feelings. It is said of him, that while at war with Egypt, he on one occasion collected a number of cats, dogs, sheep, and other animals deemed sacred by the Egyptians, and placed them in front of his army. The Egyptians dared not throw a single weapon, through fear of killing any of the animals, and Cambyses gained an easy victory. On another occasion, when told by the Egyptians, in explanation of a great rejoicing among them, that their god had shown himself to them, he begged to be made acquainted with him; and being shown the bull Apis, he was so enraged that he stabbed the animal, which was carried wounded and dying to its stable. In the reign of Smerdis (or Artaxerxes) his successor, the enemies of the Jews wrote a letter to the king, representing that Jerusalem had always been a rebellious city, and that it ought not to be rebuilt. The king, finding that this was true, gave a formal order for the stoppage of the work of restoration, and especially of the restoration of the temple.

Reign of Darius Hystaspes.—A few months later, DARIUS HYSTASPES having come to the Persian throne, the prophets HAGGAI and ZECHARIAH strongly urged their countrymen to resume the work, telling them that a recent drought and famine had been sent to punish them for permitting the house of God to lie desolate while they were ornamenting their own dwellings. The work of rebuilding the temple was accordingly resumed. Thereupon Tatnai, the Persian governor of the whole district, visited Jerusalem, and, learning that Cyrus had passed an edict sanctioning the work, he caused search to be made for it, first at Babylon, and afterwards at Achmetha, or Ecbatana, the capital of Media, where Cyrus had probably been when it was issued. The edict in question having been found at Ecbatana, Darius gave orders not only that the work should proceed, but that it should be largely helped from the public treasury.

Completion of the Temple.—The building of the temple was finished in the sixth year of Darius. After its completion, the passover was observed, with singular joy and heartiness. It was now about twenty years since the rebuilding of the temple had been begun. This gives another date for computing the termination of the captivity. From Nebuchadnezzar's first invasion, when Daniel and others were carried off, to the issuing of the edict of Cyrus, were seventy years; from the utter destruction of Jerusalem and the temple, to the rebuilding of the latter, were also seventy years. In other words, the interval from the *beginning* of the captivity to the *beginning* of the restoration, was the same as that from the *completion* of the captivity to the *completion* of the restoration—seventy years.

Haggai and Zechariah. — The prophecies of Haggai and Zechariah, which were delivered under Zerubbabel, not only stirred up the princes and the people to the duty which they were neglecting, but threw additional light on the coming of the Messiah. To comfort those who wept over the inferiority of the second temple to the first, Haggai announced that the presence of the Branch of Jesse would make the true glory of the latter house greater than that of the former. Haggai spoke of the Messiah under the beautiful title, "The Desire of all Nations"—implying that many nations were now directing, or would soon direct, their unconscious longings to the coming Deliverer. Zechariah's prophecies of Christ are, in some respects, the most remarkable in the Old Testament. In one of his visions, the Father summons the sword to awake against the Shepherd, and against the man that is his fellow; in another, men are looking in agony on the Lord whom they have pierced; in a third, Messiah rides on an ass into Jerusalem as a conqueror; and in a fourth, he is king of all the earth, and on the very bells of the horses there is inscribed "holiness unto the Lord." The divine as well as the human nature of Christ, and his office as an atoning Saviour, were thus very distinctly made known. All truly pious persons must have been deeply interested in these predictions; and an additional bond of attachment to the sacred land of their fathers must have been formed by the knowledge that its buildings and its scenery were to be so closely associated with the life of God's incarnate Son.

Intercourse with Jews at Babylon.—From Zechariah's prophecy, it appears that friendly intercourse continued to be maintained between the Jews in Jerusalem and the exiles who had remained in Chaldæa. On one occasion, Zechariah sent a solemn warning to those Jews that yet remained in Babylon, and called them to leave that devoted city without delay. It was high time that they should leave Babylon, for it was fast approaching its end. It had been most unwilling to bear the yoke of the Persians; and as the seat of royalty had been removed to Shushan or Susa, in the province of Elam or Susiana, the chagrin of the Babylonians was intense. They accordingly plotted a revolt, and, after years of silent preparation, carried it into effect in the reign of Darius Hystaspes. While their city was being besieged by the Persian army, the Babylonians suffered dreadfully from famine. In their extremity, they resolved to massacre the whole of the women and children, allowing only his favourite wife and one female servant to be spared to each man. The prophecy of Isaiah against Babylon was thus fulfilled—"Thou that art given to pleasures, that dwellest carelessly, that sayest in thine heart, I am, and none else beside me; I shall not sit as a widow, neither shall I know the loss of children: but these two things shall come to thee in a moment in one day, the loss of children and widowhood; they shall come upon thee in their perfection for the multitude of thy sorceries, and for the great abundance of thine enchantments" (ch. xlvii. 8, 9).

Revolt, Capture, and Destruction of Babylon.—Darius might yet have failed to take the city, but for a stratagem and an act of self-sacrifice on the part of one of his principal officers. Zopyrus, having cut off his nose and his ears, and mangled his body, presented himself to the Babylonians, pretending to have been cruelly treated by his master. The Babylonians believed his tale, and gave him the chief command of their armies. Zopyrus then gave the city into the hands of Darius. Its walls, formerly two hundred cubits high, were now lowered to fifty, its hundred gates were removed, its houses were given up to plunder, and three thousand of the ringleaders in the revolt were impaled. This event happened just about the time when the Jews were celebrating the completion of the temple. From that hour the glory of Babylon departed. The predictions of the Hebrew prophets were fulfilled. The great shout arose, "Babylon is fallen!" The city of Nebuchadnezzar never regained its splendour. Alexander the Great wished to make it the capital of his empire, but obstacles arose that put an end to his design. Its desolation is now so complete that its very site can scarcely be recognized. "Babylon, the glory of kingdoms, the beauty of the Chaldees' excellency, shall be as when God overthrew Sodom and Gomorrah. It shall never be inhabited, neither shall it be dwelt in from generation to generation: neither shall the Arabian pitch tent there; neither shall the shepherds make their fold there. But wild beasts of the desert shall lie there; and their houses shall be full of doleful creatures; and owls shall dwell there, and satyrs shall dance there" (Isa. xiii. 19–21).

SECTION II.—THE PERSIAN EMPIRE, FROM DARIUS HYSTASPES TO ARTAXERXES LONGIMANUS.

Darius's war with Greece—His character and work—Zoroaster, and the Persian religion—His system—Its spread—Corrupt state of Persian morals—Xerxes, and the invasion of Greece—Artaxerxes Longimanus.

Darius's War with Greece.—Soon after the capture of Babylon, Darius began a series of wars which brought Asia and Europe into contact with each other, and ultimately exercised a memorable influence on the history of the world. These were the wars between Persia and Greece. The Greek colonies settled on the shores of Asia Minor, often called Ionians, having revolted from Persia, were presently joined by the mother countries; and to subdue both, Darius mustered a gigantic force by land and sea. His first fleet was wrecked at Mount Athos; his second ravaged the Greek isles; while an immense army, landing in Eubœa, poured down with impetuosity upon Attica. The Athenians met the Persians on the plains of Marathon, and, headed by Miltiades, defeated them with prodigious slaughter. Darius spent three years in vast preparations for a new invasion of Greece, but he was prevented from prosecuting the war by a revolt in Egypt, and soon afterwards by his death. The war was continued by Xerxes, his son and successor.

His Character and Work.—Darius Hystaspes was the ablest prince that had sat on the throne of Persia. He added a few provinces to the Persian empire—India, Thrace, Macedonia, and the islands of the Ionian Sea; so that at his death it extended from the Indus to the Ægean, and from the steppes of Scythia (now Russia) to the cataracts of the Nile. But his great ability was exerted chiefly in consolidating his vast empire. He divided it into twenty satrapies or provinces, setting a satrap or governor over each. His revenues were enormous. The province of Babylon alone yielded a revenue equal to that of a first-class European sovereign.

Zoroaster, and the Persian Religion.—It was in the reign of Darius, according to some of the best authorities, that the famous Zoroaster, the reformer or restorer of the ancient Persian religion, flourished. Zoroaster lived in retirement for twenty years of his youth, in the El-burz mountains; in the course of which period, as his followers declared, he was taken up to heaven, and God's laws were revealed to him there. This tradition may have had its origin in the revelation of the law of God to Moses on Mount Sinai, a fact which must have been well known in Persia at that time through the Jewish Scriptures. Zoroaster seems to have laboured to restore the ancient religion of the Persians, which had either become greatly neglected or had been corrupted by image-worship. Sabaism, the worship of images, was the form of religion that now contended with Magianism, the ancient religion of the Persians.

His System.—Like the ancient Persians, Zoroaster taught that there was one eternal God, but that there were two principles or angels in the universe, the one of good, and the other of evil. The emblem of the good, Ormuzd, was light; that of the bad, Ahriman, was darkness. Between these opposite principles there was a contest which would continue till the end of the world, but the power of good would ultimately prevail. At the day of judgment the followers of both would be judged, and separated for ever,—the one rewarded and the other punished. Ormuzd was always worshipped in presence of a fire, as the cause of light, and especially before the sun, as the most perfect fire and the most perfect light in the universe. Darkness was held in detestation, as the element of the evil principle, whose name, it is said, was written backwards and upside down, thus, ᴎɐɯᴉɹɥⱯ. Many things in the doctrines of Zoroaster were probably derived from the Jewish Scriptures,— such as the unity of God, the doctrine of an evil spirit, the doctrine of the resurrection and of the last judgment, and the use of fire or light (as in the Shekinah) as the emblem of Deity.

Its Spread.—The doctrines of Zoroaster were set forth in the Zendavesta, the sacred book of the Persians. Everywhere, when their influence prevailed, fire-temples were erected, and image-temples were levelled with the ground.* As Darius himself adopted the creed of Zoroaster, and on his death became the archimagus or high priest, his religion spread very widely. It is still the religion of the descendants of the Persians, a colony of whom, called Parsees, exist to this day at Bombay, in India.

Corrupt State of Persian Morals. The revival of the Persian religion had little or no effect in purifying the morals of the Persian nation. The manners of the court

---

* This took place at Babylon: a number of prophecies were thus fulfilled. See Isa. xxi. 9; Jer. l. 2; li. 44, 47, 52.

were marked by excessive luxury and revolting cruelty. The barbarity of the women was frightful, and fills the Persian chronicles with the most horrid stories; their character was most depraved, and yet their influence was very great. Formerly the Persians had been remarkable for the purity and simplicity of their manners; and their children had been taught from their childhood to repeat the praises of truth and justice. But excessive wealth and prosperity were sapping the foundations of the ancient virtues, and the nation was sinking into that state of utter weakness and corruption in which it was when it ultimately fell under the arms of the vigorous and high-spirited Greeks.

Xerxes, and the Invasion of Greece.— The successor of Darius on the Persian throne was the celebrated Xerxes, whose chief object as king seems to have been to keep up the show and state of sovereignty. He is known in history chiefly in connection with his invasion of Greece. Herodotus, the Greek historian, who was born about this time (B.C. 485), says that no fewer than five million Persians accompanied him in his expedition. It is said by Josephus, and it is very likely, that the Jews, who were a numerous body of his subjects, furnished their contribution to this mighty host. It was on this occasion that the Persians were opposed at Thermopylæ by Leonidas, one of the kings of Sparta, with only three hundred followers, who drove back the mighty mass again and again, till, after they had slain twenty thousand of them, they were betrayed and cut to pieces. The Persian fleet was defeated by that of the Greeks at Salamis, under the celebrated Themistocles, Xerxes himself, from an elevated headland, witnessing the destruction of his magnificent armada.

> "A king sat on the rocky brow
> That looks on sea-born Salamis;
> And men in nations lay below,
> And ships in thousands;—all were his.
> He counted them at break of day;
> And when the sun set, where were they?"

The king was glad to return to Persia, leaving behind him his general, Mardonius, who fared little better than his royal master.

On one and the same day the Persians were defeated by land at Platæa in Bœotia, and by sea at Mycale in Asia Minor. From this time no Persian army ever crossed the Hellespont.

Artaxerxes Longimanus.—Xerxes was succeeded by his son, Artaxerxes Longimanus, whose reign lasted for the long period of forty-one years. He was called Longimanus from the length of his hands, which is said to have been such that when he stood erect they reached to his knees.

SECTION III.—STORY OF ESTHER.

Uncertainty as to the Ahasuerus of Esther—City and palace of Susa—Esther and Mordecai—Condition of the Jews in the Persian empire—Influence of Esther and Mordecai with the king.

Uncertainty as to the Ahasuerus of Esther.—It is generally believed that the king of Persia who married Esther the Jewess, and who is called Ahasuerus in the Book of Esther, was Xerxes. The supposition is supported by several considerations, including, it is said, some recent discoveries among the monuments at Susa. The name of Xerxes' queen, as given by the Greek writers, was Amestris; in which some find a resemblance to Vashti, and others, with greater probability, to Esther. The historical character of the Book of Esther has been called in question by some critics, owing to the apparently unnatural description of the events, and the absence of all corroboration from other sources. But the character of Xerxes, which was capricious and foolish, especially in his later years, explains the peculiarities of the narrative; and the known fact that the records of the Persian empire belonging to this time are extremely scanty, accounts for the silence of other histories. The picture of Persian manners in Esther is remarkably correct.

City and Palace of Susa.—In the Book of Esther we find the king of Persia living in extraordinary splendour in his palace at Shushan or Susa. This city was situated in the province of Elam or Susiana, in a mountainous part of the province, presenting far bolder scenery than could have been found either at Nineveh or at Babylon. The province is watered by several rivers, that rush down from the Zagros mountains on the east, often passing through narrow, rocky defiles, and forming scenes of picturesque beauty. Among the rivers of Susiana was the Eulæus or Ulai, on whose sequestered banks Daniel saw his vision of the ram and the he-goat, and had his first conversation with the angel Gabriel. A vast mound of ruins, still bearing the name of Shush, examined by Sir W. F. Williams and Mr. Loftus, was found to contain the ruins of the great hall of the palace of Susa, a magnificent building, 343 feet long and 244 feet broad.* The first chapter of Esther specifies "pillars of marble" among the prominent features of this magnificent palace; and now it is found that the hall must have contained "several magnificent groups of columns," elaborately carved, the capitals representing in some cases leaves of palm and lotus, and in others the figure of the half-bull, a favourite ornament for capitals at Nineveh as well as at Susa. If it was this magnificent hall that was fitted up for Ahasuerus's feast—with "hangings of white, green, and blue, fastened with cords of fine linen and purple to silver rings and pillars of marble, with beds of gold and silver, upon a pavement of red and blue and white and black marble"—the whole scene must have been one of the most magnificent ever beheld, even by Oriental eyes.

Esther and Mordecai.—The facts recorded in the Book of Esther are—the disgrace and removal of Queen Vashti, in consequence of her refusal to appear at the king's banquet; the elevation of Esther, a Jewish maiden, to the dignity, first of concubine, then of queen to Ahasuerus; the refusal of Mordecai, Esther's relation, to do obeisance to Haman the Agagite, or Amalekite, chief minister of the king; the exterminating edict against the Jews obtained by Haman; the defeat of the plot by the efforts of Mordecai, aided by queen Esther; the disgrace and execution of Haman; and the escape and triumph of the Jews. In this book, all these events are recorded with

* See Loftus's Travels and Researches in Chaldæa and Susiana; also Smith's Dictionary of the Bible, art *Shushan*.

that charming candour and beautiful simplicity which always characterize the narratives of the Bible. The crisis was one of the most alarming that had ever occurred; the unalterable nature of the decrees of the Medes and Persians made the plot doubly dangerous. Had it succeeded, the Jewish race would have been totally exterminated in Judæa as well as in other countries, and the Church of the living God would have been swept from the face of the earth. The protecting arm of God was never more plainly or signally made bare, not even in the destruction of Pharaoh or the catastrophe of Sennacherib, than it was on this memorable occasion. It became apparent once more that the promise to Abraham was true—"I will bless them that bless thee, and curse him that curseth thee."

Condition of the Jews in the Persian Empire.—Much light is thrown by the Book of Esther on the condition of the Jews throughout the Persian empire. We may observe, that it had now become common to call the children of Israel by the name of "Jews" (Esther ii. 5); also, that they were now dispersed through the one hundred and twenty-seven provinces of the Persian empire, from the Indus to Ethiopia (iii. 8); still, that they retained their national laws and usages, and continued a separate people (iii. 8); that they had many enemies (ix. 1); that they contributed such a sum to the royal revenue that 10,000 talents of silver, equal to £2,000,000 sterling, was offered as an equivalent (iii. 9); that they were so numerous as to be able, in Susa alone, to slay eight hundred of their enemies in two days, and throughout the whole empire seventy-five thousand (ix. 6, 15, 16); and that many of the subjects of the great king became proselytes to their religion (viii. 17).

Influence of Esther and Mordecai with the King.—The fact of a Jewess being queen, and a Jew prime minister (for Mordecai became next to king Ahasuerus), must have operated greatly in favour of the Jews. It is extremely probable that Mordecai and Esther continued to employ their influence with the king in favour both of their religion and of their people.

The king himself was a follower of Zoroaster, and did not embrace the Jewish religion; but the respectful manner in which he spoke of the God of the Jews, and the favour which his successor showed to Ezra and Nehemiah, may have resulted from the influence of Esther and Mordecai.

SECTION IV.—LABOURS OF EZRA.

Ezra and his company—State of Jerusalem—Ezra edits and arranges the Scriptures—Synagogues and synagogue worship—Origin of tradition: the Mishna, the Gemara, and the Talmud.

Ezra and His Company.—It was in the seventh year of Artaxerxes Longimanus that EZRA set out for Jerusalem, with a company in all of six or seven thousand souls. Eighty years had now elapsed since Zerubbabel and his company had returned to the holy city, so that he and most of those who had accompanied him must now have been dead. Ezra was a descendant of the high priest Seraiah, whom Nebuchadnezzar had put to death at the capture of Jerusalem. His chief object in returning was to reëstablish fully and firmly the laws of Moses,—a task for which his talents and training, as a ready scribe in the law, abundantly qualified him. Fortified by a strong decree of the king, in which he extolled the God of Israel as the God of heaven, Ezra set out from Babylon. He assembled his company at the river Ahava (supposed to be the modern Hit, on the Euphrates, due east of Damascus), proclaimed a fast there, and with his people earnestly called on God for protection and blessing. Four months were occupied in crossing the desert. Besides carrying with them a multitude of gold and silver vessels, Ezra and his friends had an order from the king authorizing the local treasurers of the imperial revenue to pay him what was necessary for his sacred mission.

State of Jerusalem.—On arriving at Jerusalem he found, to his great distress, that his people had paid no regard to the law which prohibited their marriage with idolaters, and that the very princes had been foremost in forming these unhallowed connections. In the deepest humiliation of spirit, Ezra deplored their offence to the Lord; and, to his great relief, found soon afterwards that the spirit of contrition had taken hold of the offenders. Measures were then devised for separating them from their idolatrous wives and for restoring the purity of the law of Moses.

Ezra Edits and Arranges the Scriptures.— Besides this important piece of reform, Ezra took a prominent part in another service, of the most valuable kind, with which his name will ever be honourably associated. This was the arranging, editing, and publishing the Book of the Law, or the canon of Scripture. It appears, from various notices, that up to this time copies of the Law were very scarce among the Jews. Now that the people had returned from Babylon, they would not only be scarce, but to many the language in which the Law was written would hardly be intelligible. Ezra's first care was to read the Law publicly in the presence of the people; and as he read he explained the meaning in the ordinary dialect of the day. In editing the Scriptures, Ezra substituted for the old Hebrew character, hitherto used, the better formed and finished letters of the Chaldee alphabet. The old character was preserved among the Samaritans, and is still to be seen in a very old copy of the Pentateuch, treasured by a small remnant of that people now residing at Nablous or Shechem.

Synagogues and Synagogue Worship.—Some of the changes thus introduced by Ezra were of the utmost practical importance. The full acquaintance with the Word of God, which the Jewish people were now enabled to acquire, must have tended greatly to discourage idolatry, and to promote that devotedness to the letter at least of the Law for which they now became so eminent. Out of the arrangements which Ezra began, two things arose that had ultimately a very great influence, partly for good and partly for evil. One of these was the institution, or restoration, of synagogues and synagogue worship; the other, the system of traditions. Although from early times there must have been local gatherings for worship, it does not appear that before the Captivity these had assumed the form of the synagogue. But after the Captivity, synagogues were set up in every direction, for the reading of the Law, for exhortation, and for prayer. The reading and expounding of the Law now became a regular profession, and it was not confined to the priests, or even to the tribe of Levi. By the "lawyers" (as the members of that profession were called) the written Word was expounded and supplemented wherever it seemed obscure or defective.

Origin of Tradition: the Mishna, the Gemara, and the Talmud.—Gradually the notion gained ground that besides the written Law there was an oral Law, which God had communicated to the fathers, but which was not recorded, the knowledge of which could be obtained and preserved only by tradition. This constituted the "tradition of the elders," in connection with which our Lord often showed so great and so just indignation. In the middle of the second century after Christ, Rabbi Judah, the son of Simeon, a celebrated doctor, collected these traditions, and committed them to writing. The book in which they were collected was called the Mishna. Commentaries on the Mishna have been written by learned rabbis: the commentary alone is called the Gemara, and the commentary and Mishna together the Talmud. The Babylonian Talmud, or the Talmud compiled by the Chaldæan Jews, is a work in twelve folio volumes. Out of this vast mass of tradition the real spirit of the Law and the Prophets has been almost entirely eliminated.

SECTION V.—REFORMS OF NEHEMIAH.

Nehemiah's family and office—His first visit to Jerusalem—Effects of his labours—His return: importance of his services—The royal family of Judah—Malachi and his prophecy.

Nehemiah's Family and Office.—Thirteen years after Ezra arrived at Jerusalem, the first of two visits was paid to it by one who became a most zealous helper in the work of reformation,—the distinguished NEHEMIAH. Nehemiah's father appears to have been one of the Jews who rose to wealth and distinction under the king of Persia: probably he resided in Shushan, where Nehemiah rose to the office of cup-bearer,— an office which was deemed highly honourable and influential, and which was also, doubtless, extremely lucrative.

His First Visit to Jerusalem.—Nehemiah, being very desirous to visit the city of his fathers, succeeded in obtaining from Artaxerxes a limited leave of absence for that purpose. He was a man of singular faith, courage, and enterprise,—one to whom no undertaking seemed difficult, because he always realized the presence of God in connection with it. He was a worthy member of the old line of Hebrew "believers;" one whose character was cast in the same mould as that of the Joshuas and Calebs, the Baraks and Gideons, the Davids and Jehoshaphats of other days. Coming to Jerusalem, he found its walls dilapidated; but, by great exertion, he succeeded in getting them built up within the singularly short period of fifty-two days.

Effects of His Labours.—Nehemiah was much annoyed in his operations by certain of his Samaritan neighbours, among whom Sanballat the Horonite, Geshem the Arabian, and Tobiah the Ammonite were notorious. Still, full of faith in the protection of God, he continued his work. By his extraordinary energy and holy courage, he reformed many glaring abuses, and persuaded the people to enter into a national covenant binding them to the faithful service of God. His disinterestedness was so great, that all the time he acted as governor he drew no salary from the State. At length the twelve years, within which he had promised to return to Persia, being exhausted, he resumed his duties at the court of Susa. (Compare Neh. ii. 1-6, and xiii. 6, 7.)

His Return: Importance of His Services.—During his absence there was a painful relapse into many of the irregularities from which he had recovered the people. After a time he came back to Jerusalem, and found too palpable evidence of the unfaithfulness of the high priest. Among other things, Tobiah the Ammonite, with whom the high priest was intimate, had got a chamber fitted up for him in the courts of the house of God. Nehemiah promptly put a stop to this profanation. In consequence of this proceeding, Manasseh, a grandson of the high priest, who had married the daughter of Sanballat, went off to Samaria, and there, it is said, began on Mount Gerizim, in a temple built for him by Sanballat, the schismatic worship which continued to be maintained there in the times of our Lord. Nehemiah laboured successfully to reform abuses arising from the contraction of marriage with neighbouring idolaters. He took full advantage of his position, and of what seemed to be the necessities of the times, to insist, even by force, on the observance of the Mosaic law. Notwithstanding, he left behind him a very noble example,—the example of one whom neither wealth, nor a Persian court, nor the service of a Persian king, had made in the slightest degree unmindful of his country or unfaithful to his God. Both he and Ezra contributed greatly to the preservation of the true religion in troublous and dangerous times.

The Royal Family of Judah.—It is remarkable that the royal family of Judah slips wholly out of view in the time of Ezra and Nehemiah. The line of Zerubbabel had not failed, but probably his descendants lacked the energy and courage needed in those times for a kingly position; and amid the troubles of the period, it was deemed unnecessary to keep up a form which had become lifeless and effete. But the genealogical records continued to be preserved; and when the great Son of David did at last appear, there was no difficulty in showing his descent. The royal line fell into greater and greater obscurity; till at length its representative was found in the humble condition of a carpenter, working in one of the most despised towns of Palestine.

Malachi and His Prophecy.—In the time of Nehemiah, or soon after, the last notes of the voice of prophecy sounded from the lips of MALACHI. The sins and abuses rebuked by that prophet were, many of them, the same as Nehemiah had laboured to correct. Malachi reproves the priests for

violating the marriage covenant and separating from their
lawful wives. He reproves the people also for their heartless-
ness and carelessness in the service of God. He foretells the
advent of a sifting time, when a vast difference should be
made between the faithful and the faithless worshipper. He
lays down very clearly the retribution of a future state. He
announces a forerunner who would go before the Lord in the
spirit and power of Elijah. He frowns on the pride that was
now too apparent in connection with the worship of God. From
the tenor of his prophecy it appears that persons of vital godliness were not numerous in his day; but such as there were
found much pleasure in speaking one to another; and, to com-
pensate for the reproach which they seem to have endured at
the hand of man, the promise was given them—"They shall be
mine, saith the Lord, in the day when I make up my jewels."

SECTION VI.—CONTEMPORARY HISTORY.

PERSIA and GREECE: At war—Eminent Greeks—Decay. EGYPT: A Persian province.
PHŒNICIA and CARTHAGE: A king of Tyre—Maritime enterprise of Carthage.
ROME: Patricians and plebeians: petty wars. INDIA and CHINA: Brahminism—
Buddhism—Confucius.

Persia and Greece.

At War.—The celebrated war between these two countries,
which (as already mentioned) Darius began and Xerxes continued, was prosecuted also by Artaxerxes Longimanus. But
his success was not greater than that of his predecessors had
been. Indeed, the losses which he sustained in the Greek wars
were so serious, that he was glad to conclude a peace, on terms
not very favourable to Persia, fifty-one years after the beginning
of the war. In the early part of the reign of Artaxerxes,
Themistocles, the Athenian commander who had vanquished
the Persians at Salamis, having, through jealousy, been banished
from his own country, threw himself on the hospitality of the
great king, and lived a short time at Susa. He was commanded
by the king to head an army which was to be sent to ravage the
Athenian territory; but, rather than consent to fight against

his own country, he put an end to his life by drinking his own blood. His position was, in some respects, analogous to that of king David at Gath; but the pagan knew not that God who extricated his Hebrew servant from the difficulty of his position. After Artaxerxes, the Persian throne was occupied by his son Xerxes II.; who was succeeded by Darius Nothus. The glory of the great empire of Cyrus was now declining.

Eminent Greeks.—Among other eminent Greeks who flourished about this time were Cimon, son of Miltiades, distinguished as a commander; Pericles, the greatest of Athenian statesmen, under whom Athens attained a splendour that made her the wonder and the envy of all Greece; Phidias, the celebrated sculptor, and a host of distinguished artists; Simonides and Pindar, eminent lyric poets; Æschylus, Sophocles, and Euripides, distinguished dramatists; and Herodotus, who has received a title due really to Moses—The Father of History. In short, this was one of the most brilliant periods of Grecian history, whether regard be had to the success of arms or to the triumphs of mind. It was during the reign of Artaxerxes that Socrates was gathering the materials of his philosophy,—perhaps getting some glimpses, through Jews, or through those who had been instructed by Jews, of that divine wisdom which sometimes glimmers among his thoughts, like pearls in the depths of the sea. Plato, too, began to flourish in this period; and, in his extensive travels in search of knowledge, he may have met with persons who had been taught from above the immortality of the soul.

Decay.—But all the progress of Greece in science, philosophy, and the arts, did not in any degree lessen the need for that supernatural revelation which God had been making, and was still further to make, on the soil of Palestine. Indeed, while Athens was at the height of its glory, the seeds of its ruin were already sown. About this time began the Peloponnesian War. It raged at first between the two great rival States of Greece—Athens and Sparta; but the flames soon caught hold of the other States. At last, Athens was taken by the Spartans, and its glory departed. Through the endless contests of this period, the way was prepared for the republics of Greece falling, first under Philip king of Macedon, a country in the more remote part of Greece, that had been little heard of till his time; and then under his son Alexander. Alexander of Macedon was the "prince of Grecia" with whom the visions of Daniel had connected so many great events.

Egypt.

A Persian Province.—Reference has already been made to the leading events in the history of Egypt. Cambyses invaded and conquered it, and reduced it to the state of a Persian province, appointing a satrap over it. Once and again Egypt attempted to shake off the Persian yoke; but, until the reign of Darius II., with little success. The Persians seem to have been very severe against the priests, whose privileges they abridged very greatly; and the rebellions which happened from time to time occurred partly by their instigation, and partly by that of the Athenians. Egypt's fame for wisdom and for learning continued to attract illustrious strangers. Lycurgus and Solon, the great legislators of Greece, had both drunk formerly from the fountains of Egyptian lore; and now two eminent Grecian philosophers, Pythagoras and Plato, came to it for the like purpose. It is very remarkable how many of the great minds, that in ancient times exerted a striking influence on the world, received part of their mental education in Egypt.

Phœnicia and Carthage.

A King of Tyre.—Seventy years after Tyre had been besieged by Nebuchadnezzar, it was restored to its former privileges by Darius, and allowed to have a king of its own. This boon was an acknowledgment of the valuable aid the Tyrians had rendered to Darius, in fitting out ships to enable him to contend with the navy of Athens. The prophecy of Isaiah thus received its fulfilment: "It shall come to pass after the end of seventy years that the Lord will visit Tyre, and she shall turn to her hire."

Maritime Enterprise of Carthage.—The Carthaginians were remarkable for their maritime enterprise, and seem about this time to have become acquainted with Britain. According to a fragment preserved by an ancient writer, Himilcon, a distinguished citizen of Carthage, conducted a fleet with settlers from that city; and, having passed through the Pillars of Hercules, reached "The Holy Island, which lies expanded on the sea, and is peopled by the Hibernian race. At hand, it is added, lies the island of Albion."* In the West, Carthage was now the dominating power, as Persia was in the East. Her trade and her conquests extended over a great part of western Europe and northern Africa. To a great extent Carthage must have spread over the West the worship of Baal and Ashtoreth, by which Syria had been so much defiled. Her intense desire to secure the island of Sicily began now to involve her in long and serious wars, which ultimately brought her into contact with the Romans, and ended in her utter ruin.

Rome.

Patricians and Plebeians: Petty Wars.—The Tarquins were expelled from Rome, the kingly government abolished, and that of consuls substituted, about the time when the temple at Jerusalem was completed by Zerubbabel. The banishment of Coriolanus happened near the time of Xerxes' invasion of Greece; and Cincinnatus was appointed dictator while Ezra was preparing to return to Jerusalem. Soon afterwards, the decemviri were appointed, and the laws of the Ten Tables compiled. This period of Roman history is characterized chiefly by two things:—a keen internal struggle between the patricians and plebeians, or the nobles and the people—the latter striving to reduce the power and privileges of the former; and a series of petty wars with neighbouring states, which developed the military genius of the Romans, and trained them in arms for their world-wide contests. But no one could have dreamt as yet of the mighty influence to be wielded over the world by the people that were now perpetually bickering about agrarian laws and popular rights; nor could it have been foreseen how all the aggressions they were now making on neigh-

* See Heeren's Historical Researches.

bouring states were ultimately to contribute to the setting up of the great kingdom of Messiah—the kingdom of meekness, peace, and love.

India and China.

Brahminism.—Although neither India nor China comes into vital contact with Bible history, it is instructive to note the phases and fortune of religion in these countries; for in them we see the human soul engaged in feeling after God, and the results of their search throw light on the need of a revelation. In India, the religion of Brahma had been established early by the Aryan invaders of the wild primitive races—a religion originally founded on the doctrine of one Supreme Being diffused as a spirit through all being—a system of pantheism, in fact. But in the course of time this doctrine had been much corrupted, and polytheism, idol-worship, and caste had become everywhere prevalent. It was held that the Deity amused himself by illusory appearances, manifesting himself in various forms; and that all things that exist, and all living creatures, are but emanations from him, and are ultimately to be absorbed into him. A priesthood, possessing great influence in the country, presided over the Brahminical religion; the principles of which were contained in sacred books called Vedas, and especially in the Rig-Veda, or Hymn-Book, the oldest and most esteemed of them all.

Buddhism.—About the time of the captivity in Babylon, Brahminism had become so idolatrous and corrupt that a great reformation of it was attempted. A young prince of the Aryan tribe of Sakyas, named Gautama, devoted himself to this undertaking. He is often known as Sakya Mouni—that is, the Recluse of Sakya; or as Buddha—that is, the Enlightened. Turning with utter dissatisfaction from the externalism and idolatry of Brahminism, Sakya concluded that true happiness lay in the conquest of all our desires; that that should be the aim of every one; and that when it was accomplished the soul would be absorbed in God, and would lose all consciousness of self. Sakya had many admirable precepts, and in his own case he attained a remarkable measure of virtue. Buddhism, as his system was called, was adopted by the Hindu people; but about the eighth century of the Christian era, whether from its having become corrupt, or from its being persecuted by the Brahmins, it was driven from India. It established itself in Tibet, Ceylon, China, and other Eastern countries, and at this day it is the religion of a great part of the human family. Weighed in the balances, however, it is obviously wanting; wanting in power to give peace and true rest in God to the individual soul, except by a process of absorption; and wanting in power to act as the preserving salt of communities.

Confucius.—In China, Confucius was a contemporary of Sakya Mouni. He too tried to reform Tauism, or the national faith, chiefly by means of a purer moral code. To this day the reverence paid to Confucius amounts to idolatry. But the state of China, and especially the position and treatment of women and female children, to speak of no other considerations, furnishes proof that Confucius was not more successful than Buddha in revealing a way for man to the favour and the moral image of God.

CHAPTER XIV.

INTERVAL BETWEEN THE OLD TESTAMENT AND THE NEW.

FROM THE TIME OF NEHEMIAH TO THE BIRTH OF CHRIST.

SECTION 1.—PALESTINE UNDER THE PERSIANS:
TO B.C. 333.

Historical chasm: Josephus: the Apocrypha—Six sections of the period—The Persian period—Events in Greece: Peloponnesian War—Rise of Alexander of Macedon—Intellectual glory of Athens.

Historical Chasm: Josephus: the Apocrypha.—A great historical chasm, about four hundred years in length, stretches between the close of the Old Testament history and the commencement of the New. During all that time there was neither prophet nor inspired writer among the Jews. Our knowledge of what took place among them is derived from the writings of Josephus,* from some of the books of the Apocrypha,† and from the notices of Greek and Latin historians. Though no further development of revealed religion took place during

---

* Josephus was a Jew of distinguished rank, born at Jerusalem, A.D. 37, and latterly a partisan of the Romans in their wars with the Jews. His work, "The History of the Jewish War," gives an account of the nation from B.C. 170 to his own time. Having removed to Rome, he published in Greek, A.D. 93, his "Antiquities of the Jews," a complete history from the creation, designed to correct the many misrepresentations of the Jews current in the Roman empire. Josephus was given to exaggeration, desiring to make his nation appear as great as possible.

† The Apocrypha is a collection of books written during the captivity and the interval between the Old Testament and the New, and relating to the events that happened about that time. There is ample evidence that none of its books belong to the canon of inspired Scripture. Some of them have scarcely the amount of credibility due to ordinary histories; but from many of them a considerable amount of useful information may be obtained.

these four centuries, they constituted a very memorable period in general history. They witnessed the fall of the Persian empire, the rise and fall of the Macedonian, and the rise of the Roman. The seat of empire passed over from Asia to Europe; and the foundation was laid of those vast social changes which have so greatly raised the western and depressed the eastern and more ancient countries of the globe.

Six Sections of the Period.—In sketching this long and important period, we shall, as heretofore, follow the thread of Jewish history, glancing right and left, as we proceed, at the leading nations that crowd the stage. The history of Palestine may be divided into six sections, corresponding to the different masters whose sway it owned.

1. The PERSIANS were its nominal masters to the year B.C. 333.

2. ALEXANDER THE GREAT conquered it in that year, and was its master for ten years.

3. On his death (B.C. 323) it fell, after a long contest, under the PTOLEMYS, or Macedonian kings of EGYPT, and so remained for more than a hundred years, to B.C. 204.

4. Then it came under the rule of the Macedonian kingdom of SYRIA, till it was set free by the Maccabees, B.C. 163.

5. It was ruled by the MACCABEES for another century, till

6. The ROMAN general POMPEY conquered it (B.C. 63), and made it tributary to the great mistress of the world.

The Persian Period.—For a considerable time after the days of Nehemiah the Persians continued masters of Judæa; but during their rule nothing of much interest happened in Palestine. The country was annexed to the satrapy of Syria, but was allowed to be governed by the Jewish high priests, acting under the Syrian satraps. The office of high priest became a great object of ambition, and in consequence several disgraceful contests for it took place. Jeshua, a brother of Jonadab the high priest, endeavoured to secure the honour for himself, but he was slain by Jonadab in the temple. For this scandalous act a heavy fine was imposed upon the Jews by the Persian governor.

Events in Greece : Peloponnesian War.—Meanwhile, in Greece, the Peloponnesian War had been brought to an end by the triumph of the Spartans and the humiliation and fall of Athens. Though partially restored afterwards, Athens never again rose to its former influence and splendour. Artaxerxes Mnemon was now on the throne of Persia; and the early part of his reign was signalized by an attempt of his younger brother Cyrus to obtain the sceptre. Cyrus was defeated and slain near Babylon; and a body of ten thousand Greeks, who assisted him, had to make their retreat along the Tigris, and through the wilds of Armenia, until they reached the Black Sea. Of this celebrated retreat, an interesting account, well known to classical scholars, was written by Xenophon, the Greek historian, who conducted the expedition. It is interesting to observe that the march of the ten thousand lay through the districts that formed the cradle of the human race, embracing, perhaps, the very land of Eden.

Rise of Alexander of Macedon.—War continued to rage between the Greeks and the Persians for many years, till at length peace was concluded. But the power of the Spartans, which had predominated in Greece since the fall of Athens, was now destined to be overthrown. First at Leuctra, and again at Mantinea, they were defeated by the Thebans, under Epaminondas. The Theban supremacy was of short duration. At Cheronæa, Philip of Macedon overthrew the combined forces of the Thebans and the Athenians, and made himself master of Greece. After this, Philip, having got himself appointed captain-general of all Greece, was preparing for a great war with Persia, when his life and reign were cut short by his assassination. His son Alexander was only twenty years of age when he succeeded him. The weapon with which the Persian empire was to be broken to pieces was now prepared. The mighty he-goat, that had been seen two hundred years before in Daniel's vision on the banks of the Ulai, was advancing from the west to overturn the two-horned ram,—the vast but now tottering Medo-Persian empire.

Intellectual Glory of Athens.—When we take a glance at

Athens during this period, we find the lustre of its literature and philosophy remaining, after the loss of military and political preëminence. Thucydides has published his history of the Peloponnesian War,—a work still unrivalled among historical compositions. In spite of the ridicule of the comedian Aristophanes, the influence of Socrates makes itself felt for half a century after his death, in a whole host of philosophers who adopt his views. Xenophon, his pupil, is keeping alive the fame and opinions of Socrates by the publication of his "Apology," besides delighting his countrymen with his own historical and other works. Diogenes, the Cynic philosopher, becomes the talk, first of Athens, then of Corinth, partly for his strange habits,—living in a tub, rolling in hot sand in summer, and embracing statues covered with snow in winter; and partly for his austere, or, as it was called, cynical philosophy. Hippocrates, a native of Cos, introduces a new era in medical science, and, travelling in different countries, spreads his views over many lands. By-and-by Aristotle, a native of Stagira in Macedonia, a pupil of Plato, and the tutor of the young prince Alexander of Macedon, becomes one of the great men of Athens. By his influence on Alexander, by his lectures and instructions in the city, and by his writings, which embrace logic, philosophy, natural history, politics, and art—in short, the whole circle of the sciences—Aristotle lays the foundation of an empire more remarkable than Alexander's, and acquires a dominion over the world of mind beyond that of any other mere man. At the time when Philip of Macedon is striving for supremacy in Greece, Athens resounds with the philippics of his great adversary, Demosthenes, the greatest of Athenian orators; while Æschines, the rival of Demosthenes, strains all his powers to commend the cause of the Macedonian. Yet amid all this intellectual life and brilliancy, the moral and spiritual darkness of Greece and of the world continues almost unbroken. Some, who held more enlightened views on religious questions than the rest, are afraid to divulge them; many, like Socrates, are longing for more light; but, for the most part, scepticism and superstition divide the empire of the soul.

SECTION II.—PALESTINE UNDER ALEXANDER:
B.C. 333 TO 323.

Alexander's career: Greece, Persia, Tyre—Jerusalem: Alexandria—Destruction of the Persian empire: death of Alexander—His character—His partiality for the Jews: their missionary influence.

Alexander's Career: Greece, Persia, Tyre.—It was in B.C. 335 that Alexander began his memorable twelve year's reign. After quelling attempts at rebellion in Macedonia, he entered Greece, and defeated the Thebans in several decisive engagements. Passing over into Asia, he encountered and defeated the forces of Darius, in the memorable battles of Granicus in Mysia, and Issus in Cilicia. Proceeding towards Egypt, which had long been in a troubled condition, he passed through Syria and Palestine. Tyre withstood him for several months, but at last fell, being reached by a remarkable mole which he constructed, between the ruins of the old city on the mainland and the modern city on the adjacent island.

Jerusalem: Alexandria.—Alexander then marched to Jerusalem. There is a tradition, that, as he approached the city, he was met by a procession of priests in their robes of office, and that the impression made on him was such, that he spared the city and granted favourable terms to the Jews. It is quite likely that the priests showed him the prophecies of Daniel, which foretold his conquests; and this may be the explanation of the story, that when he saw the high priest, he recognized in him the person who had told him in a dream that he should conquer the world. From Jerusalem he proceeded to Egypt, which he rapidly subdued; and while there he founded the city of Alexandria, which still bears his name.

Destruction of the Persian Empire: Death of Alexander.—Returning to Asia, Alexander encountered Darius in the plains of Assyria, and in the battle of Arbela, not far from the ancient Nineveh, gave its death-blow to the Persian empire, which had subsisted about two hundred years. Not content with the limits of that mighty domain, he pushed eastward into India; and had not his Macedonians positively refused to go further, he would have penetrated far beyond the countries of the Indus. He was occupied with various new projects, when he died at Babylon, of a fever brought on or aggravated by drinking to excess at a banquet. He was only thirty-two years of age.

His Character.—The early training of Aristotle is believed to have had some good effects on Alexander. Though his character was disfigured by great faults, his career was somewhat more noble than that of most conquerors. He aimed at civilizing the countries which he conquered, and especially at infusing the vigour and enterprise of the West into the indolent and luxurious East. But there was no one able to wield the mighty sceptre that dropped from his dying hand, and all his plans and projects died with himself. The he-goat from the west thus fulfilled his destined work,—smote the ram with the two horns, cast him to the ground, and stamped upon him; but that was all. It was reserved for another King to set up the only kingdom that could not be moved, and to spread over the globe a purer light and a higher civilization than those of Macedonia.

His Partiality for the Jews: their Missionary Influence.—Alexander the Great seems to have formed a highly favourable estimate of the Jews, and to have discovered, in their intelligence, steadiness, industry, and zeal the elements that make good citizens everywhere. Accordingly, when he founded Alexandria in Egypt, he encouraged the Jews to settle there, and gave them the privileges of citizens of the first class. He also encouraged them to settle in other newly founded cities, and generally throughout his empire. We have seen that, in the time of Esther, the Jews were widely scattered throughout the one hundred and twenty-seven provinces of Persia. Now their dispersion, as well as their missionary influence, became still more extensive. In consequence of their distance from Jerusalem, the *sacrificial* part of their worship became less prominent, and the study of their sacred books occupied them more. Increased attention was thus given to the Law and the Prophets in the various countries of their dispersion, and, in consequence, the expectation of a coming Messiah was more and more widely diffused.

SECTION III.—PALESTINE UNDER THE PTOLEMYS:
B.C. (ABOUT) 324 TO 204.

Division of Alexander's empire—Ptolemy Soter—Ptolemy Philadelphus—Eminent Jews: Simon the Just, Antigonus of Socho—Rise of the kingdom of Syria—Rivalry between kings of Syria and of Egypt—Persecution of the Jews: Palestine seized by Antiochus.

Division of Alexander's Empire.—On the death of Alexander, in fulfilment of the prophecy of Daniel, the great horn of the he-goat was broken; and for it came up four notable horns, " towards the four winds of heaven." His great empire was ultimately divided among four of his generals—Ptolemy, Lysimachus, Cassander, and Seleucus. Egypt fell to Ptolemy, and by-and-by Palestine was added to his share.

Ptolemy Soter.—He is distinguished in history as Ptolemy Soter. At first he treated the Jews with severity, but he soon came to see, like Alexander, that their superior character fitted them for high offices, and he sent thirty thousand of them to various parts of his dominions, including Cyrenia and Libya in Africa. Of the Jews who went to Egypt at this time, some are very honourably mentioned by Greek and other writers.*

Ptolemy Philadelphus.—The successor of Soter was Ptolemy Philadelphus, one of the most eminent of the kings of Egypt of this period, and very friendly to the Jews. The reign of this prince was signalized by many remarkable events. He built the famous light-house of Pharos, near the mouth of the Nile, which was counted one of the wonders of the world. He founded the great library of Alexandria,—a magnificent collection of the works of the writers of all nations. It was under his patronage that the Hebrew Scriptures were translated into Greek, according to the famous version of the Septuagint. This was one of the most important missionary works ever performed by man.

* Hecataeus, a native of Thrace, who went to Egypt with Alexander, and remained under Ptolemy, makes mention of a Jew named Hezekiah, with whom he became acquainted; a man, he says, of great wisdom and prudence, a powerful speaker, and thoroughly acquainted with the world. From this Jew Hecataeus got information as to the religion, polity, and mode of life of the Jews; all of which Hezekiah had with him written in a book. Hecataeus was so much interested in what he thus learned, that he wrote a history of the Jews, from the time of Abraham, which is not now extant, but is quoted by Josephus and by Origen.—*Prideaux's Connection.*

The Hebrew Scriptures, and especially the Hebrew predictions of the coming Redeemer, might now be read wherever the Greek language was known. On the coast of Palestine, Ptolemy built the famous sea-port of Acca, or Ptolemais, now called Acre, or Acho. The Ptolemys, for the most part, were excellent rulers, and under them Egypt enjoyed no small share of prosperity.

Eminent Jews: Simon the Just, Antigonus of Socho.—The most distinguished man in Judæa about this time was the high priest, Simon the Just. His character is given in the apocryphal book of Ecclesiasticus. He bore the highest reputation for wisdom, integrity, and piety; but he seems to have had not a little of the spirit of a Pharisee. The Jews have a number of traditions about him, silly and unfounded in themselves, but showing the high estimation in which he was held. A short time after Simon, flourished Antigonus of Socho, president of the Sanhedrim; one of whose pupils, Sadoc, is thought by some to have been the founder of the sect of the Sadducees. Antigonus is reported to have taught that men ought not to serve God from a servile regard to rewards, but out of love and reverence; from which Sadoc drew the unwarrantable inference that there were no rewards at all after this life, no resurrection, and no future state. These were prominent tenets of the Sadducees at a later period, but it is very doubtful whether the sect had so early an origin.

Rise of the Kingdom of Syria.—During this period, the foundations were laid of the great monarchy of Syria, or Syro-Macedonia, of which Palestine was afterwards to form a part. After various changes of fortune, Seleucus, son of Antiochus, and one of Alexander's generals, ultimately acquired nearly the whole of Asia for his dominions. It was the fashion of the time to found new cities; and Seleucus, disregarding Damascus, Babylon, Susa, and all the other ancient capitals, founded Seleucia and Antioch, making the one the eastern and the other the western capital of his kingdom. Seleucia was situated on the banks of the Euphrates, about forty miles distant from Babylon, which had now become a sort of enclosed park for wild beasts. Antioch was in Syria, on the banks of the Orontes, and was afterwards famous as a centre and stronghold of Christianity. Like Alexander and Ptolemy, Seleucus encouraged the Jews to take up their residence in his new cities; and many accepted his invitation.

Rivalry between Kings of Syria and of Egypt. — Much rivalry prevailed between the kings of Syria and those of Egypt; and the province of Palestine and Cœle-Syria formed a constant bone of contention. These kings are believed to be the persons designated in the eleventh chapter of Daniel, as the "kings of the north" and "the south." The wars, alliances, and other operations of these kings, are prophetically described in that chapter with great minuteness. In the reigns of Ptolemy Philopator of Egypt, and Antiochus the Great of Syria, the contest between the two powers came to a climax. In a pitched battle fought at Raphia, near Gaza, Ptolemy conquered Antiochus. Visiting Jerusalem after the battle, he determined to enter the holy of holies in the temple. The high priest opposed him with all his might; but Ptolemy was not to be dissuaded from his purpose. It is said, however, that when he had got so far as the holy place, he was seized with such confusion and terror that he retreated in dismay.

Persecution of the Jews: Palestine Seized by Antiochus.— Afterwards, on returning to Alexandria, he was so enraged at the Jews for having withstood him, that he deprived them of their privileges, and fined and persecuted them in the most scandalous manner. Among other wild proceedings, he brought to Alexandria all the Jews he could lay hands on from other parts of Egypt, shut them up in the hippodrome, intending to make a public spectacle of their destruction. The poor Jews ceased not to pray to the God of their fathers for deliverance. On the third day, when the king was present, and the elephants were brought forth and made drunk with wine mingled with frankincense, instead of falling upon the Jews, they turned their rage upon those who came to see the show, and destroyed great numbers of them! The king became alarmed at the evident tokens of God's favour for the Jews, and recalled all his persecuting edicts. At his death he was succeeded by Ptolemy Epiphanes, an infant of five years. Antiochus took the opportunity to wrest the districts of Cœle-Syria and Palestine from Egypt; and from this time Palestine is to be regarded as subject to the kings of Syria. The era on which we now enter is a very dark one in Jewish history.

SECTION IV.—PALESTINE UNDER THE MACEDONIAN KINGS OF SYRIA: B.C. 204 TO 165.

Progress of the Romans—Greece and Rome in conflict—Carthaginian wars—War everywhere—The Romans in the East—Antiochus Epiphanes: Greek party in Palestine—Persecutions at Jerusalem—The Jewish faith proscribed—The Maccabees or Asmonæans—Martyrdoms—Triumph of Judas Maccabæus.

Progress of the Romans.—On the accession of the infant, Ptolemy Epiphanes, to the throne of Egypt, the Egyptians sent an embassy to Rome, craving the aid of the Romans against the encroachments of Antiochus. As the Roman people now began to take a prominent part in the affairs of the East, it is necessary to glance at their history during the preceding two centuries.

Greece and Rome in Conflict.—In the early part of this period the Romans made a very narrow escape from utter destruction, in consequence of an irruption of the Gauls. The Gauls or Celts were one of the great races that spread themselves over the continent of Europe, but of whom scarcely anything is known up to the time of their coming into contact with the Romans. The Roman historians tell that after Rome had been taken and burned by them, and its inhabitants butchered, the invaders were suddenly attacked by the dictator Camillus, and driven in one day beyond the confines of Rome. Recovering power and courage, the Romans now began a career of conquest in the peninsula of Italy. While this was going on, the Tarentines, one of their foes, sought the aid of Pyrrhus, king of Epirus, one of the outlying States of Greece, on the opposite shore of the Adriatic Sea. This was the first occasion of Greece and Rome coming together. Pyrrhus was a man of great enterprise, and a very skilful general. He landed in Italy with thirty thousand men and a train of elephants. The Romans had never before faced or even seen elephants in battle, and were obliged to retire before Pyrrhus; but so great loss had been inflicted on the Greek army, that Pyrrhus uttered the memorable saying, "Another such victory, and we are undone!" He was glad of a pretext for leaving Italy.

Carthaginian Wars.—Meanwhile, the Romans enlarged their sphere of conquest. Having quarrelled with the Carthaginians about the island of Sicily, they measured their strength with that people in three successive Carthaginian wars. It was during the first Carthaginian war that the Romans equipped the first fleet they ever possessed. The campaign ended in their favour; the Carthaginians had to give up their possessions in Sicily. The aid of the Romans now began to be sought by the Greek States in their endless wars with one another; but till after the second Carthaginian war, the Roman armies did not move to the East. That campaign began very disastrously for the Romans; the victorious Hannibal seemed about to carry all before him. But it ended as much in favour of the Romans as it had begun in favour of the Carthaginians, the latter being wholly defeated just about the time when Palestine became part of the kingdom of Syria. Hannibal, hunted from refuge to refuge, at last ended his days by poison in Bithynia, in Asia. The third Carthaginian war ended about fifty years afterwards, in the total destruction of Carthage. The military power of the Romans was thus thoroughly established, and the conquest of the world lay before them.

War Everywhere. - War—war—war, is the unchanging burden of the history of those times. War in Greece, where Aratus, followed by Philopœmen, generals of the Achæan league, have been making desperate but ineffectual efforts to stir up the old love of liberty, and set their country free; war in Macedonia, where the strong Roman legion is wrestling with what remains of valour in the Macedonian phalanx; war in

Syria, war in Egypt—everywhere war; and yet all preparing the way for the establishment of the kingdom of the Prince of Peace!

The Romans in the East.—In compliance with the request of the Egyptians, a Roman army was sent into Egypt to aid Ptolemy Epiphanes against Antiochus the Great. At first the Romans were unsuccessful, but ultimately they prevailed. Antiochus was compelled by the Romans to evacuate the whole country east of the Taurus, and pay the expenses of the war. He went eastward to raise the money; but having plundered a temple of Jupiter in the province of Elymais, he was murdered by the inhabitants. Thus ended the career of Antiochus the Great.

Antiochus Epiphanes: Greek Party in Palestine.—Passing over his successor, Seleucus Philopator, in whose time little occurred in Judæa of much interest, we arrive at a dark and troubled era,—the reign of Antiochus Epiphanes. Epiphanes —that is, the "Illustrious"—was illustrious only for the grossness of his character and the wickedness of his conduct. At his accession, the high-priesthood at Jerusalem was in the hands of a worthy man, named Onias. But a brother of his own having offered to pay Antiochus three hundred and sixty talents for the office, Onias was dispossessed, and the brother installed. Onias fled to Egypt, where he built a temple at Heliopolis, and acted as high priest. The name of the usurper was Jesus; but not liking the Hebrew name, he changed it into the Greek name Jason. A Greek party now appears among the Jews. The sympathies of Jason were entirely with the Greeks; and to the utmost of his power he discountenanced the old Hebrew customs and religion. He even sent on one occasion an embassy to Tyre to take part in certain games in honour of the heathen god Hercules, and to offer sacrifices on his altar. Jason, in his turn, was supplanted by another brother, who took the Greek name of Menelaus, and was still more of a Greek than Jason.

Persecutions at Jerusalem.—Antiochus now undertook an expedition into Egypt, and was successful. While he was there, the Jews heard a report of his death, at which they showed signs of great joy. Hearing of this, Antiochus, on leaving Egypt, went to Jerusalem to chastise them. He besieged and took the sacred city, slew forty thousand Jews, and sold a like number as slaves. To show his contempt for the Jewish religion, he entered the holy of holies, sacrificed a sow on the altar of burnt-offering, and sprinkled broth made from its flesh all over the building. On occasion of another expedition of Antiochus into Egypt, he was met by Popillius, a Roman ambassador, who ordered him peremptorily to quit the country. Antiochus hesitated, on which the ambassador, drawing a circle round him on the sand, declared that he should not leave it till he had given his answer. Antiochus felt that he had no alternative but to yield. It will readily be believed that as the haughty monarch returned homeward he was in no very gentle temper. To chastise the Jews, he sent to Jerusalem a general named Apollonius, who executed his commission with terrible rigour. Waiting till the people were all assembled in their synagogues on the Sabbath, he made a frightful massacre, slaying the men, seizing the women and children as slaves, demolishing the city and its walls, and building the fortress of Acra with the ruins. The remaining inhabitants fled in consternation, and for three years and a half, till Judas Maccabæus recovered the temple and purged it from its pollutions, the daily sacrifices and all the public festivals ceased to be observed.

The Jewish Faith Proscribed. — Not content with these atrocities, Antiochus began a furious persecution against the religion of the Jews. He issued an edict requiring all the people under his sceptre to worship the same gods. The Samaritans conformed to the decree, and allowed their temple on Mount Gerizim to be dedicated to the Grecian Jove. The temple at Jerusalem was forcibly consecrated to the same heathen deity, and the statue of Jupiter Olympus was erected on the altar of burnt-offering. Two Jewish women, that were found to have circumcised their children, were led through the streets with their children fastened to their necks, and cast headlong over the steepest part of the walls.

At the feast of Bacchus, the god of wine, the Jews were forced to join, carrying ivy and taking part in the abominations of the festival. To observe any of the Jewish customs was made a capital offence,—in short, the most rigorous measures were adopted absolutely to root out the Jewish faith.

The Maccabees or Asmonæans.—But enough remained of the noble Jewish spirit of other days to resist such blasphemous tyranny. There was a family of the priestly class, sometimes called the Asmonæans, from Asmonæus, one of their ancestors, and sometimes the Maccabees. The latter name is said to have been formed of the initial letters of the motto which one of them, Judas, placed on his standard, from Exodus xv. 11, "Who is like unto thee among the gods, O LORD?" The Hebrew words are, MI CAMOKA BAELIM JEHOVAH; and from the letters M C B I was derived the word Macabi, or Maccabee, which became the surname of the family, and was applied also to all who joined their cause.* Mattathias, the father of the family, had five sons, Johanan, Simon, Judas, Eleazar, and Jonathan. They dwelt at Modin, a city to the west of Jerusalem, in the Philistine plain, near the sea-coast. When the emissaries of Antiochus came to Mattathias, urging him to conform to the pagan worship, he declared that he would never prove unfaithful to his God; and seeing a Jew presenting himself at the heathen altar to sacrifice to the gods, he fell upon him, like Phinehas of old, and killed him on the spot. Collecting his family and other like-minded persons, he withdrew to the mountains of Judæa, occupied the same caves and fastnesses which David had held nearly a thousand years before, and bade defiance to Antiochus and his armies. One body of his followers, to the number of a thousand, had taken refuge in a cave, where they were attacked on a Sabbath by a Syrian troop, and deeming it unlawful to resist on that day, every man, woman, and child was put to death. Hearing of this, Mattathias and his friends held a council, and after deliberation, came to the conclusion that resistance to such attacks on the Sabbath was lawful.

* Another derivation obtains the word Maccabees from *makkab*, "a hammer."

Martyrdoms.—Among the stories of the persecutions that took place, the martyrdom of Eleazar, and that of a mother and her seven sons, hold a conspicuous place. Eleazar was a principal scribe, ninety years of age, who, rather than taste the swine's flesh which he was commanded to eat, suffered himself to be led to torture and to death. The mother and her seven sons being required to eat the same detested food, one of the lads declared he would rather die. His tongue was cut out, and his fingers and toes were removed; and in this state he was thrown into a great vessel on a fire, while his mother and brothers looked on, comforting and encouraging one another to be faithful. One after another the noble band of brothers were tortured and put to death in the same manner. The mother, with invincible fortitude, exhorted them to meet death bravely, and to refuse all the offers of wealth and honour that were made to them on condition of their complying with the royal command. Last of all, the mother herself was added to the martyrs.

Triumph of Judas Maccabæus.—The number of the patriot army under the Maccabees gradually increased; their aged leader, Mattathias, was removed by death, but his son Judas was eminently fitted to succeed him. The war of independence is a very interesting chapter of Jewish history, but our limits compel us to notice it briefly. Three campaigns were undertaken by the Syro-Macedonians against the patriots. In all of these the Syrians were unsuccessful. One of them was undertaken by Antiochus in person. But the same loathsome disease which afterwards cut off Herod attacked and destroyed him while breathing out threatening and slaughter against his foes. A civil war having broken out in Syria, peace was at last concluded with the Jews. Judas Maccabæus became governor of Palestine, and though fresh troubles broke out speedily, a new era may be said to have begun.

SECTION V.—PALESTINE UNDER THE MACCABEES:
B.C. 165 TO 63.

Struggles and battles—Appeal to the Romans—Pompey in Palestine: Palestine tributary to Rome—State of religion: Pharisees and Sadducees.

Struggles and Battles.—When Judas Maccabæus came into power, the temple was purged and re-dedicated, and the ancient services were resumed. But Judas was not allowed to prosecute his reforms in peace. He was again attacked by the Syrians; but, though successful once and again, he began to lose ground. He then applied to the Romans for help; but before it could be granted, he fell in battle. The command now devolved on his brother Jonathan. Owing, in a great measure, to the intrigues and plots that were going on for the Syrian throne, Jonathan contrived at last to get his authority acknowledged, and was declared meridarch or commander in Judæa. But it was not long ere he was treacherously murdered.

Appeal to the Romans.—He was succeeded by his brother Simon, who, like Judas, appealed to the Romans, and, by studying their interests, he obtained a large measure of power. The sovereignty was made hereditary in the family of Simon, and he was succeeded by his son, John Hyrcanus. The sects of the Pharisees and Sadducees were now keenly opposed to each other, and Hyrcanus joined first the one and then the other. Strife and commotion again prevailed. At last, two rival Maccabees, Hyrcanus and Aristobulus, grandsons of John Hyrcanus, contended for the dignity, and a civil war ensued in Judæa.

Pompey in Palestine: Palestine Tributary to Rome.—Meanwhile the Romans, under Pompey, had extended their victories into Syria, and Hyrcanus and Aristobulus both submitted their claims to Pompey's decision. Hyrcanus was preferred. Aristobulus attempted to defend Jerusalem against Pompey, but in vain. After a three months' siege, the city and the temple were taken. Pompey impiously entered the holy of holies,—thereby inflicting an unpardonable outrage on the feelings of the Jews. It was remarked by them that after this his reverses of fortune began. He gave the government of Judæa to Hyrcanus, but would not allow him to wear a crown. A yearly tribute to Rome was imposed. Aristobulus and some others were taken prisoners to Rome.

State of Religion: Pharisees and Sadducees.—It would be impossible to narrate all the sieges, battles, murders, and massacres, that gave their dark hue to this period of history. The effect on the state of religion among the Jews must have been very disastrous. Perhaps, however, religion suffered quite as much from the bitter contests between the Pharisees and the Sadducees as from any other cause. It is not certain that the Sadducees yet held all the impious doctrines which were afterwards maintained by them. At first, their main characteristic was opposition to the traditions so strenuously upheld by the Pharisees. The Pharisees were generally the more numerous and the more powerful party. Now, as formerly, true piety probably flourished, like the ferns and the mosses of our mountains, in shady nooks and in lonely dells. Little of it can be discovered in the leaders of factions, or in any of the men who occupied prominent positions. The rose of Sharon and the lily of the valley must be sought for in more quiet and sequestered spots.

SECTION VI.—PALESTINE UNDER THE ROMANS:
B.C. 63 TO 4.

State of Rome—Rise of Julius Cæsar—Civil war in Judæa—The Parthians—Hyrcanus: Antipater—Rise of Herod—Mark Antony and Cleopatra—Murders and cruelties of Herod—His public works—Rebuilding of the temple—Time occupied by the work—Further domestic troubles and crimes.

State of Rome.—The Romans were now the real masters of Judæa. It will, therefore, be proper here to glance at the progress of their arms and influence, onward from the time when they began to interfere in the affairs of the East. In the early periods of their history, the Romans had been distinguished by a stern simplicity of character; but when they had conquered Carthage, Macedonia, Greece, and Syria, luxury and gross corruption of manners began to prevail. There is little of a pleasing kind in the succession of pictures which the subsequent period of their history presents. We see them again seriously threatened by a vast invasion of northern nations; but the military genius of a Marius saves them. We see the old hatred between the people and the aristocracy bursting out in the fierce civil war between Marius and Cinna on the one side, and Sulla on the other; each party in succession getting possession of Rome, and butchering its opponents in massacres that almost surpass belief,—one hundred thousand Roman citizens, ninety senators, and two thousand six hundred Roman knights lying in blood, under the butchery of Sulla alone. We hear the voice of the young advocate, Marcus Tullius Cicero, raised nobly in defence of the son of one of Sulla's victims, when none of the older advocates would undertake his cause; giving rich promise of that wonderful eloquence which he soon attained, and of a far higher measure of moral courage than he afterwards exhibited. We see the legions going forth to Asia to fight against Mithridates, a king of Pontus, who has seized certain provinces of the Romans, and threatens to drive them from that continent. At last, after various campaigns, in one of which Sulla acts a conspicuous part, we see the war ended under that rising general, Pompey, while Mithridates seeks refuge in death, inflicted by his own hand. Ere he returns to Rome, we see Pompey proceed to Jerusalem, settle the affairs of Palestine, restore Hyrcanus, and desecrate the holy of holies (B.C. 62).

Rise of Julius Cæsar.—Revisiting Rome, we find that city in consternation at the discovery of the frightful conspiracy of Catiline, to stir up his irresolute fellow-citizens against whom Cicero is using all the powers of his eloquence. Prominent on the stage of public life we find a young patrician, Julius Cæsar, Cinna's son-in-law, once apparently a fop and a profligate, but in whom sagacious men have discovered "many Mariuses," and found concealed a character of extraordinary strength. By-and-by we find this Julius Cæsar, along with

Pompey and Crassus, sharing among them, as the first triumvirate, the wide dominions of Rome. Then the triumvirate is broken up, first by the death of Crassus in battle with the Parthians, and then by the rupture between Cæsar and Pompey. Their forces join issue at Pharsalia, in Thessaly. Pompey is defeated, and Julius Cæsar is left sole ruler of the great empire of Rome.

Civil War in Judæa.—When the Romans conquered Judæa, they exacted a yearly tribute, but they allowed the country to be still governed by the Maccabees, in conformity with its ancient laws and customs. But between Hyrcanus and Aristobulus, the rival members of the Maccabee family, much strife and bloodshed arose. Hyrcanus was restored to the high-priesthood by Pompey, while Aristobulus, his brother, was carried to Rome to grace his triumph. But Aristobulus contrived to escape, and returned to renew the civil war in Judæa. The contest was continued by his son Alexander, who was at last defeated with terrible slaughter, at Mount Tabor, in the plain of Esdraelon, the old battle-field of Palestine.

The Parthians.—In the division of the Roman empire that had been made among the triumvirs, Cæsar, Pompey, and Crassus, Syria had been assigned to Crassus. But Crassus lost both his life and his reputation in a memorable defeat by the Parthians, near Carrhæ (Haran) in Mesopotamia—the place where Abraham sojourned after leaving Ur. The Parthians were now an important and formidable people. Formerly they had constituted a province of the Persian empire, in the neighbourhood of the Caspian; but, B.C. 250, they founded a kingdom of their own, under king Arsaces; and while the Syrian kingdom was decaying, they overran several of the countries that had belonged to Persia and Macedonia, including many of those where the Jews were dispersed. Ultimately, they fell under the dominion of Rome.

Hyrcanus : Antipater.—After the death of Crassus, Syria was administered for a time by Cassius, an eminent Roman general; but during the subsequent contest between Cæsar and Pompey, much disorder prevailed. Pompey having been killed in Egypt, Cæsar, now sole ruler of the empire, determined that Hyrcanus should rule as king at Jerusalem, and his family after him; and he appointed Antipater, an Idumæan by birth, who had made himself very useful to Cæsar, procurator of Judæa under Hyrcanus. The two sons of Antipater, Phasaelus and Herod (afterwards Herod the Great), were made governors of Judæa and Galilee. Antipater did not enjoy his dignity long—he was poisoned the following year. Three years later, his royal patron, Julius Cæsar, suffered a similar fate, being assassinated in the senate at Rome.

Rise of Herod.—In the subsequent division of empire among the new triumvirs, Octavius, Antony, and Lepidus, Syria and the East were given to Antony. Antony was on the whole favourable to Herod, and his friendship aided the latter in the ambitious projects which he was now beginning to form. Phasaelus, elder brother of Herod, had died in prison by his own hand. About this time Herod married Mariamne, a grand-daughter of Hyrcanus, of extraordinary beauty, thus securing the interest of one branch of the Maccabee family. But a new commotion was raised by Antigonus, a son of Aristobulus, who, having gained a temporary success, caused the ears of Hyrcanus to be cut off, so that, being mutilated, he might be incapacitated for the office of the high-priesthood; and he pressed Herod so hard, that he had to retire to a fortress called Massada, on the Dead Sea. In this state of things Herod went to Rome, pictured to Antony the wretched disorders of Palestine; and having convinced him and the senate that he alone could restore order, he procured for himself the office and dignity of king. Antigonus was put to death; and the rule of the Asmonæan princes came formally and for ever to an end.

Mark Antony and Cleopatra.—For some years Antony continued to be the head of the eastern portion of the empire. Every reader of history knows well the shameful profligacy to which he abandoned himself, in company with Cleopatra, the beautiful but unprincipled queen of Egypt. In Egypt, at Antioch, at Jerusalem, and at many other places, this outrage went on openly. We get a sad glimpse of the wretched state of morals in the Roman empire, when we see its highest men violating, as they did, the most sacred obligations of family life, living in open profligacy with the wives of other men, or going through the form of a divorce from their own, either to serve their convenience or to gratify their lust by a new connection. At last a war broke out between Antony and Octavius, which was terminated by the battle of Actium, in Epirus, where Antony was completely defeated. About a year afterwards, both he and Cleopatra committed suicide in Egypt, and the ancient kingdom of the Pharaohs and the Ptolemys sunk into the position of a Roman province. Octavius, now known as Cæsar Augustus, became Emperor of Rome.

Murders and Cruelties of Herod.—Meanwhile Herod, crafty, clever, and cruel, was endeavouring to consolidate and extend his power in Judæa. He was always in dread that some member of the Asmonæan family would start up to give him trouble, and he coolly planned to get rid of as many of them as possible. One of his first victims was Aristobulus, a brother of his wife, a young man of remarkably fine appearance and manners, whom he had made high priest; but as he became very popular among the Jews, Herod had him invited to his residence at Jericho, and induced to bathe in a fish-pond, where, under pretence of sport, his head was held under the water by some of Herod's officers until he was choked. The aged Hyrcanus was the next to suffer. That unfortunate prince, after his ears were cut off, had been protected by the Parthians; but Herod prevailed on him to come to Jerusalem, where he raised a false charge against him, on pretext of which he put him to death, in his eightieth year. These barbarous murders of her nearest male relatives alienated his wife Mariamne. At last she too fell under suspicion, as if engaged in plotting against him; and though Herod loved her most passionately, she was executed by his orders. After her death he was seized with fearful remorse, and became almost distracted. His temper became more cruel, suspicious, and vindictive than ever, and many new deeds of blood stained the annals of his reign.

His Public Works.—The feeling of the Jews towards Herod —never very cordial, seeing that he was an Idumæan—was becoming more and more hostile; so that he found it necessary to take steps for securing a measure of their good-will. He set about effecting important material improvements in his kingdom. An amphitheatre and a theatre were built by him at Jerusalem, for the amusement of the people. Samaria, which had lain a long time in ruins, was rebuilt, and named Sebaste, from Sebastos, the Greek word for Augustus. A magnificent palace was built for himself on Mount Zion. Another undertaking begun about this time was the building of a great sea-port, between Joppa and Carmel, called Cæsarea: afterwards it became a place of great importance and the chief seat of government, when the Roman power was more firmly established in Palestine. It is remarkable that not one of all the many towns in Palestine that had been capitals was a sea-port—not Hebron, nor Jerusalem, nor Gibeah, nor Shechem, nor Samaria, nor Tirzah, nor Jezreel, nor Mahanaim. The Jews had no love for the sea: in their view, it was the element of danger, and the emblem of strife and trouble; and in this light it is almost constantly presented in the imagery of the Bible, down to that vision of the Apocalypse where "there was no more sea."

Rebuilding of the Temple.—But the chief of Herod's improvements was the rebuilding of the temple at Jerusalem. This work was undertaken shortly after Augustus had given a decision in favour of Herod in the matter of certain complaints that had been made against his violence. Herod had signalized that decision by building a temple of white marble in honour of Augustus, at Paneas, beside the sources of the Jordan; and by this, and other heathenish proceedings, he had created great dissatisfaction in the minds of the Jews. It was therefore a very politic undertaking to rebuild the national temple at Jerusalem. It was now about five hundred years since the second temple had been built; and the natural process of decay, as well as the damage which it had sustained during the many sieges and wars that had taken place in

Jerusalem, made it exceedingly desirable that it should be renewed.

Time Occupied by the Work.—The Jews were afraid that, if Herod pulled down the existing temple before he built the new one, something might occur to prevent the erection, and their city might be deprived of its highest glory. It was accordingly arranged, that all the materials for the new temple should be prepared before the old building was demolished. A thousand waggons were employed in conveying stones and timber; ten thousand workmen in fitting the materials for building; and a thousand priests, skilled in architecture, in superintending the work. Nearly ten years passed before the building was so far finished as to be ready for dedication and divine service; but for many years thereafter, a large body of men were employed about the outworks,—justifying the remark of the Jews, "Forty and six years was this temple in building." Being regarded rather as a restoration than a new erection, it continued to be spoken of as the second temple. By such important undertakings, and by the pains he took to embellish Jerusalem, and to improve the country generally, Herod did much to mitigate the detestation with which he otherwise would certainly have been regarded.

Further Domestic Troubles and Crimes.—The domestic troubles and crimes of Herod were not yet ended. By his wife Mariamne he had two sons, Alexander and Aristobulus, whom he intended to make his successors in the government. They were sent to Rome, and introduced to Augustus, and seemed in a fair way of rising to honour and power. But the demon of suspicion haunted Herod, and he was surrounded by persons who were always trying, for their own interests, to persuade him that others were plotting for his life and his crown. At last his sons, like their mother, fell victims to his unnatural suspicion and brutal violence, and were strangled by his orders at Sebaste. Very many other persons were put to death at various times by his command, under suspicion of being engaged in conspiracies. On one occasion a large number of the Pharisees suffered this fate. These bloody and revolting deeds were perpetrated only a year or two before the birth of Jesus, and explain the suspicion which then filled Herod's mind, and which prompted him to order the wholesale massacre of the babes of Bethlehem, in order to get rid of the unwelcome rival.

SECTION VII.—THE JEWS OF THE DISPERSION.

In the countries of the captivity—In other eastern countries—In Africa—At Rome—Religious condition: Rabbinical system—Hillel and Shammai—Contrast with Christ—The Sects: Pharisees and Sadducees; the Essenes.

We must now glance at the state of the Jews in the chief countries of their dispersion, up to the time of the birth of our Lord.

In the Countries of the Captivity.—In the countries to which they had been originally carried captive large numbers of Jews still remained, and in many of them they attained to great wealth and importance. In some of these countries they kept quite aloof from connection by marriage with the other inhabitants; but in other cases they were not so strict. This gave rise to various epithets, intended to mark the degree of purity of the Jewish blood. In the district between the Tigris and the Euphrates they were "healthy;" Media was "sickly;" Elymais "in the last gasps;" and Mesene "dead." About the time of the birth of our Lord, the Jews in Mesopotamia were exposed to a terrible persecution, in which above sixty thousand of them were slain. In other districts of Asia severe persecution often befell them.

In other Eastern Countries.—In Arabia many Jews found a home; and for a long time the throne of Yemen or Seba, in Arabia, where the queen of Sheba had reigned, was filled by Jews. They even penetrated to China: according to tradition, a body of six thousand emigrated thither from Persia, fifty or sixty years B.C. Some of the Hebrews attained even to the rank of mandarins. The descendants of these Jews are still found in China, where they have a sanctuary constructed after the model of the temple of Jerusalem.

In Africa.—Egypt was long an important settlement of the Jews. At Heliopolis, where Joseph's father-in-law had been priest, they had a temple, built by Onias, the high priest who fled from Jerusalem in the time of Antiochus Epiphanes; and at Alexandria a synagogue, the magnificence of which was spoken of in the most glowing terms. In Cyrene, Libya, and other parts of Africa, their numbers were computed at about a million.

At Rome.—Rome, too, had already begun to have its Jewish inhabitants. Under Pompey, Jews were sold in Rome as slaves. They soon, however, gained their liberty. Julius Cæsar patronized the Jews greatly; and Augustus showed them favour, encouraged no doubt by the attachment which Herod had shown to him. An age or two later, their troubles and miseries began to thicken in almost all parts of the world; but at the birth of our Lord, they were not only very widely dispersed, but enjoyed no small share of comfort and prosperity.*

Religious Condition: Rabbinical System.—Little that is pleasant meets our view, when we inquire into the religious state of the Jews at this period, whether at home or in the countries of their dispersion. Indeed, it was the period now before us that witnessed the rise of what is called the rabbinical system. Allusion has already been made to the laying of the foundation of the traditions of the Jewish fathers, immediately after the restoration, under Ezra. There is a story that Ezra associated with himself in the government no fewer than one hundred and twenty learned men, who were then called the Great Synagogue, which gave rise to the supreme court or council of the Sanhedrim, by which the affairs of the Jews were conducted in the time of our Lord.

Hillel and Shammai.—Among the great Jewish doctors or rabbins of this period, there were two of special eminence,—Hillel and Shammai. Hillel was born in Babylon, about the year B.C. 112, but came to Palestine, where he is said to have lived to an extreme old age. He enjoyed an extraor-

---

* Edersheim's History of the Jewish Nation, chap. iii.

dinary reputation for learning and sanctity. Like the other rabbins, he ascribed the highest merit to the study of the Law. He was remarkable for the speculative direction which he gave to Jewish theology. Hillel allowed a measure of freedom to the minds of his followers; but Shammai, the other great rabbi of this time, adhered much more rigidly to the letter of the traditions. Hillel was a supporter of Herod; Shammai, of the party that aimed at national independence.

Contrast with Christ.--These and other eminent rabbins of this period were probably alive when Christ came into the world; some of them may have been among those with whom the child Jesus conversed in the temple; and they, or their successors, must have exercised influence in his rejection and death. There could not have been a greater contrast than that between their worship of traditions and Christ's reverence for the Word; between their theory of changing men by an influence from *without*, and Christ's, by a power from *within*; between the vain, trifling inquiries, on which their teaching bore, and the grand realities of life and death which Christ's constantly contemplated; between their pride, formality, and contemptuous spirit, and Christ's humility, simplicity, and love. It is said by some that the son of Hillel was that Simeon who took in his arms the infant Saviour. This cannot be verified; but it is known that his grandson, and successor as president of the Sanhedrim, was that Gamaliel who gave to the council so temperate advice in regard to the treatment of the apostles, and who was the instructor of St. Paul. Gamaliel was by no means so rigid a Pharisee as some others.

The Sects: Pharisees and Sadducees: the Essenes.—The contests between the Pharisees and the Sadducees continued. The great doctrine of the resurrection and the future state became prominent in the discussions of Jewish theologians. A new sect had arisen, termed the ESSENES; who, with not a few errors, seem to have had more of the spirit of true religion than either of the other two. They disliked the formalism of the Pharisees, and the worldliness of the Sadducees. They aimed at a more spiritual religion, but became almost monkish in their habits. There are said to have been four thousand of them at the time of our Lord's birth, scattered here and there over Judæa and other countries; and some have conjectured, but without evidence, that in his early life our Lord was connected with them, from a supposed resemblance between their tenets and the lessons which he taught.

SECTION VIII.—STATE OF THE GENTILE WORLD.

Britain, as described by Cæsar—Contrast with the present time—Rome under Augustus: its galaxy of literary men—State of morality—Religious longings and hopes.

We have yet to glance at the condition of the Gentile world, previous to the advent of Christ.

Britain, as Described by Cæsar.—Shortly after Julius Cæsar became one of the triumvirate, we see him leaving Rome at the head of his legions, crossing the Alps into Switzerland and Gaul, and ultimately adding these districts to the territories of Rome. He believes, or affects to believe, that the Gauls have been aided by a strange race, the Britons, living in the adjacent island of Britain; and thither he determines to go. He has gathered some information concerning this strange people. All of them stain themselves with woad, which makes them of a blue tinge, and gives them a more fearful appearance in battle; they also wear their hair long, and shave every part of the body except the head and the upper lip. Every ten or twelve of them have their wives in common. This barbarous race are very attentive to religious duties. As in Gaul, their priests are called Druids; and Druidism is believed to exist in its most perfect form among them. Cæsar's account of the Druids in Gaul is therefore probably applicable to Britain too. Besides presiding over the services of religion, the Druids were the judges of the country, settling all disputes that were brought to them for that purpose. The Druids were also the learned class of the country; but they did not commit their instructions to writing, although in other matters written records were employed, the Greek character being used. One of their chief tenets was, that souls do not perish at death, but pass into other bodies: this led the people to rise above the fear of death, and to be courageous in war. They believed that the favour of the gods could not be obtained unless the life of one man were offered up for that of another: human sacrifices were therefore often presented by the Druids. On great occasions of this kind, images of wicker-work were filled with men, who perished in the flames when the images were set on fire. Criminals were preferred for such sacrifices; but when there was not a sufficient number of the guilty, the priests did not scruple to offer up the innocent. Mercury was worshipped by them, as the inventor of arts, the guide of their journeys, and the friend of wealth and commerce; Apollo, as warding off diseases; Minerva, as aiding arts and manufactures; and Mars, as the god of war. To Mars they commonly devoted whatever spoil they might take in war. After battle, they killed all living creatures found in the spoil, and raised the rest in a consecrated heap. They were so scrupulous and conscientious in this, that it very seldom happened that any part of the spoil was carried off, either before or after the heap was raised. A very heavy punishment with torture was denounced against that crime.

Contrast with the Present Time.—How little could Cæsar have thought, when he invaded this strange, barbarous island, what a wonderful future was in reserve for it! What amazement would have filled him, if, glancing over eighteen or nineteen centuries, he had seen it the seat of an empire wider spread and more wonderful far than his; its colonies peopling continents of which he had never heard; its manufactures bearing the palm in the markets of the world; its distinguished authors read with admiration wherever books were known; and its free yet stable government the envy of every country. It would have been still more wonderful to think that it was to be one of the chief seats of a religion that should become the fostering parent of universal enlightenment, brotherhood, and love, based upon the sacrifice of its great, divine High Priest; offering a free salvation to every member of the human family, and destined one day to spread the blessings of knowledge and civilization, love and happiness, immortal life and glory, over every region of the habitable globe!

Rome under Augustus: Its Galaxy of Literary Men.—The first Roman triumvirate gave way, and left Julius Cæsar sole ruler of Rome; the second in like manner fell to pieces, and Cæsar Augustus became emperor. Glancing at the capital of the world in the days of Augustus, we find it at the very height of worldly glory. Immense riches have flowed into Rome, but have carried with them incredible luxury and frightful immorality. Virgil is delighting the lovers of letters with the fine taste and silvery flow of his "Æneid." Horace charms a large circle with the happy phrases and agreeable rhythm of his odes, and the wit and shrewd sense of his longer poems; and unhappily he does not lose caste by the licentious tone which he often shows. A host of other names, including Cornelius Nepos, Ovid, Livy, and Tibullus, brighten the galaxy of authorship that sheds glory upon Rome.

State of Morality.—But the state of morality is very deplorable. Licentiousness knows no bounds, and the love of cruel sports is carried to a terrible height. Sulla had made himself popular by exhibiting a combat where a hundred men fought with a hundred lions; Julius Cæsar had presented a show where three hundred couples of gladiators fought together; and in Pompey's shows, five hundred lions had been killed, besides elephants and other wild beasts. The same savage taste still prevails. Luxurious eating is carried to the most disgusting excesses. To support such luxury and profligacy, money must be obtained, by whatever means; and it is quite common for men to ask and obtain the government of dependent provinces, for the sole purpose of enriching themselves by extortion. We may readily understand, in this light, the intense hatred which prevailed in Judæa, and elsewhere, towards the publicans,—the persons who farmed the Roman revenues. All who are familiar with the state of morals at this time know well that the dark picture in the first chapter of Paul's Epistle to the Romans is not a whit overdrawn.

Religious Longings and Hopes.—Yet, amid all this darkness and guilt, there prevailed in many parts of the world a vague longing for a better state of things, and an expectation of the coming of a glorious prince, who was to effect a mighty change for the better. There can be no doubt that it was to the spread of the Jewish Scriptures that this feeling was due. About the year B.C. 40, Virgil composed his fourth Eclogue— a remarkable poem, in which he predicts for an infant son of the consul Pollio a remarkable career, that would realize to the world a reign of righteousness and bliss, in some degree like that which the Hebrew prophets had ascribed to Christ. Directly or indirectly he had probably come in contact with some of the Hebrew prophecies. Tacitus and Suetonius, both distinguished Roman historians, tell us that there was a common belief at that time, that one sprung from Judæa should become ruler of the world. The visit of the Magi to Jerusalem shows that the same belief prevailed in the primitive settlements of the human race. Pious Jews, like Simeon and Anna, were so full of this conviction, that they could not leave the Temple; being assured that the Consolation of Israel, for whom they were waiting, would appear before they died. At last, to the wistful eyes that were searching the Eastern heavens, the morning star was seen in the horizon. The fulness of the time had arrived, and the Desire of all Nations came.

CHAPTER XV.

GOSPEL HISTORY.*

SECTION I.—BIRTH AND CHILDHOOD OF JESUS CHRIST.

Zacharias at Jerusalem—Appearance of the city—The ancient spirit gone—The coming dawn—Annunciation of the birth of John—Annunciation of the birth of Jesus—The taxing of the people—Bethlehem—Its situation—Its sacred memories—Visit of the wise men—Flight to Egypt—Death of Herod—Christ's visit to the temple—Galilee—Nazareth—Monkish traditions—The surroundings of the town—Its associations.

Zacharias at Jerusalem.—A few years after the temple, rebuilt by Herod, had been opened for worship, a thoughtful, venerable man, might have been seen travelling slowly along the road from Hebron to Jerusalem, and at last entering the holy city. It is the aged Zacharias, a priest of the course of Abia. According to the old law requiring the priests of each of the twenty four orders to attend in succession a week at a time, his turn to serve at the temple has come.

Appearance of the City.—Jerusalem is not like the Jerusalem of former times. As he passes Mount Zion, on his way to the temple, he gazes with a mournful feeling on the palace of Herod, surmounting the height where of old king David had dwelt. A heavy sigh escapes him as he makes obeisance to the king, rolling in his Roman chariot; for in place of the gentle piety and fatherly benevolence of a David or a Josiah, he can read in that old wrinkled face little but the cruelty of an Idumæan, and the stern shrewdness of a Roman governor. Jerusalem has

---

* In the author's "Outline of Bible History and Geography" all the leading events in our Lord's life are specified and grouped; in the present work the aim rather is to convey an accurate impression of the leading features of the whole.

been greatly improved of late, and each time that Zacharias visits it he finds some new building to admire. But in no case is his admiration unmingled with pain. There, along the northern brow of Zion, are the towers of Hippicus, Phasaelus, and Mariamne, all built by Herod,—the last recalling the memory of the beautiful but ill fated daughter of the Maccabees, and the tragic end of the second dynasty of Jewish kings. There, guarding the temple, is the fortress of Antonia. It has lately got that name from Herod's friend and patron, Mark Antony; but how can Zacharias look on it without remembering the guilty life and sad death both of the Roman triumvir and of his beautiful paramour, Cleopatra? There, near the base of Mount Zion, is the circus or hippodrome, erected, in Roman fashion, for horse and chariot racing; and yonder, in the plain to the north, are two stupendous buildings, the theatre and the amphitheatre, where Herod has begun to introduce the gladiatorial fights and other savage sports of Rome.

The Ancient Spirit gone.—Everything about Jerusalem has a half foreign air. The very language is not the language of Abraham and of David. The Hebrews speak a sort of mixture of Syriac and Chaldee; others talk in Greek; and the strong-built military men, with the stern, determined countenances, speak the language of distant Rome. It gives little comfort to Zacharias to receive the salutations of the precise, formal men, with the broad phylacteries, who are making long prayers at the corners of the streets, or are carrying across the stately bridge that joins Mount Zion to the temple their tithes of anise, mint, and cummin. The Sanhedrim has still control over matters of religion; and there is something imposing in the appearance of that fine hall, reared aloft on piers and arches close to the temple, where the council meets; but Zacharias cannot have much sympathy with the Hillels, the Shammais, and the other great rabbins, who seem to love their own traditions so much, and the word of God so little. The temple is no doubt much improved; and these long colonnades, supported by Corinthian columns of purest marble, form noble coverings for its courts; but are not the money-changers and the sellers of doves usurping a more prominent place than they ought to have in them, and giving a painfully mercantile aspect to the house of prayer? And where is the *spirit* of former times? Has the glorious old line of kings and prophets come to an end? Where is the Branch of Jesse that was to bud forth in latter days? Does not communication with Heaven now seem to be entirely broken off? May not the name I-chabod be seen on each stone of these proud walls?

The Coming Dawn.—It might have been natural to give way to such feelings; but the spirit of faith would bear up against them in the believing heart. In the former history of the Church, the darkest hour of night had often been that which preceded the dawn. Man's extremity had been God's opportunity. It was to be so now, more strikingly than ever.

Annunciation of the Birth of John.—Zacharias, on this occasion, had the most honourable of the priestly duties assigned to him. It fell to him, after the sacrifice had been offered, to enter the holy place with incense, and to offer it up to God, while the people were silently praying outside. While he was thus engaged, the angel Gabriel—the same who had been sent to Daniel five hundred years before—appeared to him, and promised that a son, who should be the forerunner of Messiah, should be born to him and his aged wife Elizabeth. In token of the reality of this announcement, Zacharias was struck dumb, and remained so till after the birth of his child. In a day or two he would leave Jerusalem, and proceed southward to his usual residence, a city in the hill country of Judah; either Hebron, which was a city of the priests, or, as some think, Juttah, five miles farther south. We can fancy the look of interest he would cast on Bethlehem, as he passed near it on his way, and the feeling of curiosity that would arise in his mind as to how the prophecy of Micah would now be fulfilled—in what manner "the city of David" would send forth the "Ruler, whose goings forth were from of old, from everlasting."

Annunciation of the Birth of Jesus.—Six months roll on, and the angel who visited Zacharias is sent on a similar errand to a northern city. In the remote town of Nazareth, hid among the hills of Galilee, dwells a Hebrew maiden named Mary, the lineal descendant of king David and of the old line of the Hebrew kings, but not distinguishable from the other maidens of Nazareth, except by the greater gentleness of her spirit and the greater purity of her life. Amid the changes of fortune she and her family have sunk into poverty and obscurity; and, in one sense, they are thankful for it. If they were wealthy and powerful, they know they should excite the suspicions of the blood-thirsty Herod, and share the fate of Mariamne and Aristobulus. Perhaps it is in order to be removed as far as possible from Herod's notice that they have taken up their residence in that obscure and distant place. To that maiden Gabriel comes. He salutes her in words that intimate a career of great distinction. The poor maiden is alarmed. Does this mean that she is to be restored to the ancient honours of her family? No; it means that she is to bring forth a son, whose name is to be called JESUS. The prophecy of Isaiah is to be fulfilled,—a virgin is to conceive, and to bear a son, and to call his name IMMANUEL—"God with us."

The Taxing of the People.—On receiving this intimation, and hearing what had taken place in the family of Zacharias, Mary set off on a visit to Elizabeth, who was her cousin, traversing in her journey nearly the whole length of the country. After spending three months in fellowship with that godly and exemplary family, she returns to Nazareth, where dwells her betrothed, Joseph the carpenter, also a descendant of David, and a devout and exemplary man. Soon after their marriage, a decree of Cæsar Augustus, the Roman emperor, requiring a general taxation of the people, each in his own city, summons Joseph and Mary to Bethlehem, the city of their family. This taxing was first made when Cyrenius was governor of Syria.* Great opposition to the taxation was shown by some of the

---

* There has been some difficulty about the chronology here, as Cyrenius is known to have been governor about eight years later than the date of the birth of Christ. But recent investigations make it probable that he had been governor of Syria at a previous time, and that time corresponds precisely with that of our Lord's birth. See Andrews's Life of our Lord, p. 4.

Jews. One Judas of Galilee raised an army to resist it, and created great disturbance (see Acts v. 37); and the question whether it was lawful to pay it was still eagerly debated in the time of our Lord. In fact, it was this matter of taxation that ultimately raised the rebellion in Judæa, to quell which, forty years after the death of Christ, Titus and his legions marched against Jerusalem.

Bethlehem.—Mary and her husband proceeded southward, probably by the same route which she had traversed a few months before. Arrived at Bethlehem, they had to take up their abode in a place that seems to have been used as a stable. The tradition of the monks points, though probably erroneously, to a cave at the extremity of the town as the scene of the nativity. A handsome church and convent have been built over this cave, called the Church and Convent of the Nativity; and a silver star in the floor of the crypt, or subterranean chamber, is said, in these fanciful legends, to mark the precise spot where the Saviour was born. It was not for three centuries after Christ that the "sacred places" began to be inquired after, and in many cases the fixing of them was only matter of caprice or of conjecture.

Its Situation. Bethlehem is about six miles south of Jerusalem. The traveller going from Jerusalem over the long intervening hill, hardly loses sight of the city where Christ was killed before he comes in sight of that where he was born. On a ridge of considerable height, descending abruptly on the north and on the east, he sees a small town of a single street, half a mile long, whose houses of white stone, crowned with neat domes, contrast with the dark green of the olive groves that embosom them. The district around is exceedingly rocky, —more so than usual in that rocky country; but green spots of quiet beauty are always to be found in the nooks and hollows. Many a fig-grove and many a vineyard, each protected by its little watch-tower, adorns the terraces close to the town; and if the wild Bedouins would suffer those fine wide-stretching plains to be cultivated, the place would be again true to its ancient name—Bethlehem, "the house of bread."

Its Sacred Memories.—Never was place so rich in sacred associations. There is the spot where Jacob had his first great grief, when his beloved Rachel was taken from him. There are the fields where Ruth came to reap, and to win the heart of Boaz, and on which she and her husband afterwards made so many reapers happy. There are the plains where David kept his father's sheep, and learned to sing those songs that to the end of time are to supply the worship of all nations,—alike in the coral islands of the South, in the churches and cathedrals of Europe, and among the forests of the distant West. It was in these plains that the shepherds were keeping their flocks by night, when the announcement that has gladdened so many millions of hearts was made by the angel—"Fear not; for, behold, I bring you good tidings of great joy, which shall be to all people. For unto you is born this day in the city of David a Saviour, which is Christ the Lord." It was there, too, that the great gospel anthem fell upon their ears in all its divine beauty and thrilling force—"Glory to God in the highest, and on earth peace, good will toward men." Never, to the end of time, can Bethlehem cease to be surrounded with a halo of glory, or to awaken a thrilling interest in every Christian bosom.

Visit of the Wise Men.—A three hours' journey would at any time carry Mary from Bethlehem to Jerusalem; so that she might easily present her child in the temple, with the humble offering of the turtle-doves or young pigeons, and return the same day to Bethlehem. It must have been after the visit to the temple, when Simeon and Anna recognized the child of promise, that the wise men from the east arrived at Bethlehem. These men came from Chaldæa, or from Persia, or from some country where the Jews had settled at the time of the captivity; for their expectation of the birth of a king of the Jews was doubtless founded upon the Hebrew prophecies. Perhaps they were led to connect his birth with the appearance of a star by the prophecy of Balaam (who was himself a native of Mesopotamia): "There shall come a Star out of Jacob, and a sceptre shall rise out of Israel, and shall smite the corners of Moab, and destroy all the children of Sheth." It has been attempted to be shown by some astronomers, of whom the distinguished Kepler was one, that at the time of Christ's birth there was a remarkable conjunction of the planets Jupiter and Saturn, which they regard as "the star" seen by the wise men. This may have been; but it does not fulfil all that is said by Matthew about the star (ii. 9). It was a star that moved before them, until it rested over the very place where the infant Jesus was. It must have shed down its rays in some remarkable way, so as to indicate a particular spot —a thing which, in ordinary circumstances, the stars and planets never do.

Flight to Egypt.—The rumour of the birth of a new king aroused all the jealousy of Herod. He demanded of the chief priests and the scribes where Christ should be born; and finding that the place which had been specified was Bethlehem, he caused all the infants of that town to be slaughtered. But the warning of an angel placed Joseph and his family beyond the reach of danger. Egypt afforded them a refuge. Nothing is known of their residence there. Egypt was then a Roman province. The line of its Pharaohs and that of its Ptolemys had been alike cut short. Notwithstanding the vast antiquity of its monarchy, it could be no rival in durability to the kingdom to be set up by the infant who was now brought to it— the only kingdom that cannot be destroyed.

Death of Herod.—Herod did not long survive the massacre of Bethlehem. A few months afterwards, he died of a disease which is described as a very horrible complication. It consisted of a slow fever, with ulceration of the bowels, and other ulcerations that bred worms,—swollen feet, want of breath, and convulsion fits. Knowing how the Jews hated him, he fell upon a novel plan of securing (as he thought) a general lamentation at his death. He summoned all the principal men of the kingdom to appear at Jericho, where he lay; he shut them up in the circus; and he commanded his sister, Salome, who had instigated him to many of his murders, and her husband, to put them to death as soon as he should be dead. But the savage order was not obeyed. Herod died in his seventieth year, after having reigned thirty-seven years as king of the Jews. On his death, his dominions were divided among three of his sons. Archelaus got Judæa, Samaria, and Idumæa; Philip got Auranitis, Trachonitis, Paneas, and Batanea,—partly in Syria, partly in Palestine; and Herod Antipas got Galilee and Peræa,—this last being now the name of part of the district east of the Jordan. On returning from Egypt, Joseph, knowing something of the cruel character of Archelaus, deemed it unsafe to settle in his dominions; and therefore he returned to the obscure town where he had formerly resided, and buried himself among the hills of Galilee.

Christ's Visit to the Temple.—For well-nigh thirty years Nazareth was the earthly home of the Incarnate Son of God. Once only is that long period broken in upon in the sacred narrative; one solitary floweret is plucked for us from the enclosed garden of the thirty years. It is in connection with the Saviour's first visit to Jerusalem, to attend the passover, on his reaching the age of twelve,—the age at which the Jews considered that a boy became "a child of the law." Having missed him from the Galilæan caravan, on the way home, Joseph and Mary returned in search of him to Jerusalem, and found him with the doctors in the temple, both hearing them and asking them questions. When his mother remonstrated with him for the anxiety he had occasioned to Joseph and her, he gave the memorable answer: "How is it that ye sought me? Wist ye not that I must be about my Father's business?" When he returned to Nazareth, he continued subject to his parents; and a tradition, which derives some support from a passage in one of the gospels (Mark vi. 3), represents him as having followed the trade of a carpenter while he resided in Nazareth.

Galilee.—The silence of Scripture regarding this long period of the life of Christ deepens our interest in Nazareth and its neighbourhood, and makes us eagerly question every mountain, rock, and tree, to aid our conceptions of his early life. The district in which Nazareth was situated was of old the territory of Zebulun. The town itself is not named in the Old Testament at all, nor in the New, except as the early dwelling-place of our Lord. The upper part of the district of Galilee had been subdued and depopulated at a very early period by the kings of Assyria (see ch. x. p. 298); and from that time its population had been mixed and heterogeneous. In the New Testament it is called "Galilee of the Gentiles" (Matt. iv. 15), on account of the admixture of Phœnicians, Syrians, Greeks, and Arabs, with the Jews. From this circumstance the Galilæans acquired a strong provincial character and dialect, rough and uncouth, which made them obnoxious to the Jews. Yet for this reason their pride and their prejudices against apparent innovations in religion were less extreme, and the district was more suitable than that of Judæa would have been, both for Christ's private residence and for the commencement of his public ministry. The fierce fanaticism that prevailed in and around Jerusalem did not extend to Galilee. In most parts of that province our Lord could walk about in comparative safety and draw large audiences of at least attentive hearers. In Jewry or Judæa, on the contrary, the Jews sought to kill him, and his presence there was always viewed by his disciples with the greatest anxiety. His apostles were from Galilee. Five hundred brethren there witnessed him in his risen body at one time; whereas the whole Church at Jerusalem, even though recruited by the apostles and others, comprised but one hundred and twenty souls.

Nazareth.—The town of Nazareth lies in a small plain or basin among the hills that form the upper or northern boundary of the plain of Esdraelon. "Fifteen gently rounded hills seem as if they had met to form an enclosure for this peaceful basin: they rise round it like the edge of a shell, to guard it from intrusion. It is a rich and beautiful field in the midst of these green hills, abounding in gay flowers, in fig-trees, small gardens, hedges of the prickly pear; and the dense rich grass affords an abundant pasture. The expression of the old topographer Quaresmius was as happy as it is poetical: 'Nazareth is a rose; and, like a rose, has the same rounded form, enclosed by mountains as the flower by its leaves.' The village stands on the steep slope of the south-western side of the valley; its chief object, the great Franciscan Convent of the Annunciation, with its white campanile and brown enclosure."*

Monkish Traditions.—The present population of the town is about three thousand souls, the greater part of whom profess the Christian faith. The monks, as usual, have studded it with "holy places." The convent is said to cover the spot where the Virgin lived. Under the church is the grotto where she received the salutation of the angel, and where once stood the house which, to escape contamination from the Mussulmans, is said to have wandered through the air to Loretto in Italy. Two miles off is a hill called the Mount of Precipitation, said to be that from which the Nazarenes wished to cast Jesus down; but this is plainly an error, as the Hill of Precipitation could not have been so far off: on the hill where the city is built are several abrupt precipices, forty or fifty feet high, over one or other of which they probably attempted to force him. The Fountain of the Virgin, in the vicinity of Nazareth, may have been frequented by Mary as well as by the other maidens of the place: a Greek tradition affirms that it was here that Gabriel made the annunciation to her. But the charm of the spot is rudely broken by the scene that usually attracts the notice of travellers,—the quarrels of girls who, having come for water, contend who shall have the earliest supply.

The Surroundings of the Town.—These monkish traditions are quite unsatisfactory, and the traveller turns from them with relief to study the great natural features of the landscape, and to think how these must have appeared to the eye and impressed the mind of Jesus. "I walked out alone," says Dr. Robinson, "to the top of the western hill above Nazareth, where, quite unexpectedly, a glorious prospect opened on the view. The air was perfectly clear and serene. There lay the magnificent plain of Esdraelon, or at least all its western part: on the left was seen the round top of Tabor over the intervening hills, with portions of the Little

* Stanley's Sinai and Palestine, p 365.

Hermon and Gilboa, and the opposite mountains of Samaria, extending towards Carmel. Then came the long line of Carmel itself, with the Convent of Elias on its northern end, and Haifa on the shore at its foot. In the west lay the Mediterranean gleaming in the morning sun; Mount Carmel extending far out into the sea, and dipping his feet in the waters. Below, on the north, was spread another of the beautiful plains of northern Palestine, called El-Buttauf; beyond it, long ridges, running from east to west, rise one above another, until the mountains of Safed overtop them all, on which that place is seen,—'a city set upon a hill.' Farther towards the right is a sea of hills and mountains, backed by the higher ones beyond the Lake of Tiberias, and on the northeast by the majestic Hermon with its icy crown......

Its Associations.—"I remained for some hours upon this spot, lost in the contemplation of the wide prospect, and of the events connected with the scenes around. In the village below, the Saviour of the world had passed his childhood; and the features of nature that met our eyes must once have met his. He must often have visited the fountain near which we had pitched our tent; his feet must frequently have wandered over the adjacent hills, and his eyes doubtless have gazed upon the splendid prospect from this very spot. Here the Prince of Peace looked down upon the great plain, where the din of battle so oft had rolled, and the garments of the warrior been dyed in blood: and he looked out too upon that sea, over which the swift ships were to bear the tidings of his salvation to nations and to continents then unknown. How has the moral aspect of things been changed! Battles and bloodshed have, indeed, not ceased to desolate this unhappy country, and gross darkness now covers the people; but from this region a light went forth which has enlightened the world, and unveiled new climes; and now the rays of that light begin to be reflected back from distant isles and continents, to illuminate anew the darkened land where it first sprung up."*

* Biblical Researches, ii. 336-338.

SECTION II.—PREPARATION FOR PUBLIC WORK.

Political changes—Tiberius: Pontius Pilate at Jerusalem—State of religion—Ministry of John—Baptism of Jesus—Herod Antipas; death of John—Temptation of Jesus—End of his private life.

Political Changes.—Before our Lord left Nazareth, to commence his public ministry, an important change had occurred in the government of Judæa. Even before Christ's first passover, great complaints had been forwarded to Rome against Archelaus; in consequence of which he was deposed from his office, after having held it ten years. Judæa was now taken more directly under Roman authority and Roman law; it was reduced to a Roman province, and was administered by a Roman procurator. The seat of the supreme government was removed from Jerusalem to Cæsarea. Nothing could have been more exact than the fulfilment of the prophecy of Jacob as to the time of Christ's coming: "The sceptre shall not depart from Judah, nor a lawgiver from between his feet, *until Shiloh come.*" Had the coming of Christ taken place a few years later, this prophecy would not have been so literally fulfilled.

Tiberius: Pontius Pilate at Jerusalem.—Augustus Cæsar having died A.D. 14, Tiberius, his adopted son, succeeded him. Tiberius had shared the empire with Augustus for a few years previously, and the date of John the Baptist's appearance in public life given in Luke iii. 1, is reckoned from the earlier period. The unpopularity of the Roman governors at Jerusalem naturally gave rise to much disagreement between them and the high priests; and as the governors claimed and exercised the power of removing the high priests from office, many changes occurred. At the time of our Lord's crucifixion, the office was held in some sense by two—Annas and his son-in-law, Caiaphas (Luke iii. 2). In the year 26, according to the amended chronology, or 30 of the common era, Tiberius sent to Jerusalem, as procurator, Pontius Pilate, a man who is represented as having been a great tyrant, and addicted to every crime. Herod Antipas continued to be tetrarch of Galilee; and his brother Philip, of Ituræa and

Trachonitis. These men continued in their respective offices till after the death of our Lord.

State of Religion.—Little needs to be said here about the religious state of the nation during our Lord's early life. The condition of things was similar to what has already been described. True godliness, of the type of Samuel, David, or Jeremiah, lurked in quiet nooks and corners, but did not appear in the high places of the field. Formalism, externalism, and traditionalism were the conspicuous features of the national religion. Genuine trust in God, inward delight in his law, joyous contemplation of his works, and patient hope in the fulfilment of his promises were hardly known. Puffed up with pride in the view of the past, men believed themselves, quite apart from their character, to be the favourites of Heaven; and that the Messiah for whom they looked was one who would "restore again the kingdom to Israel," and would make the name of Israel to be honoured more profoundly and more widely than it had been even in the days of David and of Solomon.

Ministry of John.—While the Redeemer himself was quietly preparing at Nazareth for his great work, his forerunner, John the Baptist, was acquiring fitness for his office near the opposite extremity of the land. Being a priest, John would in all likelihood receive the high education which the priests usually got, embracing a very thorough training in the Law and the Prophets. Probably it was as he approached the age of thirty (when the education of a priest was completed) that, waxing strong in spirit, he retired into the deserts, and remained there till his public ministry began. This was not a very unusual course in those times. Many pious persons, as we learn from Josephus, disgusted with the corruptions and the worldly spirit of the times, retired into wilderness spots, and taught and trained followers in accordance with their own religious views. Josephus himself, "on hearing of one named Banus, who spent his life in the desert, wearing such clothing as might be had from trees, eating the food which the ground spontaneously supplied, and using frequent ablutions of cold water by day and night, for purposes of purification, took him as his exemplar; and having continued with him three years, and attained his object, returned to the city." At first the haunts of John would be those desert wilds, east of Hebron and adjacent to the shores of the Dead Sea, where David hid from Saul; and in these spots, we may believe, he would ponder the Psalms very deeply, especially those in which the Messiah and his kingdom are the subjects of the song. But when he began to preach, and especially to baptize, he would find it necessary to leave that "dry and thirsty land, wherein was no water," and advance toward the shores of the Jordan.

Baptism of Jesus.—John represented and embodied the spirit of the Law and the Prophets. That holy reverence for God, which was the great characteristic of the piety of the patriarchs and the other Hebrew worthies, raised John the Baptist far above the ordinary fears and frailties of humanity. His heart was profoundly stirred by the prevailing sins of the day. It was awful to him to think of the way in which God's authority was trampled under foot; and with a heart that neither feared nor faltered, he rebuked the manifold wickedness that prevailed. He summoned all men to repent, especially on the ground that the kingdom of heaven was at hand; and he baptized those who believed his message, and who showed signs of repentance and desire for forgiveness of sin. From the very first he declared that he was not the Christ, but that the Christ had come; and that his glory was so surpassing, that the Baptist was not worthy to loose the latchet of his shoe. Immense crowds flocked to hear him, and the sensation produced was quite remarkable. The people exhibited once more that readiness to be borne along, for a short time, by a great wave of religious enthusiasm, which had characterized them in the times of David, Solomon, and Hezekiah. After a time Jesus himself, crossing probably from Nazareth by the plain of Esdraelon, and going down to the Jordan, reached the station of the Baptist, and presented himself for baptism. The Baptist hesitated, under a sense of unworthiness; but Jesus pressed his request, and was baptized. Immediately the heavens were opened; the Holy Ghost descended like a dove, and rested on Jesus; and a voice from heaven proclaimed, "This is my beloved Son, in whom I am well pleased." After a time Jesus seems to have returned to John, who bore testimony to him as "the Lamb of God that taketh away the sin of the world." In these beautiful words John showed that he had attained a clear knowledge of Christ's work as the sin-bearer, the atoning Saviour, such as few even of the pious then possessed.

Herod Antipas: Death of John.— The career of this noble and fearless man was cut short, twelve or eighteen months later, by Herod Antipas, the tetrarch of Galilee. John had incurred Herod's displeasure by an act of noble faithfulness. Nothing was more common in those times than for princes to take other men's wives and to divorce their own, just as the fancy struck them. Augustus Cæsar had done that, and had even compelled others to do so. The horrid practice would naturally descend, in a looser form, to the lower ranks of society, spreading pollution and disorder, and corrupting society at the fountain-head. With his usual boldness, John attacked the vice in the person of its highest representative in the land. Herod had taken Herodias, his brother Philip's wife, and John declared to him that it was a sin. For this he was cast into prison; and when the daughter of Herodias pleased him at a dancing-feast, and got leave to ask what she chose, her request was for the head of John the Baptist. The king, though sorry, had not courage to resist the horrid demand. The holy man's head was given to the abandoned girl, in whom, as in her mother, those gentle and modest feelings which are the real ornament of the female sex had been completely extinguished. It has been supposed that John was imprisoned at Machaerus, on the east side of the Jordan. Canon Tristram found remains of what seemed to him to have been the prison, and a dungeon, perhaps that in which John was confined.* Herod did not long enjoy the power which he had abused so greatly. His troubles originated in this very alliance with Herodias. His former wife, a daughter of Aretas, king of Arabia, disgusted with his proceedings, fled to her father, who invaded Herod's kingdom and defeated him. Afterwards

* Tristram's Land of Moab.

Herod fell into disgrace at Rome, and was banished to Spain, where, with his family, he died in misery.

Temptation of Jesus.—Shortly after his baptism, Jesus was led up by the spirit into the wilderness, where he underwent his memorable temptation by the devil. Three times the enemy tried to turn him aside from the path of holy consecration and entire trust in his Father on which he had entered, tempting him,—first, to an act of self-indulgence, to turn the stones of the desert into bread; then to an act of self-display, to throw himself from a pinnacle of the temple; and, lastly, to an act of unholy self-aggrandizement, to do homage to him as lord of the world, and receive the whole from him. To all these temptations Jesus made a resolute resistance, replying in each case by words quoted from the Word of God. From the use of the expression "led *up*," and from the wilderness in question being called emphatically "*the* wilderness," it is likely that the scene of the temptation was that wild desert tract up from the Jordan, lying between Jerusalem and Jericho, usually called at Jerusalem "the wilderness,"—the scene of the parable of the good Samaritan. A hill in the neighbourhood of Jericho, named, from the forty days' fast, Quarantania, is pointed out by tradition as the scene of the temptation; and its peculiarly bleak, wild, and sterile character answers to the supposition.

End of His Private Life.—After the temptation, returning to the scene of John's baptism, Jesus attached to himself Andrew and John, Simon, Philip, and Nathanael, as disciples. These brethren, from listening to the gracious words of Jesus, seem to have obtained a spiritual view of him as the Son of God and the Saviour of men. "They beheld his glory, the glory as of the only begotten of the Father, full of grace and truth." It was some time afterwards that they were called to be apostles. The transition point of our Lord's passage from private to public life was at Cana of Galilee, where, at a marriage-feast, he performed his first miracle, by turning water into wine. By this he seemed to foreshadow the tendency of his gospel to sweeten the common enjoyments of life, especially in connection with the family, making common things yield all that is really good in the greatest luxuries. He showed that he was to be regarded thenceforth, not as the son of Mary, but as the public servant of God, by saying to her, when she would have used her motherly influence in the matter, "Woman, what have I to do with thee? mine hour is not yet come." It was as the Anointed One of God that he was thenceforward to be known.

SECTION III.—EARLIER PART OF OUR LORD'S MINISTRY.

Ministry in Judæa: purging the temple—Nicodemus—The woman of Samaria—Galilee: Capernaum: visit to Nazareth—The lake of Galilee: accounts of travellers—Plain of Gennesaret—Cities—Fishing—Scene of rest in the surrounding mountains—Appointment of twelve apostles.

Ministry in Judæa: Purging the Temple.—The first period of our Lord's ministry was spent chiefly in Judæa. The records of this portion of it are very scanty, and all that we know of it is from the narrative of John. His first recorded act after returning from Cana was to drive the traders out of the temple, and to protest against his Father's house being made a house of merchandise. If the miracle at Cana foreshadowed the purifying and elevating of family life which he was to achieve, the cleansing of the temple foreshadowed the purifying and elevating of the quality of worship, and the securing for God a profounder reverence than he was then receiving.

Nicodemus.—Next came his conversation with Nicodemus. Here he dealt with an individual soul. The purification and salvation of men's souls was now his theme: "Except a man be born again, he cannot see the kingdom of God." The divine provision for saving men from ruin was unfolded, under the emblem of Moses lifting up the serpent in the wilderness. How long this Judæan period of Christ's ministry lasted, and what were its effects, we are not informed.

The Woman of Samaria.—The next thing recorded of him is his journey to Galilee and conversation with the woman at Jacob's well. Here again he dealt with an individual soul, and here again he showed the necessity of divine purification and salvation. In the case of Nicodemus he dealt with a respectable and outwardly religious man; in the case of the Samaritan woman, with a disreputable and openly guilty woman. For both he had a gospel. To the woman he spoke of salvation under the figure of water, as offered with the greatest freeness: "If thou knewest the gift of God, and who it is that saith to thee, Give me to drink; thou wouldest have asked of him, and he would have given thee living water."

Galilee: Capernaum: Visit to Nazareth.—The next and the longer part of our Lord's ministry was exercised in Galilee. At an early period he removed from Nazareth as his stated place of abode, and made Capernaum, on the lake of Galilee, his head-quarters. It is not easy to identify the site of Capernaum, but undoubtedly it was situated in the plain at the north-west shore of the lake. It was a place very different from Nazareth, with more of the bustle and animation of active life. We read of at least one visit which our Lord paid to Nazareth after he had ceased to reside there. Entering the synagogue on the Sabbath day, he read from the sixty-first chapter of Isaiah, and proclaimed the spiritual blessings of his kingdom. But the Nazarenes had no taste for spiritual things, and would much rather have seen some display of supernatural power. By refusing to give this, Jesus offended them; and their passions were so roused that they took him to the brow of the hill on which the city was built, and would have thrown him down had he not miraculously escaped from them. After this, Capernaum became more emphatically "his own city;" and the waters of the lake were the familiar object with which his home, so far as he had a home, was identified.

The Lake of Galilee: Accounts of Travellers.—It is remarkable how widely travellers have differed in their accounts of the lake. In Dr. Clarke's view, it is longer and finer than any of the lakes of Cumberland and Westmoreland, and only inferior to Loch Lomond in Scotland. Dr. Robinson confesses that even the moderate expectations he had formed of its romantic beauty were disappointed. Dean Stanley does not undertake to pronounce on the question of its beauty, but dwells upon its peculiar features. In size, he says,* the lake is about thirteen miles long by six broad; but in the clearness of the Eastern atmosphere it looks smaller. What makes it unlike English lakes is its deep depression, which gives it something of the strange, unnatural character that belongs to the Dead Sea. On the east side the hills are flat, but on the north and west more varied and picturesque. Descending through the rocky walls which encompass it, the traveller meets with the thorn-tree and the palm, and other products of a tropical climate. Near the south, the steaming waters at the baths of Tiberias indicate that the volcanic agency, which in former times left such an impression on the whole district, is still at work. A strip of level sandy beach surrounds the lake, from which the hills ascend, usually in gentle grassy slopes, broken by abrupt precipitous cliffs, the bright oleander and other plants often forming a pleasant fringe along the shore. On the western side, an abundant supply of springs gives birth to a verdure and fertility not found on the eastern.

Plain of Gennesaret.—At one part of the shore, at the north-west corner, the mountains recede, leaving a level, well-watered, fertile plain, two miles wide, and three or four miles long. This plain is the "land of Gennesaret," so closely identified with Christ's teaching and labours. Four springs pour their streams through it; magnificent corn-fields show the riches of the soil; along the shore a thick jungle of thorn and oleander affords a home to a multitude of birds; and the appearance of the whole gives a vivid conception of what the vale of Siddim must have been in the days of Lot—"well watered everywhere, before the Lord destroyed Sodom and Gomorrah, even as the garden of the Lord, like the land of Egypt."

Cities.—In the days of our Lord the north-west shore of the lake was crowded with cities and villages. Here stood Capernaum and Chorazin, one of the Bethsaidas, Magdala, and many other places, the very sites of which can hardly be distinguished. Besides land occupations, fishing was prosecuted near Caper-

* See Sinai and Palestine, p. 369, *et seq.*

naum with the greatest activity. "Two of the villages on the lake (the western and the eastern Bethsaida,—'house of fish') derived their name from the fisheries; and all of them sent forth their fishermen by hundreds over the lake; and when we add the crowd of ship-builders, the many boats of traffic, pleasure, and passage, we see that the whole basin must have been a focus of life and energy,—the surface of the lake constantly dotted with the white sails of vessels flying before the mountain-gusts, as the beach sparkled with the houses and palaces, the synagogues and the temples of the Jewish or Roman inhabitants."* It must have been an amazing contrast to the present deserted condition of the lake, on the waters of which, in Dr. Robinson's time, *a single boat* was all that floated!

Fishing.—It was a sort of "manufacturing district" for Galilee,—a busy, active, bustling place. "Traders and travellers from all quarters frequented it, by whom the fame of Jesus would be quickly carried all the country round; while men and women of all classes and characters might readily be met with. Here were many 'weary and heavy laden,' toiling in that tropical clime under exhausting burdens; publicans sitting by the water-side at the receipt of custom; Roman soldiers with their slaves guarding the palace, or protecting the interests of Herod; 'women who were sinners,' attracted by the wealth or the licentiousness of the inhabitants; and hardy boatmen, filled with the faithful and grateful spirit by which that peasantry was always distinguished, who would supply the energy and docility which Christ needed for his followers. The copious fisheries of the lake now assumed a new interest. The two boats by the beach; Simon and Andrew casting their nets into the water; James and John on the shore washing and mending their nets; the toiling all the night and catching nothing; the great multitude of fishes, so that the net brake; Philip, Andrew, and Simon, from Bethsaida, 'the house of fisheries;' the casting a hook for the first fish that cometh up; the net cast into the sea and gathering of every kind;—all these are images that could occur nowhere else in Palestine but in this

---

* Stanley, p. 375.

one spot, and which from that one spot have now passed into the religious language of the civilized world; and in their remotest applications, or even misapplications, have converted the nations, and shaken the thrones of Europe." *

Scene of Rest in the Surrounding Mountains. — While Jesus was toiling amid this teeming population, with a keen sense of its spiritual miseries, he could not obtain necessary rest or retirement, except by quitting the locality and getting into quite another scene. The mountains around the Lake of Gennesaret, especially those to the east, afforded suitable and easily reached places of repose. He had but to retire a few miles from the shore, or to cross to the hills on the other side of the lake, to find a region as still and solitary as his usual residence was active and bustling. Hence the references to "the mountains," where he spent nights in prayer; and to the "desert places," where he called his disciples to rest, on the other side of the lake. An hour's walk or sail would at any time transport him from the bustle and strife of the streets of Capernaum to the stillest wilds of the desert.

Appointment of Twelve Apostles. — In entering on his ministry, Jesus took a remarkable method for increasing his influence and carrying on his work after he himself should have passed away. He instituted the college of apostles. After a night spent in prayer, he called twelve of his disciples and solemnly set them apart to be his ministers. They were mostly of the poorer class, honest and earnest, but ignorant and often wayward. Of the twelve, three were his especial attendants—Peter, James, and John. They followed him steadfastly throughout his ministry, and evidently grew in their reverence and attachment towards him. But there was one grievous exception to their fidelity—the traitor Judas Iscariot, whose earthly soul never rose to the heights to which Jesus sought to bear them all.

* Stanley, p. 377.

SECTION IV.—MIDDLE AND LATER PARTS OF OUR LORD'S MINISTRY.

Scenes of Christ's ministry: the sermon on the mount—Its imagery—Parables—"The sower"—Associations with the lake and the plain of Gennesaret—Tyre and Sidon—Cæsarea Philippi—The transfiguration: Mount Hermon—Visits to Samaria—Christ at Jacob's Well—His feeling toward the Samaritans—His imagery in the south—At Jerusalem: the family of Bethany.

Scenes of Christ's Ministry: the Sermon on the Mount.—The chief scene of our Lord's ministry was Galilee; but other districts received their share of attention. In Galilee his ministry was soon attended by multitudes. On a memorable occasion, seeing the multitudes, he went up into a mountain, and delivered the longest of all his published discourses. The mountain can hardly be identified; what is commonly called the Mountain of Beatitudes is a square hill, in the plain of Hattin, not above sixty feet high, with two summits and a platform between. This sermon was not an exhaustive proclamation of his gospel, but was rather a preparation for it. It unfolded in successive parts the character of his kingdom—its rules—its service—its spirit—its fruits or results. It abounded in gracious views for those who desired a blessing; and the very first words, "Blessed are the poor in spirit, for theirs is the kingdom of heaven," indicated clearly what a rich and glorious provision of divine blessing there was now for all who had the humility that feels and acknowledges its need. It set forth beautifully the fatherly character of God, while it showed the spirituality and searching reach of the divine law, and the impossibility of the transgressor escaping its penalty. In that earliest of his more important discourses, our Lord asserted for himself the prerogatives of Supreme Judge—"Many will say to me in that day, Lord, Lord, have we not prophesied in thy name?" It is, therefore, not correct to say that he set out merely as a moral reformer, and that it was afterwards that he assumed the position of the promised Messiah and the Son of God.

Its Imagery.—The objects of nature in the scenery around were such as to supply our Lord with many of the illustrations of the sermon. The tulips and anemones on the plain below suggested the image of "the lilies of the field;" the numerous birds, in their bright and varied plumage, fluttering over the thickets near the lake, that of the "fowls of the air;" the fields, the rocks, the sea, and the desert, had all their part in the appeal,—"What man is there of you, whom if his son ask bread, will he give him a stone? or if he ask a fish, will he give him a serpent?" Perhaps the great crowded highway passing between the cities, contrasted with some lonely mountain path, suggested the image of the broad way and the narrow way; while some stable edifice built on a rock, and some slender shed by the sandy bed of a winter torrent, may have furnished the closing image of the wise and the foolish builders.

Parables.—Of all Christ's methods of teaching, that of the parable was the most characteristic. It was an eminently Oriental method, for Christ was a thoroughly Oriental teacher. Occasionally used before, it came to perfection in Christ's hands, and it is remarkable that it was hardly ever employed by the apostles. It both culminated and terminated with Christ. Forty-seven parables are contained in the list of Christ's discourses, partly veiling and partly revealing the truth. The parabolic form was adopted to stimulate inquiry, and thus reward all who sought for truth as for hidden treasure.

"**The Sower.**"—Of the parables that derive vividness from the neighbouring scenery, that of the sower is especially remarkable. "A slight recess in the hill-side, close upon the plain [of Gennesaret], disclosed at once," says Dean Stanley, "every feature of the great parable. There was the undulating corn-field descending to the water's edge. There was the trodden pathway running through the midst of it, with no fence or edge to prevent the seed from falling here and there on either side of it, or upon it; itself hard with the constant tramp of horse, and mule, and human feet. There was the good rich soil, which distinguishes the whole of that plain and its neighbourhood from the bare hills elsewhere descending into the lake, and which, where there is no interruption, produces one vast mass of corn. There was the rocky ground of the hill-side protruding here and there through the corn fields, and elsewhere through the grassy slopes. There were the large bushes of thorn—the 'nabk,' that kind of which tradition says that the crown of thorns was woven—springing up, like the fruit trees of the more inland parts, in the very midst of the waving wheat."*

Associations with the Lake and the Plain of Gennesaret.—What precious words of instruction, what deeds of mercy and love, what glorious visions of the kingdom of heaven, are connected with this lake and that little plain! And what blessed effects may not the remembrance of the words spoken and the deeds done here have on our hearts, if we drink in the spirit of them! How many unbelieving thoughts may they rebuke, and how many distressing feelings may they remove! Are we burdened by the sense of guilt? Here stood the house through whose roof the paralytic was let down, and where the words were spoken, "Son, be of good cheer; thy sins be forgiven thee." Are we oppressed by the sense of inward disease and corruption? On yonder strand stood the Roman custom-house, where, at a feast to publicans and sinners, Jesus said, "They that are whole need not a physician, but they that are sick; I came not to call the righteous, but sinners to repentance." Are we struggling with special temptations of the devil, or with special infirmities of the spirit? It was amid these scenes that Jesus rebuked the unclean spirit in the synagogue of Capernaum,— "Hold thy peace, and come out of him;" it was here that he healed the blind and cleansed the leper; it was on yonder shore of Gadara, where the green slopes and rocky cliffs descend to the sea, and the tombs are seen hewn out of the rock at the mouth of the ravine, that the whole legion of devils, driven out of the wretched demoniac, rushed into the herd of swine; it was in this plain that the woman with the issue of blood pressed through the crowd to touch the hem of his garment, and received at last the cheering assurance, "Daughter, be of good comfort; thy faith hath made thee whole." Are we bowed down in spirit by a mingled burden of care and sin and sorrow? It

* Sinai and Palestine, pp. 425, 426.

was on these shores that the words were spoken, "Come unto me, all ye that labour and are heavy laden, and I will give you rest." Do our faithless hearts ever alarm us lest we be abandoned to want? It was in yonder desert place that the five loaves and two fishes furnished a meal for five thousand. Does it ever seem as if our Master had forgotten us, and adverse winds were about to dash us to ruin? It was over the bosom of that lake that the wild storm swept which made the disciples cry to the sleeping Jesus, "Master, carest thou not that we perish?" Then he arose, and rebuked the winds and the waves, and there was a great calm. Do we sometimes turn cold in our love to him, and languid in our service? It was on yon glistening shingle that the risen Saviour appeared to his disciples; there he addressed to Peter the searching question, "Lovest thou me?" and there, too, he gave the command, "Follow thou me." "Yes, thou lovely Lake of Galilee, though thy mountains are now barren, thy cities and villages in ruins, and thy fields and gardens desolate,—though the fishermen have disappeared from thy waters, and the inhabitants fled from thy shores, yet these naked and scorched mountains, these solitary ruins, these waste fields, and that deserted sheet of water, all speak of peace to the weary traveller. Whatever changes time has here produced, Jesus is ever the same; and we may be filled with joy and peace in believing, when every object on which the eye can rest brings to our remembrance the love and compassion of Jesus. 'Peace be unto thee,' 'Depart in peace,' are the sounds borne upon the breeze around the Sea of Galilee. 'Yes,' responds the soul, 'for He is my peace.'"*

Tyre and Sidon.—The district of Galilee was very populous. According to Josephus it contained two hundred and four towns and villages. Our Lord appears to have traversed the district several times, teaching in the synagogues, and healing all manner of disease. Besides this, he made some excursions to more distant places. On one of these occasions, deeming it prudent, perhaps, to get beyond the jurisdiction of Herod, he came to the district of Phœnicia, "the coasts of Tyre and Sidon." Notwith-

* Van de Velde's Syria and Palestine, ii. 392.

standing all the changes that had passed over it, Tyre was still a strong citadel and a flourishing port; eclipsed partly by the Greek mercantile cities, but still carrying on much of that busy traffic which, in the days of the prophets, had made its merchants princes and its traffickers the honourable of the earth. Respecting Christ's emotions in connection with this remarkable country, we have but a single hint. He seems to have found a greater susceptibility to right impressions among the people there than in his own country; so that, when he reproved Chorazin and Bethsaida for their impenitence, he added the remarkable testimony, "If the mighty works which were done in you had been done in Tyre and Sidon, they would have repented long ago in sackcloth and ashes."* The only incident recorded in connection with Christ's visit to this place, is the cure of the daughter of the Syro-phœnician woman. He tried her faith and perseverance by discouraging answers, reminding her that she was not of the house of Israel, and that it was not meet to take the children's bread and give it to the dogs. Her answers showed that with a deep sense of her own unworthiness she had the strongest faith in him. By his mercy to her he showed that even the once doomed and banned descendants of Canaan were not excluded from the sphere of his love and the reach of his blessings.

Cæsarea Philippi.—Another of Christ's more distant excursions was to the region of Cæsarea Philippi, near the sources of the Jordan. This Cæsarea had formerly been called Paneas; it had just been repaired by the tetrarch Philip, and named Cæsarea after the emperor, Tiberius Cæsar, and Philippi after himself. It was situated at the foot of Mount Hermon, at the entrance to the noble valley between the ridges of Lebanon and Anti-Lebanon. It was but a few miles from Dan, the most northerly city of Palestine in former times, and the shrine of one of Jeroboam's idolatrous calves. When the Macedonians obtained possession of the country, they built at this place a shrine for

---

* This saying is recorded in Matt. xi 21, and the visit to Tyre and Sidon in Matt. xv. 21; but it is generally understood that Matthew arranges his narrative more by *subjects* and *places* than by *chronology*; so that the visit *may* have occurred previous to the rebuke.

Pan, the god of shepherds; whence the old name of the place, Paneas, and the present one, Banias, have come. In a precipitous face of the rock is a large dim grotto, with a niche, empty now, but formerly containing the statue of Pan; and with other niches, which were the shrines of the nymphs. To this spot, where the Jordan flows out from the rock, Jesus, perhaps, would go; and there he might see the niches, and the inscriptions showing in whose honour they had been made. It has been thought by some that it was the twofold association of this place with heathenism—with Jeroboam's Egyptian calf and with the Greek shrine of Pan—that led Christ to take the opportunity of speaking privately to his followers of his Messiahship and of his approaching kingdom; for it was here that he asked them, "Whom do men say that I, the Son of man, am?" A place associated with so much misleading error was now to be associated with a great saving truth. It was here that he commended Peter for his bold and frank confession, "Thou art the Christ, the Son of the living God." It was here, too, that he began to show them how he must go to Jerusalem, and be killed, and be raised again, and thus become the fountain of a river of life, the streams of which, flowing far wider than Jordan, would spread salvation and beauty over every country of the globe. It is interesting, in this connection, to recall the old legend,—"that when the heavenly host told the shepherds of Bethlehem of the birth of Christ, a deep groan, heard through all the isles of Greece, told that the great Pan was dead, and that all the royalty of Olympus was dethroned, and the several deities were sent wandering in cold and darkness."

The Transfiguration: Mount Hermon.—It seems to have been during this visit to Cæsarea Philippi that the transfiguration took place. And certainly Mount Hermon is more likely to have been the scene of that wonderful event than the humble eminence of Mount Tabor. "It is impossible to look up from the plain to the towering peaks of Hermon, almost the only mountain which deserves the name in Palestine, and not be struck with its appropriateness to the scene. That magnificent height, mingling with all the views of Palestine from Shechem

upwards, though often alluded to as the northern barrier of the
Holy Land, is connected with no historical event in either the
Old or the New Testament. Yet this fact of its rising high above
all the other hills of Palestine, and of its setting the last limit to
the wanderings of Him who was sent only to the lost sheep of the
house of Israel, falls in with the supposition which the words
inevitably force on us. High up on its southern slopes there
must be many a spot where the disciples could be taken apart
by themselves. Even the incidental comparison of the celestial
splendour with the snow, where alone it could be seen in Palestine, should not, perhaps, be wholly overlooked. At any rate,
the remote heights above the sources of the Jordan witnessed
the moment when, his work in his own peculiar sphere being
ended, he set his face for the last time to go up to Jerusalem."*

Visits to Samaria.—During our Lord's residence at Capernaum, besides itinerating several times over Galilee, and making
occasional excursions to more distant places, such as Sidon and
Cæsarea, he went up year by year to Jerusalem, to attend the
festivals. Both in going and in returning, "he must needs
pass through Samaria," except when he preferred the route
through the plain of Jordan, when Jericho would lie in his way.
The most memorable occasion of his passing through Samaria
was early in his ministry, as we have seen, when he met with
the woman at Jacob's well, near Sychar—the ancient Shechem.
The brief reference in the Gospel to the woman's astonishment
at a Jew talking kindly to a Samaritan, throws a clear but sad
light on the state of feeling that prevailed between the inhabitants of the two districts. We have seen that from the earliest
times bitter jealousy towards Judah and every other tribe that
disputed its preëminence had characterized the tribe of Ephraim.
When Ephraim, or Samaria (as the district was afterwards
called), was depopulated by the king of Assyria, and a mongrel
race, with a worship half heathen, half Jewish, took the place
of the former inhabitants, we may believe that the feeling of
Judah towards them was not more friendly. The feeling of
the Samaritans was much exasperated when, after the Restora-

---

* Sinai and Palestine, pp. 399, 400

tion, leave was refused to them to join in building the temple at Jerusalem. And when a rival temple was built on Mount Gerizim, and a rival priesthood was set up under Manasseh, the spirit of mutual contempt and hatred reached the very climax of bitterness. Christ showed, very beautifully and nobly, how superior he was to those bitter jealousies, not only by speaking kindly to the woman of Samaria, but by offering to her, at once and freely, the richest blessings of salvation! He gave a silent but very powerful rebuke to that feeling which is so apt to be engendered by differences in race, or in rank, or in religion; and he set a fine example of the all-embracing Christian love which he so earnestly enjoined his followers to cherish.

Christ at Jacob's Well.—It would be interesting to picture the feelings of Christ as he sat at the well of Jacob, recalling, perhaps, the countless memories that two thousand years had hung around its neighbourhood. Abraham dwelling under the oak, and getting one of his first promises from the Lord, in yonder plain; Jacob forced to leave it broken-hearted, through the misconduct of his sons; Joseph, with his coat of many colours, coming unsuspectingly along the plain to look for his brethren, and never returning till his bones, carried up from Egypt, were buried in yonder field; Joshua assembling the people, first to hear the blessings and curses read out between these two hills, Ebal and Gerizim, and then to receive his last charge and blessing; the bold and bad Abimelech plotting the massacre of his brethren; the intrepid Jotham standing on yon hill-top, and in his parable of the trees giving the first example of that form of address which Jesus himself used so largely; Rehoboam coming here to be crowned, finding himself all but ruined through rash counsel and blustering words, and fleeing in terror to Jerusalem; the many wicked kings that had reigned here or in the neighbouring cities, and the many holy prophets whose words they had disregarded;—all these could hardly fail to be recalled to Christ's mind by the scenery of Sychar. His mind could not fail to be sent musing on the long period of preparation,—the two thousand years that had run on since Abraham, dwelling in this green vale, saw his day afar off, and was glad. But now, that preparatory period had come to a close, and the real business of harvest was begun. No further delay was to take place in the great work of gathering souls; hence the significance of his words to his disciples: "Say not ye, There are yet four months, and then cometh harvest? behold, I say unto you, Lift up your eyes, and look on the fields; for they are white already to harvest."

His Feeling toward the Samaritans.—Throughout his ministry, the Samaritans were evidently regarded by Christ with very different feelings from those cherished towards them by the Jews. On one occasion, when some of his disciples proposed to call down fire from heaven on a village of the Samaritans which had refused to receive them, he gave them an indignant rebuke, for not considering that the Son of man had come not to destroy men's lives, but to save them. On occasion of the cure of ten lepers, only one of the ten came back to thank him, and he was a Samaritan. The parable of the man who fell among thieves does honour to the Samaritans; and the term "good" will be associated with the name, as long as men speak of "the good Samaritan."

His Imagery in the South.—The imagery of our Lord's teaching in Galilee had been drawn mainly from fishing and corn fields; in Judæa and the neighbourhood of Jerusalem, vines and vineyards become the prominent figures. For still, as in the days of Isaiah, the "inhabitants of Jerusalem and the men of Judah," dwelling, as they did, "in a very fruitful hill," "binding their foal unto the vine and their ass's colt unto the choice vine," were most accessible to illustrations drawn from their staple employment. The parable of the labourers in the vineyard (Matt. xx. 1); that of the father and the two sons whom he sent to work in his vineyard (xxi. 28); that of the householder and the wicked husbandmen to whom he left his vineyard (xxi. 33); and that of the true vine (John xv. 1), were all spoken either at Jerusalem or in its neighbourhood.

At Jerusalem: the Family of Bethany.—During the earlier visits of Christ to Jerusalem, he held his memorable conversation with Nicodemus: he cured the impotent man at the pool of Bethesda, and performed other miracles on the Sabbath; thereby shocking the prejudices of the Pharisees, but vindicating the true character of the Sabbath as a day of blessing and privilege to man: he rescued and forgave the woman caught in adultery; welcomed publicans and sinners to salvation; and delivered the memorable parables of the lost sheep, the lost piece of silver, and the prodigal son. On occasion of his visits to Jerusalem, the loving heart of Jesus came to know, in all its depth of bitterness, the sensation of being hated, cursed, blasphemed. Each successive contest with the scribes and the Pharisees, ending, as it always did, in the triumph of Christ's superior meekness and wisdom, only added fuel to the fire of their jealousy. But now also, as he became familiar with the bitterness of human hatred, he came to know better the joys of holy human friendship. In the sequestered village of Bethany, an hour's walk from Jerusalem, Jesus had found a singularly congenial family. The holy fellowship enjoyed at night under their humble cottage-roof served to alleviate the pain arising from the conflicts of the day. Of the two sisters, Mary, who sat at Jesus' feet, has ever since been the type of the contemplative believer; and Martha, who made a feast and was cumbered with much serving, of the active disciple. It was not less as an enduring monument to the congenial spirit of that family than as a proof of his own power, that Jesus, on one of his later visits, performed the stupendous miracle of raising their brother Lazarus from the dead. This glorious display of power and love only aroused the hatred of his enemies, and led to plots being made for his death.

SECTION V.—CLOSING SCENES OF CHRIST'S LIFE AND MINISTRY.

Peræa—Banks of the Jordan; Jericho—Bethany—Jerusalem—Recollections and anticipations—Mount of Olives—Garden of Gethsemane—Christ's teaching and work—Betrayal; Peter's denial—Trial—Golgotha; death; burial—Resurrection; ascension.

Peræa.—On occasion of the last visit our Lord paid to Jerusalem before his death, he travelled by Jericho (Luke xviii.

31, 35). He had left Galilee a short time before, and spent the interval in Peræa, on the opposite side of the Jordan. Close to this neighbourhood, on the dark mountain-wall of Moab, was the height on which Moses yielded his spirit into the hands of God, and also the spot where the chariot of fire and horses of fire came for Elijah. Under the thoughts of his own coming death-struggle, it would soothe Jesus to remember the words and tones in which these two prophets, a short time before, on the mountain of transfiguration, had prepared his mind for the decease which he was about to accomplish at Jerusalem.

Banks of the Jordan : Jericho.—At last, the passover drawing nigh, he and his disciples recross the Jordan, near the place where Joshua—the Jesus of the Old Testament—and the host of Israel had crossed it, and come to Jericho with its palm groves and fountains. That enclosure contains the world-renowned balsam-trees which Antony had lately given to Cleopatra; there is the princely residence where Herod the Great died, while the wail of the Bethlehem mothers was yet resounding through the land; and yonder is the circus where he enclosed the nobles of Judæa, to make a royal mourning in honour of his death. The fame of Jesus has reached the place, and a great multitude has turned out to see him. Two blind men by the way-side have raised their imploring voices, obtained the much-sought boon of sight, and are now feasting their eyes on the glories of nature. Aloft, on the sycamore-tree, Zaccheus, the rich publican, has taken his place, forgetful of his dignity in his eagerness to get a glimpse of the great Galilæan,—little thinking how great a change his heart is to undergo, and how he is to give to Jesus a twofold welcome,—as a guest in his house, and as a Saviour in his heart.

Bethany.—Leaving Jericho, Jesus proceeds on his way, delivers to his audience the parable of the pounds, climbs up the steep mountain-pass, traverses the scene of the parable of the good Samaritan, and at last reaches the village of Bethany. It is a small hamlet lying in a rocky ravine at the eastern foot of the Mount of Olives, which at this point completely shuts out Jerusalem from view, and gives to the village an air of singular quietness and seclusion. Here, in the much-loved cottage of Lazarus and his sisters, he partakes of Martha's supper, is anointed with the precious ointment, and speaks ominously of his burial.

Jerusalem.—Proceeding next day to Jerusalem, he is met by the great crowd from the city that have heard of his arrival, and he rides in triumph over the palm-spread road. The path leads first up the eastern side of Olivet, then down to Jerusalem on the west. As it passes over the ridge, Jerusalem suddenly bursts on the view. Beholding the beloved city, the Saviour wept over it, and poured out his whole heart in the memorable lament: "If thou hadst known, even thou, at least in this thy day, the things which belong unto thy peace! but now they are hid from thine eyes."

Recollections and Anticipations.—Every traveller speaks of the view of Jerusalem from the Mount of Olives as singularly striking; even though the most prominent object now is the Mosque of Omar, which occupies the site of the ancient temple. The sudden mingling in Christ's mind of historic recollections and prophetic anticipations,—the thoughts of the past,—"this Mount Zion which God loved," and of which he said, "This is my rest, here will I dwell,"—the temple, recalling the glorious days of David and Solomon, of Josiah and Hezekiah, of Ezra and Nehemiah, and other devoted men,—these thoughts mingling with the prophetic view of Jerusalem's long desolation, guilt, and misery,—of fierce Roman assault and destruction, of Mohammedan insult and wrong, of proud error scorning truth, of wild bigotry outraging the name of religion,—filled his eyes with tears even in the midst of a triumphal procession. When he reached the city he could not refrain from giving one proof of his horror of that profanation which Jerusalem was to exemplify for ages: he entered the temple (as he had done once before) and drove from it the merchants that carried on their traffic in its very courts. A few days were then spent by him in teaching in the temple and in preaching the gospel. In the course of these, he answered the questions of the Pharisees and the Sadducees, denounced woes upon hypocrites, and foretold the destruction of Jerusalem and the end of the world. Probably at night it was his practice to return to Bethany. On one of these occasions, having gone into the house of Simon, who had once been a leper, he was anointed by a woman with precious ointment, as if in anticipation of his burial. Holy work and holy worship were his two great preparations for his approaching struggle.

Mount of Olives.—Of the localities in the immediate neighbourhood of Jerusalem specially consecrated by the footsteps of Jesus, the Mount of Olives and the Garden of Gethsemane hold a very distinguished place. The Mount of Olives is a long low ridge extending along the eastern side of the city, with three several summits, the highest only about 400 feet above the Valley of Jehoshaphat, although more than 2700 above the level of the Mediterranean. Its name was derived from the olive groves, that probably flourished at one time in much greater luxuriance than now; for it is only on one of the slopes that anything like an olive grove can now be seen, although the tree is still scattered over the hill in more or less abundance. Myrtle, pine, and palm trees seem also to have abounded in former days, but have now disappeared (Neh. viii. 14–16). The hill in our Lord's time must therefore have been more richly clothed with foliage, and better adapted for those calm exercises of soul for which Christ resorted to it.

Garden of Gethsemane.—At the opposite or Jerusalem foot of Olivet, close to the brook Kidron and the Valley of Jehoshaphat, lies the Garden of Gethsemane. It is a square of about one hundred and fifty feet. "When we saw it in May," says Lieutenant Lynch, "the trees were in full bloom; and altogether, the garden, in its aspects and associations, was better calculated than any place I know to soothe a troubled spirit. Eight venerable trees, isolated from the smaller and less imposing ones which skirt the pass of the Mount of Olives, form a consecrated grove. High above, on either hand, towers a mountain, with the deep yawning chasm of Jehoshaphat between them. Crowning one of them is Jerusalem, a living city: on the slope of the other is the great Jewish cemetery,—a city of the dead. Each tree in this grove, cankered and gnarled and furrowed by age, yet beautiful and impressive in its decay, is a living monument of the affecting scenes that have taken place beneath and around it. The olive perpetuates itself; and from the root of the dying parent stem the young tree springs into existence. These are accounted one thousand years old. Under those of the preceding growth, therefore, the Saviour was wont to rest; and one of the present may mark the very spot where he knelt, and prayed, and wept. No cavilling doubt can find entrance here. Here the Christian, forgetful of the present and absorbed in the past, can resign himself to sad yet soothing meditation. The few purple and crimson flowers growing about the roots of the trees will give ample food for contemplation,— emblems of the suffering and bloody death of the Redeemer."

Christ's Teaching and Work.—The Son of man had now all but accomplished the work given him to do. He had shown a spotless example of all excellence as a man,—and in that holy human life had exhibited the image of the invisible God. He had established his claims to Messiahship, had fulfilled Old Testament prophecies and types, wrought miracles, performed acts of beneficence, and uttered words of divine power and sweetness, that showed clearly that he was, in the peculiar sense in which he claimed to be, the Son of God. He had vindicated the Law and the Prophets from the perversions of the rabbins; had demonstrated that all true goodness must lie in the heart; had shown that a renewed will and a pure life are the only real evidence of a right state with God; and had denounced, in withering words that could never be forgotten, the hollow hypocrisy and pretentious formality of the leading religionists of the day. He had shown that a spiritual homage is the only acceptable worship of God; and had encouraged his followers to render that worship by revealing to them God's fatherly character and great love even for his lost and fallen children. While thus raising immensely the standard of holy living, he had revealed himself in his divine nature as the Life of men; and under such emblems as the Living Bread, the Living Water, and the True Vine, he had taught them where to find the inward strength required for their duty. In his conversation with Nicodemus, one of the earliest on record, he had unfolded the grand gospel doctrines—Ruin by sin, Regeneration by the Holy Spirit, and Reconciliation by the sacrifice of Himself,—"Except a man be born again, he cannot see the kingdom of God"—"As Moses lifted up the serpent in the wilderness, even so must the Son of man be lifted up: that whosoever believeth in him should not perish, but have eternal life." It now only remained, by his sacrifice on the cross, to complete that redemption which Messiah was to achieve; to grapple with the last enemy, and by conquering Death, to show clearly that he was, as he had said, "the Resurrection and the Life."

Betrayal: Peter's Denial.—It is the last evening of his mortal life. The Paschal Supper is over, the Egyptian deliverance is commemorated, and the Lord's Supper has been instituted to commemorate the higher deliverance from sin and death. The feet of the disciples have been washed; the traitor has gone out to join the high priest's band; the consolatory address has dropped like the honey-comb upon the disciples' hearts; and the incense of the intercessory prayer has filled heaven with its fragrance. Night has now fallen, and the Master and his little band seek quiet beyond the walls of the crowded city. They have passed the brook Kidron; eight of them linger in the valley, while Peter, James, and John accompany him to Gethsemane. In the course of the evening, once and again the thoughts of the Saviour must have been following Judas: he knows now that the traitor is at hand. The shadow of the hour and power of darkness falls upon him. Stretched on the hard ground, under the gnarled and twisted olives, the struggle of his great agony comes on. He who had so often said, "Fear not," now seems given up to fear. But at last tranquillity returns. And now the glare of torches is seen across the Kidron. Nearer, the din of rough voices is heard. With noisy progress they make straight for Gethsemane, for Judas knows the place. The traitor's kiss is given to the Saviour: he surrenders himself without resistance: his disciples flee: alone and helpless he goes back a prisoner to the city. He is conducted to the house of Annas, who sends him bound to Caiaphas. In his palace the rest of the night is spent. Peter and John are there; but the boldness that characterized Peter has forsaken him, and he denies his Master with oaths and curses. It is a night of weeping, and no joy cometh in the morning.

Trial.—Early next day the Sanhedrim assemble, with the chief priests and the scribes, and find Jesus guilty of a capital offence. But they have not the power of inflicting death, the Roman governor must therefore confirm their sentence; so they lead him to the Prætorium, or judgment-hall of Pilate. An unexpected obstacle to their scheme here presents itself. The unscrupulous Roman governor has become strangely scrupulous, and is most unwilling to condemn this extraordinary prisoner. As the day wears on, he occupies hour after hour in attempts to release him; for an impression has laid hold of him that this Jesus is not an ordinary criminal, and that to give him up to death would be an unpardonable crime. Anon he gets a message from his wife that she has had a dream about Jesus, and a warning to do nothing against him. Hearing that he is a Galilæan, Pilate sends him to Herod, who is at Jerusalem attending the feast; and Herod, after examining him, sends him back to the perplexed and hesitating Pilate. But at last a skilful appeal to the fears of the governor settles the question. He knows how precarious is his hold of office; and when the cry gets up, "If thou let this man go, thou art not Cæsar's friend," he has no longer courage to resist,—Jesus is delivered to be crucified, and is led away to Calvary.* The hour of retribution was not long in coming to Pilate; misfortunes thickened upon him, and at last he put an end to his own existence. There is an old tradition that his wife, Claudia Procula, became a Christian.

Golgotha : Death : Burial.—At Calvary, or rather Golgotha, the Roman punishment of crucifixion is inflicted on Jesus.

---

* Where Calvary was we cannot tell. It is nowhere said in Scripture to have been a mount, according to the popular impression; neither was the place known by that name—it is only the Latin translation of Golgotha, "the place of a skull." The most likely conjecture seems to be that of Lieutenant Conder, who places it to the north of the city, in a conspicuous position, close to the main northern road and to the ancient tombs.

The typical prophecy of the brazen serpent—"lifted up"—is fulfilled; as well as that of the paschal lamb—"a bone of him shall not be broken." Had the Jewish punishment of stoning been inflicted, such would not have been the case. Over his head the words JESUS OF NAZARETH, THE KING OF THE JEWS, are placed, in Hebrew, Greek, and Latin; for all the three languages are now spoken in Jerusalem. After hours of protracted misery, brightened, however, by the joys of a triumphant faith, the sufferings of Jesus come at last to an end. The Prince of Life bows his head and gives up the ghost. Joseph of Arimathea, a member of the Sanhedrim, goes to Pilate and begs the body; and Nicodemus brings a great load of myrrh and aloes, which he encloses in the linen cloth wrapped around the corpse. Not until it has been ascertained beyond question that he is dead is his body given up. As the hour of sunset, when the Jewish Sabbath commenced, is now drawing on, the body is hastily placed in Joseph's new tomb in the adjacent garden. And Jesus, having finished the great work of Redemption, rests in his grave till the morning of the third day.

Resurrection: Ascension.—Next day is the Sabbath. It brings no relief to the staggering faith of the disciples. Horror must have filled every heart when it was ascertained that their old comrade Judas, the traitor, had hanged himself. But the early light of the following morning shows the empty tomb of Jesus, and the Saviour reveals himself at various periods of the day to some of his apostles and followers. Notwithstanding what he had said about his resurrection, it is plain that they were not looking for it, their faith being but feeble. On the first day of the next week, still at Jerusalem, he shows himself to them again, rebukes Thomas, and removes his unbelief. A mountain in Galilee having been appointed as a place of meeting, the apostles return to their native province. First, on the shore of the lake so familiar to them all, Jesus joins the eleven, dines with them on part of the miraculous draught of fishes, and putting to Peter the threefold question, "Lovest thou me?" virtually reinstates him in his apostleship. Afterwards, on the appointed mountain, he shows himself to all his Galilæan disciples, upwards of five hundred in number. In Galilee he gives his last command: "Go ye and teach all nations, baptizing them in the name of the Father, and of the Son, and of the Holy Ghost." Last of all, Jesus again meets the eleven at Jerusalem; and when he had crossed the Mount of Olives for the last time, and had come to the well-known village of Bethany, "it came to pass, while he blessed them, he was parted from them, and carried up into heaven" (Luke xxiv. 51).

CHAPTER XVI.

APOSTOLIC HISTORY.

From A.D. [29 or] 33 to 100.

SECTION I.—THE CHURCH OF JERUSALEM.

Christ's ascension—Two streams of apostolic history—The day of Pentecost—The Jews in Jerusalem—Troubles and jealousies—Stephen—The gospel in Samaria—The Ethiopian eunuch—A new missionary.

Christ's Ascension.—The last meeting of Christ with his disciples was at Bethany. It was from amid the olive groves where he had walked with Lazarus, or near the cemetery where he had shown himself to be the Resurrection and the Life, that he was taken up, and hid by a cloud from their view. Since his resurrection, there had been so much of the supernatural about his movements, that the brethren seem not to have apprehended at once that he had left them, not to return. This announcement was made to them by two angels, who sent them to Jerusalem to prepare for their work, calling them by the almost reproachful name, "men of Galilee," to remind them that they had yet to earn their title to a more world-wide designation. They returned to Jerusalem, where they met with the converts belonging to the city and the district. The number of believers in Jerusalem was much smaller than in Galilee, where Jesus had spent the chief part of his public ministry. One hundred and twenty souls formed the entire assembly; and through the exercises of a humble prayer-meeting, after electing Matthias in the room of Judas, this feeble band prepared themselves for the conquest of the world. They continued with one accord in prayer and supplication, until the Spirit was poured upon them from on high.

Two Streams of Apostolic History.—The history of the Christian Church under the apostles runs in two streams,—the one Jewish, the other Gentile. The Jewish stream for the most part follows the track of the twelve apostles; the Gentile, mainly that of Paul. The earlier part of the Book of the Acts presents chiefly the one; the later, chiefly the other. Although there were some diversities between the two, it is evident that they held substantially the same truth —had "one faith, one hope, one baptism." Religion now becomes, much more prominently than before, a dispensation of the Holy Spirit. It is by a divine power sent from heaven,—by a baptism of the Holy Ghost,—that men are drawn to God. It had always been so, indeed, and the later prophets had dwelt much on this subject; but now the reality of spiritual agency becomes more obvious, and the third person of the Holy Trinity stands out more conspicuously before the Church, as the great agent in the conversion of men. The Acts of the Apostles has sometimes been called the "Gospel of the Holy Ghost."

The Day of Pentecost.—The first great ingathering of Jews into the Christian Church took place at the feast of Pentecost, fifty days after the crucifixion. The assemblage of Jews at Jerusalem, from different and distant countries, was very remarkable, though perhaps not unusual. Unable to pay due regard to the ordinances of Moses in the different countries of their dispersion, the Jews seem to have made very great efforts to come up to Jerusalem to the annual festivals. Probably it was thus that the foundation was laid of their wonderful commercial character; for on these occasions they could very easily obtain information, and negotiate transactions, relating to the produce of every country from Spain to India.

The Jews in Jerusalem.—The great body of the dispersed Jews had by this time ceased to use Hebrew as a spoken language, and had adopted the mother-tongues of the countries whither they had been scattered. Parthian Jews were at

Jerusalem, and Medes, Elamites, and Mesopotamians—representing the regions to which the kings of Assyria and Babylon had first carried them captive; Jews from Cappadocia, Pontus, Asia, Phrygia, and Pamphylia were there, whose fathers had been invited to settle in these provinces while most of them were independent kingdoms, or satrapies of Persia; Jews from Egypt, whither Alexander the Great had drawn them, and from Libya and Cyrene, in Africa, where they had been sent by Ptolemy Soter; Arabia had its representatives in the persons, perhaps, of high officers from the court of Yemen; Crete, too, sent its band, to do honour to the institutions of a wiser and more ancient law-giver than Minos; even Rome was not unrepresented, for the children of Abraham, or proselytes to their faith, had already their homes upon the seven hills that looked down on imperial Tiber. The conversion and baptism, in one day, of three thousand of this vast and varied multitude, furnished the first counterpart in the spiritual world to the miraculous draught of fishes in the natural. Arrangements were made, by means of a common fund, to keep the converts together for some time, that they might be instructed more fully in the doctrine and life of Christianity, and might receive more distinctly that stamp of purity and beauty which became the distinguishing mark of the primitive Church. After a short time of delightful Christian fellowship, this great army of converts separated, to tell to their countrymen and to the world at large how God had visited his people.

Troubles and Jealousies.—The Church at Jerusalem, under the charge of the apostles, grew in numbers and in moral beauty; and the humility, frankness, generosity, and love of its members, awakened general astonishment and admiration. God, by his providence, shielded it very wonderfully. On one occasion, when the influence of the high priest, who was a Sadducee, was likely to bear hard upon the apostles, the Sanhedrim were counselled to milder measures by Gamaliel, a Pharisee, president of the council, and therefore a sort of rival of the high priest. But the suppression of danger from without was followed by the occurrence of a slight disagreement within. A jealousy arose between the Hebrew and the Greek section of the Church; that is, between those who were natives of Judæa, or spoke the Aramean dialect, and those who were natives of countries of the dispersion that spoke Greek. The slight breach was healed through the appointment of an order of deacons, who were chiefly to attend to the temporal arrangements of the Church; and seven persons were chosen to it, all of whom had Greek names, and were therefore probably of the Greek section.

Stephen.—Foremost in this band was Stephen, who not only discharged the ordinary duties of the deaconship, but, "full of faith and power, did great wonders and miracles among the people." His zeal and great success roused much opposition. There were at that time in Jerusalem certain synagogues that had been founded by Jews of the dispersion, partly for their own benefit when they happened to visit Jerusalem, partly on account of their children when they sent them there to be educated. Members of some of these came forward to dispute with Stephen: probably because they alone were equally conversant with the Greek language, which he seems to have spoken. Among them was the synagogue of the Libertines, or Jews once Roman slaves, who had got their freedom; the synagogues of the Cyrenians and Alexandrians from Egypt; and what is not to be overlooked, the synagogue of Cilicia, one of whose most active members, doubtless, was the young Saul, a native of Tarsus, its capital city. Stephen was put on his defence, and delivered a speech before the Sanhedrim of great eloquence, boldness, and power. His hearers were so enraged at his bold invectives against them and their fathers, that, without a formal trial, they rushed upon him, dragged him out of the city, and stoned him to death, most probably in the Valley of Jehoshaphat. He died uttering a beautiful testimony to the exaltation and divinity of Jesus Christ, and exhibiting the triumph of Christian love and meekness, by praying for his murderers. Stephen seems to have been the morning star of the Church universal. His views of the institutions of Moses, and of the place of the Gentiles as equal to that of the Jews, were in advance of his day. It was reserved for Saul to take up his mantle, and to complete his work and testimony.

The Gospel in Samaria.—The death of Stephen was followed by a violent persecution of the Christians,—the murderous appetite of their foes having been whetted by the taste of the first martyr's blood. This persecution was overruled by the Head of the Church for the dispersion of some of its active members, who had hitherto clustered about Jerusalem. Among other places to which the light was thus carried, was a town which is called "a (not *the*) city of Samaria,"—precisely the same designation as that given to Shechem, or Sychar, in the fourth chapter of John. Very probably it was the city which had been so long celebrated in Jewish history, and whose inhabitants had first been told of Christ by the woman of Samaria. In the excited state of mind in which men then were, a designing man, named Simon, had got them to believe that he was a sort of incarnation of the power of God. Not only were the people freed through their Christian visitors from this wretched delusion, but an impression in favour of Christ appeared to be made on Simon's own mind; it was, however, only an appearance. The apostles were the only persons who had the power of conferring supernatural gifts; and when they went down to Samaria, and exercised these gifts, the hollowness of Simon's profession was shown by his proposing to buy them with his money.

The Ethiopian Eunuch.—The offer of the gospel to the Samaritans, for whom our Lord had shown so friendly a feeling, and their cordial acceptance of it, were designed to introduce a new era in the history of the Church. It was a sort of type of the reception of Gentiles and other outcasts; and it was followed by another occurrence tending in the same direction. Philip, probably one of the seven deacons, who had been the chief agent in the movement in Samaria, was directed by the Spirit to go down to Gaza, the deserted site of one of the old Philistine towns. A eunuch of Ethiopia, who held the high office of treasurer to Candace, queen of that country, had been attending one of the festivals at Jerusalem, and was returning by the ordinary road to his own country. Though an Ethiopian, or

Cushite, and therefore a descendant of Ham, he seems to have been a Jewish proselyte; and, like Ebed-melech, another Ethiopian eunuch, the friend of Jeremiah (ch. xxxix. 16), he was now about to reap the fulfilment of God's promise by Isaiah to the eunuch and the son of the stranger (ch. lvi. 4- 6). He had been at Jerusalem, the fountain-head of light, but had come away empty. Streams, however, sprang up to him in the desert of Gaza. Through the instructions of Philip, he became a believer in Christ, and was baptized; and he returned to his own country to make known the glad tidings that had cheered his own heart. This was another intimation that the door was about to be opened wide to the Gentiles; but, like the preceding one, the apostles were slow to understand it.

A New Missionary.—Meanwhile, the Head of the Church was preparing a new instrument—truly a polished shaft in his quiver—for evangelizing the Gentiles. The death of Stephen was in itself a great loss to the Church. He seems to have been a man of enlightened views and of catholic spirit,—far above ordinary jealousies and prejudices,—one who would have delighted to lead forth the Church to great catholic enterprises. Strange to tell, among the keenest of his murderers was a young man who was destined, in the wonderful counsel of God, to take up and prosecute the very task for which Stephen appeared to have been prepared. The prayers of Stephen obtained for the Gentile world an apostle still more highly gifted than himself; the mantle of the martyr fell on the young man who kept the clothes of his murderers; and the youthful and zealous pupil of Gamaliel was marked out for the task of preaching the gospel to every creature.

SECTION II.—EARLY LIFE OF PAUL.

Birth, at Tarsus—Education, at Jerusalem—Journey to Damascus: his conversion—Importance of the Event—Sojourn in Arabia- Return to Jerusalem: labours in Syria and Cilicia.

Birth, at Tarsus.—We know very little of the early life of the Apostle of the Gentiles. He was born at Tarsus, the capital of Cilicia, a province of Asia Minor, probably soon after the birth of Christ; for he speaks of himself as "Paul the aged" before his death, which took place about A.D. 68. His family was of the purest Hebrew stock, uncontaminated by the admixture of Gentile blood; and its name still stood on the public genealogies of Benjamin, although his father resided beyond the Land of the Covenant, and had obtained the privileges of a Roman citizen. Cilicia was a country of considerable importance, lying along the angle or corner of the Mediterranean, near where the range of Taurus, on the one hand, comes into contact with that of Lebanon on the other.* Its mountain wilds and its rocky creeks had long afforded shelter to robbers and pirates. More than half a century before the birth of Paul, Pompey had cleared it of these marauders, and had won the province for Rome; and one of its governors, the orator Cicero, had ruled it with more generosity and integrity than was usual in those stern and grasping Roman times. When Paul was born, Tarsus seems to have been essentially a Greek city, where the Greek language was spoken and Greek literature was cultivated. Probably Paul was equally accustomed to speak Greek and Hebrew. The one he would hear constantly in the educated circles of Tarsus; the other, sometimes, at least, in his father's house. He seems to have been brought up under the influence of the strongest feelings of admiration for his country and his nation;—hushed, as an infant, with the songs of Zion; impelled, as a boy, to noble deeds by the examples of Moses and David; and taught to regard Jerusalem and Judæa with feelings of profoundest veneration.

Education, at Jerusalem.—We cannot tell at what age he went to Jerusalem, to finish his education under Gamaliel; but we may readily fancy the intense delight with which he would examine all the famous localities both of Jerusalem and of its neighbourhood. In particular, we may fancy his interest in the celebrated localities of his own tribe;—Gibeah, where his namesake had his palace; Ramah, where Samuel judged Israel;

* See Conybeare and Howson on The Life and Epistles of St. Paul; also, The Life and Work of St. Paul, by Canon Farrar, D.D.

the passes where Joshua had beaten the confederate Amorites, Jonathan the Philistines, and Judas Maccabæus the Syrians. As a student under Gamaliel, Saul (his Latin name was Paul) seems to have greatly outstript his master in zeal and fiery ardour against the Christians. He took pleasure in persecuting them, and in forcing them to blaspheme the name of Jesus; and if his kindly nature was ever haunted by the cries of his victims, he would get rid of the pain by the feeling that he was doing God service.

Journey to Damascus: His Conversion.—Not content with carrying on his crusade in and near Jerusalem, he was willing to go to distant places to tear up the fast-spreading roots of the "heresy." In matters of religion the great Sanhedrim claimed over Jews in foreign countries the same power which they were still allowed to exercise at Jerusalem; so that it was enough for Saul to be armed with their authority. Damascus, the ancient capital of the first Syrian kingdom, had already been visited by the heralds of the Cross, and Saul obtained letters from the Sanhedrim, giving him authority to drag to Jerusalem any converts to the new heresy on whom he could lay hands. The Roman road to Damascus would carry Saul near the Lake of Galilee, and there he must have looked on some of the scenes that had been so familiar to the eyes of Him whom he was labouring to baffle and to destroy. His ears could not be altogether strangers to the fame of the mighty works that had been done there a few years before, though he would treat every such rumour as but an idle tale. But the Lake of Galilee is now left far behind; the weary Syrian desert is at last traversed; Saul and his companions have feasted their eyes on the white buildings of Damascus amid their groves of green—the "pearl gleaming in its emerald setting." Suddenly a great light shines from heaven, above the brightness of the sun. A voice speaks to Saul in the Hebrew tongue: only a few words are uttered; but they come home to him with such divine power that, in a more profound sense than the words were used of his namesake, he is changed into "another man." The persecutor rises from the ground an apostle; and all his energies are now consecrated to promote the cause which once he destroyed.

Importance of the Event.—The conversion of Paul was, in every view, a most memorable event. "It was like the call of a second Abraham." It manifested its reality from the very first in the memorable question put by Saul to Jesus, "Lord, what wilt thou have me to do?" Like the resurrection of Jesus, to which, indeed, it bore witness, it supplied an unanswerable evidence of the truth of Christianity; for what but the actual occurrence of the event narrated could have induced Paul to change so suddenly both his creed and his life? It furnished a remarkable proof of the boundless love and goodness of Him whose grace Paul was thereafter occupied in proclaiming. The mercy that had been shown in his own case to the chief of sinners was always a ready argument in his lips for any who were slow to believe the boundless grace of God in Christ. And the deep and tender sense of his obligations to Christ, and of Christ's most generous treatment of him, constantly supplied him with fresh motives to exertion, and drove away every feeling of weariness and discontent that might have stolen upon him under his unexampled hardships and sufferings in the service of his Lord.

Sojourn in Arabia.—Tradition still points out the street called Straight, and the house of Judas, where Paul lodged at Damascus; and it tells us that Ananias, who was sent to teach and to baptize him, was one of the seventy disciples sent out by our Lord, and became afterwards bishop of Damascus. But these are idle fancies. All that we know of Ananias is, that he was a disciple of Christ, "a devout man according to the law, having a good report of all that dwelt there." He was not an apostle, nor a presbyter, but only a disciple; yet he baptized the great founder of the Gentile Church. Paul remained for a short time in Damascus, zealously prosecuting Christian labours; but ere long he found it necessary to retire into Arabia. Whether his resort on this occasion was to the renowned Petra, and whether he thus became for a time one of the "dwellers in the rock;" or whether he advanced as far as to the Mount of God, and learned there to view Sinai and Zion, according to the view given in his Epistle to the Galatians, as types of the two covenants, we cannot tell. Ere long he returned to Damascus; but the Jews making a conspiracy against him, and getting the countenance of the governor, he had to be let down from the wall, and to make his escape by night.

Return to Jerusalem: Labours in Syria and Cilicia.— Retracing his former steps, he returned to Jerusalem, but with what different feelings from those with which he had left it three years before! His motive in visiting Jerusalem was to become acquainted with the apostles. At first he was received with coldness and suspicion; but the generous-minded Barnabas of Cyprus having warmly espoused his cause, he at last got the right hand of fellowship from the brethren. His zeal led him to preach Christ even in the synagogues of Jerusalem. But, as in Damascus, a conspiracy was formed against him. In a vision he was instructed by Christ, about the same time, to leave Jerusalem, and count the Gentile world his sphere of labour. His love for his countrymen was so warm, and his desire to repair his former mischief so intense, as to induce him to remonstrate and ask permission to remain. But the Lord would not yield. Accordingly he quitted the capital of Judaism, after but a fortnight's stay; and leaving Palestine by Cæsarea, he returned to Tarsus, and laboured for a time "in the regions of Syria and Cilicia."

SECTION III.—PREPARATIONS FOR CHURCH EXTENSION.

Peter's vision at Joppa—Cornelius's vision at Cæsarea—Political changes—Death of Herod Agrippa—Return of Claudius from Britain—Paul and Barnabas at Antioch: the name "Christian"—State of Antioch.

Peter's Vision at Joppa.—Meanwhile, other events were going on in Palestine designed to show more clearly how the Gentiles, as such, were to be welcomed into the Christian Church. In the course of his labours, Peter had gone down to Joppa, a very ancient sea-port on the Mediterranean.

It was, indeed, till the building of Cæsarea and Ptolemais, almost the only sea-port on the coast of Palestine. Peter had just performed his greatest miracle, by raising from the dead, in the person of Dorcas, one of the first yet ripest fruits of that loving spirit which the faith of Christ inspires. From the steep and rounded headland to which the city clings, the apostle, gazing over the blue reach of the Mediterranean, would enjoy at Joppa a wider and more varied view than the usually contracted landscape of Palestine affords. Whether this may have prepared his mind for a larger conception of the great object and sphere of the gospel, it would be difficult to tell; at all events, it was at Joppa that a vision was presented to him, intended to denote that the Gentiles, as such, were now to be freely admitted to the Church. Up to this time the universal feeling had been that they must first be circumcised—must first become Jews—before they could become Christians. Many Jewish Christians would rather have given up their lives than have questioned the binding authority of the law of Moses. The Church had to pass through a keen struggle before the door could be set open, without let or hindrance, to the Gentiles as such.

Cornelius's Vision at Cæsarea.—While Peter was thinking what this vision could mean, three men came in search of him from Cæsarea, bringing a message from Cornelius, a devout Roman officer in that city, who had been told in a vision to send for him in order to obtain Christian instruction. Setting out next morning, Peter and his companions travelled all that day over plains fragrant and beautiful with the rose of Sharon; and the next day after, the city of Herod greeted their eyes. It was a magnificent place—fresh, new, and thoroughly Roman. The very existence of such a city on Jewish soil seemed to proclaim that Judaism was gone. It was not in these purely Roman edifices that one could fight the battle of circumcision and other Hebrew rites. The Holy Ghost, falling in his supernatural gifts on the group of Gentile friends whom Cornelius had gathered to listen to Peter's discourse, confirmed the impression that had been gathering force in the apostle's mind. Peter threw aside all his prejudices; commanded the worthy friends of Cornelius to be baptized; ate with them freely, uncircumcised though they were; and when he returned to Jerusalem, vindicated his conduct, and silenced, at least for the time, those who were displeased with it. Tidings were received, about the same time, that in other places similar marks of true conversion had been shown by Gentiles; and it seemed as if the catholicity of the gospel dispensation were now in the way of being admitted by all.

Political Changes.—About ten years had now elapsed since the ascension of Christ. Various changes had occurred in the political world, in Judæa and elsewhere, at which we must now briefly glance. The emperor Tiberius was dead; the career of Caligula, with all its insane excesses of brutality and lust, had been ended by his murder, just as the Jews were in the midst of their consternation at his order to them to worship him as God. Claudius now wore the imperial purple. Caiaphas had been dismissed from the pontificate, and had been succeeded by Jonathan. Pontius Pilate, too, had been deposed from office, in consequence of a wholesale massacre of innocent Samaritans which he had caused on Mount Gerizim; and the vacant tetrarchies of Trachonitis and Abilene had been conferred by Caligula, with the title of king, upon his friend Herod Agrippa, the grandson of Herod the Great and son of the murdered Aristobulus. Soon after, Herod Antipas having been banished to Gaul, the tetrarchies of Galilee and Peræa were added to the dominions of king Agrippa. On the accession of Claudius, the Romans gave up to Agrippa Judæa, Samaria, and Idumæa, so that the whole kingdom of his grandfather was united under him.

Death of Herod Agrippa.—Agrippa had a great thirst for popularity, and to please the Jews he was induced to put to death the apostle James, and to order the execution of Peter. But the miraculous release of Peter from prison, in answer to the earnest prayers of the Church, defeated this part of his scheme. Not long afterwards, he appeared in great state in the theatre of Cæsarea, and made an oration to the people. At the close, while the sun was shining on his jewels and silver robe so as to give it a peculiarly brilliant appearance, his audience saluted him as a god. He received the impious flattery, but was immediately attacked by a horrible disease of the bowels, like that which had killed his grandfather. In a few days his career was run, and the loathsome carcass of the god was committed to the tomb. Palestine again became a Roman province, and was placed under a governor; but Agrippa, the son of the late king, ultimately obtained a part (though not this part) of his father's dominions, and when addressed subsequently by Paul, was saluted as king.

Return of Claudius from Britain.—It was in the year of Herod Agrippa's death that the emperor Claudius returned to Rome, after his expedition to Britain. He had crossed to its shores to complete the work which Julius Cæsar had begun a century before, and now he returned to enjoy his triumph. In the secret purposes of God, his expedition was designed to prepare the way for wafting to our distant shores those tidings which Paul at Tarsus and Peter at Joppa were now getting orders to spread to the ends of the earth. Little could Claudius have thought that, when the fierce Trinobantes and Iceni should become entitled to the name which people were then beginning to pronounce on the distant banks of the Orontes, the aspect of the island would undergo a change much more glorious than any which the arms, or laws, or institutions of Rome could ever have achieved!

Paul and Barnabas at Antioch: the name "Christian."— When word was brought to the apostles of the conversion of Gentiles in places so remote as Phœnicia, Cyprus, and Antioch, Barnabas, a man in whom fatherly kindness and a sound Christian judgment were finely blended, was sent to Antioch to instruct and guide the converts. It was he who had taken Paul by the hand at Jerusalem, when the other apostles were so cold to him; and now, remembering his excellent qualities, and how he had been especially called to labour among the Gentiles, he went to Tarsus to search for him; and when he had found him, he brought him to Antioch. Barnabas and he laboured for a year in that city; and it seems to have been during that year that the new and glorious name of CHRISTIANS was first given to the converts. At first, probably, it was applied in ridicule; for the people of Antioch were notorious for inventing names of derision. But no place could have been more suitable for giving birth to the name than Antioch, then the centre of the eastern part of the empire, and holding communication with the whole world. Its connection with Antioch seemed to give Christianity a metropolitan character, and to foreshadow its conquest of the world.

State of Antioch.—Mention has already been made of the founding of this Syrian Antioch by Seleucus, one of the successors of Alexander. He was the greatest city-builder of ancient times, and is said to have built no fewer than sixteen Antiochs, named after his father; six Laodiceas, after his mother; and nine Seleucias, after himself. When Paul visited Antioch, it was a great and wicked city. "Luxurious Romans were attracted by its beautiful climate......But for the most part, its population was a worthless rabble of Greeks and Orientals. The frivolous amusements of the theatre were the occupation of their life......It is probable that no populations have ever been more abandoned than those of Oriental Greek cities under the Roman empire; and of these cities Antioch was the greatest and the worst. If we wish to realize the appearance of the complicated heathenism of the first Christian century, we must endeavour to imagine the scene of that suburb, the famous Daphne, with its fountains and groves of bay-trees, its bright buildings, its crowds of licentious votaries, its statue of Apollo,—where, under the climate of Syria, and the wealthy patronage of Rome, all that was beautiful in nature and in art had created a sanctuary for a perpetual festival of vice."*

* Conybeare and Howson.

SECTION IV.—PAUL'S FIRST MISSIONARY TOUR.

Companions:—BARNABAS AND PARTLY (JOHN) MARK.

At Cyprus: Salamis and Paphos—Return of Mark: Perga: Antioch in Pisidia—Iconium: Derbe: Lystra, Paul stoned—Conversion of Timothy—Return to Pisidian Antioch—Synod of Jerusalem—Return to Syrian Antioch—Personal appearance of Paul and Peter—Paul's contention with Peter—Results of schism.

At Cyprus: Salamis and Paphos.—After labouring some time at Antioch, Paul and Barnabas were called by the Lord to missionary work in other districts, and were ordained for it by the prophets and teachers of the church of that place. Embarking at Seleucia, the sea-port of Antioch, they first proceeded to the island of Cyprus, the birth-place of Barnabas and a great resort of Jews. Originally peopled by Phœnicians, and latterly by Greeks, Cyprus was a sort of meeting-place for Greece and Asia, and its idolatrous worship combined some of the worst abominations of both. At the two extremities of the island, Salamis and Paphos, the gospel was preached; and at the latter place, Sergius Paulus, the Roman governor, became a convert. A Jewish sorcerer, named Bar-jesus, or in Greek, Elymas, made a determined effort to withstand the apostles, and prevent the conversion of the governor. The trade of sorcery was exceedingly common in those times, and the lower class of Jews, both men and women, were much addicted to it. It ministered to that eager desire to know the secrets of the future which is common to man, which was specially active in this age of general excitement and expectation, and which, now that the great heathen oracles were silent, had scarcely any other outlet. The fame of the Hebrew prophets gave Jews a preference in the practice of this art, as it was generally believed that they knew most of the future. The contest with this sorcerer was Paul's first great battle. Full of faith and power, he rebuked his countryman in language of startling vehemence, and brought temporary blindness upon him. The effect on the mind of the governor was favourable—he became a firm believer.

Return of Mark: Perga: Antioch in Pisidia.—Sailing from Cyprus, the apostles returned to the mainland, crossing the

Pamphylian gulf, and going first to Perga, the chief town of Pamphylia. Here Mark, who had accompanied them hitherto, frightened probably, in a moment of weak faith, when he learned that Paul and Barnabas meant to penetrate into the wilds of Pisidia, left them and returned to Jerusalem. At Perga they did not remain long, but climbing the mountain passes that separate Pamphylia from the elevated plain of Pisidia, reached Antioch. There is reason to believe that in this journey Paul became familiar with those "perils of robbers and perils of rivers" of which he afterwards wrote. The mountain passes were notorious for marauders, and the rivers were liable to be suddenly swollen by torrents, bursting out at the bases of huge cliffs, or dashing down wildly through narrow ravines. A great sensation was produced by Paul's first sermon in the Jewish synagogue at Antioch. The apostle offered the blessings of Christ's salvation freely to Jew and Gentile alike. The envy of the Jews was roused at the admission of the Gentiles to the same privileges with themselves. A commotion was raised, and the apostles had to quit the Pisidian Antioch, shaking the dust from their feet against their countrymen.

Iconium: Derbe: Lystra, Paul Stoned.—Proceeding about ninety miles in an easterly direction, the apostles came to Iconium. This town, afterwards called Konieh, became celebrated in history "as the cradle of the rising power of the conquering Turks...... The elements of its population would be as follows: — A large number of frivolous Greeks; some remains of a still older population; a few Roman officials; and an old colony of Jews." * The same treatment was given to the apostles here as at Antioch, and they fled to the more rural villages of Derbe and Lystra. At Lystra the miraculous cure of a lame man caused them to be mistaken for Jupiter and Mercury. This circumstance shows that the inhabitants had accommodated their religious notions to those of the Greeks. Paul deprecated their conduct, and besought them to turn from these vain idols to the living God. The fickle multitude, who had at first proposed to worship the apostles, being stirred up by Jews

* Conybeare and Howson.

from Antioch and Iconium, ended by stoning them. Paul was left for dead, but recovered.

Conversion of Timothy.—Among those who may have gazed on his seemingly lifeless face was a young Greek who had listened to his words with no common emotion. Timothy, his own son in the faith, seems now to have heard the gospel for the first time. Well instructed in the Scriptures though he had been, by his mother and his grandmother, probably till now he had never obtained the key to their meaning. After Paul's visit, the reading of the Scriptures would be prosecuted with fresh zest in that quiet domestic circle; and the young Greek would become familiar with the great "mystery of godliness," which his life was to be spent in proclaiming.

Return to Pisidian Antioch.—Paul and Barnabas now retraced their steps, and returned to confirm and comfort the churches which they had planted, amid the persecutions against which they had had to struggle. The only new place they are said to have visited was Attalia, on the sea-coast of Pamphylia. From that port they sailed to the Syrian Antioch, where they rehearsed to the brethren the tidings of the success of the gospel among the Gentiles. It now appeared more clearly than ever that God had opened to the Gentiles the door of faith.

Synod of Jerusalem.—Yet, even among those who had professed faith in Christ, there were some, originally of the school of the Pharisees, who stood out stoutly against this conclusion. These were now a large and influential body in the Church of Jerusalem. Secret emissaries came down from them to Syrian Antioch, who first insinuated their views by stealth, and then openly taught that circumcision was essential to salvation. It was resolved by the brethren at Antioch to send Paul and Barnabas and others to Jerusalem, to consult with the apostles and others as to the course to be taken in this matter. In the course of their journey, these brethren passed through Phœnicia and Samaria, where the gospel had made great progress, and where many hearts were made glad by the tidings which they carried. At last they reached Jerusalem. It was now seventeen years since Paul's conversion, and fourteen since the first visit he had paid as a Christian to that city (Gal. ii. 1). The assembly was addressed by Peter, Paul, Barnabas, and James. John was also present, but did not speak (Gal. ii. 9). No appearance seems to have been made by the Judaizing party, who preferred cunning plots to open arguments. The decision come to was entirely in accordance with the liberal views of Paul; only, on grounds of expediency, certain things were recommended to the Gentile Christians as proper to be avoided by them, to prevent needless offence. One of the things to be avoided—fornication—was immoral in its own nature, and deserved, therefore, to be avoided on much higher grounds than those of expediency; but the reference in the decree of the council seems not to be merely to the sin itself, but to certain pagan feasts and festivals with which it was often connected, especially at Antioch and Perga.

Return to Syrian Antioch.—After the council, Paul and Barnabas returned to Antioch, accompanied by Barsabas and Silas. It would seem, too, that at this time Peter paid a visit to Antioch (Gal. ii. 11), and that after a time he was so influenced by "false brethren" that came to the place, as to refuse to eat with the uncircumcised Gentile Christians. On this occasion Paul withstood him to the face (Gal. ii. 14).

Personal Appearance of Paul and Peter.—It may be interesting to hear an ingenious writer's account of the personal appearance of these two apostles at this time, though it be founded chiefly on tradition:—"St. Paul is set before us having the strongly marked and prominent features of a Jew, yet not without some of the finer lines indicative of Greek thought. His stature was diminutive, and his body disfigured by some lameness or distortion, which may have provoked the contemptuous expressions of his enemies. His beard was long and thin; his head was bald. The characteristics of his face were, a transparent complexion, which visibly betrayed the quick changes of his feelings; a bright gray eye, under thickly overhanging united eyebrows; a cheerful and winning expression of countenance, which invited the approach and inspired the confidence of strangers. It would be natural to infer, from his continual journeyings and manual labour, that he was possessed of great strength of constitution. But men of delicate health have often gone through the greatest exertions; and his own words on more than one occasion show that he suffered much from bodily infirmity. St. Peter is represented to us as a man of larger and stronger form, as his character was harsher and more abrupt. The quick impulses of his soul revealed themselves in the flashes of a dark eye. The complexion of his face was pale and sallow; and the short hair, which is described as entirely gray at the time of his death, curled black and thick round his temples and his chin when the two apostles stood together at Antioch, twenty years before their martyrdom."*

Paul's Contention with Peter.—The scene at Antioch was a very remarkable one. "Judaism and Christianity, in the persons of the two apostles, were for a moment brought into strong antagonism. The words of Paul contain a strong statement of the gospel as opposed to the law: 'If thou, being born a Jew, art wont to live according to the customs of the Gentiles, and not of the Jews, why wouldst thou now constrain the Gentiles to keep the ordinances of the Jews? We are by birth the seed of Abraham, and not unhallowed Gentiles; yet, knowing that a man is not counted righteous by the works of the law, but by the faith of Jesus Christ, we ourselves also have put our faith in Jesus Christ, that we might be counted righteous by the faith of Christ, and not by the works of the law. For by the works of the law shall no man be counted righteous.' These sentences contain, in a condensed form, the whole argument of the Epistles to the Galatians and Romans."

Results of Schism.—The schism in the Christian Church was not permanently healed by the decision of the Jerusalem Synod; it showed itself afterwards, as the Epistle to the Galatians proves. But one good effect arose indirectly out of the schism,—namely, the singular clearness with which Paul was

* Conybeare and Howson.

led to expound the way of acceptance for sinners under the gospel, and the great strength of argument which he brought to bear on the doctrine of justification by faith alone. This prominent doctrine in St. Paul's writings, which has explained the way of salvation to millions of perplexed inquirers, might have received much less elaborate vindication had no Judaizing teachers arisen to bewitch "foolish Galatians," and even shake the steadfastness of St. Peter. It is to be remarked, at the same time, that there is no real ground for the theory which some German critics have framed, that the Church was formally divided into two, and that the breach was not healed till towards the end of the second century. History gives no hint of such a state of things, and the theory is now generally felt to be untenable, even by those among whom it originated.

SECTION V.—PAUL'S SECOND MISSIONARY TOUR.

Companions:—SILAS, AND PARTLY TIMOTHY AND LUKE.

Separation of Paul and Barnabas: Paul and Silas in Asia Minor—Syria and Cilicia: Derbe and Lystra: Timothy joins Paul—Galatia—Troas—Classical associations: Luke joins the party: vision of man of Macedonia—First gospel campaign in Europe: Philippi—Thessalonica—Berea: Paul's voyage to Athens—State of Athens—Paul's three appearances there—Paul at Corinth—Sails to Jerusalem: Returns to Antioch.

Separation of Paul and Barnabas: Paul and Silas in Asia Minor.—After a short time spent at Antioch, Paul proposed to Barnabas that they should make a tour of inspection, visiting and watering the churches which they had formerly planted. An unhappy quarrel took place between them, occasioned by the desire of Barnabas to take his nephew Mark along with them, and Paul's want of thorough confidence in Mark, caused by his having left them in Pamphylia. As the two apostles could not agree, they took separate routes, Barnabas and Mark going to Cyprus, while Paul, accompanied by Silas, traversed a large portion of the provinces of Asia Minor. The record in Scripture even of matters so little creditable as this, is a clear proof of the honesty of the narrative and the truth of the history.

Syria and Cilicia: Derbe and Lystra: Timothy Joins Paul.
—The first visits of Paul and Silas were paid to the districts of Syria and Cilicia, the provinces where Paul had laboured and preached the gospel soon after his conversion. Doubtless his native Tarsus was among the places which he now visited; but no details have been preserved of his actings there. Next, striking up in a north-westerly course, through one of the "gates" or passes of the Taurus, he returned to Derbe and Lystra. Great must have been his joy to find his young friend Timothy so strong in the grace that is in Christ Jesus, and so well reported of by the brethren both at Lystra and Iconium. It would be with mingled emotions of joy and sorrow that his grandmother and mother saw Timothy depart with Paul and Silas into the wild regions of Galatia and Phrygia;—joy, that he was going on so holy and honourable an errand; sorrow, at the loss of so like-minded a member of their family.

Galatia.—Striking into Galatia, Paul entered on new ground, and came among quite a new race. The Galatians, as the first syllable of their name implies, were of Gallic origin; four centuries before, their ancestors had worshipped under the oaks of Gaul. They had been borne along in an emigration that at last brought them from the west of Europe to the west of Asia. The invasions of Rome and Greece by the Gauls are familiar events of history. The Galatians, or Gallo-Grecians, were connected with the latter event; but, repulsed from Greece, they crossed the Ægean, and settled in the centre of Asia Minor. It seems to have been in a time of sickness that Paul visited them (Gal. iv. 13). Their reception of him was most affectionate,—they would have plucked out their eyes and given them to him (Gal. iv. 15). But they were soon after perverted and bewitched by Judaizing teachers. Like the rest of the Gallic or Celtic race, they were "susceptible of quick impressions and sudden changes, with a fickleness equal to their courage and enthusiasm, and a constant liability to that disunion which is the fruit of excessive vanity."

Troas.—After traversing Phrygia and Galatia, it would have been natural for Paul to direct his course to the great sea-port of

Ephesus, or to the scarcely less important towns of Pergamos, Sardis, Philadelphia, Laodicea, Smyrna, and Thyatira; but the arrangements of God for these places were different,—"they were forbidden by the Holy Ghost to preach the word in Asia," —proconsular Asia, as a district near the coast was called. Bithynia, too, seemed closed against them. The only place to which they had access was Troas, which still preserved the classical name of Troy.

Classical Associations: Luke Joins the Party: Vision of Man of Macedonia.—It must have been with deep interest that the apostle gazed upon the famous plain where, at the dawn of Grecian history, according to the popular story, the whole forces of that country had spent their strength for ten years in the siege of Troy, and whose every locality had been invested by the genius of Homer with an interest that would survive to the end of time. But still more intense must have been his feelings when he looked across the Hellespont, and, for the first time in his life, beheld the summits of the European hills. The mountains from which the Macedonian "he-goat" had come down against the "two-horned ram" of Persia, would interest him greatly; and, as he lay down at night, the form and figure of the great conqueror would be full in his mind's eye. In his sleep, "there stood a man of Macedonia, and prayed, saying, Come over into Macedonia, and help us." That cry of distress was not to be disregarded. Next day Paul and his companions, of whom the beloved physician Luke was now one, might have been seen on the quay of Troas, inquiring for the first ship to Macedonia. The wind wafts them over the waters that, five hundred years before, had borne on their bosom the magnificent armada of Xerxes. The story of the shepherd's sling and stone is again about to be realized. These four humble men in the Trojan ship are to accomplish what the millions of Xerxes failed to accomplish—to conquer not only Greece, but all Europe.

First Gospel Campaign in Europe: Philippi.—The first campaign of the gospel of Jesus Christ in Europe was fought in Macedonia; Philippi, Thessalonica, and Berea were the principal battle-fields. Philippi was a Roman "colony;"—

the word denotes a sort of epitome of Rome itself, where the privileges of Romans were held peculiarly sacred. Being more of a military than of a commercial city, it had no Jewish synagogue; but devout proselytes and Jews assembled in a *proseuché*, or prayer-meeting, by a river side. A woman engaged in commerce,—a girl possessed by a demon,—and a jailer, whose character suited his office, were the first persons converted at Philippi, and became the nucleus of the first church in Europe. The influence of Christianity in Europe, in elevating woman and then in making use of her gentle instrumentality for promoting the cause of Christ, as well as in subduing the most rugged passions of man, seems to have been foreshadowed by these conversions. The freeness of the salvation of the gospel was at the same time gloriously exhibited in the brief and memorable reply to the jailer's question, "What must I do to be saved?"—"Believe on the Lord Jesus Christ, and thou shalt be saved." The sustaining and consoling power of divine grace was also beautifully exhibited by Paul and Silas, who prayed and sang praises by night, in the gloomy vaults of the prison, while suffering the agony of the scourge and the stocks. Philippi could have borne sad testimony to the opposite course to which misery and disgrace drive unconverted men; for it was there that both Brutus and Cassius had destroyed themselves. When the jailer was about to follow their example, the voice of the Christian apostle was heard saying, "Do thyself no harm."

Thessalonica.—From Philippi Paul proceeded to Thessalonica, an important and busy sea-port, with a Jewish synagogue. Here a delightful little Christian community was gathered together, whose "work of faith, labour of love, and patience of hope," lived long in the memory of the apostle. From this busy place the fame of the new religion, which was embraced by many of the old pagans, sounded out through all the neighbouring regions of Macedonia on the north and Achaia on the south.

Berea: Paul's Voyage to Athens.—But persecution drove Paul from Thessalonica, as it had driven him from Philippi.

He took refuge in the provincial town of Berea, where, through the diligent study of the Scriptures, many Jews were converted, and also some of the principal Gentiles. The signs of another gathering storm led the brethren to send Paul away in haste, while Silas and Timothy remained at Berea. A ship bound for Athens conveyed the apostle from the shore, where "Olympus, dark with woods, rises from the plain to the broad summit glittering with snow, which was the home of the Homeric gods......The shepherds from the heights above the vale of Tempe may have watched the sails of his ship that day, as it moved like a white speck over the outer waters of the Thermaic Gulf. The sailors, looking back from the deck, saw the great Olympus rising close above them in snowy majesty." The white speck was wafting to the classic shores of Athens the Hebrew preacher, through whose doctrine the gods of Olympus were to be dethroned for ever, and a purer heaven, a holier life, and a brighter immortality presented to Grecian eyes than had yet been dreamt of in all their philosophy.

State of Athens.—It would occupy too much space to describe all the objects that Paul would see, or to fancy all the emotions that would fill his mind, when his ship rode into the harbour of Piræus, and he himself, after passing between the Long Walls that connected the port and the city, found himself fronting the Acropolis of Athens. One thought can hardly have been absent from his mind: In Athens he would see mankind in the circumstances most favourable to the natural man; for if mental culture could enlighten, if the fine arts could purify, if philosophy could elevate, if poetry could sweeten, if the pagan religion could transform, the Athenians could not but be an enlightened, a pure, a noble, a genial, a holy people. As he walks through the city he sees everywhere statues of deified heroes and of the older gods; shrines and temples of every size and form, from the niche in the rock to the magnificent Parthenon; groups of statuary representing the old legends of mythology; and, among the rest, that altar of which he made good use in his speech—"To the unknown God." But Athens is the seat of philosophy, as well as the head-quarters of mythology. Two sects especially were encountered by him—the Stoics and the Epicureans. The Stoics enforced a sort of stern virtue, a high disregard alike of pleasure and of pain, that sometimes led to noble deeds in those evil times; but oftener to such mournful results as the suicide of their first two leaders, Zeno and Cleanthes, and of their most illustrious Roman adherents, Cato and Seneca. Pride was the great characteristic of the Stoic. The Epicureans were the children of pleasure—almost deriding the notion of a God, and encouraging men to live and die in indifference and ease.

Paul's Three Appearances there.—On three different spots Paul bore testimony to the truth at Athens. The first was the synagogue of the Jews; the next was a more public platform —the Agora, or market-place, the common meeting-place of the Athenians, to which they were always drawn when there was anything to gratify that craving for news and excitement which even four centuries before had been rebuked in them by Demosthenes. Some of the philosophers who heard Paul there, wishing to listen to him in a quieter and more solemn place, took him to Areopagus, or Mars' Hill—the place where the judges had sat from time immemorial, to decide causes civil and religious. "It was a scene with which the dread recollections of centuries were associated. It was a place of silent awe in the midst of the gay and frivolous city. No place in Athens was so suitable for a discourse upon the mysteries of religion." * Here, gazing on the splendid temple of the Parthenon, Paul taught that God dwelleth not in temples made with hands. Under shade of the colossal statue of Minerva, armed, as the champion of Athens, with spear, shield, and helmet, he declared that the Godhead is not like unto gold, or silver, or stone, graven by art and man's device. Here he taught the scoffing Epicureans that the world was not an accidental concourse of atoms, but that it was created by God. Here he summoned the proud and haughty Stoic to repent of all his wickedness, and foretold the coming of a terrible day of retribution by God's Son; of which the certain pledge had been given to all men, in

* Conybeare and Howson.

that he had raised him from the dead. It is probable that Paul would have gone on to speak more of Christ, and of salvation through his blood; but he seems to have been interrupted and obliged to close abruptly. The philosophers derided his doctrine, or treated it with indifference; and Paul, in one of his after letters, could only speak of the gospel as "to the Greek, foolishness." Dionysius, one of the judges of the Areopagus, believed, and a few others; but Athens—polite, refined, intellectual—was not one of the places where the gospel triumphed.

Paul at Corinth.—Paul had paid his visit to Athens alone; but at Corinth, to which he next proceeded, he was joined by Silas and Timothy. On his way to Corinth he determined that he should make "Jesus Christ, and him crucified," the subject of his preaching there. Corinth was now the actual capital of Greece. The celebrated peninsula, the strifes and struggles of whose republics form so large a chapter of ancient history, had been formed by the Romans into the province of Achaia, with Corinth, situated on the isthmus or "bridge of the Peloponnesus," for its capital. Corinth was a place of great commercial activity. By its sea-port on the west it communicated with Europe, and by that on the east with Asia. It was preeminently noted for its licentiousness. In a temple dedicated to Venus, a thousand harlots were supported in honour of the goddess, at the public expense. It abounded with fornicators, and idolaters, and adulterers, and effeminate, and abusers of themselves with mankind, with thieves, with covetous, with drunkards, with revilers, and with extortioners (1 Cor. vi. 9, 10).

Sails to Jerusalem: Returns to Antioch.—At Corinth Paul took up his abode with Aquila and Priscilla, a countryman and countrywoman, who, with the rest of the Jews, had lately been expelled by Claudius from Rome. According to Suetonius, the Roman historian, the Jews were always exciting tumults, at the instance of one Chrestus. The origin of this charge probably was, that the unbelieving Jews were exciting tumults against those who worshipped Christ. Doubtless Aquila and Priscilla would give Paul much information about Rome, and perhaps excite that desire to visit it which he began to feel. At Corinth Paul had great success. Crispus, ruler of a synagogue, became a convert—a circumstance that must have caused great excitement. Yet Paul's spirit was burdened and depressed. That which distressed him was the bitter and blasphemous opposition to the truth which the Jews were ever exciting. But the Lord mercifully encouraged him in a vision, and for a year and a half he continued to labour at Corinth. It was now that he wrote his two epistles to the Thessalonians—the earliest of all his recorded letters. At last, having a strong desire to be present at one of the festivals at Jerusalem, he set sail for the holy city, taking Ephesus on his way. Promising to try to return to Ephesus, he went on to Jerusalem, and after his visit, returned to Antioch,—thus completing his second great missionary tour.

SECTION VI.—PAUL'S THIRD MISSIONARY TOUR.

Companions:—TIMOTHY, TITUS, SOPATER, ARISTARCHUS, SECUNDUS, GAIUS, TYCHICUS AND TROPHIMUS, LUKE.

At Ephesus—Tumult and departure—At Troas: in Macedonia: at Corinth—Voyage to Jerusalem: reception there.

At Ephesus.—The third missionary campaign of the apostle, during the whole of which he had Timothy for his companion, opened in Phrygia and Galatia, where he had been before. But the chief place to which his attention was directed in this tour was Ephesus. There the way had been prepared for him by the preaching of Apollos, an eloquent Jew of Alexandria, well versed in the Scriptures; who, however, was only a disciple of John the Baptist, and had to be instructed in Christian truth. Ephesus, situated at the mouth of the Cayster, was the chief city of the region to which the name of Asia was first restricted. Its inhabitants were half Greek, half Asiatic; and their religion and superstitions were a compound of the East and the West. Sorcery or magic, an importation of the East, was exceedingly common. Diana, a goddess of the West, was the great object of worship; but the style of worship had in it much of Oriental mystery and magnificence. The temple of Diana, or Artemis, at Ephesus, was renowned over the whole world. It had been 220 years in building. Its roof was supported by 126 columns, 60 feet high, the gifts of as many kings. The image of Diana, believed to have fallen from heaven, was but of wood, and thus formed a striking contrast to the magnificence around. Ephesus was notorious, besides, both for its luxury and for its licentiousness.

Tumult and Departure.—Yet, from the materials which this wicked place furnished, one of the most beautiful and interesting of all the ancient churches was formed (Rev. ii. 2, 3). No epistle glows with more satisfaction and joyful remembrance than that of Paul to the Ephesians.* Even from among the exorcists many converts were obtained; and the value of the books of magic, which they committed to the flames in token of their sincerity, exceeded £2000 of our money. The religious change was becoming so great that the craftsmen who gained their living by making silver models of the image of Diana became alarmed, and raised an insurrection. The apostle and his companion were rescued from the danger through the eloquence of one of the magistrates of the place; but they were not able to remain in Ephesus. After bidding the church farewell, Paul proceeded to visit the churches of Macedonia. It seems to have been at Ephesus that he wrote his First Epistle to the Corinthians (1 Cor. xvi. 8).

At Troas: in Macedonia: at Corinth.—On leaving Ephesus, Paul first went to Troas, where he preached with great success (2 Cor. ii. 12); then he proceeded to Macedonia and the countries of Greece lying to the north. At Philippi he wrote the Second Epistle to the Corinthians. He was now actively engaged in a scheme for collecting money for the poor believers in Judæa, designed to show the good-will of the Gentiles, and to soften down the bitter feeling of the Jewish church towards their uncircumcised brethren. Titus, to whom one of the pastoral letters was afterwards written, was specially employed by him

* Yet it is right to mention that it has been questioned, on pretty strong grounds, whether this epistle was originally sent to that church, there being some reason to think that it was a circular letter intended for several neighbouring churches.

in promoting this collection. Hearing that Judaizing teachers had been corrupting the church of Galatia, he wrote the Epistle to the Galatians, powerfully refuting and remonstrating against the errors in question. Three months were then spent in Corinth; and the Epistle to the Romans was written, and despatched by Phœbe. It is remarkable that no mention is made of any apostle, or other celebrated man, having founded the church at Rome. It was probably quietly formed by converts to Christianity, who either had left the Jewish synagogue at Rome or had come as Christians to the city from other countries. Paul returned to Macedonia, and sailed thence to Troas.

Voyage to Jerusalem: Reception there.—From Troas, he directed his course to Jerusalem. He proceeded by sea, and his voyage was full of interest. After spending a week at Troas, after taking a most affectionate farewell of the Ephesian elders or bishops at Miletus, and after touching at Coos, Rhodes, and Patara, the apostle and his companions sailed to Tyre. A church had existed there since the persecution at the death of Stephen, and there were now not only Christians but prophets in what had once been a great stronghold of Baal and Ashtoreth. Leaving Tyre, the party saluted the brethren at Ptolemais or Acre, and at length reached Cæsarea. From that place, in opposition to the remonstrances of the evangelist Philip, and other friends, who dreaded the excited feelings of the Jews, Paul travelled to Jerusalem, where he was received kindly by James and the elders, and refreshed them by telling what God had been doing among the Gentiles.

SECTION VII.—CLOSING SCENES OF PAUL'S LIFE.

Arrest at Jerusalem: sent to Cæsarea—Scenes on the way—Felix, Festus, Agrippa: appeal to Cæsar—Voyage to Rome: the shipwreck—Paul's behaviour—Malta: Puteoli—View of Rome—State of Rome—Missionary labours—Trial and acquittal—Journey to Spain—Second arrest—Second trial; condemnation: execution—His companions.

Arrest at Jerusalem: Sent to Cæsarea.—We can only refer in general terms to the occurrences that took place while Paul was in Palestine. The hatred towards him of that part of the Church which was leavened with the spirit of the Pharisees found a speedy outlet. On a false clamour being raised, he was beaten by the people in the temple; he was rescued, however, by the Roman soldiers, and carried to the neighbouring fort and barrack of Antonia; there he was about to be put on the rack, but escaped the torture by declaring himself a Roman citizen; he was tried before the Sanhedrim, as Stephen had been twenty-five years before, when he was himself a virulent persecutor; he received in a vision a cheering promise of protection from God; and, a plot against his life being discovered, he was sent, with a large escort, by night, to the Roman capital, Cæsarea.

Scenes on the Way.—The places through which he passed were fitted to encourage faith and fortitude. It would be interesting to fancy his feelings as about midnight he passed Bethhoron the nether, and gazed perhaps on the moon looking down on the valley of Ajalon, where, fifteen hundred years before, it had lingered to witness the triumph of Joshua. The light of the morning sun, rising behind the snowy crest of Hermon, would find him in the plain of Sharon; and as he rode along, the rose of Sharon and the lily of the valleys at his feet, and the young roe sporting on the mountains of Bether on his right, might carry his mind to the Song of Solomon, and assure him both of the love and of the presence of his Lord. In the after part of the day, he and the seventy troopers that accompanied him, after passing the colossal statues of Julius Cæsar and Rome that adorned the new capital, would dismount from their weary horses at the barracks of Cæsarea.

Felix, Festus, Agrippa: Appeal to Cæsar.—The Roman governor, resident at Cæsarea at this time, was Claudius Felix, an unscrupulous, sensual profligate, whose wife Drusilla was a daughter of Herod Agrippa I. On his first appearance before Felix, Paul was remanded, under pretence that he would be tried again; the next time, in presence of Drusilla, he made Felix tremble, as he reasoned of righteousness, temperance, and judgment to come; after that he was kept a prisoner at Cæsarea for two years. At the end of that period Felix was recalled from Palestine, and Porcius Festus was sent as governor in his room. Paul was now tried again, and on this occasion took his memorable appeal to Cæsar. In the meantime, Herod Agrippa II., king of Chalcis, in Syria, with his sister Bernice, having come on a visit to Cæsarea, Paul was brought before them, and in another powerful address, "almost persuaded" Agrippa "to be a Christian." His appeal to Cæsar could be heard nowhere but at Rome; and soon afterwards, under charge of a centurion of Augustus's band named Julius, Paul, with other prisoners, set sail, in a ship bound for Adramyttium, for the metropolis of the world.

Voyage to Rome: the Shipwreck.—The record of Paul's voyage to Rome, in the twenty-seventh chapter of Acts, is remarkably interesting, partly for the incidents that occurred, partly for its minute information respecting the seamanship of the time, and partly also for the wonderful verification of the narrative, in its minutest particulars, which modern inquiry has supplied. The vessel, on leaving the great dock constructed by Herod at Cæsarea, touched at Sidon; then passing to the north of Cyprus, through the gulfs of Cilicia and Pamphylia, it afforded the apostle a view, probably his last, of his native mountains. At Myra, in Lycia, a ship was found chartered for Rome, to which the prisoners were transferred. After creeping along slowly as far as to Cnidus, adverse winds forced the ship out of her direct course, compelling her to pass southward, under lee of the island of Crete, as far as to the harbour called Fair Havens. After waiting long for a favourable breeze, the vessel set sail, but had not proceeded far when she was caught by a furious gale from the north-east. The crew seem to have turned round the right side of the vessel to the wind, and allowed her to be carried along, on the starboard tack, in a westerly direction. In the circumstances it is reckoned that she would drift at the rate of about a mile and a half in the hour. After a fortnight of discomfort and terror that can hardly be conceived, the sailors became aware, one midnight, that they were approaching land. The ship was immediately anchored astern, and daylight anxiously waited for. When it came, it was observed that a creek ran into the shore. Into this creek the vessel was attempted to be run; but in the attempt her bow stuck fast on the bottom. Partly by swimming, and partly by the aid of boards and broken pieces of the ship, all the passengers, who were two hundred and seventy-six in number, got safely to land.

Paul's Behaviour.—In the course of this fearful voyage, Paul distinguished himself very greatly by his presence of mind, his sagacious advice, his regard for the welfare of his fellow-passengers, and his boundless confidence in God. At an early period of the storm he had relieved many hearts, by telling of a vision in which God's angel had assured him that the lives of all should be preserved. He had prevailed on the party to refresh themselves with food after a very long fast, and had prevented the stealthy escape of the sailors when their approach to land was first discovered. The wonderful influence which the poor prisoner in chains acquired in the ship was a proof, not only of his native vigour of mind, but of the calmness and wisdom, in the hour of danger, which he had got from fellowship with God.

Malta : Puteoli.—The island on which the ship was cast was Malta—now a possession of Great Britain. The bay where the shipwreck occurred still bears the name of St. Paul; and all the circumstances of the shipwreck, as recorded in the Acts, agree wonderfully with existing appearances. The island was inhabited by a people of Phœnician origin. After spending three months among them, Paul and his companions embarked in another vessel; touched at Syracuse in Sicily; had to wait at Rhegium for a favourable wind to carry them through the Strait of Messina; and at last, having passed the smoking crater of Vesuvius and the lovely scenery of the Bay of Naples, they landed at Puteoli.

View of Rome.—From this sea-port to Rome, a distance of one hundred and fifty miles, the apostle travelled by land. Advancing by the Appian Way, he would pass countless localities memorable by associations with the mythology and the history of the Romans. At Appii Forum, fifty miles from Rome, and again at the Three Taverns, deputations from the Christians of the city came to offer to the great apostle the expression of their deep regard and affection. From a height about ten miles distant from Rome he would catch his first view of the imperial city. At last he is in the streets of Rome. Its palaces, its temples, its aqueducts, its theatres, and its columns, rise on every side. The long cherished desire of his heart is fulfilled—he is to hear the echoes of salvation reverberate among the seven hills.

State of Rome.—Never was a city in greater need of a transforming gospel. Corruption and profligacy in every form were at their height. Crimes too abominable to be named were openly committed in the houses of the first families. The emperor Nero, though only in his twenty-fourth year, had begun his awful course of crime—had already stained his hands in the blood of his mother and his wife, and was living under the influence of his mistress, the infamous Poppæa, a proselyte to Judaism. The free citizens were more than a million, the slaves about the same in number.

Missionary Labours.—At first Paul endeavoured to make impressions on the Jewish inhabitants; but his efforts were in vain. He then turned to the Gentiles, with whom he had much greater success. For two years he continued a prisoner, dwelling in his own lodging, but constantly chained to a Roman soldier. Some of these soldiers seem to have been converted to Christ—won, very probably, not less through the influence of his consistent example and loving spirit than by the force of his arguments. Even in Nero's palace converts were made through his instrumentality. It is certain that the Roman church increased largely; for a year or two afterwards, the number of Christians who were slaughtered by Nero was enormous. During these two years were written the epistles to Philemon, the Colossians, the Ephesians, and the Philippians.

Trial and Acquittal.—At last Paul's trial came on: most probably it was conducted in the immediate presence of Nero. The narrative of Acts comes abruptly to a close before telling the result. It is from Paul's epistles we learn that he was set free. How the remaining portion of his life was spent can be gathered only from indirect notices in his letters, and from the statements of uninspired writers.

Journey to Spain.—It is generally believed that from Rome he went to Asia Minor, and thence to Macedonia. He seems then to have gone to Spain, where he is thought to have spent two years (Rom. xv. 28). Returning to Ephesus, he found matters in a somewhat critical condition. In Crete, too, which he visited about the same time, he found much cause for anxiety. False teachers were busy perverting the truth and sapping the foundation of Christianity. The First Epistle to Timothy and the Epistle to Titus seem to have been written about this time, instructing the faithful men who were labouring respectively in Ephesus and in Crete to resist all false doctrine and zealously to maintain the truth.

Second Arrest.—Paul had hoped to spend the winter at Nicopolis in Macedonia; but he was not allowed to remain there. He was arrested on a new charge, and was hurried to Rome to stand a second trial. Since he had last been at Rome, Nero had conducted himself in a very shameful way. More than half the city had been burned by an awful fire, which lasted for six days, and which some ascribe to Nero himself. The blame was laid by him on the Christians, who were now an exceedingly numerous body. A frightful persecution raged against them. "Some were crucified; some were disguised in the skins of beasts and hunted to death with dogs; some were wrapped in robes impregnated with inflammable materials, and set on fire at night, that they might serve to illuminate the circus of the Vatican and the gardens of Nero, where this diabolical monster exhibited the agonies of his victims to the public, and gloated over them." The number of those who perished was very great.

Second Trial: Condemnation: Execution.—Paul's privileges on his second confinement seem to have been much smaller than on his first. The Second Epistle to Timothy was now written by him, in the full expectation of being speedily "offered up." When brought to trial, in presence of a large number of leading men, he was enabled to make a bold statement of the gospel. But no defence could avail against the will of Nero. The apostle, on being called a second time, was condemned. Near the spot now occupied by the English cemetery, his head was struck from his body. His friends carried the headless corpse to the catacombs, or subterranean vaults below Rome, to which in after times the martyrs used often to flee for concealment. There, in some unknown vault, rests the body of the greatest of apostles, awaiting the fulfilment of his own words, "Death is swallowed up in victory."

His Companions.—Very little is known respecting the future history of Paul's more immediate companions. Timothy had been summoned by him to Rome in his second epistle; probably he immediately complied with the summons, but of his future history nothing is known with certainty. At one time he was a prisoner of Jesus Christ (Heb. xiii. 23); and, according to tradition, he suffered martyrdom under the emperor Domitian. Of Titus, all that we know is told us in a single clause in 2 Timothy,—that he departed into Dalmatia. Whether this was by Paul's instructions or at his own instance, we cannot tell. Silvanus is mentioned in 1 Peter as the bearer of that apostle's letter to the strangers scattered throughout Asia Minor. Mark, who regained Paul's confidence, and became again his companion (Col. iv. 10), and whom he wished Timothy to bring with him to Rome (2 Tim. iv. 11), was also associated latterly with Peter, to whom he is said to have acted as secretary and interpreter. Tradition sends him afterwards to Alexandria, where he is said to have founded the Christian church, and to have suffered martyrdom. Luke was at Rome immediately before Paul's death, being apparently the only trusty friend that was present to cheer him in the last scenes of life. Of Luke's after life history contains no record, and the accounts of tradition are improbable and contradictory. Respecting the less prominent of Paul's fellow-labourers absolutely nothing is known with certainty.

SECTION VIII.—LABOURS OF THE OTHER APOSTLES.

James (1) the son of Zebedee—James (2) the son of Alpheus—Peter—Thomas—Andrew—Bartholomew—Philip—Matthew—Simon—Jude—Matthias—John—The Seven Churches of Asia—Patmos—Anecdotes of John.

James (1) the Son of Zebedee.—This apostle, as has already been mentioned, was put to death by Herod in the early years of the church (Acts xii. 2).

James (2) the Son of Alpheus.—This apostle, known in history, from the strictness of his life, as James the Just, is universally represented as having continued to labour in and about Jerusalem. Opinion is divided as to whether this James or another was "the brother of the Lord." He directed his efforts mainly to counteract the loose morality of those who abused the doctrines of grace. In his later years he seems to have given countenance to the Pharisaical section of the Church, notwithstanding the tendencies which Paul had to denounce so strongly in the Epistle to the Galatians. Yet this very weakness is said to have proved the occasion of his death. Provoked at the success of his doctrine outwardly, in drawing their countrymen to acknowledge Jesus as the Messiah, the basest and most bigoted party leaders among the Jews resolved to sacrifice him to their rage. Taking advantage of the interval between the departure of the Roman governor, Festus, and the arrival of Albinus, his successor, Ananus, the high priest, caused him to be condemned by the Sanhedrim; and, in conformity with the sentence, he was cruelly stoned to death.

Peter.—It is more difficult to trace the career of Peter. The tradition that he went to Rome in the reign of Nero, and was condemned at the same time as Paul, is now generally abandoned, ancient though it be. There is much more probability in the opinion that, when he left Palestine, he published the gospel in Parthia, especially in the region of Mesopotamia. Many Jews were settled there—the descendants of those who had been carried captive in the days of Daniel and Ezekiel; among them the apostle would find abundant scope for his ministry. In his first epistle he writes of Babylon as if he were either in or near that ancient city, which had not yet been quite obliterated (1 Peter iv. 13). From near this place he wrote his first epistle, "to the strangers in Pontus, Galatia, Cappadocia, Asia, and Bithynia." If he had not visited these churches in person, he had at least heard about them from Paul's former comrade, Silvanus, who was then with him; and foreseeing that the great wave of persecution which was then breaking against Paul at Rome, would soon be borne to the churches in Asia, he wrote his epistle to confirm them in the faith and nerve them for the coming trial. An ancient tradition tells that when Peter saw his wife led to martyrdom, he called out to her, mentioning her name, "Oh remember the Lord!" Whatever place was the scene of Peter's death, it seems pretty certain that he died as a martyr, though the tradition of his being crucified, at his own request, with his head downwards, that he might thus suffer a more humiliating death than his Lord, is probably unfounded. The apostles had themselves been taught, and had taught others, that while suffering inflicted by unrighteous judges was to be patiently borne, it was never to be courted.

Thomas.—According to some accounts, Thomas preached the gospel in Parthia. As that term embraced Persia as well as Mesopotamia, Thomas may have had a separate sphere from Peter. Pursuing the scattered tribes into Afghanistan (the Afghans are thought by some to be their descendants), he may thus also have verified the tradition that makes him the apostle of India.

Andrew.—This apostle had Scythia for his district. He traversed the shores of the Black Sea; and among other places where he preached, Sinope, Sebastopol, and Byzantium (Constantinople), are all mentioned by ancient writers. It is said that he was condemned to die on a cross formed like the letter X, hence called St. Andrew's cross. That his death might be lingering, he was fastened to the cross with cords; and he is said to have exhorted the bystanders for two days, till at last death came to his relief. This account is improbable; and it may be remarked that the most trustworthy of the ancient writers mention only the two Jameses, Peter, and Paul, as *martyrs* among the apostles.

Bartholomew.—Bartholomew is said to have laboured in "exterior India;" which an ancient writer explains to mean Seba or Yemen in Arabia, over whose people it has been already mentioned that a Jewish family reigned. Tradition brings back Bartholomew, in his later years, to Phrygia and Armenia, and asserts, probably without foundation, that he was put to death by being flayed alive.

Philip.—It is reported that Philip laboured in Phrygia; but the accounts of his death that have been handed down are so mingled with what is plainly fabulous, that little reliance can be placed on them.

Matthew.—It is said that Matthew went into the Asiatic Ethiopia, and laboured there, as well as in Macedonia and Asia. His Gospel seems to have been written at an earlier period, for the benefit of the Jews in Palestine.

Simon.—To Simon, Egypt, Cyrene, and Mauritania have been assigned, and even Great Britain, where he is alleged to have been crucified by the natives. Most of these stories of the martyrdom of the apostles were invented in a later age, when martyrdom was regarded with such superstitious and idolatrous veneration, that any one who did not die in this way was hardly counted a proper saint.

Jude.—With the name of Jude, or Thaddeus, is connected a story of one Agbarus, or Abgarus, ruler of Edessa in Mesopotamia—the Greek name of Orfah or Urfah. This Agbarus is said to have corresponded with Christ about the cure of a disorder, and the reputed letters have been preserved; but they bear evident marks of forgery. Afterwards, it is said, Agbarus was converted by Thaddeus—either the apostle Jude or one of the seventy disciples. In the reign of Domitian, a rumour had reached that emperor that some of the line of David and of the kindred of Christ still survived, and might one day dispute his empire. Two grandsons of Jude, "the brother of the Lord," were sought out and brought to Domitian; but their condition of life was so poor, and their answers indicated such a simple, unambitious spirit, that they were dismissed without molestation.

Matthias.—This apostle has been assigned by some writers to Ethiopia, and by others to Cappadocia. One ancient writer says that he died at Sebastopol, and was buried there, near the Temple of the Sun.

John.—The only apostle whom we have now to notice is John. The records of the life of John are more trustworthy than those of the other apostles. He had left Jerusalem before Paul's last visit to it, but where he was labouring at that time we cannot tell. It is probable that soon afterwards, the threatening state of things in the churches of Asia Minor, which led Peter to write his first epistle to them, induced John also to take up his residence among them. It is affirmed on good authority that he resided for a long time at Ephesus. Thence he was banished by the emperor Domitian to Patmos; he returned, under Nerva, to Ephesus; and there his death took place, under Trajan, in extreme old age.

The Seven Churches of Asia.—The name of John is inseparably associated with "the seven churches of Asia," to which our Lord commissioned him to write short epistles in his name. Of most of these we have not yet had occasion to speak; a brief notice of them may be conveniently introduced here:—

1. *Ephesus.* The state of this town, and the history of the introduction of Christianity into it under Paul, have been noticed already. It was the capital of Ionia, and was famed for its Temple of Diana, its philosophy, its magic, and its sensuality. The first condition of its church was singularly beautiful, but there had been a falling off. In the epistle to this church a warning was conveyed—unless they should repent, their candlestick would be removed. The warning has been fulfilled. "The whole place is now utterly desolate, with the exception of the small Turkish village of Ayasaluk. The ruins are of vast extent, both on Coressus and on the plain."*

2. *Smyrna* lay forty miles to the north of Ephesus. No word of blame was spoken to this church; but a day of trial

---

* Smith's Dictionary of the Bible.

was foretold. The trial was nobly endured. The confession of the aged Polycarp of Smyrna is one of the noblest on record. He was faithful unto death, and received a crown of life. When ordered to blaspheme Christ's name, he made the memorable reply—"Fourscore and six years have I served him, and he hath never wronged me at all: how then can I blaspheme my King and my Saviour?" Smyrna is still a large town, numbering 130,000 inhabitants. The American and other missionaries there have met with much encouragement.

3. *Pergamos*, about sixty miles north of Smyrna, was the capital of an ancient kingdom, and was famous for a royal library of 200,000 volumes. Divine honours were paid in it to Æsculapius, under the form of a living serpent. There may be a reference to this, as well as to the wickedness of the place, in the expression, "I know where thou dwellest, *even where Satan's seat is.*" The modern town, in which magnificent ruins are mingled with wooden hovels, contains a population of but 14,000.

4. *Thyatira* was in the northern border of Lydia. It was famed for the skill of its inhabitants in dyeing cloth. Its population now is between 6000 and 7000. In vain does the traveller search for the "works, and charity, and service, and faith, and patience" of apostolic times.

In the notices of these four churches in the Apocalypse, we can see evidence of the realization of what Paul had dreaded—that "grievous wolves would enter in, not sparing the flock; and that of their own selves should men arise, speaking perverse things, to draw away disciples after them." The Nicolaitanes and "that woman Jezebel" had done infinite damage under a Christian guise,—inviting and attracting believers to the revels and abominations of heathenism,—destroying their influence, and sapping the very foundations of piety.

5. *Sardis* was the capital of the ancient kingdom of Lydia, whose king, Crœsus, was reputed the richest of men, and whose treasures, when seized by Cyrus, were reckoned at above £120,000,000 sterling. Nothing now remains of Sardis, except ruins. Its present desolation seems a fitting memorial of the

state of its ancient church—"Thou hast a name that thou livest, and art dead."

6. *Philadelphia* was the second city of Lydia. The epistle promises that its people should be kept "in the hour of temptation, which should come upon all the world, to try them that dwell on the earth." This promise was fulfilled. Gibbon, the historian of the Decline and Fall of Rome, says: "The captivity or ruin of the seven churches of Asia was consummated [by the Ottomans] A.D. 1312; and the barbarous lords of Ionia and Lydia still trample on the monuments of classic and Christian antiquity. In the loss of Ephesus, the Christians deplored the fall of the first angel, the extinction of the first candlestick of the Revelation. The desolation is complete..... The circus and three stately theatres of Laodicea are now peopled with wolves and foxes; Sardis is reduced to a miserable village; the God of Mohammed is invoked in the mosques of Thyatira and Pergamos; and the populousness of Smyrna is supported by the foreign trade of the Franks and Armenians. Philadelphia alone has been saved, by prophecy or courage. At a distance from the sea, forgotten of the emperors, encompassed on all hands by the Turks, her valiant sons defended their religion and freedom above fourscore years, and at length capitulated with the proudest of the Ottomans. Among the Greek colonies and churches of Asia, Philadelphia is still erect—a column in a scene of ruins—a pleasing example that the path of honour and safety may sometimes be the same."

"One solitary pillar," says Dr. Kitto, "of high antiquity, has been often noticed, as reminding beholders of the remarkable words in the Apocalyptic message to the Philadelphian church—'Him that overcometh will I make a pillar in the temple of my God, and he shall go no more out.'"

7. *Laodicea*, the capital of the greater Phrygia, was a place of very great size and splendour. An amphitheatre, of which the remains still exist, must have accommodated from twenty to thirty thousand spectators. The hills are of volcanic origin, and in the neighbourhood are still several hot springs, of different degrees of warmth, the proximity of which may have

suggested the comparison, "Thou art lukewarm, and neither cold nor hot." Laodicea is now quite desolate. "For centuries," says a traveller, "it has been a perfect mass of ruins.... Laodicea is even more solitary than Ephesus; for the latter has the prospect of a rolling sea or of a whitening sail to enliven its decay, while the former sits in widowed loneliness. Its walls are grass-grown, its temples desolate, its very name has perished. We preferred hastening on, to a further delay in that melancholy spot, where everything whispered desolation, and where the very wind swept impetuously through the valley somewhat like the fiendish laugh of Time over the destruction of man and his proudest monuments."

Patmos.—Of the island of Patmos, to which John was banished by Domitian, there is little to be said. It is a rocky, barren island, in the Ægean Sea, indented by many bays and gulfs. Its principal town is built on the summit and steep sides of a high hill which overlooks the harbour. Half way down the hill is a jutting rock, where, according to tradition, John was in the Spirit, and saw the visions of the Apocalypse.

Anecdotes of John.—Many anecdotes are told by ancient writers illustrative of the gentle heart yet burning zeal of John. Hearing that a convert had become captain of a band of robbers, he went to him unarmed, and never ceased till, by prayers and tears, he brought him back to the true fold. On another occasion, having gone into a bath, he observed there the heretic Cerinthus, and, turning hastily away, exclaimed, "Let us flee from this place, lest the bath should fall while this enemy of the truth is within it." When too infirm and aged to be able to preach, he was accustomed to be carried into the church; and, after stretching out his arms and saying, "Little children, let us love one another," he would retire from the assembly. He is believed to have lived to an extreme old age.

SECTION IX.—DESTRUCTION OF JERUSALEM, AND CONTEMPORARY HISTORY.

Events in Judæa—Titus takes Jerusalem—Reigns of Titus and Domitian—War in Britain: Agricola's conquest—The work of Christ and of his apostles—Close of Bible History.

Events in Judæa.—The Roman governors of Judæa, after Felix and Festus, governed the country ill, and excited great discontent among the Jews. Frightful massacres of the people sometimes took place: on one occasion many thousand Jews were massacred in the streets of Cæsarea. Partial insurrections at length swelled into a general rising. About the time when Paul suffered martyrdom, Nero sent Vespasian, his ablest general, against the Jews. Vespasian, everywhere victorious, was advancing towards Jerusalem, when, being proclaimed Emperor by the army, he went to Rome, and left the prosecution of the war to his son Titus.

Titus Takes Jerusalem.—When Titus appeared before Jerusalem, frightful dissensions raged within the city, but for which, he used to say, it could not have been taken. The Roman army gradually took part after part of the city. Titus was most desirous to save the temple; but a soldier having, on the 5th of August, thrown a brand into it, it was burned to the ground. After the destruction of Jerusalem the Jews still held out in various neighbouring strongholds, in some of which most tragic scenes occurred; but Judæa was thenceforth a captive land. The holy and beautiful house where the fathers had worshipped was burned with fire; the long era of desolation began; Jerusalem was to be trodden down of the Gentiles, until the times of the Gentiles should be fulfilled. We can easily conceive how earnestly the apostle John, with the remembrance of Jerusalem's calamity full in his mind, would warn the churches of Ephesus and of Asia generally to beware lest *their* candlestick, like that of Jerusalem, should be removed out of its place.

Reigns of Titus and Domitian.—Little occurred of great interest in the general history of the world during the latter half of the first century. Vespasian reigned creditably for ten years, when he was succeeded by Titus, who earned for himself the title, "The delight of the human race." During his brief reign occurred that frightful eruption of Mount Vesuvius which buried in ashes and lava the cities of Pompeii and Herculaneum. Titus, after three years, was followed by his brother Domitian —one of the greatest tyrants that ever sat on a throne. It was during his reign that the persecution raged under which (as is most generally believed) John was banished to Patmos. Domitian was succeeded by the aged Nerva, and he by Trajan —a prince of talent and energy, who did much to restore the ancient vigour of the empire.

War in Britain: Agricola's Conquest.—From the time when Augustus shut the Temple of Janus, before our Lord's birth, there had been comparatively little of foreign war. The Germans, the Parthians, the Britons, and other tribes that lay along the outskirts of the Roman empire, were the chief sources of employment to the arms of the legions. In Nero's reign a bloody campaign was conducted in Britain. About the time when the apostle Paul was dwelling in his hired house in Rome, and writing his epistles to the Philippians, the Ephesians, and the Colossians, Suetonius Paulinus was burning Druids in the Isle of Man, and shamefully scourging the warrior queen Boadicea. While John was exhorting the Christians of Ephesus to love one another, Agricola was completing the conquest of Britain, —was erecting his forts across the island, and encountering the warlike Caledonians in their Highland wilds. Among the Roman soldiers who came about this time to our shores there can be little doubt that there were some whose hearts had been filled with the love of Christ, and who would use their best endeavours to instruct the poor natives in the knowledge of salvation. It is probable that, before the first century had closed, there were Britons, both south and north of the Tweed, who had learned to love and bless the name of Jesus.

The Work of Christ and of His Apostles.—To delineate the changes that had now taken place in social and religious life would require a volume instead of a concluding page. The glorious truth that had been so dimly announced to Adam and

Eve in paradise was now set in the clearest light of God. The promised Deliverer himself had come; he had fulfilled his work; and he had gone back to his Father. While living and working among men, he had appeared chiefly in the character of a great Benefactor,—a source of pardon and life, of joy and peace, of love and holiness, of liberty and progress, and of every other blessing precious to perishing men. The impression which his life was fitted to produce was, that living contact with him must somehow heal all the diseases of the spirit,—all must come right through union to him. It was reserved for his apostles more fully to reveal the great mystery of his atoning death, to establish doctrinally the way of salvation for the guilty, and minutely to apply the principles of Christianity to the practical business of daily life. It was reserved for them also to throw light on the details of the Jewish dispensation, and bring out clearly the purport of its many symbols and mysteries.

Close of Bible History.—All this having been done, the canon of the Scripture was closed, the power of miracles was withdrawn, and the gospel was left to fight its way and achieve its triumphs under such supplies of grace as God ordinarily grants to the prayers of the faithful. The Christian Revelation being now completed, and the Christian Church set up as a witness for Christ, Bible History comes to an end.

GENERAL INDEX.

AARON, Jewish high priest, 125, 129, 137, 139, 142.
Abel, son of Adam, 26.
Abigail, 237.
Abihu, 134.
Abijah, or Abijam, king of Judah, 304.
Abimelech, son of Gideon, 201.
Abiram, 139.
Abner, 240.
Abraham, his birth-place, 55; his early life, 56; his call, 57; at Mount Moriah, 69; his death, 71; his character, 72.
Absalom, son of David, 247.
Accad, ancient city, 48.
Accadian poem, 68.
Accadians, the early, 48.
Achan and his crime, 174.
Achor, valley of, 174.
Actium, battle of, 402.
Adam, 19.
Aden, port of, 259.
Adullam, cave of, 235.
Agricola in Britain, 494.
Ahab, king of Israel, 276-281.
Ahasuerus (Cambyses), 361.
Ahasuerus (Xerxes), 368.
Ahaz, king of Judah, 311.
Ahaziah, king of Israel, 282.
Ahaziah, king of Judah, 308.
Abijah, 260, 268.
Ai, pass and town of, 60, 173, 179.
Ajalon, valley of, 176.
Akabah, gulf of, 138.
Alexander of Macedon, 378, 384, 386.
Alexandria, town in Egypt, 386; Jews in, 387.
Altar, eastern, 190.
Amalekites, the, 124, 138, 198, 226.
Amaziah, king of Judah, 309.
American traditions of the Flood, 36.

Ammonites, the, 75, 145, 152, 188, 201, 224, 348.
Amon, king of Judah, 320.
Amorites, the, 144, 145.
Amos, prophet of Israel, 295.
Andrew, apostle, 427, 487.
Annunciation, the, of John, 354, 414.
Annunciation, the, of Jesus, 414.
Antigonus of Socho, 389.
Anti-Lebanon, or Hermon, 170.
Antioch in Pisidia, 465.
Antioch in Syria, 389, 463.
Antiochus the Great, king of Syria, 390.
Antiochus Epiphanes, 393.
Antipater, 400.
Antony, Roman triumvir, 401.
Aphek, battles at, 280.
Apis, or sacred bull of Egypt, 99, 133.
Apocrypha, 382.
Apostles, the twelve, 432.
Apostolic history, 451.
Aquila, 476.
Arabah, wady el, 143.
Arabia, Jews in, 405.
Arad, king of Canaan, 143.
Ararat, mountains of, 18, 33, 37, 341.
Araxes (Gihon?), a river of Eden, 17.
Arbela, battle of, 386.
Archelaus, tetrarch of Judæa, 419.
Argob, region of (Bashan), 147.
Argonautic expedition, 218.
Aristobulus, murder of, 402.
Aristotle, Greek philosopher, 385.
Ark, building of, 32.
Ark of the covenant, 135; taken by Philistines, 205; placed on Zion, 243.
Armenia, highlands of, 17.
Arnon, river, 144.
Aroer, ancient city, 146.
Artaxerxes, king of Persia, 359, 368-371.

Asa, king of Judah, 273, 304.
Ashdod, siege of, 319.
Asher, tribe of, 183.
Ashtoreth (Astarte), image and worship of, 162.
Asia, Western, the centre of life, 39.
Asmonæans. See *Maccabees*.
Asshur, son of Shem, 43.
Assyria, 216, 244, 331, 339.
Assyrian idolatry, 120.
Assyrian invasions of Israel, 298.
Athaliah, daughter of Omri, 307, 308.
Athens, rise of, 335; intellectual glory of 384; Paul at, 473.
Augustus Cæsar, 410.
Ayin Mousa, wells of Moses, 122.
Azariah, or Uzziah, king of Judah, 310.
Azoff, sea of, 37.

Baalath, or Baalbec, 185, 261.
Baal-peor, worship of, 154.
Baal-zebub, god of Ekron, 282.
Baasha, king of Israel, 223, 305.
Babel, tower of, 44; city, 48; Chaldæan traditions of, 45.
Babylon, 216, 332, 333, 343, 353, 363.
Babylonia, Jews of dispersion in, 405.
Balaam, prophet of Mesopotamia, 152, 153.
Balak, king of Moab, 152.
Barak, deliverer from Canaanites, 194, 196.
Barnabas, apostle, 463.
Bartholomew, apostle, 488.
Bashan, kingdom of, 146, 188; stone cities of, 147.
Bath-sheba, 245.
Beatitudes, mount of, 433.
Beer, the well at, 144.
Beer-sheba, 62, 101.
Beke on Sinai, 123.
Bel, or Belus, Babylonian god, 344.
Belshazzar, king of Babylon, 351, 353.
Ben-hadad I., king of Syria, 274, 280.
Benjamin, tribe of, 179.
Berea, Paul at, 473.
Bethany, 441, 443.
Beth-barah, battle at, 199.
Beth-el, 60, 61, 76, 283.
Beth-gamul, in Bashan, 149.
Beth-horon, pass and towns of, 176, 179.
Beth-lehem, 78, 178, 230, 416.
Bethsaida, 431.
Bezer, 189.
Birs Nimrood, 46.
"Blast," the, that destroyed Sennacherib's host, 314.
Boaz, 214, 230.
Bozrah of Edom, 141.

Brahminism, 380.
Brick-making in Egypt, 106.
Britain, Britons, 408, 463, 494.
Brugsch on Egyptian monuments, 50, 103, 268.
Buddhism, 380.
Buffon on longevity, 31.
Burning bush, the, 112.

Cæsar, Julius, 399, *et seq*.
Cæsarea Philippi, 184, 437.
Cæsarea Palestina, 463.
Cæsarea, Paul at, 479.
Cain and his race, 26, 27.
Caleb, 138.
Calvary, or Golgotha, 448.
Calves at Dan and Beth-el, 272.
Cambyses, king of Persia, 361.
Cana of Galilee, 427.
Canaan, son of Ham, 41, 43.
Canaan, land of, 58, 164.
Canaanites, 138, 145, 195; judgments on, 191.
Capernaum, 429, 430.
Capitals, Jewish, 403.
Captivity of the ten tribes, 299, 338-342, 342-347.
Captivity of Judah, 324.
Carmel, Mount, 182, 237, 278.
Carthage, empire of, 334, 378.
Carthaginian wars, 392.
Caspian Sea, 37.
Cassius, Roman general, 400.
Catherine of Alexandria, 136.
Ceremonial law, 129.
Chaldæan Genesis, 13.
Chaldæan traditions of the Fall, 21, 22.
Chaldæan traditions of the Flood, 35.
Chaldæan traditions of Babel, 45.
Chaldæan Empire, the early, 47.
Chaldæan idolatry, 120.
Chaldæan learning, 343.
Chedorlaomer, 63.
Cherith, brook, 277.
Chesney, Colonel, his expedition to Euphrates, 18.
China, 380.
Chinese traditions of the Fall, 24.
Chinese traditions of the Flood, 36.
Chorazin, 430.
"Christian," the name, 463.
Chushan-rishathaim of Mesopotamia, 195, 216.
Cicero, Roman orator, 399.
Cilicia, province of, 471, 460.
Cincinnatus, Roman dictator, 379.
Cinna, Roman general, 399.
Civilization, primitive, 29; early, 88.

GENERAL INDEX.

Claudius, emperor, 463.
Cleopatra, queen of Egypt, 401.
Codex Sinaiticus, 137.
Cœlo-Syria, province of, 170, 185.
Confucius, 351.
Corinth, Paul at, 476, 478.
Coriolanus, Roman general, 379.
Cornelius of Cæsarea, 461.
Cosmogony, science of, 11.
Crassus, Roman general, 400.
Creation of the world, 10, 11; order of, 12.
Creator, doctrine of One, 11.
Crœsus, king of Lydia, 352.
Cush, son of Ham, 17, 41, 42.
Cyaxares, or Darius the Mede, 333.
Cyprus, Paul and Barnabas at, 465.
Cyrenius, governor of Syria, 415.
Cyrus the Persian, 333, 351, 354.

Damascus, 58, 63, 186, 289, 458.
Dan, city of, 63, 179, 184.
Dan, tribe of, 178.
Daniel in Babylon, 323, 344, 352.
Danite migration, 213.
Darius the Mede, 342, 354.
Darius Hystaspes, 359, 361, 364.
Dathan, 139.
David, king, 226, 227, 229-257; his character, 253.
Dead Sea, 61, 66.
Deborah the prophetess, 194, 196.
Delilah, 204.
Delta, the, 89.
Derbe, Paul at, 466, 471.
De Saulcy's ruins of Sodom and Gomorrah, etc., 68.
Dispersion of man, 40.
Domestic life, time of the Judges, 208.
Domitian, Roman emperor, 493.
Dothan, 79.
Druids and Druidism, 408.
Dura, image in, 345.

Ebal, Mount, 59, 174.
Eber, father of the Hebrews, 43.
Ecbatana, capital of Media, 341.
Eden, garden of, 16; rivers of, 17; trees of, 18, 21; east gate of, 25.
Edom, 74, 140, 309, 348.
Edrei, battle of, 147.
Eglon, king of Moab, 195.
Egypt, Abraham in, 60; Joseph in, 80; Jacob's removal to, 81; physical aspect of, 89; Upper and Lower, 90; relations of, to the East, 91; the Hyksos period, 92; in Scripture, 96; domestic life, 96; religion of, 98; temples and worship, 100; effects of, on Israelites, 101, 105, 117; in time of Judges, 215; of David, 244; of Solomon, 258; subsequently, 330, 348, 378; in time of Christ, 418.
Egyptian Empire, the early, 47.
Egyptians, origin of, 49.
Ehud, deliverer from Moab, 194, 195.
Elah, king of Israel, 274.
Elam, son of Shem, 43.
Elamites, 216.
Eleazar, the high priest, 177.
Eleazar, the scribe, martyrdom of, 396.
Eli, high priest, 205.
Eliakim, counsellor of Judah, 320.
Eliakim (or Jehoiakim), king of Judah 323.
Elijah and Mount Horeb, 136, 279.
Elijah's career, 276-285.
Elim in Sinai, 122.
Elisha's career, 279.
Elymas, the sorcerer, 465.
Empires, the two early, 47.
En-dor, 182; witch of, 227.
En-gedi, 237.
Engineering, talent of Uzziah for, 310.
Enoch, 28.
Epaminondas, 384.
Ephesus, Paul at, 477; John at, 489.
Ephraim, or Samaria, 169.
Ephraim, tribe of, 180; jealous spirit of, 200, 202, 267; war with Gilead, 202.
Ephraimites killed in Egypt, 102.
Epicureans, sect of, 475.
Erech, 48.
Er-Râhâh, plain of, 127.
Esarhaddon, king of Assyria, 332.
Esau, 74.
Esdraelon, plain of, 181; its battles, 181, 197, 205, 278, 280, 321.
Essenes, 407.
Esther, story of, 368.
Etham, 116.
Ethiopia, or Cush, near Eden, 17.
Ethiopian eunuch's conversion, 454.
Euphrates, 16, 17.
Europe, the gospel in, 472.
Eve, 19.
Evil-merodach, king of Babylon, 351.
Ezekiel, prophet of Judah, 334, 347.
Ezion-geber, gulf of Akabah, 138.
Ezra, labours of, 359, 371-376.

Fables, Grecian, and Hebrew miracles, 219.
Fall, the, 16, 19; traditions of, 20, 21, 24.
Farms, time of the Judges, 208.
Feirân, in Sinai, 126, 136.
Felix, governor of Palestine, 480.
Festivals, religious, 130, 209.

Festus, governor of Palestine, 480.
Flood, the, 25, 33; traditions of, 35, 36

Gad, settlement of, 155, 187.
Galatia, Paul in, 471.
Galilee, 169, 419, 429.
Galilee, Lake of, 176, 429.
Gamaliel, 453, 457.
Gath, David at, 235.
Gauls, the, at Rome, 391.
Gedaliah, ruler of Judah, 325.
Gehazi, 288.
Genealogies, preservation of, 356.
Genesis, first words of, 10.
Gennesaret, plain of, 430, 435.
Geography, scriptural, value of knowledge of, 10.
Geology and Genesis, 13.
Gerar, 69, 305, note.
Gerasa, 188.
Gerizim, Mount, 59, 174.
Geshur, kingdom of, 186.
Gethsemane, garden of, 445.
Gibeah, Saul's capital, 223; David at, 234.
Gibeah, tragedy of, 213.
Gibeon, battle at, 175, 240.
Gibeonites, their fraud, 175.
Gideon, deliverer from Midian, 194, 198.
Gihon, (Araxes?) a river of Eden, 17.
Gilboa, Mount, 182, 228, 239.
Gilead, 150, 155.
Gilead, war with Ephraim, 202.
Gilgal, Elisha at, 287.
Golan, 189.
Golden age, the classical, and paradise, 21.
Golden calf, 133.
Golden calves of Jeroboam, 272.
Golden fleece, legend of, 17.
Golgotha, or Calvary, 448.
Goliath of Gath, 226, 233.
Gomer and his descendants, 42.
Gomorrah, 61, 66.
Goshen, land of, 101.
Government, method of, 210.
Granicus, battle of, 386.
Greece, 217, 220, 335, 376.
Greek traditions of the Flood, 36.
Greek traditions of Babel, 46.
Greek literature, 335.
Greek religion, 336.

Habakkuk, prophet, 326.
Hachilah, David at, 237.
Hagar, 65.
Haggai, prophet, 361, 362.
Ham and his descendants, 40, 42.
Haman, 369.

Hamath, entering in of, 185.
Hanani, prophet, 305.
Hannibal, 392.
Haran, or Carrhae, ancient city, 57.
Haran, son of Terah, 56.
Haurân, district of, 170.
Havilah, (Colchis?) near Eden, 17.
Hazael, king of Syria, 279, 289, 309.
Hebron, 62, 178, 189, 239.
Hellenes, the, 218.
Hermetic, or sacred books of Egypt, 109.
Hermon, Mount, 150, 184, 438.
Hermon, Little, 182.
Herod the Great, 401, 418.
Herod Antipas, 419, 426.
Herod Agrippa I., 462.
Herod Agrippa II., 481.
Herodotus, 37, 47, 91, 335, 367.
Heroic age in Greece, 218.
Heshbon, in Bashan, 157.
Hesperides, garden of the, 22.
Heth, founder of the Hittites, 43.
Hezekiah, king of Judah, 311.
Hiddekel, or Tigris, a river of Eden, 16.
High priesthood, contests for, 383.
Hillah, 46.
Hillel, Jewish rabbi, 406.
Hindu traditions of the Fall, 23.
Hippocrates, 385.
Hiram, king of Tyre, 258.
History, object of Bible, 9; relation of Bible to general, 10.
Hittites, the ancient, 71, 105.
Homer, Greek poet, 335.
Hophni, son of Eli, 205.
Hophra, king of Egypt, 330.
Hor, Mount, 147.
Horace, Latin poet, 410.
Horeb, Mount, 126.
Hosea, prophet of Israel, 295.
Hoshea, king of Israel, 297.
Hûr, (Ur of the Chaldees?) 55.
Hur, 125.
Hyksos in Egypt, 92, 102.
Hyrcanus, Jewish high priest, 397, 400.

I-chabod, birth of, 206.
Iconium, Paul and Barnabas at, 466.
Idolatry, rise and spread of, 51, 86, 120; Syrian, Milton's sketches of, 161.
Idumæa, 140.
India, 380.
Isaac, his birth, 69; his offering, 71; his character, 73; his death, 78.
Isaiah, prophet, 316.
Ish-bosheth, rival of David, 240.
Ishmael, 65, 74.
Isis, Egyptian god, 99.

Israel, kingdom of, 267; tabular view of, 270.
Issachar, tribe of, 181.

Jabal, 27.
Jabbok, river, 77, 145.
Jabesh-gilead, siege of, 224; men of, 228.
Jabin, king of Hazor, 170.
Jabin, king of Canaan, 196.
Jacob, 74; early history, 75; at Beth-el, 76; at Padan-aram, 76; meeting with Esau, 77; in Egypt, 81; his sons, 81; his death, 81.
Jacob's Well, Christ at, 440.
Jael, 197.
Jaghi Tagh, "mountain of flowers," 18.
Jahaz, battle of, 145.
James, apostle, 432, 486.
Japheth and his descendants, 41, 42.
Jazer, land of, 145.
Jebel Haurân, 150.
Jebel Heish, 150.
Jebel Mousa, 126.
Jeconiah, or Jehoiachin, king of Judah, 323, 351.
Jehoahaz, king of Israel, 290.
Jehoahaz, king of Judah, 308, 322.
Jehoiada, high priest of Judah, 309.
Jehoiakim, king of Judah, 322, 343.
Jehoram, king of Israel, 283.
Jehoram, king of Judah, 307.
Jehoshaphat, king of Judah, 305.
Jehu, king of Israel, 279, 289, 290.
Jehu, prophet, 306.
Jephthah, deliverer from Ammon, 194, 202.
Jeremiah, prophet, 321, 323.
Jericho, 167, 168, 170-172, 282, 284, 443.
Jeroboam I., 260, 268, 271.
Jeroboam II., 291.
Jerusalem, capture of, by David, 240; situation of, etc., 241; destruction of, by Nebuchadnezzar, 324; in time of Ezra, 371; Alexander at, 386; at birth of Christ, 412; synod of, 467; taken by the Romans, 493.
Jesse, David's father, 230.
Jesus Christ, birth, 416; transfiguration, 438; betrayal, 447; death and burial, 448; resurrection and ascension, 449, 451.
Jethro, priest of Midian, 110, 125.
Jewish farms, 208; employments, 210; government, 210.
Jews, reason of their prominence in sacred history, 10.
Jews of the dispersion, 405; in Jerusalem, 452.

Jezebel, wife of Ahab, 276, 290.
Jezreel, plain of, 181.
Jezreel, city of, 182.
Joab, 247, 249.
Joash, king of Israel, 290.
Joash, king of Judah, 309.
Job and his times, 86.
Job, book of, 87, 88.
Joel, prophet, 315.
John Baptist, 414, 424, 426.
John, apostle, 427, 432, 489.
Jonah, prophet, 292.
Jonathan, son of Saul, 224, 234, 238.
Joppa, 169, 181, 460.
Jordan, 61; its depression, 166; the valley of, 166; Elijah and Elisha at, 284; east side of, 144.
Jordan, fords of the, Moabites defeated at, 196; Midianites defeated at, 199.
Joseph, his early life, 79; in Egypt, 80; his treatment of his brethren, 80; his death, 82.
Joseph, the carpenter, 415.
Josephus, 49, 195, 367, 382.
Joshua, 138; in command, 164; divides the land, 177; his final charge, 190; his death, 191; his character, 191.
Josiah, king of Judah, 320.
Jotham, king of Judah, 310.
Jubal, 27.
Judah, or Judæa, the country, 168.
Judah, tribe of, 177.
Judah, wilderness of, 236.
Judah, kingdom of, 300; table of kings of, 301.
Judah, Rabbi, 373.
Judas of Galilee, 416.
Judas Iscariot, 432.
Judas Maccabæus, 396.
Jude, apostle, 488.
Judges, the, 193.
Judicial law, 130.

Kadesh-barnea, 137, 140.
Karnak, temple of, 103, 303.
Kedesh-naphtali, 189, 197.
Kenites, 125.
Keturah Abraham's wife, 71; her sons, 74.
Kishon, river, 182.
Kizil-Ermak (Pison?), a river of Eden, 17.
Knowledge of good and evil, tree of, 18.
Korah, rebellion of, 139.
Kuhi Nuch (Ararat), 38.

Laban, 76.
Lachish besieged by Sennacherib, 313.
Lamech, 31.

GENERAL INDEX. 501

Lane, Mr., on Egypt, 101.
Language, the primitive, 46.
Languages, confusion of, 44.
Laodicea, church at, 491.
Law of Moses, 128.
Law, purpose of the, 131.
Leah, 76.
Lebanon, 170.
Lepidus, triumvir, 401.
Leuctra, battle of, 384.
Levi, tribe of, 129, 188.
Libnah, revolt of, 308.
Life, length of, 29.
Life, tree of, in Eden, 18, 19, 21.
Livingstone, Dr., on the fig-tree, 21.
Livy, Roman historian, 410.
Longevity, traditions of, 30.
Lot, 56, 61; his sons, 75.
Luke, the historian, 472, 485.
Lycurgus, Spartan lawgiver, 335.
Lynch's expedition to Dead Sea, 67.
Lystra, Paul at, 466, 471.

Maccabees, the, 395.
Macedonian kings of Syria, 391.
Machpelah, cave of, 63, 70.
Magi, the, 343.
Mahanaim, 187.
Malachi, prophet, 375.
Malta, or Melita, Paul at, 482.
Mamre, oak of, 62.
Manasseh, east half of, 155, 188.
Manasseh, west half of, 180.
Manasseh, king of Judah, 318.
Manasseh, priest of Gerizim, 375.
Manetho, Egyptian historian, 49, 50, 108.
Mankind, common parentage of, 28.
Mantinea, battle of, 384.
Maon, David at, 236.
Marah (Huwârah), 122.
Marathon, battle of, 365.
Mareshah, battle of, 304.
Mariamne, wife of Herod, 401.
Marius, Roman general, 399.
Mark, evangelist, 465.
Mary, the mother of Jesus, 415.
Massada, fortress of, 401.
Mattathias, head of the Maccabees, 395.
Matthew, apostle, 486.
Matthias, apostle, 489.
Media, country of, 333, 340.
Medo-Persian Empire, 354.
Megiddo, plain of, 181; battle of, 321.
Melchizedek, 64.
Memphis, capital of Lower Egypt, 91, 99.
Menahem, king of Israel, 297.
Menes, king of Egypt, 50.

Merodach-baladan, king of Babylon, 315, 322.
Merom, lake of, 166; battle of, 176.
Mesopotamia. See *Assyria*, *Chaldæa*, etc.
Messiah, expectations of a, 411.
Methuselah, 29.
Micah and his images, 212.
Micah, prophet, 317.
Michmash, Jonathan's exploit at, 225.
Midianites, 74, 154, 198, 199.
Miracles, Hebrew, and Greek prodigies, 219.
Miriam, sister of Moses, 107, 137, 140.
Mithridates, king of Pontus, 399.
Mizpeh, 206, 235, 325.
Mizraim, founder of Egypt, 43, 62.
Moab, 144, 151, 156.
Moabite stone, 282.
Moabites, 75, 145, 195, 306, 343.
Moral law, 129.
Mordecai, 369.
Moreh, plain of, 59.
Moriah, Mount, 69, 257.
Moses, birth of, 107; his youth and education, 108; at Sinai, 110; contest with Pharaoh, 113; at Rephidim, 140; striking the rock, 140; his last charge and his death, 157.
Mount, sermon on the, 433.
Mugeyer, or Hûr, 55.

Naamah, 27.
Naaman the Syrian, 286.
Nabal, 237.
Nabonadius, 351.
Nabopolassar, king of Babylon, 332.
Naboth and his vineyard, 281.
Nadab, son of Aaron, 134.
Nadab, king of Israel, 273.
Nahor, son of Terah, 56.
Nahum, prophet, 317.
Naphtali, tribe of, 183.
Nathanael, apostle, 427.
Nazareth, 183, 419, 420.
Nebuchadnezzar, 323, 333, 343, 344, 348, 349; purpose of his conquests, 350.
Neby, Samwil (Mizpeh), 206.
Necho, king of Egypt, 321.
Nehemiah, reforms of, 359, 373-376.
Nepos, Cornelius, Latin writer, 410.
Nero, emperor of Rome, 483.
Nicodemus, 428.
Nile, the, 89; its water, 90; plague of, 113.
Nimrod, 35, 43, 48.
Nineveh, its rise, 48; in time of Jonah, 293; destruction of, 322, 333.
Nitocris, mother of Belshazzar, 353.

No, No-Ammon (or Thebes), 90.
Noah, 28, 32; his vine, and its fruits, 40; his prophecy, 40.
Nob, David at, 235.
Noph (or Memphis). 91.
Numbering of the people, 251.

Obadiah, prophet, 326.
Octavius, triumvir, 400.
Oded, prophet of Israel, 244, 251.
Og, king of Bashan, 146.
Olives, Mount of, 242.
Omri, king of Israel, 274, 275.
Oreb, prince of Midian, 199.
Orfah, or Urfah, 48, 55.
Osiris, Egyptian god, 99.
Othniel, deliverer of Israel, 194, 195.
"Outcasts of Israel," 209.
Ovid, 410.

Palestine, origin of name, 164; boundaries of, 165; two mountain ranges, 165.
Palmer's exploration of Sinai, 112, 128.
Palmyra, or Tadmor, 260.
Parables, Christ's, 434.
Paradise and the Fall, 16.
Parthians, 400.
Passover, festival, 116, 130.
Pathros, or Upper Egypt, 90.
Patmos, John at, 492.
Patriarchs, the Hebrew, 55.
Patriarchal religion, 85, 117.
Paul, apostle, 456-485; his personal appearance, 468.
Pekah, king of Israel, 297, 310.
Pekahiah, 297.
Peloponnesian war, 377, 384.
Pentecost, festival, 130; day of, 452.
Penuel, or Peniel, 78, 187, 200, 271.
Peræa, 129, 442.
Perga, Paul and Barnabas at, 465.
Pergamos, church at, 490.
Persecution of Jews, 394.
Persia, precious stones of, 17; war with Greece, 364, 367, 376; Jews in, 405.
Persian traditions of the Fall, 23.
Persian religion—fire-worship, 52.
Persians, Palestine under the, 382, 383.
Peter, apostle, 432, 447, 460, 468, 486.
Petra, 75, 141.
Pharaoh, the title, 91.
Pharaoh's host, destruction of, 117.
Pharaohs, kings of Egypt, 92, 115; statues of, at Thebes, 115.
Pharisees, 398, 407.
Pharsalia, battle of, 400.
Philadelphia, 188; church at, 491.
Philip of Macedon, 384.

Philip, tetrarch, 419.
Philip, apostle, 427, 488.
Philippi, Paul at, 472, 478.
Philistines, land and cities of, 150.
Philistines, the, 179, 203, 225, 226, 227, 250, 348.
Phinehas, son of Eli, 205.
Phœnicia, 184, 217, 258, 333, 378.
Phrygia, Paul in, 471.
Pilate, Pontius, governor of Judæa, 423.
Pisgah, Balaam on, 153; Moses' view from, 156.
Pison (Kizil-Ermak), a river of Eden, 17.
Plagues, ten, of Egypt, 113.
Polytheism, origin of, 52.
Pompey takes Jerusalem, 397.
Primitive state of happiness, 20.
Priscilla, 476.
Promise of a Saviour in Eden, 20.
Prophets of judgment, 291.
Psalms, classification of, 256.
Psammiticus, king of Egypt, 330.
Ptolemys, Palestine under the, 388.
Pul, king of Assyria, 298.
Pyramids, early origin of, 50.
Pyrrhus, war with Rome, 391.

Quarantania, mountain of, 427.

Rabbah, 188, 245, 348.
Rabbinical system, 406.
Rabshakeh, 313.
Races, the two—Cain's and Seth's, 27.
Rachel, 76, 78.
Rainbow, the, 34.
Ramah, 273.
Rameses II., 105, 106.
Ramoth-gilead, 189; sieges of, 280, 306, 308.
Râs es Sûfsâfeh, 127.
Rebekah, 71.
Red Sea, passage of, 116, 121.
Refuge, cities of, 156, 189.
Rehob, 138.
Rehoboam, king of Judah, 267, 303.
Religions of man, 51.
Religious life under Patriarchs, 85, 117; under Moses, 159; under Joshua, 192; under the Judges, 211; under Solomon, etc., 265; under the Kings, 328; during the Captivity, 356.
Rephidim in Sinai, 124.
Restoration, the, 359.
Reuben, settlement of, 155, 187.
Rezin, king of Syria, 311.
Ritter, Carl, on Sinai, 127.
Rizpah, 250.
Rome, Romans, 336, 337, 379, 398.

Rome, church of, 479.
Rome, Paul at, 481, 482.
Ruth, story of, 214.

Sabaco, or So, king of Egypt, 298.
Sabbath, its antiquity, 15.
Sacrifice, origin of, 25.
Sadducees, 398, 407.
Salamis, battle of, 367.
Samaria, 169, 275, 439.
Samaria, woman of, 428.
Samaritans, the, 299, 360, 441.
Samson, his country and exploits, 194, 203.
Samuel, 206, 207 ; at Ramah, 223.
Sarah, 56, 70.
Sardanapalus, 332.
Sardis, church at, 490.
Satan, the tempter, 18.
Saul, first king of Israel, 222-229, 234, 238.
Saviour, promise of the, 20.
Schools of prophets, 224.
Scriptures, edited by Ezra, 372.
Sebaste, 343.
Seir, Mount, 77, 140.
Seleucus, 389.
Sennacherib, king of Assyria, 312, 331.
Septuagint translation of Bible, 388.
Serbâl, Mount, 126.
Sergius Paulus, 465.
Serpent, the instrument of temptation, 22, 24.
Serpents, the fiery, 143.
Seth, his race, 27.
Seventh day blessed, 12.
Shallum, king of Israel, 296.
Shalmaneser II., king of Assyria, 297, 298.
Shalmaneser IV., king of Assyria, 298.
Shammai, Jewish rabbi, 406.
Sharon, plain of, 181.
Sheba, insurrection of, 249.
Sheba, queen of, 259.
Shebna, 320.
Shechem, 59, 174, 180, 189.
Shekwet el Khudr, "high hill of Bashan," 150.
Shem and his descendants, 41, 43.
Shepherd kings of Egypt, 92.
Shibboleth and Sibboleth, 203.
Shiloh, 181, 189.
Shinar, plain of, 44.
Shishak, king of Egypt, 268, 303.
Shunammite woman, the, 286.
Shunem, 182.
Shushan. See *Susa*.
Sidon, 184, 436.
Sihon, king of Amorites, 144.
Silas, Paul's companion, 470.
Simeon, tribe of, 178.

Simon the just, 389.
Simon the sorcerer, 455.
Simon the apostle, 427, 488.
Sin, wilderness of, 124.
Sinai, Mount, the Israelites at, 125 ; subsequent history, 135.
Sinai, peninsula of, 110, 111.
Sinai, the wilderness of, 123.
Sisera, Jabin's captain, 197.
Smerdis, 361.
Smith, George, on Chaldæan traditions, 14, 35, 45, 56.
Smyrna, church at, 489.
Social life after Flood, 39; under Patriarchs, 87; under Moses, 158; under the Judges, 208; under Solomon, etc., 262; under the Kings, 327; during the Captivity, 355.
Socrates, 336.
Sodom, 61, 66.
Solomon, 257-262.
Solon, Athenian lawgiver, 335.
Spain, Paul's visit to, 484.
Sparta, Spartans, 335, 377.
Spies, the twelve, 138.
St. Catherine, Mount, 126 ; Convent, 127, 136.
Stephen, proto-martyr, 454.
Stoics, sect of, 475.
Succoth, 116, 200.
Suetonius, Roman historian, 411.
Suez, 116.
Sulla, Roman general, 399, 410.
Sumir, 48.
Susa, palace of, 359, 363.
Sychar, or Shechem, Christ at, 430.
Synagogues, 372.
Syria, idolatry of, 161 ; kingdom of, 389; wars with, 274, 280, 288, 309, 348.

Tabernacle, the, 135.
Tabernacles, feast of, 130.
Tabor, Mount, 182, 197.
Tacitus, Roman historian, 411.
Tadmor, or Palmyra, 260.
Talmud, the, 373.
Tarquins, the, banished from Rome, 379.
Tarsus, Paul's birth-place, 456.
Temple, David's desire to build, 243, 252; Solomon's, 257; rebuilt by Zerubbabel, 362; by Herod, 405.
Temptation of Jesus, 427.
Ten tribes—captivity of, 338; ultimate fate of, 341.
Terah, father of Abraham, 56.
Theban supremacy in Greece, 384.
Thebes, capital of Upper Egypt, 90, 332.
Themistocles, Athenian general, 367.
Thermopylæ, battle of, 367.

GENERAL INDEX.

Thessalonica, Paul at, 473.
Thomas, apostle, 487.
Thotmes III. of Egypt, 103.
Thucydides, Greek historian, 385.
Thyatira, church at, 490.
Tiberius Cæsar, 423.
Tiglath-pileser, king of Assyria, 298, 310, 311.
Tigris, or Hiddekel, a river of Eden, 17.
Timothy, conversion of, &c., 467, 485.
Tirzah, 274, 275.
Titus, Paul's companion, 485.
Titus, Roman general, 493.
Tobiah, the Ammonite, 374.
Tobit, book of, 340.
Tongues, confusion of, 44.
Tradition, Jewish, origin of, 373.
Traditions, of the Fall, 20; of the Flood, 35.
Transfiguration, Mount of the, 284; the, 438.
Troas (or Troy), Paul at, 471, 478.
Troy, siege of, 218.
Tubal-Cain, 27.
Two brothers, Egyptian story, 95.
Tyre, 184, 333, 348, 378, 436
Tyropœon valley, 241.

Um el Jemâl, 149.
Ur of the Chaldees (Urfah, Orfah), 48, 55.
Uriah and king David, 245.
Usdam (Sodom), 61.
Uzziah, or Azariah, king of Judah, 310.

Van, Lake, probably in Eden, 18.
Venus, polluting effects of her worship, 53.
Vespasian in Palestine, emperor, 493.
Vine, Noah's, 40.
Virgil, Latin poet, 410, 411.
Von Haller on longevity, 31.

Wady el Arabah, 143.

Wady el Kelt, 277.
Wady Er-Râhâh, 126.
Wady Feiràn, 124, 126.
Wady Ghurundel, 123.
Wady Mokatteb, or "written valley," 150.
Wady Shu'eib, 127.
Wales, Prince of, at Machpelah, 70.
Week, the, and the Sabbath, 15.
Wilkinson's ancient Egyptians, 96.
Wise men, visit of the, 417.
World, the, before the Flood, 25, 32.

Xenophon, and retreat of the Ten Thousand, 384, 385.
Xerxes' invasion of Greece, 367.

Yemen, or Sheba, 259.

Zachariah, king of Israel, 296.
Zacharias at Jerusalem, 412.
Zalmunna, prince of Midian, 199.
Zandevesta, 366.
Zarephath, Elijah at, 184, 277.
Zebah, prince of Midian, 199.
Zebulun, tribe of, 183.
Zechariah (1), (son of Jehoiada), prophet, 309.
Zechariah (2), prophet, 312.
Zechariah (3), prophet, 361, 362.
Zedekiah, king of Judah, 324.
Zeeb, prince of Midian, 199.
Zemaraim, battle of, 304.
Zephaniah, prophet, 320.
Zerah, Ethiopian, invasion by, 304
Zerubbabel, governor of Judah, 359, 360.
Zimri, king of Israel, 274.
Zion, Mount, 242, 243.
Ziph, wilderness of, 236.
Zoan, antiquity of, 62; or Tanis, 102.
Zopyrus' stratagem in taking Babylon, 364.
Zoroaster, reformer of Persian religion, 365.

www.ingramcontent.com/pod-product-compliance
Lightning Source LLC
Chambersburg PA
CBHW051200300426
44116CB00006B/380